The Wo

THE WORLD RUSHED IN

The California Gold Rush Experience

J. S. HOLLIDAY

Foreword by Howard R. Lamar

University of Oklahoma Press

Norman

for
Sara Sabrina Swain   1860–1953
Edward Eberstadt   1883–1958
Dale L. Morgan   1914–1971
Craig Wylie   1908–1976
and
Nancy, Tim, Brett, and Jack, who also
waited many years for "the book"

Library of Congress Cataloging-in-Publication Data

Holliday, J. S.
  The world rushed in : the California gold rush experience / J. S.
Holliday.—Red River Books ed. / foreword by Howard R. Lamar.
    p. cm.
  Based on the diary of William Swain.
  Originally published: New York : Simon and Schuster, c1981.
  Includes bibliographical references and index.
  ISBN 0-8061-3464-X (alk. paper)
    1. California—History—1846–1850. 2. California—Gold discoveries.
3. Swain, William, 1821–1904. 4. Overland journeys to the Pacific. 5.
Pioneers—California—Biography. 6. California—Biography. I. Swain,
William, 1821–1904. II. Title.

F865 .H695 2002
979.4'04—dc21

                                                    2002069594

1   2   3   4   5   6   7   8   9   10

Contents

Illustrations

MAPS

Foreword

When J. S. Holliday's *The World Rushed In* was first published in 1981, it was immediately hailed as the most outstanding single book on the 1849 gold rush ever written. Ray Allen Billington, the dean of western historians, called it "a unique book, destined to take its place as a classic in our literature," a tribute echoed in many hundreds of reviews across the nation and in Europe over the next decade.

The publication of a new edition of *The World Rushed In* in 2002, twenty-one years after the original volume appeared, is cause for a double celebration: first, it marks the continued availability of what is undoubtedly one of the best gold-rush diaries ever found. In Holliday's own words, it was "so inclusive, so complete as to be a rarity among the hundreds of eyewitness accounts, published and manuscript, that tell the gold-rush story." The public must have agreed, for it has been one of the most popular gold-rush diaries ever published.

Second, Holliday's own impeccable, exhaustive editing and supplement to William Swain's account with that of other diarists who also went west in 1849 is a marvel of historical scholarship. His innovative coverage of this saga has resulted in no less than a whole new understanding of the entire gold-rush experience. These breakthroughs deserve recognition and high praise as this new printing by the University of Oklahoma Press comes to press.

■

The most significant event to occur in the American West in the nineteenth century was James Marshall's discovery of gold in the race at Sutter's Mill on Coloma Creek, California, on January 24, 1848. The multiple impact of the additional fabulous gold finds that quickly followed are almost impossible to measure. Within two years, more than one hundred thousand goldseekers had come to California, enough population to make it a state of the Union by 1850. The discoveries transformed the nation's own vision of itself and its future by marking the passing of America as a largely agricultural nation.

Although thousands of goldseekers came by boat from Asia, Europe, and Latin America, nothing captured the American imagination more completely than the overland rush across the continent in 1849 and 1850. Thousands of young men made plans to take the overland trail to get rich quick and come home. The overlanders themselves were so convinced of "the uniqueness and the historical significance of their travels," writes John D. Unruh in *The Plains Across*, "that in the entire American experience perhaps only the Civil War has called forth a commensurate cornucopia of letters, journals, diaries, memoirs, and reminiscent accounts; a veritable folk literature of one of the nation's greatest achievements." Devoted scholars and students of that "folk literature" have collected and published over one thousand overland journals and diaries since 1849. Almost all tell the same story: a saga of grueling physical hardships, of loneliness, and of the danger of death from accident, disease, and Indians. To most overlanders it was the quintessential American frontier experience. But was this the real and complete story?

Virtually all the older versions of the gold rush—by both scholars and popularizers—stressed its frontier qualities: the rampant individualism of the goldseekers, armed with guns and quick to take offense, and the fighting, drinking, gambling, and thievery in the outfitting towns of Independence and St. Joseph, Missouri. In contrast to these generalizations, Holliday found that William Swain was a well-educated, responsible young man from a loving, deeply religious family. Moreover, Swain and three neighbors joined a company of overlanders from Michigan called the Wolverine Rangers who were much like themselves and included, in its sixty or so members, two doctors, a minister, a newspaper editor, farmers, and mechanics. In contrast to more stereotypical portrayals, Wolverines actually contracted with one another to elect officers, obey rules on the trail, observe the Sabbath, and take turns as cooks in their separate messes. The important fact is that the company organization was the most common form of going west. William Swain and his fellow Wolverines were far more representative argonauts than the much-touted wild frontiersmen.

To test his findings Holliday consulted more than five hundred diaries and two hundred sets of letters written by goldseekers who, as noted before, went west in the very year that Swain and the Wolverines did. By interspersing excerpts from their accounts in brackets, he fleshed out the accuracy of Swain's narrative. As one awed reviewer of *The World Rushed In* noted, Holliday has actually written a group biography of five hundred argonauts. In the process he discovered, as Swain and his companions frequently did, that far from being alone on the trail, they always seemed to be in company with hundreds of caravans and travelers. It is revealing that no less than 42,000 goldseekers set out from the Missouri frontier to travel overland in the spring and summer of 1849.

As full and vivid as this larger narrative seemed to be, Holliday concluded that he had uncovered only half of the gold-rush story. The other half involved what was happening to the families back home, and in particular to William Swain's wife, Sabrina, his brother, George, and their relatives. To his great good fortune Holliday discovered that Swain wrote many letters to his wife and brother back in New York state and that they, in turn, sent Swain letters, all of which had been preserved. These letters portrayed an acutely lonely wife who had opposed his going to California, a loving brother who wrote him comforting letters, and an aged mother who was always fearful that Swain had died of cholera and lay dead in an unmarked grave. Swain's own letters further identified him as a sensible middle-class Victorian full of concern for his wife's and daughter's health. In short, his family was never out of his consciousness.

Once in California, Swain (like other overland diarists) gave up his diary entries in favor of sending letters to his wife and brother back home in Youngstown, New York. These letters, covering the period from his arrival in the mining camps in November 1849 to his departure by ship from San Francisco in November 1850, tell the robust story of Swain's experiences in California. To enrich these letters, Holliday interpolated scores of other eyewitness recountings of that masculine society. Thus we have details of his life in the diggings, his lack of success as a gold miner—again a representative experience of thousands of others—and his disappointment in the excesses of California society. Without being a puritan, he was disgusted with the money-grabbing merchants, gamblers, saloons, and prostitutes that seemed to be everywhere. Here again we must thank Holliday for providing a succinct description of life in California by describing the mining camps, cities like San Francisco and Sacramento, and the fast evolution of mining techniques from the simple rocker to sophisticated hydraulic mining. But the most overwhelming theme was the frustration of tens of thousands of miners like Swain who never hit it lucky.

Disappointed yet strengthened by his California experience, Swain gave up his hopes of making a fortune. With only five hundred dollars to show for his efforts, he joined thousands of other ex-goldseekers and headed for home, boarding a ship in San Francisco, bound for Panama City, on November 4, 1850. In this last chapter of *The World Rushed In*, Holliday once again drew on a vast array of letters, diaries, and newspaper reports, all of which fill in details that Swain—in his brief, almost telegraphic letters—overlooked during the dramatic voyage to Panama and across the isthmus.

Racked by a Panama fever, Swain finally reached New York, so weak he was bedridden in a New York hotel until his ever-caring brother, George, came to take him back to Youngstown in early February 1851. There the entire town turned out to welcome him—not as a failed goldseeker but as someone who had survived and returned.

Here again we must be grateful to Holliday for continuing to follow the fortunes not only of William Swain and his family but also the careers of a number of the Wolverines after 1851. Some returned home, some died early, others succeeded in California or back in Michigan. These accounts provide a broader perspective on the gold-rush experience, in contrast to many other narratives. With that perspective, Holliday highlights one of the most moving themes of William Swain's diary and his life: a poignant love story in which he and Sabrina and their four children basked in the sunny joy of his return, celebrated each February with readings from the diary and a toast from Sabrina to her "forty-niner." William Swain's diaries, among other things, chronicled a true love story,

However intimate and personal the Swain experience, it was part of a larger national event that changed America itself. It was also a traumatic time: in one year (1849), more people died of cholera than during the entire Mexican War (1846–48). The gold rush also brought 89,000 people to California in one year: 42,000 over land, 6,000 from Mexico, and another 40,000 by ship via Cape Horn or across the Isthmus of Panama. But the overland trail story remains the most significant in that it constituted the largest voluntary mass migration of people in modern history. The adventurers who set out on the more than 2,000-mile trek were wholly dependent upon oxen, mules, and horses for transportation and the land itself for grass, water, and often food. Their traumatic, sometimes fatal experiences inspired a nation to erase time and distance in the next two decades with stagecoach lines, the pony express, the telegraph, and—in 1869 at Promontory Point— the joining of the Union Pacific and Central Pacific railroads. It was a reminder that however glorious and significant a role the frontier had played in American history, the argonauts of 1849 symbolized the conquest of the frontier rather than defeat by it.

■

The World Rushed In remains a classic today—more than twenty years after its first appearance—for many reasons. Undoubtedly the most unique feature of *The World Rushed In* lies in how Holliday transformed his painstaking research into a wonderfully lively and beautifully written narrative. His uncanny ability to capture the heady atmosphere of California and his penetrating insight into the goldseekers' lives and thoughts will move readers to feel that they are caught up in the gold rush themselves and that they know Swain, his companions, and his wife and family intimately. The result is one of the most vivid, gripping, and thorough accounts of this defining moment in the American experience.

HOWARD R. LAMAR

Yale University
March 2002

Preface to the Red River Books Edition

Through more than five decades of research in public and private libraries (and exploration of attic trunks and basement boxes), I have found—to the enrichment of my writing—letters and diaries by the many hundreds. In the course of this quest an aphorism has often come to mind: "The strongest memory is weaker than the palest ink."

Reminiscences have been written and published for centuries, but how much more impulsively truthful, and inadvertently revealing, are letters and diaries to be read only by a wife or husband or other dear person. However pale or smudged, these voices from the past have the power of immediacy, like conversation that carries us—the unexpected interceptor—to a distant scene, a forgotten emotion. Exemplary of such rewards, I recall this sentence from a letter written by Sabrina Swain, the wife of the central figure in this book: "O William if I could see you this morning I would hug and kiss you till you would blush."

In our unblushing world of 2002, that cry of longing carries no erotic message. But in 1849 that sentence challenged traditions and mothers' warnings that taught restraint and stifled emotions. When received many months later by her lonely, weary husband, Sabrina's hug and kisses so urgently promised, so tempting to imagine set to work in William's mind, competing with his resolve to remain in California until his promise of a fortune in gold could be fulfilled.

Later in this preface you will read how in 1950 I found this letter and persuaded Sabrina and William's daughter (Sabrina Swain, born 1860) to allow me to use her parents' correspondence as a vital part of this book. But first I want to consider how personal records like those of the Swains, though of "the palest ink," have the power to carry us into the homes and minds of times long past, to affirm and vivify the expectation of 1849 and later years that fathers, husbands, sons, brothers, and fiancés would return from California's "gold fields" with treasure enough to pay off debts, to buy new land, to afford previously unimagined luxuries—to create a new life, say, in Michigan or Maryland. And more than validating that contagion of optimism, I found in these diaries and letters a less familiar dimension of this national experience. For many men their months and years in California proved to be an escape from the moral authority of mothers and wives, from the constraining traditions and Sunday admonitions that had ruled for generations. Thereby America felt the first impact of California's unfolding influences.

The goldseekers first sensed their new freedoms while traveling the overland trails and sea routes to the Pacific land of wonders. Coarsened by those months surrounded by men, most of them strangers, they gained a full awareness of their liberation in the continuing masculine world of California's burgeoning cities and wildly free mining camps, the latter with names like Rough and Ready, You Bet, Red Dog, and Gouge Eye. (As we have learned to exclaim: where else but California!)

This sense of escape from the rules and predictability of life at home found expression in many letters and diaries but seldom with the candor of this free spirit who wrote from San Francisco in January 1850 to his wife in Massachusetts: "I feel bad sometimes when I think of home and the comfort I am deprived of by being away. Then again, come to think of how dull it is at home, I do not want to be there."*

When I read that bold revelation (in a library in Old Lyme, Connecticut), I thought there could not be another husband so candid, so crudely thoughtless. But just yesterday I found in my files an even more daring assertion of freedom. This husband wrote to his wife from Sacramento City on December 23, 1850: "I cannot tell the time when I shall be home. It may be one, two or three years. I long to see the time when I shall land safe home and find you all well. But wife, don't be uneasy about me. I enjoy myself better than you might think, for I spend my time hunting, gambling, drinking, smoking, etc."**

From letters like this there spread among many families a sense that while in the "new Golgotha" their men faced temptations far worse than drinking and gambling. In response, Sabrina Swain and thousands of other "California widows" sent their pleas and biblical warnings. Few wrote with more spirit than Mary Mills of Easton, Connecticut, who in December

---

* *Manuscript letter by James I. Maxfeld, January 24, 1850, in the collection of Matthew R. Isenberg, Old Lyme, Connecticut.*
** *Manuscript letter by James C. Riggin, December 23, 1850, in the Henry E. Huntington Library, San Marino, California.*

1849 addressed her fiancé: "Henry, I did not think you meant to stay away two whole years when you went away and now you write that you think of staying still longer. Forget the nuggets. I do not care to have the strength of my affections tested by a much longer absence."*

Voices like these tempted me to continue research for this book, long past many fervently promised deadlines. Despite even the deaths of those to whom it would be dedicated, I stubbornly searched through hundreds of diaries and letters, determined to find the vivid description, the impulsive revelation that would carry my readers to a critical scene—the ferrying of ox teams and wagons across the treacherous currents of the North Platte River, or to an emotional moment—a husband's confession that he would not be coming home.

Though extended over many more years than the efforts of William Swain and thousands of other goldseekers, my perseverance was similar to their search for nuggets, grains, and specks hidden in gravel and sand, buried beneath rocks along the banks of the Sierra's streams. I was like the husband who wrote, "O Caroline, I can't bear to think of going home with so little money as I have got now when there is a fortune so near. If I was to go now, I know that I could never be contented."**

Contented or not, I finally had to accept in 1980 the edict to stop my searching and rewriting or there would be no publication of this book. Now as I write the preface for the new edition of *The World Rushed In*, I recall my sense of vindication gained from this wonderfully perceptive comment from a review in the London *Observer* at the time of the 1983 British edition:

> It is right of Holliday to interpolate the records of other '49ers into Swain's chronicle, for American literature has always felt an obligation to be choral and collective. . . . He has written a group biography for five hundred men and by extension has done even more than that: reading these letters has enabled him to eavesdrop on the dream life of all Americans.

That eavesdropping, that exploration of our nation's first California-inspired dreams so strengthened and enriched this book that it has now gained for its Red River Books edition the prestigious imprint of the University of Oklahoma Press. How lucky I am, like a miner whose claim yielded rewards far longer than forecast by its initial assay.

---

* *Roland D. Crandall, ed.,* Love and Nuggets *(Old Greenwich, Conn.: Stable Books, 1967), 50.*
** *Manuscript letter by Andrew M. Orvis, February 1850, in the Beinecke Library, Yale University.*

Some who read this preface may wonder why (as Professor Howard Lamar states in his foreword) more than one thousand books about the California gold rush have been published since 1849. Why did so many thousands of Americans make the considerable effort to keep diaries and write letters describing their experiences? What energized such a national response, comparable in the nineteenth century only to the Civil War?

I believe the answers are not as obvious as may be presumed, nor have they been adequately pursued and analyzed, either in the first edition of this book or in other publications—though I hasten to express my admiration and respect for several recent studies. For example, Malcolm J. Rohrbough's *Days of Gold: The California Gold Rush and the American Nation* (1997) focuses on the relationship, nationwide, between the goldseekers and their families back home. Persevering in his research and refreshing in his narrative, Rohrbough created an impressive interpretation that expands and enriches the theme first explored in this book.

In *Roaring Camp: The Social History of the California Gold Rush* (2000), Susan Lee Johnson places a revisionist emphasis on ethnic, gender, and sexual relationships and intolerance as she presents a revealing picture of life in California's southern mining region, an area less studied than that to the north. In her detailed narrative she studies the crises in Anglo-Americans' relations with South Americans, Mexicans, African Americans, and Chinese goldseekers, and, too, the native Californians.

A third recently published study that deserves special recognition is that of Brian Roberts, *American Alchemy: The California Gold Rush and Middle-Class Culture* (2000). While expanding on the relationship between those who rushed to California and their families at home (in the process dismissing this book and others as contributing to the gold rush's historiographic "decline into anecdotalism"), Roberts digs more deeply and surveys more broadly, thereby achieving what I judge to be the most ambitious reconsideration of this persistently studied subject.

Valuable and enlightening as these interpretations are, with new revelations from diaries and letters that are powerfully presented and thoughtfully contextualized, these books and many others continue to place traditional emphasis on the goldseekers as victims of their own great expectations and self-imposed burdens, a story that has become legendary—the goldseekers' disappointment and departure. Supporting that interpretation are statistics (seldom used) that reveal on average 20,000–25,000 men (very few women) left California each year during the 1850s—by ship from San Francisco, bound for the States and other countries. And yet (here is the contradiction), California's population by 1860 totaled 380,000. Obviously, many more arrived than departed. The world rushed in, not only in 1849 but throughout the years and decades thereafter.

I think we need a new perspective to explain that magnetic pull, why so many more ex-miners stayed than left, why so many of their successors found California attractive, despite the news of the 1860s and '70s of social disorder and economic depression. Why did Oregon's population total only 54,000 by 1860, when its image was one of social stability (families) and economic opportunity (plenty of fertile land)?

As an opening consideration, let us recall that during the 242 years preceding the discovery of gold in California, the westering pressure of American families pushed the frontier of settlement from the shores of the Chesapeake Bay (1607) to the banks of the Missouri River (1849). Sustained and hastened by the rewards of the virgin continent—fertile soil and vast forests watered by innumerable streams amid a profusion of natural bounty, this migration of husbands, wives, children, and bibles pushed ever westward, across the Appalachian Mountains and into Pennsylvania and the Northwest Territory of Ohio and Indiana and on to Missouri and Texas. Despite Indian hostility, disease, and suffering, the settlers' perseverance and land hunger had created by 1849 the thirty United States.

Throughout those more than two centuries of westward expansion, the presence of women and children affirmed their menfolks' confidence that the wilderness promised a better living, to be earned as years of labor yielded ever more bountiful harvests. That was the lure of "the West": cheap if not free land, available to anyone ready to plow new furrows.

To temper the hope and optimism that nurtured westward migration, no one set forth a more realistic assessment than the West's own first president, Andrew Jackson, who admonished in 1834: "The planter, the farmer, the mechanic and laborer all know that their success depends on their industry and economy and that they must not expect to become suddenly rich by the fruits of their toil."*

In 1849 the news of gold in California—free for all—challenged the ethos pronounced by President Jackson and known for generations before him to be true. Suddenly California promised that those who journeyed there would be "rich by the fruits of their toil." And just as amazing, that toil would be brief, for the news from the gold fields reported the treasure to be not only free for the taking but abundant and easy to dig up, if not simply to pick up.

---

* *Arthur M. Schlesinger Jr.*, The Age of Jackson *(Boston: Little, Brown, 1945), 126.*

Therein lay the true motive force of the rush to California—that the gold belonged to no one, in contrast to the world's storied past. For thousands of years gold had been sought and found and controlled and plundered by pharaohs and kings and emperors and czars and pirates and whomever else had swords and power: Egyptians, Persians, Greeks, Romans, and, more close at hand, the Spanish in Mexico and Peru. But California in 1849 had no ruler, no governing authority, no institutions or property owners to claim possession of this most sought-after treasure. The world rushed in, free to find California's gold, to dig for it and to take it home—no license needed, no tax to be paid. Gold free for all, in an easily accessible terrain, in a benign climate with native people known for their peaceful ways. The wonder of California!

How different if "gold mines" had been discovered in France or Spain, in New Jersey or Illinois, in the middle of the nineteenth century. The news would have told of government authorities, soldiers, and landowners, all proclaiming "keep out." How different if discovered in Africa or South America where, if not governments to resist goldseekers, the climate and deserts and jungles and hostile natives would have projected a world image of danger and deprivation, in strong contrast to the image of California.

How could it be that California remained in the mid-nineteenth century so virginal, so unprepared to resist the onslaught of one hundred thousand strangers and many thousands more for years thereafter? The intriguing answer is found in the prologue of this book. For now, suffice to say that this image of unprotected gold, free for the taking, became the lure of California, reinforced and validated by eyewitness reports describing the first goldseekers' freedoms and successes during the year 1848, in a country newly acquired by war with Mexico and beyond the control of Washington's regulations and the rules of home.

And so it was that California in 1849 and for many years thereafter attracted an immigration unlike the westward settlement of previous centuries. Men from all regions of the nation left their families at home and set off for the distant land, promising to return, surely within a year. That was the central fact, the all-shaping influence—they would be separated from their mothers and wives and sisters and thereby freed from the moral authority that had ruled the societies of their fathers and grandfathers and, too, ruled the Oregon Territory. First settled in the 1830s and attractive through the 1840s to hundreds more pioneering families, this Pacific northwest territory offered land and thereby attracted and developed the traditional society—one dominated by families and the church.

In striking contrast, California would be a masculine society, free for several years from the authority of women and Sunday sermons.* A place not of settlement with the toil of cultivating new land but rather of immediate gain, sufficient to finance a better life back home: gold to pay off the mortgage on a farm in Indiana, to pay back money borrowed from a father-in-law in Baltimore, to provide escape from the subservience of being a younger brother in Massachusetts, to win the hand of a sweetheart in Georgia.

From San Francisco, from towns like Dutch Flat and French Corral, and from mining camps even more startling like Murderers' Bar and Timbuctoo, letters told of a new world where men made money, often astonishing sums of money, not only from digging for gold but—even more surprising—from businesses that would never be allowed in Michigan or Maryland: gambling "palaces," dance halls, tents where the proprietors sold liquor of all kinds, even on Sunday. And never mentioned, but implied and rumored—brothels. More comfortable came the news of big profits from more familiar businesses, like bathhouses, laundries, restaurants, boarding houses, mule packing, freighting, and lumber mills. Such reports of freedom and opportunity captured the attention of thousands of city men who had never before envisioned "going west." Lawyers and doctors, clerks and bakers, preachers and professors, even lighthouse keepers on the coast of Maine—greenhorns who had never fired a rifle, followed a plough, or cut down a tree—decided that the chances of striking it rich in California would be equally rewarding for the soft-handed as for the callused.

In an age when the discomforts, dangers, and expenses of travel confined all but a few Americans to live their lives in their counties and cities, the departure of scores of thousands of men could only be compared to a call to war. In 1849 the entire nation shared in the leave-takings, from barn yards and village squares, from riverside wharves and big-city docks. Newspaper editorials and Sunday sermons echoed the farewells. For the first time in the nation's history (only sixty years since 1789), a common, unifying interest competed with the regional differences that contradicted the concept of united states. The vast emigration of men and the even greater number of relatives left at home created a shared expectation and anxiety. In California's promise the people of Connecticut and Alabama felt a common bond.

---

* *Exemplary of the statistics that affirm the scarcity of women, the harbor master in San Francisco estimated that 599 women disembarked there during 1849 (and one can be certain that every female was counted at least once). This compared to more than 31,000 men who landed at that port during the same year. Comparable contrasts prevailed on the overland trails to California.*

Within hours of their last goodbyes, the men felt a new sense of themselves, a slipping free from the past, an escape from the authority of fathers and employers. For the first time in history (other than in times of war), thousands of men were released by mutual consent from their filial or other social obligations, set free to act entirely on their own responsibility. Day by day and especially at night, they felt more aware of the new world created by their California quest, surrounded by men cursing and carousing with an unexpected abandon, strangers who shared the same expectation and eventually would be competitors, maybe even before reaching El Dorado.

In giving their fervent promises to return, the men had assured their wives, parents, and friends that meantime letters would be sent whenever possible, describing what everyone knew would be a risky journey, whether by overland trails or sea routes. Received throughout the thirty states, these letters by the many thousands described the wide world as seen for the first time by hometown eyes. In times past, the wonders of the western wilderness had been reported in the publications of famous writers, like Washington Irving and Francis Parkman, and in the official reports of government explorers like John C. Frémont. Similarly, ocean voyages and foreign ports had been made known through the books of famed travelers. Beginning in 1849, New York farmers, Virginia planters, and Wisconsin brewers scrawled their own word pictures of encampments of Sioux and Pawnee, vast herds of buffalo, snowcapped mountains, and sterile deserts. These California-bound travelers were, in fact, the West's first tourists—eager to scratch their names on Chimney Rock, proud to boast of shooting a buffalo, quick to complain of irksome companions. And so it was with the thousands who journeyed by ship. Their letters and diaries told of the freezing blasts at Cape Horn or the fevered jungle trail across the Isthmus of Panama. Abroad in the world for the first time, these ordinary folk ventured ashore at Rio de Janeiro, Valparaíso, Callao, and Panama City, where like "ugly Americans" of a later century they often wrote with scorn of "lazy . . . cheating . . . backward" foreigners.

From foreign ports previously unknown to their families and from equally obscure western outposts on the trails to California, letters were sent home by the thousands. More than family connections and promises motivated this effort to communicate. The men and their families, indeed the entire nation from President Polk in Washington to editors of weekly newspapers in Arkansas, sensed the unfolding of a historic event that should be reported by its eyewitness participants. Because letters often could not be sent back, many travelers tried to keep diaries as records to be shared when their authors returned from the great experience. But unlike the letter writer who believed his efforts would be read in a few weeks, at most months, the diarist's reader was far more distant—many months, maybe a year or more. That sense of separation, of uncertainty, weakened their resolve, and many diarists gave up the tiresome task, which should make us all the more appreciative of the more than six hundred manuscript and published diaries of 1849 and the 1850s that somehow survived their long journeys and often casual care of later decades.

Certainly the diaries maintained were few in number compared to the letters sent back to the States. And equally certain, most of those letters have disappeared—maybe never delivered, probably thrown away, or (to be hoped) yet to be discovered. Whatever their fate, their total number is impressive. For example, the Pacific Mail Steamship Company's twice-monthly sailings from San Francisco bound for Panama City each carried a reported 40,000–45,000 letters. That would be at least 90,000 per month or 1,080,000 in a given year in the 1850s, most of them addressed to relatives in the States.

As California became an ever more familiar yet exceptional place, a sense of curiosity, even envy spread across the nation and around the world. The following excerpt from a June 1850 letter—written by a young, unmarried woman in Plainfield, Illinois, to her father in California—suggests how news from that new world nurtured impatience with the predictability and limitations of life in that town, as in many others:

> We have no news of much importance. The dull monotony is seldom interrupted. Everything passes along in the old routine. No weddings— nothing. It was with the greatest reluctance I gave up the idea of going to California. . . . I should have liked a few thousand of its glittering ore. Plainfield looks lonely, very. And all its young men, nearly, have started for your El Dorado.*

That attraction held strong through the 1850s and the decades beyond. In 1854 the number of passengers landing at San Francisco totaled 64,000, despite the surfeit of bad news from mining camps, cities, and small towns: news of miners by the thousands in debt, among them many giving up and heading for San Francisco to seek passage home. Too few mining claims available for old-timers, much less for newcomers. Murders, vigilance-committee hangings, and bank failures. Floods and fires (Marysville burned six times in the years 1851–56). Disappointment and disaster seemed to dominate the news from the thirty-first state. Like Gresham's Law, bad news drove out good. Then as now.

---

* *Isaac Foster,* The Foster Family, California Pioneers, *ed. Lucy Foster Sexton (Santa Barbara, 1925), 82–83.*

Competing with this drama of disorder, letters (and books) described California as constantly changing—an appealing contrast to Connecticut and Illinois. Written in 1851, a letter sent back to Ohio by an ex-miner projected California's ever more alluring image: "The independence and liberality here and the excitement attending the rapid march of this country make one feel insignificant and sad at the prospect of returning to the old beaten paths of home."*

There it was, why so many thousands could not keep their promise to return, why so many in the States felt impatient to pursue their luck in that tumultuous arena. Where else had luck favored so many ordinary folk? Where else could a boarding house or a freight wagon produce more— much more—than a living?

But it was more than the hope for money. California offered a chance to break free, a new kind of freedom—where a man could take risks and fail and not feel a failure, not feel ashamed, certainly not feel "different" or an outcast. In the mining regions and the transient, careless world of San Francisco and lesser towns, amid drunkenness and despair, even suicide, failure was commonplace, almost a given, a part of the way of life, of the process of seeking success. In mining (and at some time everyone tried mining), you failed each day you failed to strike it rich, each time you gave up a claim and sought another. Each time a merchant's debtors disappeared. Each time an unexpected shipment of liquors undercut the value of the shipment purchased yesterday. Unlike home, the loss of money here could be offset by new opportunities, easy credit, offers of partnerships. Reports heard in gambling halls and boarding houses told of as many successes as failures: the string of pack mules that earned $6,000 on one trip to the isolated mining camps along the Mokelumne River, the toll bridge opened at Downieville that collected big profits its first month. California: world of risk-taking.

Possibly no one expressed the power of this psychology better than California's first economic historian, J. S. Hittell, who in 1863 offered this assessment:

> The business of California is conducted boldly. Men make money rapidly, spend it freely and hastily. Changes in occupations are frequent and in wealth rapid. Hazardous speculation is the body of our commercial system. Most of our businessmen are young, and they are still under the influence of the feverish times of '49. Hereditary wealth is unknown. Our rich men all came to California poor, and they are prominent advertise-

---

* *Manuscript letter by Charles Plummer, March 14, 1851, in the Huntington Library, San Marino, California.*

ments of the victories that may be achieved by enterprise and bold speculation. . . . It is no uncommon thing to see men who have been wealthy
on three or four occasions and then poor again. . . . When men fail, they
do not despair . . . they hope to be rich again.*

There it was, another affirmation of freedom and opportunity, rewards for
risk-takers, optimism in the face of failure, in a society unlike any other, this
time heralded in 1863, only fourteen years after Mexico lost its fragile hold
on what had been a sparsely settled, backward, peripheral province. What a
transformation. I think we forget the rapidity, the uniqueness of this state's
progress. Consider these fundamental characteristics, created and shaped
by the impact of the gold rush.

Urban. Unlike all previous frontiers, California's rapidly expanding
population built towns, soon to be cities—first San Francisco, which immediately boomed to the stature of a world trade center with prosperous manufacturing and cultural attainments. A population of 115,000 by 1863. And
the state's second city, Sacramento, thrived as the transport hub for receiving thousands of tons of everything from shirts to nails, champagne to pickaxes, delivered by steamers overnight from San Francisco up the Sacramento
River for transshipment by hundreds of freight wagons to the many towns
in the Sierra foothills and from there by pack mules to more distant mining
camps. In sum, an urban society, economy, and culture—in sharp contrast to
the traditional gradual evolution of scattered settlement along an extended
frontier.

And affluent, most remarkable. Within a few years more wealth per
capita than any other state or nation. During the decade of the 1850s, mining produced gold worth $594 million ($1.2 billion in today's dollars).
While most of that gold was removed from California, to the East Coast
and around the world, many millions circulated through the state's economy, as innovative technology and engineering skills extracted more treasure from the tortured landscape.

And a unique society, at first dominantly masculine. By 1860 the population statewide was 72 percent male, in many counties still 90 percent. The
transient men lived in hotels and boarding houses, free to drink and gamble
and otherwise indulge an exceptional life while sensing their freedom of
anonymity would be temporary, given that everyone knew, in time, they
would return "home," or that wives and mothers and young women would
arrive in numbers sufficient to reform California's carelessness. More important, the state's population from the outset was marked by a degree of diversity

---

* *J. S. Hittell*, The Resources of California *(San Francisco: A. Roman, 1863)*,
333–34.

far greater than any other, with scores of thousands arriving from all the eastern states and from Europe, Latin America, and Asia. Where else did men from New Hampshire and Louisiana, from Wisconsin and Texas stand side by side at a liquor bar; Chinese and Irish compete for the same jobs; men from France gamble with men from Chile? The world rushed in, creating a global society one hundred and more years before that concept was conceived.

And consider another dimension of California as "the great exception" (Carey McWilliams's phrase). From their very first plantings, farmers raised their crops for the purpose of selling to the nearby urban markets, where the demand and affluence yielded astonishing prices. This surplus-crop economy was in striking contrast to the tradition of subsistence agriculture that had characterized and prevailed for many years on previous frontiers. As early as the mid-1850s farms, orchards, and wheat ranches produced enough to supply California's demand, and by 1873 wheat exports to Liverpool, England, totaled 29 million bushels. Similar progress marked the advance of manufacturers.

All this derived rapidly, carelessly, wastefully, often cruelly from the attraction and production of gold, that much-sought commodity without any utilitarian value. Yes, far more than gold made it all possible, but as Carey McWilliams asserts: "Examine any phase of California's life— agriculture, labor, government, industry, social organization—and the examination inevitably involved some consideration of the gold rush."

I hope this preface reaffirms McWilliam's judgment—and more, that the diaries and letters of those genetic years translated a personal into a national experience. Like the Civil War, the California gold rush deserves to be a vivid part of our shared sense of America.

■

As the person through whom the reader of this book will relive the cycle of the gold rush—leave home, travel to a distant land, experience a new life, return a changed man (as in a war)—William Swain will prove to be an admirable alter ego. As I came to know him—first through his personal records and my talks with his daughter, later through relatives and in years to come by comparing him to hundreds of other goldseekers revealed through their diaries and letters—I felt ever more admiring of his discipline and self-restraint, though I must admit that as a writer, I did hope on many an occasion that William would succumb to temptation and join so many others in the gambling dens, dance halls, and other "lewd" places. But no, he never deviated from his prescribed course and returned to Sabrina the truly good man he had always been.

I first read William Swain's diary in February 1948. Eminent New York book dealer Ed Eberstadt and I were standing in a vaulted room of the Yale University Library surrounded by stacks, crates, and shelves of books, manuscripts, and maps that made up the William R. Coe Collection, then not yet cataloged. From this vast gathering of personal and government records of the exploration and settlement of the American West, Ed selected two leather-bound notebooks. He handed them to me and with his inimitable ability to dramatize, declared that I held the most graphic and literate—"most important"—diary of the many written by the men who rushed to California in 1849.

I turned a few pages and read aloud several entries. Ed commented on the quality of language; I marveled that the one-hundred-year-old diary had survived in what seemed almost perfect condition. On most pages the hand-writing, in brown ink, was legible, with only here and there a smudge or blot, each day's entry boldly dated. When I found a page dense with lines neatly crowded together, I could imagine the writer by an evening campfire carefully recording that day's events. On other pages the writing scrawled carelessly across the narrow space, and I thought of him weary and hurried, with only a few moments to spare for his record.

Ed told me he had met William Swain's surviving daughter, Sara, in Youngstown, New York, in 1938. She had proudly preserved her father's gold rush diary and the letters he had sent home during his two-year odyssey. Eberstadt persuaded her to sell these treasures by promising to publish them. Well acquainted with the diaries published up to that time, he believed the Swain record would make an important contribution to the history of the American West.

During the remainder of that afternoon we looked at a score or more gold rush diaries, published and manuscript, none of which, Ed assured me, had the human appeal, the quality of language, and the descriptive detail that distinguished the William Swain diary.

That evening at dinner, Ed told me of his hopes for the Swain diary, hopes unfulfilled because of the press of his business and his ill health. He asked if I would take up the task of preparing the diary for publication. At first surprised, I realized that had been his plan all along.

I had just graduated from Yale, with a major in history. For me to write history seemed outlandish—but for Ed's sake, I agreed to make a start. I went to work in the Coe Collection, first reading (two or three times)

Swain's diary and letters. I did not appreciate Ed's judgment of them until I had spent several months studying all the other gold rush records collected there. Many of them offered little more than daily recitations of miles traveled and weather conditions, with an occasional complaint or observation about food, dust, or some other discomfort. Nonetheless, I took notes from each, searching for arcane details, informative observations, vivid descriptions, and poignant personal revelations. I read the histories of California and of the gold rush by Bancroft and more modern historians. Week by week I knew that the book I wanted to create would differ in style and scope from what Ed had envisioned; and would differ, as well, from the established tradition of scholarly editing of historical documents. By that tradition I would be confined to reproducing Swain's diary and letters word for word as they appeared in those two notebooks—and that would be all, except for footnotes to clarify confusions and make corrections of Swain's mistakes, grammatical or substantive. I had read several diaries brilliantly edited for publication, with scores of footnotes that explained what the diarist had left out. But in each case, despite the work of the editor, the reader was restricted to experiencing only as much of the gold rush story as the diarist felt like writing—perhaps he was sick or just too weary to write more than cursory entries for days, even weeks; perhaps on reaching California he gave up his diary, as was the case with most goldseekers.

Unlike so many others, Swain as diarist and letter writer was remarkably disciplined and descriptive. During the overland journey he wrote in his diary every day (except for a three-day illness) and sent letters home whenever possible. Then after a blizzard in the Sierra Nevada forced him to end his diary, he wrote lengthy letters throughout his months in California, even continuing to write during his return voyage. In all, his record is so inclusive, so complete, as to be a rarity among the hundreds of eyewitness accounts, published and manuscript, that tell the gold rush story.

I wanted my book to reach beyond Swain, to create a record more descriptive of each day's happenings, more fully reflective of the total gold rush experience than any one person—even Swain—could have written: a book that would be an authentic, vicarious experience for the modern reader. When Swain, inevitably, wrote brief or repetitive entries, when he concentrated on himself to the exclusion of the larger scene around him, I would quote other diarists and letter writers who were at the same place, at the same time, who wrote more descriptively, observantly, and factually; I would use their accounts to enrich and balance the Swain record.

Building on Swain, I envisioned a book that would encompass the total experience—the cycle of the gold rush, from leaving home to returning home. Swain's diary would tell of the overland journey, his letters from California would describe life in the mining camps, and his final letters would allow me to develop the dramatic conclusion so long ignored: the return of tens of thousands of goldseekers to their homes back in the States.

From Yale I went to other major libraries in the East, to read every available diary and letter of 1849 and 1850, the climax years of the rush to California. By spring of 1949 I was ready to take my search to the Midwest, but first I wanted to talk with Miss Sara Swain, to learn all I could about her father. She was still living in Youngstown. Eighty-nine years old, a retired schoolteacher, never married, she was a lady with zest, humor, and a great interest in my expanding plans for publication of her father's diary and letters. She answered my questions in abundant detail. She gave me genealogical documents and other records and photographs.

To my most important question—Had her father brought back any of the letters sent to him by his wife Sabrina and brother George?—she told me that she had them all but felt they were too personal for publication. I begged to see them, several still in their envelopes, simply addressed: "William Swain, Fort Sutter's, On American River, California."

Rich in the formal language and emotions of mid-nineteenth-century America, filled with the daily details of childrearing and farm chores typical of thousands of families whose men had gone to California, the letters revealed as well the longings and anxieties of a wife—a "California widow"—waiting for her husband to return.

I had to have those letters. But Miss Swain stubbornly held to her conviction that publication would violate her sense of family privacy. I knew better than to press too hard. Months passed. I wrote to her and telephoned. I visited her again in October 1949, not to persuade but to share with her my progress and my great hopes for her father's story. We met for the last time in January of 1950—and as she presented the treasured letters, she gave me a pat of encouragement and a smile to cover her regret that she would not see our book.

The Swain family letters represented a major discovery: they opened a new dimension to the gold rush story—the back-home drama of thousands of families waiting and worrying, like families in wartime. Through Sabrina and George's letters I could create a more complete view of the gold rush, not only of the tens of thousands of men on the overland trails and in the mining camps and cities of California but also their families on farms and in villages and cities in all the thirty states—the gold rush as a profound national experience that changed America's awareness and expectations of the West.

For families in the town of Marshall in south-central Michigan, those expectations centered on the return of sons and husbands who had gone to California as members of a company called the Wolverine Rangers. William Swain and his three companions from Youngstown joined that company of fifty-eight men in spring 1849 and traveled all the way to the Sacramento Valley with them. Therefore, I went to Marshall and surrounding towns one summer to search for diaries and letters written by the Rangers. I found some of their letters and a diary—not in attics and old desks, but on the pages of the *Marshall Statesman*, a newspaper published daily in 1849 and the early 1850s. I read informative letters sent home by young men named Horace Ladd, Herman Camp, and James Pratt, all Swain's companions. Pratt had been the editor of the *Statesman* prior to leaving for California, and, as a good newspaperman, he sent back not only letters but also extensive excerpts from his vividly written diary.

Encouraged by these discoveries, I sought other local newspapers, the *Detroit Daily Advertiser* and the *Marshall Democratic Expounder*, where I found more letters by Wolverine Rangers and by other goldseekers from Michigan, describing life on the overland trail and in the mining camps and cities of California.

With Pratt's letters and diary, the letters of other Rangers, and Swain's diary and letters, I had a more complete records of a gold rush company than had ever been found—and I realized that my ambition to create the most authentic eyewitness account of the entire gold rush could be achieved.

From the Rangers I took descriptions and specific information to augment and expand Swain's daily record. For instance, when Camp recorded in greater detail the excitement and dangers of a buffalo hunt, when Ladd described the Rangers' elaborate celebration of the Fourth of July in the wilds of present-date Wyoming, when Pratt reported the success and failure of Rangers in the mining camps and cities of California, I selected the best sentences or paragraphs and, with connecting phrases, blended them into Swain's diary and letters on the appropriate date.

In applying this technique of interpolation, I pursued my search in libraries, historical societies, and here and there an attic, looking for the diaries and letters and newspaper accounts written by men whose experiences paralleled Swain's. Often my hours of reading the scrawl of manuscript diaries or hundreds of pages of newspaper on microfilm revealed only a sentence or two of value to me. But if that sentence enlivened or illuminated a weak or obscure passage in Swain, if it filled in what he had left out, if it looked beyond his view to reveal a broader scene, I was willing to keep on prospecting.

As the years passed, I selected from hundreds of diaries and letters the most intimate and revealing statements about goldseekers' moods and conditions of life on the trail, in the mines, in San Francisco, and on the voyage home. Hundreds of these excerpts were added to the Swain diary and letters, as extensions of his sentences or as new paragraphs.

Exact rules and standards were established and applied. Each interpolation had to come from a diarist or letter writer who wrote what Swain himself might have seen, experienced, or been told. To make certain that the reader would always know exactly what had been added, each of these interpolations was set apart from Swain by brackets and quotation marks, identified in the notes with its original source.

In the course of my searching, it seemed at times that fate was with me. Not only did I find the writings of Swain's companions, the Rangers, I found two prolific diarists (Lord and Bruff) who traveled for weeks within a few days of the Rangers and often mentioned them; and several others (including Lord again and Delano and Baker) who mined on the South Fork of the Feather River near Swain's claim; and one (Batchelder) who traveled at the same time as Swain when he gave up mining to go to San Francisco. As well, one of the Wolverine Rangers, Oliver Goldsmith, published a book about his experiences. Though he wrote from memory, I used Goldsmith occasionally because I had so much evidence to corroborate his statements.

My good luck was reinforced by Ed Eberstadt. In 1956, two years before he died, he called me in Berkeley, where I was a graduate student at the University of California. He asked how I was progressing on the book and then told me he had purchased a manuscript diary by a man named Middleton who had traveled much of the overland trail close to the Rangers and sometimes actually camped with them. Middleton's diary provided a number of important interpolations for both Swain's overland account and his life in California.

By the 1970s my manuscript had become more an encyclopedia than a readable narrative. I had not only added to Swain more than eight hundred reinforcing, enriching, clarifying, augmenting, and tangential interpolations, I had developed a complex system of footnotes as well as notes for the back of the book; and, too, an array of commentaries for the back, on every subject I thought might need elaboration or explanation—in sum, what amounted to a psychological effort to justify how and why I had spent so many years on "the book." Friends who criticized the massive manuscript warned me that I had burdened even the most dedicated reader with far more than anyone would ever want to know, much less read.

And so I began a long process of cutting, pruning, and simplifying. First, I eliminated years of footnotes and commentaries, reducing those that survived to a necessary, publishable many. A few commentaries refused to succumb—and I swear they are of immense value! And then came the more painful task of selecting the interpolations to be removed—sentences, paragraphs, entire pages, by the score, that had required months, even years to find and to weave into their exact place in the narrative. After major surgeries, I completed the restructuring in 1980.

In its final form the book's first nine chapters tell the story of the overland journey based on Swain's diary, April to November 1849. During the first weeks of the trip Swain wrote a number of letters to his wife and brother. These letters appear chronologically with the diary entries. Inevitably, diary and letters sometimes described the same scenes and circumstances and reflected the same feelings. When a diary entry told the story best, I cut out the duplicative sentences or paragraph(s) in the letter. When a letter told it best, I excised the equivalent portion of the diary. Occasionally, to advance the narrative more smoothly, I substituted a portion of a letter for part of that day's diary entry.

Chapters 10, 11, and 12 tell what happened in California from November 1849 to November 1850. The structure and tempo change from the discipline of Swain's day-to-day reporting to the more personal tone of letters to Sabrina and George, letters that tell of life in the mining camps and of his changing moods and expectations. Supporting Swain, woven into his letters, are the observations, descriptions and commentaries of scores of other miners.

The return from California, November 1850 to February 1851, is recounted in chapter 13, based on six letters by Swain. Because these letters are limited in their information, they required substantial interpolation. Recreating the experience of crossing the Isthmus of Panama proved to be a major challenge. Most goldseekers could not be bothered to write inasmuch as they expected to be home in a few weeks. However, I was able to find several remarkably graphic diaries and other reports written at the time of Swain's return. These enabled me to re-create the heretofore unpublished story of what the goldseekers experienced on their homeward journey.

Although it took many years of research to find exactly the quotations I needed to strengthen Swain, I knew from the start that the letters Sabrina and George sent to William could stand alone as a unique record of a family waiting for their man to return. These letters, edited in accordance to the standards set forth below, are gathered in chronological order at the end of each chapter, under the heading "Back Home."

Throughout the book, the following editorial standards have been applied:

1. All interpolations are set off by brackets and quotation marks, with the source of each identified in the notes.

2. All spelling, including geographic and scientific names, has been modernized. Swain spelled many words differently each time he used them—sometimes close to correct, other times so imaginatively as to require bracketed corrections. Spelling for all interpolations has also been modernized.

3. Correct punctuation and logical paragraphing have been provided throughout.

4. I have revised and untangled sentences where necessary for logic, clarity, and consistency. I have gathered in proper sequence sentences that were originally scattered but relate to the same subject, and I have deleted all sentences (occasionally paragraphs) that are repetitive or otherwise confuse or retard the narrative flow.

Additional commentary and explanation as to editorial method are provided as required within the text and notes.

Carmel, April 2002
San Francisco, May 1981

The World Rushed In

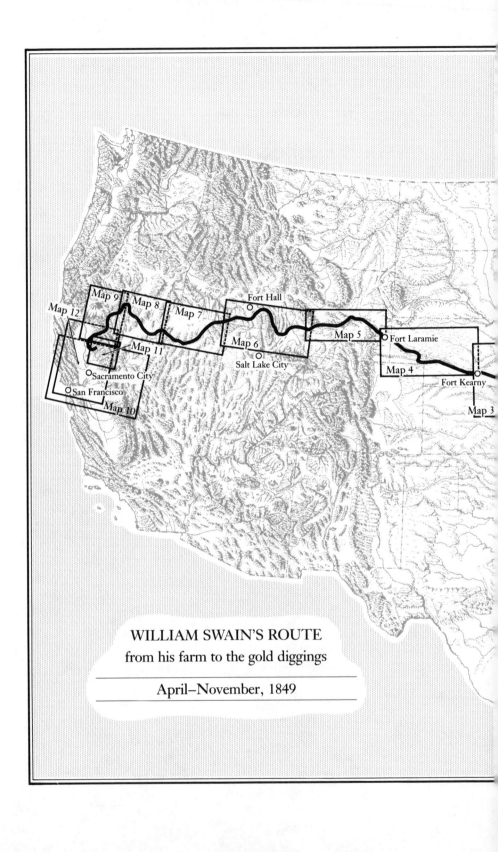

Fort Hall

Map 9 Map 8 Map 7

Map 12

Map 5 Fort Laramie

Map 6

Salt Lake City

Map 4

Fort Kearny

Map 11

Sacramento City

Map 3

San Francisco

Map 10

WILLIAM SWAIN'S ROUTE
from his farm to the gold diggings

April–November, 1849

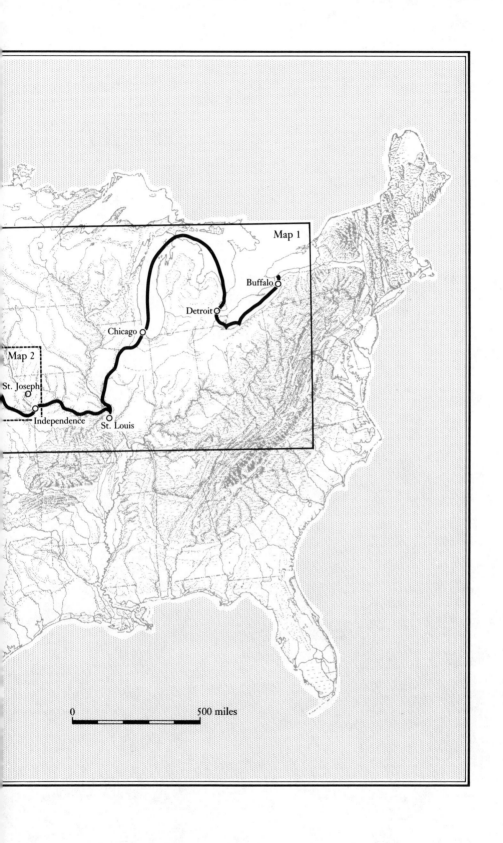

Map 1

Buffalo

Detroit

Chicago

Map 2

St. Joseph

Independence

St. Louis

0   500 miles

Prologue

*"How long the gathering of gold by the
handful will continue here and the future
effects it will have on California, I cannot
say. . . . A complete revolution in the ordinary state of affairs is taking
place. . . ."*

After two years of war, the United States and Mexico on February 2,
1848, signed a treaty which ceded to the victor the vast expanse west from
Texas and north to Oregon. With this territorial acquisition, President
Polk achieved for his country its Manifest Destiny—one nation from
Atlantic to Pacific.

Nine days before the treaty signing, a native of New Jersey, a carpenter named James Marshall, chanced to find several pieces of gold at a
place called Coloma, in what was yet Mexican California. His discovery
the morning of January 24, 1848, might have been made at some far
earlier date by one of the Spanish explorer-looters who had found gold
from Aztec to Inca cities and searched the continents for more. Or Mexican soldiers in pursuit of Indians might have uncovered the first nugget
and thus have provided Mexico City the means and the will to resist
Yankee expansion. Instead, California's gold remained hidden through
seven decades of Spanish and Mexican rule, a historical irony and a
testament to Yankee luck. Some Protestant preachers proclaimed the discovery to be the work of God, who had hidden the gold as long as Popery
—the Catholics—held sway over California.

That gold should be found in a place so difficult to reach by land or
by sea was foretold in 1510 when a romantic novel published in Seville
described "an island called California very close to the Terrestrial Paradise." Ruled by an Amazon queen named Calafia, "the island everywhere
abounds with gold and precious stones and upon it no other metal is
found." The faraway land stirred Spanish imagination. Fiction seemed
more like fact when Cortez, following his conquest of the Aztecs in 1521,
wrote of an island northwest of Mexico which he called California. But

the fable did not come true until by God's design, destiny or luck, a few gold specks caught the eye of the American carpenter—who worked for John Sutter, native of Switzerland, Mexican citizen, a man whose ambitious plans for an agricultural empire would be destroyed by the gold found on his land.

Everything about California would change. In one astonishing year the place would be transformed from obscurity to world prominence, from an agricultural frontier that attracted 400 settlers in 1848 to a mining frontier that lured 90,000 impatient men in 1849; from a society of neighbors and families to one of strangers and transients; from an ox-cart economy based on hides and tallow to a complex economy based on gold mining; from Catholic to Protestant, from Latin to Anglo-Saxon. The impact of that new California would be profound on the nation it had so recently joined.

But nothing about the old California, except the fable of Queen Calafia, vaguely hinted at its future. Reports of the first Spanish explorers told of a bleak coastline with natives so primitive as to have no knowledge of gold. After 1602, exploration ceased. California remained Spanish only by the work of royal mapmakers who often showed it as an island.

One hundred and sixty-seven years later, Spanish interest revived, not in hope of gold but from fear of Russian expansion south from Alaska. To thwart that presumed threat, the viceroy in Mexico City determined to create an outpost of empire on the California coast. In 1769–70 a sickly expedition built a mission and a presidio, frail structures, at both San Diego and Monterey. To Christianize and control the Indians, the vice-regal government in 1771 sent ten Franciscan priests and sixty soldiers; that same year three new missions were established. Thus Spain sought to colonize California—at the very time England's colonies on the Atlantic Coast were beginning their struggle to break free.

More than missionary zeal and courage, California needed colonists. But a far frontier without prospect of gold held little attraction for the citizens of Mexico. With few exceptions, only the most miserable and ignorant from city streets could be induced to emigrate. To augment the policy of shipping "idle, undesirable people," convicts from Mexican jails were exiled to California. Most of the soldiers conscripted for the protection of the expanding mission system were drunkards, assorted criminals and deserters from the regular army. Faced with such colonists to intermarry with the Christianized Indians and such soldiers to protect and control the Indians living at the missions, the head of the Franciscan padres, Junipero Serra, begged the government "not to look upon California and its missions as the China of exile. . . . Being sent to our missions should not be a form of banishment, nor should our missions be filled with worthless people who serve no purpose but to commit evil deeds."

Toward the end of the century, the feeble hold that Spain had placed on California earned the scorn of a British sea captain, George Vancouver, who sailed along the coast and visited several presidios in the 1790s. In his report he noted that "should any civilized nation" have the ambition to seize California, the Spanish military "could not make the least resistance." The weakness he observed forecast the collapse of Spain's New World empire, not from the ambition of her imperial enemies, France, England and Russia, but because of internal disruption. From 1808 into the 1820s, Spain's colonies were in revolt, with Mexico gaining independence in 1821.

California drifted through those years of turmoil so isolated that little was known of political affairs in faraway Mexico City. In 1822 the province quietly came under the rule of the new Mexican government. Relations with the capital changed little from Spanish days. For most Mexicans, "to speak of California was like mentioning the end of the world." And so the policy of exporting convicts as colonists continued. Called *cholos* (rascals or mongrels) by Californios, the thieves and political prisoners settled in the towns of Los Angeles and San Jose and in the villages attached to the presidios. Their brawling, drunkenness, gambling and abuse of Indians gave those places a rough character.

During the Mexican period, 1822–46, the policy that had the most profound effect on California was the secularization of the twenty-one Franciscan missions, a process by which millions of acres of land and herds of livestock were to be allotted to the Indian converts, with the Franciscan padres reduced to curates of the parish churches. Given the wealth to be distributed, the pitiful unpreparedness of the Indians to manage their own affairs and the political rivalries in Mexico and California which produced a succession of bickering governors, it was inevitable that the vast holding of the missions should end up not in the ownership of the Indians but sold, leased or granted to retired soldiers, government officials and anyone else with the right connections. By the mid-1840s, 8 million acres of mission lands and the authority of the Franciscans had been transferred to some 800 families who made up the new social order. They lived on ranchos, some of them encompassing more than 250,000 acres, where their cattle grazed unfenced over quiet valleys and rolling hills.

For the mission Indians who had been ruled for decades by the Franciscan padres, the breakup of the mission system was disastrous. Dispossessed of land that was supposedly theirs, unready for their homeless freedom, they were demoralized by liquor and violence, with large numbers of them exploited as servants of townspeople and rancheros. They suffered as well from white men's diseases, especially syphilis, which had spread as an epidemic for years within the missions and beyond to the unconverted Indians. By the late 1830s the missionized Indians had declined to fewer than 4,000 from an estimated 30,000 in 1820.

A new California evolved, a pastoral society of large families living on vast ranchos, far from their neighbors. Blessed with a comfortable climate, plenty of land and cheap Indian labor, the ranchero, patriarch of his realm, enjoyed a good life, celebrated in history and legend as a "pastoral Arcadia." A household might include nineteen or even twenty-nine children, plus a number of poor relatives and transient strangers enjoying unstinted hospitality, all supported by Indian servants grinding corn for tortillas, serving in the kitchen, washing clothes and sewing or spinning. One rancho had 600 Indians as servants and field hands.

Through the years of rule by Mexico, California remained an isolated and neglected province. Political turmoil in Mexico City reflected the instability and poverty of the new nation. By the 1840s the United States government feared that England or France might easily take control of the Pacific province, or that a Mexican president might decide to cede California to England in payment of long-overdue debts. In October 1842 a bizarre episode proved how easily California might be captured.

To keep watch on English and French naval vessels in Pacific waters not far from California, Washington sent Commodore Thomas Ap Catesby Jones (Welsh ancestry) to take command of the U.S. Pacific squadron. Well aware that critical relations between Mexico and the United States might lead to war, Commodore Jones feared that the British fleet might use such a crisis as an opportunity to seize defenseless California. When the commodore received intelligence that his country was at war with Mexico, he sailed two of his warships into Monterey Bay and landed 150 marines without encountering any resistance. He hauled down the Mexican flag and ran up the Stars and Stripes over the capital village. The next day he learned there was no war; peace prevailed. The commodore lowered the U.S. flag, graciously apologized to the Mexican officials, fired a salute to the Republic of Mexico and exchanged official visits of courtesy. Later he reported that "no angry words or unkind expressions have been used by either party." The American warships sailed away, having found in Monterey evidence of the Arcadian simplicity of the Californios.

From the time of the first Spanish settlements and later under Mexican rule, California's colonists lived along the coast and in the coastal valleys. In a land so broad, with so few people (non-Indian population 2,000 in 1810 and 6,000 by 1840), there was no need to push inland, to explore the great Sacramento and San Joaquin valleys or to probe the foothills of the Sierra Nevada. Spanish military forays had chased Indians who escaped from the missions and fled eastward, but the pursuers found nothing more than a vast open country—oak groves, tule swamps, and primitive aborigines. No gleam of gold, no reason to think there might be treasure in the crude villages.

The coast held the colonists as well because casually enforced Mexican import regulations allowed greatly increased trade with foreigners whose ships, some from England, most from Boston, brought necessities and luxuries to a country that produced only simple clothes from cowhides and rough cloth and a few other handcrafted products. Everything else, all manufactured goods, was imported—boots and shoes, tools and agricultural implements, bright cloth and jewelry, coffee and tobacco, mirrors and furniture, wine and brandy. For all this, so welcome on that crude frontier, the Californios could pay with the one product they had in abundance—cowhides. From the vast pastures where thousands of animals grazed without restraint, the vaqueros rounded up those to be slaughtered, and the hides, crudely cleaned and dried, were squeezed into ships' holds (as many as 40,000 to 50,000 in a single vessel) for the voyage around Cape Horn to Boston, there to be cured as leather. A year or so later, Boston-manufactured shoes and boots tempted the Californios when displayed in the harbors and coves north from San Diego to San Francisco.

The imports from this trade eased the isolation and roughness of life in California. More important, the trade brought to this remote shore Britishers and Yankees with skills and education unknown to the Californios. Sea captains, shipping agents, representatives of trading companies and sailors received land grants, prospered and became influential in the affairs of the province. By 1840 these foreign residents numbered 380, including Americans, who swore allegiance to Mexico, adopted Catholicism and married into prominent families. Abel Stearns won the hand of Doña Arcadia Bandini and in time acquired several ranchos totaling 200 square miles. David Spence through his marriage into the Estrada family gained 25,000 acres and 4,000 head of cattle. Henry Fitch and his wife, Josefa Carrillo, owned 14,000 cattle and 10,000 sheep. These maritime settlers belonged to a way of life soon to be swept aside.

Far more important to California's frantic future, there came into the Sacramento Valley late in the fall of 1841 a party of overland emigrants from Missouri and other western states. Frontiersmen, farmers, they were the kind of people who had moved America westward from Virginia to the Missouri River. Setting out from Independence, Missouri, in the spring, they had found their way through the wilderness of deserts and mountains by following trails opened in the 1830s by fur trappers ("those men who made the unknown known"). Though it had taken this first overland party six months to make the journey, they had survived—the first of hundreds of land-seeking American pioneers who would follow their route along the Humboldt River to the passes through the Sierra Nevada and down to the warmth of the Sacramento Valley. After 1841 this route would be known as the California Trail.

Though California was not as well publicized through the 1840s nor as much a part of the nation's political rhetoric as Oregon (that territory attracted 11,500 Americans by 1848), the Mexican province had its boosters. They were visitors who wrote in praise of the mild, healthful climate, the fruits and vegetables, the "horses that retain their vigor past thirty years." Despite their enthusiasm, these Yankees could not hide their morality and nationalism when they came to describe the Californios: "Miserable people who sleep and smoke and hum some tune of Castilian laziness, while surrounding Nature is inviting them to the noblest and richest rewards of honorable toil."

The most popular account of California, Richard Henry Dana's *Two Years Before the Mast*, was published in 1840. A sailor on a Boston ship that traded for hides along the coast in 1835 and '36, Dana described how the trade was managed and told of the Californios, their character and society. He reflected America's sense of superiority and a feeling for the special mystique of California: "In the hands of an enterprising people, what a country this might be! Yet, how long would a people remain so in such a country? If the 'California fever,' laziness, spares the first generation, it is likely to attack the second."

Whatever its appeal, a place of agricultural wealth or a country ready for Yankee know-how, California attracted 2,700 overland emigrants between 1841 and 1848.

Through the decade of the '40s, before the world rushed in, the American farmers who settled in the Sacramento and San Joaquin valleys pursued farming and hunting and animal husbandry. Unlike the maritime Americans who converted to Catholicism, became Mexican citizens and merged into the Californios' society, the valley folk kept largely to themselves, isolated from the Mexican government at Monterey. While they developed their primitive agriculture, the rancheros expanded their herds of cattle and the hide trade. The missions, sorry reminders of Spain, crumbled, ravaged by neglect and theft. The "tamed" Indians sank ever deeper into economic dependence, while their wild brethren remained free of the white man though devastated by his diseases. In the villages and towns from San Diego, Los Angeles and Santa Barbara in the south to Monterey, Yerba Buena (later renamed San Francisco) and Sonoma in the north, the number and influence of foreigners, especially Americans, increased year by year.

The quiet and ease of California were dramatically interrupted in the summer of 1846. Motivated by their fear that the Mexican government was going to evict them from land they occupied without title, encouraged by the presence of John C. Frémont and his semimilitary band of Topographical Engineers, the American settlers in the valley staged what they called the Bear Flag Revolt. They captured the town of Sonoma and declared California a republic; but before their impulse and ambition could lead them they knew not where, news reached California that the United States had declared war on Mexico.

The U.S. Pacific squadron was once again in coastal waters in anticipation of war. On July 7, 1846, the flagship *Savannah* entered Monterey harbor, 250 men landed, the flag was raised, and American occupation was announced.

With the Republic of California put out of business by this more impressive action, the Bear Flaggers enlisted in the United States Army, Frémont received a commission as a major, and the conquest of California proceeded. By mid-August the province was declared entirely free from Mexican dominion.

Though the Californios in Los Angeles revolted against this presumed conquest, peace and quiet returned to all of California in January 1847. Meantime, a more serious war continued in Mexico, ending with the American occupation of Mexico City and the treaty of peace signed February 2, 1848.

While waiting to become a legitimate part of the United States, California was ruled by a series of military governors. During 1847, the last year before gold finally took charge, California drowsed along at its old tempo. However, two places changed and grew rapidly, as if preparing for their central roles in the next year's drama—Yerba Buena on the shores of San Francisco bay and Sutter's ranch on the banks of the American River in the Sacramento Valley.

After years as a scruffy village of adobe huts, one store and a few tents where hide traders and whalers did some business, Yerba Buena gained a sudden population boost when a ship from New York, via Cape Horn, dropped anchor in July 1846. Two hundred and thirty-eight Mormon men, women and children came ashore under the leadership of a printer named Sam Brannan. They had sailed from the East Coast hoping to find in California a haven from American persecution, possibly a place to which Brigham Young could bring the other Saints. Faced with the unwelcome news that California was under United States rule, Brannan sent some of his men into the Sacramento Valley (where they settled near Sutter's ranch), while the others took shelter in the Mexican custom house or shivered in tents. In January 1847, the alcalde (an elected position that combined the duties of mayor, judge, lawyer and marshal) renamed the town San Francisco. He also authorized a plan with streets to be laid out American-style, intersecting at right angles. That same month Sam Brannan started printing a newspaper, the *California Star*. By the end of 1847 San Francisco had 200 buildings and 800 inhabitants—one year later it would be the great metropolis of the Pacific coast.

Out in the valley, John A. Sutter ruled over a prospering ranch. He had landed at Monterey in 1839 and within a year had applied for Mexican citizenship and received a land grant of nearly 50,000 acres in two parcels, one at the junction of the American and Sacramento rivers, another to the north along the Feather River—names soon to be familiar to thousands of gold miners. Near the south bank of the American, on a knoll high enough to stand free from floods, Sutter built an adobe-walled fort to control the surrounding land, all of which he called New Helvetia, a place to which he would bring colonists from his home country. Furthermore, the Mexican governor appointed Sutter alcalde for the entire Sacramento Valley.

In January 1848, the fort with its dozen cannons overlooked fields cultivated and ditched by Indians in Sutter's employ, a ten-acre garden, horses, cattle and sheep, and a nearby river landing where Sutter's sloop was tied up when not sailing the Sacramento River or all the way to San Francisco. It was a lively place, the center of trade and communication for all the settlers in the valley. At once a fortress, inn, granary, warehouse and retail store, Sutter's Fort and environs had a white population of about 290, most of them frontiersmen and farmers from the United States. As well, there were a number of Hawaiians—Kanakas—and 450 Indians who worked as servants and in the fields. A man of vision to match his ambition, Sutter laid out a town, Sutterville, along the banks of the Sacramento River. Some distance up the South Fork of the American River, several of Sam Brannan's Mormons worked for Sutter in building a flour mill. Most important for Sutter's plans and for California's future, about forty-five miles from the fort James Marshall served as construction superintendent of a sawmill at a bend of the South Fork, in a gentle valley called Coloma.

While work on the sawmill continued, the millrace had to be deepened to increase the flow of water and thereby provide a greater force to turn the wheel. The morning of January 24, 1848, Marshall walked along the race to inspect the flow of water. Recalling the moment, he later reported: "My eye was caught by something shining in the bottom of the ditch. . . . I reached my hand down and picked it up; it made my heart thump, for I was certain it was gold. The piece was about half the size and shape of a pea. Then I saw another. . . ."

Buried there for endless centuries, those glittering granules and flakes of gold that Marshall held in his hand had been freed from their hiding by the digging of the race and the action of water running through, loosening and separating the rocks, gravel and sand. This very process of digging and washing, so innocently accomplished by Marshall and his workers, would be the method used by tens of thousands of men working with picks and shovels and crude mining machines in their search for gold, first along the South Fork of the American River and then, as the months passed, along scores of rivers and streams and up canyons and gorges along the western slope of the Sierra Nevada.

But first Marshall had to determine what, in truth, he had found. When he ran back to the mill with his particles of gold, he shouted, "Boys, I believe I have found a gold mine." The workers were doubtful. After testing the metal, biting and hammering a piece and finding it not brittle, several men went down to the tailrace to look for more. Work continued on the mill, but each day they found more gold. On January 28, Marshall rode over to Sutter's Fort and met with Sutter, and after more careful testing, they agreed Marshall had found gold. Excitement in Marshall, uncertainty in Sutter; the one returned immediately to the mill, the other waited until the next day. On the 29th, Sutter, Marshall and several workers examined the race, found gold all along it and more along the banks of the fork.

The growing excitement aroused in Sutter a new vision, but he could not turn easily from his plans for New Helvetia. Fearful that work on the sawmill would be interrupted, possibly stopped altogether in the face of a greater cause, he asked his workers to stay on the job, and though they could continue in their spare time to dig for gold, would they say nothing to outsiders about the discovery?

Such startling news could not be contained. Sutter himself talked of it, and in a letter he boasted: "I have made a discovery of a gold mine which, according to the experiments we have made, is extremely rich." Inevitable talk by the workers also spread the news. The Mormons working on Sutter's flour mill a few miles down the South Fork of the American River came up to the sawmill on February 27. A few days of digging and they too found enough gold to make them believers, and when they returned to their work site and noted the similarity of the riverbed and gravel bars, they scratched and dug and found more. The second "gold mine" became famous as Mormon Island.

Sutter could not hold his workers. The flour mill stood unfinished, hides rotted in the warehouse. All his plans depended on a staff of assistants, field workers, carpenters, tanners. Suddenly they were gone, with plans of their own.

While Sutter's world changed quickly, the news traveled slowly to the rest of California. In March and April a few outsiders came to the diggings along the South Fork and at Mormon Island, from San Francisco and ranches in the valley. Sam Brannan was there in early April, and he found some gold. Another who came to see what truth there might be in the rumors was a man named Isaac Humphrey. He had been a miner in Georgia and would soon show the greenhorns how to use the tools of his trade.

But mostly the news met with doubt and skepticism. Talk, legends, boasts of gold were part of California's history, heard at some time by most everyone. In fact, gold had been found in the mountains north of Los Angeles in 1842, but the deposit was shallow, limited in area and productive for only a short time. Possibly Coloma would be the same.

The two weekly newspapers in San Francisco, the *Californian* and the *California Star*, first mentioned the Sutter mill discovery rather casually in mid-March. Another report of gold appeared on March 25, and a more informative article followed on April 1. Then on May 12 the tune and the tempo changed. On that date, Sam Brannan returned from Coloma and brought to San Francisco's streets the kind of evidence and the kind of excited announcement needed to brush aside the doubters and the collective restraint. Holding high a bottle full of gold dust, Brannan shouted: "Gold! Gold! Gold from the American River!"

The man's enthusiasm, the electrifying words, the sight of gold, the accumulated force of rumor and expectation now released, all combined to create a contagion of belief and of impatience to get to the American River. As the agriculture of the Sacramento Valley had nurtured visions in Sutter's mind, now the gold of that place spawned dreams and concepts in the minds of hundreds of San Franciscans. One of those entranced recalled: "A frenzy seized my soul. . . . Piles of gold rose up before me. . . . castles of marble, thousands of slaves . . . myriads of fair virgins contending with each other for my love—were among the fancies of my fevered imagination. The Rothschilds, Girards, and Astors appeared to be but poor people; in short, I had a very violent attack of the gold fever."

Others less wildly imaginative but all serious in their purpose set out from San Francisco and San Jose, from Monterey and later that summer from Los Angeles and San Diego. But California was a backward place. There were no roads, no ferries at river crossings, no steamers on the rivers, no hotels or inns along the few trails. The rush to the gold region came by horse- and muleback, on board whatever craft could navigate up the Sacramento River, some with ox-drawn wagons and a great many on foot with backpacks.

On May 29, the *Californian* finally caught the spirit and reflected the scene: "The whole country from San Francisco to Los Angeles and from the seashore to the base of the Sierra Nevada resounds to the sordid cry of gold, gold!, GOLD! while the field is left half planted, the house half built and everything neglected but the manufacture of shovels and pick-axes." In fact, there was no manufacturing, only handcrafting and impro-vising. Like everything else, shovels and picks and pans, blankets and buckets, the essentials for mining were in desperately short supply. As in the past, these and other necessities would have to come from the East Coast.

By the middle of June, San Francisco stood half empty, with three-quarters of the men off to the mines, most stores closed, the alcalde's office shut, the newspapers suspended, outbound ships at anchor deserted by their crews. News from San Jose, Benicia, Sonoma, all the same— empty streets, abandoned businesses, fields of grain opened to roaming cattle.

At Monterey the alcalde kept a diary which, beginning in June, told of the news reaching there and of initial disbelief. "Doubts still hovered in the minds of the great mass. They could not conceive that such a treasure could have lain there so long undiscovered. The idea seemed to convict them of stupidity." Samples of gold arrived on the 20th, more on July 15 and finally on the 18th the alcalde reported: "Another bag of gold from the mines and another spasm in the community. It was brought down by a sailor from the Yuba River and contains 136 ounces. . . . My carpenters at work on the schoolhouse on seeing it threw down their saws and planes, shouldered their picks and are off to the Yuba. Three seamen ran from the *Warren*, forfeiting their four years' pay; and a whole platoon of soldiers from the fort left only their colors behind."

Commodore Jones, back again on the coast, reported to the Secretary of the Navy: "For the present, and I fear for years to come, it will be impossible for the United States to maintain any naval or military estab-lishment in California, as at the present no hope of reward nor fear of punishment is sufficient to make binding any contract between man and man upon the soil of California. To send troops out here would be needless, for they would immediately desert."

The comments of the alcalde in Monterey and of Commodore Jones pointed up the fact that the United States had no military power and barely any presence in California, a situation somewhat ironic in view of the outcome of the recent war, but in the best tradition of California under its two previous rulers.

In any case, the situation was more important than ironic; indeed, it was unique in American history and had within it the potential for anarchy. What was the legal status of California after the treaty of peace? Congress had passed no law for the formation of a territorial government, yet that treaty had ended the war and thereby deprived the appointed military governor of his legal power. If he sought to claim such power, where were the soldiers to enforce it? Who should govern this suddenly vigorous and growing population? In the absence of a territorial government and given the illegality of a military government in a time of peace, were the people to govern themselves? And what of the fact that all the land in California now belonged to the United States, at least until legal proceedings had legitimated land grants and other contracts? The miners were all trespassers, taking gold for themselves from public land, taking it without any laws that gave them the right and certainly taking it without any requirement that they pay fees to the government or seek title to the land they mined. In fact, the government had no more power to prevent trespassing than John Sutter, who watched an ever-growing horde camp on what he considered his land, to mine his gold.

The first goldseekers and most of their successors from the valley and other parts of California, later from Oregon and then from the United States, knew nothing of mining or of geology. With their farming heritage, their sense of the wilderness as a place to be tamed for planting and for homes, the idea of the earth providing sudden wealth, free, was an astonishment. Possibly they knew of the Spanish and how lucky they had been in their exploration and conquest. But by comparison, American mining experience was paltry—some mining for gold in North Carolina in 1799 and Georgia in 1828–29; lead mining in Galena, Illinois, in the 1820s that produced a mining rush. But those local excitements were incidental to the national agricultural experience, in no way suggestive of quick and easy wealth for all.

Like almost everything in California, the gold had special characteristics. Compared to past and future discoveries, the gold at Coloma and for hundreds of miles beyond was unequaled in its availability—not known to the natives; free to everyone because no government had control of the territory; in a mild, comfortable climate and in a reasonably accessible terrain. More important than this welcoming environment were the fortunate geological circumstances. The gold found by Marshall and soon by many thousands far beyond the millrace had been eroded and abraded through eons of time by glacial and climatic forces until it was freed from the rock formations in which it had been encased in veins and fissures. Further abraded and swept along for thousands of years by the wild power of torrents racing down river canyons and gorges, the larger pieces of gold sank upstream, to lodge among rocks and in cracks of the river bottoms or in sandbars and gravel banks, while the lighter flakes, scales and grains were carried farther downstream until the slight current finally released them in quiet eddies and behind giant boulders.

Many of these prehistoric rivers with their gold deposits were later thrust upward by violent earth movement which left the riverbeds hidden beneath a layer of rocky debris. Called dry diggings, they often proved immensely rich.

These deposits of endless centuries enriched the lucky men of 1848. Sometimes as nuggets of five and eight ounces, often as grains the size of pumpkin seeds, usually as flakes and granules, the gold was found first in the millrace cut into the flood plain of the South Fork and from there in myriad places—rocky bars where streams turned sharply in a canyon; widespread rock and gravel islands exposed by the low water of midsummer; narrow ravines dry after the spring runoff.

When they dug in those places, the first goldseekers generally found "color," bits of yellow exposed when they washed the gravel in their pans or stirred the dry pebbles and sand. If such prospecting proved rewarding, then more serious digging would begin. Their searching and digging required frying pans (or any kind of shallow bowl), shovels, picks, knives, buckets, blankets, tents—the simple tools and needs of men impatient to find their fortunes. Setting the pace for the years ahead, merchants (what few there were) made their fortunes more quickly than miners. Sam Brannan's store at Sutter's Fort grossed $36,000 between May 1 and July 10. Sutter himself seemed helpless to cope with the abounding opportunities.

Through April and May, many miners continued to work with only their knives or whatever improvised sharp instruments they could obtain, picking into rocky crevices, searching under large boulders along the rivers, or digging in nearby ravines. Because they were skimming off the surface accumulations, even such simple methods produced thrilling results, always an ounce, sometimes a pound.

Among the growing number of goldseekers along the American River, Isaac Humphrey had previous experience in mining. Impatient with panning, he introduced to California a machine of ancient origins called a rocker or cradle. Like the pan, it utilized the action of water and the weight of gold, but it vastly increased the volume of dirt that could be washed. Built of wood, this simple contrivance was four to six feet in length and had an open box or hopper at its upper end and a series of cleats along its sloping bottom. When gold-bearing dirt was shoveled into the hopper and water poured on top, the sievelike bottom of the hopper held back the rocks and most of the gravel; the lighter gravel and muddy, sandy water fell through and ran out the lower end, leaving the heavier particles and scales of gold behind the rows of cleats—and all the while one of the miners rocked and shook the simple machine to hurry up the distintegration of the gold-bearing dirt.

With Sutter's agreement and assistance, Humphrey rounded up some of the ranch's Indians to work as laborers. Presumably they received more in geegaws, food and liquor, or possibly in gold-dust wages, than had been their reward as field hands. With some of the Indians digging, others carrying dirt and water to the rockers, Humphrey and his partner greatly increased the quantity of dirt they could wash each day. Their success caused others to imitate their methods. One of Sutter's ranch neighbors brought fifty Indians to Coloma in early April and, after watching Humphrey, moved down the forks of the American and set up his rockers. In five weeks, with his Indians carrying the dirt in willow baskets, this ex-rancher washed $16,000 in gold.

An even more dramatic expansion of the gold region soon followed with a gold "strike" on the Middle Fork of the Feather River at a place called Bidwell's Bar. In April another rancher visited Coloma, returned to his primitive home far to the north and, with Indians to help, worked the Trinity River, which was not even a part of the Sierra drainage system—yet he too found spectacular amounts of gold. The mining region had expanded northward 200 miles.

In the rush and excitement, few goldseekers bothered or had reason to keep records or otherwise report what was happening as they searched ever farther from Coloma. Fortunately Thomas O. Larkin, one of the most influential Americans in California and a successful merchant in Monterey, was in the habit of writing letters to his business associates and to Colonel Richard B. Mason, the military governor of California. On May 26, 1848, Larkin, at Pueblo de San Jose, wrote to Mason at his headquarters in Monterey, "We can hear of nothing but gold, gold, gold. An ounce a day, two or three. Last night several of the most respectable

American residents of this town arrived home from a visit to the gold regions. Next week they will go with their families, and I think nine-tenths of the foreign storekeepers, mechanics or day laborers of this town and perhaps of San Francisco will leave for the Sacramento. . . . Baskets, tin pans, shovels, etc. bring any price imaginable at the gold washings."

On June 1 from San Francisco, Larkin wrote to the Secretary of State, James Buchanan, in Washington: "I have to report to the State Department one of the most astonishing excitements and state of affairs now existing in this country that perhaps has ever been brought to the notice of the Government. On the American Fork of the Sacramento and Feather rivers . . . there has been within the present year discovered a placer, a vast tract of land containing gold in small particles. . . . It is now two or three weeks since the men employed in these washings have appeared in this town with gold to exchange for merchandise and provisions. I presume near $20,000 of this gold has as yet been so exchanged. . . . I have seen several pounds of this gold and consider it very pure. . . . Fourteen to sixteen dollars in merchandise is paid for it here. . . . Common spades and shovels one month ago worth one dollar will now bring ten dollars at the gold regions. I am informed that fifty dollars has been offered for one. Should the gold continue as represented, this town will be depopulated. . . ."

Writing to Buchanan again on June 28, Larkin perceived the future: "If our countrymen in California as clerks, mechanics and workmen will forsake employment at from two to six dollars per day, how many more of the same class in the Atlantic states earning much less will leave for this country under such prospects?"

Through the spring and summer of 1848 the gold did continue as represented. Seven men from Monterey working fifty Indians on the Feather River dug out 273 pounds of gold in two months. Many Indians worked for themselves, but it was a risky choice, for there were Americans who thought nothing of driving the natives from any productive area.

The pace of success quickened and the mining region expanded week by week, not only north from Coloma along the many tributaries of the Sacramento, but south to the rivers and streams that flowed from the Sierra foothills into the San Joaquin River.

In June, military governor Mason, traveling with his chief of staff Lieutenant William Tecumseh Sherman, left Monterey to visit the gold regions. When they came to the Mormon Island diggings on July 5, they found 200 men living in scores of tents and brush shelters, a store and several "boarding shanties." Many of the miners worked rockers and washed $100 each day. In the diggings along the North Fork they found "a small gutter not more than 100 yards long by four feet wide and two or three deep . . . where two men had a short time before obtained in seven days $17,000 worth of gold. . . . They employed four white men and about 100 Indians. . . . Another small ravine was shown me from which had been taken upwards of $12,000. Hundreds of similar ravines . . . are as yet untouched."

Mason judged there were about 4,000 miners in the gold district, and of these, 2,000 were Indians. He estimated the total production at $30,000 to $50,000 per day "if not more." His report continued, "I was surprised to learn that crime of any kind was very infrequent and that no thefts or robberies had been committed in the gold district. All live in tents, in bush houses or in the open air and men have frequently about their persons thousands of dollars' worth of this gold. . . . Conflicting claims to particular spots of ground may cause collisions, but they will be rare as the extent of the country is so great and the gold so abundant that for the present there is room and enough for all. . . ."

Mason concluded, "Many private letters have gone to the United States giving accounts of the vast quantity of gold recently discovered, and it may be a matter of surprise why I have made no report on this subject at an earlier date. The reason is that I could not bring myself to believe the reports that I heard of the wealth of the gold district until I visited it myself. . . . No capital is required to obtain this gold, as the laboring man wants nothing but his pick and shovel and tin pan with which to dig and wash the gravel, and many frequently pick gold out of the crevices of rocks with their butcher knives in pieces of from one to six ounces."

Mason was certainly right in emphasizing the simplicity of mining methods and the quick gains during the summer of 1848. In one of the more spectacular examples, a group of goldseekers who traveled overland from Los Angeles took over an Indian mining claim in the dry diggings not far from the newly settled town of Sonora, on a branch of the Tuolumne River. (Named after Mexicans who had come up from the province of Sonora earlier that summer, the town and its surrounding diggings marked the southern limit of mining activity in 1848.) After driving out the Indians, the Angelenos went to work. One quickly dug out forty-five ounces of coarse gold, another dug down three feet and found a pocket of gold. More than fifty-two pounds came from that geologic bonanza. In another hole dug four feet deep, one of these greenhorns spent the day digging with a spoon, piling the nuggets in a wooden bowl, until by evening he strained to lift it out. Weary, he turned the treasure hole over to a companion, who eagerly continued the cramped work that would be described again and again as the story of this strike spread throughout the mining regions and eventually far beyond.

By the fall of 1848 the energy and ambition of the miners had expanded the known gold regions a distance of 400 miles, from the Trinity River in the north to the Tuolumne in the south, a kingdom at last for Queen Calafia.

While her fabled domain had only women, in this California women were rare—a few wives of ranchers and mothers with children. Probably they settled at Coloma and Mormon Island, where some semblance of civilization slowly developed. But beyond those shanty villages, it was a world of men, where fifty or sixty miners might camp together on a river bar or under some sheltering trees along a river flat. A few mining camps had as many as 200 men. Nearby they dug and washed each day, hearing on all sides the shaking of rockers, the rattle of stones thrown out of hoppers, and now and then a shout that told of sudden success. Slipping and slogging in the rocks, gravel and icy water of streams pouring down from snowbanks up above in the Sierra, or digging in some otherwise quiet ravine where the stifling heat bore down at 110 degrees in the shade, these bearded goldseekers labored and cursed, sweated and shivered through July, August and September, hoping to make their fortunes before the rainy season, which might set in any time after September and cause the streams to rise and ravines to flood.

Reporting once again on these men who had transformed California, Larkin wrote a letter to Buchanan on July 20. "Some of those who first made the discovery of gold, after working a month and obtaining $1,000 to $3,000, have left the place [planning] to return when the weather is cooler. . . . A few who are working thirty or forty Indians are laying up $1,000 to $2,000 a week. None of these men had any property of consequence to commence with. . . ."

There was plenty of gold but very little to buy—a classic supply-demand crisis. Brannan grew rich from his stores at Sutter's Fort and Coloma. Larkin, so successful as a merchant and trader before the discovery, sold goods to the miners on the Yuba River in August making a 300 to 500 percent profit. One of his agents wrote to him in July from San Francisco to report that he had been unable to buy any blankets or clothing, both in great demand. He said that Brannan had purchased almost $12,000 worth of such supplies, hence the shortage and high prices. Then the agent urged Larkin: "If you can have it done within a month, you had better have a large lot of pants made up of flannel, jeans, osnaburg and cotton goods." What the miners needed more than pants was shoes and boots to replace those that rotted and wore out from sloshing in the stream beds. But, as another agent reported in August: "There are no shoes on all the Sacramento. They are worth $10, ready sale. If you can buy some and send up to us, we can do well with them."

Orders for everything California needed went by ship to Honolulu. By July the gold fever raged there. Each ship for San Francisco was crowded with expectant miners and whatever goods could be found for the fevered California market. When the news reached Oregon in August, thousands of men determined to head south for the mines. Some came by ship to San Francisco, many left with wagons, some with their families. The *Oregon Spectator* reported that by the end of the year "almost the entire male population has gone gold digging in California." Though this newspaper's estimate was exaggerated in tune with the excitement, the number of Oregonians in California could not have been fewer than 4,000; most of them ended up in the Trinity River mines in northern California.

Another rush came from northern Mexico. A long trail across deserts made the journey difficult and dangerous, but several thousand from Sonora, Sinaloa, Chihuahua and Durango reached the southern mines during the summer and fall of 1848; they continued to crowd in thereafter. By late fall the stories of gold made their impact in Peru and Chile, and hundreds, eventually thousands, came by ship from Callao and Valparaiso, bringing more hopeful goldseekers to a California that had set off the first international gold rush in history.

While the news from Coloma and other mining camps spread to various Pacific ports, the United States government and the American people remained unaware that the war with Mexico had won far more than the long-coveted control of the Pacific Coast. Knowledge of a new California that no one expected would be revealed by Governor Mason's official report and Thomas Larkin's letters. With his eyewitness account, Mason sent solid evidence to support his enthusiasm—230 ounces of California's future. The special courier carrying this powerful message sailed out of Monterey Harbor on August 30 and finally arrived in the capital in late November. Larkin's letter of June 1, carried across Mexico, reached Secretary of State Buchanan in mid-September.

While these fateful messages made their way to Washington, the number of miners and the production of gold rapidly increased. Hawaiians, Oregonians, Mexicans and Latin Americans joined the American settlers and Californios who, since spring, had been discovering new river and dry diggings. From an estimated 2,000 in July, the non-Indian goldseekers increased to 5,000 by October, and by year's end these men with pans and rockers and high hopes had grown to possibly 8,000. No one knew how many, or cared—there seemed to be plenty of gold for every-one.

For the American farmers who had come overland since 1841 and most of all for the 400 emigrants who arrived in the Sacramento Valley in the fall of 1848, what a wonder California turned out to be. Letters from these ex-farmers sent to their relatives back in the States sounded very much like the first reports from Sutter's mill and the South Fork in the spring of 1848—so boastful that they aroused skepticism. A survivor of the Donner party wrote to friends back in Illinois in early August: "We in this country live and move on beds of the richest minerals. . . . We are in our infancy in wealth. It is but dawning so far as mines and rich ores are concerned. We have them for picking up. . . . I pledge upon my sacred honor that I shall not state anything to you but what is true to the letter and spirit. The poor man in the course of sixty days is raised into comparative ease, and many become wealthy. All who work but from four to six hours per day have $800 to $2,000 in their possession, and many from that sum up to $10,000. Plenty for all, for years to come."

However boastful and aureate, this and other letters sent to the States did reflect the dramatic change in California's economy—from hides by the thousands to gold by the pound. So much gold, in fact, that it declined in value. By fall 1848, an ounce of dust and granules from a miner's pouch would buy not $14 to $15 but $8 to $10 in provisions, tools and whiskey at the few trading tents and shanty stores in the mines, and even less in the stores at Sutter's Fort or San Francisco.

Other changes affected the ever-increasing number of men searching impatiently, expectantly. Through the spring and summer there had been so many places to look for gold that no one much bothered about staking claims or establishing rules to control who could mine where. But by fall the well-known river bars and flats and dry diggings were crowded, and simple rules became necessary to protect the old-timers from the ignorant newcomers. On some bars a claim would be limited to ten square feet. At other places fifty square feet or more were allowed. Everywhere it was understood that a miner's pick, shovel or pan marked that area as off limits to the roving prospector.

For many hundreds of miners just getting started, the greatest prob-lem was to decide whether to stay put and wash for gold or search for truly rich diggings. This uncertainty was fed every day by stories of richer diggings a few miles upstream or over the ridge in the next canyon. Consequently the transient population was large, composed of those who had been disappointed after a few days or weeks of washing, those who had just arrived and were looking for a place to start, and more serious prospectors who had been around long enough to know where to search for new diggings far from the crowd.

While this restless searching produced far more disappointment than reward, it also contributed significantly to the rapid expansion of the known mining district. A major motive for climbing ever higher up the boulder-crowded canyons and gorges was the persistent belief among many of those men that the gold had been washed down from a single source, a place where the precious metal had erupted out of the earth in a solid flow from which one could chisel off great chunks. Beguiled by this geologic myth and knowing that others were looking for this fountainhead, there were fortune hunters in 1848, as there would be in later years, who forsook the gold immediately at hand to search for the ultimate El Dorado.

These searchers would be joined one year later by tens of thousands from cities, towns and farms across America. After centuries of responding to the pull of the West, the siren song of rivered forests and wide prairies, the American people were about to find beyond the Great American Desert, beyond the snows of the Sierra Nevada, what the Spanish had hoped for so long ago.

■

CHAPTER I

A Migration of Strangers

*"Great talk about California gold region
and I don't know hardly what to think of
it. I have at times a mind to go. . . ."*

In midsummer 1848, city and small-town newspapers in the United States told of political debate in Washington over a plan to prohibit the expansion of slavery into the West and specifically into the territories recently conquered from Mexico. Fearful of angering voters on both sides of the controversy, the candidates in the upcoming presidential election, Democrat Lewis Cass and Whig General Zachary Taylor, hero of the war with Mexico, avoided making any statements on the subject.

In early August a more interesting story began to appear. A St. Louis newspaper on the 8th printed part of an article brought overland from San Francisco, where it had appeared in the April 1 issue of the *California Star*. The news told of gold "collected at random and without any trouble" on the American River. A letter from California in the New York *Herald*, August 19, predicted "a Peruvian harvest of precious metals." Other major newspapers—the Baltimore *Sun*, the New Orleans *Daily Picayune*—printed similarly colorful letters and reports from "the gold regions." Editors across the country impatiently sought whatever news of California could be found. The New York *Journal of Commerce* ran a letter from the alcalde of Monterey which told of miners digging "eight to ten ounces a day." He concluded by characterizing the miners as "men who open a vein of gold just as coolly as you would a potato hill." On September 14 the Philadelphia *North American* printed another letter from the exuberant alcalde in which he boasted, "Your streams have minnows and ours are paved with gold."

Across the country Americans read and talked of gold and felt in-

WILLIAM SWAIN'S ROUTE
from
YOUNGSTOWN, NEW YORK
to
INDEPENDENCE, MISSOURI

April 11–May 2, 1849

Sheboygan

WISCONSIN

Lake Michig

Milwaukee

Racine

IOWA

Chicago

Kanesville
(Council Bluffs)

Iowa City

Michigan-Illinois Canal

Peru

Peoria

Illinois River

INDIAN TERRITORY

St. Joseph

Springfield

Oregon-California Trail

Independence

ILLINOIS

Wabash River

Santa Fe Trail

Missouri River

St. Louis

Jefferson City

Mississippi River

MISSOURI

0   100 miles

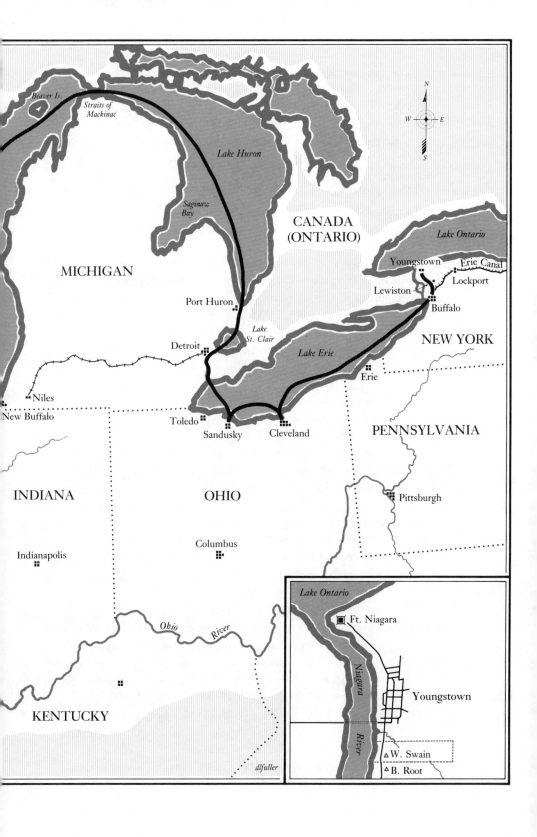

creasingly envious of miners who could dig their fortunes in a matter of days or weeks. For farmers in Massachusetts or Kentucky and city folk in Cincinnati or Savannah discouraged by their prospects, for others restless after returning home from the war with Mexico, or those weary of marriage or fearful of growing debts, these first reports of gold and the resulting expectations of quick fortune might have been enough to send them on their way to El Dorado. But for most potential goldseekers in the thirty states, far more tangible evidence was needed to overcome doubts and scoffing neighbors—evidence strong enough to justify to wives and creditors, parents and business partners the expense and the danger of the long journey to California.

What the American people needed was an official endorsement of the California news. It came in December, directly from the two most trusted authorities in the nation: the President and the United States Army.

Having received Colonel Mason's official report of the diggings, President James K. Polk was prepared to speak with authority and confidence about the astonishing events in California. Mason had sent dramatic evidence (the 230 ounces of gold) to back up his report, and he set forth his judgment of California: "I have no hesitation in saying there is more gold in the country drained by the Sacramento and San Joaquin rivers than will pay the cost of the war with Mexico a hundred times over." Thus encouraged and more than willing to find additional justification for the recent war of conquest with Mexico, President Polk on December 5, 1848, delivered his message to the second session of the 30th Congress. Of the news from California, he stated: "The accounts of the abundance of gold in that territory are of such extraordinary character as would scarcely command belief were they not corroborated by authentic reports of officers in the public service." With this endorsement of the seemingly incredible, with the gold on display at the War Department, and with the full details of Mason's report published throughout the nation, skepticism gave way to unrestrained enthusiasm.

After December 5 and through the winter and spring of 1849, there appeared in literally every newspaper in the country continuing reports of the ever-increasing emigration to California. Whether in New York or Iowa, editors wrote of the national drama in florid phrases and excited tones, as if the wonder and impact of the news might not otherwise be fully appreciated.

On January 11, 1849, the New York *Herald* trumpeted its judgment: "The spirit of emigration which is carrying off thousands to California so far from dying away increases and expands every day. All classes of our citizens seem to be under the influence of this extraordinary mania. . . .

If the government were under the necessity of making a levy of volunteers to the amount of two or three hundred thousand men for any purpose in California, the ranks would be filled in less than three months. . . . What will this general and overwhelming spirit of emigration lead to? Will it be the beginning of a new empire in the West, a revolution in the commercial highways of the world, a depopulation of the old States for the new republic on the shores of the Pacific?

"Look at the advertising columns of the *Herald* or any other journal, and you will find abundant evidence of the singular prevalence of this strange movement and agitation in favor of gold digging on the Sacramento. Every day men of property and means are advertising their possessions for sale, in order to furnish them with means to reach that golden land. Every city and town is forming societies either to cross the Isthmus or to double Cape Horn. . . .

"Poets, philosophers, lawyers, brokers, bankers, merchants, farmers, clergymen—all are feeling the impulse and are preparing to go and dig for gold and swell the number of adventurers to the new El Dorado.

"The spirit which has been thus awakened in this country by the discovery of the gold mines in California and by the authentic facts published concerning them under the authority of the government in Washington exceeds everything in the history of commercial adventure that has occurred in many ages and can only be paralleled by that which sprang up in Spain and other parts of Europe by the discovery of the mineral wealth of Mexico and Peru by the expeditions of Cortez and Pizarro."

More influential than such editorial fervor, what nurtured hopes on farms and in villages and challenged the faint-hearted were personal reports direct from California—letters sent home by settlers who had become California's first gold miners. Eagerly sought by local newspapers and then reprinted again and again by dailies and weeklies in other states, these statements written in the language of neighbors told of digging for gold along rivers called the American, Feather, Yuba and Mokelumne, where in a matter of months young men using methods that sounded simple, even haphazard, gathered fortunes totaling thousands, tens of thousands of dollars.

A letter from a man named McClellan written to his family in Jackson, Missouri, concluded: "You know Bryant, the carpenter who used to work for Ebenezer Dixon, well, he has dug more gold in the last six months than a mule can pack." In family councils at day's end, in churchyards after the Sunday sermon, in country stores and city saloons, men used Bryant's triumph or similar reports to argue in favor of going to California. Week by week the news gathered force, more men believed and their families agreed that if they could get to California success would be assured, success that required no knowledge of mining and only a few months' work.

As the frugality of generations gave way to a contagion of optimism and ambition, responsible family men found their jobs and prospects unrewarding when set against all that California could provide. They figured how much they could bring home after a year's sojourn in the gold fields and justified the cost of the journey and the length of their absence as an investment that would guarantee financial security. And it was not just ambitious men who dreamed. In January 1849 the wife of a struggling shopkeeper wrote to her parents: "Joseph has borrowed the money to go; but I am full of bright visions that never filled my mind before, because at the best of times I have never thought of much beyond a living; but now I feel confident of being well off."

In East Coast ports, shipowners announced sailing dates for steamers, schooners, brigs and old whaling ships resurrected to meet the sudden demand. Newspaper advertising columns announced the sale of businesses by men "overtaken by the gold fever." Manufacturers of money belts, tents, India-rubber wading boots and clothing, medicines, and gold testing and smelting devices proclaimed their products essential to success in the land of gold. And inventors attested to the infallibility of their patented mining machinery, including a "hydro-centrifugal Chrysolyte or California Gold Finder" and an "Archimedes Gold Washing Machine." Equally imaginative entrepreneurs announced an "aerial locomotive" capable of carrying fifty to one hundred passengers from New York to California "pleasantly and safely" in three days at a cost of $200—and they assured their readers that two hundred tickets had already been sold.

Those more aware of the realities of geography and commerce knew that the journey would require many weeks—even months—of arduous, possibly dangerous travel by wilderness trails or ocean voyages. For those on the Atlantic Coast with seafaring traditions, the ocean routes seemed the only way to go. For forty years New England merchants and whalers had sent their ships around Cape Horn, an 18,000-mile voyage, to the coves and harbors of California, there to trade or obtain fresh food and water. This commercial tradition helped build confidence in the Cape route (despite the distance and four to six months on shipboard), so much so that all but twenty-two of the 124 gold-rush companies that organized in Massachusetts during 1849 sailed around the Horn, taking a total of 6,067 emigrants from that state alone.

In contrast to the time that would be spent on board a ship sailing around South America, goldseekers could reach California in a matter of weeks by taking a steamer from New York to the town of Chagres on the Atlantic side of the Isthmus of Panama. From there it took two or three days through dense jungle to reach the ancient Pacific port of Panama City, where another line of steamers tried to accommodate the ever-pressing demand for passage to San Francisco. If they sailed from New York to Panama in January, February or even March, they could be in the diggings before the first overland emigrants even set out from the western frontier. In all, about 6,500 emigrants took the Panama route in 1849; but disease, exorbitant costs, overcrowding and too few steamers on the Pacific route caused delays of weeks and sometimes months throughout that first year of the rush.

For those who lived inland and had farming as a background, the ocean voyage seemed fearful, the overland trails practical, even familiar. The well-known history of travel from the Missouri frontier to Santa Fe and to Oregon increased their confidence. During the winter and early spring of 1849 tens of thousands of men throughout the United States prepared for the overland trek that would begin with the first good weather in April or May. In cities and country villages they organized joint-stock companies, each member paying an equal amount to provide funds for the company's purchase of wagons, teams and provisions. Organized as the Pittsburgh and California Enterprise Company, the Illinois and California Mining Company, the Sagamore and Sacramento Mining and Trading Company and many more, goldseekers joined together more as ambitious businessmen than as carefree adventurers. In Ithaca, New York, a company of fifty men, with a capital of $25,000 and a credit of $25,000 more at a local bank, planned to leave the western frontier in early April and reach the gold country in June. There, as the Ithaca *Journal* reported on March 21, 1849, "they will select a suitable location, erect cabins and proceed to rake in the dust."

In addition to reporting the financial arrangements of the overland companies, the local newspapers often printed each company's membership lists and their lengthy constitutions, or "Rules of Regulation," which more often than not prohibited swearing, drinking and violation of the Sabbath. Some companies issued uniforms, elected officers with military titles and drilled their members. Some purchased ships which carried cargoes of supplies and trade goods around Cape Horn to San Francisco, there to await the members' arrival by overland trail. One company included in its equipage eleven "gold finders" and a machine for making gold coins.

To raise money to join an overland company or to purchase a wagon, team and other "California fixings," goldseekers mortgaged or sold homes and farms, took out life savings, or borrowed from friends and fathers-in-law. The financial impact of this money raising caused concern in several states, with editors lamenting the loss of capital withdrawn from the local economy to support the sudden needs of men afflicted with gold fever. On March 27 a newspaper in Ann Arbor, Michigan, estimated that $30,000 had been taken out of Washtenaw County alone, with each man spending an average of $400 to pay for his outfit and transportation to the frontier. Many had to find additional money to provide for their wives and children until their return. A man in Ann Arbor, father of six daughters, sold his home to his brother for $1,200; a farmer on February 24, 1849, sold his acreage to his father-in-law for $1,300. More often, such funds came from mortgages, but some would-be goldseekers found that a mortgage was not always enough—they had to enter into a contract to share equally with the moneylender the gold that would be found in California. Such contracts suggest the contagion of optimism that spring of 1849.

Ignorant of guns and camping life except for what they had heard or read in legend and literature, thousands of city and rural men studied John C. Frémont's famous *Report of the Exploring Expedition to the Rocky Mountains in the Year 1842 and to Oregon and North California in the Years 1843–'44* and the accounts of other western travelers. In part motivated by such reading and by the traditional fear of Indians, these emigrants purchased a remarkable number of guns, an impulse encouraged by the U.S. War Department's February 1849 offer to sell pistols, rifles and ammunition at cost to California (and Oregon) emigrants.

In further preparation for their long journey, they probably bought one of the several "emigrant guides" issued that spring to tell the greenhorns how to find their way through the vastness of mountains and deserts. These publications, along with newspaper articles describing "Travel in the Far West," gave the goldseekers advice on what equipment and food they should purchase, whether oxen or mules made the best teams, where the Indians would be most dangerous. There were even tables of distances which set down the specific mileages from point to point—water sources, river crossings, major topographic features. All this information reflected the fact that the trails from the western frontier across the wilderness half of the continent had been explored and traveled for many years—by fur trappers and traders to Santa Fe since 1822, and to Oregon since 1812. Exploration or trailblazing would not be necessary for the crowds of inexperienced goldseekers or Californians as they were often called.

They had a choice of two primary routes: the Santa Fe Trail through territory newly acquired by conquest from Mexico, with various branches leading to southern California; or the far more publicized Oregon–California Trail, which since 1841 had been traveled by settlers headed for the Willamette or Sacramento valleys. Both of these well-established trails started at the major outfitting towns on the frontier, Independence and St. Joseph.

The goldseekers came to the frontier from every state in the Union, even from East Coast cities where the sea routes would have a strong appeal and from southern states where the routes through Texas and Mexico were open year-round. In all, at least 30,000 men, with possibly 1,000 women, traveled to the Missouri frontier. Never before had this country, or any other, experienced such an exodus of civilians, all heavily armed or intending to purchase rifles and pistols, mostly young men on the road for the first time, many organized into formal companies, others alone or with a few friends from their neighborhood. Impatient, curious, somewhat fearful of the uncertainties and dangers ahead, yet buoyed by their common expectations, they were not unlike a great volunteer army traveling from all parts of the nation to mobilize at the frontier.

Many who lived on farms and in villages and cities in Illinois, Wisconsin, Iowa and Missouri packed their gear in their wagons and rolled down the nearest road, headed for the Missouri river towns. Thousands from farther east began their journey on river steamers down the Ohio and Mississippi, with typical cost $9 per man (including stateroom) for seven days from Pittsburgh to St. Louis. Others traveled west on the great Erie Canal across northern New York or across Pennsylvania on the Portage and Canal System. On Great Lakes steamers they often experienced their first bout of seasickness, while from East Coast cities they rode in crowded railroad cars to connect with river and canal transportation to the West.

Along the way some of these men kept their promise to write home, and thus began a dynamic process by which the entire nation was emotionally involved in the rush to California. Scores of thousands of Americans who stayed home—wives, parents, sweethearts, relatives, friends who doubted the California stories, business partners and bankers who had helped finance the enterprise—received, shared, or read in local newspapers letters sent back by the goldseekers. The first of these letters reached homes in March and April; they continued to come from St. Louis, then from the frontier, and later from military posts in the Far West; some from the Mormons' embryo city at Salt Lake, and finally from California. For some families, the letters came for years from husbands and sons who could not give up their quest for gold. Through these letters (and after the men came home, through their diaries) America saw the great West—Indians, buffalo, deserts, the Rocky Mountains—for the first time through hometown eyes and vicariously experienced life in the Sierra mining camps and in the astonishing cities of Marysville, Sacramento, Sonora and San Francisco.

One of the thousands who set out that spring of 1849 promising to write letters and to keep a diary was a man named William Swain, aged twenty-seven, from a farm near the village of Youngstown, New York, north of Niagara Falls. He had read of California's gold in the local newspapers. By February, California had become the focus of his future.

Swain's past, his family history and his pre-gold-rush prospects were representative of a large class of Americans who lived a rural life as comfortable inheritors of their fathers' frontier enterprise. Swain's father, Isaac, born in England in 1759, emigrated to eastern Pennsylvania in 1794 and finally settled in western New York in 1805 with his first wife and children on eighty acres near a cluster of cabins later known as Youngstown. After serving two enlistments in the Army during the War of 1812, he returned in 1814 to find his farm had been burned and pillaged by British troops. With $200 he received from the state of New York "for the relief of the late sufferers on the western frontier," he built a cabin near the ruins of his old home, and there two sons were born to his second wife, Patience: George in 1819, and William in 1821.

With summer help from his boys, Isaac slowly reestablished his farm, and in the spring of 1836 he hired two masons to help with the construction of a new home. Using cobblestones George and William had gathered and red clay from the shores of the Niagara River, the masons, sons and helping neighbors labored all summer under the supervision of Isaac, aged seventy-seven. With the two-story house completed before the first snow, Isaac imbedded in the hearth a relic found in the ashes of the first home he had built on this site—the door to the Franklin stove that had warmed his first wife and children. In 1838 Isaac died, leaving the farm to Patience, George and William.

In April 1840, William graduated from Lewiston Academy. Having given up his military ambitions, he studied for his teacher's certificate and spent his winters as a schoolmaster in Niagara County. At his school's spelling bee in the spring of 1846, he met Sabrina Barrett, dark-haired, slim, twenty years old. A seventh-generation American (her ancestors settled in Connecticut Colony in 1640), she had graduated from Leroy Academy in Theresa, New York, east of Youngstown. Through the summer of '46 William often left the work of the farm to George so that he could ride his horse to the village of Lewiston and up the ridge to the

Barrett farm. There he courted Sabrina. Often they walked through her father's fields to a secluded place which commanded a sweeping view of the Niagara River Gorge and north across the valley to Youngstown. They talked of their future, and William told Sabrina of his and George's plans to enlarge the Swain farm, plant scores more peach trees and become major farmers in the valley.

Married July 6, 1847, William and Sabrina moved into the cobblestone house with Patience and George; and there on June 18, 1848, Sabrina gave birth to Eliza Crandall Swain.

Through the summer of 1848 William and George worked the farm, repairing fences around their fields and clearing part of the surrounding forest to enlarge their orchard. George's ambitions in Niagara County politics took him with increasing frequency to Buffalo and the towns of Niagara Falls and Lockport during the political campaign. He brought back the local newspapers and sometimes New York City papers, which were shared with neighbors when they came to the Swain home, a center for political discussion. Following the November elections, the newspapers and neighborhood talk returned to more mundane affairs. Then on December 5, 1848, President Polk delivered his endorsement of the report from California.

The newspapers in Buffalo, Niagara Falls and Lockport carried the President's message. During the weeks thereafter they reprinted whatever the New York papers reported about California. On January 26, 1849, the Buffalo *Morning Express* published an editorial entitled "The Gold Excitement": "We are quite sure that it is the duty of newspapers to use all the means in their power to repress rather than stimulate the prevailing excitement on the subject of gold in California. But we must publish all the authentic intelligence from that region and of what avail is sedate or sage or admonitory comment in the face of the glittering, dazzling news? According to the New York papers the inhabitants of that city are wild with excitement. The New York *Express* says 'We have seen in our day manias, fevers and excitements of all sorts, but it can easily be said never were people so worked up, so delirious as they were here and elsewhere yesterday when they read the gilded telegraphic dispatches from Washington chronicling the reception there of intelligence from El Dorado. . . . The fact is, this last gold news has unsettled the minds of even the most cautious and careful among us.' "

The January 30 issue of the New York *Herald* carried a dispatch datelined Liverpool, England: "The gold excitement here and in London exceeds anything ever before known or heard of. Nothing is heard or talked about but the new El Dorado. Companies are organizing in London in great numbers for the promised land. Fourteen vessels have already been chartered."

Most eagerly awaited through the winter of 1849 were the astonishing reports direct from California. The Buffalo *Morning Express*, February 8, published a letter dated "Monterey, California, November 16, 1848" which explained that "gold is found pure in the native soil here and is worth more, just as it is taken from the ground, than an equal weight of coined gold from any mint. It occurs in the form of small leaves or irregular masses. . . . The stratum of gold is unbroken and extends over a tract 120 miles in length and seventy miles in breadth."

Such was the dazzling news that appeared in newspapers during January and February 1849. The Buffalo *Daily Courier*, February 7, ran a column with the heading "Ho! for California" which advised that "another company of emigrants to California started from our city on Thursday evening. We learn that several sober-minded citizens, businessmen not before 'suspected,' are also making preparations to start for the gold country."

Day after day columns in the newspapers carried headings that read "Routes to California," "From the Gold Country," and "Gold Regions: Highly Important to Emigrants!" Here were discussed the best routes by land and sea, the proper equipage and the cost of a "California outfit." As well, there were reports of success direct from the gold fields. One such letter advised: "Many men who began last June [1848] to dig for gold with capital of $50 can now show $5,000 to $15,000."

In the stores and streets of Youngstown, Lewiston and other farming towns in western New York, as in cities and villages across the nation, passing conversation turned from the weather, farming or business problems to the thrilling subject of gold in the Sacramento Valley. At the Swain farm George and William came in from their chores and talked at dinner and later before the fire with Sabrina and their mother about the latest newspaper reports. Through George's political contacts and from salesmen and others arriving by the Erie Canal at Lockport, sixteen miles to the east, they kept informed of the latest reports and rumors from Washington and New York City. News from western states, from the frontier and St. Louis, came with passengers on lake steamers that docked each day in Buffalo from Chicago.

Given the Swain brothers' educational background and the fact that since student days they had read the novels of Sir Walter Scott and the poems of Wordsworth, had memorized long passages from Shakespeare and each Sunday had read from the Bible, it was natural for them to turn to books for further information about California and the West.

One of the most widely circulated books of the time, *What I Saw in California* by Edwin Bryant, published in 1846, told in vivid detail what it was like to travel through the vast territory which most maps called "The Great American Desert." But more than any other account of trails and travel in the western wilderness, John C. Frémont's *Report* spoke to thousands of families about life in the West—about the Platte River, Fort Laramie, South Pass and other places that a few months later would be seen by men whose reading of Frémont had helped them decide to go. The Swains owned a copy of Frémont, and they must have turned its pages many times during January and February. Their talk centered ever more sharply on William's growing determination to go to California on the overland trail.

Sabrina pleaded with him to stay home—reminded him of the needs and demands of Eliza, not yet one year old. She turned to Patience Swain for support. But the mother left the decision to her sons. George favored William's ambitions, and it was his willingness to take full responsibility for the family and the farm that freed William to plan his journey.

With George he figured the costs of getting to California and the equipment that would be needed, and most important, they talked of who should accompany William on this dangerous expedition. As the older brother, a bachelor, a man of spirit and imagination, George would have been the ideal partner. But someone had to stay home to watch over Sabrina and her baby and their elderly mother and maintain the farm. In any case, George had hopes of a political appointment through his Democratic friends.

First, William and George approached their friend Frederick Bailey, Youngstown resident, aged thirty, married and father of a young son. He was eager to join William. Then they met with their neighbors on River Road, Dr. Benjamin Root and his wife Elizabeth. They agreed that their son, John, nineteen and a bachelor, could go. A few days later a longtime friend, Michael Hutchinson, came to Youngstown for one of his periodic visits from his farm south of Buffalo. A widower without children, he would be the oldest of the group, forty-three.

To reach the Missouri frontier, Swain and his three companions decided to take passage from Buffalo by lake steamer to Detroit, and then by rail and canal boat to connect with river steamers down the Illinois River and on to St. Louis. After considering the difficulties of taking their wagons and supplies from their homes, they concluded it would be far less expensive and much quicker to buy wagons, teams and necessary equipment and food at the frontier. The newspapers encouraged this plan with reports that merchants in the frontier towns of Independence and

St. Joseph had large stocks of tents, kettles, rifles, flour, rice, wagons, mules and oxen, and all other "California fixings."

Swain and his family knew that when he left home he would be exposed to dangers that could cause sickness, injury or death. Of primary concern was the ubiquitous pestilence cholera. Little was known about the disease in 1849. Its cause was a mystery, its treatment a matter of choice. The suggested causes varied from "evening mists" to "a lack of electricity in the victim's system." The preventives were equally imaginative, including "Captain Paynter's Egyptian Cure for Asiatic Cholera" and "Dally's and Connell's Magic Pain Extractor."

Of course cholera might attack Sabrina or George or Patience, even Eliza, while William traveled westward; but somehow the danger seemed greater for him, far from home, in a migration of strangers. And there was news of cholera on Mississippi River boats and in St. Louis.

There were other dangers, more subtle, more ill-defined, but of great concern. William's moral health might be undermined during his absence by the influence of new companions, the snares and lures of sinful people and places. Without moral support and the elevating influence of his family and their religious commitment, without regular reading of the Bible, William might succumb to temptations of gambling, swearing, drinking, worse. Patience and Sabrina admonished him to read his Bible every day. To that end, his mother gave him a Bible with certain pages marked for his special attention.

Of importance almost equal to Bible reading, William would keep a diary—a daily record of his life and all that happened. This discipline would serve as a reminder of family obligations and shared values and would attest to his purpose to return home. When the diary was read by his family, his adventures would be relived through its pages. Meantime, there would be letters Swain promised to write to Sabrina, George and his mother, to be sent home during the journey to the frontier, and especially from St. Louis and Independence. Then once on the trail, he might be able to send letters from one of the military forts in the Indian Territory.

Many thousands left home the spring of 1849 promising to keep diaries, write down each day what they had seen and what had happened. Setting out for the far side of the continent, they shared not only financial ambitions, but as well a sense of history in the making, a sense that they were part of an epochal event, with the whole nation looking on. Their diaries would record crossing the fabled Rocky Mountains, digging gold from the streams of the Sierra Nevada, and they would return home not only wealthy, but distinguished by their participation in an event that commanded everyone's attention and respect. Each man's diary would be a history of the whole story, to be shared by family and grandchildren.

And yet once on their way, most soon gave up their assigned task. To find time and a quiet place to write at the end of each day became ever more difficult. Furthermore, as the weeks passed their experiences seemed too big, too demanding, to be told in daily diary entries. Possibly this sense of frustration and inadequacy was best expressed by a doctor from Michigan who wrote to his wife in July 1849: "It is impossible for me to give you an account of the interesting incidents that occur on this route, but when I have an opportunity I will give you enough to satisfy you that 1849 will ever be a memorable epoch in the history of our country. Neither the Crusades nor Alexander's expedition to India (all things considered) can equal this emigration to California."

William Swain did persevere; he wrote each day in his diary and wrote letters home as well. Possibly his journalistic ambition came from his education, his reading of history. But most of all he was motivated by George. William felt a sense of obligation to his older brother, not only because he had agreed to stay home to protect the family and manage the farm, but also because William knew how much George would have enjoyed the adventure of journeying to California. So William had George in mind each day when he took time to write the record that would later give his brother a chance to share the great experience.

And too, William wrote his diary for Sabrina, so that she would know how her husband, though absent for so long, had suffered and struggled for her well-being.

As the newspapers through the winter had reported what was known of California, now in March and April they reported the news of thousands of men leaving cities, villages and farms all over the nation. Public attention focused on the Californians, who carried with them the hopes and ambitions of so many who would wait for their return. Like soldiers off to do their duty, with a sense of excitement and adventure, the gold-seekers left from train stations in Philadelphia and Baltimore, from docks in Boston and New Orleans, from river landings in Pittsburgh and Memphis, from barnyards in Michigan and Alabama. For many, especially those in organized companies setting out from cities, the goodbyes were eased by sounds and colors of pomp and circumstance—flags waving, bands blaring and speeches and editorials that sent the boys west with hearty wishes for their "success on the Pacific shores."

Wednesday morning, April 11, William Swain embraced his mother and then Sabrina one last time, shook hands with George and climbed onto Dr. Root's wagon. Riding down the River Road, he looked back at his family standing in front of the cobblestone house; he passed the orchard he had helped plant as a boy; he rode away from his past in search of gold.

John Root and Frederick Bailey rode with William as Dr. Root drove the two horses thirty-two miles to Buffalo where they would meet Michael Hutchinson.

That night in a hotel room near the Buffalo waterfront William started to write in his diary, a task he would attend to almost daily until his plight in the Sierra Nevada would force him to give up the effort 203 days later.

■

April 11, 1849. All my things being ready last night, I rose early and commenced packing them in my trunk, preparatory to leaving home on my long journey, leaving for the first time my home and dear friends with the prospect of absence from them for many months and perhaps for years. Among these are an affectionate wife to whom I have been married less than two years, and an infant daughter ten months old, to both of whom I am passionately attached; an aged mother who from her great age —seventy-one years—much probability arises of never seeing again on this side of the grave, to which is added the painful reflection that she is now under the charge of the family physician from a sickness brought on by taking cold; and last but not least, an older brother to whom I am deeply attached, not only by the common ties of brotherhood alone, but also by a long course of years of common hardship, disappointment and neglect, and by a high moral and mental character, a manly and dignified deportment. Being two years older than myself, he has been my adviser and guardian from youth up, at once a father and a brother.

The leather-bound diary has survived in remarkably good condition, with original linen tie-strings attached. Each page, approximately four by six inches, is firmly sewn to the spine.

This volume contains entries for April 11 through August 6. The second volume (in rather tattered condition) contains August 7 through last entry, October 31, 1849.

Opening pages shown here read: (left) "The property of William Swain, Youngstown, Niagara Co. N.Y. April 11, 1849." (right) "Journal of Rout to Calafornia from My Home in Youngstown via, of Buffal, Detroit Chicauga St. Louis & Independance: comencing April 11 1849."

All these complicated ties of affection were broken by the sad stroke of separation. I had fortified my mind by previous reflection to suppress my emotions, as is my custom in all cases where emotion is expected. But this morning I learned by experience that I am not master of my feelings in all cases. I parted from my family completely unable to restrain my emotions and left them all bathed in tears, even my brother, whose energy of mind I never saw fail before.

I left home at eight o'clock with Mr. Bailey and the two Mr. Roots and arrived in Buffalo at half past four in the afternoon.

We had bad roads and altogether a gloomy day of it, the thoughts of leaving home frequently filling my bosom with emotions which I was unable to suppress. This evening reason has assumed governing power, and I calm my feelings with the reflection that duty and the interest of my family call for this separation. I feel that I have left behind all that I hold dear, and henceforth the thought of those loved ones will call up pleasing reflections.

Buffalo, April 11, 18

Dear Sabrina, George, and Mother,

I am now in my bedroom with John and Dr. Root at Huff's Ho
We had a good but slow passage down here today, arriving at about half past four with time to do considerable looking around. We can get gold, plenty of it, for 1 percent.*

I have bought a trunk for $3 with two straps on it. I have priced all the rifles in town and find that I can get one that will answer for about $15 and good revolvers at the same price. I have had my likeness taken and cased for $2 and shall send it to Sabrina by Dr. Root, with a token of fond remembrance. My coats I have not looked after yet, it being darkish when I got through at the daguerrian rooms, but shall see to it probably before Dr. Root leaves for home.

Mr. Hutchinson bought a double-barrel fowling piece for $18 to take along.

We intend to leave here for Detroit at ten o'clock tomorrow on the *London*, cabin passage $5. ["About twenty steamers of the largest class run between Buffalo and Chicago, besides many others of less size to Detroit

---

* *By paying a premium of 1 percent, the paper currency issued by local New York State banks (there was no national currency in 1849) could be converted to universally accepted gold coins.*

and the other intermediate ports on Lake Erie. There is a steamer for Chicago generally every evening at seven."]

I have been in better spirits on our route today than I expected. After mastering my feelings, I have felt generally lighthearted, with the exception of now and then a sad thought. I have no concern of mind for myself, I shall get along finely. But I have much concern for Mother's health. I hope that when I get to Independence, I shall receive news of her recovery.

Dear Sabrina, I am afraid that your feelings will be too severe upon you, unwell as you already are, and that you will be taken down altogether. But I hope that you will govern your feelings by reason and that I shall hear at Independence that you enjoy yourself tolerably well. Kiss Little Cub for Papa. Take care of yourself, my dear, for I am coming back again with a pocket full of rocks!

Dear George, I think it quite necessary that you should feed the curly heifer a few messes of potatoes and turnips. Our company are in good spirits and expect a pleasant trip tomorrow. I hope to be seasick, as I think it would be good for me. I shall have a buckskin belt made in the morning in which to carry my "yellow boys."

I will write from Detroit. Do not fail to write to me at Independence, and Sabrina must write too. You can write tomorrow and then every day until you think that your letters would not get there until the 4th or 5th of May, and then I can know all about home.

Yours truly,
William

April 12. Last night stayed at Huff's Hotel, and this morning commenced completing my outfit. I was with the rest of the company busily engaged until twelve o'clock, when the outfit was completed. [Delayed by these activities, Swain and his companions missed their planned departure on the *London*.]

At half past two o'clock we took passage for Detroit on the steamer *Arrow*.

The lake is very smooth, and the boat shoots along like an arrow, and as she leaves far in the distance objects familiar to me and bears me on to those that are strange, I feel that she bears me and my destiny.

April 13. This morning we are coasting along the banks of the lake in the state of Ohio. Stopped at Cleveland, Sandusky, and Toledo.

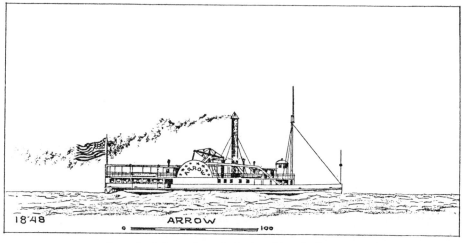

Launched in spring 1848, the side-wheel steamer *Arrow* was in its second season of service on Lake Erie when Swain and his companions boarded her in Buffalo.

Steamer *Arrow*, Lake Erie
April 13, 1849

Dear George,

Here we are going along among the numerous islands of the upper end of Lake Erie with a fine rolling billow, over which the steamer bounds like an Arrow. I have just been trying to make myself seasick, but cannot. Our boat is the swiftest on the lake, passing those which left Buffalo six hours before we did. Our party are all well, none being seasick, although some on the boat are.

We left Buffalo yesterday at three-thirty o'clock after finishing our outfits, which occupied us very busily through the forepart of the day. I obtained a good outfit, notwithstanding my money was as we supposed rather short. But I have plenty left, I think, for the journey, having $250 in my pocket, which I intend to take particular care of as I am convinced that I can make better use of it than any common pickpocket.

My outfit cost as follows:

One trunk with two straps	$ 3.00
One good, heavy cloth frock coat	$ 6.00
One heavy pilot-cloth overcoat	$ 5.00

These coats I had at my own price, and it was a good bargain. Both are of middling-fine wool and well made, and could not have been bought in Niagara Falls for less than $16.

Percentage on $250.00 in gold	$ 2.50
One rifle and two pair [bullet] molds	$16.00
One revolver, one steel rod, two pair molds, one large powder flask, and five boxes of caps	$14.00
Suit of oilcloth	$ 2.25
One pair of blankets	$ 3.50
One pair of gloves	$ 1.00
One cap	$ .25
One quart of alcohol	$ .18
Tavern bill	$ 1.00
Passage to Detroit, in the cabin	$ 3.00

I obtained laudanum and some other notions with the assistance of Mr. Hutchinson. Many articles which I neglected he has in abundance. . . .

We have touched at all ports. Cleveland has a fine harbor made at great expense by the government. The piers are made of large-cut stone, forming fine stone wharves with cast-iron spikes one foot in diameter. . . .

We are now, at dusk, within five miles of Toledo. As it is dark, I shall not see much of the rest of the route as we shall be in Detroit by twelve o'clock where I shall mail this. Our passage up the lake has been very pleasant. We have all our things snugly packed in a trunk apiece; have nothing but my overcoat out of the trunk and have packed Mr. Hutchinson's double-barrel fowling piece in with my rifle. So we have nothing to trouble us, plenty of leisure time, live on the best, first-rate sport and fun.

Our passage from Detroit to Chicago will be $5. At Chicago I shall endeavor to see Dr. McArthur [family friend from Youngstown]. Mr. Bailey sends his love to his family and says he is well and in good spirits. And by the by, George, we are all true philosophers—our polar star is ahead, saddening thoughts of home do none any good, but deprive us of enjoyment. Therefore, we take the world gaily and have our laughs and fun.

We find many persons on the way to California, and the crowd at Independence may raise the prices there.

I feel concern for Mother's health and am anxious to hear from her. Sabrina must take her comfort and have as much fun with little Eliza as possible. George, you must kiss Mother for me. And Sabrina must kiss Little Cub for me. And you must go and see Mrs. Bailey and Mrs. Root. If anything occurs between here and Detroit, I will note it before I mail this. I will write from Chicago. O! George—kiss Harriet for *me*.* John Root sends his love to his mother and says he is getting along well and will write from St. Louis or Independence.

Your brother,
William

P.S. We are now at Toledo wharf. If you can read this, "you'll do," as it is written in a blow.

April 14.   This morning we awoke and found ourselves in Detroit City. ["The dock is full of hotel runners with their cries. . . . Almost the first thing that meets your eye is the black roof of the locomotive house . . . built of brick and about 600 feet long."] We left the *Arrow* early in the morning to take our passage on the [Michigan Central] railroad. But after learning that the fare to Niles, 180 miles to the west, was $6; that we would have to travel from there by stage forty miles to New Buffalo and thence from there by steamboat to Chicago for $6 more; that it would take three days on that route; and that the cars and boats did not run on Sunday, we concluded to take the lake route on account of its cheapness. The steamer *Michigan* was to leave at two o'clock and would carry us cabin passage for $6 and complete the route in four days. We concluded that $6 or $8 saved in one day was better than gold-digging, and we took our passage on the steamer.

While in Detroit I expended 91 cents for a compass and $1 for a bottle of sarsaparilla. [As advertised, this remedy "purifies the blood and cures the scrofula, rheumatism, stubborn ulcers, dyspepsia . . . liver complaint . . . consumption, female complaints, loss of appetite, debility, etc."]

We left Detroit at two o'clock, passed through the Detroit River, Lake St. Clair and part of the St. Clair River before dark. Today I took my first lesson in tailoring by putting a pocket in my vest.

In the evening we spent our time conversing in the saloon. I retired rather early.

April 15.   This is Sabbath morning and we are in the St. Clair River, "wooding" [taking on fuel] on the Canadian side.

---

* *Harriet Barrett, one of Sabrina Swain's sisters and a favorite with William and George, lived on the Barrett family farm at Lewiston Heights, six miles south of Youngstown. During William's absence, Harriet often came to the Swain farm to visit Sabrina.*

We were soon on our way up the river, slowly passing numerous sawmills and some villages. The river is clear and has numerous flocks of ducks on it. At twelve o'clock we landed at Port Huron, which lies about two miles from the entrance to Lake Huron.

Mr. Hutchinson and self went into the village and attended church and were nearly left by the boat. The captain, however, waited a few minutes for us and we put in our best licks and got on board, determined not to leave the boat again.

We put out into Lake Huron which had a tremendous swell, making the boat hop and pitch like any "hoss." Our company spent the evening debating upon the moral binding force of conscience and in reading the Bible. Today I read the Bible presented to me by my wife upon leaving home and have read with attention the two parts marked by Mother and Sabrina.

April 16. About sunrise we crossed the edge of Saginaw Bay, and we had a time of it: a rough sea and all on board were sick. Hutchinson and Bailey cast up old accounts. I ate hearty this morning and pitched out Jonah once, but not enough to do any good. John, the rogue, stood it like an old salty and was all the time making fun of us.

All day we wallowed through it, and at bedtime it was still the same. Passed Thunderbay Island just at sunset.

April 17. Last night our course was along the coast of some land [the south channel of the Straits of Mackinac] and it was not rough. I slept well all night, the first night's sleep since leaving home.

I awoke at daybreak refreshed and found the boat gliding smoothly over Mackinac Bay, and before I arose she was moored at the wharf. We breakfasted here. The waters of Lake Huron and the Straits are the clearest and most transparent waters I have ever seen. In the bay a six-pence can be distinctly seen at a depth of twenty feet. And the fish, which are here in great abundance, are as good as the waters are clear. This I know experimentally, for the steward bought a full barrel of fresh white-fish and trout—large, fat, and sweet!

We left at eight o'clock [A.M.] without being able to go to Fort Mackinaw, which, being on high ground, made a good appearance from the bay.

We dodged the ice as well as possible and made our way into Lake Michigan through a heavy snowstorm, driving winds and big waves. We had fairly got out on the lake when the captain told us that a heavy blow was approaching, as his barometer told him, and that he would make for a small harbor in Beaver Island which we had just passed. So we about-ship, ran along the coast of the island about twelve miles and entered the best-shaped little harbor in the world. We cast anchor within a stone's throw of the shore, secure from everything but the falling snow. Here we lay the rest of the day and all night, living on whitefish and trout and good potatoes and plenty of other necessities.

April 18.   This morn we left our retreat about ten o'clock and resumed our course. In crossing the lake in the afternoon the sea was heavy, and the boat rolled and pitched until the tables, chairs, stands and settees all took to themselves legs and danced in great confusion around the room. It was with difficulty that we could keep our seats or feet by holding on to the posts and other parts of the boat. None seasick, however, and all took a hasty meal.

This evening I am sad, having spent part of the evening in thinking upon my family at home.

April 19.   Today we coasted along the shores of Wisconsin between Sheboygan and Chicago.

April 19, 1849
[On board the *Michigan*]

Dear Sabrina,

I wrote from Detroit, or rather mailed a letter from there, early in the morning on Saturday [April 14]. . . .

The *Michigan* is a large and good sea boat, but the slowest on the lakes. She has every convenience, staterooms in particular, one of which each of us has occupied. The captain, who is a very fine and prudent man, sets a first-rate table. . . .

We have touched at Sheboygan, Milwaukee, Racine and Southport. We have had a heavy sea all the way and are heartily glad that our journey on the lake is so near ended, being as I write within forty-five miles of Chicago. We are all well and in good spirits and strong in the belief of the success of our expedition.

[At this point the letter is temporarily concluded, to be resumed and completed on April 20.]

April 20.   This morning we are in the Chicago River where it is full of crafts. After dressing ourselves a little extra, we secured our passage on the Illinois Canal and moved our luggage on board the canal boat. We paid $2.50 for our passage to Peru [a town on the Illinois River, 250 miles above St. Louis].

Mr. Hutchinson and I walked all over Chicago to view its location. It has many fine buildings, churches in particular, and a great business section. ["It is a large city of some 20,000 inhabitants. There are several delightful residences, particularly along the beach of the lake. The river is full of shipping. . . . There are some splendid public houses, among them the Sherman House, the City Hotel and the Tremont House. . . . There are four daily papers, the *Journal*, *Democrat*, *Advertiser* and *Tribune*. Including daily, weekly and monthly papers, there are nineteen published in the city."] But it is most horribly located and the streets are literally slough holes.

[Continuation of the letter started the previous day]

Chicago, April 20, 1849

We are just going to start down the canal. [The Illinois–Michigan Canal, one hundred miles in length, connected Chicago with steamboat navigation on the Illinois River and thus with the Mississippi.]

We have met a company returning from Independence. Great crowds there, discouraged and selling out their outfits. Just what we want.

I have not time to finish my letter as I had expected. I have only time to mail this before we leave.

Kiss little Sister for me. Give my love to all. Tell Mother that I am very anxious about her and look for a letter from home at Independence.

Farewell till I get to Independence.

Yours affectionately,
William

[*Evening, April 20.*]   We left the wharf at ten o'clock and I walked along on the tow path. As it led by Dr. McArthur's office, I called to see him and found him there. It was with a great deal of trouble that I could get off from staying with him until the next day. I had to go up to his house and see the family. I saw them all. He has grown old very fast, and Harriet [Mrs. McArthur] looks like an old woman, having been unwell ever since she was down at Youngstown.

["When I told him that I was going to California for gold, he laughed

and asked me if I had enough money to get back with. He advised me—
and urged me—to put the money I had into land in Chicago and go home
again."]

I left as soon as possible and overtook the boat and was soon out on
the pleasant prairies, which were a new and pleasing sight to me.

[Towed by teams of mules or horses, the canal boats moved slowly
through the channel of the Chicago River from Lake Michigan to the first
lock four miles south of the city where the canal itself started. Sixty feet
wide, the canal was built with a tow path on one side, about ten feet
wide, for the teams. Beyond the first lock the canal ran alongside the Des
Plaines and Illinois rivers, often separated from the river by only a narrow
embankment.

[Passengers on board the canal boats "sleep, eat, and live" in a cabin
"fifty feet in length, nine feet wide, and seven feet high. . . . Baggage is
secured on the roof of the boat and covered with canvas to screen it from
the effects of the weather." In the evening the cabin "is transformed into
a bedroom. . . . No less than fifty sleeping places are rigged up in this
small space, and twenty more are spread upon the floor. . . . These sleeping places consist of shelves placed three deep, the entire length of the
cabin on either side, with a height of two feet between each."]

April 21.   Today we are moving slowly along the canal through the
prairies, which present the most beautiful landscapes. The level lawn,
stretching away as far as sight, is dotted with herds of cattle, which
assume all shapes in the undulations of the air and fog or haze, sometimes
running and dancing and sometimes looking like buildings almost out of
sight. The beautifully rolling landscapes form the most beautiful building
spots. The hollows are frequently covered very thinly with large white
oaks with small streams coursing at their feet, in which are thousands of
ducks of every variety, wild geese, prairie hens, plover, sandhill cranes,
woodchucks, muskrats, and all sorts of small birds. Our company improved the opportunity to shoot these as we passed along and were shooting all the time, but with little success, as we were on the boat and the
game on the shore.

[On another boat bound for the frontier, a Californian reported: "We
have amused ourselves all the way down the river shooting at wild ducks,
and when no men were around, we would shoot at hogs, dogs, etc. on
the shore. Thirty or forty rifles fired all at the same time would hurry a
dog some! By the time we get among the Pawnees, we will be able to take
their eyes out without much trouble."]

Toward night we struck the Illinois River, which in the rays of the setting sun mirrors everything on its edges and has the most beautiful scenery I ever beheld.

April 22.   Today is Sabbath, and we are on a boat whose crew knows no Sabbath, although all nature around us is keeping the holy day in an appropriate manner.

We arrived at Peru at eleven o'clock [A.M.] and took passage for St. Louis on board the steamer *Avalanche.*

Peru, Illinois
April 22, 1849

Dear Mother,

Although far from home, I feel a great deal of anxiety about your health and am impatient to get to Independence, as I feel sure of getting a letter there. My only concern is about home, and I am rather glad that circumstances delayed me so long on the lakes as I am the more certain of getting news from home before I leave Independence.

We are all well and enjoy ourselves and are encouraged rather than discouraged as we near the scene of our fitting out. We learn that great numbers have set out and that many are getting tired on the journey and giving up. We have heard considerable about the cholera at St. Louis, but as we are nearing the place we hear less about it. I have conversed with the captain of the steamer *Avalanche,* on which we have taken our passage to St. Louis, and he says that there is nothing heard about cholera at St. Louis, no cases among the inhabitants of the place. It is among the emigrants who come up from New Orleans as steerage passengers—filthy, dirty, and corrupt from all manner of disease. We have no fears. However, we are careful of ourselves, for one ounce of preventative is worth a pound of cure. We are careful to have our meals regularly, our sleep ditto, and eat nothing that we deem improper.*

We arrived in Peru about noon today, after having spent two hard nights on the canal boat, which was very crowded. We immediately

---

* Contrary to Swain's assurance, cholera killed twenty-six people in St. Louis during the week of April 23. The disease reached epidemic proportions in May and claimed 1,900 lives in June.

The causes of this almost always fatal disease were not known until 1883, when the German bacteriologist Robert Koch isolated the causative organism, Vibrio cholerae asiaticae. The Vibrio bacteria enter the body through the mouth and cause an infection in the small intestine. Death results, often within a few hours of the first indication of illness, from dehydration caused by severe diarrhea and vomiting.

engaged our passage to St. Louis for $4 apiece and are to have our dinner and supper on the boat, as she won't leave until tonight.

These boats are comfortable, but the awkwardest-looking things that ever navigated. They have flat bottoms and are very wide and very high, the first story being open. The *Avalanche* draws less than two feet of water and has some of its load on board. These boats run like prairie fires, calculating to run from here to St. Louis by Tuesday morning. . . .

And now dear Mother, I must leave writing until I get to St. Louis. Give my love to Sabrina and George, and kiss dear Sister.

William

April 23. This morning we are laying at Peoria, which has a beautiful location. We walked over the city and admired its pleasant situation.

At twelve o'clock we started down the Illinois River, which is a dirty-colored stream with flats on either side covered with cottonwood, elm, swamp oak, and soft maple. These flats extend back from the river a quarter of a mile to three miles, with alternately high rocky bluffs and beautifully rolling prairies forming the back-lands.

April 24. This morn we are still on the Illinois, which preserves its former appearance with the exception of the bluffs, which, as we near the mouth, are rocky and closer to the river.

We entered the Mississippi River at eleven o'clock. It has the same appearance as the Illinois, only wider. We soon passed the mouth of the Missouri River, whose waters are like the waters of a mud hole.

At three o'clock we arrived at St. Louis. [The city "looks beautiful from the river, situated on high ground and skirted all along the levee with steamboats. . . ." "Every boat that comes up is completely loaded down with freight and passengers en route for the gold diggings. It is really amusing to see what a variety of outfits, etc. are strewed about upon the landing. . . ." "Steamboats are discharging their freight, hundreds of drays are endeavoring to load and unload, and a motley crowd of all colors and speaking all languages are using every exertion to pass and re-pass among the sugar hogsheads, flour barrels, stacks of hemp, bales of cotton, etc. The puffing of the steamboats, the swearing of five hundred draymen, the noise of horses' hoofs on the pavement, the rattling of wheels—all make up this modern Babel."]

We took lodgings at the Missouri Hotel, which is a poor house, having plenty of bedbugs.

April 25.   We spent the day in pricing the articles of our outfit and have concluded to purchase it at Independence.

["St. Louis is a great city numbering 65,000 souls, and it is growing rapidly. . . ." The rush of goldseekers "is tremendous. Hundreds . . . arrive here every day. Hotels, boardinghouses, and steamboats are filled with them." This impatient throng "has given a wonderful impetus to certain kinds of business. Placards are seen all over the city calling to the attention of Californians every variety of Gold Washers, California outfits, etc. Blacklegs, swindlers and pickpockets are as thick as the locusts of Egypt. Many a green'un who has started for the gold mines has been relieved of his 'tin' by the time he has been in St. Louis three days and has had to forgo his golden dreams and return to the 'old diggings.' "]

St. Louis, April 25, 1849

Dear George,

Here we are in St. Louis at the Missouri Hotel, paying $1 a day for our board and very comfortably situated too. We arrived here yesterday at three o'clock and are agreeably surprised both by the health and the market of the city. Of the latter I can only say that everything is much lower in price than at Buffalo and as extensive as five such places, in proof of which I counted fifty-six steamers lying at the shores as we came in yesterday. I have not heard of a case of cholera, nor have I heard a word spoken of it since we came here.

I have been busily engaged this forenoon in pricing things in this market. . . . We find upon thoroughly investigating the subject that the number of persons going to California has been quadrupledly exaggerated. The emigration has not kept pace with the supplies sent to the Missouri frontier, and the markets here are abundantly supplied: bacon at $4.50 per hundred pounds, mules from $50 to $80, wagons ready to hitch and start from $70 to $100. We have therefore concluded to purchase our outfit at Independence, buy six good mules, take a light wagon, carry grain enough to last two weeks, crack through, and be among the first wagon trains, if possible.

We are all well and enjoy our journey. For myself I can say that I have not enjoyed life for many years as I have the last week. Free from care!, enjoying good health, mind contented, enjoying constant change of spring scenery, a mild spring climate, and living on the best of wholesome food. Who could, if I could not, take comfort? My only wish on the passage down the Illinois River was that the whole family might be with

me to enjoy the same pleasures that we enjoyed. . . .

We have made up our minds to get out of this city as soon as the steamer will carry us. I drink no water, unless necessity drives me to it. This morning I drank a quarter of a cup of coffee at breakfast and two swallows of water at dinner. I eat dry food and such as I have been used to. . . .

The public buildings here are the most splendid specimens of architecture I have ever witnessed, and many of the private buildings are splendid habitations. But the business part of the city is dirty, with black, narrow streets filled with carts drawn by mules. It is a bare heap of stone and brick, covered with coal smoke, with which the air of the city is black all the time.

This, as you know, is a slaveholding state, and yet not one in twenty of the laborers of this city is black. There was one sold at auction at the courthouse today, but we had not time to witness the spectacle.

[Advertisements for the sale of Negroes appeared in St. Louis newspapers almost daily. For instance: "Four Negroes for Sale. Woman, twenty-seven years old . . . A Girl, sixteen years old, likely; and one twelve years old; a Boy twelve years old. All black and just from the country, sound and fully warranted. Also a good work horse, cheap.

St. Louis riverfront, with steamboats tied up along the levee.
MISSOURI HISTORICAL SOCIETY

Apply at 104 Locust Street where they may be seen."

["The upper part of the city is pleasant, many fine dwellings. The ladies tread the street freely and ride horseback; they generally dress very richly. . . . All possess an air of dignity and self-possession peculiar to the slave state, arising perhaps from conscious superiority to those who attend to all menial affairs for them."]

I shall be glad to hear from Mother at Independence, and I think it almost impossible that there will not be a letter there for me from home.

Mr. Hutchinson and Mr. Bailey have just returned from the steamboat, and we have concluded to stay here until tomorrow.

We have seen many companies bound for California, but I have seen none that I would prefer to our own, or whose prospects are better than ours. We have uniformly had respect paid to us as being a company of respectable persons and have had proposals to join our company, which we have declined.

John Root and Hutchinson are arguing the slave question. Hutchinson is making our India-rubber blanket with needle, thread and thimble.

Tell Sabrina that she must be happy and take her comfort. I would be glad to be wealthy and be able to travel with my family and enable them to enjoy the pleasures of an easy life; therefore I take my way to the mountains to get the rocks. If health and success crown my exertions, my family with myself will equally share the benefit. May Heaven grant that success, and may the overruling hand of Providence guide me and you, until we enjoy a happy meeting in our own dear home.

Give my love to Mother and Sabrina, and you must all kiss little Sister for me and learn her to think of her Papa.

Your affectionate brother,
William

April 26. This morning we engaged our passage to Independence [387 miles up the Missouri River] on the steamer *Amelia* at $6 and moved our baggage on board the boat. We leave John here in St. Louis to await the arrival of his rifle which he forgot in Detroit.

We left St. Louis at twelve o'clock. The *Amelia* was crowded to overflowing with 250 tons of freight and one hundred passengers.

[Other river steamers were equally crowded with "a dense medley of Hoosiers, Wolverines, Buckeyes, Yankees, and Yorkers, including black-legs and swindlers of every grade. . . . The decks above and below exhibited a stupendous assortment of wagons, horses, mules, tents, bales, boxes, sacks, barrels, and camp kettles; while every cabin and stateroom was an arsenal of rifles, fowling pieces, bowie knives, hatchets, pouches, powder horns, and belts." "Every berth was full, and not only every settee and table occupied at night, but the cabin floor was covered by sleeping emigrants. . . ."]

April 27. This morning the monotony of our journey was early broken by the sight of three deer standing on a very high bluff, looking at us as though we and our boat were intruders. A number of shots were fired without even arousing their fears or starting them from their repose.

["Geese, ducks, turkeys, etc." were frequently seen along the shore. "Speaking of game . . ., *gaming* is a business very extensively followed on the river steamers." On board the *St. Paul* "two Californians . . . had what means they possessed taken from them in double-quick time. There is more or less gaming day and night. . . . Poker is much followed on this river. . . ." "Many passengers engage in some kind of reading, principally of the trashy, obscene kind of stuff offered for sale on all the boats on leaving any of the cities and towns where they stop."]

We stopped at Herman, a German village of some size situated on the right bank. Here we found the first water which was fit to drink that we have seen since we left the Illinois River.

We passed many picturesque farms which would be beautiful places to spend leisure time. ["The Missouri is decidedly a finer river than the Mississippi, as far as scenery is concerned. The short bends and the wooded banks prevent one from seeing too far ahead, and the numerous little creeks and shaded coves . . . have an air of quiet wildness about them. . . ."]

April 28.   This morning we went aground at the mouth of the Osage River, though we got off early and soon arrived at Jefferson City. The passengers went to view the state capitol which is situated on a beautiful hill fronting the town. It has a grand appearance, being a design like the national capitol at Washington. . . .

Having taken on an extremely heavy lading, we left Jefferson City at two o'clock and proceeded slowly on our way, having on board a company of emigrants from that city. Here we heard of a man dying of cholera.

[Other reports told of cholera raging "with great violence on board several steamers, one of which . . . was entirely abandoned and left tied to the shore." On another, cholera broke out "with virulence" the very first night out of St. Louis: "Under the unfavorable circumstances of irregular diet and a crowded and dirty steamer, its effects were quick and deadly. A great panic ensued, and many of the noisiest braggarts became suddenly endowed with a lamblike meekness. Some eighteen or twenty poor fellows died and were laid on the deck till enough corpses accumulated, when they were buried, wrapped only in their blankets, in shallow holes hastily dug by the deck hands on the river islands, the boat barely stopping long enough for the purpose."]

April 29.   Today is Sabbath, and I am on the Missouri River far from the home that keeps my relatives. They are now preparing for divine services while I am surrounded by the hum and noise of travel, the wild scenery and the uncultivated shores of this great river. The influence of the accustomed repose of the day has its effect upon my mind and disposes me to reflections which ever turn to those I have left at home and wake the strongest feelings in my bosom—feelings which require the greatest self-command to control.

This morning we are a few miles from Rocheport. The banks and scenery of the left bank are very grand, the bluffs being close to the river and rocky, high and broken. We touched at Rocheport which is situated in a valley of the bluffs. . . .

A company from Marshall, Michigan, is on board and has two ministers in its number. At eleven o'clock we attended public service conducted by Rev. Hobart, one of the ministers from Michigan. All the passengers attended and presented a singular appearance. Far from the endearments of home, about ninety men, with but two females who were steerage passengers, filled the saloon. The deepest solemnity pervaded the company during the service, which was the regular Methodist service. The singing, which was good, the prayer and the reading of the Scripture were all very solemn and listened to attentively by the assembly. Whenever those we had left behind us were mentioned, the audience was in tears, which gave proof that those on board had brought with them the tender ties of kindred which they had but lately torn asunder. The afterpart of the day we spent reading, reflecting and conversing.

Today I have lost the mark presented to me by Mother and placed in my Bible at Christ's Sermon on the Mount, a circumstance which I deeply regret. I have been very unwell yesterday and this forenoon from living too high and taking too little exercise, but this afternoon I am much better.

April 30. This morn we had heavy wind which drove us ashore and blew heavily for an hour and a half. We improved the time by loading wood which we had to carry twenty rods. The passengers all helped and had a good exercise which we all needed. It was pleasant to have the chance to walk on land after being shut upon the boat for three and a half days.

May 1. This morning we are only five miles from where we were last night, and the slow progress of our boat is discouraging to all on board. The sandy deposits of river banks, the unbroken cottonwood forests on the river flats, the dirty water, and the confinement on board with so many persons have become completely disgusting. We have been on board two times as long as the captain told us we would be on this trip. The truth is that they have loaded too heavily for the depth of the river and the strength of the engines. On this river they may abuse the traveling public with impunity, but in civilized countries they would receive a severe reprimand.

Today one of the company from Michigan was taken sick, thought at first to be cholera but proved to be a bowel complaint. Toward night he was better, but still very sick, supposed to be turning into intermittent fever. He has good attention, the attendance of two physicians. His sickness has caused great concern on board. ["It is surprising to see how many doctors are going to California. Every company has two or three."]

I am resolved to take all easy, to be prudent in diet, careful not to expose myself, and to leave the rest to the Ruler of the destiny of all mankind. Many on board have not had beds to sleep on and consequently have had no rest. But we have had our regular sleep every night and intend, if possible, to continue to do so.

May 2.   This morning we are still twenty-five miles from Independence, having made only fifty miles in thirty-six hours.

About nine o'clock the pilot ran the boat on a sand bar, where we are now lying as easily as can be. We have been aground two hours. All hands and passengers have labored to get us afloat, but it won't go. How long we shall lay here I cannot say, but certainly the prospect is anything but encouraging.

[Sometimes passengers had to go ashore and "walk, in order to enable a boat to cross a sand bar."]

We got off the sand bar about three o'clock and made slow progress, having no wood and being obligated to stop along the banks and buy rails from the farmers.

I forgot to mention that the two doctors of the Michigan company have both been sick for the last three days. They were better yesterday. I saw one of them at breakfast this morning, and the other is comfortable. The man taken sick yesterday has a high fever.

We arrived at the Lower Independence Landing at eight o'clock and lay there all night.

Back Home

"O, William, I wish you had been content
to stay at home, for there is no real home
for me without you. . . ."

After saying goodbye to his son, John, and to Swain, Bailey and Hutchinson at Huff's Hotel the morning of April 12, Dr. Root drove his wagon and team from Buffalo back to Youngstown. Late that afternoon he pulled into the Swain farm, where Sabrina and George had been waiting for a final message. The doctor gave Sabrina her letter, and then came the surprise—the daguerreotype portrait William had sat for the previous evening.

Thus began William Swain's reaching back to his family through his letters, first from Buffalo, later from the frontier, and finally from the gold mines. At the same time Sabrina and George sought to keep William close to their lives through their letters, the first sent to Independence, Missouri.

During the three weeks that Swain spent traveling to Independence —April 12 to May 2—his wife and brother wrote three letters. He received them on May 7. He would not hear from home again for almost a year.

Through the summer and fall of 1849 and through 1850, Sabrina and George wrote at least once each month, addressing their letters to Sutter's Fort, California. Failing eyesight prevented William's mother from writing.

In all, from the three in Independence to the last that reached him in California, William received twenty-nine letters from home. He saved each one, as Sabrina and George treasured all of his.

Sunday evening, April 15, 1849

Dear, dear William,

I want very much to describe my feelings as near as I can, but in doing so I hope not to crucify yours. I feel as though I was alone in the world. The night you left home I did not, nor could not, close my eyes to sleep. Sis slept very well, awoke in the morning, and looked over at me seemingly to welcome a spree with her father, but to her disappointment the looked-for one was absent. She appears very lonesome, and seems to miss you very much. She is very troublesome and will not go to anyone, but cries after me and clings to me more than ever.

I received your daguerrian. . . . I think I never saw anything but life look more natural. I showed it to Little Cub, and to my astonishment and pleasure she appeared to recognize it. She put her finger on it, looked up at me and laughed, put her face down to yours, and kissed it several times in succession. Every time it comes in her sight she will cry after it.

William, if I had known that I could not be more reconciled to your absence than I am, I never could have consented to your going. However, I will try to reconcile myself as well as I can, believing God will order all things for the best.

I must stop now and take Sis.

Monday morning, 8 o'clock

Good morning, William.

I feel pretty well this morning and in better spirits than I have since you left. Sis is pretty well. Mother Swain is better. She is now eating some toast, and George is sitting to her back, whilst Harriet has Sis. Breakfast is waiting for us. . . .

It is almost nine o'clock and I must close.

My dear, take good care of your health, keep your spirits up, and think as little about home as possible; read your Bible, and put your trust in God. He alone can protect you and bring you in safety to your family. Some people here think you will not go any further than Independence. I almost hope you will not. If you are taken dangerously sick between here and there, or at Independence, write for me to come.

Write often, tell us all, keep a journal and preserve it for me. Harriet joins in love to you. Sis kisses me for you.

Farewell,
Sabrina

At Home
Swain Farm, Youngstown
April 19, 1849

Dear Brother William,

Last night we received your letter of the 13th mailed at Detroit, and we were right glad to hear that you were in good spirits and enjoying your journey. We have been at the post office every day since you went. . . . I have been at the post office tonight. I tell you we shall keep a watch there as long as you are in the bounds of civilization. But when you get beyond that into the land of "Sweet botheration and shillalah law" we shall look for letters from you like angel's visits, few and far between. . . .

Mother is better, but still keeps to her bed most of the time. She sits up two or three times a day for twenty or thirty minutes. She appears now to be in a fair way to recover. I feel quite easy about her now. . . .

Sabrina is, I think, some better than when you left. Eliza is better also, I think. She was very noisy and disturbed Mother badly, and so Sabrina took Sis up to her family this morning [the Barretts' farm at Lewiston Heights, four miles to the south] where she will stay three or four days. If Mother was well, I should not want Sabrina to go away at all unless it was her choice. Little Cub is full of her fun and prate, and we like her all the more that her father is gone. . . .

Everything is after the old sort here. Many are inquiring about you and what you write. They all knew that there was a letter in post office from you. Some are saying you will be back in less than a month. I tell our folks that such persons don't know the man. We hear that there are 4,000 persons at Independence and that cattle are $200 per yoke and other things in proportion, which will make it bad for you. But William, look the ground over calmly, and if you think there is a fair prospect of getting through with life and health, go ahead. But if you can see no prospect ahead but want and misery, don't go. Come back rather, and wait the moving of the waters. I would rather you would go now, as you are started, if you can; but I wouldn't have you hazard everything with chances strongly against you—that would be folly.

If you go, do not make any dependence on provisions at the Mormon settlement [Salt Lake City], mind that. If you do, you fail. They have none to spare. You should take at least three or four weeks' more provisions than you think you will want, so that in case of accident or detention you will not run short. You had better get a good quantity of little articles of medicine and little comforts . . . hot drops, peppermint sauces, blister plasters, strengthening or sticking salve, opium and laudanum, etc., and don't depend on Mr. Hutchinson, although he has a "good supply of things which you forgot." Make each one provide sufficient, and more than that, for himself; then you will not be short. . . .

The neighbors are very kind to Mother and all of us. I saw Mrs. Bailey and Dr. Root today. Both families are well.

I am so sleepy that I cannot keep my eyes open. I have fallen asleep three or four times already and made the blots you see. Now past twelve o'clock—must have some sleep.

Good night, Will. May God protect you from all harm.

Friday morning, April 20

Good morning, my lad. The top of the morning to you, wherever you be.

Well, Will, I was so fast asleep last night I don't know what I have written, and I slept so hard that I don't know what to write. Mother says she is better this morning and says: "Tell William that there is now a prospect of my getting well and put him in mind of his Bible." Lorayne [a cousin, visiting the Swains] says: "Give William my respects and tell him I wish him success and happiness and that he may come home with a pocket full of rocks." . . . Philena [one of Sabrina's sisters, also visiting] sends her respects and wishes you good luck. Be sure to write us two or three long letters from Independence.

O, Will, one word of scandal. Old Mrs. Washburn has told some of her "confidential" friends that our friend Michael Hutchinson, Esq. was paying attention to, or courting, her. Perhaps you'll catch him dreaming on the prairies of his "Nora Crena." Just rally him a little. It may make a bit of fun for you in tent or on the march. . . .

If you go on the prairies, I hope you will have lots of fun and sport with those rifles. Give the buffalo "Jesse." I'd like to be with you, my old boy, but I believe I have done some good at home, and I shall do all I can. Tell Mr. Bailey that whatever I can do for Mrs. Bailey, I will. I told her yesterday to call on me for whatever assistance I could render her and it would be forthcoming.

Give my best wishes to all the company. Tell them I am with them in spirit and should like to take a stampede on the prairies with them in body. It is now a quarter after eight. I must hold on. So goodbye, Will. God bless you.

Your brother,
George

Sunday, April 22, 1849

Dear Husband,

It is with pleasure that I seat myself to converse with you a few moments today, would that it were verbally. I am now at Father's and am weaning Little Cub. She is very unwell and consequently she is more trouble to wean. I left home Thursday. . . .

O William, I wish you had been content to stay at home, for there is no real home for me without you. This is woman's weakness. O, that the days, weeks, and months might roll rapidly on and speed you back again. . . .

I saw Mrs. Bailey last Wednesday. She was well and little Frank also. He says his Papa has gone to California and is coming home again with a lump of gold for him. Mrs. Root and family are well.

We received your letter of the 13th last Wednesday, the 18th, and were glad to hear of your pleasant ride and good spirits. I shall look strong for another from you today. I have no news to write, only that the curly cow has calved and got a fine heifer calf. We shall try to raise it for you. . . .

Most of the people tell me that I am a fool for letting you go away and that no man that thought anything of his family would do so. They say that I need not indulge a hope of seeing you again. I tell them you are

Sunday 9th 22nd 1849

Dear Husband

It is with pleasure I seat myself
to converse with you a few moments to day;
(would that it were verbally) I am now at Father's
and weaning little cub, she is very unwell and
consequently makes her more troublesome to
wean, I left home on thursday Mother is getting
better slowly, Lorayne is there now, Geo went to
Lockport after her last tuesday, she intends to
return next week, to Rochester, Mother is trying
very hard to persuade her to spend the summer
with her, if she succeeds in doing so, I suppose my
room will be considered better than my company.
Oh William I wish you had been contented to staid
at home for their is no real home for me without you
(this is womans weakness,) O that the days weeks and months
might roll rapidly on and speed you back again.
Philena is at your place and will probaly stay untill they
can get someone, They have Eben McClun engaged.
I saw Mrs Bailey last Wednesday she was well and
little Frank also, he says his Papa has gone to Calapoix
and is coming home again with a lump of gold for him
Mrs Bird and family are well.

in the hands of God and that your life is as precious in His sight there as here. . . .

I feel as though this would be the last letter you may ever read from me. God forbid that it shall be so. . . . Remember your Bible and your God. Put your trust in Him and all will turn out for good in the end. My anxieties for you are beyond description, but I will and must leave the result with God.

Our people join in love to you and wish you Godspeed. I hope you will not keep anything back concerning your journey. If anything happens that you cannot write, get someone to write for you. . . . Write how far it is to the Sacramento River from Independence.

I hope we shall meet again. How can I be reconciled if we do not? Farewell, farewell, my dear.

Yours affectionately,
Sabrina

Opening page of Sabrina's second letter. Her first is so faded as to be almost illegible.
AUTHOR'S COLLECTION

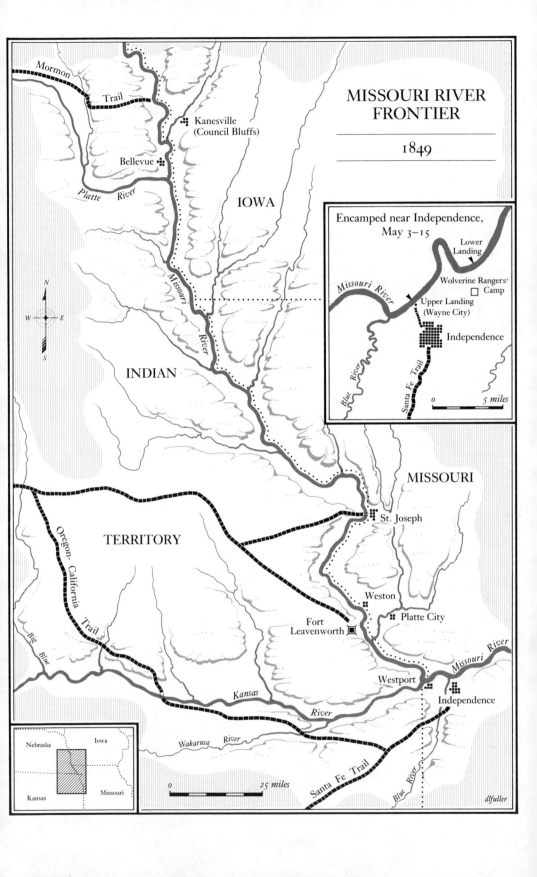

MISSOURI RIVER FRONTIER

1849

Encamped near Independence, May 3–15

Lower Landing

Wolverine Rangers' Camp

Upper Landing (Wayne City)

Independence

Missouri River

Blue River

Santa Fe Trail

0   5 miles

Mormon Trail

Kanesville (Council Bluffs)

Bellevue

Platte River

IOWA

Missouri River

INDIAN

N
W   E
S

MISSOURI

St. Joseph

TERRITORY

Oregon-California Trail

Weston

Platte City

Fort Leavenworth

Big Blue

Westport

Missouri River

Independence

Kansas River

Wakarusa River

Blue River

Santa Fe Trail

Nebraska   Iowa

Kansas   Missouri

0   25 miles

dlfuller

CHAPTER II

Fitting for a Start

"The mustering of Californians on the frontier is like the marshaling of the hosts of our empire for a military invasion."

By mid-April some 30,000 goldseekers had reached the outfitting towns along the Missouri River. In meadows and forest groves they camped on the outskirts of these jumping-off points, packing and rearranging their wagon loads and training their teams. Each day hundreds more pushed ashore at the steamboat landings at Independence, Westport, Weston, St. Joseph and Council Bluffs. Others who had come overland from farms and villages in Illinois, Wisconsin, Iowa and Missouri could find space to set up camp only on the outer edge of the vast sprawl of tents, wagons, mules, oxen and horses. At night the campfires looked like those of besieging armies.

After the months of anticipating and planning and then the journey to the frontier, the goldseekers wanted to get started for California. But everyone had to wait, those who had set up camp in early April and the stragglers who arrived in May. With the prairie trails soggy from spring rains and the grass yet too sparse to provide forage for the thousands of animals, the emigrants spent their days attending to camp chores or wandering into the towns to make purchases or just to look at the crowds. The first companies broke camp the week of April 15; the great majority rolled west by the first week of May.

Like William Swain and his friends, many landed in these towns without teams or wagons, unsure whether to travel by themselves or to join a larger organized company. Decisions had to be made as to the best route—the Santa Fe Trail or the Oregon–California Trail. For the great majority of Californians this period of decision-making, buying, organizing and then waiting for good weather took place at Independence or St.

Joseph, the centers and rivals for the overland outfitting business.

Founded in 1827, Independence was widely known as the eastern terminus for the wagon trains that traveled to Santa Fe for trade with Mexico. Through 1846 the town had the reputation as the best place for Oregon and California emigrants to buy their animals, wagons and supplies. In 1847 St. Joseph, about a hundred miles north, and Kanesville, farther up river in Iowa, became serious competitors. The latter town, also known as Council Bluffs, developed that year as the point of departure for the Mormons, who traveled west along the north side of the Platte River bound for their haven on the shores of the Great Salt Lake.

What had been a traditional rivalry between the frontier's major commercial centers changed in the spring of 1849 to a strident contest for the profits to be made in outfitting the sudden influx of Californians, many of them inexperienced city folk and all of them impatient. In this competition, the merchants of Independence and St. Joseph resorted to every device to attract customers and at the same time to frighten them away from the rival. Independence ran advertisements in the St. Louis newspapers, and in Louisville and Cincinnati, emphasizing the town's experience in the Santa Fe trade and boasting of the eighteen wagon-maker shops, the blacksmiths, gunsmiths, saddleries, numerous equipment and provisions stores and the large stock of oxen, mules and horses —all at low prices. The St. Joseph *Gazette* accused the Independence *Expositor* of printing "many thousand lies about St. Joseph and its facilities to accommodate the emigrants." The *Gazette* was especially outraged by reports of rampant cholera and extortionate prices in St. Jo, supposedly spread by Independence agents in St. Louis and other river towns. One of the best arguments used to favor St. Joseph was the town's location eighty miles farther west than Independence, an advantage that could save the impatient goldseekers at least a week's travel time.

Given the "hard lying," the misleading advertising and testimonials and the many rumors of disease and delays, the emigrants found it difficult to know which town would be preferable. As it turned out, St. Joseph emerged as the more successful outfitting post. More than 17,000 Californians started from there, while about 15,000 set out from the encampments that surrounded Independence.

Most of these thousands came to the outfitting towns on board Missouri River steamboats. There were thirty-seven of these wood-burning side- and stern-wheelers that ran between St. Louis and Council Bluffs. Exemplary of the traffic that spring, the *Consignee* stopped at St. Joseph on March 31 to disembark 240 goldseekers, most of them from Pittsburgh, with a hundred tons of gear, seventy wagons and eighty to ninety mules.

During the week-to-ten-day trip upriver from St. Louis to Independence or St. Joseph, the crowded passenger quarters and ignorance of sanitation provided grimly ideal conditions for the spread of cholera. On board the *Monroe*, the virulent disease swept through the 300 passengers, killing fifty-three and causing such panic that on May 11 the boat was deserted in Jefferson City.

Through April and the first two weeks of May, the Californians crowded the streets of Independence, St. Joseph and the smaller frontier towns. Some of these greenhorns in their western outfits tried to look like the rough mountain trappers who in previous years had ruled the bars and whorehouses; others looked for friends from back home, and a good many explored the gambling houses. But most were busy buying salted bacon, salertus, hard bread, dried fruit, pistols, rifles, percussion caps, medicines, tin stoves, India-rubber blankets, bowie knives, rope, lanterns and a score of other recommended necessities. At nearby corrals they debated whether to buy oxen or mules.

Of all their decisions in preparing for the overland journey, the choice of teams was most important and difficult. Many complained that every resident of Independence and St. Joseph seemed to have either oxen or mules to sell or sought to promote the interest of friends who had one or the other. Despite the contradictory recommendations, decisions were made, sometimes with such certainty that arguments broke out between members of the same company, some demanding purchase of oxen, others insisting on mules. A few companies split over the issue.

From information and general discussion heard in Independence, Swain and his friends judged that oxen were preferable to mules, in part because they sold for $40 to $50 per yoke, while mules cost $50 to $70 each. As well, the perversity of mules, especially for a city man, dissuaded many from choosing the long-ears. For those who did, Mexicans could be hired in Independence and St. Joseph to break the wild mules that had been sold with the assurance "they would be as handy as sheep."

Better than half of the companies chose oxen. Only a few hitched up horses to their wagons. Some companies bought pack saddles for their mules to carry food and supplies, thus saving the cost of wagons. But packing was known to be a demanding experience without a place to rest or, if necessary, to carry a sick comrade. And worse, with pack mules the companies could not carry the array of equipment they expected to need in the mines—everything from underwater diving suits and bells to gold-washing machinery, in addition to all the food and gear required on the trail. Wagons would allow room for everything.

There was another alternative for getting to California that seemed to offer the fastest and certainly the easiest journey. Called "passenger service," there were on the frontier several stagecoach lines that tried to get started in the spring of 1849. The best-known and the only one that eventually reached California was appropriately called the Pioneer Line. Operated by a company in St. Louis, this outfit proposed to carry passengers across the plains in "twenty elliptic spring wagons, covered and fitted up comfortably for six passengers each. . . . Price of passage, including rations, $200. We expect to make the trip in 55 to 60 days but we take provisions for 100 days. . . . All that the best kind of mule teams, the most complete outfit and experienced conductors can accomplish, we promise to do." Announced for a hundred passengers, the Pioneer Line sold 120 tickets by the end of April and set out with twenty carriages and twenty-two baggage and supply wagons.

For all but a few, the tradition of earlier travelers to Oregon and California showed the way to go—by wagon and in organized companies or associations. No one faced the vast distance with just one wagon and four or five companions. Though motivated by individual ambition, indeed by an independence of spirit that had sent them off from home, the goldseekers knew that the journey would require joint effort and cooperation, that collective security would be needed in the face of wilderness uncertainties and dangers. Therefore, back home or at the frontier they organized joint-stock companies that served not only as business partnerships to meet the costs of purchasing wagons, teams and supplies, but also provided governmental or military decision-making authority and leadership. For defense against Indian attack, regulation of guard duty to protect the animals, decisions as to where to camp each night, it had been proved in years past that officers with authority, sometimes enhanced by uniforms, could best manage a company of greenhorns.

Swain and his friends had either to gather together a company of their own from the many strangers in the town or to join a group of Californians already organized. Fortunately, during the river trip from St. Louis they had come to know the well-organized company of fifty-eight men from Marshall, Michigan, who called themselves the Wolverine Rangers. On May 5, Swain, Bailey and Hutchinson walked to the Rangers' camp at the Lower Landing and asked about joining. (John Root had gone up to St. Joseph.) With payment of $100 each and agreement to provide their own wagon, they became members of a company which to a remarkable degree represented the nationwide exodus. This association of farmers, blacksmiths, carpenters, lawyers, preachers, clerks, gunsmiths, physicians, machinists, tanners and other residents of small towns and farms in southern Michigan had set out for Independence on April 18. Heralding their departure, a Detroit newspaper published an editorial which revealed the impact of the rush to California:

Almost every village in this state has sent or is about to send forth to this new land of promise its company of young, active and enterprising men. . . . The members of these companies take with them as a general rule from three to five hundred dollars in money . . . principally raised by mortgages on their farms or homesteads at a high rate of interest. . . . Not less than 6,000 men have already made arrangements to leave this area. . . .

In planning their departure from Marshall, Michigan, the Wolverine Rangers had sent ahead an agent, James Pratt, who had been editor of one of the town's two newspapers, the Marshall *Statesman*. Prior to his leaving for the frontier, Pratt's paper had published the names and occupations of all members of the Wolverine Rangers and their "Articles of Association and Agreement" which set down the rules for organizing and managing the joint-stock company, including the election of a board of directors and a captain, lieutenant, secretary, treasurer, and steward.*

James Pratt was important not only as the company's advance agent who purchased supplies and selected oxen at the frontier, but also as the reporter whose letters sent to his newspaper provided the people of the town and surrounding country an accounting of the Rangers' experiences in Independence and later their life on the trail to California. Several other members of the company wrote letters home, also published in the *Statesman*.

That the *Statesman* and its rival the *Democratic Expounder* regularly printed letters from Marshall's citizens on their way to El Dorado was in no way unusual—almost every newspaper in the United States printed letters "From the Frontier" and from those "On the Trail," letters that provided personal and general information about the great emigration. Back home amid 17 million Americans in thirty states, thousands of families waited eagerly, anxiously, for news from their men on the trail to California. Some letters brought evidence that the gold fever raged as strong as ever. A young man encamped near Independence on May 12 wrote to his wife back in Boston: "The reports here of the gold regions are as encouraging as they were back in Mass. Just imagine yourself seeing me return with $10,000 to $100,000."

This Bostonian's optimism, like that of many others camped around Independence, was encouraged by news of a letter from California's gold fields written by ex-Governor Lilburn W. Boggs of Missouri. James Pratt heard of this letter and reported: "Governor Boggs has written another letter to his friends here and he tells them, no matter what may be their business, to leave immediately for California. Gov. Boggs left the state

---

* *The "Articles" are reproduced in the Appendix.*

poor and has found an immense fortune, as have several others known here who went with him."

More than optimism and youthful exuberance, this news inspired poetry. Pratt told of meeting a young goldseeker from New York "who scratched off the following for us to sing. It is so appropriate and breathes so much of the right sentiment, I give it to you." He copied all six stanzas of verse, with chorus, to be sung to the tune "O, Susannah, Don't You Cry." Two of them read:

> *We're sons of gallant fathers, boys,*
> *And mothers kind and true,*
> *Who whispered as they wrung our hands*
> *"God bless and be with you."*
> *Wives, scores of sympathizing friends,*
> *Who wish us hearty speed,*
> *Besides the <u>world</u> to back us, if*
> *Our steps to fortune lead.*

> *Chorus: Oh California!*
> *Thou land of glittering dreams,*
> *Where the yellow dust and diamonds, boys,*
> *Are found in all thy streams!*

> *And all of us—have we not left*
> *Our best of life for this?*
> *But cheer we up! we will return*
> *Laden with gold and bliss!*
> *Then saddle our mules! away we go*
> *With hopes by fancy led,*
> *To where the Sacramento flows*
> *Over its glittering bed!*

Possibly William Swain heard this song. If he did, his literary background caused him to forsake repeating it in his letters from Independence, written to Sabrina, his mother and George. As eager as they were to hear from him, to know of his health, his prospects, even more he hoped to hear from them before leaving the frontier. Though a transient in a town swarming with thousands of strangers, he did receive on May 7 three letters postmarked Youngstown.

Through the rainy days of early May, the Wolverine Rangers worked at their campsite near the Lower Landing, six miles from Independence. One of the largest companies on the frontier, they numbered sixty-two men as of May 5 when Swain, Bailey and Hutchinson and a man they did not know from Milwaukee each bought a share and became equal owners of the company's property. They had much to learn, even those among them who had been farmers. Oxen were common draft animals, but training them to work as a team of six to pull a heavily loaded wagon and knowing how to guide and command them were skills that required some days of trial and error.

The Rangers' success in reaching California would depend first on the health and strength of their teams and second on the durability of their wagons. James Pratt, as the Wolverines' agent, had purchased their wagons in Chicago and had them shipped to Independence. Like those of other companies on the frontier, they were simple farm wagons, such as had been used in earlier years by Oregon and California settlers. They were not at all like the heavy, sway-backed Conestoga wagons used in Pennsylvania in the mid-eighteenth century and adapted for the Santa Fe trade where the cargoes required size and heft. The gold rush wagons were standard vehicles, common on farms across America—and seldom, if ever, were they called "prairie schooners." Light but sturdy, they had three basic parts—the bed, the running gear, and the top. The bed was a wooden box about nine or ten feet long and four feet wide, with the sides and ends about two or three feet high. The axles and tongues were made of well-seasoned hickory, ash, oak or other hardwood; many companies carried extras, for these parts were known to snap and give way at stream crossings and steep declines. The wheels had to be extremely tough, and the rims or tires were made of iron. The tops or covers, made of canvas or some other thick cloth that had been waterproofed with linseed or other oil, were stretched over five or six bows of hickory. Inside the "covered wagon" an enclosed space about five feet high from bed to peak provided storage space and shelter. Because these simple wagons had no brakes (and, of course, no springs), the teamsters learned how to tie chains around the rear wheels to lock them, and thus provide a drag when the teams started down a steep slope.

There was much to learn, not the least how properly to load the wagons, each to carry one ton. While learning and organizing, the members of the more militarily inclined companies wore uniforms and guard duty was started in preparation for the Indian country to the west.

The Wolverine Rangers spent their days hard at work and in the evenings sought the shelter of their tents or wagons to escape the chill and rain. In other camps around Independence and the other outfitting towns, arguments and fights, even shootings, sometimes caused organizations to collapse, with the dissidents taking their wagons and whatever supplies they could agree belonged to them and leaving to find another company to join. Men grew bored with the routine or the laziness of camp life and sought excitement and possible reward in gambling. Card playing in tents or beside wagons, roulette, monte and faro in the towns' gambling halls, and liquor in saloons enlivened the chilly nights.

Spending his days and nights in the Rangers' camp, seeing only the crowd nearby, Swain could not have known or even guessed the magnitude of that vast gathering. In one of his letters to George he estimated the total number to have been 10,000.

On the roads leading to the ferry crossings of the Missouri River at St. Joseph and Council Bluffs, long lines of wagons, oxen and mules and cursing men moved slowly day after day down to the riverbank, there to board the crude ferryboats. At these crossings part of the great migration could be counted. On May 18 the St. Joseph *Adventure* reported 4,350 wagons, 17,400 men and 34,500 animals had crossed at the several ferries. Adding those who crossed after the 18th, those who crossed at Council Bluffs and the crowd from the Independence area who took either the Santa Fe or the Oregon–California trails, it is clear that at least 35,000 goldseekers set out from the western frontier in the spring of 1849.

Not all who reached the jumping-off points shared the excitement of breaking camp and rolling onto the prairies. In scores of camps men lay in tents and wagons suffering the agonies of cholera while their companions waited helplessly for the inevitable task of digging their graves. At steamboat landings the bodies of victims were dragged ashore and pushed into shallow graves. Rumors multiplied the deaths, intensifying fear of the pestilence and impatience to move west. Every man who kept a diary during the weeks of preparation and delay at the frontier told of companions dying or burial ceremonies in nearby camps. Swain reported the death and formal burial of two Rangers and wrote his family that "a solemnity or rather gloom" had settled over the camp.

For a few of the families whose fathers, husbands or sons died on the Missouri frontier, farther west or in California, the financial impact was eased by life insurance policies their men had purchased before they left home, in St. Louis or at the frontier. A woman in Michigan received in late 1849 from the New York Life Insurance Company the sum of $400, "the full amount for which my husband was insured." And a goldseeker in 1850 wrote to advise his wife that he had bought a policy that would bring her $2,500 if he died.

Most who died along the Missouri frontier were victims of cholera. A few died from gunshot wounds in fights or accidents. There were others who would not be part of the great caravan across the prairies— the backtrackers, those who became discouraged, sold out and headed for home. Their number would grow in the weeks ahead. But the vast majority in the great crowd waited, loaded and reloaded their wagons, argued and waited, impatient to break free from the States. By the second week of May most of them were struggling over the first miles of the long trail to California.

■

May 3, 1849. This morning our boat started for the Upper Landing, which is twelve miles from the Lower.

We arrived about nine o'clock after a pleasant run of three hours. This landing has a hard appearance, being at the bottom of a very high bluff and close to the shore. ["It is known by the pompous name of Wayne City . . . a most uninviting and dismal-looking hole."]

We landed the trunks and hired a man to take them to the city for 25 cents apiece while we walked, the distance being three miles. On arriving at the top of the hill, we had a grand view of the river below us. The road from the river to Independence runs through rolling woodland, which resembles our own forests at home. The oaks, hickory and other forest trees seemed like familiar friends. The sweet notes of the familiar birds —robin redbreast, mourning dove, and yellowbird—brought to my mind pleasing reflections of home. The walk was a delightful one, and we relished it the more as we were just freed from the confinement of the boat.

We arrived at Independence and took board at Mr. F. H. Hereford, Esq.'s house at $4 per week. ["The Noland and Independence Houses are full as eggs, as is also every other house in town where boarding and accommodations may be had, and almost every hour in the day the landlords are compelled to refuse applicants for admission."]

We find this to be a business town, presenting the most businesslike appearance of any town we have seen since we left St. Louis. Here are many fine buildings, stores, taverns, and dwellings. In fact, it presents the appearance of a northern village of some 1,500 to 2,000 inhabitants, situated in a good place for mercantile pursuits. We spent the afternoon in getting information, pricing mules, wagons and oxen. ["You have only to let it be known you are a Californian . . . to have the price raised 100 percent higher than that charged any other person."

["Considering the large number of strangers that are congregated together here, the contentions pervading and quarrels arising, and the reckless manner in which firearms of all descriptions are used . . . a person passing among the throng and witnessing the excitement and hearing the deadly threats exchanged would be inclined to pass the same way again to ascertain the extent of injury or who was killed in the affray. Happily, however, the great majority of such broils end in 'gassing.' "

["There are two gambling houses here, open day and night, where some of the Californians stand a good chance of being so fleeced that they can neither return home nor go farther." "One of these establishments is located on the public square. . . . So large is the company congregated in this small room, both day and night, that it is necessary for ventilation to keep the windows hoisted. This enables the passerby and stranger readily to see where his fortune is to be made, while the music of jingling coin attracts his ear and inclines him to venture in to see the doings. To make the thing more attractive and seducing, at each table will be found some honest-looking better who wins heavily . . . and daily and hourly you can hear reports on the street of such a one beating the bank out of six hundred or a thousand dollars. This heavy winner is a quiet partner, and his success is a bait to others."]

I visited the post office this afternoon, looking anxiously for letters from home, but found none. ["The little seven-by-nine post office is crowded when open. It takes a long time to be waited upon, so great is the rush. The mail comes tri-weekly and by land at that, which takes four and a half days from St. Louis." "They have rather singular rules at the post office. When mail is received, they open it and then make a list of the letters . . . and hang it out at the door. If you want a letter, you must examine the list and if you find your name . . . an ugly, sour and lazy looking individual who acts as postmaster . . . will, if convenient, hand you your letter; or if not convenient, tell you that he can't find it. The Californians in this place say they will petition Zachary {President Taylor} to have him removed."]

We find the cholera prevalent here in a virulent form. [A doctor with a company from Chicago "recommends a dose of laudanum with pepper, camphor, musk, ammonia, peppermint or other stimulant. . . . The medicine is aided by friction, mustard plasters and other external applications."]

Today I have felt unwell, have had some dysentery and some disagreeable feelings, and slight griping. This afternoon I took two doses of Mr. Bailey's dysentery medicine, at evening took a dose of peppermint and laudanum. Tonight I feel better; my dysentery has stopped.

May 4.   Today it is muddy, having rained heavily through the night. It is a poor day for business; there are but few persons in the streets.

We find that the most experienced in trading advise the use of oxen in the journey across the plains. ["They can be managed with much more facility and with one-half the trouble that is required by mules and with far less damage." "Mules are so stubborn and will not do what is wanted of them and are more apt to stray off on the prairie, while oxen will stay near where they are turned loose." "The Indians will not steal them as they care nothing for an ox, but they will steal a mule wherever they can catch him. Oxen will probably require some fifteen days more on the road, but what is that compared with the safety of an ox team?"]

I have felt better today than I have for some days previous, although I confess that I had the blues when I found that I had the prospect of being one hundred days on the plains. I had a mind to start home. But upon reflection, I think that duty to myself and *family* and relatives will not permit me to look back. This evening my spirits are higher, and I feel better than for a week before.

The cholera continues here, and today has been very bad for it, one death and two new cases. ["The alarm among the people is excessive. . . . The public houses are strewn over with lime and other precautionary measures are taken to prevent diffusion of the disease. . . . It has not confined its ravages to the emigrants, but has been very severe upon the citizens. At the hotels it is most strongly developed, resulting doubtless from the mixed character of those crowded and illy ventilated houses. . . ." "Cholera is the prevailing topic, and you hear but little else spoken of. As for rumors, there is no end to them."]

May 5.   Today it is still damp and gloomy, the weather being foggy. The cholera is still raging, and a gloom appears on the countenances of all persons in this community.

Today at noon we left Independence to go down to the camp of the Wolverine Rangers at the Lower Landing to see about joining that company.

We found that we could join by paying $100 into the company funds and furnishing a wagon, which we and a Mr. Lord of Milwaukee have agreed to do. Accordingly we have done so and paid over the money and are now Wolverine Rangers.

It was too late to go back to Independence tonight, and we have commenced boarding and lodging with the Rangers. ["All hands are making . . . sacks, wagon covers, and tents, except a few who are cooking by the side of an old log preparing coffee, bacon, beans and hard bread. The boys stand up or sit down on the logs to eat their grub and drink their coffee from their tin cups. They crack their jokes and enjoy it all."

[In a nearby camp a man wrote to his sister back in Kentucky: "You

would be amused to see us in our operations, cooking and washing—but never washing our hands. . . . I feel greatly the want of counsel and advice from you or others in biscuit-making and in some approved, or improved method of brewing coffee. I have improved in all the arts pertaining to man's vocation; but in sewing, cooking, and washing I must confess myself at fault. I have always been inclined to deride the vocation of ladies until now. But I must confess it is by far the most irksome I have ever tried. By way of taking lessons in sewing, I have often examined your stitches in my work bag. And then the cooking! I wish you could take supper with me, that you might judge the hardness and durability of our biscuits. I must at some time send you a recipe for making this lasting sort."]

Drawn on May 6, 1849, by J. Goldsborough Bruff, captain of the Washington City Company (Washington, D.C.), this scene depicts Bruff's company encamped near St. Joseph. The setting and conditions are remarkably similar to those described by Swain at the Rangers' camp near Independence.

Of the few diarists who attempted to illustrate their records, Bruff was by far the most skilled and consistent artist. His pencil drawings provide a unique depiction of life on the trail and in California. Bruff traveled near the Wolverine Rangers, sometimes mentioning them in his diary. Seventeen of his drawings appear in this book.

HENRY E. HUNTINGTON LIBRARY

Independence, Mo.
May 5, 1849

Dear Sabrina,

Here I am in a tent six miles from Independence, encamped on the banks of the Missouri River, in tolerable good health, as are all our company. And you are at home some two thousand miles from me, but I trust enjoying the comforts of home and health. Although we are now parted, I have the joyful reflection that the separation is only temporary, and that we are both in the line of duty. I have the reflection, too, of our connection, which brings to mind pleasing emotions and remembrances of our days passed in one another's company, filling my bosom with joy and thankfulness for the connection. Indeed, my dear, I have been hitherto a stranger to the strength of my feelings by separating myself from those I love. You can judge something of my feelings when I tell you that a transient thought of yourself, little Sister, or of home fills my mind with emotions that require my greatest self-command to suppress. But I solace myself with the thought that you are all at home in comfortable circumstances, and I am in the post that duty calls me to fill.

I have been tolerably well ever since I left home, concerning which I shall write George. . . . I have felt some concern for your health, and I wish you to pay particular attention to your dress, food and all things that will in any way affect it. I wish you would refrain from wearing skirts in such a way that they will hang their weight around the waist and do not wear tight-waisted dresses. I wish that you generally wear loose dresses made after the fashion of your white loose dress. I hope you have some good sarsaparilla before this time. I want you to thoroughly get rid, if possible, of that humor in your blood.

You will have some leisure time, and I want you to take your comfort, be cheerful, buy yourself clothes, and make them in the most comfortable way. . . . I think that you had better get shoulder braces and abdominal supporters and wear them. I am very desirous that you should exercise a great deal in the open air, go to bed early and rise early.

As I am absent, the duty of taking care of our child will devolve upon you more than before, which was, I am aware, even then a great task to one in poor health. But I have not the least concern but what that duty will be properly discharged. This cannot, however, be properly discharged without the knowledge of the human system necessary to form an enlightened judgment. I would recommend therefore that you supply yourself with books on the subjects of teething, teeth, food and its effects on the system; and on dress and its effects. If you wish, get George to assist you in choosing these books. Form your own opinions from what you know; do what you think is your duty to the child; and leave the rest to the Almighty, remembering always that the *chest* should be developed as much as possible, that dress, and coarse but nutritious food, not rich food, will best contribute to the health and strength of our child. . . .

The health of the inhabitants of Independence is not very good. The cholera is raging to some extent and is very fatal, but we apprehend little danger from it. We have a good physician and are prudent and careful not to expose ourselves. I have not taken any cold since I left home.

I hope to get letters from home before I leave. You must write to me directed to Sutter's Fort and San Francisco. If anything occurs before I leave, I will write.

Kiss dear little Sister for me.
Adieu for a long time.

> Yours with affection,
> William

May 6.   Sabbath. Today we are at camp busy in the arrangement of the tent. All the company are well and enjoy themselves. In the evening we listened to a sermon by Mr. Rawson, a minister and member of the company. I have not read in my Bible today, as I left it in my overcoat pocket at Mr. Hereford's, my boarding place.

> Sabbath, May 6, 1849
> Six miles from Independence

Dear George,

Here I am in camp with arrangements made for my start across the plains. I wrote from St. Louis and I will start from there. . . . We arrived at Independence on the 3rd of May. . . . We were glad to exchange the deck for the fine rolling woodland of this country.

We have spent our time in getting all the information we could, and the result is that we have concluded to cross the plains with ox teams. All those experienced in prairie life think this the best way. . . . And packing on mules is so laborious that we will not think of it.

We came up from St. Louis with a company of Californians from Marshall, Michigan. They are got up on the joint stock principle and are going with ox teams. On learning that we were going with oxen, they proposed that we should join them by paying $100 each into the fund, furnishing a wagon and thus becoming members of their company, having one equal share in the company, which we have done.

This company was got up last January. We now consist of sixty-three members, Americans, mostly eastern and some western men, but mostly smart and intelligent. There are among them two ministers and two doctors, one of whom is said to be well educated and very successful in his practice. There are also blacksmiths, carpenters, tailors, shoemakers and many other mechanics. They are men of good habits and are governed by the regulations of civilized life. They are not to travel on the Sabbath and are to have preaching on that day. They have had agents here buying their teams and their outfit for the last six weeks. Their outfit has been purchased at the lowest rates. For instance: the wagons were bought and fitted out at Chicago—except for the covers—at $48 apiece.

The cost of transporting them here was $6.50 apiece, making $54.50. They would sell here for $115.

We have the best outfit I have seen since we arrived here. We have eighteen wagons, fifty-four yoke of oxen, sixteen cows, and nine months' provisions, allowing one-third more per day than other companies. We have one large tent and two wagons for each mess [eating group] and three teams to each wagon. We have nine messes in all, each with seven men. We have rice, beans, flour and dried meal; two tons of bacon and 4,400 pounds of dried beef; and all other things in proportion. Our camp equipage is good, among which is a stove for every mess. Mr. Bailey is a first-rate cook, and we live as well as at a tavern.

If the country is as pleasant as it is here, we anticipate a pleasant journey. Although it has rained some today, our tents are perfectly dry. We expect to start on Wednesday, and unless we are disappointed, this will be my last letter to you in all probability, for which I am sorry. It will take at least one hundred days to complete our journey, but we look forward to its completion with confidence. . . .

There is some cholera here, in fact considerable, there being four deaths among the inhabitants on the 4th, which was wet and rainy. The physicians of the place appear not to have success in the treatment of the disease. We have but little fear of it, however, and hope to escape it by care and prudence, which we constantly observe. The physician of the company is a very kindhearted, skillful, and attentive doctor. We all keep cholera medicine in our pockets, which we are directed to take immediately upon the first premonitory symptoms.

We have been a long time coming but we are early enough for the grass on the prairies, as the emigrants have but just commenced leaving for the plains.

It is estimated that some five thousands will leave this place for California this spring and as many more from all the places on the western frontier.

Dear George, I have seen many lonely hours since I left, and many times when I think of our family I can hardly restrain my feelings. However, my company are all very kind to me and my lot could not be cast with kinder persons. As I am away longer from home, my spirits are lighter, and I enjoy myself better. As have you, I have had some hard feelings at different times. I wish to say that I am aware that I have often been petulant and ugly to you, for which I ask your forgiveness.

Mr. Hutchinson sends his best to all our family.

William

May 7.   Today we went into Independence to buy a wagon, which we got for $115. I settled my board bill and wash bill and other little notions and took our trunk into the wagon and went back to the camp. I drove the oxen going home—or to camp—for the first time.

[In Independence "noise and confusion reigned supreme. . . . Traders, trappers, and emigrants filled the street and stores. All were in a hurry, jostling one another and impatient to get through with their business. . . ."]

Today I have felt very well. Cholera very bad in the city.

May 8.   We are engaged in fitting up the wagons. [The covers "are made of osnaburg with one coat of linseed oil and beeswax mixed by boiling, giving them a color of light sand. . . . They shed rain well."]

Felt hollowness at the pit of my stomach and pain in my bowels and in my left breast. I have been troubled with the same feeling more or less for two weeks past. This afternoon I took some peppermint essence, and it relieved me; this evening I feel very fine.

May 9.   I slept soundly last night and feel well this morning. We have been busily engaged fixing the wagons and loading them, a ton in each.

Tonight our camp looks like "going out": eighteen covered wagons all standing around and seven large tents pitched among them.

On Monday [May 7] I received three letters from home [dated April 15, 19 and 22], but my feelings were too deeply affected to allow me to read them without sorrowful feelings at the thought of the family's health. Today I have read them all through, and I am happy that Mother is better, but fear that Sabrina may not enjoy herself while I am absent.

May 10.   We all begin to feel alarmed about John [Root], as he has not come up from St. Louis, when he should have been here on Sunday. The cholera may have prevented his coming.

> Owen's [Lower] Landing, Independence
> May 10, 1849

Dear Sabrina,

I received your affectionate letters on Monday and rejoiced to hear from you and from home. I am glad to hear that you are all well, or better. That is a great blessing for which we cannot be too thankful. We are also well.

Today is Thursday and we shall not start until tomorrow or Saturday on account of our teams not being ready. Our camp is ready to move, our wagons being already loaded. From appearances, we have the prospect of a pleasant journey and as comfortable a one as any other caravan. We have been engaged all this week in fitting for a start and are now about ready.

We live tolerably well at present. This morn we had meat fried in batter, boiled beans, pancakes, pilot bread [ship biscuit] and coffee. This noon we have tea, rice, meat and pilot bread, making out a good dinner. Occasionally we have fiddling and fluting and singing to regale our spirits.

You would scarcely know us if you should see us in our camp, we are so altered in our dress with our California rig on: our woolen or striped shirts and broad-brimmed hats. You might pass us by without particular notice. You would say we were a parcel of old country immigrants. [In several camps "mustachios are becoming quite fashionable, and everyone who can turn out a hair on his face makes a parade of it."]

I shall write after we get out of Independence if I can send a letter back by any means and will write every chance I get. You must not fail to take your comfort this summer. Remember not to give yourself any anxiety about the cholera, for that is very likely to predispose yourself to it. Eat wholesome food, that which is easily digested; have your meals regularly; and go to bed at nine o'clock. . . .

I am glad to hear that you have more confidence in the protection of the Almighty than those who say that I will not get home alive. Thank them in my name and tell them that they have not soul enough to comprehend the intentions of one who would risk all for the sake of his family.

Give my love to all. Kiss Little Cub for her Papa. You will believe me when I say that I write this letter sitting on the ground and use my trunk for a desk.

May God grant us a happy meeting in our dear home. May God bless you, my dear.

William

May 11.   Today we have finished the wagons, and this afternoon I ran up [poured] some bullets. Mr. Hutchinson and I went out and shot some rabbits and plovers and had a fine soup for supper. The camp is all tolerably well. I, however, am not very well, being troubled with pain in my stomach which makes me feel weak and tremulous.

This evening as we were all eating supper and saying that we were afraid we would never see John again, he came in sight to our great satisfaction. He has had bad diarrhea and looks as though he had been sick. He was at Independence last Sabbath, but did not find us and went up to St. Joseph looking for us.

[News from St. Joseph told of "wagons perfectly rammed, jammed, crammed in among the cattle and mules that crowd the streets. Teams are formed in a line by the hundreds . . . awaiting their turns to cross the river." "Fighting for precedence is quite common . . . and two teamsters in one of those disputes killed each other with pistols."

["There are only two flatboats at St. Joseph, crossing night and day. These are rowed across by the persons owning the teams. Some have waited their turn three weeks and others have gone out in the suburbs and camped, almost discouraged. . . . The grog shops and gambling houses are full. The hotels are crowded to excess, and steamboats are constantly arriving up the river with more teams and Californians. . . ."]

May 12. Today we have been breaking the oxen. It is a mean job. ["By noon our steers were quite tame and would haul old logs about and not run away—unless they found a good chance." Another company "had quite a rich scene in yoking up the oxen. . . . Of all shapes and tangles cattle were ever known to be guilty of getting themselves into, they certainly performed them." But it was the mule companies which had the real trouble: "A wild, unbroken mule is the most desperate animal . . . ever seen. . . . They kick, bite and strike with their forefeet, making it very dangerous to go about them." One company "had a high old time breaking the mules to harness. . . . They were lassoed, thrown, harnessed, and dragged into place by sheer and simple force. . . . Each animal had a rope with a choking noose around his neck, at the other end of which was a mad and excited individual who walked, ran, jumped, fell, swore and was dragged. . . ."]

John went out hunting today and got squirrels and doves, of which we had a good supper. I took a portion of rhubarb and soda to loosen my bowels, they being too costive. It has worked well.

At half past ten I attended divine service which was held in the woods close to the camp; preaching by the elder Hobart. There is something about these services more solemn than I have ever felt when at home. I feel a deep interest in them. Attended another service at four o'clock.

Our company doctor [Dr. Joseph H. Palmer] has got the cholera very bad. He is out of his head this evening and will probably die before morning. ["He is being rubbed constantly with brandy, hot drops and tincture of lobelia; but his pulse is down, and he cannot be brought up."]

Sabbath, May 13, 1849
Six miles from Independence

Dear George,

I received your kind letters all at once last Monday and was glad to hear from home and especially glad to hear that Mother is getting better. I hope that it may be a permanent return to health and that I may see her well when I get home. . . .

I have given you the prices of things in this market, the number crossing, and a description of our company. In addition I would say that we take along a barrel of alcohol and spirit lamps to cook with in rainy weather when the [buffalo] "chips" are wet. Our mechanics all have their tools with them; the doctors their libraries; and our medicine chest cost $200. We are ready to roll out. We have eighteen well-covered wagons, nine large wall tents, fifty-four yoke of oxen, ten cows for milk, and four ponies. We have many things for our comfort and convenience and expect that we shall get through if any company does.

[Each of the nine messes "has two wagons and each is drawn by four yoke of oxen. One wagon is called the mess wagon and contains the mess chest, cooking utensils, and rations. The other, called the provision wagon, carries the supplies to be dealt out by the commissary." "Each mess has a little stove and furniture, also table furniture such as knives and forks, plates, spoons, basins, etc., all plain but good. Our plate is neither silver nor gold, but real tin. We shall have to wait for the gold plate until after we return from California!"]

We are all enjoying good health at present. John left his rifle at Detroit and stopped in St. Louis for it to be brought by express. He came after us, missed us and went up to St. Joseph and has at last found us and we are all together again. I refrained from saying anything about John's absence by his own request.

My mess consists of Bailey; Hutchinson; Root; a Dr. Wells of Genesee County, New York; a McAllister; and a McClellan. Wells is a fine fellow, McAllister a poor coot.

Last Friday [May 11] was the first day I have had any leisure. I went hunting. The first time I shot the rifle I got a rabbit. Mr. Hutchinson killed another and we had a fine soup. We live well and enjoy ourselves tolerably well. Pancakes, eggs, butter, milk, chickens, tea, and pilot bread was our dinner today.

I shall write to Mother before I leave for the plains and shall write every day after we leave if I can send the letters back to Independence. . . . We expect to roll out by Tuesday [May 15].

Your brother,
William

Camp, six miles from Independence
May 13, 1849

Dear Mother,

Although absent from you and home, still the tenderest feelings of my heart are on my relations. Distance, absence, and time for reflection unfold to my mind the true value of those dear connections, the family circle and the ties of nature from which I have so lately separated myself. Dear Mother, that separation has doubly endeared yourself to me. The memories of my childhood and of the tender and watchful care you exercised over me in my youth have been overlooked in the care of business. But now leisure and reflection have restored those memories to their proper place in my mind. I acknowledge that I have failed to hold your advice and counsel in proper estimation, which I deeply regret; and I hope you will not hold anything for it against me.

I am glad to hear that you are getting well again, for your sickness has been a source of anxiety to me, as I was afraid that you might not recover. I feel a great anxiety about Sabrina and Sis in my absence, and I also feel afraid that George will work too hard this summer. I think that he had better hire a strong, good hand. . . .

The new scenes in this wild country are not pleasing to one who has been in civilized life, especially one who has left home under the circumstances in which I have. The fact is, the western country has its charms, but they are not equal to those of our own civilized, settled, enlightened country. I think that I should not want to "go west" if I was at home, although I think favorably of my California expedition. . . .

Dear Mother, I hope to see you yet again. Although I am engaged in a perilous and tedious journey, I am consoled by the reflection that if God crowns my enterprise with success we shall all reap the benefit of my toil and peril. I feel anxious that Sabrina and little Sis should live with you and George most of the time while I am gone [rather than go to stay with Sabrina's family at Lewiston], for I feel that your and George's care for them in my absence will in some degree make up for the want of a father and a husband. Sabrina will undoubtedly feel lonesome, and the reflection that kind friends are feeling for her will be a source of great comfort to me.

[This letter was concluded on May 15.]

May 14.   This morning Dr. Palmer is dead. Died at three o'clock [A.M.]. ["Dr. Wells and E. S. Camp stayed with him until midnight and worked faithfully. At that time Dr. Carr was called and several others, who stayed with him until he was dead. He had the best care and attention and the best wishes of all his brethren in this expedition. No man stood higher in the affections of all the company than Dr. Palmer."]

There is a solemnity, or rather a gloom, on all countenances in the camp. Dr. P. was buried at ten o'clock in the burying ground on the top of the hill. It was a solemn sight to see one of our number carried to his last resting place far from home and relations. Only thirty-six hours ago he was joyful and mirthful with bright hopes, glowing in his prospects. His relatives little think he is no more. What sad hearts will be at his home when the news reaches them.

Our business today is yoking the steers, branding them, and getting them ready to start tomorrow. The day is rainy, with thunderstorms, and it is quite cold and chilly. Today our camp is all well. I feel well myself, but sad.

May 15.   This morning Mr. Nichols, who was taken sick with the cholera last night, is dead. He was attended by Dr. Carr [who succeeded Dr. Palmer as company physician]. Mr. Nichols was carried past the camp by the Directors of the company to the burying ground just as we were ready to start. So although we have been here but ten days, two of our number are no more, and their remains are deposited beside the Missouri in a lone spot where many exiles from home have been deposited before.

Today our camp is all bustle in preparation for starting. Breakfast was out of the way early, and all hands busily engaged in getting steers together into the shape of teams, which done, the scene of driving the oxen commenced. The tents struck and all things packed into the wagons, we were ready for the move.

At ten o'clock we at our tent were ready and led the company by starting the first two wagons out of the camp. Mr. Hutchinson, Bailey and John have the baggage wagon, and myself, Dr. Wells and McClellan the other or mess wagon.*

Our oxen went remarkably well by having drivers on both sides. I had the luck to have one of my wheel oxen fall in crossing a bridge, and I expected to see him and everything else fall into the valley some twelve feet below, but fortunately we stopped the team and he regained his feet, and we passed on unharmed. The road was slippery from the recent rains. We had to double-team up a large hill but got on without any extra trouble, while many of the other messes were troubled in every way by their steers. We kept close to our teams on both sides and took great pains not to let them get the advantage of us and in that way learn them to know and do what we want them to. We got along without whipping the team much; and as we go slow, we are not fatigued ourselves. We traveled four miles and encamped two miles east of Independence.

The spirits of our camp are entirely changed by the excitement of the day. All appear cheerful as they sit around their tents at tea and round the blazing camp fires. Our mess as usual is the first in having supper, and our meal really relishes well and all seem happy.

[Conclusion of letter started May 13]

Two miles from Independence
May 15. Tuesday evening, eight o'clock

Dear Mother,

Here I am in our camp wagon writing to you by candlelight and using the tops of our trunks for a stand, while John is writing to some "Nora Crena," and Dr. Wells is writing to his folks. Bailey and Hutchinson are snoring in the tent by the side of the wagon.

We arranged things this morning as soon as possible to start on our long journey. We were a long time getting started, as so large a body does not move quickly. Our teams are all young, mostly steers, and you can imagine that we had "fun" with two yoke of steers for leaders and one yoke of old oxen for "wheel horses." We yoked them on Monday [May 14], got our teams together this morning, and finally got them hitched to the wagons. They look slim enough. Our folks [the other Rangers] thought we would be greenhorns, but they had no fun over us. We rolled out of camp ahead of any other mess, and although we had steers, heavy

---

* *The seventh member of the mess, McAllister, apparently had either joined another mess or left the Rangers. He is not mentioned again by Swain or by any other member of the company.*

loads and bad roads—as it had rained heavily for some days past—we have made a start. Got six miles, encamped, and had to go back and haul the boys up a hill.

We are very comfortably rigged and look forward to the journey with pleasure, believing that we shall have lots of fun. We will pass through Independence in the morning, when I shall get a number of little articles for my comfort, after which I shall have from $120 to $125 in gold to take with me, which will leave me in better circumstances than I expected.

When once we are past the bounds of civilization, we may not have an opportunity to write home. But whenever we do, I shall improve the chance.

Of our prospects you can judge. Here are some sixty men, 120 cows and oxen, all yoked and hitched to eighteen covered wagons, with a rope to the head of every yoke, and a Californian at the end of the rope with a large whip in his hand, plodding along at the rate of three miles per hour, pantaloons in boots. Never mind, this is the most comfortable way, and the longest way round is the surest way home.

Give my love to all inquiring friends and tell them I am going to California with my gold washer in a box, and I'll try to bring home a pocket full of rocks.

I told George in his letter that 5,000 persons would leave this place for California, and I think that a large estimate, so that the report of 40,000 going is all moonshine.

Kiss little Sister for me and give my love to George and Sabrina. It is now ten o'clock and this is so uncomfortable writing that I can't stand it.

> Your affectionate son,
> William

Back Home

During the time of Chapter II—May 3 through May 15, while Swain was in Independence—Sabrina and George did not write any letters. For May their first letter was dated the 27th; it is printed at the end of Chapter III.

CHAPTER III

The Great California Caravan

"The road is literally filled with two weeks' travel. . . . The trouble is to get out of the way or to pass others."

By the third week of April, emigrant scouts reported to their company captains that the prairie to the west looked dry enough for the wagons to pass and the grass high enough for the teams to graze. Sounds of breaking camp echoed through the ravines and forest groves, teamsters yelling, whips cracking, wagons creaking as they rolled slowly from the camp-grounds. Most companies had packed and repacked their wagons; with few exceptions they loaded them too heavily—extra axletrees and wheels, sheet-iron stoves, anvils, chains, personal clothing, boxes of medicines, shovels, pickaxes and gold-washing machines; and quantities of foodstuffs —barrels of flour, sacks of sugar, salt, cornmeal, beans, coffee, salt pork and saleratus. Under the traffic of hundreds of wagons pulled by six and even eight oxen or mules, the trails became deeply rutted, in some places quagmires. Axles cracked, wheel rims tore loose from spokes, wagons sank too deep in the mud to be pulled out and were abandoned. Within a few miles of the camps and westward for many miles, companies began what would be a continuing process for many weeks—they lightened their loads. Some companies left entire wagons when they consolidated weary teams. News of this booty just to the west attracted townsfolk from St. Joseph and Independence who went out in their wagons to take back what the Californians had purchased only a few weeks before.

On May 16 the Wolverine Rangers broke camp, their oxen slowly pulling the eighteen wagons onto the rutted trail crowded with other companies' wagons, headed for Independence, where the Santa Fe Trail led southwest across the sweeping prairies. Swain and his sixty-one companions knew from rumors and various reports from St. Joseph that they

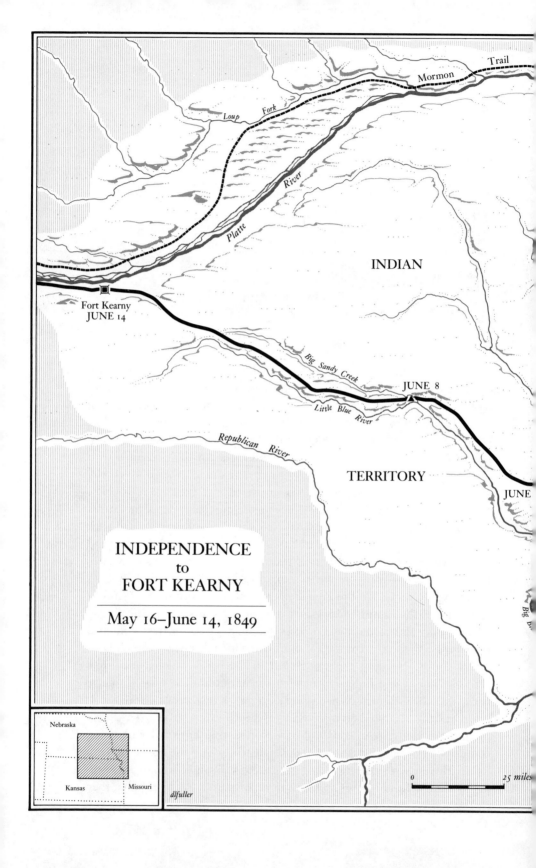

Trail

Mormon

Loup *Fork*

River

Platte

INDIAN

Fort Kearny
JUNE 14

Big Sandy Creek

JUNE 8

Little Blue River

Republican River

TERRITORY

JUNE

INDEPENDENCE
to
FORT KEARNY

May 16–June 14, 1849

Big bl

Nebraska

Kansas   Missouri   dlfuller

0   25 miles

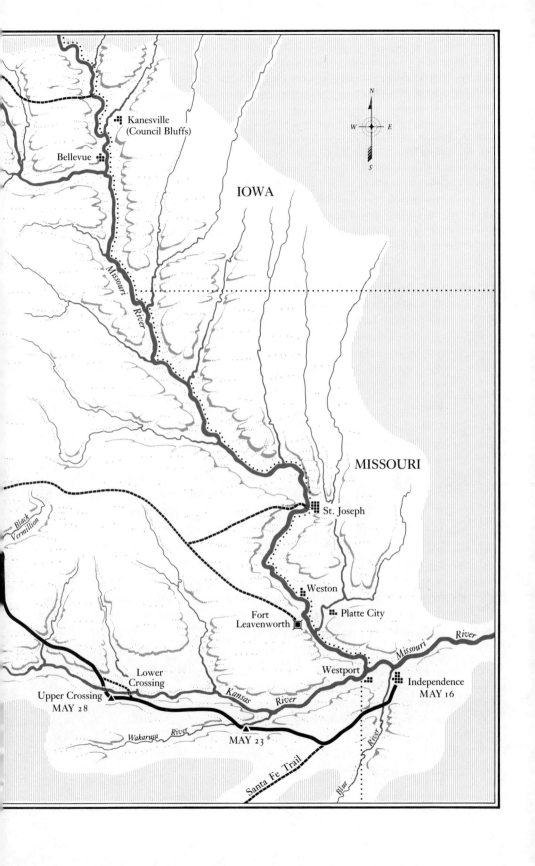

were making a late start—they did not know the lead companies had passed Fort Kearny (315 miles to the northwest) on May 7 and 8.

There seemed no need to hurry, no reason to feel anxiety about their place in the migration. West of Independence they could see for miles across the oceanlike swells of prairie. The trail ahead was marked to the horizon by an undulating line of white-topped wagons and to the rear back to Independence. No dust obscured the astonishing scene; mud and the crowd of wagons slowed the advance. At night the glow of campfires nearby and far off to the west gave everyone a sense of security.

Forty-five miles southwest of Independence the trail forked. The Santa Fe Trail led southwest through Arkansas, on to present-day New Mexico, Arizona and finally to southern California. Relatively few gold-seekers chose that route—at most 3,000. Like the vast majority, the Rangers turned north, heading for the crossing of the Kansas River and on to the first military outpost, Fort Kearny.

The emigrants who set out from St. Joseph traveled a trail that led due west, to merge with the Independence crowd at a junction about one hundred miles from the Missouri River. Farther north at the Council Bluffs crossing of the river, another trail followed the north side of the Platte River. This route, generally known as the Mormon Trail, attracted about 2,500 emigrants in 1849.

On leaving the western settlements, these trails entered what maps labeled "The Indian Territory," a vast area intended by the government to be a permanent location for western tribes and for those Indians removed by the government from their traditional homes in the States. The first Indians the emigrants encountered were the "civilized" Shawnee and Potawatomis—peaceful, poor, altogether a contrast to expectations. But farther west, to the north of the Kansas River, the trail entered the country of the Pawnee, a tribe much feared by travelers on the plains. By spring 1849, the once-powerful Pawnees had been sadly weakened by frequent attacks by their old enemy, the Sioux. As well, during the spring and summer of 1849 they suffered over 1,200 deaths from cholera brought to them by the invading goldseekers.

Having so long anticipated the danger of Indians and consequently equipped themselves as if an army, most goldseekers experienced the ironic disappointment of not seeing any "wild" Indians. Where were the Pawnees? One of the Rangers explained: "We are armed to the teeth but on account of the consternation among the Indians because of cholera, we could hardly get a sight of them. . . . Our arms are useless, for we carry with us in their imagination a protection more formidable: the dread scourge which has spread among them."

The emigrants armed themselves not only as protection from Indians but as well in eager anticipation of hunting in the Far West, an area long described in government reports and by travelers as a sportsman's paradise. Buffalo, antelope and elk promised excitement and tests of skill. Given the fact that many, probably most, goldseekers were inexperienced or even quite ignorant about the use of guns and yet were "so eager for sport that they will discharge their pieces no matter if they fire in the direction of a whole train," the number wounded or killed by other emigrants far exceeded the few killed by Indians east of the Rocky Mountains.

The real killer was cholera. The crowded trail became a breeding ground for the highly infectious disease. Thousands of hurrying, careless men left the campsites littered not only with trash and rotting food but, far worse, with the fouled clothing and bedding of those who had died. The deadly bacilli were spread by flies, contaminated water, human excrement and even pathetic cholera patients abandoned by their frightened comrades.

The number of graves mentioned by diarists suggest that cholera killed at least 1,500 on the trails east of Fort Laramie. Ignorant of its causes, fearful of its prevalence, the emigrants hurried westward hoping to escape the enemy in their midst.

But there would be no escape until they reached the mountains west of Fort Laramie. As they crossed the green prairies on the way to Fort Kearny and west of that fort through the valley of the Platte, the disease killed every day. Hoping to get ahead of the crowd, some companies lashed their teams and rumbled past the rut-bound lines of wagons. Such efforts widened the trail so that in some places the caravan spread out to a width of ten and twelve wagons abreast. Rivalry for position was most intense at approaches to narrow ravines or stream crossings. But often teamsters who had whipped their teams to get ahead watched that evening or early the next morning as a rival company rolled past. And sometimes in the rush and excitement of trying to pass a line of wagons, inexperienced teamsters fell beneath wagon wheels, escaping at best with broken legs or painful lacerations.

Among the other surprises of the first weeks on the trail, the emigrants found that they needed money. Most everyone carried some money, usually gold coins to buy supplies and equipment when they reached California. But as one traveler warned: "It was generally supposed that after we left the frontier money would be of no use. It is the greatest mistake possible. I know of no part of the world where money is of more use than in crossing the plains and where a man is more helpless without it." The truth of this judgment became ever more apparent the farther west they traveled, especially at the crossings of wild rivers. In addition, food supplies, at first abundant, later scarce, could be obtained only by purchase or theft. There was little charity along the wilderness trail. For the Wolverine Rangers, their first need to pay money came at the ferry crossing of the Kansas River where the operators charged $2 to $4 to carry each wagon on primitive scows.

Life on the trail discouraged some goldseekers. If they gave up and headed for home, they were said to have "seen the elephant." This special phrase, used by almost every gold rush diarist, had been a part of the American language before 1849; but it took on a poignant meaning for the tens of thousands who experienced getting to California and then life in the mining camps. As the goldseekers' moods and expectations changed, so they used "the elephant" in different ways. But the essential idea remained dominant as revealed in the story from which the expression is presumed to have originated. By 1837 circus parades commonly included one or two elephants. The story goes that "a farmer who had heard of elephants, but had never seen one, longed to do so. When a circus, complete with elephant, came to a nearby town, he loaded his wagon with eggs and vegetables and started for the market there. En route he met the circus parade led by the elephant. The farmer was enchanted but his horses were terrified. They bucked, pitched, overturned the wagon and ran away, scattering broken eggs and bruised vegetables over the countryside. 'I don't give a hang,' said the farmer. 'I have seen the elephant.' "

As the universal expression of the gold rush, "seeing the elephant" symbolized the great adventure of going to California to dig a golden fortune. On the way "the elephant" revealed himself in the many unexpected difficulties and dangers that beset the goldseekers, and "to see the elephant" became the expression for suffering a severe ordeal, facing one's worst expectations, overcoming the meanest realities; in a word, knowing the Truth.

For William Swain and thousands of other men who only a few weeks earlier had been working on farms in New York or Alabama or in buildings in Indianapolis or Baltimore, life on the overland trail was an astonishment, not only because of the contrasts with their home routine —guard duty in wind and rain at night; food prepared by careless, impatient, grumbling men; the crude, loud campfire talk of men without women—but equally because they began to feel a sense of freedom in their traveling life. A Pennsylvanian expressed it all in writing to his brother: "I wish you were with me. It is far more pleasing to me, and I know it would be to you, than to sit daily locked up in a dirty office.

Besides the pleasure of the thing, it gives us health and strength. I can sleep in the tent or wagon far better than I could in a bed, no roaches to disturb us at midnight here and no bell to call us at breakfast."

Swain experienced some of this freedom, but he felt constrained by his sense of obligation to George, Sabrina and Little Cub and by his mother's admonitions to read his Bible. He held close his memories of home and the promises that had justified his leaving.

The goal for the first stage of the journey was Fort Kearny, located on the south shore of the broad Platte River, near the western end of Grand Island. Established by the U.S. Army during the summer of 1848 to protect the emigration to Oregon and maintain peace between the Pawnee and the Sioux, this outpost was known by a confusion of names —Fort Childs, New Fort Kearny, and Fort Kearny, the latter title being correct, in honor of Brigadier General Stephen Watts Kearny, hero of the Mexican War. Here the Californians mailed letters, rearranged loads, made repairs and generally prepared for the long pull through the valley of the Platte. While Swain looked to the fort as a place to mail a letter, many other emigrants sought from the Army officers information on how many companies had already passed. Their curiosity derived both from their anxiety not to be left too far behind the leaders and from their sense of being part of a historic migration. How many of us are there?

Knowing this question concerned families throughout the States, newspapers from St. Louis to New York printed letters sent from Fort Kearny. Many of these writers estimated the size of the emigration, in all cases suggesting a total far more accurate than William Swain's surprisingly low estimate of 7,000 to 10,000. Other reports on the emigration came from travelers who had journeyed eastward from Fort Kearny and claimed to have counted the passing throng. One newspaper in St. Louis sent its own correspondent to Fort Kearny.

Beginning the first week of May, Army officers at the fort counted the wagons that passed along the south side of the Platte River. As of June 23, by which time all but the slowest stragglers (a few hundred at most) had passed, their count totaled 5,516 wagons. But their effort had been casual at best with wagons rolling by unnoticed at night or at some distance from the fort. And they ignored the goldseekers who traveled with pack mules.

Considering the Army's count and other estimates, figuring four to five men per wagon, adding in some 1,000 members of pack companies, the emigration passing Fort Kearny must have totaled at least 29,000. A crowd indeed, but stretched out by mid-June as a line of wagons that reached west to present-day Wyoming.

How that passing crowd during May and June must have disrupted

Army life at Fort Kearny! In addition to all the questions they asked and all the food and equipment they dumped in the area, the emigrants burdened the military with thousands of letters they confidently expected to have delivered back to the States. William Swain wrote from there, as did several other Rangers, including James Pratt. His letters in the Marshall *Statesman* occasionally had the tone and broad viewpoint of the editor he had been before the spring of 1849: "This California movement if it does nothing else cannot fail to open the eyes of the people to the vastness and richness of the land over which we move, and cannot fail to bring about a reconsideration of that policy of the government which restrains the white man from occupying and cultivating it."

Another letter written May 17, 1849, not far from Fort Kearny and published in the Oquawka, Illinois, *Spectator* caught the mood of many of the young men far from home: "Tell Charles that I have not been chased by a squaw nor bit by an antelope, yet!"

■

May 16, 1849.   This morning we started for Independence—breakfast over and all ready by eight o'clock. We traveled smoothly into town where we stopped about three hours while the company all went shopping. With our wagons all regularly numbered, we made a grand appearance. [Using axle grease, the members had printed "Wolverine Rangers, Mess No. —" on each wagon cover. In other companies "the wagon covers are nearly all painted with the names of owners, and their residences. Many of them have various mottoes and devices. . . ." such as Wild Yankee, Rough and Ready, Live Hoosier, Never Say Die, Patience and Perseverance, and Have You Seen the Elephant? "Others have drawings—a sprawling eagle or a huge elephant, a tall giraffe, a rampant lion, or a stately ox, done in charcoal or black paint with an artistic skill that is bold if not accurate."]

I went to the post office and got a letter from George, in which he advised me to come back home if we had the prospect of having cholera on the plains. If I had received his letter before I had made my arrangements for going, I think that on account of the prevalence of the sickness on the route I would have done it, although it would be crushing to my feelings to give up the route now. But trusting in the Almighty, I will go on, nothing daunted, with courage and high hope.

We left Independence about noon on the Santa Fe road, which for four miles is very hilly. The road, wet at this time, is very bad.

We crossed bad bridges and a short pitch without any accident and came on to the most pleasant locations for farms that I ever saw. The country is very undulating and . . . grand in its conceptions and gives light countenances to all our mess who are commenting upon its grandeur.

We encamped eight miles from Independence.

May 17.   This morning the camp was tardy in its movements, wishing to give the teams a chance to eat. . . . We traveled through a country similar to that of yesterday. . . .

The road is getting hard, and if it was not for the ups and downs it would be good. Just at sunset we passed a deep, thickly wooded hollow and then raised a long hill, where we encamped just on the border of the plains and just on the line of the Indian Territory. To the west we have nothing in sight but the vast open prairie, while on the east we are leaving the line of civilization on this continent. I am much disappointed in not having been able to get time to write a letter to send back by the inhabitants of this country.

May 18.   ["Last night our wagons were formed in what is called a corral. Into that space . . . we drove the cattle and set watches upon them. . . . The watches were continued until half past four this morning, when the cattle were let out and herded. This is a custom we shall keep up all the way through.

["It is now about ten o'clock A.M. We are still encamped, on the edge of timber on one side and the prairie on the other. Our blacksmith forge is erected and the smiths are fastening chains to the wagons for locking the wheels. . . . It is a warm, lovely day, and the breeze on the prairie ground is cool and refreshing. Some of our men are cutting hickories to make some extra axles and tongues. Blankets and coats and clothes are all spread out in the air. We lay by most of the day for these purposes."]

This afternoon the property of the deceased members of the company [Dr. Palmer and Chauncey Nichols] was sold at auction, which took until four o'clock, when we struck our tents and moved about seven miles on the prairie.

I have felt unwell all day and have neglected to write a letter home, which I might have done if I had not attended the sale. I feel guilty for not having done it, as I could have sent one from here.

One of our company, Mr. Ives, is sick with cholera.

May 19.   Mr. Ives is dead. We have buried him on the plains.

This morning the company moved in regular order, which we have not done before. It rained and we dressed in our oilcloth suits which are very comfortable. We traveled all day with only now and then a tree in sight.

The plains are good pastures and covered with beautiful flowers. If I ever get home and have the means to do it, I will travel through the whole western country with my family.

This evening we encamped on Bull Creek. ["We are traveling through a country which for its vastness and beauty calls for exclamations of astonishment and delight. . . . Our train is so large that we seem like a village whenever we stop. We are scarcely out of sight of emigrants at any time, though the throng is in advance of us.

["Here at Bull Creek . . . the Santa Fe road and the one usually traveled by the California emigrants separate. When we move again we shall leave the Santa Fe road to our left."]

May 20.   Sabbath. This morning I was called at four o'clock to assist in taking care of Mr. Highly, who is sick but will, it is thought, get well.

The wind is quite high on the plains, like that on our own lakes, and the clouds look like rain. We have had no preaching today. I have spent most of the day in writing to Sabrina, and I shall send it home by the first opportunity.

This afternoon we had a heavy thundershower, which makes camping disagreeable both for men and beasts. We are obliged to turn the cattle out of the corral onto the plains and keep guard around them all night. I had my watch from two until four-thirty in the morning, being my second watch since we left Independence.

["We were joined today by Mr. Smith, a young man from Battle Creek, with two companions. They are to travel under our regulations but own their wagon and outfit."]

This is a place of general camping for the emigrants, and the amount of death among them is plainly told by the number of newly made graves in the vicinity, it being no less than ten which I have seen. Poor fellows! They little thought that this would be their fate when urged on by the laudable hope of benefiting themselves and their families. They left their homes and friends to endure hardship and toil, hoping to meet again the loved ones and to make them comfortable through life. Sad is their fate, buried here in this wild of wastelands, where not a mark will denote their last resting place far from loved ones.

Sabbath, May 20

Dear Sabrina,

We are all well and encamped on the plains forty-five miles from Independence. . . .

Our teams have given us but little trouble, and we shall soon be able to ride in the wagon and take our comfort. We encamp at sunset and have supper ready soon. Our stoves are a great convenience.

The grandeur of these boundless plains can only be realized by the thoughtful eye traversing their bosom. . . . The extent and grandeur of the scene will forcibly remind you of the almighty source of creation and evoke the thought that you yourself are but a speck in the midst of the grand scene. Sabrina, when I get home we will have a route through all this western country and enjoy ourselves together and have Little Cub with us. We could take real comfort contemplating the beautiful scenery.

We have had a high wind today, which we generally have on this ocean of plain, accompanied by a heavy rain which beats through our tent and has dampened my paper so that I can hardly write. I shall send this by the first chance to Independence and will write every opportunity. . . .

I got George's letter of April 25 when we passed through Independence and was glad to hear from home. . . . Tell George that my prospect brightens as I near the land of golden promise, and if good luck attends me, I am confident that the enterprise will be one of advantage to us all.

> *O friends, don't you cry for me*
> *For I am going to California*
> *With my wash bowl on my knee,*
> *And a pocket full of rocks I'll bring home.*

Mr. Hutchinson sends his best respects. John Root is well and hearty. Mr. Bailey says tell his folks that he is hearty and well. As to myself, I am growing better all the time. I enjoy myself far better than I expected I could when absent from my family, although my strongest feelings are entwined around the family circle. Tell George to take his comfort this summer, if possible.

As for you—eat, drink, laugh, be merry, and have your fun as much as anybody around you.

As ever, your affectionate husband
William

May 21.   Today our company are all well enough to travel, and we rolled out of camp at eight o'clock and traveled through an unbroken tract of prairie.

The roads were slippery from the recent rain; but the wind, which often blows on these vast plains, blew from the east, and as we traveled to the west our wagons rolled along very easily, the wind blowing so hard that we had to brace ourselves against it as we walked along. [When the wind blew from a less favorable quarter, some companies removed their wagon covers to ease their advance.]

We had plenty of company today. Many mule teams were stuck in the mud, and it looked hard to pass them by and leave them in difficulty, but if we should stop to help all in trouble, we would stop all the time.

We saw Indians today for the first time. ["Many of them obtain quite a livelihood by begging from the emigrants. They make use of every pretext imaginable to filch money. . . . Some will pretend to be chiefs who are on their way to Washington to have a talk with the 'Great Father,' and they solicit alms to bear their expenses. They get some white men to draw up a begging paper for them. . . . One paper presented by a chief pretending to be on his way to Washington was nine years old, as evidenced by the date. But he pretended it was drawn up for the present occasion, and many gave the scamp money. There are similar begging papers in the hands of different Indians. . . ."

[Some of the women practiced their own money-making schemes. One emigrant "saw more than one white man pay a squaw and start for the bushes. She would lead the way for a short distance, then turn and run to a gang of her own people. . . . The squaws would clap their hands and laugh as if they would split their sides. . . ." "Such was the amativeness of some of the train boys that they were glad to hug even a lousy squaw. They called it 'otter hunting.' "]

We found wild garlics along our road today. At noon we stopped to take dinner and feed the cattle on the banks of Mud Creek which is here a large creek and runs rapidly. It looked good to see the cattle stand in the stream up to the brisket as they were drinking. The creek has a narrow flat covered with heavy timber. We moved on after dinner about one mile, and going down the bank of the river one wagon broke an axletree and another broke a tongue. The rest of the company crossed the stream; and some two members being taken with cholera, we encamped on the west bank and commenced doctoring them.

May 22.   We are encamped on the west bank of Mud Creek forty rods from the line of woods which winds along the east bank as far as we can see, while to the west nothing but the unbroken expanse of dark green prairie stretching away to the horizon greets the eye. Certainly the scene is grandly beautiful.

We were in camp all day mending the wagons, fixing the ox yokes and bows, and doctoring the sick, who are on the whole some better; but some others are complaining.

I have not felt very well myself today. I think my feelings arose from indiscretion in eating or from eating too much, as my appetite is voracious and our cooks, Mr. Bailey and Dr. Wells, are the finest cooks out and our living is pretty good.

Today we saw a drove of horses that appeared to be perfectly wild. They had long tails sweeping the ground and heavy, flowing manes. As we came near them, they moved off and circled around us in a most graceful manner, seeming to tread lightly upon the green carpet of the plain and to scorn the thought that we could catch them.

We are getting into Indian country, and tomorrow we are ordered to carry sidearms. ["It is said by alarmists that different tribes intend opposing the emigrants. They might as well oppose the whirlwind. . . . All emigrants are armed to the teeth. It is like one continual glorious 4th of July. . . ."]

Today the officers of the company are to be elected for three months.

[Up to this time the Rangers were under the command of Jesse Baker, captain; S. S. DeArman, lieutenant; three other officers; and the board of directors. However, before departing from Michigan they "had adopted a set of bylaws. One of these provided for an election of officers when ten days out on our journey. This proved a very wise arrangement, for before that time had passed we made the discovery that our first captain was not a good one. Although an English Methodist class leader of excellent reputation, he and some others got at the whiskey, which was private property, and kept 'full' as long as it lasted. . . ."]

[Therefore, on May 22, a second election was held. "Our . . . choice for Captain was Judge J. D. Potts. We also appointed a Lieutenant, Frank Cannon, and elected a Secretary, George Alcott . . . whose duties were to keep a record of all the doings of the company, from the health and conduct of its members down to the number of miles traveled each day which we ascertained by means of an Odometer attached to the hind wheel of one of the wagons.* We also appointed Reverend Randall Hobart of Marshall as steward to the company commissary."]

---

* Also called by other companies "roadometer" and "miledrometer," this was a device attached to a wheel of known circumference. With each turn acting on sets of cogs, the mileage was recorded with impressive accuracy. Some such mechanism, homemade or purchased, was used by most companies to determine their rate of advance.

This evening a company from New York City with mule teams is encamped thirty rods north of us, and they appear to be men of standing and character. They came into our camp and invited us to see them in the evening. We did not go, but our bugler commenced playing on his bugle and played some time. I had lain down to sleep and just closed my eyes when I heard a splendid song commenced close to our tent. It was an old familiar song, the "Canadian Boat Song," sung in well-cultivated voices carrying the four parts. It was our New York friends serenading us, and certainly they sang well. Here in this wilderness country such a treat was soul-stirring and called up associations of past enjoyments in the same recreation. They sang many good glees and closed with the old song "Good Night." Then they gave three cheers for our company, which was returned by our boys for them, and they went to their camp and we to sleep.

May 23. This morning it rained, and we spent the forenoon in camp because of the sick men. Had dinner early. I have lived on scalded milk and hard bread mostly today, with cayenne pepper in it on account of irregularity of my bowels. I have also drunk steeped white oak bark.

We struck tents and started about noon, crossing fine rolling prairies and two small streams [the Little Wakarusa River and Spring Creek], and pitched our tents on a rolling knoll six miles from our last camp, in sight of two good-looking farms with good fences and comfortable buildings— withal a comfortable-looking place. They belong to some Indians from eastern tribes who have settled here.

We have a beautiful campground, one which my noble brother would glory in seeing.

May 24. This morn our camp was well enough to travel, and we started early from campground. We had before us one half-mile away the Wakarusa River, a considerable creek, and then three miles of bad road which we expected would give us great trouble. We stopped on the east side, while some of the party fixed the west bank [by cutting a grade for easier ascent of the wagons]. Here an Indian named Logan has settled and established a grocery where John Root and I bought twenty pounds of sugar for extras. ["This Indian, a Shawnee, makes money by the handful out of the emigrants. He is a shrewd, agreeable man and understands well how to trade."]

By doubling the teams, making six yokes per wagon, we crossed the river with but little trouble and traveled the three miles of bottom land by noon, making noon halt on the prairie.

In the afternoon we made good way over very bad roads till four o'clock, when we began to ascend a series of high plains. About five o'clock a thunderstorm commenced as we were ascending a hill or bluff about two hundred feet high. Our captain rode forward to reconnoiter and viewing him through the mist from the vale, he looked like a sentinel posted on the lone watchtower overlooking the destinies of the wilderness.

As we raised the hill, thunder, lightning, rain, hail, and tremendous wind made the elements "war." I gave the team into the charge of Mr. McClellan and Dr. Wells and walked to the northern edge of the tableland and stood for some time enjoying the view below and beyond us. It was the first time the Kansas River had greeted my eye, and I shall not soon forget the scene. I longed for George to enjoy the same. I turned with reluctance from the sight and walked after our teams, wading through flowers and through the peltings of the storm, which, with our oilcloth suits on, were harmless to us. We traveled about an hour and then formed our corral and pastured our teams in a wind that prohibited pitching tents. We stood it out, and about sundown it cleared off and gave a good chance to pitch tents, cook, and make beds.

May 25.   This morn we are all soaked out by last night's heavy rain. About midnight the wind commenced a rookery such as you find nowhere but on these "land seas," and the rain fell in streams, literally. Tents blew down; the boys yelled, sang, laughed, swore, and turned out of their beds in their shirts, pants, and socks, drenched in rain. Our tent was strongly staked and stood the storm, but the rain found the bottoms, and we were lying in the water before we could get up. Beds wet, shirts and stockings, too. We scratched up, put on clothes, and stood it till morn, when we changed clothes, made fires and had a fine day.

In the afternoon we traveled about eight miles over a series of ascending rolls, the road good. We are probably six hundred feet higher than yesterday.

May 26.   We started early and have made twenty-two miles, the best time and distance made on any day's travel before. The country presents the same appearance as yesterday, only in place of gradually rising, we are slowly descending. Today we have crossed some two large creeks, one of which was Otter Creek.

May 27.   Sabbath. In violation of our principle, we travel today on account of the sickness on the route. The health of our company is improving, and it is thought advisable to keep the company in active operation to keep their minds from getting engaged on cholera. I hope we may not have to break the Sabbath again.

Today we have had uneven and bad roads and many gullies in which many of our teams got stuck in the mud. We have traveled part of the day and made eight miles.

May 28.   This morning Mr. Lyon, who was taken sick with the cholera last night, is dead. His mess and the doctor who attended him seemed to take but little care of him; otherwise he might, in all probability, have been saved.

A gloom appears on the company. We started late, leaving some of the company and Mr. Lyon's mess behind to bury him.

Traveled over broken roads, crossing many small creeks, and about twelve o'clock arrived at the trading post one half mile from the Kansas River ferry.* [Called Uniontown or Union Village, this settlement "contains fifteen or twenty log and shingle buildings for dwellings, a number of stores, and a kind of market place, where goods are distributed to the Indians." "The shops are kept by white men, licensed to supply the Indians with the flimsy, fantastic and trumpery articles they require; liquor being specially interdicted and very properly so. . . ."]

Here I wrote a letter to George in great haste and left it at the stores to be sent as soon as possible to Independence. At the trading places here, they sell goods as reasonably as at Independence. I purchased a butcher knife, case knife, fork, small tin pail with cover, nutmegs for the mess and one half-yard of duck [a cotton fabric, lighter than canvas].

We arrived at the ferry landing at two o'clock, swam the cattle across the river and prepared to take the wagons over tomorrow. There are some fifty wagons waiting to cross. ["Two boats are constantly employed carrying over two wagons each."]

It really looks singular here in the woods to see the banks of the river lined with wagons, men, and cattle, and Indians riding on fine ponies decorated in the finest-style saddles, bridles, martingales, and breast straps. Many of the Indians have strings of small bells around their horses' breasts. They wear leggings, blankets or shawls, turbans around their heads, and make a grand appearance as they prance around the camp. They are splendid riders.

---

* *There were two ferry crossings of the Kansas River, the emigrants divided about equally in their use of them. This one, located near what is presently Willard, Kansas, was called the Upper Crossing; the second, approximately twenty miles to the east at the site of Topeka, was known as Papin's ferry or the Lower Crossing. (See map, p. 113.)*

["This land of the Shawnees and Potawatomis will soon be on the market, it is inevitable. . . . It is well wooded and watered, and the rich soil invites the labor of the husbandman. Some of the Indians do a little farming, but they will never develop the resources of a great state that might lie directly west of Missouri. . . . The Shawnees, the Delawares . . . and the Potawatomis are a peaceable, inoffensive people, fond of ease and display. If they could live with the whites without imbibing their vices, they might become good citizens. The Indian in the course of years has either to become exterminated or else he is to be taught to cultivate the soil, read, write, and pursue industrious and laborious occupations.

["We shall soon be among the Pawnees. . . . Stories have been circulated here and elsewhere that emigrants have been attacked, plundered, and slaughtered by them. . . ." On May 26 "news arrived that the Pawnees have surprised and slain seventy emigrants one hundred miles from this ferry." "The stories have alarmed some timid men, who retrace their steps. The best intelligence from the plains is that the emigration moves on safely."]

Banks of the Kansas
Indian Territory, May 28

Dear George,

Here we are on the banks of the Kansas, ready to be ferried over, which we shall probably accomplish by tomorrow noon. We are all well and hearty as bucks, eat everything that comes before us and hungry at that. You will probably be surprised at our being so long in getting such a little way, 120 miles from Independence. In explanation let me say we have had a great deal of rainy weather, swelling the streams and making the roads bad, and making us lay in camp. The roads are getting better and so is the weather. . . .

["The whole emigration is wild and frantic with a desire to be pressing forward. . . . Whenever a wagon unluckily gets stuck in the mud in crossing some little rut, the other trains behind make a universal rush to try to pass that wagon and to get ahead of each other. Amid the yelling, popping of whips and cursing, perhaps a wagon wheel is broken, two or three men knocked down in a fight, and twenty guns drawn out of the wagons. All this is occasioned by a delay of perhaps two minutes and a half."]

We have found the feed good, and our teams have "fatted" on the way already. Water has been plenty, as has wood. I think there is a fair prospect of getting through without as much hardship as we anticipated, and in better circumstances as to money than I expected as I have on hand now $115, which will be handy when I begin to sift gold.

Our teams are starting and I have not time to finish my letter so good-bye. Give my love to Sabrina and Mother, and kiss little Sister. I mailed a letter to Sabrina on the 24th [written on the 20th, mailed at the "grocery" on the Wakarusa]. I shall write every opportunity.

Your brother,
William Swain

May 29.   This morn I wrote a letter to Mother as we were waiting for the other companies to cross which had got in ahead of us. About nine o'clock we got our wagons down to the ferry and then waited until ten before we commenced crossing the Kansas which is here some thirty rods wide, runs six or eight miles an hour and is muddy like the Missouri. Unfortunately for us, the ferrymen sank one of their scows last night, and we shall hardly get over today.

Today three of our company are sick, two with cholera. They will probably recover.

About one o'clock we commenced ferrying our boats across the river, and I labored all the afternoon getting the wagons on the scows, towing the scows upstream along the south bank, and I twice rowed over and back again. It was near sundown when we finished, and that was accomplished only by the help of a company [from Plymouth, Michigan, with four wagons] who wished to travel with us. The scow which had sunk last night had been raised, and we paid the ferryman for the use of it.

We have had a hard time of it, and it was late when we got to eating supper. We eat like men who have had a hard day's work, and we were not well pleased with Mr. Bailey for not having supper ready when we arrived on the north bank, as he had been over here since three o'clock.

[Bailey probably shared the opinion of another Ranger: "The duties of the cooks are the hardest of all. They have to get over as many miles as the others. On coming into camp they have to procure water for coffee, let it be a long or a short distance from camp, and secure fuel and make it burn, rain or shine. And regardless of their fatigue or the distance traveled, they have to go to work at once, while others having turned out their teams to feed can rest." To compensate for their extra work, the cooks were relieved from guard duty.]

I find that I have worked too hard, as I am very stiff this evening and have pains in my breast and side. I went to bed and covered myself very warmly, took a dose of cayenne pepper, got into a fine sweat, and slept nicely till morning.

> Indian Territory
> South Bank of the Kansas
> May 29, 1849

Dear Mother,

It is with pleasure that I seat myself in my tent this morning. . . . I have just risen from breakfast, which was eaten just at the edge of the river bank, on the cover of our mess chest for a table, we sitting at the time on our camp stools. Breakfast consisted of fried bacon, boiled rice, pancakes made of flour and Indian meal, nut cakes, pilot bread, flour gravy, apple sauce made of dried apples, sugar and coffee. You will think this fine living for the wilderness, but we have a great supply of these articles, enough to last nine months; and best of all is that the farther we go the better the victuals taste, in fact our appetites are voracious. However, we are warned by discretion not to injure ourselves by gratifying our appetites, as we might burst the boiler. . . .

We are getting among the Indians. They come into camp with all their native rigging on, all mounted on ponies splendidly rigged out, for which they ask from $30 to $50. They are Potawatomis from Michigan and have made considerable improvements here. But they dislike this country and say they will go back again to their homes because there is no game, no wood, and bad water here.

Day after tomorrow little Sis is one year old, and you must all keep her birthday and whip her for Father. I wish I could see her and all of you. Give my love to all and tell them I often think of my dear home. Although there are pleasures here, there are also hardships and privations which I would not advise anyone to undergo.

I wrote a line to George yesterday and left it at the trading place. . . . I have stolen the time to write to you this morning, as I ought to be helping to get the train over the river. I shall have a chance to send this up to the stores, as we shall not leave the river until tomorrow morning.

I shall write Sabrina the first opportunity.

> Your affectionate son,
> William Swain

May 30.   This morn I am much better than last night. As we leave all civilization today, I thought it best to go to Uniontown and get some articles for the convenience of the mess. Accordingly I purchased a bake kettle, stew pan, jug, small dipper, and for myself, a bake kettle and small boiling kettle. Dr. Wells accompanied me, and we returned to camp about one o'clock, just as the company was starting. We traveled about six miles over high, dry roads and encamped early, as it commenced raining before sunset.

May 31.   Today we have traveled over rolling plains, high and dry, and have crossed a small stream, name unknown but a bad crossing. Traveled the remainder of the day over good roads.

I was attacked with dysentery at noon very badly. I took medicine from Dr. Wells and got Reverend Hobart to make me a composition tea which I drank after going to bed. It sweat me, and I thought I was better the next morning.

June 1.   Still taking medicine, opium and astringent powders. I rode John's horse this forenoon. This afternoon I walked and rode in the wagon.

About noon today we crossed the Red Vermilion. It is a fine, clear stream running over a stony bottom. It was delightful to see the little minnows glide through its swift, clear water; to hear its murmur and taste its cooling draught. Some of the men bathed in it.

Today I have thought much of home and of my little girl, who is today one year old. She is probably making much fun for her mother, with some trouble, as she must run about and talk considerably by this time.

June 2.   Today I feel some better. I have concluded to take a dose of rhubarb, which I did in the forenoon. I rode on horseback most of the day, which I find very tiresome.

We encamped without wood and with very bad water, but as we had carried a supply of wood along with us we got along very well. My physic worked very hard tonight, and I took medicine to stop it. I am getting very weak and am in fact very sick. All the mess, Mr. Hutchinson in particular, are very kind to me; and the doctor is as attentive and kind as though I was his own brother.

June 3.   Sabbath. Today we traveled to get to the creek between the Red Vermilion and the Big Blue River. We arrived at its banks about noon and encamped and unloaded all our loads to air them.

I am very unwell, and my physic is still running me. This afternoon Dr. Wells and I went to the creek to wash some shirts. We bathed ourselves, but I was so weak that I could not do anything toward washing, or even stand on my feet. So he washed my woolen shirt, and we went to the tent, where I lay till night. The doctor put a mustard plaster all over my bowels, which I wore till morning although it was very severe.

I have had chances to send letters home, but I am unable to write and would not at present if I could.

June 4.   This morn I am very unwell. I am very weak, having eaten nothing to speak of for a long time, and I dare not drink much of the water. The mess fixed a good bed for me in the wagon, where I rode all day and find it much easier than riding horseback. I am better than yesterday.

We crossed the creek and traveled over high, fine prairies. Just at night we crossed the Big Blue River, here a fine large stream over twenty yards wide and four feet deep; has fine fish and very large fresh-water clams. We encamped on its west bank, having come eighteen miles.

June 5.   Today I am very sick, and it jolts me to ride over these knolls and valleys.

Our road is still over the high prairie. We encamped at night without wood or water.

[Nine miles beyond the crossing of the Big Blue River the trail from St. Joseph joined the trail from Independence. "In looking behind over the road just traveled, or back over the St. Joseph road, or forward over that to be taken, for an indefinite number of miles there seemed to be an unending stream of emigrant trains; whilst in the still farther distance along these lines could be seen great clouds of dust, indicating that yet others of these immense caravans were on the move. It was a sight which, once seen, can never be forgotten; it seemed as if the whole family of man had set its face westward."]

June 6.   Today I am much better than yesterday; I am very weak, but can ride comfortably. If I had been able to write, I could have sent a letter home today via some emigrants who have given up the chase and are going back to the states. ["They have seen the tail of the Elephant and can't bear to look any farther. Poor, forsaken looking beings they are. . . . Some are on foot and some on horseback, and we see now and then one with wagon and oxen. But our motto is 'Go Ahead!' I don't think there is a man in our company today who would sell his interest for $500." The backtrackers "see worse times coming back than they did going, for the emigrants plague and pester and interrogate them so much that they cannot look a man in the face. Some of them actually turn off the road in order to avoid the trains." They "are very useful to the emigrants as they supply the place of a mail service and can always tell how far ahead to wood and water."]

June 7.   Today our road, water, and country are the same as yesterday. I am still on the gain, but very weak. I rode on Mr. Hutchinson's pony a short time this afternoon, and I think it did me some good. My appetite is good but I cannot eat hearty for fear of consequences.

["We are traveling through one of the most beautiful countries the eye ever rested upon. . . . Our hour of rising in the morning is four o'clock, hitch up and start at half past six, drive until eleven, rest until two, and drive until six in the evening. The roads are now first-rate, and we are making from seventeen to twenty miles per day. We have been driving slow heretofore, in order to recruit our cattle. They are now in fine order, and we begin to push ahead."]

June 8.   Today our road lay over rolling prairie. Water bad and wood none. About four o'clock we came in sight of the Little Blue River. It is a large muddy creek with bottoms covered with cottonwood timber. We encamped as soon as we came to its banks, watered our teams, and many of the men bathed. Some few caught fish. . . .

June 9.   This morn we got an early start. I rode Mr. Hutchinson's pony for three hours and walked two or three times through the day. Our folks have seen antelope for two days past and today are going out in small parties to hunt.

This afternoon the road lay over the upland, and we had to travel till dark to get to the river to camp. We made a long day's travel, twenty-seven and a half miles.

[Along the trail "every bone or horn . . . is endorsed with numerous individuals' and companies' names . . . with the date of passing. Papers are stuck up on sticks, recording unfortunate circumstances, encounters with Indians, and cautionary advice."]

June 10.   Sabbath. Today we are enjoying ourselves by laying abed late to rest. The sun was high when we got up and got breakfast, which we all enjoyed well, as we got some extras: pudding, apple pie, etc.

["We are now forty miles from the Platte and about sixty from Fort Kearny. We learn that the Pawnees, in whose country we now are, but

Typical pages of Swain's diary. Entries for June 8, 9, and 10. Upper
left "8F." translates: Eighth of June, Friday.

none of whom we have seen yet, and the Sioux who have been at war
with each other, meet at the fort today . . . to make a treaty of peace. We
hope they will continue together at least two or three days, so that we
may have a look at them in council."]

I am not quite so well as yesterday, but well enough to patch my
pants, fill out my journal, bathe in the river, and wash a shirt and drawers.

Towards evening I wrote a letter to my wife, which I sent by a train
of traders bound for St. Joseph with buffalo hides.*

Today one of the Plymouth company met with a serious accident
when his gun [which he had set up against the side of his wagon] was
discharged by a bundle of clothing which he threw out of the wagon, the
bullet passing through his knee and breaking the joint and bones badly.
["His wound will probably cripple him for life and prevent him from

---

* This was the fourteenth letter Swain had written since leaving home. Sabrina or George
received every one—but somehow this letter of June 10 was subsequently lost.

prosecuting his trip. . . . We shall leave him at Fort Kearny under the charge of the surgeon."]

June 11.   This morn we were all aroused before daybreak by a heavy storm of wind and rain, which blew down many of the tents and wet the beds and clothes of many of our people. Our tent stood the storm but we got well soaked, though took no cold. We started at ten o'clock, the road bad from the recent rain. We stopped at noon one hour.

Traveled all the afternoon along the valley of the Little Blue River, which is here becoming clear and gives signs of its head being not far distant. We made fourteen miles and encamped for the last time on the banks of this river whose waters have yielded us so many comforts.

Today we had a feast on antelope which our men had killed, being the first fresh meat furnished by our hunters. ["It created quite a sensation. The messes had a sufficiency to make a stew-pie, which relished well, for we have regaled ourselves on no other meat than bacon for a month."]

I am taking oxide of iron, which Dr. Wells prescribed. He made me some composition tea last night, and I feel much better.

June 12.   This morn we started early and traveled about ten miles along the flat, and then struck over the prairie to the northwest for the Platte River.

Yesterday we passed nine graves of persons buried along the road, with boards or posts at their heads on which were written the name, place of residence, years of age, and date of death. Today we have passed but one, showing that on the lowlands there is more disease than on the uplands.

We encamped on the prairie where there was no wood or water, but our previous supply was still good. Today we have divided and apportioned the duties of our camp. Mr. Hutchinson and I have our duty together, which I am well pleased with.

June 13.   Last night was rainy. This morn we rose late and broke corral at seven o'clock. I am not as well as yesterday, probably exercised too much. Our road is wet.

We traveled on and encamped early three miles from Fort Kearny, a place where the government has established a fort for the protection of the emigrants. It is situated on the south side of the Platte, near the head of Grand Island.

June 14.   We have a fine, pleasant morning, and we were up early and had breakfast over and were started from camp by six o'clock. Stopped at the fort for two hours to get some information concerning the route ahead. I occupied my time in writing to George and had little time to look around, but enough to learn that the fort was commenced a year ago this last April in conformity with an act passed the winter before to establish a line of posts to California [Oregon]. . . .

We halted to noon about five miles beyond the fort. Our road is two miles from the river and there is no wood short of it. We have traveled nineteen miles and encamped early. The weather is fine.

[This afternoon several Rangers went to a nearby camp of a Massachusetts company, the Sagamore and California Mining and Trading Company. Their purpose was reported by a member of that company: "Some of the Wolverine Rangers visited us today and tried to buy some liquor. Did not succeed."]

Fort Kearny, June 14, 1849

Dear George,

Here I am at Fort Kearny. . . . It is built of turfs and covered with bushes and sods for roofs and situated near the upper end of Grand Island on the Platte, which island was spoken of by Frémont in the journal of his expedition on about the 29th or 30th of June, 1842. There are some one hundred and twenty troops stationed here, all busily engaged in building the fort. . . .

["There is a store, blacksmith shop, a horse-powered saw mill and a boarding house kept by a Mormon. The soldiers' tents are scattered around with less regularity than in any ordinary encampment. We saw a few pieces of cannon, but no fortifications." "The sutler's store . . . is built in the same style as the other buildings and has a ground floor. His shelves are arranged with a pretty good stock of notions—cigars, sardines and some extras for officers' use. . . . Well might the sutler say . . . that if he had on hand all the articles Californians inquired for, he could make more money than by going to the gold region itself. As it is . . . few merchants in the States do better than those who are appointed sutlers."]

We are all well and by the letter I wrote to Sabrina last Sunday you will think we are doing first-rate business in the line of living and enjoying ourselves. I was unwell then but have picked up my crumbs greatly since. . . .

We are now some 380 miles from Independence [actual distance: 325

Ft Kearney June 14th 1849

Dear George

Here I am at Ft Kearney a place commenced last spring by government as a fort built of turfs & covered with bushes & sods for roofs & situated at the upper end of grand Island on the Platt spoken of by Fremont in the journal of his expedition about the 2[?] or 30 of June there is some 126 troops situated here all busily engaged in building the ft. here is a settlers shop and things look something like civilization, but the gathering of the Natives which we expected here is not to take place

We are all well and by the letter I wrote Sabrina last Sunday you will think that we are doing a first rate business in the line of living & enjoying ourselves It was unwell then but have picked up my crumbs greatly since then, We left the little Blue on tuesday crossed the high parare 25 m in yesterday, about 1600 we came in sight of the platte & today we encamped last night about 3m from the Fort & this morning we stop the train here in front of the ft. to write from this post as the mail leaves here every 2 weeks for Independence

We are now some 3 & 0 m from Independence making about 20 miles a day & having good easy times & enjoying ourselves very well & although we get along slowly we are provided for any emergency that might arise & on the whole I am well suited with our choice in mode of traveling & would not wish to be any otherways situated on this rout nor would I wish to be at home On the contrary I am glad that I am on the way to a place where I have a prospect of benefiting

miles], making about twenty miles a day, having good easy times and enjoying ourselves very well. Although we get along slowly, we are provided for any emergency that might arise, and on the whole I am well suited with our choice in the mode of traveling and would not wish to be any otherwise situated on this route, nor would I wish to be at home. On the contrary, I am glad that I am on the way to a place where I have a prospect of benefiting myself and my family, although absence from home often makes me sorrowful for the moment; and dangers, hardships, and toils often beset my way. . . .

We are now passing through the territory of the Indians and buffalo, but neither have been seen by our train, although the bones and horns of the buffalo line the track of our road. But we have seen and killed some few antelope. The number of trains passing has scared the buffalo from the road; but we intend having a lick at them before leaving the plains. We are truly out of civilization, never hearing from the States and knowing nothing at all about things in our own country. . . .

["There was a rumor that a treaty was in contemplation between the Sioux and the Pawnees to come off soon at this fort. It turns out to be merely a fable. We now learn that the Sioux decline any compromise with their ancient enemies. . . . A few days since we met some emigrants returning and we bought seventy pounds of coffee at seven cents per pound. The rest of their traps they had disposed of. Every day we meet some one, traders or emigrants, returning to the States."]

Tell Mother that she would be delighted with the rare specimens of vegetation in this country, the prickly pear in beds of acres and a small species of globe cactus having numerous spurs covering its whole surface.

The number of persons who have passed the fort is variously estimated from 7,000 to 10,000; but no certainty can be arrived at in judging the number.

Give my love to Sabrina and tell her that I am determined to have my share of the rocks, if possible. Give my love to all my young friends.

Your affectionate brother,
William Swain

[Hundreds of companies stopped at Fort Kearny to lighten their wagon loads. "The great majority . . . were profoundly ignorant when starting of what was before them, had no idea of what an outfit consisted of. . . . The result of such want of experience was that almost every wagon left the frontier overloaded, not with articles absolutely necessary but with such things as each might fancy he would want while on the prairies or after he reached the end of the journey. Sawmills, pickaxes, shovels, anvils, blacksmith's tools, featherbeds, rocking chairs, and a thousand other useless articles filled the wagons. . . . The loading was too great for the teams, and now overboard goes everything."

[An army officer who visited Fort Kearny at the height of the emigration reported that "men come in at every moment, bringing letters for the States (which are dispatched from here twice a month by government express), making thousands of inquiries on every conceivable subject . . . and asking for every sort of assistance. . . ." "Every state, indeed almost every town and country in the United States, is now represented in this part of the world. Wagons of all patterns, sizes and descriptions, drawn by bulls, cows, oxen, jackasses, mules, and horses are daily seen rolling along towards the Pacific, guarded by walking arsenals. Arms of all kinds must certainly be scarce in the States, after such a drain as the emigrants have made upon them."

["The great California caravan has swept past this point, and the prairies are beginning to resume their wonted state of quiet and loneliness. Occasionally, a solitary wagon may be seen hurrying along like a buffalo on the outskirts of a band; but all the organized as well as disorganized companies have cut loose from civilization and are pushing towards the Pacific."]

Back Home

"Every day we wonder where poor William is, and we wish we could send you pancakes, baked potatoes, beans, and beef by telegraph."

Sabbath, Youngstown, May 27, 1849

Dear William,

Here I am at home with Mother, George, Delia [William's cousin], and dear little Sister, with rather poor health for myself and the child. However, I have reason to rejoice rather than to complain as regards Eliza's health. Four weeks ago I thought she would be no better, but now, by the providence of God, good care, and doctoring, she is better but still very unwell. I am giving her a syrup made of dandelion roots. . . .

While I am writing to one she has already forgotten, Eliza is trotting about the house with her playthings and coming to me occasionally to be taken up, which I have to do; and I let her oversee the writing, which she does with good grace by knocking my elbow now and then.

As to my own health: it is no better, if anything I think it is not quite as good as it was when you left. Not only my back, but my stomach

The number 40 in the upper right corner in ink signifies forty cents postage.
AUTHOR'S COLLECTION

---

troubles me very much; also I have a great deal of pain in my head, particularly on the top. I have not as yet had any of the sarsaparilla, but am taking a syrup compound of different roots which may be as good as sarsaparilla. Dr. Creswell tells me that I cannot get well until I am willing to lie on my back for two months. My appetite is very poor and has been ever since I weaned Sis. The fact is, William, I feel bad every way, not only poor health but low spirits which I cannot get rid of. I cannot be reconciled to my lot. If I had known that I could not be more reconciled than I am, I should have tried hard to have kept you at home. My feelings are such that I cannot describe them, and more than that, I try to conceal them as much as I can. I am quite confident that it wears on me. But let my feelings be what they will, I hope it will not trouble you.

Dear William, when I think of our separation, for a moment it seems like a dream, but a second thought and it is so. How could I endure it, I ask myself, if you should never return? I could not live. As you say, hitherto I was a stranger to my attachment.

I received your letter of the 6th. Some one of us has been to the post office every day for two weeks. We began to think something had happened. I can tell you, my dear, that my soul rejoiced with unspeakable joy to read . . . your letter. May God bless you, my dear, in your undertaking. . . .

Dear William,

We have just been to tea. Delia and I washed the dishes. Mother is reading in the Bible. George is upstairs writing, and Sis is asleep—all here but you, and why should the loved one be gone? . . .

I do not much expect that you will ever read this letter. O! If I could only hear from you every week, I could content myself much better.

Eliza is getting so she thinks a great deal of George. She calculates to have a play with him whenever he comes in. I stayed at home three weeks. Eliza appeared to be very glad to get back here. I enjoy myself full as well here as at Father's, and in accordance with your request I shall be here a good share of the time.

William dear, it is now half past nine and I must close and retire. And I have got to go without you, saddening thought. But I am to go to a bed of feathers, while you to a cold, damp ground. Yet I have one thing to comfort me: I think you have things as comfortable as you could on such a journey.

I have many things to say to you, but cannot. May God guide and bless you in our separation and hasten your return. If we are never permitted to meet on earth, may Heaven grant us a happy meeting in that world where parting is never known.

I shall write you again by the next steamer. We are looking every day for another letter from you. Mrs. Bailey received a letter from Mr. Bailey the same time as I got yours. I saw her yesterday. She and Frank were well.

Good night—and farewell,
Sabrina

Youngstown, Sabbath afternoon
May 27, 1849

Dear Brother William,

Your letter dated Independence May 6 and 7 came to hand on Thursday, May 24, and gave us great pleasure to hear that you were "tolerably well." . . . We expect to get a full description of your outfit and company in your next.

We—the Roots, Baileys and Swains—were in a perfect fever of anxiety about you on account of the cholera. We watched the mail every day, and I never saw so long a two weeks as those between your St. Louis letter and your Independence letter. The latter has slightly relaxed the anxiety, but we still almost hold our breath, for we know the cholera will be with you in crossing the plains and probably in California. Do write as soon as you get there. . . .

The tenor of your last letter to Sabrina lacked the enthusiasm of former ones, although showing that your fortune thus far and your prospects for the future were good. I suppose the reason for this is that as it was Sabbath you had nothing else to do and surrendered yourself to thoughts of home and those you left behind you. But courage, William! We'll meet again, and I hope in better circumstances, although the parting and separation produce pain and anxiety. I wish I could telegraph you now, and tell you how we are, though I suppose you are three hundred miles out on the prairies. . . .

Sabrina is now back with us after her visit with her family and has been for two weeks, and I give you my honor I will do all I can to make her and Little Eliza comfortable and happy. Sabrina's health is, I think, some better than when you left. Little Sis is decidedly better. . . . She is quite cheerful and playful. But as Sabrina is writing, I will leave that story for her to tell. . . .

I wish I could this evening talk to you in your prairie tent. You are thought of here every day, and I may say every hour. Every day we wonder where poor William is, and we wish we could send you pancakes, baked potatoes, beans, and beef by telegraph. All this of course will do you no good, but nature will have her course.

Dr. Root and family are all very well. You must have John write his mother regularly, as she and all the family feel anxious about him. Mrs. Bailey and her boy are in good health, but Mrs. B. feels anxious about her husband. Tell Mr. Bailey to be sure and write. Let everyone of you mention each of the others' names and their health and success, so that if one letter comes here we shall hear of you all, though the other should be miscarried. . . .

William, I beseech you not to give yourself uneasiness about home. I will not leave anything undone to make each of the family comfortable, and I think we shall be as comfortable in regard to bodily wants as if you were here. True, we shall still be thinking and talking and dreaming about you. I shall write every month. . . .

Will, I want you to write me everything about the country. Keep a pencil and paper in your pocket and note down everything, and when you write send it along. . . .

Mother says, "tell William that I am rejoiced to hear of his determination to read his Bible, and I hope he will persevere till he finds the pearl of great price. Tell him I often see him and converse with him in my sleep and that my sincere prayer to God is that He will protect and bless him and return him safe to us." And that, William, is the feeling of us all. I never dreamed that I could feel such anxiety as I have felt and must continue to feel for a long time to come. I beg of you, be careful of yourself. If you feel unwell, attend to yourself. . . . And especially if you have a cough, stop it if possible; if you can't, come home *immediately— don't stay there if you cough.* . . . May God give you wisdom to conduct yourself discreetly and wisely in this and all other matters. Remember, William, we would all rather you would come home without a cent, with health, than that you should come loaded with gold and disease and but a short lease on life. It is needless for me to say more, but still I can hardly stop.

May God in His mercy protect and guide and bless you and all of us, is the prayer of your affectionate brother,

George Swain

[The next morning]

Please give my particular respects to Mr. Hutchinson. Tell him that although he has no family here, still he has friends who want to hear from him, and the same to Messrs. Bailey and Root. When I think that this letter will not reach you till the last of August, it seems a long time; but it may be some satisfaction to you to get news from home even at that distant time.

All well and join in love to you. May God bless you. Goodbye, William.

CHAPTER IV

Tracks of the Elephant

"There is much to vex and try the patience of men on such a long trip. . . . The tongue is allowed to run too much by many."

Though the wilderness stretched off to the horizon, though they were moving each day twenty miles and more through a vastness they had imagined or read about since childhood—the very places that Frémont had described, they could not escape the sight and sound of hundreds of other emigrants. At night as they waited for sleep, in the morning as they crawled from their damp blankets, they could hear and see on all sides the great crowd of cityfolk and farmers. Where was the silence of the wilderness, the solitude they had imagined? Nearby they heard the friendly banter of campmates, farther away the angry yells of strangers in argument, the impatient cry of the cook for more firewood, the stamping and pushing sounds of mules and oxen corraled within the ring of company wagons, the bark of a dog chasing a horseman in pursuit of a vagrant team. After dark, songs and fiddle playing aroused thoughts of wives and sweethearts. Morning duties might be punctuated by the rifle fire of hunters target shooting in expectation of seeing on that day's route a herd of buffalo.

Through May and June the 29,000 men (here and there a company with women and children) moved west from Fort Kearny through the valley of the Platte. For 336 miles to Fort Laramie, they would advance along the south side of the mud-colored river which in some places sprawled two miles wide.

Except for the crossing of the South Fork of the Platte, a mile of quicksand, and the steep descent at Ash Hollow where the trail entered

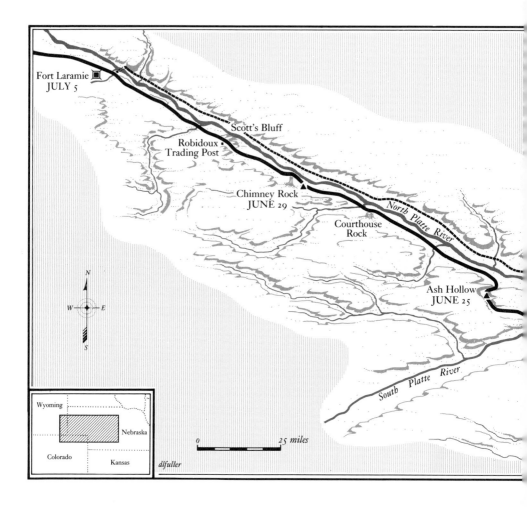

Fort Laramie
JULY 5

Scott's Bluff

Robidoux
Trading Post

Chimney Rock
JUNE 29

Courthouse
Rock

North Platte River

Ash Hollow
JUNE 25

N
W—E
S

Wyoming

Nebraska

Colorado

Kansas

South Platte River

0   25 *miles*

dlfuller

the level plain of the North Platte, there would be no obstacles to delay their progress. Along the way they passed well-known landmarks named in earlier years by fur trappers and explorers and described in all the books about the West. Like tourists anticipating what they had been told or had read, the thousands of goldseekers felt a thrill when far to the west they saw the narrow spire they knew to be Chimney Rock, or when they camped beneath the architectural mass of Courthouse Rock or the looming bulk of Scotts Bluff.

Anxious to get away from the crowds and curious to see the wonders of the West, many of these men had enough energy at the end of a day's march to take long hikes, going miles from the trail to climb a ridgetop, there to see the surrounding country. Or they dared to climb the sheer sides of Chimney Rock or Courthouse Rock not only for a better view but to carve their initials in the soft sandstone. One climber was astonished to

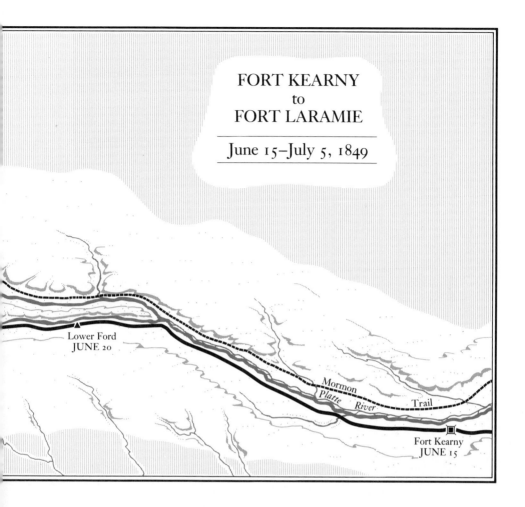

FORT KEARNY
to
FORT LARAMIE

June 15–July 5, 1849

Lower Ford
JUNE 20

Mormon
Platte Trail
River

Fort Kearny
JUNE 15

find at the uppermost point he could reach a miniature windmill whirring in the breeze, a testament to the ambition and imagination of a gold-rush Kilroy.

More purposeful, they also left messages on rocks and abandoned wagons and tied to trailside sticks. Almost everyone had friends or relatives or at least hometown acquaintances marching west in that ever-lengthening emigration which as of June 15 stretched all the way from Fort Kearney to South Pass, a distance of 600 miles.

Whether prompted by friendliness to advise and direct those coming along behind or by rivalry to show who was ahead in the race to the Sacramento, the goldseekers used all sorts of devices to communicate. The walls of a trading post at Scotts Bluff "were plastered with paper so that the emigrants could inform their friends . . . when they had gone by this point and that they were well, etc." Another diarist complained:

"Not a buffalo skull or elk antler along the road but has a notice on it." This communication continued all the way to California and became more important farther west where two or more trails diverged. At such forks hundreds of messages would be posted or left in a barrel marked "post office."

Though many had lightened their overloaded wagons at Fort Kearny, the process continued even on the gentle westward slope of the Platte Valley. More and more they realized the need to care for their teams. Other values changed as well. In the face of the continued threat of cholera, their often frantic fear of the disease caused the healthy to give their sick companions less than gentle care. Many wagons kept moving through the heat and dust with dying men suffering inside; and sometimes graves were dug before death brought surcease. Diarists reported a callousness that would have shocked and frightened families back home. "It would make your heart ache to see how some of the companies buried their dead. I have visited graves where the person was not buried more than twenty inches deep and found them dug up by wolves and their flesh eaten off and their bones scattered to bleach upon the plains."

The changing morality found expression in other ways less tragic but with lasting consequences. Quarreling, fighting, shootings and stabbings may have been inevitable among so many men living an exceedingly communal life wherein one man's failure to do his duty affected the well-being of so many others. "If there is anything that tries a man's patience and brings out his combativeness . . . it is a trip across the plains. . . . If there is any inclination to shirk or do any little mean trick or the slightest tendency to hoggishness, it will soon develop."

Few companies reached California, or even Fort Laramie, without serious disputes that often caused division into two or more angry groups. The causes of dissension were cited by many diarists, with some of the more unexpected being card playing, dogs that frightened teams into a stampede (in one company two dogs were shot) and arguments over the observance of the Sabbath. Though many companies' rules or constitutions called for strict observance of the Sabbath as a day of rest, the realities of life on the trail often made that impossible. The needs of the teams increasingly took precedence over back-home customs, with the day of rest being chosen when ample grass and water could be found. But some stubborn adherents to the Sabbath rule refused to travel on Sunday, forcing the division of their companies.

To control these greenhorns, to make decisions as to where to camp each night, whether to lay over or push ahead, how to punish men who fell asleep on guard duty—these and many more crises tormented the captains of overland companies. "To be the leader of an emigrant train through the wilderness is one of the most unenviable distinctions. . . . Some may think the children of Israel in the wilderness were a clamorsome set, but they were nothing more than what folks are now."

The strains of enforced companionship, of cooking for impatient grumblers, of coping with a balky mule or sick ox were lessened by the moments of excitement and high adventure that fulfilled the previous winter's expectations. Most memorable was the first sight of buffalo. Everyone wanted a chance to kill one of the legendary beasts. Most companies had a few horses or ponies, and hunting parties usually brought back great chunks of meat for the cooks. But accidents were common. In one chase an old bull charged and gored Wolverine Ranger Horace Ladd's horse, with Ladd escaping uninjured. Other hunters lost their pistols and rifles and sometimes their horses, leaving the bruised sportsmen a lonely hike back to camp. If camp duties or too few horses kept most men from joining the hunt, everyone could enjoy the campfire luxury of broiled buffalo steaks which inspired diarists to extravagant praise. "Oh, if I could only send this great, tender piece of tenderloin to my friends at home! Such delicious, juicy meat I have never before put under the operations of my masticating organs."

The Sioux Indians ranged through the valley of the Platte during May and early June. But, as in Pawnee country, many companies never caught sight of this famed tribe. "They are much wilder than the buffalo and antelope. The traders have told them that the emigrants have the cholera and smallpox, and they keep shy of us." When they did come to the trailside, they were invariably friendly and sometimes profit-minded. One company encountered a band of Sioux who had stationed themselves by the trail, raised an American flag and asked the intruders to pay tribute. Of special interest to many in the passing throng, "the pretty young squaws certainly are beauties of Nature and will compare very well with some of the young ladies of the States who think themselves handsomer. . . . They are what Nature designed them to be, women without stays or padding."

The Wolverine Rangers did not reach the forks of the Platte, an area where emigrant companies most often met the Sioux, until late June; by then the tribe had followed the buffalo northward. Bringing up the rear of the emigration, with consequent disadvantages—grass generally overgrazed, campsites littered, the trail rutted and lined with cast-off equipment and rotting foodstuffs, the Rangers advanced under careful leadership. They frequently rested on Sunday and generally maintained an adherence to their "Articles of Agreement" and an amicability among their sixty-seven members that was ever more uncommon the farther west they went.

Captain Potts' leadership probably contributed to the orderliness of the Rangers' trail life, as did the subtle influence of knowing that letters were being sent back to Marshall and other nearby hometowns by the Reverend Randall Hobart, Horace Ladd, James Lyon and the Camp brothers, Herman and Elmon. Most prolific was James Pratt, whose many letters often included lengthy excerpts from his diary.

Carried to Independence by backtrackers, these reports (regularly published in local newspapers) kept anxious families informed of life and health in the Rangers' camps. Unlike Swain, whose letters and diary are largely devoted to describing—often eloquently—the scenery and natural environment of what is now Nebraska, the other Rangers took more interest in the human story. Pratt wrote about individual Rangers and how they were adjusting to camp life, and he revealed how difficult it was to find time to keep up a daily diary. Horace Ladd told how the company was managed, and fortunately he took a special interest in how the meals were prepared. He reported that each mess received its weekly food supplies from the main commissary on Sunday, and if the company was encamped that day, then the cooks had time to vary the menu with "good light biscuits, dried applesauce, stewed gooseberries, hard bread, dried beef and tea. So you see, we are not starving." The more usual weekday meals consisted of quickly prepared frying-pan-sized flapjacks with bacon and coffee.

Like a great highway, the valley of the Platte opened the way west and then more and more northwest, a naked plain five to fifteen miles wide reaching out to scattered buttes and distant bluffs. The river (so muddy it was said to flow "bottomside up") was named La Platte by French fur traders who had visited this region as early as the 1720s. For gold rush companies, travel through this valley would be the easiest part of the entire journey—the upward slope so gentle they hardly felt the grade, the terrain so open that the trail widened in places to several miles, and always water nearby, though so muddy someone said you had to chew it.

At the western end of the Platte Valley where the Black Hills (eastern Wyoming) forewarned of more difficult travel conditions up ahead, the trail came to the second military outpost, Fort Laramie. Purchased by the U.S. Army from a fur-trading company for $4,000 in June 1849, this adobe structure carried a name known to most emigrants, for the place had been described by Frémont, Bryant, Parkman and the lesser writers who had shaped America's awareness of the Far West. Important as it had been to the fur trade and would be to the Army, in 1849 the fort could not help the thousands of passing emigrants. They could not buy there, at any price, what they needed most, goggles to protect against the sun and dust and fresh oxen or mules to replace those that had died or looked as if they could not survive much longer. News of the size of the emigration up ahead, and that the lead company (from Ithaca, New York) had passed the fort on May 27 caused some mule companies to abandon their wagons and set out as pack companies. Many more companies responded to their growing fear of what lay ahead—"We are told that the Elephant is in waiting"—by throwing away everything they could agree was unnecessary.

When the Rangers visited Fort Laramie in early July, they probably learned how far behind they were. But Swain and his companions remained unperturbed, as emphasized by their elaborate celebration of the Fourth of July.

To celebrate Independence Day was a matter of pride, even obligation, for most gold-rush companies. One diarist, no doubt remembering how hot it always was in Pennsylvania on the Fourth, told of an exotic celebration: "We had a pail full of punch made and cooled it with a lump of snow from a deep snowbank. . . . Having drunk our punch and given three cheers for our Glorious Union, we resumed our march." Another company made ice cream and flavored it with wild peppermint, while another filled a barrel with explosives, buried it on a mountainside and blew it up. Heavily armed and without Indian dangers to justify their armaments, many companies found in the Fourth an excuse for firing their rifles and pistols. One company "fired a gun for every state in the Union and a volley for California and for the gold diggings. In this salute one of the Rovers got a thumb shot off. The firing kept up till a late hour. . . ."

Such exuberance suggests the character of this great army of hopeful men. They were indeed like soldiers, freed from family restraints, sharing physical discomforts and challenges that became a test of their manhood. In a far land they gathered around campfires—an American ritual—to talk of home, of women, to complain about their food, their officers and their duties. They considered the dangers ahead and turned them aside with talk of California. Seeing so many on the trail, they felt an ever increasing impatience to get to the gold mines. Sometimes their talk explored the possibility of disappointment, but such doubts were easily replaced by recalling the reports of fortunes found in 1848.

■

June 15, 1849.   [In camp at Fort Kearny.] This morning we were up early and on the march by six o'clock. I had the lead today and wished to make a good day's travel. [The favored lead position, dust-free in the line of twenty-three wagons, rotated among the messes.].

The road was dry and cool; pleasant breeze from the south. John Root went to the bluffs to hunt antelope, saw fifteen, shot at two, and came to the train in noon halt without any game. Today near evening an antelope started from the river and ran ahead and around our train to the bluff. It was the first one I have seen.

["Antelope are very shy as well as fleet. . . . You cannot slip up on an antelope, but you can excite their curiosity and entice them up to you and shoot them. One would think they were all females on account of their curiosity. . . . All that is necessary is to hide behind a sage bush, draw your ramrod from your rifle and fasten a red handkerchief or shirt on the end of it and move the red object back and forth. As soon as it is seen by the antelope, he will circle round it, gradually approaching nearer and nearer until within good shooting range."]

Shortly after noon Mr. Hutchinson rode his pony up on the bluffs to have a look at the plains beyond and when he returned I took the pony to visit the Platte River which lay about a mile across the flat from the road. Although we have traveled some days along the river, I had not visited its shore before. On arriving at its edge it lay before me, a muddy stream at least two miles wide, its surface about two or three feet below the level of the flats.

The reflections produced by the sight were pleasing to me, and I allowed myself the luxury of letting my mind recur to past days. The interest with which in youth I had contemplated the great American wilderness with its streams, its plains, its mountains, its inhabitants, and all connected with it, was fresh in my thoughts. Now I am in the midst of these themes of so much interest, by the shore of the Platte with its sweeping tide, its fine plains, its islands, and its bluffs all in my gaze. Although thoughts of youth, home, family, and friends blot half its grandeur, still there is a pleasing beauty in its scenery. The river thus far averages one half mile wide, its bottoms four miles wide. Its bluffs are conical hills some sixty feet high. Wood is almost entirely confined to the islands. We are now burning buffalo chips.

["It is the duty of the cooks on arriving at a camping place . . . to sally forth and collect chips for cooking. . . . It would amuse friends at home to see them . . . jump from the wagons, gunny bag in hand, and make a grand rush for the largest and driest chips. The contest is spirited and always fun-provoking. . . ." "It takes an average of about five bushels

Bruff titles this scene: "On the plains, preparing to feed, [with] buffalo chip fuel."
HENRY E. HUNTINGTON LIBRARY

---

to cook supper and breakfast for twelve persons." "The chips burn well when dry but if damp or wet are smoky and almost fireproof." "They emit a delicate perfume. . . ."]

June 16.   This day we have a fine road and day for traveling, the wind being high, as it always is on these plains and dead aft so that it helps us along greatly.

This afternoon when I was in the rear I observed a commotion in front. The horsemen galloping along the train, the footmen, the drivers, all seemed anxiously inquiring for something. Soon the train formed a telegraphic line, on which the word "buffalo" was transmitted. All hands seized their guns and every man at liberty started for the head of the train. The drivers all mounted the wagon tongues and drove with one hand, having hold of the wagon cover with the other, while eyes and mouths were wide open in search of the subject of the commotion. I was driving and from the tongue on which I stood, I soon fixed my eye on the

When Swain stood on a bluff June 18 to look across the valley of the Platte, the Rangers' camp may have looked much like the Washington City Company shown here. Unfortunately, Bruff chose to ignore the scores of other wagons traveling over these plains.
HENRY E. HUNTINGTON LIBRARY

object of all the feeling and interest of the company: a troop of some twenty buffalo who had come across the river and were making for the bluffs across the head of our trail. They had far the start on our boys and were doing their best. Footmen ran and horsemen put the ponies under whip and spur. The plain was three miles wide, and the chase was very even for the first half way; but the buffalos' wind proved the best and all but three of the horsemen gave up the chase, one of whom came up with the buffalos. He was far in advance of the train when he saw them and had no arms but his revolver, and from that he shot four balls, two of which took effect but only made the buffalo run the faster. Thus ended our first buffalo chase. I confess I was much displeased, as I had made up my mind for some steak this evening.

We encamped early on the river bank, where we found some water willow which had been killed by the fires of the prairie and which answered to good purpose for cooking on the Sabbath. Wind very high. Distance, twenty-three miles.

June 17.   Sabbath. Today in camp all day. I spent the day in doing little necessary chores which I cannot do on other days. First I washed the dishes and gathered chips for the next three days; then went in swimming, which I found very much fun. On plunging into the river,

which I supposed three feet deep, I found I could but just stand on the bottom, which being of sand, would slip away from my feet as soon as the force was applied to it necessary to sustain myself against the current, which was very strong; and in place of standing where I expected, I found myself sweeping along down the river. I was obliged to swim with the current, which took me along like fun.

After having a fine swim, I washed some clothes, and then I made a bag to keep my clothes and gun in. Attended preaching at seven o'clock.

Three of our boys forded the Platte with horses to chase the herds of buffalo we have seen all day. They brought one home this evening and we had our first buffalo meat.

[After watching the hunters from his company and those of other companies, one diarist observed: "Not less than fifty buffalo were slaughtered this morning, whereas not three in all were used. Such wanton destruction of buffalo, the main dependence of the Indians for food, is certainly reprehensible. But, the desire by the emigrant of engaging once at least in a buffalo chase can scarcely be repressed."]

June 18.   This morning we started early and had a fine day for traveling. The bluffs are still high and picturesque. Through the day we saw many deer and antelope and some wolves. The river is becoming wider and more full of islands, which are tolerably well wooded and are truly beautiful. They are small, and many of them rise just out of the water covered with fine grass, while others are covered with woods. The river, some two miles wide and very full of these islands, certainly forms a perfect model of water scenery.

This afternoon I had the use of Mr. H's pony, and my curiosity led me to scour over the bluffs to our left. I selected the highest one in sight and rode over the plains some three miles to its base and ascended its steep side till I stood on its pinnacle. The top was marked by footprints, which had lately been imprinted by some adventurer before me. On its top I found a species of wormwood and some three or four kinds of flowers, specimens of which I have placed in my flower book. On the north, the river with its islands, flats and bluffs was before me, and from this point formed a splendid scene. ["As far as the eye can reach, you see to the east and west a continuous line of wagons moving quickly westward. . . . On the opposite bank of the Platte is the trail from Council Bluffs, on which a long line of teams is creeping westward like so many caterpillars. . . ."]

June 19.   Today fine. The scenery of the river changes to a clear channel, and I think that we are past the mouth of the Forks [the junction of the North and South Forks of the Platte]. The bluffs change to rolling highlands and the flats descend gradually from the uplands to the shore.

[Along the river flats "races between trains are very common." "The excitement of an ox race, where the utmost speed is an ordinary walk, is as great as it is at a racecourse. A race sometimes continues for a half day, and the cracking of the whips and the hollering of 'Close up, Close up' makes no little noise. After a while the race is terminated by the coming to a place where but one wagon can go at a time, when the train which strikes it first, if well closed up, prevails, and the other goes behind."]

Twenty-three miles today.

June 20.   We left camp early and coursed across the plain, the road running along the foot of the highlands. About eight o'clock the cry "buffalo" ran along the line, and on looking ahead I saw a drove of nine buffalo coursing along the flat between us and the river. Our horses had run off in the night and all our horsemen [one of whom was John Root] had left camp early to go after them and had not returned. So we did nothing but content ourselves by looking at them. They ran abreast, as they always do and formed a fine troop. The back end of our line, supposing that they would run close to them, took guns in hand; but the herd changed course and ran towards the river. A horseman of the Plymouth company dashed across the plain and headed them off. They changed their course again and came directly towards the center of the train. All hands snatched their rifles, ran to the top of a roll in the plain over which the buffalo had to come and sulked till the herd came within ten rods. The line of fire was then opened on them and some thirty shots blazed at them. They sheered and hobbled on their course as fast as broken shoulders, legs, and ribs would allow. They came rushing across our road and ran two wagons behind our mess. They certainly presented a fine appearance. They were all large, fine bulls and ran abreast with heads up. Their deep, large shoulders, which with the hump, head, and neck were covered with long hair in contrast to the short, smooth hair on the rest of their bodies, appeared much higher than their hind parts and gave them a proud and haughty appearance. Every man who could gave them his fire as they passed, and almost every one of the herd went off giving evidence of being wounded. Our horsemen arrived just in time to pursue them to the bluff, and every man who could run gave chase.

And now the interest of the chase commenced. Men and horses became excited. The horsemen soon stopped two of the noble animals on the plains, and the footmen coming up were all anxious to have a dead shot at them. Some thirty shots aimed at the head of the first one finally brought him to the ground, and the other was soon dispatched. Then all hands fell to skinning and cutting away the choicest parts, while the horsemen pursued the herd and dispatched two more on the hills. We judge these animals would weigh twelve or fourteen hundred pounds. The first one killed was of age, for I counted nineteen wrinkles on his horns.

All returned to the train loaded with buffalo meat, which we cut into pieces and hung along the sides of our wagons, on the reach, and along the tops of the covers. In such a fix we look like living.

We stopped to noon early and all hands struck a fire and had a fine buffalo steak for dinner, which certainly is the sweetest and tenderest meat I have ever eaten.

After traveling about three miles, a line of clouds in the west which had been advancing some time gave evidence of an approaching storm of no ordinary character. The men all clad themselves in India-rubber or oilcloth, preparatory to a rainstorm. The wind, which had blown all day from the southwest, suddenly changed to the northeast, and the clouds changed their course with it and came directly upon us. The train was advancing in fine order and all things looked likely for a cooling thunderstorm. But as the clouds advanced, a noise like the rushing of heavy wind grew louder and louder, until the whole air resounded with a noise resem-

bling a shower of stones falling on a floor of boards. In an instant the air ahead appeared full of falling white spots, and in an instant more the pelting of heads and the bounding of ice balls convinced us that a tremendous hailstorm was upon us. The fury of the storm can only be imagined by a minute description of itself and its effects. In a moment after the first hail fell, the air was literally *filled* with balls of ice from the size of a *walnut* to that of a *goose egg*, falling like drops of rain and rebounding from whatever they struck; while bursts of thunder broke out in tremendous peals and forked lightning shot through the sky, streaking it with vivid lines of light.

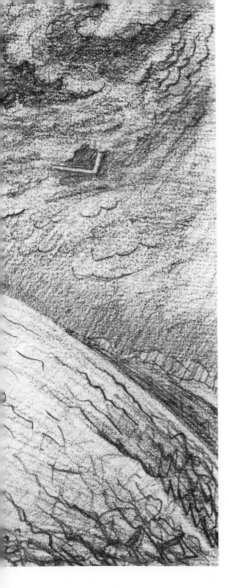

Bruff's illustration of the hailstorm described by Swain on June 20.
HENRY E. HUNTINGTON LIBRARY

The train, proceeding on its course, first stopped for a moment. And then commenced the crisis of the incident. The teams, unacquainted with such punishment inflicted by an unseen hand and frightened and writhing with the pain inflicted by the strokes of the hail, bellowed and reared and sprang from its fury, wheeling their heads from the storm. The drivers, seeing the teams and wagons wheeling, sprang forward to guide the teams in turning and thus saved the train from destruction. The bellowing of the cattle, the shouting of the teamsters and others, the crack of breaking tongues, the crash of upsetting wagons, the rattling of wheels urged on by the teams maddened by the strokes of the storm, the groans and strong curses of the men, the vivid flashes of lightning, and the crack of thunder, all mingled with the tumultuous noise of the hail striking upon the earth, formed a moment of terrific suspense, the termination of which might have decided the success of our enterprise. But another moment showed that the determined and prompt action of the men, even at their own peril, had triumphed over the danger of so uncommon and terrific a storm, for it saw our wagons and teams flying in tolerable safety over the plains at full speed before the storm. All who could, sought safety in the wagons, and those who could not shielded themselves from the fury of the descending ice by any means in their power. Some clung to the reaches of the wagons and allowed themselves to be drawn along under them; others crowned themselves with camp kettles while the horsemen who were lucky enough to retain their animals placed the saddles over their heads and awaited as best they could the termination of the storm. It lasted about fifteen minutes. During that time our teams had scoured over the plains in every direction, at first running, then walking, and finally, as they became convinced there was no running from the storm, stopping.

When the storm had subsided sufficiently to permit investigation, it was found that the damage done to our train consisted of only one wagon upset, two tongues broken, and one wheel smashed, with sundry bruised and gashed heads, black eyes, pounded and swollen backs, shoulders, and arms, which with a little attention from the doctor and considerable liniment soon became sound. ["All the wagon covers, which were either painted or oiled, looked as if they had been used during the Mexican War as a breastwork. . . . The cattle were many of them cut through on the hips and back by the hail. . . . This storm was decidedly severe, a touch of the terrific, something of the Elephant."].

We soon repaired our breaks and were on our course again in good spirits, remembering the past with many a hearty laugh over the various freaks of fortune in her dealings with us. "No great evil without some good" was our motto, so we filled our pails and kettles with hail and had icewater the rest of the day, a luxury we little expected on this route.

We traveled fifteen miles today and encamped about three miles west of the Lower Ford, which is just where the High land commences between the forks of the North and South Platte River.*

---

* *There was another well-known crossing place fifty-three miles west of this Lower Ford, called (inevitably) Upper Ford. Companies crossed the South Platte wherever they found it practicable, although these two fords were the ones most frequently used. The Rangers chose the Upper Ford.*

June 21.   The day is fine. Good roads lined with a variety of gay flowers.

Made nineteen and a half miles and encamped. This evening Dr. Wells, Mr. Hutchinson, and I bathed in the Platte.

["When we halt at night, we are usually too tired for games or sport of any kind. We smoke our pipes, talk when we feel like it, and before we examine the Odometer, we do some guessing about the number of miles made during the day. In true American fashion, if we have anything to bet, and there is sometimes a little extra tobacco, we back our opinions regarding the speed of the train with a wager. This is about the extent of our gaiety."].

June 22.   Traveled today along the valley, which still has the same gently rising flat and rolling highland and no timber. Game in abundance —antelope, buffalo, and prairie dogs; flora beautiful, especially the cactus and prickly pear, which are in bloom. Some have as many as seven blossoms on a leaf.

We encamped near the Upper Ford, having made twenty-two and three-quarter miles.

[Along the route several prairie dog villages were seen, "sometimes of several acres in extent, where innumerable little heaps of earth show the entrances to the subterranean cells of the inhabitants, and the well-beaten tracks, like lanes, show their mobility and restlessness." The prairie dogs "come out of their burrows by thousands, and standing perfectly erect on their hind feet, impudently bark with their sharp voices at the passing multitude." "They are very hard to get, as they are never found far from their holes, and when shot fall immediately into them. . . ."]

June 23.   We started early for the ford and prepared to cross by raising our wagon boxes six or eight inches above the bolsters by means of blocks. We doubled teams and started into the river, which is here about three-quarters of a mile wide and from one to three and a half feet deep. I stripped off all but my shirt, tied a belt around me, and drove the leaders both times crossing. ["To plunge the wagons into the river was a strong act of faith as from its looks it might well be a hundred feet or any depth. But it had to be crossed and the mounted men scattered out on a wide front to feel the way and plunged in, the wagons in a long line following close. The bottom was sandy and shifting, making constant motion necessary to prevent settling down in it, besides the incessant attention to the teams, which, alarmed by the swirling current, rushing noise, unstable footing and deep holes, were with difficulty prevented from being swung around and forced downstream."]

We were all on the north bank by noon, where we halted. And then we commenced our journey across the bluffs to the North Fork. On approaching the highlands, our Directors wisely determined that we should camp on the bank of the South Fork till Monday morning [June 25]. A day of rest was needed, and we camped willingly.

Mr. Hutchinson and I had a fine spot of fun this afternoon in getting wood from an island in the river. We tried to ride double on the pony to the island, but in wading to it we came to an unexpected channel so deep that the horse swam; his hind parts sank, and I slipped off into the water, head and ears, but swam with one hand to a log we were approaching, having an ax in the other hand.

Later we took a bag and filled it with buffalo chips, which we find in great abundance all through the Platte country. The rest of the afternoon I spent in mending my vest.

June 24. Sabbath. Today the weather is warm and clear. After breakfast Mr. H. and I bathed and washed and spent the leisure time in mending our clothes. Today our camp appears more like Sabbath than any other Sunday before. All things are still, and the scenery around us partakes of the same stillness. It disposes me to think of home and the dear ones there; of what they are probably doing now, and of the appearance of things at their place of worship. It now being twelve o'clock, they are probably in the meeting house at Youngstown.

We have had two sermons today, which is the first time since leaving the Independence Landing. ["A fairly good pulpit was made by setting a mess chest on end, from which the dominie delivered his sermon. Looking upon the motley congregation, he saw gathered close about him a few cutting hair and performing the offices of barbers for each other, several doing their mending, others washing out a few shirts, and the cooks taking the opportunity to bake soda biscuit and boil beans. He saw that no disrespect was intended and that though they were not all in devotional attitudes, they were seldom inattentive and always joined lustily in the singing of the hymns."]

I have had a headache today. In the evening we all assembled and had an old fashioned sing, everyone singing the tunes he knew and all who could assisting him. We carried three parts to many tunes of my acquaintance, and I was highly pleased at the full, swelling tones of some of the voices of the Plymouth company. The effect of the singing as it sounded along through the stillness of the plains was electric on me, and I suppose on the wolves, for they set up a most horrid pow-wow on the plains beyond our camp.

June 25.   This morning I was awakened by the cry of "Breakfast!" from Dr. Wells, who had it ready and wanted someone to eat it. We answered the call by promptly seating ourselves around the table and doing duty.

We left camp early and ascended the bluffs, which rise gradually to a height of two hundred feet. The plain is rolling and gradually ascends as we advance towards the North Fork.

About four o'clock we arrived at the edge of the bluffs on the south side of the North Fork. . . . We commenced the descent by a series of gradually descending hills, hill after hill, till Ash Creek valley was but one more hill below us, down which we let our wagons by locking all four wheels. Then the sand bed of the creek was our road for three miles. The creek has small, scrubby ash and some red cedars. We found a fine spring of good water in this ravine, the only good spring on this route— for they are all bad, giving the traveler diarrhea.*

We encamped on the North Platte at the mouth of Ash Hollow, with good grass.

June 26.   We started early this morn and had a good day's work over sandy roads. I bathed in the North Platte at noon. Elk are along the road today. Graves are also frequent.

["During the forenoon the road passed through many steep ravines and sandy bottoms just under the line of the bluffs, which are high and rugged and are properly named Castle Bluffs for they appear like ruined castles. The road is almost all sand, the day hot, the mosquitoes abundant and unmerciful. The bones of buffalo as usual are bleaching on the plains. Records are made on them by travelers. . . . We have just recorded our arrival, all well at this spot."

["All the accessible faces of cliffs are marked with names, initials, and dates. . . . Nothing escapes that can be marked upon. . . . Even the slabs at the head of graves are all marked by this propensity for penciling by the way."]

---

* *Except for the one at Ash Hollow, Swain was not referring to springs as such but rather to seep wells dug near the trail by the emigrants. Most of the way up the Platte the trail ran some distance back from the river, and since water quickly filtered into holes dug two to four feet deep, the emigrants found this source preferable to packing water from the muddy river. However, the thousands of animals and men traveling and camping along the route contaminated this water source, with resulting sickness in almost every train. The Wolverine Rangers chose to avoid these holes and used only river water, which they knew to be safer.*

We encamped early on the river, having made seventeen miles and the hardest day's work we have yet done.

June 27.   Today our road is better, and we have a fine prairie to pass over, though somewhat sandy. The bluffs are as high as Ash Hollow. We made nineteen miles today.

At noon, when at halt, we discovered something in a lone tree growing at the river edge. When we started again, Mr. Hutchinson went to see what it was and on his return to the train he lent me the pony. I rode over and saw for the first time an Indian woman buried after their manner of burial, which is to place the dead body in a tree. This is done by making a staging upon the limbs of the tree and then placing on it the body, wrapped in blankets, skins and other articles of fine apparel, with the person's cup, ladle, etc. It was a revolting sight to me, but they [the Sioux] probably consider this method as sacred as we do that of burying in the consecrated grounds at home.

[An emigrant who visited a Sioux village on June 5 described them as "a proud, noble-looking race, of good proportions, tall, strong, athletic, and good horsemen. They dress with little clothing. . . . They wear a great many ornaments, the tusks of animals, pearls, and strings of beads. . . . One Indian prided himself in having about a dozen Pawnee scalps a-wearing over his shoulders. . . . Old and young, the Sioux stood outside their tents watching the long line of emigrant wagons that passed through their village. They evidently are much wonder-struck at the crowds going past. . . ."]

June 28.   Today our road is still some sandy, better than yesterday but wet from last night's rain. The grass along this plain and country is very good and fresh on account of the abundant rains of this season, which have been very heavy and frequent. Usually this region is dry, barren, and parched; but now it is moist, the brooks running, and the pasture green and good.

We made twenty miles and encamped opposite the noted Courthouse Rock, which Frémont speaks of.

We also have a view this evening of Chimney Rock. We have a fine camp ground near the river, and I have had a good swim this evening. Yesterday and today we have been badly troubled by mosquitoes and gnats, which poison us by biting and bloat us very badly as their bite swells, and many of us have our eyes and ears badly swollen.

["Mosquitoes can't be beat. Day and night they swarm around completely covering the animals. At night they are worse, and if you do not

Chimney Rock, with Courthouse Rock in the distance.

---

almost suffocate yourself with smoke inside the tent, they would eat you up. . . . There is not room on this river for another mosquito. And they bite, O Mercy!"]

Courthouse Rock stands six miles south of the road, and from here it looks like a large edifice with columns, roof and dome.

June 29.   This morn we have Courthouse Rock behind us, and on the left have many other curious-shaped mounds. But the object of attraction with all of us is the celebrated Chimney Rock, which we came opposite to when we encamped for noon halt. . . .

This column will not probably stand long, as it is badly scaled, cracked, and falling fast. Frémont makes it three hundred feet high. From a distance it appears like the high tower of a steam factory. I have put a specimen of the marl, limestone, and sandstone in my trunk, which I intend shall be a part of my cabinet if I ever arrive at my home again.

["There is but one point, the southeastern, where the emigrants can climb up the chimney, and every part of this singular structure has names upon it, at the base and even as high as thirty feet up the chimney. To accomplish this, men first cut places to put their feet, and then cut places to hold by, and each venturesome climber seems to wish to put his name above the last one. . . . One poor fellow fell and was killed."]

The deception in judging distances here is very remarkable; for instance, the bluffs or other objects at an apparent distance of, say, a mile, prove when tested by approaching to be three or four miles. We also experienced the same deception in judging the height of the bluffs.

Nineteen miles today.

June 29, 1849

Dear Sabrina,

Here I am by the side of the road, writing a word to you just to say that we are all well and that we are doing well, having good roads, weather, and fine times. We are on the North Fork of the Platte River approaching Scotts Bluff, one hundred miles from Fort Laramie. I send this by a trading wagon just passing by. I must send this now, or not at all.

William Swain

Looking east to Chimney Rock, Bruff drew this scene on July 6 when he was about two days behind the Rangers. Though he succeeded in depicting the vast distances of the North Platte Valley, he failed to show the scores of wagons traveling west in early July, across a plain littered with abandoned supplies and the remains of numerous campsites.
HENRY E. HUNTINGTON LIBRARY

[This trading wagon was "a government express on its way from Fort Laramie to the frontier. . . . They told us that the mass of emigrants was some 200 to 250 miles ahead of us. After examining our train they told us we would get through in good season. This encouraged some, who imagine a thousand difficulties ahead." "We frequently meet disheartened emigrants, even at this point, who say they have certainly found 'the Elephant' and are returning. But we have heard this so many times that we begin to discredit them entirely. Our course is still onward and upward, ever hoping that we may soon commence descending toward the golden valley."]

June 30. We left camp at six this morning. We filled our water barrel on leaving the river, as we would not touch it again in thirty miles.

Encamped near Scotts Bluff for noon halt. These bluffs run quite close to the river and force our road through a ravine in the bluffs.

Encamped this evening at a spring spoken by of Frémont. Twenty-one miles today.

July 1. Sabbath. This morn at sunrise we saw a grand spectacle on the bluffs, clouds resting on their tops in rolling masses, leaving a narrow line of bright sky, above which they lay in dark and massive lines of mist.

In camp today. I visited the bluffs in company with Dr. Wells and

John Root for the purpose of getting my first glimpse of the Black Hills [the Laramie Mountains, in southeastern Wyoming]. Here in this wilderness of plains, on the broken bluffs of the Platte, at an elevation of six or seven hundred feet, we stand and admire the beauty, the grandeur and the extent of the scene. . . . This sight calls up with a magic influence all the thoughts and interests connected with these objects heretofore known to us only by the page of the voyager. Our distance from home, our passage across the hills' rugged brows, our prospects beyond their line, all these thoughts pass quickly across the mind; and these passed over, the mind rests upon the time when "Homeward Bound" shall be our song.

[At the western end of the valley back of Scotts Bluff, the trail passed close by a trading post operated by Antoine Robidoux, a member of the famed frontier family. Of this trader and his post, one of the Rangers wrote: "A man has a blacksmith shop here and keeps certain supplies for the emigrants. He has an Indian wife and family and seems to live much at his ease, making money plentifully." Another Ranger added that the proprietor, "a Frenchman, shoes horses for $1 a shoe and sets the tires on a wagon for $8, all other work in proportion."

[He "lives in an Indian lodge and has erected a log shanty . . . in one end of which is the blacksmith's forge and in the other a grog shop and sort of grocery. The stock of this establishment consists principally of such articles as he had purchased from the emigrants at a great sacrifice and sells to others at as great a profit. Among other things . . . he had purchased an excellent double wagon for 75 cents. The blacksmith shop is an equally profitable concern. When the owner is indisposed to work himself, he rents the use of his shop and tools for the modest price of 75 cents an hour. . . . The forge is in constant use by the emigrants."]

July 2.   We started late this morn. Our road lay over gradually rising hills and vales for about six miles, after which we struck the river bottom, which was very wide.

We kept near the highlands where the road was very good and encamped near the Platte this evening with good grass. Mr. H. and I had a fine bath in the river. Made nineteen and three-quarter miles today.

July 3.   This morning we left camp early. Our road lay along the bottom which begins to be dry, sterile and sandy. The feed is bad and the road intolerably dusty, which flies like ashes covering ourselves, the teams, and the wagons with a coat of grayish dust.

We encamped this evening eight miles from Fort Laramie, opposite

Fort Bernard. ["It has been burnt and abandoned. It formerly consisted of eight small houses in a semi-circle."] Here we shall celebrate the birthday of our nation tomorrow. I bathed today. Made twenty miles.

[This evening, after forty-nine days on the trail, the Rangers experienced their first dissension. James Pratt, one of the directors, reported that "the Board decided we should stay over tomorrow to celebrate the Fourth of July. Many of the members were dissatisfied and met in a tumultuous meeting to overrule the decision. The turbulent spirits spouted and seemed about to succeed. I was cooking. Leaving my beans and applesauce on the fire, I explained the reasons that had induced the Directors to conclude to stop and succeeded in procuring a vote affirming our action."]

July 4.   ["At sunrise a salute of thirteen guns was fired."] We lay abed late this morn and after a late breakfast set about getting fuel for cooking our celebration dinner.

Our celebration of the day was very good, much better than I anticipated. We had previously invited Mr. Sexton of the Plymouth company [which had joined the Rangers on May 29] to deliver an address, and we had appointed Mr. Pratt to read the Declaration of Independence. We had one of the tents pitched at a short distance from the camp, in which was placed a table with seats for the officers of the day and the orators. The table was spread with a blanket.

At twelve o'clock we formed a procession and walked to the stand to the tune of "The Star Spangled Banner." The President of the day called the meeting to order. We listened to a prayer by Rev. Mr. Hobart, then remarks and the reading of the Declaration of Independence by Mr. Pratt, and then the address by Mr. Sexton. We then listened to "Hail Columbia." This celebration was very pleasing, especially the address, which was well delivered and good enough for any assembly at home.

We then marched to the "hall," which was formed by running the wagons in two rows close enough together for the wagon covers to reach from one to the other, thus forming a fine hall roofed by the covers and a comfortable place for the dinner table, which was set down the center.

Dinner consisted of ham, beans, boiled and baked, biscuits, john cake, apple pie, sweet cake, rice pudding, pickles, vinegar, pepper sauce and mustard, coffee, sugar, and milk. All enjoyed it well.

After dinner the toasting commenced. The boys had raked and scraped together all the brandy they could, and they toasted, hurrayed, and drank till reason was out and brandy was in. I stayed till the five regular toasts were drunk; and then, being disgusted with their conduct,

I went to our tent, took my pen, and occupied the remainder of the day in writing to my wife, in which I enjoyed myself better than those who were drinking, carousing, and hallooing all around the camp.

Many thoughts of home have crowded upon me today—the state of things there, and if they are as they usually are; what enjoyment George is in; how Mother is; my dear Sabrina, how she is enjoying herself; my little girl, how she looks, how much she can talk, how large she is; where they are; whether they send a thought or a wish after me; and what they think of my Fourth here in the land of the desert. I am afraid that they will be greatly concerned about me, as they will unquestionably hear that the cholera is on the route. But I hope this will not reach their ears and that their cup of enjoyment may be running over and that I may arrive safely at home again to enjoy their society.

At night the boys danced by moonlight on the grass or rather on the sand.

> July 4
> in camp for celebration,
> eight miles below Fort Laramie

Dear Sabrina,

I have just left the celebration dinner table, where the company are now drinking toasts to everything and everybody and cheering at no small rate. I enjoy myself better in conversing with you through the medium of the pen. It is now some time since I wrote home, or at least since I wrote at any length, having written to you a line [on June 29] by a returning emigrant whom I met on the road and had just time to say that we were all well. But there is no certainty in sending letters by such conveyance. You may or may not have received some of the many letters I have sent you by traders and others, on many of which I have paid a postage of 25 cents.

I last wrote to George from Fort Kearny [June 14], and I will give you a sketch of our journey from that point. . . . We shall pass Fort Laramie tomorrow, where I shall leave this to be taken to the States. It will probably be the last time I can write until I get to my journey's end, which may take till the middle of October.

We have had uncommon good health and luck on our route, not having had a case of sickness in the company for the last four weeks. Not a creature has died, not a wagon tire loosened, and no bad luck attended us. ["While many other companies have been entirely broken up with internal dissatisfaction, the loss of their cattle, the breaking of their wagons, and the loss of their provisions, ours has been steadily pursuing its way with the most eminent success. Our wagons and provisions are in excellent order and repair, our cattle daily improving, and in our company harmony prevails. . . . It is no uncommon thing to meet returning parties—it is almost a daily occurrence, even after they have accomplished more than a third of the whole journey."]

The country is becoming very hilly; the streams rapid, more clear, and assuming the character of mountain streams. The air is very dry and clear, and our path is lined with wild sage and artemisia.

We had a fine celebration today, with an address by Mr. Sexton, which was very good; an excellent dinner, good enough for any hotel; and the boys drank toasts and cheered till they are now going in all sorts around the camp.

I often think of home and all the dear objects of affection there: of George; of dear Mother, who was sick; and of yourself and poor little Sister. If it were consistent, I should long for the time to come when I shall turn my footsteps homeward, but such thoughts will not answer now, for I have a long journey yet to complete and then the object of the journey to accomplish.

I am hearty and well, far more so than when I left home. That failing of short breath which troubled me at home has entirely left me. I am also more fleshy. Notwithstanding these facts, I would advise no man to come this way to California.

Give my love to George and Mother and tell them that I am well and enjoy myself. Kiss my little girl for me, and when I get home I will kiss you all.

> Your affectionate husband until death,
> William Swain

*July 5.** We started late this morning and in eight miles we forded the Laramie River and came to Fort Laramie. ["The site of the fort is quite picturesque, the Black Hills being in the near background and Laramie Peak looming up grandly back of these."]

Stopped to noon without grass for the cattle, as the feed was parched by a long drought and eaten up by the numerous trains in advance of us. Fort Laramie [on the north bank of the Laramie River near its junction with the North Platte] was built by the American Fur Company and purchased by our government about two weeks ago for a military post. U.S. troops are in occupation of the fort and encamped in tents around it. The American Fur Company is camped at the mouth of the Laramie River.

[As at Fort Kearny, "this is a great resting place for emigrants. Most of them by this time have seen enough of the elephant to know what they really want and what they can dispense with. . . . A great many parties are abandoning their wagons at this point and take to mule packing, on account of rumors of no grass and bad rocky roads. . . ." "Every mode of conveyance ever invented is put into use here—men on foot with their packs on their backs, two-wheeled carts, etc." "You see piles of bacon and hard bread thrown by the side of the road; wagons are left here and many burned . . . trunks, clothes, boots and shoes, lead by the hundred, spades, picks, and all other fixings for a California trip. . . ." "Rifles are thrown by the dozen into the river and worthless white beans almost cover the ground and old stoves almost without number are thrown away." The emigrants "must either lighten up or lay their bones upon the plains."]

I tried to buy a horse at the fort, but the prices asked were so extravagant—ranging from $100 to $200—that I gave up the idea. I purchased a buffalo skin for my bed for $3 and left a long letter, well

---

* *The morning after the Fourth probably found many celebrants feeling much like one who awoke amid the wilds of the Black Hills and scrawled in his diary: "Arose with a bursting headache. O! for a glass of soda water. Remained in camp."*

filled, at the office of the fort for Sabrina. It is discouraging to think that it will not reach her until September. ["Bushels of letters are daily being sent back to the States through the agency of an individual at the fort, at a charge of 25 cents each."]

We left the fort about two o'clock and took the road over the hills and between the North Platte and the Laramie River. We were soon gradually rising over the hills. The soil is sandy and poor, and what little grass has grown this spring is dried up and turning brown.

We stopped to camp in a ravine, where we found a little grass but no water. Sixteen miles today.

Back Home

> "O! William, if I can once hear that you are at your journey's end and well and doing well, then I can rest contentedly and begin to hear about your coming home."

Youngstown, Sunday: June 24, 1849

Dear William,

I have seated myself by the stand in my bedroom to write a line to my absent but much loved husband. It is now twelve o'clock, all is still around me except for the stomping feet and prattling noise of our dear little daughter, who is trotting around and now and then comes to chat a bit with her Ma. Mother is in her rocking chair reading the Bible. George is upstairs on the bed, unwell with the headache. . . . Father's folks are not any of them well. The weather has been very warm for a few days back and most of the people are complaining more or less. As to myself, I am very unwell, scarcely able to sit here and write, and for that reason you must excuse me if I do not write but a few lines to you this time. My head reels so I cannot collect my thoughts enough to write anything that will pay you the trouble to try to read it. I hope my being unwell will not give you any uneasiness, for I think when the weather becomes cooler I shall feel better.

Eliza is better and grows like a weed. She is rather troublesome nights yet and needs a great deal of care and attention both day and night, more than I feel able to do many times.

I have not been to church today, not being able to go to [choir] practice. . . . Mother has just been out in the garden and brought in a handful of strawberries, and Sis is running after her crying for them. She is now sitting on the floor eating them. They are not sweet yet, but taste very well.

For two mornings back I have gone out before breakfast and weeded out your mammoth Alpines. However, I do not do much at weeding, and the reason why is because it makes my back sore. I exercise in the open air as much as I conveniently can, but not as much as I would like to on account of caring for Sis. It is too much of a task to put upon Mother to take care of her. . . . So you see I am very much confined in the house on her account. But I do not murmur nor complain at this, for withal she is a source of comfort to me, and I hope she will be more so as she grows older. On her birthday [June 1], I rode out with her; we had one of father's horses and our buggy, and brother Ozro to drive. She enjoyed it very much, as she always does a ride. We did not give her a whipping, but I think we should if we had your letter in time.

We received your letter of the 24th of May on June 13th, and my dear if I was ever glad to hear from anyone in my life, it was then. I hope we shall hear often from you on the plains. I need not tell you to write as soon as you get to your journey's end, for I am sure you will realize our anxiety to hear from you. . . .

I can assure you I was glad to hear that no bad accident had befallen you and that you were getting along as fast as could be expected. We have abundant reason to be thankful to the Source from which all blessings flow.

My dear, I must leave this to finish in the morning. Sis is crying and I must take her.

It is now Monday morning, and I have again attempted to finish this scrawl. I had a very bad night, being this morning anything but a fit subject to write. I was up with Sis till twelve and sick the rest of the night myself.

O! William, I wish I could see you this morning. I dreamed about you last night with my eyes wide open, which I often do, and sometimes with them shut. However, I cannot derive pleasure from my dreams, for you will not have anything to say to me.

We received your letter of the 29th of May on June 22nd. I was somewhat surprised at your slow progress, but was glad to hear of good health and good luck. May God grant that it might be so until your journey is through.

The next morning [Tuesday]

After getting your letters, I took them and went down to see Mrs. Bailey, and I read some parts of them to her. She said Mr. Bailey had mentioned some sickness amongst them, but from what she said, I took it to be nothing serious. I hope you will not keep anything back, let it be ever so bad. Nothing could make me feel worse than I do now. I am all the time framing up something that will befall you. I do not place that confidence in God that I ought to; still, I feel that His arm is able to protect you in your absence. But the loss of your society is great, and the longer you are gone the less reconciled I feel. My dear, I feel sometimes as though I should sink under it. I am confident that it wears on me. You know, William, that I am of a very nervous temperament and for that reason I cannot get along with it as well as I could were I not.

I assure you of one thing, and that is, if God spares you to get home again, I shall hang on to you as long as there is any of you left. However, my dear, I never have been sorry that I acted the part I did in letting you go, but I think I should act otherwise were it to be done again. This may, as I hope and trust, be a good lesson for us both. It may learn us to be contented with what we have and to enjoy ourselves better when together. I, however, have one thing to comfort me, that we always did live agreeably when together, and often does my mind revert to the times and places that we have been and enjoyed ourselves together. Yet with all this, we cannot realize our attachments and fondness for one another until we are deprived of the society of those fond ones.

It is with reluctance, and yet with pleasure, that I attempt to address you. With reluctance because I feel as though there was a great chance of your never getting my letters, and again it is with pleasure, for me to write to one I love and adore, and at the same time assuring myself that I am doing my duty. O! William, if I can once hear that you are at your journey's end and well and doing well, then I can rest contentedly and begin to hear about your coming home. But it is a long time before I can hear that.

You are very kind in wanting me to take my comfort this summer, but I cannot in your absence. . . .

Mother's health is better than it has been since last Fall, which George will tell you at length. She and George are very kind to me and Sis, for which I have a great reason to be thankful. Had I not kind friends I do not know how I could live.

Father's folks do all they can to make things pleasant for me. Ozro comes down every little while with a horse, takes our buggy, and we take a ride. . . .

Mrs. Bailey and child are well; we see them often. We have not had cholera any nearer than Lockport, and only one case there. I do not give myself uneasiness about it. I only think of it on your part. As for myself I think nothing about it.

It is getting time for the mail, and I must say adieu.

From your affectionate wife,
Sabrina Swain

CHAPTER V

Black Hills and Sweetwater

"Any man who makes a trip by land to
California deserves to find a fortune."

West of Fort Laramie the scenery changed abruptly. From the broad plain of the North Platte the trail climbed onto the steep ridges of the Black Hills, so named because of the growth of juniper and pine, a dark contrast to the bleached plains to the east. The river narrowed and swirled through canyons, the once far-distant horizon disappeared behind surrounding hills. To the south snow-capped Laramie Peak stood as an outpost of the mountain ranges farther west.

In this rough hill country the trail forked about twenty-one miles west of the fort. The hill road traced its way through the Black Hills several miles distant from the North Platte while the river road (followed by the Wolverine Rangers) held to its name only to the extent that it was often in sight of the river's canyons and gorges and twice passed along its banks. But there were numerous tributaries flowing from the higher hills to the Platte, and the emigrants crossed these streams, finding an abundance of fresh water and often good grass. They were headed for the northerly bend of the North Platte, where they would have to ferry the turbulent stream and finally leave it after so many weeks.

Beyond the Platte they would follow and depend on several other rivers, first the Sweetwater, then west of the Continental Divide the Bear River, and finally, most important of all, the Humboldt. But for now, through present-day Wyoming, the North Platte and the Sweetwater assured the thousands of men and their teams fresh water, grass and a generally benevolent environment for their advance.

In the Black Hills trail life changed dramatically. Suddenly, inexplicably, cholera disappeared. Probably the higher altitude, the fact that the

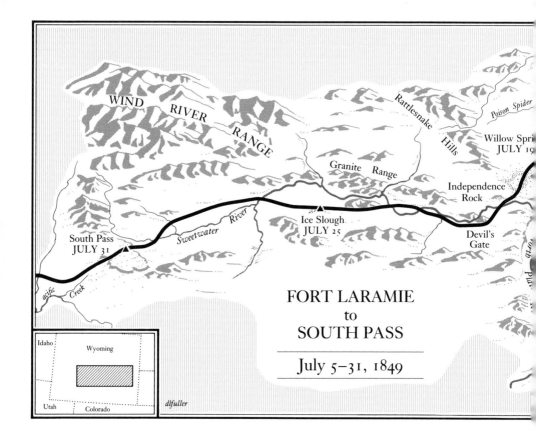

WIND RIVER RANGE

Rattlesnake

Poison Spider

Willow Spri
JULY 19

Granite Range

Independence
Rock

Hills

Sweetwater River

Ice Slough
JULY 25

Devil's
Gate

South Pass
JULY 31

acific Creek

FORT LARAMIE
to
SOUTH PASS

July 5–31, 1849

Idaho

Wyoming

Utah   Colorado

dlfuller

emigration was less congested and the availability of fresh water combined to eliminate the circumstances that had spread the disease. This
part of the journey was marked as well by the absence of Indians. Most
goldseekers had not seen any of their presumed enemies east of Fort
Laramie; now to the west they assumed that danger had passed—and
they grew casual, even confident of their living arrangements in the once
feared wilderness.

Other changes marked trail life west of Fort Laramie. While traveling
through the broad valley of the Platte the emigrants had relied upon
buffalo chips for fuel. In the Black Hills, where chips were scarce, they
found enough scrub timber to suffice. Farther west, all the way to the
Sierra Nevada, they would depend on sage and greasewood for their
campfires. Abandoned wagons provided another source of fuel. "The
number of vehicles that share this fate would be impossible to calculate.
Thousands of fine trunks, boxes and barrels are also burnt for cooking
purposes. Property that cost $100 in the States is none too much to make
one comfortable fire in an evening."

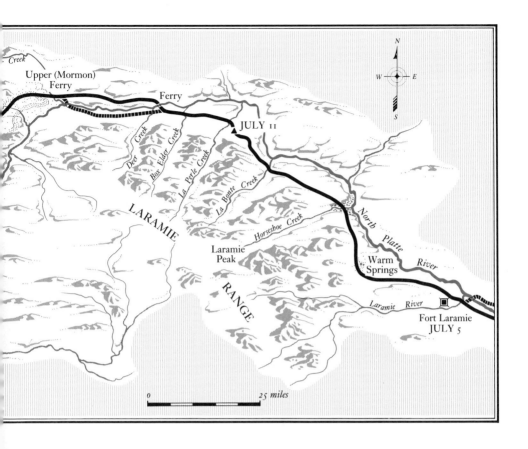

Anticipating the more than one hundred miles of rugged Black Hills country, most companies had lightened their wagon loads at Fort Laramie. But as the miles seemed longer and the rocks bruised and cut their animals' hooves, company property—a gold-washing machine, a bundle of shovels—had to be left by the trail with other gear that had once seemed so important. While parting with jointly owned property might be distressing to ambitions born back home and sustained so many miles (one company finally abandoned in the Black Hills an entire sawmill they had planned to operate in California), even more anguishing for the individual emigrant was the process of deciding what personal possessions to give up at the third or fourth wagon-lightening.

The Wolverine Rangers managed to pull their full loads until July 16 near the ferry crossing of the North Platte. On that day for the first time they sorted through company and personal property to select what could best be left behind. Passing each day what hundreds of companies had long since discarded, Swain and the other diarists and letter writers among the Rangers might well have expressed some anxiety about the pace of their advance. Instead they seemed to enjoy their trail life more than ever.

They were too far west to expect to meet many more backtrackers, but other means of sending mail became unexpectedly available. On the Sweetwater west of the Black Hills "a Yankee turned his wagon around . . . and a large placard announced the pleasing fact that it was an express to carry letters back to the States. . . . The price for transmission of each letter was 50 cents, and the Yankee must have realized a large fortune in a few weeks."

The great opportunity for money-making on the overland trail was found at the crossing of the North Platte River (in the area of present-day Casper, Wyoming). Far too deep to allow the wagons to be forded, the river could be crossed only by ferrying—rolling the wagons onto some sort of raft and floating them across to the north bank.

Fortunately the Mormons in 1847 had pioneered ferrying wagons across the North Platte. Each summer thereafter they operated their ferryboat as a business, charging Oregon settlers and then in 1849 the Californians $3 per wagon and 50 cents per man. As one goldseeker enviously noted: "The Mormons . . . have as good a gold mine here as any in California."

They would have made far more if they could have accommodated the demand for ferriage. The emigrant companies arrived in such numbers as to overwhelm their single ferryboat. The lead companies reached the ferry on June 3; by the 6th sixty wagons were waiting to cross, by the 10th the number was 175, and by the 14th the jam at the Mormon Ferry was so great that companies were camped for twenty miles along the river, all the way to Deer Creek. Impatient at the delay of two or three days, a few companies determined to ferry themselves across the 200 yards of cold, swift-flowing water. Some cut down cottonwood trees to make rafts, others removed the wheels from their wagon beds, caulked the cracks and floated them across, using ropes to hold their swaying crafts upright and keep them from being swept downstream.

Seeing their success, other companies quickly set about building rafts. By late June there were ferrying operations all along the North Platte from Deer Creek up to the Mormon Ferry. Several of these improvised ferries were run as a business by companies that stopped for a few days, even a week or more, to make money, charging $3 to $5 per wagon. Many companies that built their own rude ferryboats sold them to the next company for $25 to $30.

The animals were all driven into the river "to ferry themselves." But often they refused to swim across and turned back or downstream. Teamsters dove into the icy water to direct them. In the watery melee of wagons and rafts, yelling teamsters and frightened, thrashing oxen, mules and horses, men drowned each day—at one crossing a total of twenty-eight drownings was reported. What a sad irony on a trip through the Great American Desert.

When the Rangers reached the Deer Creek crossing on July 12, Swain mentioned "innumerable camps," which suggests that the struggle to get across continued even at that late date. Anticipating a delay in getting their wagons ferried, Captain Potts decided to use the time to the advantage of the oxen. Swain and twenty-five other Rangers were ordered to drive the teams up Deer Creek to find grass and pasture them while the men cut hay for the barren miles beyond the river. Thus Swain did not see the ferrying drama. When he and the others reached the riverbank with the oxen on the 14th, they found the last wagon about to be landed on the far shore. They drove the oxen into the water, herded them across without loss and rolled on, having passed one of the most dangerous places on the trail with only a casual comment by Swain.

Beyond the crossings of the North Platte the country changed—more barren, the hills blue-gray, a few dwarf cedars but mostly sagebrush in a desertlike region pocked with poisonous pools of alkaline water. Oxen (less often mules and horses) that drank from these tempting springs quickly collapsed, soon to putrefy and add to the stench from older carcasses. The sight of these fallen teams must have given the Rangers a renewed sense of their dependence on the lumbering, docile animals. But some companies failed to care for their teams, driving them too hard, pushing ahead when a day's rest would have been wise and kind, failing to guard them from poison water.

Swain and others may have shared the emotions felt by the owners of teams seen lying along the trail—anger at the loss and consequent inconvenience, fear that the remaining teams might not survive, sadness for animals they had lived and walked with for so many weeks, so many hundreds of miles.

Like most diarists, Swain did not mention how he felt about his oxen or those fallen along the way. There seems to have been an almost universal insensitivity to the suffering of the animals pulling wagons till day's end and then foraging in sage and greasewood that had been chewed and trampled for weeks. Carcasses by the trail, others bloating around the dark pools were noted and sometimes counted; several diarists recorded day after day their count of dead oxen and mules. But rarely did they express concern for the torment of their nonhuman partners.

One man who did think about the importance and welfare of his teams reflected his empathy in a judgmental statement on the character of most overland teamsters. "There are but few who know the worth of their oxen. I am confident that if a team of cattle is treated with humanity, they will travel across the continent at the rate of 400 miles per month. But the inhuman treatment by drivers is enough to destroy a number of teams. Men are in ox driving like they are in everything else, some not fit to carry a whip within a mile of a team. Driving is reducing to system, and he that drives to let others know he is driving will soon have no team to drive. The fact is, every attention to your cattle is actually necessary to take you through this trip. Oxen are the central object on this route, and you belong to them instead of them to you."

After crossing fifty miles of alkaline desert west of the North Platte, the trail led the grumbling, weary goldseekers to the Sweetwater River, named years earlier by fur trappers who welcomed its water after the poisons nearby. Through this open valley gradually rising to South Pass in the Rocky Mountains, the entire emigration moved west on a single trail. For the first time since leaving the Missouri River, every company traveled the same route; there was no other.

On the banks of the Sweetwater they once again found dramatic evidence of their country's long history of reaching ever westward—Independence Rock. Probably the best-known landmark on the entire California Trail, this massive rock on the north bank of the river was supposed to have been named by a party of American fur trappers who camped by it on July 4, 1829. It was described by most early explorers and travelers (and by every gold-rush diarist), and Frémont wrote of the rock in 1842: "Everywhere within six or eight feet of the ground where the surface is sufficiently smooth and in some places sixty or eighty feet above, the Rock is inscribed with the names of travelers. Many a name famous in the history of this country and some well known to science are to be found mixed among those of fur traders, travelers for pleasure and curiosity and missionaries among the savages."

By the end of July 1849, the dark sides of the rock carried the names, slogans, graffiti of thousands of passing goldseekers. Not only scrawled along the base where by July there was hardly room to squeeze in even a short name, but on top as well, the names were daubed in tar or carved with knives—among them William Swain and Michael Hutchinson and, presumably, the names of other Rangers. Winters' snow and summers' sun have worn and faded away most of those marks so pridefully placed on that historic monument by men who felt a part of history that summer of 1849.

Among the names on that great rock were those of mountain men who had trapped beaver along the Sweetwater in earlier years. Some of their clan still lived in that valley and farther west. Occasionally gold rush companies met those trappers and talked with them, men who had lived a way of life about to be ended by the influx of emigrants, the 1849 crowd being the vanguard of tens of thousands to follow each year thereafter.

After visiting the camps of these survivors of another era, goldseekers often revealed in their diaries and letters a sense of envy, a realization that their city lives had put constraints on them which they had not thought about before. "The trappers say there is more real pleasure in one year in the mountains than a whole life time in a dense, settled country. There are no political pursuits to tire and weary, and last but not least no law or lawyers to pettifog among them or mar their peace and sow discord among them. Their duties are confined to the horse and gun, and when they become tired of one place, they remove to another, their squaws performing all the labor." Another young diarist hurrying to California wrote in his diary: "Their mode of getting through life is, I think, rather captivating. . . . They seem not to have a care and are free from the petty annoyances and scandal of civilization. Money is no object, nothing to sell and nothing to buy with it. Game of all sorts in abundance. . . . They all have their wives and some not satisfied with one, have two. They purchase them from their fathers, a young squaw being valued as a good horse."

At the west end of the Sweetwater Valley the trail climbed onto a broad plateau, undramatic in appearance, yet powerful in its geographic and symbolic importance. In the midst of those barren hills, the goldseekers' wagons would roll through South Pass, the halfway point on their great trek and the first place where they could drink from a stream whose waters flowed west toward the Pacific.

July 6, 1849. [In camp eight miles west of Fort Laramie.] We left camp at seven. Drove slowly over the gradually but highly rolling hills, which present a desolate appearance. The prickly pear is in great abundance but very small, and the china aster lines our road both yesterday and today. The weather is very hot and sultry in the daytime, especially when we are in the hollows of the hills; but on the hilltops a breeze generally cools the air. The nights are generally chilly.

About eleven o'clock we entered a deep ravine or bed of a creek and in a few hundred yards came to the Warm Springs [about thirteen miles northwest of Fort Laramie]. They are the largest springs I ever saw, boiling up just at the lower edge of a ledge of limestone rock and clear as crystal. They form a large pool which runs off in a small creek where we watered the oxen. A cool draft out of my hand from this fountain was most delightful. I have selected a few specimens of fine pebbles from the springs, which I intend to take home if possible.

Today we passed the place where the Platte cuts through the Black Hills. We followed a ravine to its source, ascended a very steep hill, and stopped to halt for noon about one o'clock where we had no water and only a little poor, dried grass. While here a smart shower of rain began to fall, which laid the dust and cooled the air. If showers will only precede us on the way to South Pass, they will insure the success of our journey. . . .

The features of the country are entirely changed. East of Fort Laramie the bare prairie, naked and level, was the feature, but here it is that of a broken, rocky, mountainous country. The broken ledges of bare rock and sparse, scrubby pine rising hill upon hill is the ever-changing scene that meets the eye.

Our road has been strewn with articles left by the emigrants to lighten their loads.

Our camp [in the hills beyond Bitter Cottonwood Creek, some twenty-four miles west of Fort Laramie] is very healthy, and we enjoy ourselves finely.

July 7. This morn we left camp early, our cattle having had good grass but no water. The face of the country is more level than yesterday, with the strata of rocks less bare and a little more pine on the surface of the hills. The Platte is here a mountain stream, quite clear, often cutting through deep rock.

I am quite unwell today. Had no sleep yesterday or last night, having been on guard last night. There is something pleasing and exhilarating in viewing the starry heavens when on guard alone by myself. These "eyes of heaven" are the friends of my childhood, the lights that glowed on me when at the door of my home and on which my relatives probably frequently gaze from the same sacred spot. They speak to me of family and of home, when none but God knows of my thoughts. In the darkness of the night watch I can roam in imagination the haunts of home and see the dear loved ones there, sleeping and resting sweetly through the peaceful hours of the night without thought of keeping guard over their home.

[This day the Rangers advanced to Horseshoe Creek about forty-four miles northwest of Fort Laramie, forded the stream, and camped on the banks of the North Platte in a meadow praised for its beauty by many who passed this way.]

July 8.   Sabbath. This morn we are in camp for Sabbath. My duty is that of herdsman, and I have spent the early morn on the flats near the foot of the bluffs a mile from camp, watching the cattle. I watched the rising sun with much interest as it gilded the tops of the rugged peaks, while we in the vale were still in the twilight. The rising smoke and the stir and bustle of our camp on the edge of the little plain, the rushing of the Platte in its rapid course, the sunlight gilding the hilltops, and an occasional quack from wild geese along the river are the objects of interest this morning. After sunrise the cattle lay down to rest, and I sat down to take my ease and soon fell asleep. When I awoke, the sun was midway in the heavens. I scrambled up and got what breakfast I could, for the mess had had breakfast long since.

Later I went to the river, which here cuts a long canyon through the red sandstone standing five hundred feet perpendicular from both shores. . . .

News of short feed along the trail ahead induced our captain to search for a good spot of grass at which to cut hay to take with us. So we all went down the Platte two miles from camp, where fine redtop and wild wheat were growing in great abundance. Here we spent the rest of the day in making hay.

At sunset I visited the Platte just below and found the finest spring I have found on the route. It ran from its source to the river up a stream four feet wide and two feet deep, clear and pure. Tracks of wild geese, antelope, and elk lined its edge.

I returned to camp at dusk well tired and ready to do duty in good style at the table.

July 9.   This morn we started early. Our road is good and soon led across the flat where Frémont in 1842 fed his mules on cottonwood. The stumps and trunks of the trees are still lying in sad confusion.

We soon passed a flat of good grass, and then, leaving the Platte, commenced our way across the hills.

The appearance of the soil, vegetation, and road changed with our ascent. The soil, sandy and gravelly, was dried to powder and the vegetation crisped. Nothing but the bloodless wild sage showed its head, and the road was macadamized with sharp gravel which wore the cattle's feet badly.

Breaking Mules. Nº 2

The mule understands breaking better than being broke.

["In some trains animals had to be left, being too lame to proceed, while in others rough boots were made and fastened over the foot . . . to keep the dirt and sand from the foot which was smeared with tar and greese." These boots, or moccasins as they were often called, were cut from buffalo skins or from the hides of dead oxen found along the way. In some cases leather pieces were nailed to the hoofs, and another remedy was to apply "boiled tar and resin, hot as possible, to the tender feet. This fills up the cracks and forms a coating over the hoofs, protecting them from the sand, which grinds like emery."

[At least one mule company shod their animals while passing through the Black Hills: "As with few exceptions none of our mules were ever shod before, and as not one of us had ever shod a mule, our process of shoeing would probably astonish a blacksmith as much as it does the mules. It is counted cowardly to throw the animal, and the favorite method is to lash him up, head, body, and legs, alongside a wagon. The tools are a drawing knife, with a sharp Bowie for the finer touches; a hatchet, and an axehead for clinching."]

We halted on a barren hill to noon, at the foot of which the cattle got some water and some little picking. Our road through the afternoon was a succession of ups and downs. At dark we reached La Bonte Creek, where we encamped without feed for the teams.

July 10. This morn at three o'clock we started the teams up La Bonte Creek in search of grass. After driving the herd until sunrise, we found tolerable good grass on which we let them feast till ten o'clock, when we started back for camp. Arrived there by noon and soon began the afternoon tramp. . . .

We made a long afternoon's drive and encamped by the roadside late in the evening where we found a small, dry stream but in which some springs welled out. Our cattle have very poor feed tonight and are out on the plains with guards set around them.

July 11. This morn we left camp in good order. Traveled two hours, when we came to [La Prele Creek] and camped for the day, having to drive the teams down the stream five miles to feed. I bathed in the stream. We then unloaded the wagons and I spent the day in mending the wagon box and cover and reloading the wagon. Had supper early. The cattle being brought in, all hands yoked, hitched on, and prepared for a night drive.

We left camp at seven o'clock and made our way along in fine, comfortable style till nightfall, which set in cloudy, with no moon. The road was fifty percent better than for the last three days, but it required all the attention of the men to keep on it as it was still hilly, frequently crossing deep ravines and creeks and turning short knolls through the first half of the night. At noon of night we stopped and had a lunar dinner, for the moon rose at twelve o'clock. Our road the rest of the night was on an inclined plane, sandy to the depth of three or four inches, through which the wagons rolled without the least noise at a good rate. The teams caught the spirit of the night and almost ran during the whole drive. [During the night the Rangers traveled about fourteen miles, crossing Fourche Bois Creek.]

We reached the valley of the Platte by daybreak Thursday morning [July 12] and mighty glad were we to once again behold the good stream which had so long furnished us good roads and fine grass, and so many times quenched our thirst with its healthy waters.

July 12. Our road for the last ten hours has been sandy and dusty, or rather chalky, for the dust is white and soft and rises in the air in thick clouds, thick enough to make breathing difficult. We traveled along the valley of the Platte till eight o'clock [A.M.], when we came to innumerable camps on a stream now almost dry, which we crossed and turned down its left bank one and a half miles till we came to the banks of the Platte. We are at the Lower Ferry, at the mouth of Deer Creek, where we intend to cross the Platte. We formed a corral, pitched tents, cooked and ate breakfast and turned the teams loose to eat what best they could from a sod a hundred times grazed already.

We found feed all used up, and in the afternoon twenty-six others and I were detailed to drive the teams up Deer Creek to pasture and to cut hay enough to load two wagons, which was to be taken along to feed on the road in case we found no grass on the way to the Sweetwater River. The rest of the company were to ferry the wagons across the Platte on a craft of eight canoes fastened together by poles and pegs. The river is some twenty rods wide and runs very fast, which makes difficult ferrying.

We left camp with the cattle at three o'clock and drove till dusk, when we got above where the emigrants had pastured and found grass good for both cutting and grazing. We took a cold supper, as it was too late to allow the cook to get supper. After making a large fire, we all wrapped in our blankets and lay down around it to rest. Wrapped in my buffalo robe, I slept warm and soundly.

July 13.   We rose early and prepared to commence haying. Some of the boys found a deer in a thicket near the camp and shot it; and Lieutenant Cannon, while looking for a place to hay, shot a large antelope, so that we had fat living today. Our cooks made us a good breakfast and then all hands commenced haying and worked till noon, when we began laboring at another kind of business—destroying a fine venison stew, which was delightful employment.

We had the two wagons loaded with hay by four o'clock and they started back to the river. Our cattle were losing nothing by resting and being in good feed; the train would hardly be ferried across the Platte today; and aside from these considerations, we all wanted a hunt in this land of game. So we concluded to keep the cattle here till morning and have our fun. We took the horses and hied away to the bluffs and shot two buffalo, cutting the choicest pieces of the carcasses and packing them home on the horses while we walked by their sides. We arrived at our camp at ten o'clock, after picking our way in the dark for three hours over hilltops and through deep ravines. We ate supper with good appetites such as hunters frequently know, and soon, wrapped in our blankets and buffalo robes, laid ourselves down by the fire to sleep.

We had intended to start with the cattle at three o'clock [A.M.] for the

Using this ferry boat, Bruff's company crossed the North Platte at Deer Creek on July 20. The Rangers used a similar emigrant-built ferry when they crossed on July 14.
HENRY E. HUNTINGTON LIBRARY

---

ferry, but we were so fagged out that the first guard on calling the second gave him the watch and lay down and instantly fell asleep. His successor put the watch in his pocket, asked where the cattle were, rolled over, and grunted. That was the last noise our band made till the sun was up, shining clear and bright the next morning. There we slept in this wilderness, amid the howl of the wolves, without a guard.

July 14.   I awoke and on looking at the bright daylight I sprang to my feet and spoke to Lieutenant Cannon, who jumped up and called the boys. We were soon driving the cattle to the river. We found our train just crossing the last wagon, so we swam the herd across the river and at twelve o'clock rolled away from the ferry.

[For miles along the wooded shore of the North Platte, "a general crossing was going on with canoes, wagon beds, and rafts for a distance of twenty-five miles or more up the river as far as the Upper [Mormon] Ferry, probably farther."

[At these makeshift ferries "men are daily drowned. . . . If one of these frail boats oversets, all on board are lost. Not one in a thousand can save his life by swimming, no matter how expert a swimmer. The water is cold, being formed from the melting snows, and the current rolls, boils, and rushes along with a tremendous velocity." One company lost "six men . . . drowned by the upsetting of a raft. . . ." In addition to ferrying accidents, many companies were troubled by their animals "swimming about in the river, refusing to cross and constantly turning back."]

The road from the ferry leads directly over the bluffs, which are very high, steep, and sandy; these are the heaviest roads we have passed on the route. The sand is dry and mixed with the dung of numerous trains which have preceded us. In this dust the wheels and the cattle sink three or four inches, and clouds of it rise till the air is thick. In breathing, the breath seems impregnated with the powdered excrement of the cattle.

We traveled five miles and found some small grass on a flat of the river, where we camped.

July 15.   Sunday. Necessity compelled us to move in search of grass. Our road lay along the valley of the Platte and is still sandy and dusty beyond endurance. The men and beasts are choked and covered with it.

Near night we rose a very high knoll, and finding no grass, we traveled on in the sand until dark, when our cattle began to sink with the fatigue of the day. Our captain had gone ahead in search of a camping ground and had advanced too far for us to drive up to where he was. At eight o'clock we stopped. Leaving the wagons in a line in the road, we turned the teams loose on the sand to rest. We took a cold bite, pitched the tents, and laid down to rest.

July 16.   This morn we hitched up and started off for a feeding place. Crossed a high, sandy bluff and at ten o'clock camped to feed the teams.

Spent the day in lightening our loads, throwing away the articles in the company property that could best be dispensed with and such personal baggage as we had been allowed to carry.

July 17.   Today we traveled along the river. At ten o'clock we arrived at the Upper [Mormon] Ferry where the road leaves the Platte, heading for the bluffs and the Sweetwater River.

["Some thirty or forty Mormons are camped here, having come from Salt Lake . . . to make money by ferrying, blacksmithing, and selling various articles necessary to emigrants, and well has their time been put in. They have realized $3,500 from the ferry, $1,500 from the blacksmith shop, and I don't know how much from sales of sundries. But judging by the price of whiskey, sugar, etc., it must have been profitable also. Whiskey was 50 cents per pint and a great demand for it. . . ."]

We passed over the bluffs, and our road, having been heavy and sandy, became hard and gravelly. We passed many saline lakes which were dry, their beds covered with alkali. Those with water are dangerous for the teams, as they often die from the effects of drinking it. ["This water seems to affect an ox much more seriously than a man or horse. . . . It seems to eat the lining of their stomachs. They lie down and soon commence bleeding at the nose, in which state there is no hope for them."]

The grass of this region is also unhealthy for cattle. ["Mules instinctively or with better judgment reject either grass or water which is bad."]

We encamped at the Mineral Springs spoken of by the Mormons, about fourteen miles from the Platte. Here we found fine grass and turned the cattle out to luxuriate.

[The *Latter-day Saints' Emigrants' Guide*, published in 1848, described this spring as a "mineral spring and lake. Considered poisonous. No bad taste to the water, unless the cattle trample in it. In that case it becomes black and is doubtless poisonous. No timber near."]

July 18.   This morn we started late and soon found our cattle sick from the effects of drinking from the saline springs. We doctored them by giving them large pieces of fat pork and had the good luck not to lose any of them. [The poisoned oxen "were immediately unyoked and chained to the wagon wheels. We then tied pieces of fat bacon to the ends of sticks or whipstocks and shoved it down the throats of the suffering creatures. It formed a sort of soap in their stomachs which neutralized the effect of the alkali."]

We traveled late and encamped in a driving storm of wind, which took up the sand and gravel and carried it along like shot. [In these storms "it is impossible to look up for a moment, as the eyes become immediately filled with sand, so that the teamsters are obliged to fasten their handkerchiefs over their faces to enable them to see where they are going. . . . The wind, in addition to its furious violence, is so very hot and dry as to render respiration . . . quite difficult. The throat and fauces become dry, and lips clammy and parched, and the eyes much inflamed from the drifting dust."]

We almost made our supper from sand tonight, as the wind had spiced our victuals.

July 19. This morn we rolled out early. Traveled three miles to Willow Springs, where we breakfasted and fed the cattle.

[Willow Springs, twenty-seven miles from the Mormon Ferry, "is an Eden spot in a desert. . . ." "There are several springs and some considerable pasturage. . . . More wreckage here: a sheet-iron stove, sidesaddle, wagon tires, bolts, wheels, burnt wagons, a jack screw, boots, shoes, etc. . . . Playing cards are often seen about camps and along the roadside."]

At ten o'clock we rolled on [beyond Willow Springs the road ascended a high hill "from the summit of which is a grand prospect of the surrounding country, and hence it is named Prospect Hill. . . . Westward lies the valley of the Sweetwater River, bounded by the pale blue jagged line of the Rattlesnake Mountains. . . . On the left is the serpentine, silver line of the Platte River and rising beyond in dark and bold grandeur, the Black Hills wall in the scene."]

Westward view of the Sweetwater Valley from the top of Independence Rock.

At noon we found a bog on which we cut grass for the teams. The whole country along here is pregnant with alkali. We encamped on Crooked Creek, which presents the appearance of being a small, clear mountain stream, the first one we have seen. Here we found fine grass and water.

July 20.   This morning we left camp and traveled over the heart of the saline territory. Lakes of saleratus, two of which I visited and found dried up, with a crust over their entire beds, appear on all sides of our road. These crusts are from one-half to an inch thick, and white as snow.

[While crossing this alkaline area, a diarist estimated that he saw "more than one hundred dead oxen and two or three horses." "As soon as an ox dies, he bloats as full as the skin will hold, and sometimes it bursts, and his legs stick straight out and he smells horrible. . . . When they are nearly decayed there is frequently three or four bushels of maggots about the carcass."]

We arrived at the Sweetwater River at noon, where we encamped till four o'clock and then rolled on till night. About sundown we passed Independence Rock, on which, with Hutchinson, I wrote my name in large letters. We forded the river and camped one mile from the rock.

["Independence Rock at a distance looks like a huge whale" or "some huge monster rising from the ground." Standing isolated from the surrounding hills and rock formations, it "is about two hundred feet in height and oblong in shape. It is composed of solid granite. . . . Near the foot of this rock flows the winding and silvery Sweetwater. . . ." "Thousands of names are upon it, some painted well, others tarred, and many cut in the rock. You can see names not only from the U.S. but from all parts of the world."]

July 21.　　This morn we left camp early and traveled along a good, hard road, which is here a luxury. We passed Devil's Gate, a cut 400 feet deep through a spur of the granite hills on the north of the Sweetwater, through which the stream runs.

During the afternoon we passed a fine, clear creek, on which was good feed. We camped eleven miles from Devil's Gate with good grass.

July 22.　　Sunday. Today we travel on to get better grass. Our road was most horrible, being light sand. [To avoid the meanderings of the river in this area, the trail led away from the Sweetwater and crossed low, sandy, sage-covered hills.]

I have been very unwell today. Fortunately for me our train camped at two o'clock. Soon after we had pitched our tent, a cold rain and wind from the mountains came up. I got wet and took cold, with a chill, fever, and diarrhea. Was very sick all afternoon and night.

July 23.　　This morn we started late, giving the teams time to eat and, if possible, to recruit while along this river. Our road was sandy and hard.

Towards night we came into an open place in the valley where the Wind River chain is visible, on which the rain of yesterday had fallen in snow. It still lay glittering in the sun.

[During the next three days, Swain's illness prevented him from making daily diary entries.* "It is indeed hard to be sick in a wagon while

---

* *Entries for July 24, 25 and 26 have been created from other diarists' accounts.*

traveling under the burning sun, with the feeling of those around you so blunted by weariness that they will not take the trouble to administer to your comfort."

[*July 24.*   During this day's advance the Rangers probably reached the second ford of the Sweetwater. Here they crossed to the north side of the river and entered a canyon, about thirty miles west of Devil's Gate. This canyon was "a very narrow and rugged pass . . . with perpendicular rock walls from 400 to 600 feet high . . . and a thick growth of willows on the banks. Plenty of remains of wagons here, as well as some dead oxen. . . . This pass is one and three-quarter miles long." Within the canyon the trail crossed the river twice, while another trail led over the hills and thereby avoided this hazardous canyon passage.

[West of the canyon the two trails joined and then continued along the north side of the Sweetwater. The Rangers probably camped near the next ford of the river.

[*July 25.*   After fording to the south bank to avoid following a long northerly bend of the Sweetwater, the Rangers traveled westward across a desert of sage and alkaline ponds for sixteen miles before again returning to the river.

[In the midst of this desert region, the trail passed near Ice Spring, or Ice Slough. Mentioned by many diarists, this was "a morass perhaps a mile in length by half a mile in breadth. Some of the boys, thinking that water could be easily obtained, took a spade and going out on the wild grass commenced digging. About a foot from the surface instead of water they struck a beautiful layer of ice, five or six inches in thickness. . . . This natural ice-house is . . . a great curiosity . . . in this dry, barren, sandy plain. . . . The morass is either a pond or a combination of springs covered with turf or swamp grass, and at this high altitude the temperature of winter is very severe, converting the water of the morass to solid ice. Although the sun of the summer is intensely hot in these mountain valleys, the turf and grass intercept the intensity of its rays and prevent the dissolution of the ice, on the principle of our domestic ice-houses." "The surface is dug up all about by the travelers, as much from curiosity as to obtain so desirable a luxury in a march so dry and thirsty."

[Four miles beyond Ice Slough the trail passed two alkali lakes and a small spring and then continued through the sage and sand to a steep bluff overlooking the Sweetwater. From such a vantage point "the view is beautiful and grand. On one side of the Sweetwater the banks are speckled with white tents and wagons and cattle and horses. The road can be seen winding over the plain for many miles like a great serpent, and train after train of white-topped wagons can be seen either way as far as vision can extend; and then beyond the scope of vision dust can be seen rising in clouds. . . . One side of the river presents this scene of animation, with distant sounds arising from it, whilst on the other side the plain reposes in silence, and there is not a vestige of animal life about it—not even an Indian lodge, or elk, or antelope."

[*July 26.* Having traveled across the sixteen miles of desert, the Rangers again returned to the banks of the Sweetwater and forded to the north side. The river in this region was lined with small groves of willows.]

July 27. Yesterday I had my first spot of fun fishing in the Sweetwater. We fished with a net and caught fifty-three good-sized suckers. It was fine sport to drive them into the net and then pull them, floundering, to the shore. The exercise was too much for me, and I paid dearly for it today, for I was attacked with the old complaint and had a sick day.

July 28. We left camp late and rolled across rolling hills of fine-grained dark sandstone. Struck the Sweetwater at eleven o'clock and nooned.

This afternoon we are within ten miles of South Pass. Our road lies along the gradually rising valley of the Sweetwater.

["A Mormon from the Salt Lake settlement passed today with a wagon. He is going eastward to pick up old iron or anything valuable that he can find along the trail and take it back. He will not have to go far before he gets his wagon filled."]

This afternoon we left the road and drove up towards the mountains, where there is good grass, to stop to let the teams recruit till Thursday [August 2], while the Captain goes forward to explore the road ahead.

July 29. Sabbath. Today I am getting quite smart. The company are all resting, while the oxen are feeding. The cooks are cooking, and many of the men are out towards the mountains hunting antelope, elk, and sage hens, plenty of which they have found.

July 30. Today Lieutenant Cannon has gone haying with a part of the company. Others are hunting and many are mending clothes, boots, etc.; I have been making a belt for my rifle, revolver case, and accouterments. The cooks are cooking the game caught by the hunters and the camp lives high, but I, being no better, cannot enjoy it with them.

July 31.   Haying. Myself taping boots and patching pants. Captain Potts came back from the Little Sandy [about twenty-seven miles west of South Pass] and reports good feed on the route, but no water.

Back Home

> *"The stories of returning emigrants make the plains sound like a kind of golgotha, inhabited by savages and armed with storms, pestilence and famine to obstruct your passage to the golden land."*

Youngstown, July 26, 1849
Wednesday morn.

Dear Brother William,

I snatch up my pen in haste to write you a few lines to go by the August steamer to the Isthmus. We are all well as usual. Mother is quite comfortable and able to go out in the buggy. . . . She talks a great deal about "Will" and "Poor Will" and wishes she could see him. She is now busy with the rest of the women of our family drying cherries. They often wish they could send a cherry pie to you on the plains—aye, and many other little comforts with it too.

Sabrina and Sis . . . are in about their usual health. Sabrina's health is about the same, I think, as when you left. It cannot be called good, and the doctor says it will not be good till she lays on her back two or three months to cure the spinal infection with which she is afflicted. . . . She seems as contented as could be expected in your absence. She talks of "William," wonders where he is, and how he is today. All perfectly natural, you know, William. And by the bye, we all help her along in that before we know it, for we have felt a great deal of anxiety on your account, for we have had such terrible accounts from the plains of cholera and suffering—and from men who ought to tell the truth: officers of the U.S. Army and others, who say the road was lined with new graves and that sufferings of emigrants had just commenced and would increase as they advanced. The stories of returning emigrants make the plains sound like a kind of golgotha, inhabited by savages and armed with storms, pestilence and famine to obstruct your passage to the golden land. (This is a free version of what we hear, but almost literally true.) After throwing out three-quarters of newspaper reports, there is enough still left to make it sure that you run great risk, must encounter disease, bad weather, and fatigue in no stinted measure. But I hope for the best. I can't and won't believe that you were made to be left on those plains till I am obliged to do so.

Your letter from the Blue River dated June tenth and eleventh and received the twentieth of this month, forty days after it was written, gave us some relief, though it made us sure that you too had suffered from disease. I hope you may be spared the rest of the way. But be assured, William, the same cause, overexertion, which you say was the cause for your sickness, is the principal thing which I apprehend you will suffer from at the diggings. *You will overwork yourself* and won't know it till you are flat on your back or in the grave. *Do you hear*, boy? Keep cool! Go at it moderately, and if you can't get quite so much gold in the same time, don't kill yourself.

Give my particular thanks and respects to Mr. Hutchinson for the very kind and brotherly attention which you say he bestowed on you in your sickness. May God bless him for it, so say we all. And tell him I request him to take you under his particular care and not let you overdo yourself.

I told you of Sabrina. Now of Sis. She grows tall; her health has not been good for two or three weeks past. She has had some diarrhea consequent upon cutting her back teeth, which are just now cutting. She walks all around the place; comes out to the barnyard gate, takes hold of the pickets with both hands, puts her face up to the gate, and sings out for me to let her through which I sometimes do, and then she has great times. She is very fond of fruit and of apple and cherry sauce on the table, and the way she will make a hurrah for it until she gets it is not slow, I can tell you. She pitches potatoes into her face like rags into a rat hole! She wages exterminating war on cherry pie and "bags" mother's dried cherries in the most approved and scientific manner, the warnings of all the physicians in Christendom to the contrary notwithstanding. It is fun to see her: she is just tall enough to reach cherries on the edge of boards across the banisters of the front stoop, and I have laughed to see her walk carefully onto the stoop and reach up on tiptoe over her head and get a cherry, one at a time. She will go out into the back yard and get the cherries off the boards on the logs, and as she goes, she will look back to see if any of the folks are watching; if she finds they are, she will walk by the boards and as she goes will reach up and grab what she can and keep right on. We frequently say she is her father's girl. She is very fond of riding in a wagon, and she and I have great times dancing round the house when I am at leisure. . . .

The cholera is making havoc all over the country in all large places. Cincinnati and St. Louis have as yet been the greatest sufferers, but it is severe in New York City and all the business places of the whole country. It has carried off many of our great men, as well as many of the lower classes. It is in Buffalo, Rochester and Toronto. In Lockport [eighteen miles east of Youngstown] there have been two or three cases, but these were passengers on the [Erie Canal] boats going through. As yet we have been healthy on the [Niagara] river and hope we shall continue in the same blessing. The President of the United States has recommended Friday the third day of August as a day of fasting and supplication to the Almighty to arrest the destroyer and restore health to the nation. I think the day will be extensively observed throughout the U.S. The papers are filled with cholera, cholera, cholera. On account of it business has become very dull; a great part of the lake craft are laid up until the Fall trade commences.

I will send you some one or two papers that will give you a glimpse of the States and of the world. I feel very anxious to hear from you and know whether *I am going out next Spring*. . . .

Goodbye, William. May God bless you and protect you. Mother sends a hearty kiss.

I am as ever,

Your brother,
George Swain

Youngstown, July 26, 1849
Wednesday, six o'clock P.M.

Dear William:

In haste I take my pen in hand to drop a line to you and in consequence of having been away from home I shall not have time to say but little. . . . But suffice it to say that it is through the mercies and blessings of an all-wise Creator that I am permitted, when deprived of one of the greatest earthly blessings—a truly worthy friend and companion—to write to you, although it seems as though I could not dwell upon your absence long enough to write to you.

I have just come from Father's; they are all well and join me in love to you. I went upon the mountain yesterday to see Harriet. Papa is harvesting his wheat and Harriet waits upon the men. . . .

William, I am enjoying myself this summer as well as I can in your absence. However, I do not want you to leave home again for the sake of leaving me to ease and comfort. My health is poor, more so I think than our folks are aware of. Not only my back is bad, but I have a pain in my chest and left side, palpitation of the heart, and dyspepsia. But do not give yourself any uneasiness about me, for I am getting better and the doctor says I may be cured by being prudent and careful. . . . I must undress and go to bed. Good night, my dear.

Thursday morning

William, how are you this morning? O! that I could see you or even know where you are and how you are. It would be a great relief to my mind. O, my dear, the separation is bad. When shall we meet again? Yet two long months must pass if success crown you before you shall reach your journey's end, and then the space of time before I can expect to see or even hear from you! William, I cannot endure it. Time hangs heavily. May God hasten your return.

I received your letter of June 10th in forty days after it was written. I rejoiced to hear from you, but was sad to hear of your sickness caused by diarrhea; I was thankful to God Almighty for your recovery. Give my warmest regards to friend Hutchinson and may heaven's blessings rest upon him for his kind and brotherly attention to you during your illness. . . .

Sis is quite well with the exception of teething. She grows tall and runs all over; tries to say some words, one is "Ma," another "Papa," and third "Ganma." She is full of mischief, plenty of grit, and upon the whole rather a fine girl. She is great for making us understand, especially when she wants anything to eat or drink. I think we might well say that she is her father's child.

George has just been in and says it is time for the letters to go, and so I shall have to bid you goodbye until next month.

Sabrina Swain

CHAPTER VI

The Pacific Side

"I do not know where we are, nor do our maps. . . . We have concluded to throw away the maps, trust to good luck and when we arrive in California, we shall probably know it. . . ."

At South Pass the goldseekers paused to consider and some to celebrate their having reached the Continental Divide, 1,000 miles from the frontier. In contrast to their expectations of a Rocky Mountain pass, they could see for many miles to the west across a sweeping, sage-covered plateau.

Unable to locate the pass, most companies could not enjoy the symbolic moment when their wagons rolled onto the Pacific side of the continent. But William Swain knew when he and the Rangers came to "the spot where half of our toils would be over." He remembered Frémont's *Report*, which said the pass lay "between two low hills arising on either hand fifty or sixty feet."

Though obscure rather than dramatic, South Pass inspired some colorful descriptions: "This elevated and notable backbone of Uncle Sam," "the summit of the continent." Aware of the geographic and emotional transition that the Californians would experience at this place, one diarist stood near the trail "to take a parting look at the Atlantic waters which flow towards all I hold dear on earth." He watched "long trains of wagons with their way-worn occupants bidding a long, perhaps a last adieu to eastern associations, to mingle in new scenes on the Pacific coast."

In June, six weeks ahead of the Rangers, another diarist described a more spirited reaction: "I got out the Star Spangled Banner and planted it on the South Pass. A breeze waved it, our folks met around it and

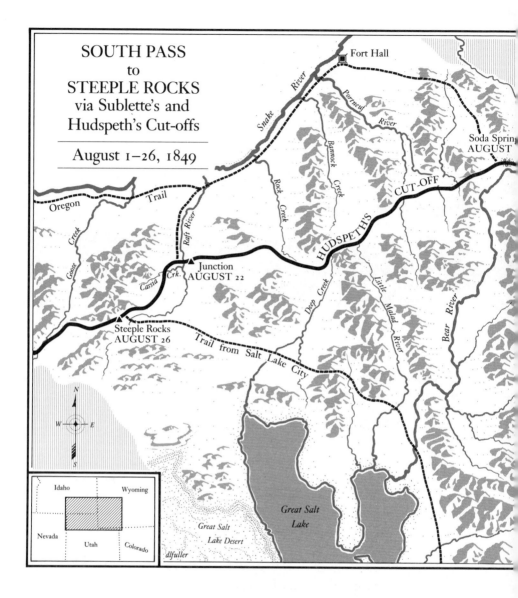

SOUTH PASS
to
STEEPLE ROCKS
via Sublette's and
Hudspeth's Cut-offs

August 1–26, 1849

passed a cheerful evening fiddling, singing and dancing on a sheet of zinc."

Beyond South Pass for over 400 miles there would be no river valleys such as the Platte and the Sweetwater to open the way. Except for a brief interlude of easy travel down the valley of the Bear River, the trails led westward across north-south rivers and mountain ranges.

Since there was no single best way through this vast mountain wilderness, by 1849 several routes had come into use. About twelve miles west of South Pass the trail forked at a stream named Dry Sandy. One

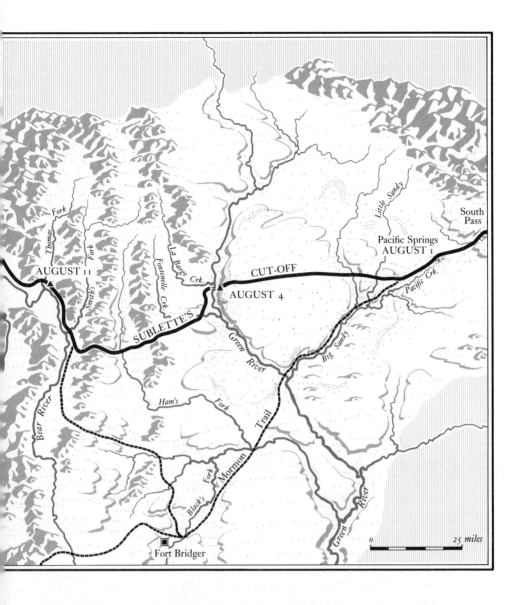

set of wagon ruts led due west (a route generally called Sublette's Cut-off) and another (the Mormon Trail) south 220 miles to the settlement at Salt Lake. This choice of routes fortuitously divided the emigration in the mountain desert country of west-central Wyoming. About one-third of the companies chose to go via Salt Lake, thus easing on both routes the competition for grass and fuel. Another factor that significantly helped the goldseekers as they entered an ever more inhospitable, demanding terrain: the emigration by August 1 had thinned out, stretched across the western wilderness for more than 1,000 miles—from the Rangers who reached South Pass that day and hundreds of emigrants who were still farther back on the Sweetwater to the lead company which had reached the Sacramento Valley on July 24.

For the companies that chose the southern route, Salt Lake City proved to be a haven of rest and plenty, even a place for some fun. Several diarists told of meeting Mormon girls, hinting at romance and telling of swimming parties on the lake shore. For the Mormons two years after the founding of their infant city, the Californians were an economic blessing. The North Platte and Green River ferrying operations prospered; at Salt Lake City the emigrants eagerly bought vegetables, milk and cheese. If they had no cash, the emigrants traded cooking utensils, tools of all sorts, flour and bacon and clothing, all of which might later have to be dumped but had unexpected value at the Mormons' wilderness city. Many companies consolidated teams, trading two or three weak and sickly oxen or mules for one that might survive to California. Thus the Mormons acquired hundreds of animals which a few weeks later would be healthy while their prior owners suffered in the Nevada deserts.

When the goldseekers reluctantly left the Mormon oasis, they traveled north around Salt Lake and then west to a junction with the main trail at Steeple Rocks, 185 miles northwest of the city.

For all its known benefits, the Mormon Trail seemed to most companies an unnecessary southerly detour, and certainly so with Sublette's Cut-off offering a direct route to the west from the Dry Sandy. The Rangers chose the cut-off and immediately faced a dry run of fifty miles across rough desert country to reach the first water at the Green River. From that river, where during June and July the crowds of goldseekers once again experienced the dangers and expense of ferrying a deep mountain stream, the trail continued west across mountainous terrain and finally down to the lovely Bear River Valley. There for the first time they found a place that matched their expectations of the Rocky Mountain West: a valley with rushing streams, luxuriant grassy meadows, geese, ducks, songbirds, wild berries, trout in clear waters—a place to restore men and animals. In this valley they met bands of Shoshoni (also called Snake Indians) whose friendly begging and curiosity made them more bothersome than threatening. Many companies, the Rangers included, met another resident of the Bear River Valley, Pegleg Smith, who, like the other fur trappers along the trail, sought in 1849 to adapt to the consequences of having about 18,000 easterners pass through his part of the wilderness during June, July and August. After talking with Smith, a number of diarists once again expressed a sense of respect and envy for those fiercely independent Americans of whom it was later said: "They had mastered the last, the biggest, and the hardest wilderness . . . the land of little rain, the Shining Mountains. It was theirs before the movers came to blemish it. . . ."

Swain and the Rangers enjoyed six days of leisurely advance up the Bear River Valley, an interlude of eating the rewards of fishing and hunting—trout, ducks and geese, of finding plenty of grass, and even of bathing and washing. Swain washed some shirts and presumably himself, though cleanliness had obviously long since been forgotten. The appearance, habits, manners and smells of these men had changed drastically since leaving Youngstown, Marshall or Baltimore; and yet the changes were not noted or commented on, any more than the diarists spoke of private matters such as arrangements on the trail for bodily functions. One diarist did tell of his reaction to his first bath in many weeks. "Changed my underclothes . . . got out my glass and looked at myself. But for certain unmistakable evidence of identity would have as soon believed myself almost anybody else."

On August 15 at the north end of the Bear River Valley the Rangers came to another choice of routes. Until mid-July there had been only one trail to follow, the old Oregon Trail, which led northward to Fort Hall on the Snake River and then west to the Raft River, where the Trail to California branched off to the south and the Oregon Trail continued northwest across Idaho. To avoid this northerly detour, a company of goldseekers on July 19 broke free from the rigid routine of following the wagon companies up ahead. This company left the established trail and drove its teams due west into rough, mountainous country. They blazed a new trail through southeastern Idaho, the first and only part of the entire overland route that was explored and opened by goldseekers.

That same day other companies followed the thin wagon tracks westward through the sage. Like sheep, almost every company thereafter took what came to be known as Hudspeth's or Emigrant's Cut-off. By the time the Wolverine Rangers chose this route, it was advertised at the forks by notes and cards stuck on sticks, some of which promised that the cut-off would take them to the Humboldt River in only one hundred miles.

For 134 miles this cut-off led through unknown, unnamed territory, and the Rangers and other companies often felt lost with only wagon ruts to prove that someone had been there before. Not that they were alone. A diarist traveling ahead of the Rangers on August 11, midway on the cut-off, wrote that fifty to one hundred wagons could be seen up ahead or to the rear. But in contrast to the previous trails, here the mountains, streams and topographic features had no names. No trappers, no explorers, no Oregon pioneers had passed this way. One diarist lamented: "We feel puzzled to know our locality. We are here but do not know where here is." They followed the cut-off hoping to find water and grass somewhere along each day's advance, hoping that when they rejoined the old trail they would find that the cut-off had saved miles, maybe days of travel.

On August 6 a young man about to start on Hudspeth's Cut-off sat down by the trail and wrote a letter to tell his people back in Missouri about the realities of the West: "Senator Benton and other big men may talk and humbug the country and you greenhorns about a railroad to the Pacific, but if you and I live a thousand years, we will never see the resemblance even of such a thing. There is not timber along this route to lay the track half part of the way; and if there was, it would cost more money to build it than there is in the U.S. Men who could build a railroad to the moon perhaps could build one over these mountains, but I doubt it. You may think you have seen mountains and gone over them, but you never saw anything but a small hill compared with what I have crossed over, and it is said the worst is yet to come. But never mind, Gold lies ahead."

How much less sanguine might this Missourian have been, and the Rangers too, if they had known that while they struggled to find their way over the cut-off, a number of the lead companies had crossed the Sierra Nevada and were by the end of July actually at work digging for gold. If such news had reached them would the Rangers have continued their leisurely pace? Would they on August 24 have held one of their monthly company meetings and at this meeting have listened to formal reports from the officers and then have appointed a committee to consider such reports? How remarkable that after ninety-nine days on the trail, quite uncertain where they were, the Rangers persisted in maintaining the formalities of reports and committees. What a contrast to the disagreements and anarchy that had long since fragmented many other company organizations.

While dissension and fights were common, crime of any kind was rare. Everything once valued enough to be packed in the wagons could be picked up along the trail. Farther west food would be scarce, but stealing flour or bacon was unlikely. Theft of animals was surely a temptation, but a man's mule or ox could generally be identified; in any case, could one be sure the animal had not strayed off? Money was not a temptation —there was very little of it, and gold lay ahead. Women—there were very few. Anger, sudden or smoldering, did cause shootings, stabbings and bludgeonings, with death the consequence in several cases, as headboards recorded. But given the size of the emigration, the anonymity of life on the trail once beyond one's own company and the improbability of punishment (few were willing to stop long enough to consider evidence against an accused person), the incidence of crime was far lower than it would have been among a similar number of people back in the States.

If companies held together under the same captain despite the inevitable arguments and fights, they nonetheless often lost a few men here and there along the way. The farther west they advanced, more and more members decided to set out as back-packers, carrying their possessions and what food their companies would allow them to take. These impatient men, traveling sometimes alone, more often in twos and threes, calculated they could hike the trail faster than their slow-moving, dust-shrouded train of ox- or mule-drawn wagons. John Root made such a decision while the Rangers were about midway on Hudspeth's Cut-off.

Swain, Bailey, Hutchinson and the sixty-three other Rangers stayed with their wagons and gaunt oxen and struggled through the desert-mountain country near the Utah–Idaho border north of the Great Salt Lake. When they passed the point where Hudspeth's Cut-off joined the trail from Fort Hall, they, like others before them, may have compared travel times and distances with those who had stayed on the old trail. Like an Illinois company, the Rangers may have been "thunderstruck" to learn that the cut-off had saved, at most, only a few miles. Farther west, another cut-off would tempt them again.

August 1, 1849. [Near South Pass.] This morn we made preparations for starting. About eleven o'clock we rolled out of camp and I walked ahead to cross between the identical twin mounds which form South Pass.

We have looked forward to this pass with anxiety for weeks, as the spot where half our toils would be over. That anxiety was fully repaid when I stood on top of a mound and traced the streams forward of us in a southerly direction. I have placed a sample of the formation of this pass in my trunk. We have gradually risen to this point without experiencing any sudden elevation on the road. Here the Wind River Mountains, at a distance of fifteen miles to the northwest, rise in high, broken masses. . . . The ravines between the peaks are covered with snow. To the south, at a distance of three miles, the hills rise rather steeply to a great height for hills. They are covered with sage at the bottom, above which a green mountain bush from one to two feet high covers their sides. . . . The

whole chain of mountains in the south appears to partake of a rolling character.

The Westward descent to Pacific Springs, which are two miles distant, is quite steep. We passed the Springs which form a small brook [Pacific Creek]. The feed here is nothing, nor can be. The flats are narrow, the other lands sandy and covered with sage and very alkali. ["The

Looking east to South Pass, some eighteen miles distant.

marsh and road are strewed with dead oxen, those on the road greatly swelled by the sun and putrescence and highly offensive in passing."]

Six miles from Pacific Springs we stopped to get supper and feed the teams, and at sundown started our night's travel. Reached Dry Sandy, nine miles from the Springs, and watered the cattle from our casks.

We took Sublette's Cut off. ["At the forks there was a stick driven in the ground with a board nailed on it, plastered with notices of what companies . . . and when had passed on either route and desiring friends in the rear to hurry up, etc. A notice requested travelers to throw stones up against the base to sustain the stick." "This kind of post office is very common at different points on the road. . . . Every person looks to see who the notices are from and goes on, leaving all as he finds it."]

August 2.   Reached the Little Sandy at daylight. ["A beautiful mountain stream, a little brackish but cooled by the melted snows at its source in the Wind River Mountains. . . . The bottom is about a quarter-mile wide, bounded by clay hills and cliffs twenty-five to thirty feet high."]

Great deal of alkali here. No feed, all eaten up. Plenty of water. Fed the teams hay and meal [a mixture of flour and water].

Started at eight o'clock [A.M.] for the Big Sandy [seven miles] where we camped at eleven. [The camping ground "is a nasty, dirty place, where the many who have camped here before have left all their filth and offal."]

Afternoon in camp.*

August 3.   Camped till four [P.M.] and with casks filled, started for the Green River.

["Quite a sandy and dusty trail; first few miles level . . . and perfectly arid. . . . Dusty sage bushes scattered over the country and hosts of dead oxen. . . . Ox trains rolling along enveloped in a cloud of dust. Men and oxen suffering much from dust, heat, and sandy trail."]

Moon up all night. Roads good, latter part of night hilly. ["There is something very unique and exciting in a night march—the long trains of wagons and oxen scarcely to be distinguished in the darkness and the indistinct forms of their drivers and men belonging to the trains, all moving along quietly, without noise except an occasional word of encouragement to the animals. . . . It is . . . easily imagined to be the stealthy march of an army upon some slumbering town."

[The "thirsty and dusty route . . . trended generally west-south-

---

* *Most companies traveling Sublette's Cut-off camped at the Big Sandy. From their guide books and information posted at the forks, they knew that a long stretch of arid, rough country had to be crossed to reach water at the Green River. Therefore, they gave their teams a chance to rest and filled every available container with water.*

A short distance from the Rangers' camp the Washington City Company also rested in preparation for the desert crossing. Their captain, J. Goldsborough Bruff, recorded in his diary that the Rangers "broke up a wagon, leaving the sides, etc. for the benefit of our cooks. We also found on their campground several hundred weight of fat bacon, beans, lead, iron, tools, a cast-iron stove, etc."

west. . . . Country now becomes more irregular, sand deep; crossed several ravines and deep hollows and over high, round hills of sand and slate." "Such a rough and barren country is enough to kill the Devil, much more the cattle. . . ."]

August 4.   Stopped at sunrise to feed, water, and get breakfast. The feed was good here. Very tired today and slept all the forenoon in the wagon.

[After resting by the side of the trail, which was "smoking with dust and heat," the Rangers hitched up about noon and set out for the last pull to the Green River.]

Road hilly but hard and good.

[Rolling on through the sun-scorched midday, through a fog of dust, the Rangers by early afternoon reached a line of "very high and steep clay and sand bluffs, some parts perpendicular and even overhanging. . . ." From these bluffs the Green River "appeared like a curved, silver thread. . . . It was a grand sight."

["Before we reached the river, our cattle became aware that we were nearing water and showed signs of great impatience. . . . When the stream was actually in sight, we found it necessary to unyoke the teams and let them loose to prevent them from stampeding with the wagons. The approach was down quite a steep mountainside. As soon as they were free, they rushed pell-mell down into the river. It was a beautiful, clear stream, and they stood in it drinking and cooling their feet for a long time. It required a good deal of urging to get them out, drive them up the hills, and reyoke them."

[One by one the twenty-one wheel-locked wagons were haltingly eased down the descent behind the teams of oxen stumbling and sliding in the sand and stones, until at last the entire company reached the valley floor.]

Reached Green River at five o'clock. Forded and camped.*

August 5.   Sabbath. Traveled eight miles ["over high, narrow and very crooked ridges of gray and brown sandstone"] to a creek among the hills of the Bear River Mountains where we found good feed.

[The Rangers camped in "the beautiful valley of the Fontenelle, a tributary of the Green River. . . . A delightful, fertile valley. The creek

---

* *Through June and most of July the only way to cross the then-swift and deep Green River had been by one of several primitive ferries. By August 4, however, the snow at the headwaters had melted and the dryness of the summer had made the river fordable for the companies bringing up the rear of the emigration.*

Descent at the Green River.

is very sinuous, about ten feet wide and three feet deep, sparkling and rapid." "Crowds of wagons are constantly arriving and stopping here. . . ."

[A short distance up Fontenelle Creek several Rangers and members of other companies found "a camp of some old mountaineers and Indian traders. They had adopted the native custom of taking as many wives as they could feed. Each man had from three to six wives. . . . They were all crazy for whiskey and offered us any one of their wives for a drink." "The camp was composed of conical skin lodges, tents, bush houses and about ten blue ox-wagons. Here was a mixture of white women and squaws and children of every age and hue. The men were in a tent playing Monte on a skin. . . . Indian goods of every description, mingled with horse trappings, were scattered around amongst the wagons. In the fine meadow on the opposite side was a large band of fat horses and ponies. . . . About a mile and a half higher up the creek is another camp of these traders. . . . They ask high prices for their horses, few less than $300. . . . Great feats of horsemanship by the traders riding at full speed over plain, stream, ditches and irregular and elevated places in pursuit of a run-away pony."

[The captain of a company traveling near the Rangers climbed to the top of a cliff above Fontenelle Creek "and was well compensated by the magnificent bird's eye view of the stream and the valley. . . . The beautiful silvery stream meandering in every variety of curve . . . bright green grass and willows and little groves of bright willows . . . cattle grazing, the camps and people and blue smoke curling up in delicate and graceful spirals from the campfires, the warm tints of the bluff, darker hills above and the distant blue mountains made a picture I gazed on with admiration for some time."]

August 6. [This day a group of emigrants from Ohio with four wagons camped with the Rangers.*]

[West of Fontenelle Creek the trail led through the rugged foothills of the Bear River Mountains, winding along dusty ridges and descending through "deep sand and dust, loose stones, and projecting rocks" to the bottoms of numerous ravines.]

Traveled fifteen miles over hills and camped on a bare knoll. Drove the teams three miles to feed down a creek.

August 7. Left camp early and ascended a high hill, the second range of the Bear River Mountains, then descended two long, steep hills. The verdure of the country begins to assume the look of Spring. Some grass green, vegetation generally fresh, and flowers in bloom. At the bottom of the second mountain we found good grass, green and luxuriant, which we have not found since we left Deer Creek on the Platte [July 13].

In the afternoon we crossed the backbone of the Bear River Mountains. We descended the ridge and encamped on Ham's Fork, a branch of the Green River, clear as crystal and full of trout. The flats are large and covered with a luxuriant growth of grass.

---

* *While they never formally joined the Rangers, these men (their number is uncertain but presumably about sixteen, four per wagon) traveled with or very near the Rangers for the rest of the journey. One of them, Dr. Joseph Middleton, kept a diary which is frequently quoted hereafter.*

August 8.   Left camp early and immediately commenced raising the first ridge west of the backbone, which has a very bad pitch at the top. We traveled but a short distance and nooned. The afternoon's travel was tolerably level till near night when we ascended the second ridge. Its descent was five miles, very steep and intolerably dusty.

Camped in a very narrow, deep chasm, on a small spring stream on which we found ducks. The feed good. Twelve miles today.

August 9.   Had great trouble in finding our teams this morn on account of their rambling among the bluffs. Finally found them and crossed the last ridge and descended a bad hill to the Bear River bottom, which has a luxuriant growth of grass and abounds in wildfowl, ducks, geese, plovers, and snipe, which we enjoyed ourselves in hunting during the afternoon while our teams were indemnifying themselves for their past privations.

August 10.   Our company is in camp today on account of the sickness of Mr. Seymour. It is no loss to our teams.

This morn I and friend Hutchinson started hunting before daylight, but had bad luck. His gun would not go off, and my rifle would not kill. So we returned to camp with but one duck.

Captain Potts has gone forward to examine the road. The river here has a breadth of five rods and depth of three feet, with considerable current. The water is muddy, and the banks are lined with willows.

I washed some shirts and attended to other camp duty, and Mr. H. and I went hunting and fishing until night with good success. Caught a good string of trout and got five ducks, two of which I shot with one shot with Mr. H's shotgun, which kicked me most outrageously. John Root also got lots of fish and ducks and one wild goose, so that we had a fine feast on wildfowl. Mr Seymour is no better this evening.

[Bands of Shoshoni or Snake Indians lived in and near the valley of the Bear River. One of the Rangers described a man and woman as "the finest-looking 'redskins' I ever saw. Both young, stalwart, and clean, for Indians. . . . They invited us over to their village. Some of our men went."

[The Shoshoni "speak many English words, as 'good,' 'very good,' 'horses,' . . . etc. Camps and moving bodies of them are in all directions; plenty of fine horses, colts, squaws, papooses, warriors (old and young), dogs, etc. The young men are continally begging for 'powdree,' 'balle.' They stand and sit around the messes while dining, anxiously waiting for a morsel and picking up every crumb. . . . An Indian . . . traded some fine trout for an old cotton shirt. They are very fond of cloth and fancy caps; one had a perforated tin door of a lantern attached to a Scotch bonnet for a visor. Another had a fine, silver-mounted bowie knife and held in his hand a new and bright claw hammer, no doubt stolen from some of the emigrants."]

August 11. We started in good season this morn and traveled down the river bottom, which affords a good, level road. It abounded with wild currants of three kinds—yellow, black and red. Five miles from camp ground we crossed Smith's Fork, a large mountain stream, cold and clear and abounding with large trout, a mess of which we caught. . . .

Mr. Seymour is worse this evening.

August 12. Sabbath. Mr. Seymour is dead. We have buried him beside the road with all the decency that we can here on the wilderness plain. I was a guard last night and had the care of him. He was insensible when I first saw him, no pulse, arms cold to the elbows. I tried to administer some medicine, but it only made his breathing worse, as he did not swallow it. His breath grew shorter, and at half past twelve he ceased to breathe, gasped three times, and the soul had taken its departure without causing the slightest motion of a muscle. The funeral service was performed by Mr. Hobart. All the company appeared very solemn, and a solemnity has rested upon the camp all morning.*

We left camp late and started across a point of hills twelve miles to the Bear River. Our road was very hilly, particularly two bad hills soon after leaving Thomas Fork.

Today is Sabbath, and my family is probably worshiping God in the congregation at the church while I am here in these wilds traveling as though there was no Sabbath. Although traveling because the company does so, I still feel a sacred stillness in the day and can feel with a little reflection a part of the feelings of my family as they enjoy the benefits of religious rites and join in observing the day: enjoying rest, reading, and conversing together, perhaps about me. I would that I could send them some intelligence of my health and my whereabouts, but that I cannot do for two long months. But I shall probably have news from them at Sutter's. I hope I may soon be there. May God grant that I may meet them again in health and by this absence be able to make their lives happy. And may not the sad intelligence be borne to them that I am left on these

---

* *Seymour probably died from the disease mentioned most frequently along this part of the trail, the sometimes fatal "mountain fever." A collective designation for several possible fevers, it was most likely the tick-borne infection now known as Colorado tick fever.*

plains or rest from the troubles of life in California. For how could my dear Sabrina endure the sad news were she in the place of Seymour's wife, or who would have the care of a father for my dear little Eliza Crandall. May God bless them and George and Mother and protect them from cholera and all other sickness and grant us all a happy meeting. I am now enjoying good health, for which I trust I am thankful to Almighty God.

After noon halt we descended the western side of the ridge up which we had ascended in the forenoon. ["The descent down gravel, rocks, down long and almost precipitous steeps, was attended with much difficulty. . . . This descent must be some 3,000 feet."]

From the summit we had a splendid view of the Bear River valley, which was truly beautiful.

We traveled six miles along the river bottoms and encamped on a small mountain creek, clear, cold, and hard. Twenty miles today.

[A few miles beyond the point where the trail returned to the Bear River Valley, "Pegleg Smith, or Rocky Mountain Smith, has a cabin across the river, a squaw for a wife and is quite rich. . . . He is a man of about fifty or fifty-five years of age, rather portly, round-headed. . . . He has lived in the mountains twenty-five years, seems to be a very hospitable old man, has a large number of cattle and horses and two pigs. Last winter was a very cold one, snow on a level four feet deep. He fed a great many Indians on his beef and horses and saved them from starvation." "His squaw is . . . about sixteen, rather bulky than otherwise. She has one child, a boy. . . . Smith is fond of company and treats them on the best he has and in great abundance, almost to wastefulness. . . . He appears happy as a lord."]

August 13. Left camp early and traveled along the river valley, which affords a level road. Towards night we crossed a spur of the bluffs, and it was eight o'clock before we arrived at the river and camped. Twenty-two miles.

August 14. We had an early start this morn. Our road was over rolling hills between the river and the mountains. We made slow progress through the dust which rose in clouds and is very disagreeable, coating everything in and around the wagons. About ten o'clock we crossed a clear stream and drove up its right bank some eighty rods and stopped for noon halt at the famous Soda or Beer Springs. They are situated along the valley of a clear mountain stream, which runs down from the northeast and empties into the Bear River just where it changes its course from a northerly to a southerly direction.

These springs, resembling in appearance the effervescence of combining alkali and acid, issue from the earth in channels of various size and blubber as they come into contact with the air. Their sediment usually forms cones, through the top of which the springs usually flow. . . .

One spring . . . presented the appearance of a pot of boiling water and made a noise like lard boiling violently. Another named Steamboat Spring, one mile below on the bank of the Bear River, was still more of a curiosity—boiling and foaming from six inches to three feet with a noise and appearance of the foam behind a steamboat wheel; while one foot from it, gas was issuing at intervals with considerable noise from a crevice in the rock.

We traveled three miles in the afternoon and encamped early.

August 15. We started late and traveled along a level road. At two miles from camp we arrived at the point where the Fort Hall and a cut-off road separate, which is just at the point where the river takes a direct course south. [The Rangers chose the cut-off—later known as Hudspeth's Cut-off—which led westward from the forks.

["There were at the forks innumerable notes and cards stuck up for the benefit of the various companies behind. Several . . . stated that 'by this cut-off it is only 100 miles to the Humboldt River.' "]

We crossed the plain between the mountains and stopped to noon without water just as we were about to ascend the mountains.

["The road having been opened this season, no written mark describes it, and no one has returned to tell of its peculiarities." "Whether it is one, ten, or fifty miles to the next watering place is a fearful secret."]

August 16. We had an early start. I equipped myself with my rifle and revolver for a mountain tramp with Dr. Wells, McClellan, and young Vitts. We descended the stream to a point where it ran around the base of a high peak and emptied into a larger stream [the Portneuf] which has a fine mountain valley. We climbed over this peak by the easiest ascent we could find, which was very toilsome. On arriving at the summit, we had a splendid view of the little valley, winding stream, some of the nearest hills, and our train which was winding its way among the hills below.

On descending I found some June cherries which grew on bushes about eleven feet in height and are larger than those at home. I doffed my hat and picked it full to take to the train. My costume reminded me of my childhood, when bareheaded and barefooted I used to pick berries in the fields of the old home of my youth. I am sure that any one of my friends arriving in sight and seeing me bareheaded, with hair disheveled and tossed in the wind, belted and with a rifle on my shoulder, would have taken me for an Indian.

August 17.   Left camp at seven o'clock, traveling six miles across the valley and ascended a high range. Four miles beyond these hills we stopped to noon on a small stream [part of the watershed of the Little Malad River].

In the afternoon ascended another range by good road and after traveling along the stream for four miles, camped in its valley. . . .

August 18.   We were up early and on the road, which leads directly over the hills by a good road that is remarkably level for so hilly a country. Our camp is in good spirits. All begin to look anxiously for the time when the Sierra Mountains shall be at the head of our train, for we think of them as the end of this tedious and irksome journey.

Our road runs south far more than we expected and must lead us near the Salt Lake.

At ten o'clock we crossed a fine mountain stream running through a small mountain valley; and at quarter past ten we commenced the ascent of a high ridge [on the west side of the Little Malad Valley] by a mountain pass such as we have not met with before. . . . At four o'clock we arrived at the top and commenced the descent, which was down another defile, very steep and so narrow that the teams and wagons were often times eight or ten feet below the feet of the drivers. We reached the bottom of the mountain at sunset.

["When we commenced the journey, trifling hills were considered great obstacles. But now we lock our hind wheels and slide down a thousand feet over rocks and through gullies with as much sang-froid as a school boy would slide down a snowbank."]

After driving in the dark and through clouds of dust, which we do all the time, at eleven o'clock we arrived at a spring sufficient to afford water for the train and sat down in our tents to a midnight supper, tired and weary after a day's travel of twenty-nine miles [to Rock Creek].

["The dust is one of the greatest if not the greatest annoyances of this journey. It not only arises around you, filling your nose, eyes, lungs, etc., but there seldom being any rain here to lay it, it becomes very deep so as to render walking through it very tiresome." "The soil is of a light volcanic character and the least breeze or trampling of the cattle is sufficient to raise it in such clouds as to envelop a whole train to such an extent as to render it difficult to distinguish the wagons at a few yards distance. Sometimes, too, a whirlwind will come sweeping up a ravine carrying the dust spiraling mountain high, almost smothering teams and teamsters in its passage."]

August 19. Sabbath. Today we are in camp. Teams and men are resting from their labors. Washed four shirts, drawers, socks, and mended pants, and bathed in the cold brook-water. This brook, and also the one passed yesterday, runs into Salt Lake, which lies distant twenty to thirty miles and can be seen from the bluffs along our road. ["The lake looks white as the driven snow, with now a dark, now a green, now a blue spot in the center, stretching away toward the southeast to a high, black-looking island.. The white expanse is pure salt. The dark streak is the water. . . . Beyond the white expanse rise high, black, barren looking mountains. It is a sublime but melancholy sight."]

At seven o'clock attended preaching by Mr. Moore. The sermon was on the death of Mr. Seymour and was good. Our company, with many others camped near us, listened to it with great attention.

August 20. This morn the road leads directly among the hills. At nine o'clock we struck another pass or defile of stone, winding among the hills and rising gradually, smooth and clear. No art could make a better pass. We found water at noon. . . .

We found two good springs this afternoon. At five o'clock we struck the source of a fine stream, which runs along the side of our road; it is cool and clear. We find good grass along the hills.

We encamped early and had a pleasant evening before a large camp-fire made of dry poplar, which we often find among the hills.

August 21. This morn I was on the last guard and commenced my first lessons in cooking by starting breakfast: making coffee, frying meat, cold mush, and by mixing up some nut cakes and frying them.

We traveled along the little creek for some time and found the road good. But the fires of the emigrants have run over the flats and the hills to their summits and have destroyed the feed. We hear that the Indians have burned the valley of the Humboldt River, which will make it bad for our teams as they are now failing from the hard driving we give them.

At noon halted on the creek, which sinks in the sand one half-mile below our noon halt. There is no feed on the creek here.

We ascended a low hill to the left of the creek, from which we saw a large valley to the west lying between the Salt Lake and the Snake River and between us and the mountains west of the valley. At the foot of these mountains there appeared to be a large stream of water. Where we were

The Swain diary for August 19, 20, and 21. These entries are part of the second volume (about the same size as the first), which has been crudely resewn to hold its pages together; many are torn and badly smudged.

or on what streams we had been since we left the Bear River, we knew not; and all of us were at once conjecturing where we were and what stream we saw.

The plain which appeared three or four miles across proved to be sixteen miles, and the "stream" nothing but the grayish appearance of the air across so level a plain. We found, however, good spring brooks and camped at sundown with abundance of good feed for the teams.

[While crossing this same plain, "arid and dusty with naught growing thereon except wild sage," another company on August 14 was similarly deceived by a mirage, "wonderfully realistic and beautifully exhibiting far distant mountains in the most fantastic shapes. It was hard to believe we were not looking at an actual scene. But it slowly faded away after fifteen or twenty minutes."]

August 22. Moved the train six miles to a head branch of the Raft River, where we are now lying with the finest camping ground since we have been on the cut-off; good water and splendid green feed for the teams. We have decided to recruit the teams till Saturday [the 25th].

The company voted to buy John Root's interest.

[Root was "discouraged by our slow progress . . . and thought he could make better time by himself. . . ."]

August 23. In camp with nothing doing. I made a pair of suspenders and spliced a whiplash.

August 24. This morn I assisted Dr. Wells in cooking and made my first bread. I had good luck and turned out three nice, light loaves!

[In the camps along the Raft River "fresh-water lobsters are boiled and eaten by many, said to be good. They are about four inches long. The emigrants, or some of them, cook and eat rattlesnakes. They call them *bush fish*. Prairie dogs are nice eating. . . . Marmots are used for food. They are very fat and good. Rabbits are abundant here. Ravens are very numerous and tame. . . ."]

Afternoon attended the [monthly] company meeting and heard the Agents' and Directors' reports to the company. I was appointed one of the Committee to consider the Reports. Met in committee to appoint the Chairman and called for reports and vouchers.

I spent the remainder of the afternoon and evening in writing a letter to my wife to send to California by John, who packs in the morning, thereby hoping to send a letter home three weeks in advance of my arrival.

August 25. Rose early this morn and got all ready for tramping. John packed his horse. Breakfast over, we left camp at seven o'clock. Rolled directly up the valley of a branch of the Raft River, which leads into the mountains directly west three miles from camp.

Just where the stream [Cassia Creek] issues from the mountains, the Fort Hall road unites with the cut-off.

The valley of the little stream is narrow. The creek is lined with water willows and the creek bottoms have good feed.

A number of our company are sick today with diarrhea. John leaves the train at noon.

We nooned on a small stream or creek which comes in from the north bluffs. John purchased the gray pony from the company and will not leave till tomorrow morning.

We met a Mr. Ottaway today, who is an old trader. He says that we are now not more than four hundred miles from California and that we are not on the Fort Hall road but on a cut-off leading from the Fort Hall road to the Mormon road to the Humboldt River. Amid this confusion of statements we know not where on the route we are.*

We traveled until two o'clock along this little stream. Then the road led through a valley of a dry creek to the south and struck another valley, large and covered with good feed. We camped by the side of a clear mountain brook. . . . The small hills at the bottom of the range of mountains west of us are masses of fine marble, and they appear like gothic structures—columned, terraced and domed. [These were the first of a cluster of freakish formations known in 1850 and ever since as the City of Rocks.]

Our feed was good and our water pure. This whole country is destitute of game, and we are obliged to live on our salt provisions.

August 26.   Sabbath. This morn John left the train. [Taking "two ponies . . . and a few pounds of provisions, he started off alone."]

We got a late start and traveled directly across the valley before us, amidst the best scenery we have seen since we have been among these hills. South, a high range of mountains speckled with snow. East, a range of high bluffs with a level plain at the foot. West, the marble buildings; and in the background high, broken and detached cragged mountains speckled with pure white marble cropping out in ledges.

Halted to noon in a ravine bounded with the most splendid rock scenery I ever beheld. . . . Here was a mass of common buildings, the streets, the town pump, the taverns with their chimneys, the churches

---

* *Ottaway's estimate of 400 miles as the distance to California was at best an "as the crow flies" guess, and his statement that they were "not on the Fort Hall road but on a cut-off leading from the Fort Hall road to the Mormon road to the Humboldt River" can best be untangled by consulting the map of the trails in this area (see p. 200). All in all, Ottaway was as confused as the Rangers. Swain's diary makes it clear that the Rangers had completed passage of Hudspeth's Cut-off, rejoined the main California Trail earlier this day at Cassia Creek and were now moving west from Cassia into the valley called "City of Rocks" described in the following paragraph.*

Although Swain calls Ottaway "an old trader" and implies that he had been over the trail before, the diary of Dr. Joseph Middleton clearly identifies him as just another gold-seeker.

with their spires, the monuments of the graveyard, the domes, the cornices, and the columns. These all had their representations in this wild scene of Nature. Some emigrants had appropriately inscribed on one of the large castles "Castle City Hotel," which was certainly a very appropriate name for the place.

[After ascending through the valley of the City of Rocks, the trail passed Steeple Rocks, "two tall and sharp-pointed columns two or three hundred feet in apparent height." "Opposite these two rocks the Salt Lake road comes in through another valley. . . ."]

Mr. Rice, who traveled with us to the Platte ferry and went by way of the Mormon City, is camped by us tonight.*

["This evening a Boston mule company of about seventy is said to be broken up and destitute of provisions and are . . . troubling emigrants to sell provisions to them. They say if people will not sell to them, they will take by force. Yesterday we nooned near where they camped, and some of them . . . came to our wagon and pressed hard to buy bacon, but got none. There were, very fortunately, about forty wagons camped nearby. . . . Such men as these are to be dreaded and must be sharply watched."]

Back Home

"O! William, if I could see you this morning, I would hug and kiss you till you would blush."

Youngstown, August 25, 1849
Saturday morning

Dear Brother William,

After a hard day's work yesterday, I did not wake this morning till six o'clock, and then I thought that if I did not write you today, you

---

* Mr. Rice and several thousand other goldseekers who chose to travel via Salt Lake City rejoined the mainstream of emigration at Steeple Rocks. The total distance from South Pass to Steeple Rocks via the Mormon settlement was about 420 miles, or about eighty miles longer than via Sublette's and Hudspeth's cut-offs. That Rice had camped with the Rangers at the North Platte ferry (July 14) and was now camped nearby suggests he had made as good time as the Rangers on their cut-off trails.

would not get a letter by the September mail. So I pitch right at it. . . .

Sabrina has been visiting at her father's for two or three days past, and I have sent Walter [a hired hand] post haste after her. Mother went with him for the ride.

We are all well and doing pretty well, for which blessing we should be thankful to the giver of all blessings. Little Cub grows finely and runs all around the yard, having great times with her dog pup; and if I begin to whistle she runs up to me laughing, with both hands up for me to take her and have a dance. I can whistle her out of her mother's arms when she is eating or going to sleep in a minute. She is larger than any of the children around her age—taller I mean. . . .

All are very anxious to hear from you. We have received your letters up to the line you wrote beside the road one hundred miles this side of Fort Laramie, June 29, and are glad to hear that you are well. But the same mail that brought that letter brought news of four persons dying of cholera out of a Buffalo company of twelve at Fort Laramie ahead of you, so that we are now anxious as ever about you. . . . We all had the horror about you till your June 29 letter came and cheered us. . . .

We shall not have any fruit except apples. Peaches are an entire failure. There are a few pears and a very few plums. We had about four bushels of early apples, and I tell you I wished I could send you some of them. They'd make you sing "Carry me back to old Niagara." . . . The cholera is raging all over the country. . . . We have not been visited here, though there have been some premonitory symptoms, but no deaths [in Youngstown]. Many cases among the inhabitants at Lockport. . . .

If you have good luck and want me to come out, you must send the word. If you have bad luck and want to come home, let me know and I will send you the means. . . .

Mother and I have been reading Frémont to become acquainted with your route and the distances. I hope you will have kept a journal and will send home extracts, for we want to hear every little particular.

We have been reading the secret memoirs of the Empress Josephine, *written by herself*. She was an extraordinary woman, a compound of goodness and greatness, of love and jealousy, of benevolence and avarice, of monarchist and republican, liking unbounded power and yet afraid of it, clinging to Napoleon till her last breath, and he to her. She pleaded with him to give up the war with Russia. . . .

But it is now time I should be at the post office. May God be with you and protect you and return you safely to us.

I asked Mother what she says to Will. "O, say everything that is good. Kiss him well for me in the letter, tell him we think it a long time since we saw him, and that with every good apple and tomato and melon we wish he had a part of it, and that every hour in the day we wish that God may bless him."

I am in a great hurry, Will, I can't read my letter over to correct it. Good-bye. God bless you. Give my respects to Messrs. Hutchinson and Bailey and Root.

Your affectionate brother,
George Swain

Youngstown, August 24, '49

Dear William,

I again seat myself to write a line to an absent husband, and it is as usual in a hurry—only half an hour to write all I would like to say. . . .

Little Eliza C. has been bad with diarrhea this week past, but I have at last succeeded in checking it in a small degree. She is not by any means a healthy child, although she appears to be pretty well and grows. She has three double teeth, which she has cut through lately, which may be the cause of her diarrhea. She tries to talk a great deal and does in her fashion. She can say "poor Pa" as plain as any one. She is a great deal of company for me, and I often think if she should be taken away, I could not be reconciled to it under my present affliction. May God grant that I may not be called to pass through the trial.

We received your letter [of June 29] on August 14. I began to feel very anxious about you and conjured upon a thousand things that might have befallen you. . . . O, what glorious news that you were getting along so well and above all in health. May God grant that it may continue so, while amidst sickness and death. Thus far we have been spared—how thankful ought we to be to a kind and merciful Providence in watching over us and keeping us under His protection.

Dear Husband, this is only the 25th of August—what a long summer. O!! how I want to see you. Sometimes I almost imagine myself with you, but alas it is only the dream of fancy. May Heaven endow us with patience and grant us a happy meeting in His own due time. I long to hear from you at journey's end, which I hope will be soon. I often think what a tedious summer you have spent, makes me shudder and think you have had to exercise a great deal of patience to endure all you must have had to pass through. May God grant that this absence and journey may prove to be a wise lesson to us both. O! William, if I could see you this morning, I would hug and kiss you till you would blush.

When you get where you can write with comfort, write me a great, long letter and tell me just how you feel, all the hardships of your journey. Do not keep anything back.

I shall have to bring this note to a close and write the next time, when I intend, if health permits, to write a long one.

Father's people join in love to you. . . .

So goodbye for this time.
Sabrina Swain

CHAPTER VII

The Humbug River

*"Our cattle are getting so poor it takes two
to make a shadow. . . . Their feet are
sore, their backs are sore, and we are sore
all over."*

At Steeple Rocks the two main streams of travel came together—one
from Hudspeth's Cut-off and Fort Hall, the other from the Great Salt
Lake valley. Beyond this junction a single trail opened the way for the
entire emigration, west and south to a dangerously steep mountain pass
that dropped 2,000 feet to the bluff-lined valley of Goose Creek, then
through Hot Springs valley, where clusters of boiling springs watered
marshy turf and sent up plumes of steam. At last, some ninety miles
southwest of Steeple Rocks, the wagon trains reached the Humboldt
River.

From a variety of names—Swampy, Ogden's and St. Mary's, some
of them dating back to its discovery in 1828, the river was officially
named by Frémont in 1848 to honor Baron Alexander von Humboldt,
the most distinguished geographer of his time. Whatever its formal name,
gold rush diarists complained bitterly about this "meanest and muddiest,
filthiest stream," "nothing but horse broth seasoned with alkali and salt,"
and several called it "Humbug River."

No matter what they thought of the Humboldt, it was the most vital
stream of the many followed on the trail to California. Its water and grass
sustained men and animals through 300 miles of arid, hostile wasteland
from the northeast corner of present-day Nevada to the Reno area. Without this thin (some suggested providential) lifeline, the goldseekers would
have had to travel first to Oregon and then to California, with consequences that would have radically changed the history of both states.

Whether in July and August for most companies or September for

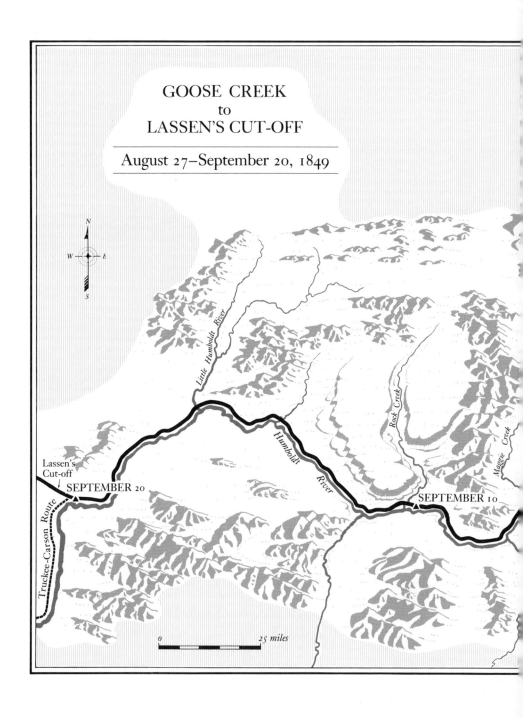

GOOSE CREEK
to
LASSEN'S CUT-OFF

August 27–September 20, 1849

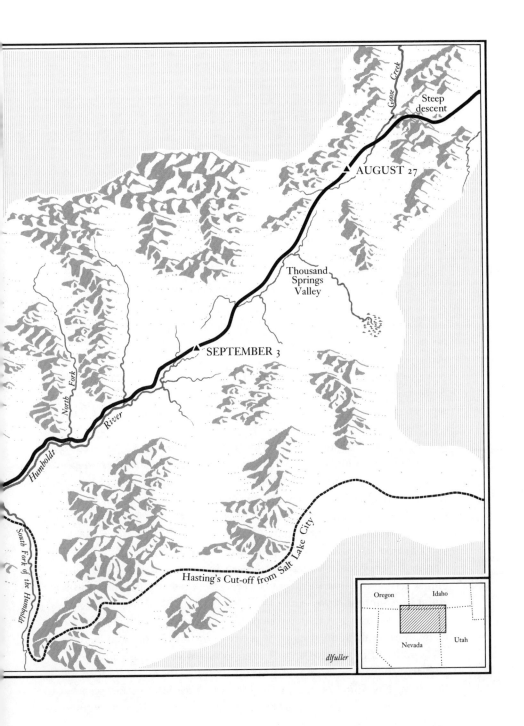

Goose Creek

Steep descent

▲ AUGUST 27

Thousand Springs Valley

▲ SEPTEMBER 3

North Fork

River

Humboldt

South Fork of the Humboldt

Hasting's Cut-off from Salt Lake City

dlfuller

Oregon | Idaho

Nevada | Utah

the Rangers and others farther back, the three weeks and more spent moving down the valley of the Humboldt seemed to compound and intensify the worst of the long trek: the wearying, endless walking day after day under the scorching sun, breathing and tasting dung pulverized and mixed with dust; the increasing disgust with meals that looked and tasted shriveled and dry; the inescapable day-and-night sounds of messmates complaining and cursing, oxen squealing and groaning; the monotony of sandy plains rising onto sage-covered hills blending into naked mountains; the dreariness of it all, plus the knowledge that tomorrow's miles promised more of the same. "Where the hell *is* California?"

Far worse than discomfort or boredom, the Humboldt revived the emigrants' forgotten fear of Indians—not Indians like the Pawnee or Sioux, but a far different wilderness people whom the fur trappers long before 1849 derisively called Diggers. Hunting with crude weapons in a country where game was scarce, these small, stealthy people lived on roots, seeds, small animals and insects. They belonged to the Shoshoni and Paiute tribes, but the goldseekers, like the trappers before them, had no tribe in mind; they used the term Diggers to identify any of the skulking marauders who killed or stampeded their animals. Companies posted guards to watch over their grazing teams, yet each night oxen or mules were driven off in the darkness, or at dawn herdsmen found them with arrows deep in their gaunt sides. Emigrants mistaken in the dark for Diggers were shot by jumpy guards.

Except for the increasing torment of dust, no subject received more repetitious attention from diarists than the Diggers and their depredations. Yet Swain made no mention of them. His silence suggests that the Rangers once again did not see the enemy, while their guard system succeeded in protecting the teams. Other diarists, even those whose teams also escaped attack, almost daily reported rumors and firsthand accounts from nearby camps of animals that had been stampeded or killed. Less frequently they told of guards and herdsmen wounded or killed, of emigrants setting out in armed forays to retrieve their teams and of full-scale emigrant counterattacks.

Loss of oxen and mules stolen, killed or felled by exhaustion forced companies to abandon wagons that had somehow held together through 1,500 miles of mountains and deserts. Personal possessions and company property that had escaped all previous consolidations were sadly left in the dust. Unwilling to accept such losses, some goldseekers resorted to stealing animals. The menace of these "white Indians" became an increasing concern along the Humboldt.

Edible provisions no longer littered the trailside. So much had been thrown away that food supplies were fearfully short. Many companies subsisted on "rancid bacon with the grease fried out by the hot sun, musty flour, a few pinoles, some sacks of pilot bread broken and crushed and well coated with alkali, and a little coffee without sugar."

More and more back-packers were seen trudging along some distance from the fog of dust stirred up by the passing teams and wagons. If these packers traveled alone like John Root, or with only one or two companions, they had to find a safe place to sleep each night, and maybe they even had to beg for a meal. Sometimes their requests met with hostility. A diarist with a small wagon company complained: "We have a great many that call to stay all night. . . . Some propose paying, but they are mostly on the begging order and endeavor to pay by telling some great tale respecting the route."

There must have been many times along the Humboldt when Swain's determination to keep his diary faltered, when he questioned the value of reporting each day's advance, so much like the day before—more heat, dust and problems with the teams. He not only maintained his remarkable standard of informative reporting, he had the spirit, the energy of mind to appreciate and vividly describe scenes of beauty and moments when his thoughts carried him to Youngstown.

Other diarists persevered—scores, in fact, but few with Swain's care and style. Among the Rangers, James Pratt and Horace Ladd had written frequent letters while traveling east of Fort Laramie. But west of there they had no means of sending their reports back home, so they were silent. Two men who traveled close to the Rangers and sometimes camped with them, Dr. Joseph Middleton and Dr. Isaac Lord, both kept diaries and often mentioned the Michigan company. Another neighbor of the trail was J. Goldsborough Bruff who maintained one of the most detailed of all 1849 diaries. On September 9, Bruff told of visiting the Rangers' camp: "Conversed with some very respectable and intelligent people there. All well and looked so." On the 11th he reported that Captain Potts with two Rangers came to his camp and "very politely invited me to dine with them tomorrow should we noon near each other."

Aside from the back-home habit of sociability that survived their tiredness on the trail, the goldseekers visited each other's camps because they felt reassured when they could compare disappointments and problems and talk over the latest rumor about the trail up ahead or reports of Indian attacks. There was pleasure in walking over to a nearby camp to squat down by the evening fire and just get away from one's own campmates. In the course of the summer's nightly campsites, it was almost inevitable that a man would meet an acquaintance from his hometown or a fellow Hoosier, Buckeye, Badger or Green Mountain Boy. As one diarist put it: "Overtaken by our fellow townsman, M. P. Ewing. Not fond of him at home, but here the sight of a familiar face, even though doggish, is welcomed."

Camp visiting also allowed for trading to obtain what the cook did not have, or maybe there would be some singing with fiddle or banjo. But by September sounds of music were no longer common; instruments had been ruined by the heat and voices were too sorrowful for song.

Now and then one of the diarists in that long train of creaking wagons and sweating men scrawled a line that caught the pathos of it all. One such man recalled an evening when he was writing in his diary and one of his companions exclaimed: "My God, McKinstry, why do you write about this trip so you can remember it? All I hope is to get home alive as soon as possible so I can forget it!"

For all the misery along the upper Humboldt, staying alive was more assured than back at the outfitting towns or along the Platte. Cholera had long been forgotten; few men carried guns—in fact, most rifles had been thrown away. Mountain fever was far less common. Bowel complaints persisted, but there were few fatalities. Writing of one, a diarist told of an Indiana company which had stopped to dig a grave near the banks of the Humboldt. "I looked in one of the wagons and saw him still alive and smothered with dust and blankets. They buried him in a most inhuman manner, perhaps alive."

As the Rangers and other companies advanced down the Humboldt in mid-September, reports filtered back along the trail telling of the horrors suffered by wagon trains and packers crossing the desert south of the Sink, a marshy area where the Humboldt finally expired in the surrounding desolation. From the Sink two trails led across forty miles of absolute desert, one to the Carson River and along its banks to a pass through the Sierra Nevada and then down to California. The first goldseekers to reach the Sink in early July and those that followed throughout the month took the Carson route. By early August, news of suffering on that route caused most companies to try the other trail across the desert to the Truckee River, along its twisting course, over the Sierras and into the mining camps.

By mid-September when the Rangers were still some distance north of the Sink, the news that traveled back along the trail told in frightening detail what could be expected on the desert crossings: wagon wheels hubdeep in the hot sands, hundreds of oxen and mules too weak to move, left to rot with other carcasses in the blazing sun, men with lips cracked and tongues swollen begging for water. Halfway on the route to the Truckee a hot spring offered some surcease; not even boiling water relieved those on the crossing to the Carson.

With their teams sadly reduced in number and strength, the Rangers and others listened eagerly to more welcome news from up ahead: a new trail called Lassen's or Lawson's Cut-off led due west from the Humboldt, avoiding altogether the terrible desert. Furthermore, it was reported that on the cut-off "the Sierra Nevada Mountains could be crossed with but little difficulty, while on the other it was a work of great labor and some risk." Adding to their hopes and their uncertainties, they heard of another possible choice which Swain called "a middle route," to the Feather River in northern California, a distance of only 110 miles.

More confusion than knowledge circulated along the Humboldt. There were in fact three routes through the Sierra Nevada: the Carson, the Truckee, and Lassen's Cut-off which started fifty-eight miles north of the Sink. The first gold rush company to try the cut-off did so on August 11, by which time at least 15,000 goldseekers had already passed down the Humboldt. After the 11th, the frightening news from the south and the appeal of a cut-off caused most companies to take the new route.

By the second week of September, when the Rangers heard of Lassen's Cut-off, it had been traveled for a month. On September 14, one week before they reached the forks, Swain reported that Captain Potts had "decided to take Lawson's pass," believing it would lead in less than 200 miles to the Sacramento Valley.

Sick of the Humboldt, hopeful about the new trail and fearful of the old, the weary Rangers and other bedraggled companies pushed onward through the heat of September to the junction where the new trail promised an early arrival in the mines.

■

August 27, 1849. [At Steeple Rocks.] This morn we left camp early and ascended the hills through which the ravine leads. We had before us an extensive view of hills which promise a very rough road. The scenery has changed from that of yesterday to the accustomed rolling, gray, barren, bare, and desolate mountain hills. The country ahead is far lower than we are and appears to decline to the north. Along this morn's road the descent was stony and very steep and leads into Goose Creek valley.

[The road "would not have been practicable to any but a California emigrant. . . . The descents were frightful. . . . To look up at wagons coming down, it did not seem as if they could be held back. . . ." To slow the wagon's descent, "the hind wheels were chained, the wagons steadied with long ropes held by the men and thus prevented from sliding against the teams, which were scarcely able to retain a foothold on the rocks."]

We struck Goose Creek just at the junction of Goose and Muddy Creeks, where we nooned without feed for the teams. Our road along the valley after noon was very smooth. The creek is a hard stream, lined with willows. The feed is all eaten up.

We camped early, which was very pleasing to me as I was unwell. Feed bad. I am afflicted with pains in my chest.

August 28.   This morn I rode Mr. Hutchinson's pony in company with Mr. Rice and conversed with him about the Mormon settlements, where he had just been. ["Those who came by Salt Lake say that the celebration of the 24th of July by the Mormons {commemorating Brigham Young's arrival there in 1847} was a grand affair. All were invited, not less than five thousand dined, speeches were made, and all passed off glibly. . . . They are represented as cheerful and happy, possessing an abundance of the necessities of life. The climate is salubrious."]

At noon we passed some St. Louis boys, who have had their team stolen by the Indians. John stayed with them last night.

In the afternoon we passed through a canyon which was very narrow and high. The road was full of large fragments of rock, which made traveling a "slam jam" business and taken with the storm of wind which raised solid clouds of dust and filled the canyon, the afternoon's drive was a most horrid one.

["How times change and men change with them. We look in vain among the ragged, grave, and bronzed codgers dragging themselves wearily along for those dashing, sprightly, gay, young fellows full of song and laughter, whom we saw in the valley of the Blue and on the banks of the Platte two months ago."]

August 29.   We left camp in good season. Our poor, hungry, starved teams are fagged out by hard pulling without feed or water. [An ox belonging to another company "took it into his head to lie down in the middle of the road. . . . One man whipped him and another screwed his tail. That would not do, so he scraped it in two places till the blood came. That too had no effect. . . . Poor ox, he had done his best and his last."]

We arrived at the Warm Springs after a drive of seven miles across a barren lawn of sage. Here we expected to find feed for the teams but were obliged to drive till three o'clock down the valley of a spring stream, where we found poor feed.

[This valley, variously known as Warm, Hot, or Thousand Springs Valley, "is about thirty-five miles in length and varying in width from one to three miles. It is enclosed on both sides by a range of low mountains. . . ." Through the northern end of this valley the trail passed "marshes, sinks, ponds . . . alkaline water predominating. Some of these springs are cool and remarkable, and some are warm springs in soft, elevated mounds surrounded with wet turf, very dangerous for animals."]

I am unwell from the cause before mentioned, which has changed to a severe pain and intense heat in the forepart of my head and eyes, assuming the character of mountain fever. I am also afflicted with severe pains in the small of my back. . . .

This morning I left camp on the pony ahead of the train. We were in a large mountain plain. It was early. The sun had just risen above the eastern range of brown and rolling hills and his morning rays lit up the sky along our morning track. . . . The elements appeared lulled to perfect tranquillity, and the resemblance of the morn to our Indian summer brought fresh to my mind those days, that home with its relatives and its friends. I can but think of happy hours spent in their society at my peaceful and happy home. I have thought much of my wife and child lately, and it appears hard to be deprived of their society so long, and it is still worse to be sick here on these desolate plains, deprived of any intelligence of them for months, and maybe my life will not be spared to benefit them by this tour.

We left the Warm Springs valley at sundown and traveled across plains of sage with some low hills till ten o'clock, when we camped on the banks of a dry creek without water for the teams and only dry grass.

August 30.   We had a good level road and found water at ten o'clock, where we watered the teams with the pails. We entered the Hot Springs valley at eleven. Feed appears better and water is occasionally found in the bottom of the stream.

Nooned on tolerable feed. Afternoon, had a good, smooth road. At night found good feed, and there is a running stream in Hot Springs Creek.

August 31.   Left camp early and traveled along the valley. Passed excellent feed, and at ten o'clock we arrived at the Hot Springs which covered an area of three acres. ["Clouds of steam rise from the surface and this is seen some distance before you reach the springs."]

I tried to hold my finger in these springs, but found them of the heat of boiling water and was obliged to take it out instantly. The stream running from them is large enough for a millstream, and at one half mile distant is hot enough to boil eggs. The water possesses chemicals, and it is probably their union or disunion which causes the heat.

We left the head of the valley at six o'clock and crossed a ridge to the Humboldt Springs, where we arrived at eleven at night. Here we had good water, but the teams fared hard as all the feed had been eaten up.

September 1.　　Today traveled down the Humboldt Springs valley. Found good feed at noon. Corralled early in good feed for Sabbath. I am still unwell, unable to do duty.

[Scattered through this valley were numerous springs or "wells," in which the water was "several feet below the surface and the bottoms so deep as to be invisible." At the western end of this cluster of springs "a grassy and willowy rivulet" traced its course through the plains of sand and sage. This was the headwaters of the Humboldt River, a watercourse "long looked forward to and which seemed, when we left home, to be at the outer edge of Nowhere."]

September 2.　　Sabbath. In camp. Men and animals recruiting and en-joying a rest from so hard a tour. Attended preaching by Mr. Moore at two o'clock.

We have determined to travel nights going down the Humboldt. We started tonight at six o'clock. Being unwell, I rode in the wagon.

[The sweltering heat of the desert sun and the fading strength of their teams caused other companies to resort to night traveling along the Humboldt. During the day the men tried to sleep in the shade of the wagons and tents, while the animals grazed on patches of withered grass. Then in the coolness of evening the teams were hitched up and the advance continued through "the sterile, barren and sandy plains grown over with nought but wild sage."

[Two and three men "often struck out ahead of the trains to avoid the dust." Two of the Rangers—the Reverend Mr. Moore and a compan-ion—followed this procedure. They "would serve supper to the men and start out walking ahead of the train, a man being able to go much faster than the train could move. At about ten o'clock they would lie down by the roadside, get a good sleep, then overtake the train in camp and cook the men's breakfast."]

September 3.　　This morn we find ourselves on the Humboldt, which is here a good creek lined with willows. ["It is too deep to wade, with little current, keeping mostly near the center of its valley, which varies from two to five miles in width, bounded by rocky, dismal and barren hills. . . ."]

We lay in camp, the men sleeping and the teams eating and resting. [Many emigrants "never tie up their bedclothes [to air] in the daytime but sleep in them with their clothing on and often in the daytime, either in wagons or in tents. It is astonishing to contemplate how many millions of living creatures must be emigrating to California in close contact and partnership with these human beings."]

Started at six. Cold night. Crossed a fine stream, probably the main northern stream or branch. Came twenty miles.

September 4. [This morning the Reverend Mr. Moore and his companion told "how the Indians had shot at them last night. Captain Potts advised them to keep with the wagons, but a good many of the men made fun of their story and joked at them."]

We are camped on the river, where there is plenty of willows for the teams to get lost in. Sage hens are flying in all directions, one of which I shot on the wing. We intend to have a pot pie. ["These birds are the size of a chicken and have much the color and appearance about the head of a guinea fowl. They are very fat and tender, and certainly are the greatest of all delicacies."]

We had a late start on account of losing some of the teams in the willows. The road during the night was rough, yet we drove fast and made twenty miles.

September 5. All sleeping to indemnify for last night's lack of sleep. Feed is bad. The stream is here quite a fine creek.

Today quite an excitement in camp on account of news from California by a train of Mormons. ["Eight wagons, several women and children, and plenty of stock, among them some very fine California horses. . . ."] They state that the feed is bad for forty miles, then good for six days' travel; that we must cut hay at the Sink to feed [the teams while crossing the desert] to Salmon Trout [Truckee] River; that there is good feed over the mountains; that the gold diggings are as good as ever; that prices of all articles in California are lower; and that steamers are now running [from San Francisco up the Sacramento River to Sacramento City].

["Every emigrant feels an increased anxiety at this stage of the trip to hear some account from the gold mines, by which he may judge whether or not he is to receive any recompense for the toils he is enduring."]

Left camp late. Traveled slow through a canyon. We moved on over a steep sandy hill. Deep dust.

September 6.   We are three miles above the South Fork of the Humboldt.*

All asleep, as is all Nature. The sun is very hot, the country perfectly a desert. ["The heat is fiery, intense, sultry, oppressive, suffocating, parching and scorching the earth, air, water, and everything green— Californians included."]

We made a start at seven o'clock [P.M.] and traveled along in dust, or rather volcanic ashes, from six to twelve inches deep and light as mist, filling the air with clouds which enveloped the teams, wagons, and men, making the traveling most horrid. This same difficulty we have found along the whole of this valley, and we are getting disgusted with this dirty, dusty, tedious killing of time. We find none but dry feed, and that has been used up by the emigration preceding us.

In the latter part of the night we struck a ravine and followed it to the river, where we arrived at nine o'clock [A.M.].

September 7.   [During the night drive "an ox fell down in the yoke and had to be left. Another dropped this morning. . . ."

["There is not a particle of dew or moisture on the grass in this valley in the mornings. . . . At sunrise all the long grass and rushes are as dry as if it were noon. . . . The grass here is very scarce, and the cattle have to spread out and stroll to great distances and prowl into the labyrinths of willows on the river banks and bottoms. As a consequence it is very difficult and laborious to get them together, and often they cannot all be found. Then the emigrant immediately says that the Diggers have stolen them. This may be true or it may not, but it is asserted."]

Resting the teams. Men sleeping. Mr. Hutchinson talks of packing. ["The heat today greater than yesterday. Not a living thing to be seen at twelve noon, except what belonged to the trains. The lizards disappeared and the ants, which usually run over one by the dozens every time you lie down on the ground."]

Started late on account of hunting cattle in willows. Rolled out at dark and traveled till eleven o'clock and stopped on a sand bank to rest the teams. Had supper at twelve. Pitched tent and slept till late, when we

---

* *This stream marked an important point on the trail to California. Here the Donner party on September 30, 1846, finally reached the main trail along the Humboldt after four weeks of suffering on Hastings' Cut-off, which had led them west from Salt Lake City across the Great Salt Desert.*

    In 1849, few gold rush companies dared to take this infamous cut-off; a surprising number faced its challenge in 1850.

were called to take an ox out of the mire at nine. ["The river is very winding . . . with dangerous sloughs and lagoons. . . . They are impassable, and cattle are often mired in them and even go over-head in them."]

September 8.   Hunted cattle till nine o'clock [P.M.] and then rolled out of camp down the valley. Found feed and camped to stay till tomorrow night.

Tonight Mr. Hutchinson called a meeting to make proposals to leave the company and to pay us $15 for [release from] his services to California. Rejected. A motion [was then passed] to allow him and all who wish to, to leave by signing over their interest in the company stock to the Company, whereupon Mr. H. rejected the offer. Nine others accepted it and are going to pack.

I watched the cattle tonight.

September 9.   Sabbath. Got to camp late from watching the cattle and found all ready for breakfast. Washed today.

Today we let one of our wagons go to Mr. Ottaway to take through to California, to be delivered to us when he gets through. We have unloaded another and are going to yoke up the poor, loose cattle and draw along the empty wagon with them. This arrangement breaks up one mess and gives us six yokes of oxen to put on with the other teams.

Started at six o'clock and traveled till twelve. Had supper and started at one. This night driving is hard upon both men and beast. It is hard but honest.

September 10.   This morning in camp twenty miles from yesterday's camp. Tolerable feed. All sleeping. ["Our grass has been wretched for some time back. . . . It is a matter of astonishment that our cattle can live, much less work, on apparently no grass."]

This afternoon the nine packers left camp at four o'clock. ["They each took about twenty-five or thirty pounds of provisions and one blanket." Two of the packers, Oliver Goldsmith and Almon Frary, had complained of "marching by night" and not being able to sleep by day. They set out each with a pony to carry their packs.]

Started late and had to leave the captain to find six oxen that could not be found this evening.

September 11.   Traveled eighteen miles last night. Our teams are wearing out fast, but we find good feed among the willows along the river. The captain arrived with the oxen at four o'clock [P.M.].

September 12.   Last night eighteen miles.

By neglecting to keep it daily because of sickness, I have made a mistake in keeping my journal.*

Tonight we could not find four of the oxen, and one of the men has got lost hunting among the willows. After having the teams all hitched up, we are obliged to turn the cattle into the corral and to stay here till morning. As this will probably end our night driving, I am glad of it.

The man came in at nine o'clock [P.M.] with two of the cattle. The poor fellow had lost his course in the dark and had been driving over the river, back and forward, some seven times.

September 13.   This morn while getting up the cattle, the men saw a catamount, but as they had no firearms with them they allowed the fellow to go off unmolested.

Left camp this morning at eight o'clock and traveled until eleven, when the weather became rainy and finally turned into a hard rain and hailstorm. It is the first rain of any account since we had the big hailstorm on the Platte River [June 20]. The mountains appear dusky and dim, the clouds assume the aspect of winter, and the air, filled with mist and smoky duskness, is chilly. The winds are cold and the nights cold, especially towards morning. Our cloth tents are poor habitation in such weather.

The river here is nothing more than a mud ditch winding through the alluvial deposit of the valley in the most crooked course that could be marked out for it. The water is considerably alkali, but quite clear. . . .

Sixteen miles.

September 14.   Last night our teams had good feed, and this morn we left camp at eight and a half and rolled along down the valley, which has the same appearance as heretofore. The mountains are still very high, steep, and are more broken and cragged. The day is very cloudy and thick coats are necessary to comfort. The air is very dusky and the mountains are dimly seen through the smoky atmosphere.

Today one of our teams gave out and I was obliged to drive along with two yoke of oxen.

My health, which has been poor for some time past, is getting better; and I am better than for weeks past, but still not very well.

The afternoon was rainy and misty, and oil clothes were worn. Hare

---

* *Swain refers to a chronological mix-up. He had dated his September 13 entry the 12th, then crossed it out, redated it the 13th and squeezed in a new entry for the 12th. The confusion has been corrected.*

and rabbits are frequently seen, and duck are found along the river. The stream is still losing itself in the sand and is this evening no larger than a good creek.

Our captain has decided to take Lawson's [Lassen's] pass through the mountains, which leads us into the upper part of the Sacramento valley by a gradual ascent like the South Pass. The valley is less than two hundred miles from here [via that route], but there is seventy miles of road without feed, and we will have to cut hay to take along for the cattle.

About five o'clock we found a place to cut hay and camped to stay two days. We had a fine scene at sunset: the clouds were broken and settled on the tops of the mountains, and in the rays of the setting sun they were gilded most brilliantly.

September 15. The camp is preparing slowly to commence haying. We find that most of our cattle have the "hollow horn" and we have corralled them and all hands are engaged in boring their horns, cutting tails, and currying the teams.

[The full treatment for this undefined but common ailment was described by another diarist: "Bore the horn and put in salt, pepper and water until it runs out of their noses. For another disease called 'hollow-tail,' we split the tail where it is hollow."]

At noon we commenced haying with four scythes in wild grass which would turn one and a half tons to the acre. By night we had cut and spread out to dry enough and more than we could take. The day was a fine hay day. Here in this pleasant spot of rich marsh with haying going on, the men all around the marsh with forks and rakes and scythes in hand, little swallows skimming over the new-mown hay, the herds of cattle scattered over the lawn with bells tinkling, and the smoke rising from numerous encampments along the river, we present a rural appearance, one so familiar in civilized lands that it brings fresh to mind the familiar scenes of our happy homes far away in the habited parts of creation. May those homes and dear ones there still be alive and happy. The scene contrasts badly with the barren plains and mountains and shows up the grayish sage and bare sand hills in their true character of barrenness, desolation, and dreariness. I find that swinging the scythe is healthy work still, and I feel well this evening after having swung it almost all afternoon.

Our teams are luxuriating, but we have great trouble to drag them out of the mire holes.

September 16. Sabbath. This forenoon the committee on which I am chosen and whose business it is to report to the company upon the reports of the Agents and Directors met and spent the forenoon in examining its papers and making out its report. We recommend a reception of J. D. Potts', James Pratt's, H. Ladd's, and F. Cook's reports, and a rejection of Thomas Rawson's and R. Hobart's reports and of the report of the Directors, for reasons set forth in our report.*

Afternoon, gathered hay and got ready to make our last push for the Sierra Nevada. We learn today that there is a middle route, which leads to the head of the Feather River and brings us to that stream in one hundred and ten miles. Our camp is talking of taking that route.

This afternoon a train camped by us in which there is a family of eight brothers with their mother with them. One of the brothers had his family of five small children and his wife.** She has been sick since she left the Kansas River and is now supposed to be struck with death. She has her rational mind and is a professor of religion, in the hope of which she is happy in death. She sent a request to Mr. Moore to preach at their camp this evening, and he complied with the request. Most of our company went over and attended the service. The elder stood by the side of the dying woman and among her five children, while he conducted the worship and spoke from Deuteronomy, thirty-third chapter and twenty-eighth verse: "The Almighty is thy refuge and underneath are the everlasting arms." The circumstances affected the speaker much, and altogether it was an affecting and solemn scene.

September 17. Last night was cold—ice an inch thick in the wash basin. The day is clear and the sun shines out warm. The lady in the neighboring camp is no more.

We left camp at eight o'clock with cheerful spirits, hoping soon to see an end of this tedious and monotonous journey. If we take the middle pass [Truckee River], a week will bring us over the mountains; and if the northern [Lassen's Cut-off], two weeks will do it. And then, Ho! for the gold!

The roads are very dusty and heavy and some sandy. Feed is tolerable good. The valley is narrow, the mountains low. The weather is fine in day, but cold nights. I feel quite well today, better than for three months past.

---

* *None of the papers, reports, or records survive; they were formally burned by the Rangers on October 14, 1849. See Chapter IX, p. 277.*
** *The rarity of women and children should be emphasized once again. The fact that women and children will be seen more frequently, and mentioned especially on Lassen's Cut-off, reveals the sad fact that they had fallen farther and farther to the rear, so that they made up a disproportionate percentage of emigrants in September and October.*

We made sixteen miles and camped where there was plenty of dry willows to make fires, a great pile of which I brought to camp.

September 18.   I am herdsman today and had a fine tramp after the cattle. Our camp is in fine health and spirits.

We left camp early and traveled along the valley. The road is heavy, full of pitch-holes, and jerks the teams considerably. We had to double teams to raise a hill this forenoon. The road . . . along the river bottom . . . is worn from one to two feet deep by the large amount of travel on the route. It is six inches deep with dust and full of ruts, all of which makes it bad traveling.

The flats of the river, unlike those of other rivers, grow smaller as they approach its termination. Here, twenty miles from the forks of the northern [Lassen's Cut-off] and southern [via "the Sink"] routes, the flats are no more than one-half to one-quarter mile wide. The plains are perfect deserts on which nothing but the desolate wild sage grows, together with some small greasewood.

September 19.   This morn we left camp at eight o'clock, and our road lay along the bottoms. The early morning was cold, and while I was herding, the frost made my hands ache. But the day as usual will be hot. This valley of cold nights and hot days will soon be among "the things that were" with us, as today is our last day's travel in it. We expect to come to the forks of the road today, when we shall make our debut for the mountains. It will be a hard tramp, but let it come, the sooner the better.

Our noon halt is on a flat with nothing but dry feed. ["The sand hills, wind-piled and seamed with chasms, glitter in unrelieved barren-ness. The river stands still in sluggish mudbanks . . . the sky is of copper or brass . . . the whole is a scene of unmixed, stark, Saharian desolation."]

We encamped on the river flat at sundown, having made twelve miles. The feed was among the willows and the willow boughs them-selves. They are green and the cattle like them, but they are bad feed as they scour the cattle.

I was herding till eight o'clock when the night guard was set and I released.

[Despite the posting of night guards by most companies, "scarcely a night passes without the Diggers making a raid upon some camp. . . . If they cannot drive the animals off, they creep up behind the sage bushes in the night and shoot arrows into them, so that the animals have to be left. . . . During the night it is a common practice for those on duty to discharge their firearms frequently, to show the Digger banditti that they are on the alert. . . ."

["These fellows are really the Arabs of America. They are thieves, nothing conciliates them and no amount short of *all* will satisfy them. Their hand is against every man, and every man's hand will be against them." "They are seldom seen on or near the road but keep themselves concealed during the day and in the night leave their ambush and sally forth in search of plunder. . . . Passed several wagons that had lost their stock by the Indians and were unable to pursue their journey."]

September 20.   We left camp at eight. The road led five miles across the bluffs but was partly marl and not so bad as most of the bluff roads.

Such a thing as a tree I have not seen since we struck this Humbug River, which is nothing more than a ditch with bottoms in the shape of oxbows, through which a good-sized creek runs.

We nooned without feed and traveled across another bluff till four o'clock, when we struck the river flat and camped one and a half miles from the forks. We are a little disappointed in not finding these forks sooner, but in the morning our first steps will be towards the Sierra. We have no feed, or but little for the teams tonight.

I bathed this evening in the river, which is very cold, to try to wash off the alkali dust which eats our skin and makes us itch and scratch dreadfully.

[" 'A man can get used to anything' is an old saying, the truth of which is pretty clearly demonstrated on this journey. . . . We have seen a man eating his lunch gravely sitting on the carcass of a dead horse. And we frequently take our meals amidst the effluvia of a hundred putrescent carcasses. . . ." "We see some of the most grotesque figures, living caricatures of the human species, some of them mounted on poor, dusty looking mules, others on miserable looking worn down horses, all dressed in dusty, ragged clothes, as most of us are." "Well, they say misery loves company, so we can have some enjoyment after all, for there is plenty of that kind of company here."]

Back Home

*"O, my dear William, when I contem-
plate my loneliness and your absence I am
ready to exclaim: 'Would to God you had
never left me,' for what is gold in comparison to my constant anxieties. . . ."*

Youngstown, September 19, '49

My dear beloved Husband,

The time has again arrived which announces to me the pleasure of
addressing you, my dear friend and husband. It is now seven o'clock.
Mother has just come home from Mr. Hall's and is now getting Sis to
sleep so that I can have a chance to write. Sis has been very unwell all
day, and I have scarcely had her out of my arms. I am in hopes it is
nothing more than teething. She has got three double teeth, and her eye
teeth are very badly swollen. She grows and appears to be very well,
except for her teeth. She tries to talk a great deal and some words she
speaks very plainly. She continues to be quite restless nights yet.

Mother's health is better than it was last winter, notwithstanding she
is quite feeble and often wishes she could see you. . . .

My health is some better than it has been through the summer,
although it is very far from being good. My back troubles me very much
yet. As to my mind, it is rather more at rest as far as anxieties concerning
yourself, which have been relieved very much by hearing from you on
your long and tedious journey more often than I expected. Your last letter
was received on the 10th [of September], dated the 4th [of July].

As to the loss of your society, I feel it more keenly the longer you
are away and feel as though I could not wait for the time to come around
when I shall again see you. O! may it prove to be a good lesson to us
both; may it teach us to place our confidence in Christ and to lean upon
Him for guidance and protection, and may I learn better to appreciate
your worth and society and be better qualified to fill the place of a wife.

O, my dear William, when I contemplate my loneliness and your
absence I am ready to exclaim: "Would to God you had never left me,"
for what is gold in comparison to my constant anxieties of mind, which
must necessarily be, considering the length of your journey and the dan-

gers and hardships you must constantly be exposed to. My dear, does not your mind often revert to the scenes of home and friends and the many pleasant hours spent in one another's society?

It is now ten o'clock and I must retire by bidding you good night and pleasant dreams.

Good Morning, William—

We have just got through with our breakfast, and I now have time to finish my letter. We are well as usual and Sis is better than yesterday. Two deaths of cholera at the fort yesterday, soldiers. There have been two or three deaths amongst the citizens of Lewiston and one in the east part of town. It is as a general thing abating. As to myself, I have no fear of cholera but often think of you, as you are amongst it.

I want to get hold of that journal of yours very much and get a full account of that storm [of June 20]. I feel as though there was a Providence in it. We would naturally think that the whole train would have been destroyed. John Root did not mention it. Mr. Bailey spoke of it as being beyond description. Tell Mr. Bailey I often see Mrs. Bailey, and she appears to enjoy herself tolerably well, but with the rest counts the time long.

Ozro [Sabrina's brother] was in here a few minutes ago and wishes to be remembered to you, as do all our folks. All the people around appear to have a great deal of anxiety about you and want to know the news whenever we receive a letter.

I often dream about you, but cannot have any satisfaction, for you treat me with disdain.

Now William, it is time to put this in the office; I shall write you again by the next steamer.

Take good care of yourself and do not overdo, *is* the sincere wishes of your affectionate wife,

Sabrina Swain

Youngstown, September 20, 1849

Dear William,

We are threshing today and I steal a moment from the barn to drop you a line, and but a line. . . . The men are calling me. . . .

You will see by the four papers I sent you yesterday that Hungary is crushed and political freedom is almost ruined in Europe. Russia is *the Monster* power of Europe now. If she is saucy, she may unite Western

40

William Swain Esq
Sutters Fort
    on American River
        California

Youngstown Sept 20th 1849

Dear William

We are threshing to day & I steal a moment
from the barn to drop you a line & but a line. We are all well
& doing well.— Mother Sabrina & little Sis are better
I think than when you we wrote last. the men are
calling me, but they may do as they can till I get there
We wrote last month on 24th & started it on the 25 & the Falcon
left N.Y. on the 27th so that it did not probably get off with that
mail. we want to be in time this month.
Everything as usual You will see by L. papers I sent
you yesterday that the Cholera has almost subsided
No one has died in Youngstown. 8 soldiers have died at
the fort. Political matters in all kinds of fix Barnbur
ners have united with old Hunkers. Administration
still making removals. Race is to have Ported place &
I am to take Babcocks our nominations was sent to
Washington & will be here in a day or two. I have
almost done seeding. I sowed on the 25 Aug. & 6 & 7
Sept— I shall sow 4 or 5 a. more corn & buckwheat ground
I shall then have some 20 acres in. We may have 8 to 40
bu. Winter apples, not more. No oats a little corn & Buck
Enough potatoes for ourselves. Wheat is now $1.00 pr bu
first quality & down to 75c for shrunk corn 30c Barley 50c
oats 25c Peaches $1.50 to $2.00 Apples 25 to 50c.
You will see by th papers that Hungary is crushed

Europe against her. We have had a bit of a stir in relation to Cuba, but it is all smoke. General Taylor makes a good executive so far. . . .

Give my respects to Messrs. Hutchinson, Bailey, and Root. And in your letters home, we want each of you to tell about all the others, so that if only one letter gets here we shall hear from you all by name. . . .

Your affectionate brother,
George Swain

Mother sends her best love to Will.

CHAPTER VIII

Meeting the Summit

*"Every nerve seems to be sprained, so that
I feel I will be an old man from this time
on."*

They had tried Sublette's and Hudspeth's cut-offs, and now a third hoped-for short-cut required a choice. If they stayed with the old trail, south along the Humboldt River, they would come to the Sink, where the river expired in a vast slough surrounded by a desert. Crossing that desert to the Carson or Truckee rivers was the great danger and the source of stories of dreadful suffering and of death. To avoid that danger they could leave the Humboldt and head west on the new route, Lassen's (or Lawson's) Cut-off, which according to reports promised arrival in the diggings in just ten days.

Prior to August 11, the thousands of sweaty, grumbling goldseekers had all followed the only route they knew—south to the Sink. After that date the newly opened cut-off lured almost every wagon company and backpacker. At least 10,000 entered one of the most formidable desert-mountain regions in all the West. Why did they make this choice which so dramatically and sadly changed not only the course but the well-being of the emigration?

Certainly what was known about the old versus what was hoped for the new played the major role. But there were other influences. The first company that turned off from the river to follow faint west-heading wagon tracks was captained by Milton McGee, a man who had helped to pioneer trails to California in 1843 and thus in 1849 had a reputation for knowing how to get there. His wagons were immediately followed on August 11 by other companies, and when a few days later Benoni Hudspeth's company chose to follow the cut-off, the new route gained an

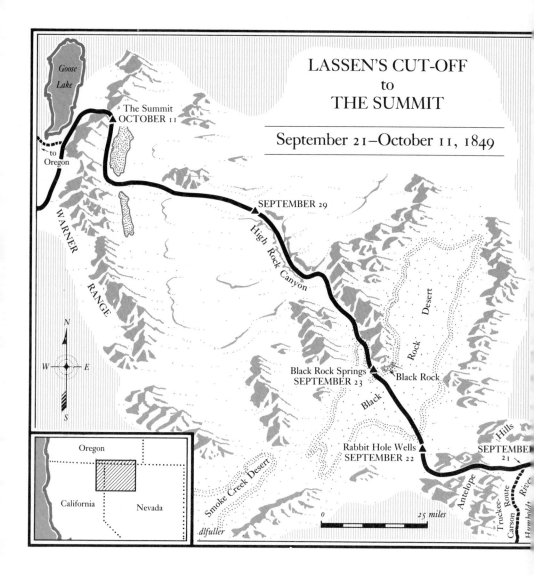

important confidence-building endorsement. But the truth was that the first company to take the cut-off on August 11 and the last in the darkening days of October did not know where or how far they would travel to reach California.

Most companies paused at the forks to read notices posted on sticks or to fish through the barrel of notes and letters left by those who had passed days and weeks earlier, some warning against, most strongly favoring the cut-off. The forks became a meeting place where each day wagon companies and men with only packs on their backs stopped to talk, standing amid wagons and animals, trying to learn the news from those ahead, questioning, arguing which way to go. Nearby, the Humboldt River meandered southward, promising at least a source of water, while the wheel tracks westward led through scrawny sage toward dust-colored hills in the distance. Clearly this was a moment of final choice. Without maps, with only rumors and guesses as to distances, they had to choose between the old trail with its well-reported suffering and the new trail with its promise of a quick arrival in the diggings. Anxiety, impatience and the sight of wagon after wagon starting out on the cut-off shaped the decision for most men standing on that bleak plain.

More than most of them, William Swain had a sense of the geography and history of the West. Time and again his reading of Frémont and his interest since childhood in western themes had helped him that summer of 1849 to know the rivers, mountains and passes. As the Rangers started on Lassen's Cut-off leading into the most desolate of all the wilderness they had crossed, Swain's reference to "a middle route" to the head of the Feather River in California must be remembered, for he makes anguished mention of it later; and such a middle or left-hand (to the west) route was clearly the expectation of McGee, Hudspeth, Potts and other captains that sustained them while moving ever farther and farther north.

The Wolverine Rangers' oxen pulled their wagons onto the broad, dusty cut-off Friday morning, September 21, 1849. Certainly each of those fifty-six men had thought on leaving home that they would be "in the diggings" by that date. For Swain this would be the 163rd day since he had left his farm. And yet he, Bailey, Hutchinson and their friends from Michigan found themselves with the fearful Sierra Nevada waiting for them somewhere to the west. Even if the cut-off proved to be as direct as advertised, they would still have to cross the mountain barrier in the late fall. And already the cold nights warned of worse weather ahead.

Cracking their whips, goading their gaunt oxen, the Rangers rolled west from the forks, other companies following close behind. The first water oozed to the surface at Antelope Springs, a tiny spot of green in the rough desert country. Nineteen miles to the north, they came to the next water at Rabbit Hole Wells or Springs (named in 1846 by Oregon pioneers because scores of rabbit tracks led to this meager source of water). A few miles farther on, the trail dropped down from the hills to Black Rock Desert, a vast naked plain, its dirty-white surface baked hard by the sun, cracked and crusty. To the west, beyond this level whiteness, rose the craggy outline of Black Rock, where water could be found, more than twenty miles away.

The crossing of Black Rock Desert would never be forgotten. Both sides of the trail were lined with swollen carcasses, equipment piled and scattered, skeletons of burned wagons, wagons pushed off the trail and toppled over, wagons left in line where they had been unhitched from teams driven ahead for water.

Each day through September and into October the emigrants widened the trail, seeking to escape the sights and smells of death, only to leave a parallel fringe of wagons and dead or dying animals.

To save their oxen from the baking heat of day, the Wolverine Rangers decided to make the grim crossing at night. Their wagon wheels crunching through the brittle crust, each mess moved ahead at its own pace, and in the darkness Captain Potts lost contact with his company. In the confusion Swain took charge of the desperate effort to reach water at Black Rock. This harrowing desert passage and Swain's sense of pride and relief in having made the right decision in leading the Rangers are poignantly reported in his diary. He tells as well of his realization that instead of finding a "left-hand route" (a middle trail to the west as expected), they were traveling ever more to the north and thus away from California—in fact toward Oregon. But in the crisis of getting most of the wagons and teams across the twenty miles of desolation and rescuing other Rangers marooned on the desert, there was no time to debate or to explore.

Later with the torments of the desert behind them and revived at Black Rock by the boiling water that cooled in a nearby swamp, Swain and the Rangers could only move on; it was too late to turn back to the Humboldt Trail. They continued on the cut-off, north through a sheer-walled canyon, farther north around a dry lake bed, until at last they began the ascent of the Sierra Nevada, which rose dark and misty above them.

Swain not only survived the miles of struggle and disappointment, he had the energy and curiosity on September 30 to take "a mountain tramp" up to a high place where he could see far ranges and peaks that "exceeded" anything he had seen in the Rocky Mountains. He continued to write in his diary every day, entries that were descriptive, often dramatic, sometimes personal. One night he crawled into his bedroll "and for a moment my little girl, and my big one too, filled my mind with pleasing recollections."

It is a marvel that he persevered in his writings, day after day. Probably by now he did so for Sabrina, so that she would one day know, mile by mile, how he had faced so many challenges and had prevailed. Indeed, as if inspired by adversity, Swain recorded the days and nights on Lassen's Cut-off with more detail, more concern for the other Rangers and for the human scene around him than in all the weeks before.

All the Rangers persevered, even finding time to fuss with reports from their officers. On October 2 Swain tells of "making a report upon the Directors' Report"! Equally in character, they finally began to dump along the trail the kind of heavy gear everyone else had long ago discarded. Swain reports that the "company voted to throw away the blacksmith tools and many other articles which we can do without." They voted first, and then unloaded. A rare company.

A different kind of unloading took place in the camps of a few other companies. Graves were dug to hide valued possessions carefully packed and wrapped; then the gravesites were closed with rocks and headboards were placed on top stating the name and date of persons who had "died." Several such graves were noted on Lassen's Cut-off. These caches both evidenced the remarkable optimism of Californians who thought they would and could come back to such a wilderness and retrieve their possessions and attested to the ingrained materialism of these easterners who carried with them the values of home.

Ice an inch thick in the morning, wolves howling at night, dark clouds looming over the mountain peaks—signs of winter that warned the Rangers and all the other rag-tag goldseekers that they must hurry. But there was no strength for hurrying, scarcely enough for slow plodding ahead.

On October 11 the Rangers started their climb to a pass that would lead through a range of mountains with peaks up to 10,000 feet high. Like all the companies ahead of them, the Rangers thought they were about to reach the summit of the famed and feared Sierra Nevada—in fact they faced a separate massif known today as the Warner Range. By the time the Rangers started their ascent, at least 20,000 other goldseekers had completed their journeys and were camped in the gold regions, having followed the Carson or Truckee trails. By October 11 many of them had been at work as miners for several weeks, even for months. And some had already experienced the satisfaction of sending gold to their families back in the states.

The Rangers knew nothing of such good fortune. Lured by the promise of a short route from the Humboldt into California, they would spend the last week of September and all of October pushing, hauling, cursing their way over the terrible miles of Lassen's Cut-off.

■

September 21, 1849. [Near the start of Lassen's Cut-off.] Left camp in good season and soon passed the forks. [From the forks "the two trails or roads are broad and as well beaten as any traveled thoroughfare can be. . . . In the forks of the road . . . a red-painted barrel stands. . . . It is a nice, new barrel, about the size of a whiskey barrel with iron hoops and a square hole cut in the head; and neatly painted in black, block letters upon it, 'POST OFFICE'. . . . It is half full of letters, notes, notices, etc. Near this is a stick and billboard, also filled with notices. These notices are chiefly directed to emigrants in the rear, hurrying them along, giving information about routes, telling who had taken this or the southern route."]

Commenced the tramp over the desert, and desert it is truly, not a spear of anything but stunted sage no more than a foot high which grows in the spring to wither in the summer.

[Across this sun-cracked plain "people are driving their poor, exhausted cattle . . . and when they lie down from exhaustion, they will sometimes wait awhile for them to rest. At other times they will beat them or split the skin on their tails or set a dog on them if they have one, or go through all these operations in succession, and if the poor creatures can bear all these operations without moving, then they are abandoned. This has been . . . and continues to be a daily occurrence."]

At noon we fed hay, without water.

[Toward evening the Rangers entered a ravine leading through the sterile, rugged hills now known as the Antelope Mountains.]

Arrived at some springs at eight o'clock in the evening, where we got a scanty supply of water for ourselves and teams. [These three springs, a few hundred yards apart, "are mere drippings, percolating from small clay cliffs in the hollow slope of the mountain. Travelers had dug out hollow reservoirs below each spring, which, filling, enable the animals to drink."]

We fed the teams heartily with hay, had our suppers, wrapped ourselves in our blankets and buffalo skins, and lay down in and under the wagons to sleep. But I slept none, as the boys were making noises in watering their teams. Fourteen miles today.

September 22 [and 23]. We rose from under the wagons, hitched on the teams, and started at three o'clock, and by daylight we had raised by a gradual rise to the top of the mountain. The descent was gradual into a mountain vale, where we arrived at eight o'clock and halted to feed and get breakfast. This over, we commenced the ascent of a long hill gradually rising over the top of a low range, beyond which appear high, cragged

Rabbit Hole Wells or Springs, as drawn by Bruff on September 20.
The Rangers passed here two days later.

mountains looming to a great height in the smoky atmosphere, though it
is clearer here than on the Humboldt. From the top of the low range our
road lay along a descending canyon all the way to the springs, or Rabbit
Hole Wells, which were nineteen miles from the springs in the side of the
mountain.

We arrived at the Wells at four o'clock, where we stopped to water
and feed meal and the last of the hay. We supped here and waited for
those of our wagons which had not kept up with the train.

[One of the Rangers wrote of Rabbit Hole Wells: "I had associated
with the name 'wells' a vision of an oasis—verdure, trees, and cooling
water. The whole environment as far as the eye could reach was simply
an abomination of desolation . . . ash heaps of hills into which slowly
percolated filthy-looking, brackish water. More than half the wells were
unavailable as they were filled with the carcasses of cattle which had
perished in trying to get water. To add to the natural horrors of the scene,
about the wells were scattered the bodies of cattle, horses, and mules
which had died here from overwork, hunger, and thirst; broken and
abandoned wagons, boxes, bundles of clothing, guns, harness, or yokes,
anything and everything that the emigrant had outfitted with." "Two of
these springs were about four feet apart. In one was a dead ox, swelled
up so as to fill the hole closely, his hind legs and tail only above ground.
Not far from this was another spring similarly filled. There was scarcely

space for the wagons to reach the holes because of the ox carcasses. . . .
Here and there around the other springs in an area of one tenth of a mile
. . . eighty-two dead oxen, two dead horses, and one mule. Of course,
the effluvia was anything but agreeable."]

At eight o'clock [P.M.] some packers came up and informed us that
the teams behind were camped on the top of the hill which we had raised
in the morning. On hearing this we determined to go on to Muddy Creek,
which we supposed was seven miles ahead and where we supposed we
should find feed, as those behind would not come up till morning. We
rolled out of camp, all but one mess, at half past eight.

The moon was some two hours high, the night cold with a fresh
wind blowing from the northeast. Our cattle walked quickly along and
our train moved more gaily than for weeks past. Our Captain and Mr.
Hutchinson went ahead prospecting, and after two hours' travel we expected every fire ahead was the end of our tramp for the night. But no
Captain was found. I had observed that our course through the day was
northwest, and in the night it was nearly north. We found no left-hand

Looking west across Black Rock Desert on September 21, two days ahead of the Rangers.

[middle] route, although we were twenty-five miles past the point where we expected to find one.

After traveling till midnight, I pointed out our course to Mr. Bailey by calling his attention to the North Star. I told him my convictions were that we were on Lawson's road to Oregon and that we had to make seventy-five miles of desert; as we were then forty miles on the desert. If we could make ten miles by daylight by pressing forward, we would be safe, for by eight o'clock we should find water. But those teams behind were gone-for if they could not cross the desert. My surmise proved true. So strong were my convictions that this was the fact and that we should cross successfully that I fairly triumphed over the feelings of danger around me, and no part of the journey has been more pleasing to me. We had traveled against the Captain's orders, and I looked upon it as the salvation of the train.

When morning broke [September 23] our triumph was complete, for in the gray of dawn the mountains [Black Rock] lay five miles ahead. This would soon be passed and, excepting the three teams and the mess which refused to come with us, our teams and wagons would be across the desert—making five teams which we little expected would ever cross as the day's heat upon the teams in their weakened condition would cause them to suffer and die.

On this night's route [across Black Rock Desert] a destruction of property beyond my conception lined the road. Wagons and carts were scattered on all sides, and the stench of dead and decaying cattle actually rendered the air sickening. Some idea can be drawn from the fact that in one spot could be seen 150 dead creatures, as I was informed by one who came through in daytime. [Another who said the plain "in the sun looks like a vast field of ice" reported seeing "a very beautiful mirage in the southwest . . . in which appeared a long lagoon of blue water bordered with tall trees and small islands reflected in its delightful looking bosom. . . . Oxen had stampeded for it, hoping to quench their burning thirst and left their swelled-up carcasses over the plain in that direction."

[During the night's advance the Rangers passed "parties sleeping under their wagons with their cattle standing, lowingly complaining of their hunger and thirst. Or we would have to turn out for some unfortunate whose team had just given out, whose answer to our query as to what he was going to do was: 'God only knows.' When there were women and little children among them, as was sometimes the case, it was very distressing. But it was everyone for himself, for no one could tell what was yet to be encountered."]

Many of our cattle tired on the road and were left to perish by hunger and thirst. One of my team tumbled down two miles from the [Black Rock] Spring, but by allowing him to lay and rest an hour and by feeding him the rest of the meal, I got him up and went on rejoicing and arrived at the Spring at nine o'clock [A.M., Sunday, September 23].

Here I found boiling hot water in great abundance. By going down the creek the cattle could drink. We found some little feed two miles ahead, where we drove the teams to get something to sustain life. We lay down to recruit our wearied bodies, now worn down by two nights' successive toil, and to think upon the condition of our folks still behind. Twenty-seven miles last night.

[The Rangers remained encamped this day on the western side of the desert near Black Rock Spring which took its name from "the great basaltic promontory of Black Rock frowning in dark majesty over the dreary scene." The spring "is a deep, circular pit like the mouth of a small volcano. . . . The water looks green and is constantly sending up bubbles, just like a pot beginning to boil. . . . To the west it forms into an extensive, shallow pond, say seventy-five by one hundred feet, and runs out at an opening there . . . spreading over a broad meadow to the west."]

Mr. Hutchinson [who with Captain Potts had gone ahead of the train during the night of the 22nd] went out early this morn [September 23] to meet us on the desert. On raising the sand bank beyond where we were camped, he beheld the teams of Mess No. 4 [Swain's mess] and in view of our arriving so unexpectedly, he was fairly triumphant in his feelings as he rode up to the wagons, for he had given up hope that we could get across with the teams. His feelings were more elated than I ever saw them before.

At night the Captain with a picked team started with relief to the folks behind. They took provisions for the men and two barrels of water and meal to give the teams.

September 24. Today the teams are feeding on dry grass and drinking brackish water. The camp is resting.

The Captain and rear guard came up this afternoon in sad plight. The Captain met the men ten miles from the springs. They had left two wagons and lost eleven oxen, thrown away most of the medicines of the company and much of their loading. They were fourteen hours without water and had suffered much from hardship.

Rolled out of camp at seven [P.M.] and crossed a plain six miles to good water and grass. The teams traveled well.

September 25. Laying in camp. Teams doing well. Cattle and camp recruiting. Our location is in a valley between two mountain ranges running northwest, six miles from the boiling springs where we first found water after crossing the desert. The valley, from six to ten miles wide, is a bed of volcanic ashes with occasional ridges of sand. The plain is dotted with the abominable greasewood, and around the foot of the mountains boiling hot springs and cold, pure springs occasionally break out. Around the line of these springs we find bunch grass which is very coarse and some fine rushes. This constitutes the grass our animals are recruiting on.

The water here becomes highly alkaline by soaking on the surface of the earth, which is covered with a white coating of alkali resembling a thin covering of snow or ice, from beneath which the water has fallen. In walking on this crust the feet make a rattling resembling that made by walking on thin ice. . . .

["Half an hour before sunset the thermometer in the sun was 105°."]

September 26. Today we are in camp. This afternoon Mr. Hutchinson and I went haying, taking our washing with us and washing while the hay was drying.

We left camp at dark, rolled six miles and camped on the last spot of grass for twenty miles.

September 27.   I am some unwell today on account of drinking sulphur water. The camp is generally troubled with diarrhea from its effects. Am taking burnt rhubarb.

I have been having my first siege at darning my stockings. All are preparing for the twenty-one mile stretch tonight. Our teams are doing tolerably well.

At five o'clock supper was over and the cattle brought into camp, and at six we were on the road. We found six miles of heavy, sandy road and much deep marl through the forepart of the night; in the afterpart the road was very stony and rocky. At daybreak we struck the valley of a little marsh where there was feed. Rolled along three miles and encamped just at sunrise, twenty-one miles from yesterday's camping.

September 28.   Camped in a small valley some eight miles in diameter, in the middle of which is a marsh and the edges sage land, all surrounded by very high and picturesque mountains.

This morn we had a rare opportunity to have a warm bath, and Mr. Hutchinson and I improved it by having a swim in a small lake of hot water laying just by the camp. The bath was very pleasant to the feelings, making the veins extend and increasing the circulation; but the effect was not so beneficial as that of cold baths, for I experienced a languid feeling in the muscles during the day. I have spent some hours in sleeping today. Had the soundest sleep I have had in the daytime on the route.

Our teams are growing weak very fast. The men are all becoming more or less weak and unwell.

["Thermometer 94° in the shade of wagon at four P.M."]

We had supper early and left camp at dusk. Traveled one mile, where we met Captain Potts who had been forward and was unwilling to try the road in the night on account of its roughness. So we camped and turned the teams on the marsh, where they did well.

[Another company continued its advance at night by burning grease-wood bushes along the trail. "This produced quite an illumination. The direction of the wind would not endanger anything, and the fire ran along the dry grass catching from bush to bush, and the tall flickering flames lit up the adjacent hills. . . ."]

September 29.   We left camp at eight o'clock and rolled along our course, which is directly northwest across a ridge of mountains. The road rises gradually and is very stony and rough, which makes it hard for our weak teams.

Our folks are getting discouraged and begin to talk of divisions of the provisions, divisions of the Company, and also of leaving some of the wagons. I hope and believe we can get through with nearly all our property. But if some must be left, why, let it.

At dusk we entered through the rocks [High Rock Canyon] a gorge of the most interesting kind. The bottom was level, probably three hundred feet wide, and covered with thick, fine grass. The sides, which rose perpendicular to the height of five hundred feet, stood in massive towers between which openings ran up to the back hills. The moon was shining vertically as we passed through, and the spirits of our people were enlivened by the sublimity of the scene. Singing, whooping, and halloing to one another were resorted to, to test the reverberating power of the cliffs which walled us in. The mocking rocks were apparently ready to join the glee of the boys, for they answered back their words and sent them ringing along from cliff to cliff. In the soft and strange light of the moon these regions have the grandest appearance.

[The members of another company in High Rock Canyon fired their rifles to hear the echoes "like thunder close above our heads. . . . A mule took up the chorus in her own dulcet strains, and we could almost believe that those of her kind we had left on the road behind were still accompanying their mates in spirit."]

We issued from the gorge and found water in a little valley, where we camped at ten o'clock. Thirteen miles today.

September 30.   Sabbath. This morn our train intends to move three miles to feed. I took the opportunity to have a mountain tramp. I shouldered my rifle and left the train as they rolled out of camp and had a hard tramp, found no game but was well-paid by the grand view of the mountains around. . . . This tramp has been the best I have had on the journey, for the extent of the mountain scenery around me was a rare treat, and the rocky, broken, and elevated ranges and peaks looming in the distance far exceed anything of the kind that I saw among the Rocky Mountains.

I arrived at camp at noon. After shaving and dressing, I attended the funeral of a child of Mr. Smith's, the man whose wife died two weeks ago where we were haying. The child was one of twins, eighteen months and seven days old, and has died of the same disease which caused its mother's death. The sermon was preached by Mr. Moore from these words: "Suffer the little children to come unto me." He spoke very feelingly upon the death of children, and I thought of my own dear wife and child and Mother and brother, from whom I have not heard these five months. God knows what is their condition. May He protect them from all harm.

October 1. This forenoon the camp is still and all are resting as are the teams, which are feeding on tall, coarse grass which grows thick and some of it very high, say six feet. It is perfectly ripe and dry, but standing upright. From the fact of there being no rain during the summer months in this region, the grass retains considerable of its nutriment, though bleached very badly by the sun. The teams look poorly. They have got rid of the bloat caused by the alkali, but are very weak.

The sides of the canyon [Little High Rock Canyon] are here very high and rise from the level canyon floor eight hundred to twelve hundred feet. They appear to have been tumbled together in one great confused mass when in a half-liquid state, for many of the rocks seem composed of thin layers which are bent in every way and would be well represented by a mass of molasses candy, laid in layers and bent and twisted when warm and allowed to cool in that form.

Our water here is excellent, and I am growing better fast.

We left camp at two o'clock and traveled three miles along the canyon. The road here is very level and good, the grass very thick and large. If we had been here when it was green, we would have had good feed.

October 2. In camp till noon. I employed my time in making a report upon the Directors' Report.

After noon we rolled out of camp and traveled all the afternoon, say ten miles, along the canyon, which grows narrow. The wind was very high and blew the dust badly.

Mr. Hutchinson returned to camp tonight from searching after the company horse. He was thirty miles ahead and has brought the intelligence that we are eighty miles from the summit and that the summit is 260 miles from the first settlements. ["At one time we hear the distance to the mines is not more than twenty miles, and perhaps in an hour we will hear it is between two and three hundred. The one will encourage while the latter will greatly discourage and not a day passes but what we hear similar reports. . . ." "Some of the travelers, among other rascalities, are in the habit of putting up erroneous notices to mislead and distress others."]

The cold continued all night. Overcoats and large campfires were necessary.

Little High Rock Canyon.

October 3.   This morn the Company voted to throw away the blacksmith tools and many other articles which we can do without.

    [A diarist near the Rangers reported: "The Wolverines are lightening their loads. They have much need to, for their cattle are extra inferior. . . . They threw away one pair blacksmith's bellows, large anvil, large vise, other blacksmith tools, a bar of cast steel five feet long and inch square, seven large iron-bound casks, one iron-bound ten-gallon keg, some log chains, ropes, saddles, and various other things."]

We left camp at ten o'clock and had to pass a canyon two miles long. It had the roughest, crookedest road we have passed. ["Thank Jupiter! this incomparable route was only about two miles through."]

We traveled seven miles and camped with bad feed and poor water. The wind still blows from the northeast and the air is disagreeably cold. Campfires are necessary. The ground was frozen this evening and ice formed over the little brook by our camp.

October 4. ["A very cold night. Ice an inch thick this morning. . . . The wolves made a tremendous racket last night howling among the hills."]

This morn we put on our underclothes and rigged for winter, as the air is cold and the frost severe. We left camp early and crossed the side of a plain five miles to a camping ground, where we drove the teams to a hillside to feed. Good water. The sun shines warm but the air is cold and chilly. Black glass [obsidian] abounds here.

[A diarist encamped near the Rangers reported this day: "Got a present of about eight pounds of sugar and a small piece of bacon from one of the messes of the Wolverines, which was received as a Godsend. A pony which we had found was claimed today by a man that was with the Wolverines. . . . He was a mean fellow. . . . He claimed to have found it himself some way back. . . . Most of the Wolverines were in our favor and none spoke against us. So as to settle the difficulty, one of our men and the fellow played a game of euchre, the best of three games. The fellow won."]

Today is the first time we have seen any timbered hills, except for some fir and juniper groves, since leaving South Pass where the Wind River chain was timbered with pine and poplar. This evening a mountain range covered with evergreen trees is to be seen eight miles to the north. The sight is indicative of a better country than that passed and tells a pleasing tale of a clime far away. Today I had my first view of the summit range of the Sierra, from which we are sixty-five miles distant. The peaks which rise to a great height are covered in spots with snow.

We drove the teams to the mountain ravines and tablelands to feed, where we found green grass for the first time since we left the Humboldt.

Game is beginning to make its appearance, some antelope and sage hens and signs of elk.

October 5.   ["Thermometer at sunrise 18°."] Today in camp. Teams recruiting on the mountain grass. Many of the men hunting but get no game. Mended my coat. Teams doing well.

October 6.   This morn got a late start and commenced our tramp across a sixteen-mile desert. The road was heavy for eight miles, where we found some feed and turned the teams out an hour.

Afternoon we crossed the valley and found it a good ten miles with a middling good road. We reached camp at eight o'clock and found pure water, good marsh, and buffalo grass, the latter being partly dry. Two sage hens were killed by Mr. Hutchinson today.

This evening we supped at nine o'clock after a good day's work and lay down to sleep soundly in our frail little "white house." Eighteen miles.

October 7.   Sabbath. In camp all day. Drove the teams two miles to good feed and took breakfast at ten o'clock. The teams begin to gain, though but a little.

Afternoon mended coat and went hunting among the mountains, which have a stunted juniper forest on them. Lieutenant Cannon killed an antelope today, which is a great treat to the company as no large game has been killed since leaving the Bear River.

Today is cloudy and looks like a storm. The mountains here rise to a great height and have quite a growth of buffalo grass on their slopes, which makes good feed. Near the tops vegetation is quite green, and in the ravines many fine springs are found. Upon the general, the country is changing from a desert to a land of vegetable growth.

October 8.   ["Last night flocks of wild geese flew over going south—a sign of severe weather at hand."]

Afternoon passed through Little Mountain Pass. Road stony but level.

Arrived at Dry Creek at eight o'clock. Supped, and I drove the cattle two miles up creek to water and feed. I camped out all night.

Today was cloudy with raw, cold air. The clouds emitted light showers during the last part of the night.

Fourteen miles.*

October 9.   Rose at daylight. I started up the creek to gather the teams

---

* *On this day Dr. Joseph Middleton recorded in his diary a "review of the Wolverine Train." According to this inventory, the train consisted of twelve wagons pulled by thirty-three yoke of oxen, most of which Middleton described as "poor."*

together and found them scattered over the bluffs and through the ravines. I finally got them together on the creek four miles from camp at nine o'clock. Arrived at camp at eleven and took breakfast.

We left camp at twelve o'clock and arrived at Warm Creek at two. Nooned one half hour and started for the summit ridge, nine miles distant. Arrived at camping at eight o'clock, after traveling five miles of lake bottom.

We are now under the bluffs of the summit ridge, which looms up to a height of three thousand feet above us. Thank God that we are so near it.

The weather has been cloudy, and dense clouds and fogs have hung along the mountain tops all day. This evening they portend an autumn storm. At nine o'clock the clouds emitted a gentle rain and thunders were rolling among the tops, while we were safely ensconced in our tent and joyfully keeping time with the knife and fork over a smoking supper to the patter of the rain on the tent roof. We had some dark forebodings of the passage of the summit this evening, but the spirit of the camp is high; and I only say to this labor and hardship: "Thou Elephant of the route, though wrapped in the storm clouds thou art now within my grasp."

We soon lay down to a sound night's sleep which I was particularly fitted to enjoy by the loss of sleep last night, so all the novelty around me was soon forgotten and for a moment my little girl, and my big one too, filled my mind with pleasing recollections. The next object that reason recognized was the sunlight of the morn and the hum of the rising camp.

*October 10–11.** This morning my eyes are heavy and my limbs tired from watching the teams all night. I was placed on guard with Vitts and Pratt, the one a drone and the other a "gentleman of the bar." As today is the day when both men and teams in particular are to try their mettle in scaling the summit, I was unwilling to trust the teams to their care and therefore kept busily engaged in guarding, herding, and feeding them all night.

Our camp is immediately at the foot of the hill. From it the road lays winding over the summit whence we shall take our first march. Today is to be the one that places us on the Sacramento side of the mountain.

At daybreak thick, dense, dark, rolling clouds enveloped the summit peaks above us [nine to ten thousand feet in height], and some of the

---

* *Swain's entries dated October 9, 10 and 11 were not written chronologically—a result of his falling behind in keeping his diary each day. The resulting inaccuracies have been corrected, in part by combining October 10 and 11 as one entry.*

southern peaks in sight had on their "nightcaps" from the rain of yesterday. The early morning air was cold and chilly. Though gloom saddened the mountain brow, the eyes of hopeful ambition never droop, and this morning, though tired and worn, I exult in the day's business before me.

The clouds and wintry gloom vanished from the mountain tops as the rays of a clear morning sun rested upon them, and a fine southwest breeze blew gently down from the hills and gladdened the joyful hearts of all the people in our camp. I tended carefully to the teams till the sun was one hand high, and then went to camp to breakfast.

All the camp was soon ready for the ascent. The teams, full of tricks, were hitched on, and the first that left the camp was No. 4, closely followed by all the train. The passage of the Sierra Nevada was fairly commenced.

Up, up we wound our way, over the hills and around their bases and along the mountain ravines and among the scattered yellow pines, whose very leaves played tunes old and familiar to my ears. Sometimes we were doubling and sometimes rolling along the slopes with single team. After thus traversing two miles of mountain road, we arrived at the foot of the summit ridge, the top of which lay one mile distant and over two thousand feet above us. Here we nooned by a fine spring brook and soon commenced the toilsome ascent, doubling teams. Up we ascended, slowly but surely, by the toilsome climbing of the teams and by the lifting of the members of the mess at the wheels. Dreadful was the lashing our poor teams received, and many a drop of sweat was lost by our men.

[Swain pridefully told only of his own mess's ascent. But the summit trail was crowded with wagons of other Rangers as well as those of other companies. A diarist described what was probably a typical scene at this climactic point on Lassen's Cut-off: "In the center of the very broad, sandy, dusty road men were urging their heavy ox-trains up the steep hill with lashes, imprecations, and shouts. . . . Across the road about midway up . . . lay an ox on his knees, dying and covered with an old gum {oilcloth} coat by his compasssionate owner. But it was unavailing, the dust was suffocating and the animals and wheels went over him in the haste and trouble of the steep ascent. . . . Women were seen with the trains, occupied at chocking the wheels while the oxen were allowed to blow. . . . Some wagons had as many as twelve yoke of oxen on them. One wagon . . . when near the summit became uncoupled and down the hill it ran, stern foremost, with great rapidity. . . . Men shouted and with all the rest of the fuss, there was a great clamor. A dead ox a short distance in front of a heavy team and the men by it stopped the backing vehicle, most luckily without damage to anyone."]

Four hours of this toil saw us with our teams' wagons on the highest point of the pass. To the south, peak after peak rose to the sky. To the north the hills were less elevated, and behind us were the desolate hills and dry lake bed we had crossed. Before us, two hundred feet below [to the west] was a fine valley covered with white grass, while the hills beyond were thickly wooded with tall yellow pine.

Encamped two miles from the summit in good feed and with fine water and rejoiced in having accomplished the pass in so good a style.

Back Home

"We feel a degree of anxiety for you which you can never realize, and no doubt you feel anxiety about 'home' which we can never know. But courage, my boy!"

Youngstown, October 7, 1849
Sunday afternoon, 4 o'clock

Dear Brother William,

I again take up my pen to write you. And how the deepest feelings of my soul are stirred as I trace a line that shall express but feebly the feeling of anxiety and love that reigns here for my only brother, now three thousand miles from home in a strange land, and we obliged to wait two long months before we can hear from him, and it is already two months since we have heard from you. [The last letter was received September 10, written eight miles east of Fort Laramie on July 4. See p. 243.] We don't know what vicissitudes you are exposed to, and that makes our imaginings all the worse, "Since never yet was shape so dread, but fancy thus in darkness thrown could frame more dreadful of her own." We feel a degree of anxiety for you which you can never realize, and no doubt you feel anxiety about "home" which we can never know. But courage, my boy! There is no need or cause of anxiety to you. Here we are all well, thank God healthier than we used to be when you were here, with a fair prospect of a continuation of health. Aye, and doing tolerably well too. I have received my appointment as Inspector and am getting my $2 per day. I began last Tuesday, October 2. . . .

There have been two schooners started from Lake Erie for California loaded with lumber, merchandise, and passengers, via Quebec. . . .

We calculate that you will get to the diggings about this time and will write by the November boat which we shall get early in December. So write everything; fill one and a half sheets. . . .

Dr. Root's family are well, and Mrs. Bailey and boy were well a week ago. . . . Our friends are well, as far as I know. If I have time, I shall write more before I mail this.

[This letter was mailed unsigned.]

Youngstown, October 9, 1849

My Own Dear William,

It is now three o'clock in the afternoon and I have again seated myself to drop a line to you. George is writing, and I presume will write at length, and as it has been but a short time since I wrote you a long letter, you will I doubt not excuse me if I am very brief this time.

I am now at Father's and have been since last Tuesday. My health is better, with the exception of a very bad cold caught last Saturday quilting in the chamber, which makes me very unfit for writing. Sis is here by my elbow and is quite well, grows finely and is full of her laugh and fun. She does not learn to talk very fast but will imitate almost anything. She will say "tato," which is her favorite food; "mich," which is her favorite drink; and "Uncle," meaning George, whom she is very fond of, as well as her Grandma. She can speak some other words quite plain, which I cannot mention, one being "poor Papa." I think you would be amused to see her cut up her mischievous capers, which is not seldom and she is not at a loss to find mischief when she can. She appears to enjoy herself here, for there is a number of us and she likes company; but she does not stay long enough to become very much attached to them. . . .

We have not received any intelligence from you since yours of the 4th, and I can tell you, my dear, I want to hear from you very much. I long too, to hear of your arrival in California, which I hope will not be longer than next month. . . .

I shall endeavor to write you a long letter by the next steamer.

Our people all join in love to you and wish you success.

Do not fail to write all the hardships and particulars of your journey, when you shall write from California.

Goodbye for this time, from your affectionate wife till death.

Sabrina Swain

Youngstown, October 9, 1849

Dear William,

It is now ten o'clock at night. . . .

We are all well today, and if we are not well in the morning I will tell you. Sabrina is at her Father's. She went up there last week to have the girls help her quilt a quilt, as the story ran. But I suspect there is some wedding matter on the carpet, as G. Myres is at the Barretts' pretty often, though I know nothing about it, merely suspicion. But the good book says "Where the body is, there will the Eagles be gathered together."

. . . Please remember me and each of your family to our friend Mr. Hutchinson. May he enjoy health, happiness, and prosperity. And also remember us to each of the Messrs. Bailey and Root. May God bless you, William, and protect and prosper you and return you safely home, is my strongest wish. Mother wishes you to write her how your mind is affected in a religious view. She sends all sorts of love to you and says it is a long, long time since she has seen the poor boy; she says she prays God to bless you in mind and body.

It is now past eleven o'clock, P.M., but a little after seven with you. . . .

October 10. A.M.

All well. God bless you, boy.

George Swain

CHAPTER IX

A Perfect Labyrinth of Mountains

"The emigrants are . . . now scattered, broken, selfish stragglers . . . many of them thin with hunger as well as anxiety."

At what they thought to be the summit of the Sierra Nevada, the Rangers were at last in California. But instead of a view of the famed Sacramento Valley, they looked west and south across endless miles of mountain ridges and gorges. How bitterly disappointing—the cut-off had delivered them they knew not where or how far from the mines.

The first Californians they met were not miners but men from Sacramento City sent to rescue them. General Persifor F. Smith, commander of the Pacific Division, U.S. Army, had learned in August from newly arrived overlanders the serious plight of the companies crossing the Carson and Truckee deserts. Of even greater concern were the emigrants far back on the Humboldt River who would be dangerously late in trying to cross the mountains. October in the northern Sierra Nevada brought to mind the snowdrifts that had trapped the Donner party back in 1846. To prevent a catastrophe that could dwarf the fearful tragedy of the Donners, General Smith in late August set in motion a major relief and rescue effort.

The first plan centered on sending food and other supplies to the passes on the Carson and Truckee routes. On September 14, Major D. H. Rucker, charged by General Smith with organizing and directing the relief expeditions, received the first warning that conditions on Lassen's Cut-off would be far worse than on the other trails. More emphatic was a report from Milton McGee, who had captained the first wagon train over the cut-off. On September 17 when he reached Sacramento

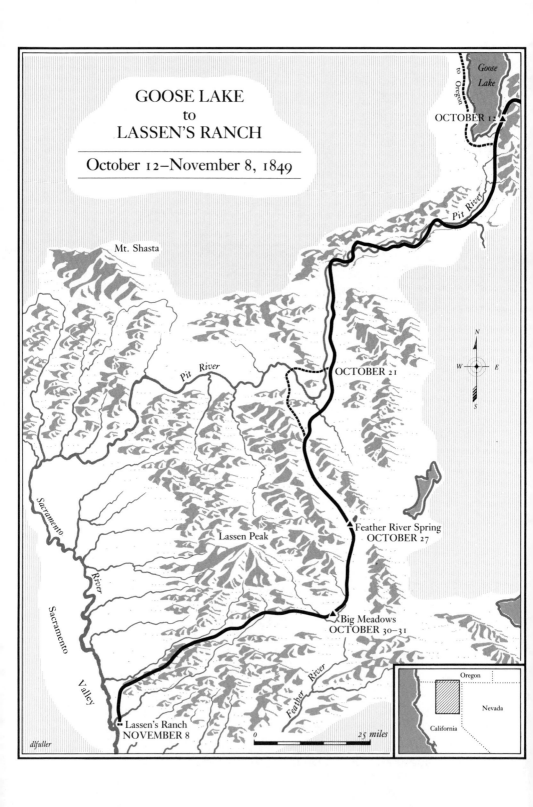

GOOSE LAKE
to
LASSEN'S RANCH

October 12–November 8, 1849

Goose Lake

to Oregon

OCTOBER 12

Pit River

Mt. Shasta

Pit River

OCTOBER 21

N
W   E
S

Feather River Spring
OCTOBER 27

Lassen Peak

Sacramento

River

Big Meadows
OCTOBER 30–31

Sacramento

Feather River

Valley

Lassen's Ranch
NOVEMBER 8

dlfuller

0   25 miles

Oregon

Nevada

California

City, McGee reported to Rucker: "I have just come in from the northern route and can assure you . . . that many are now entirely destitute of provisions, while others will not have a sufficiency to bring them within many days' travel of the Sacramento Valley."

Neither McGee nor Rucker knew—no one did—that there were still, in mid-September, at least 8,000 men and several hundred women and children out there in the desert-mountain wilderness. Many had advanced over the cut-off and were approaching Lassen's Ranch; they would get through safely, without assistance. Many more struggled over the terrible miles of Black Rock Desert, and far to the rear several thousand were still moving south along the Humboldt River trail. They had not yet even reached the start of the cut-off! Among them were the Wolverine Rangers, who made the Lassen turnoff on September 21.

Acting on what information he had, Rucker decided to send immediately a well-provisioned party to the Lassen route, with the intent of going as far east as necessary to be certain of helping those at the rear. He planned to lead the Lassen rescue party himself, but supervision of the efforts on the Carson and Truckee trails delayed him in Sacramento City. So Rucker instructed a civilian named John H. Peoples to proceed to the cut-off, having first procured "fat beef cattle" and other provisions. Once on his way, Peoples became so sick with mountain fever that he had to turn over his command to E. H. Todd.

With six men Todd reached the summit on October 8, established a camp on the west side and set about following his instructions to issue provisions sparingly "and remember that persons can live on half rations for fifteen or twenty days. . . . Use every exertion to bring the emigrants into the settlements. Admonish them of the lateness of the season and the great possibility of a snowstorm and urge them to throw away everything of any weight that may not be absolutely necessary. . . . See that all women and children have the means of riding to Lawson's even if you are obliged to make your own men walk."

The Wolverine Rangers pulled the last of their wagons over the summit on October 12. That evening several of them walked over to the nearby camp of the relief party. After talking with Todd and his men, they returned to their wagons with some meat for their first meal in California, a pot of smoking beef soup. Sitting around their campfires, the Rangers must have talked over Todd's warnings, for the next day they called a company meeting.

Camped on the rocky slopes west of the summit, the smoke from their fires blowing through the tall pines of the vast forest, they faced their prospects. From Todd they had learned the mileage facts of their great mistake in taking the supposed cut-off. If they had stayed on the old trail down the Humboldt and then over either the Carson or Truckee trails, the distance from the turnoff at Lassen's to Sutter's Fort would have been 260 miles. Instead they learned that they still had to make 219 miles from their summit camp to reach Lassen's Ranch.*

With his usual calm, Swain on October 13 commented that this "intelligence" made "many of the company uneasy."

On October 14, James Pratt wrote in his diary that Todd and his men had warned that "it is useless for us to try to get our teams through. We should hurry on for our lives." He further warned that the road ahead would be "the worst in all the world."

With this information, the Rangers made a Ranger-type decision. Accepting that it would be impossible to travel together over the mountain trail with their twelve wagons, they determined to separate into small groups and strike out independently for Lassen's Ranch—but each group would keep one or two wagons. They were not alone in their tenacious desire to save their possessions—many other companies defied Todd's warnings, not only at the summit but later when the dangers would be even greater.

One hundred and fifty-one days after leaving Independence, these remarkable men from Michigan and New York voted on October 13 to dissolve their company and divide wagons, teams and remaining company property among the fifty-six members. At the conclusion of another meeting on the 14th, they burned all the company records. No one explained why—possibly the act symbolized the freeing of the Rangers from further obligations.

Swain's diary entries for October 13 and 14 are brief, bare-bone sentences which report without comment the orderly business of dissolving the company. Pratt on the 14th noted that "the government agents tell us we should hurry on for our lives." But like Swain, he said nothing that suggested an awareness of their desperate plight. Dependent on the relief party for food, Pratt reported the Rangers "luxuriated" on government beef. The final division of company property he described as "an animated scene."

Even more typical of the Rangers' surprising sangfroid, Swain mentioned on the 13th—almost as if referring to a social event back home— that the Ranger "boys" with another company nearby and "the Smith

---

* Even Todd was incorrect in his mileage information. The actual distance from the turnoff to Sutter's Fort via either the Truckee or Carson routes was 350 miles. He was close to right as to the distance from the summit to Lassen's Ranch: 250 miles.

girls" joined in a fandango that lasted till ten o'clock that night. That the Smith family (the eight brothers, some with wives and children, who had camped with the Rangers on September 16 and 30) felt up to dancing after suffering two deaths suggests that all of them—the Rangers, the Smiths and others—sought in music and dancing a momentary escape from their anxieties.

Neither Swain, Pratt nor other Rangers described the fandango, but it must have been an unforgettable scene—more than seventy men and a few women gathered around campfires in a forest of soaring pines; wavering shadows on the tattered remains of wagon covers; men and women, with children watching, dancing to improvised music—a moment that drew them all together before facing separately the next day's realities.

Hurried by Captain Todd and by their hopes for warmth and an end of their toil and disappointments, the Rangers started down from the summit on October 15, moving out from camp in groups of four, six or more, some with only backpacks, others with a wagon or two pulled by the surviving oxen. Assigned one wagon and a team of four oxen, Swain, Bailey, Hutchinson and S. H. McClellan (a farmer from Galesburg, Michigan) headed down the trail, through brush and around rocks, to Goose Lake far below.

The next day, October 16, Todd and his men helped the last of all the emigrants to cross the summit. Possibly Swain and the scattering Rangers sensed the drama of their circumstance. Of all the thousands who had set out from Missouri way back in May, the Rangers were just *one* day in advance of the last stragglers to reach California in 1849.

At Goose Lake the trail turned south at last, toward the Sacramento Valley. But immediately ahead they entered the barren watershed of the Pit River, a topographical chaos of ridges, gorges and sharp-edged plateaus. This was a California never imagined.

Here the Rangers and other scattered bands of emigrants faced a new danger, the Pit Indians. Named because of the deep pits they dug as traps for animals and their enemies, they were known to the emigrants by the recurrent epithet Diggers. They were in no way related to the tribes along the Humboldt River, but they were even more hostile. Captain Bruff of the Washington City Company, a few days in advance of the Rangers, wrote frequently in his diary of the Indians, noting that "the emigrants have such a reluctance to guard duty or neglect it so that they are constantly losing their animals. The Indians . . . all along the Pit River . . . are known to be most hostile, occasionally murdering people and continually shooting and stealing animals." Bruff reported that they attacked the relief party led by Peoples and stole his mules.

Working their way over the rocky trail that followed the Pit River and farther south reached the headwaters of the Feather River, Swain and the refugee-like Rangers passed scenes of suffering and anguish—men straining desperately, angrily at the wheels of their last wagon as it sank in the mud; pathetic camps of men stricken with scurvy, too weak to move; carcasses of oxen bloody from butchering by emigrants hungry for meat; rifle fire ringing through the forest as men hunted game to allay their hunger. Hundreds of emigrants escaped starvation or death from exposure only because of the supplies passed out by the relief expedition, which in early October was enlarged by the arrival of Major Rucker, who came up from Sacramento City to establish a camp on the Feather River.

By November Rucker had returned to Sacramento, where in one of his orders he expressed his impatience with what he had seen on Lassen's Cut-off: "You must tell all the emigrants that they must be more active and get to the valley at once or they may perish. I cannot conceive what they are thinking of. Their own lives and the lives of their families are certainly worth more than their wagons and effects."

As suggested by this angry admonition, Rucker, Peoples, Todd and their men must often have wondered about the people whom they so heroically sought to rescue. One company from St. Louis with twenty-five women and children lost most of their oxen in an Indian raid, and when they came into Peoples' camp for assistance, the men squabbled over what they would abandon and what they would drag along.

The Rangers' behavior continued to reflect their unwillingness to face reality, to give up old values and expectations. For instance, Swain in his diary entry for October 30 made the astonishing comment: "I am badly put to it to fix up our food so that we can live well. Making puddings and making dressing for the breadstuffs is hard business with the material we have." Pratt on the 27th tells of sitting around a dying fire one morning before starting on the trail, "while Ladd and Mansur are shooting at a mark." While Swain and his friends continued to be held back by the struggle of their oxen to haul their wagon, several other groups of Rangers also stubbornly stayed with their wagons.

Rain the night of the 30th turned to snow. In the morning it melted on the trail but the mountains stood white, and a cold wind carried snow from the treetops. More snow on the 31st and November 1—a threatening reminder for the people on Lassen's Cut-off who, praying or cursing, stumbled over the roughest, most precipitous miles of the entire journey.

Swain does not explain why, but October 30 is the last entry in his diary. For 203 days, with only one brief interruption, he had diligently maintained his record. Even through the worst days and nights of September and October he had remained calm and stoic, his attention directed not to the physical discomforts and the toilsome miles of walking and climbing but rather to the wilderness scene around him and to the circumstances of his company. Without self-pity, without bemoaning his fate or even expressing more than mildly what must have been his deepening disappointment, he had held to his task and reported each day for Sabrina, George and his mother. After October 30, the best he could do was to hang onto the two leather-bound journals, hang on to them when everything else was abandoned in the final rush to safety.

Fortunately, one of the men in Swain's band of Rangers—James Pratt—kept his diary each day. Several other diarists struggling over the trail within a mile or so also continued to write, including Bruff, who maintained his regimen of remarkably detailed daily entries. And the official reports of Rucker, Peoples and Todd told much of the story, including a specific mention of William Swain.

To provide a daily record of what happened to the Rangers after Swain stopped writing on October 30, the diary of James Pratt has been used for each day for the period October 31 through November 4. Additional information has been drawn from Bruff, Rucker and other diarists.

Beginning November 5, Swain himself returns as the main narrator. His account of the last four days on the cut-off was written many weeks later in a letter to Sabrina and his mother. To augment Swain's recollections, Pratt and others continue to be drawn upon.

Carried by a fierce wind "whistling through the pine forest like the roar of Niagara," a snowstorm swept across the western slopes of the Sierra Nevada during the night of November 1. Thereafter the nights of snow and days of cold rain turned Lassen's Cut-off into a place of chaos —deep mud amid great rocks, animals, people and wagons confined to the winding trail that led down into ravines and steeply up onto narrow ridges. In his official report, Peoples told how he and his men struggled during the five days of the storm to advance their wagons crowded with women, children and sick men. On November 5 most of his best mules were killed by the storm, "rendering it impossible to move the wagons the next morning." Peoples therefore rode down to the Sacramento Valley to get help; some days later he sent back several men with mules and beef cattle.

Summing up the relief party's efforts, Peoples later stated: "In justice to the men in my party, I cannot omit to mention . . . they did everything that men could do . . . and although not one of them had a dry blanket or dry clothes for half a month, there was no complaint. . . . At every river or slough they stood ready to wade over with the women and children in their arms. . . . I must remark that had the men of the rear emigration thought less of their property and more of the lives of their families, I could have brought them all to the valley before the storm."

In passing out provisions to the destitute along the trail, Peoples, in accord with his orders, kept a careful record of each person or company that received beef, rice, flour and other food. For November 1 he noted in his record of "provisions, etc. to Overland Emigrants": "Capt. Potts & Comp. Michigan, 24 lbs. beef" and "Mr. Swain, Michigan, 10 lbs. beef."

Through the rest of his life William Swain remembered with pride that he had survived the fearful days and nights at the end of Lassen's Cut-off, struggling through snow and rain, abandoning everything in a final dash for safety. His diary told most of the story, beginning back at the summit on October 12 when he and the Rangers enjoyed a brief moment of triumph before facing their ultimate challenge.

October 12, 1849.   [On the west side of the summit.] This morning we left camp late and recrossed the summit to pack over the loading of the remaining teams. It was hard work to climb the hill "pack on back." Our appearance would have excited a hearty laugh from our friends at home could they have witnessed our trudging as we ascended the hill with bags, trunks, and other articles of all sizes and descriptions on our backs. We had all the things on the summit by four o'clock, and the teams came up with the empty wagons which were soon loaded again.

We bid a long and hearty goodbye to this team-killing, back-breaking, leg-soring mountain and arrived at camp at sundown, where we indemnified ourselves in part with a pot of smoking beef soup, the material for which was received from a relief train sent out on the route by Governor P. Smith with a drove of beef cattle to be distributed among the emigrants as their necessities required.

October 13.   Today many of the company are uneasy on account of the intelligence we have received from the government folks who inform us that we are yet 380 miles from Sutter's Fort. To Lassen's location will be 219 miles over considerable bad roads and one desert of forty miles.

Many of the company are talking of packing and of dividing the company. Finally a meeting was called for the purpose of passing a vote to dissolve, which was carried, and today we are in camp dividing the company property. The teams are resting and doing well on dry grass.

This evening our boys, and those of another train lying here, joined with the Smith girls and had a tall time in the way of a fandango, which lasted till ten o'clock.

October 14.   Sabbath. Today still in camp, finishing the division of the company which goes off very smoothly. ["The teams were equalized . . . each four persons being entitled to a team. Several members today packed and left for the settlements. . . . The supply of government beef is plentiful and we all luxuriated upon it."]

Mr. Hutchinson, Mr. Bailey, Mr. McClellan and self drew a team and wagon together and shall travel the remainder of the way on our own hook.

This eve Mr. Moore preached and we had a company meeting at the same time to complete the settlement of the company business. This was arranged and a vote taken to free any member from all company dues or business by paying to the Treasurer $2 for which the Secretary must give a receipt. [At the end of the meeting "the papers and records of the company were formally burned."]

October 15.   ["All feel well that a division has been made, and all are satisfied with themselves by reason of the harmony prevailing. Each association is on the move."]

This morn Mr. Hutchinson packed for the diggings for the purpose of finding a location. He will proceed down to Sutter's and return to the diggings with a stock of provisions for himself, Mr. Bailey and myself who have agreed to work together and share the proceeds of our labor equally.

We left camp at nine o'clock. Our road lay along the valley and soon struck over the ridge of a pine hill west of the valley toward Goose Lake. The road was stony and ran through pine timber where the limbs grow to the ground.

We arrived at Goose Lake at noon. [The trail led around the south end of the lake.* At this season of the year "the water has nearly disappeared, having receded several miles from the shore. . . . The bed of the lake . . . appears like a vast plain of sand. A thin sheet of water is barely visible in the distance. . . ." "The whole shore is white with carbonate of soda and the beach is a perfect quagmire. . . ."]

---

* *Here Lassen's route forked, the road to Oregon continuing northwest with the "cut-off" leading southwest, at last toward the Sacramento Valley.*

Along the lake to Cow Creek the road was very good. Arrived at Cow Creek at dark, having made twenty miles.

We have traveled today with four of the messes of the company and at night camped together. They let their teams feed out on a plain at night while we tied ours to the wagon, being afraid that they might be stolen by the Indians who are very thievish here.

[Notices "posted on trees by the road caution travelers to be particularly watchful of their animals. A large number are reported to have been stolen or disabled in this neighborhood. The Indians disable oxen by shooting them with their bows and arrows and the owners are obliged to leave them, and the Indians help themselves to the beef at their leisure."]

October 16.   We left camp early today and found our road good. Nooned on the head branch of the Pit River.

In afternoon had stony road over some low hills and camped on the Pit River.

We formed a corral tonight, and after herding the cattle on the bunch grass of the hills, the other messes corralled their teams, but we chose again to tie ours to the wagon.

October 17.   This morn we were ready to start early, but the other messes had lost eight head of cattle which were probably driven away by the Indians. They had set a guard over their teams but had allowed the teams to get out of the corral in the night.

Captain Potts' mess passed us early, and as our mess was ready, we left camp, leaving the rest of the boys to hunt for their teams. I stayed and helped hunt for them for two hours and then I left them to find their cattle themselves, which they never did. I overtook my mess at noon just as they were having dinner. The team had green grass from the edge of the river, and we enjoyed our meal with good appetites.

["Frequent deep pits are seen along the roadside." "They are some ten or fifteen feet deep. . . . The dirt has been carefully carried off. . . . They are traps to catch some kind of game."]

Having passed the Smith family in camp just at dusk, we overtook Captain Potts at seven in the evening. Twenty-four miles.

[The group of Rangers traveling under the command of Captain Potts consisted of eleven men with three wagons. One of these men was James Pratt. In his diary he told of Swain, Bailey and McClellan coming into camp that evening. "After dark when our campfire burned brightly and our cattle were tied up and our supper had been cleared away for some time and most of our little company had retired to rest, the roll of wagon wheels was heard. It proved to be Captain Bailey's team. He brought us news from the Wolverines behind. He said they had lost eight head of cattle the night before on account of insufficient guard. He had saved his by tying them up and had started off in the morning determined to overtake us. We were glad to receive him, for he is a noble gentleman and a first-rate companion. There were two others with him."

[After this evening's reunion, Swain, Bailey and McClellan remained with Captain Potts' group.]

October 18.   We rose this morn at three o'clock and herded the teams till daylight while the cooks got the morning meal. All was ready to leave camp at daylight and on we went.

I shot a goose in the river and had to swim to get it—and it was COLD. Mr. Crosby shot two deer. I rambled along the river a long time and only overtook the train at noon when they were cooking the venison, which was excellent.

["Far to the west of us, solitary, rises to an immense height a gigantic mountain {Mount Shasta}, the top and sides clear to the base covered with snow—a magnificent sight. . . ."]

Camped at the mouth of a canyon [of the Pit River] in company with the government train, which is returning tu Sacramento City.*

October 19.   ["Last night Mr. McClellan on our second watch saw an Indian and shot at him, whereupon two others sprang up and ran. No one was hurt."]

Left camp at sunrise and commenced the passage of the canyon, which occupied all day. The fords of the river, which are eleven in number, are very stony and rough and the water frequently came up to the wagon hubs. We accomplished the passage by sundown, but it was a hard day's work for the teams. Fifteen miles.

["We have a good camp tonight, plenty of firewood, our fire burns brightly, and we keep a most vigilant watch all night and are well prepared to give the Indians a warm reception if they visit us."]

October 20.   Left camp early and traveled along the valley, which is wide here.

Had a fine view [to the south] of many lofty snow peaks [including Lassen Peak]. We are getting far from the summit ridge.

Drove late and camped without feed for the teams. Roads good.

---

* E. H. Todd and his men with eleven riding and pack animals were traveling down the Pit River to rendezvous with the main relief expedition.

Though this is a scene on the Carson Trail far to the south of Lassen's Cut-off, this drawing depicts the kind of terrain that the Rangers and thousands more had to struggle through during the last weeks of their journey. Note the plank bridge in the foreground and, beyond the wagon wheel, a wagon lurching through the giant boulders.

CALIFORNIA HISTORICAL SOCIETY

Twenty-two miles. [On the trailside "were vestiges of a recent camp of emigrants accompanied by the usual garnish of wheels, hubs, tires, chains, yokes, clothes, old boots, and lastly—an *empty* liquor case."]

October 21.   Sabbath. Left camp at four o'clock this morning and traveled till seven, when we found grass and halted to get breakfast and rest the teams.

In the afternoon we met Captain Peoples' company of the government relief train, going up to meet the emigrants with hard bread, pork, and beef on foot for their relief.*

At three o'clock we took the left-hand road ["because we saw the government relief party come that way"] and left the Pit River.

[In the evening Peoples' relief party "killed a beef and distributed it. Some Wolverine Ranger packers stopped to get some of it."]

October 22.   This morn we left camp early, and Mr. Crosby and I went

---

* *John H. Peoples joined forces with E. H. Todd this day. For the next four weeks they remained on the trail, distributing food and directing the rescue of families.*

to the canyon of the river to get cans of water. We descended a rocky bank equal in height and roughness to the gorge between Niagara Falls and Lewiston. We reached the train at nine o'clock.

Today has been busily engaged in passing twelve miles of the roughest road we have traveled on the route, literally a rock road. The country is becoming a finely timbered one.

We arrived at a creek at four o'clock, and I occupied the time till eleven in cooking.

October 23.   This morn we were up at three o'clock, and as there was no feed for the teams we left camp at four, our road lit by a pitch torch carried ahead of the train. We ascended a mountain and by a gradual rise through pine forests we arrived at the top by sunrise. Doubling teams over the top pitch, we passed on one mile, where we stopped to feed the teams on good grass and to breakfast.

[In his diary for this date, James Pratt reported: "Our party under Captain Potts now consists of . . . seventeen men, five wagons and fifteen yoke of cattle. Our old train is scattered all along behind, some near us and some quite remote. We are all well pleased with the division, for all are well satisfied that it would have taken double the time to move the great train over this road that it takes to pass over it in small parties."]

October 24.   Left camp early and traveled all day through a fine forest of pines over gently rolling hills and along ravines. We found no water and about three o'clock halted to let the teams rest and to take a luncheon ourselves.

We soon started and met Lt. Cannon who had been to water four miles ahead down the mountain side, which we descended till dark and found water but bad grass.

Today we have made twenty-four miles.

October 25.   Our feed was poor this morn, and we left camp and found feed in two miles and camped till noon.

We camped at dark in a small mountain valley where we found good grass and a fine creek.

["Evidences of a large emigration through here are seen in the blackened trees which have been set on fire, many of which we see burning every day, as well as in the condition of the road and the camping grounds. . . . It is strange that we have passed so far through a country swarming with Indians, where they commit so many depredations and where we see their fires all around us, without getting a sight of any of them."

[At another campsite "the Indians carried off sixteen head of oxen. . . . A party started out in pursuit . . . trailed them up the valley and were so close on them that they found the meat of several oxen hanging on limbs of trees in the process of drying."]

October 26.   Left camp late and drove over the roughest kind of road. We found this morn two men sick with scurvy and not able to move their teams, as they were too weak to drive them. ["They wanted us to take them through. But distressing as is their condition, we declined, because the government train sent here for the relief of the emigrants will be back here in a few days, and they will be proper objects for them to provide for. They have one noble ox, which will probably enable them to make some bargain to get through even before that train returns."

["It is now evening. Supper is over and some are in bed, others sitting or standing around our blazing campfire. . . . Our cask supplied water for supper, and we are to take breakfast before starting in the morning. Our boys shot a brace of ducks this afternoon from the shore of a clear pond of water, about four miles back where we watered our cattle. We shall put them with some beans and have a soup in the morning. . . . The moon tonight shines through a hazy atmosphere."]

October 27.   ["Our duck soup this morning was excellent. The cattle were turned out on the rising of the morning star and are now soon to be yoked up for another day's work. The sky is not clear as it has been and it behooves us to make the best of our way to the settlements."]

Left camp at sunrise, and the road lay across a fine level, but was very stony and rough. We arrived at Feather River Spring at four o'clock, having made twelve miles. This spring is a small lake of cold, clear water, two hundred yards in diameter, which has its source around the edges of the lake where water issues in large quantities from the rock.

October 28.   Sabbath. Today we left the teams to feed till noon, and I improved the time to have a good bath in the springs, which was much needed. We are now living upon our vegetable food without any kind of meat, but we can live better than we expected.

[Many emigrants killed their own teams "as a last and only resort to avoid a visit from that lank, lean, old monster, Starvation." With the pangs of hunger, there were also the torments of disease. "Many emigrants were afflicted with scurvy—swelled, blotched legs and ankles, and stiff joints." Graves were frequently seen along the trail; one near this spring was marked:

Sacred to the memory of
W. Brown
of the Rough and Ready Company
of Platte Co. Mo.
Died with skervy Sept. 19, 1849
Aged 35 years.

[Midst the suffering there were grim touches of humor. A diarist told of "an Irishman and his wife with an ox-wagon, to the rear of which was attached a large hencoop, full of chickens and roosters. And Pat swore by the 'howly mother of Moses' that he'd starve before he'd kill one of 'em, intending to make a grand speculation on them in California."]

At one o'clock we left camp and traveled seven miles and struck a branch of the Feather River where we met a Captain Rogers who is stationed twelve miles from here with supplies of provisions for the emigrants. By his advice we drove six miles farther in the night and encamped in the big marsh.

Our drive tonight was through a forest of pines of great size and height, some of them twelve paces around at the foot and at least two hundred feet high. We camped at one o'clock at night and had a cold bite and lay down to rest.

October 29.   [Swain and his companions were camped this morning in what was generally called the Feather River Meadows or Feather River Valley, "very nearly round and about six miles across, very swampy, covered with heavy grass, surrounded by a heavy belt of timber, and on the east and south are mountains reaching up into the regions of everlasting snow. On the north a mammoth spring breaks out . . . and feeds a pool from which a large stream . . . runs off. This pool is from ten to twenty feet deep and of such crystal clearness that the smallest gravel may be seen on the bottom with perfect distinctness. Myriads of speckled trout and mountain suckers are sporting in the limpid water. . . . Thousands of dollars' worth of property is buried at or near this place by persons who have lost all or most of their teams and are unable to take it farther. . . . There are few articles of a full and complete outfit but what can be picked up here, besides many nonessential and useless ones that were hauled here to be thrown away after breaking down the teams. . . ."]

Our cattle were on the marsh feeding till ten o'clock, where many of them got mired and we had to go to great trouble to get them out.

We left camp at one o'clock and traveled seven miles by the side of the marsh. We camped on the Feather River by Rogers' camp in the big

Last entries in Swain's diary. His dates are incorrect by one day. His entry dated "M 30" (Monday, October 30) on the second line of the left page should have been October 29 and has been corrected in the text. Similarly the entry "M 31" (top line right) has been changed to October 30.

marsh. Here we have to cut hay to feed the cattle on the desert. [It "begins twenty miles ahead and is described as awful." "It is not a desert in other respects than lack of grass, for there is water . . . and very heavy timber." "Water occurs, it is said, at points often enough, but we are advised not to let our cattle go into the ravines after it but to go down ourselves and bring up water in pails. It is said that the carcasses of hundreds of dead cattle lie in the ravines, the results of the emigrants having driven them down for water and the cattle not having the strength to return. Rough, rocky roads and grizzly bears go to fill up the pleasing description of the desert we have to cross before arriving at Lawson's."]

Many emigrants are camped here recruiting, very destitute of bread-stuffs and leaving upon meat received from the government train. We have them every hour in our camp begging, and we cannot refuse them a part of our small stock.

[In contrast to the charity of the Rangers, at least one company sought to profit from the needs of hungry emigrants. This company "sold bread at 50 cents per pound, sugar at 75 cents, and bacon at 50 cents. . . . They sold several hundred pounds of flour to a pack company, and it was said that at the same time they were selling provisions at such high rates, they recruited their stores by begging from the government relief party."

[At one of the relief stations the officer in charge "was surrounded by begging emigrants. . . . He had to serve out the fresh beef, pork, flour, bread, etc. as judiciously as possible, subject of course to much imposition. Some emigrants greatly in need, some meanly bent on an increase of stores, and others who would steal a dying man's shoes. His stores were insufficient to serve those actually in want, but how was he to discriminate? He had to contend with impudence, etc. from the disappointed and rude applicants. It was one of the most delicate and troublesome duties ever entrusted to anyone."]

October 30.   In camp all day cutting hay.

This evening three messes of our Wolverine brethren came up. I am badly put to it to fix up our food so that we can live well. Making puddings and making dressing for the breadstuffs is hard business with the material we have.*

[The morning of October 31 found Swain and his sixteen companions, with five wagons and thirty-two oxen, still camped in the Feather River Valley.**]

[*October 31.*   "We remain here getting hay for the desert. . . . The day is cold, the sky obscured with clouds. To add to our discomfort it is now raining. Who can tell what we may have to endure if the rainy season should commence now?" "In fourteen miles we will reach an altitude of 5,000 feet above the Sacramento plain and descend to it in forty miles by rugged ridge travel!"

[*November 1.*   "It rained hard all night—a cold, comfortless rain! This morning the mountain tops are sprinkled with snow. It is a bad day . . . snowing, cold, and cheerless. We started late this morning. . . ."

---

* *With this entry Swain's diary abruptly ends. The story is continued by using James Pratt's daily entries, information from other diarists and part of a letter Swain wrote some months later.*
** *Also known as Big Meadows, this valley is today largely covered by Lake Almanor in Plumas County.*

[At the ford of the North Fork of the Feather River "the banks are steep and slippery. . . . The stream is here about sixty feet wide, generally only a few inches of water but some deep holes. . . . Current rapid."

["It is night. We have encamped six miles from our starting point. . . . We have some large logs burning for our campfire. It is now snowing hard."

[*November 2.*   "This morning . . . at four o'clock our campfire was burning brightly, and the moon shone clear upon the valleys and mountains covered with snow. It was a beautiful sight, but one calculated to excite fearful doubts of our being able to make the settlements with our teams.

["It is now six o'clock and Potts has gone to bring up the cattle. Daylight is just dawning. Clouds obscure the sky. Our little party are in the main in good heart, and what man can do, we can effect. The road here leaves the river. . . ."

[The trail led from the North Fork of the Feather River over steep hills and through a thick forest some six or seven miles to the headwaters of Deer Creek. "For twenty miles wagons are buried in the mud up to their beds, and cattle are lying all around them."

["This evening we arrived at Deer Creek. Our cattle were driven two miles over the mountains to feed."

[*November 3.*   "It rained and snowed all last night. We lay here until noon today. We moved on about five miles up the valley and encamped. Rained hard all afternoon."

[*November 4.*   "Daylight dawned on the lifeless carcasses of sixteen of our oxen . . . fallen by the chilling blasts of the merciless storm." "The rest of our teams are unable to move. Snow covers the ground. We lay here all day.

["Rogers and one of the government employees stopped and dined with us at three P.M. They are hurrying on to Lawson's. They bring distressing news of the rear emigration. They say there are forty women and children behind yet, some sick men also, who must perish. Also that General Wilson and family are behind yet, in a great straits.*

---

* *General John Wilson, recently appointed "special agent for California Indians," was traveling to his new post with his wife, three sons and two daughters. Having lost all but seven of their mules to the Indians, Wilson had cached most of their baggage and struggled on with one wagon.*

["The evening clears up, but it is cold! We have concluded to move Captain Bailey's wagon and one other in the morning, leaving the other three here. We will all have to pack our clothing. We will have to leave about everything."]

*November 5.** Early this morning each man with his pack on his back commenced his way through the snow to the Sacramento, with our provisions in two wagons drawn by the remaining oxen. Our outfits, which we had labored hard to bring so far over the plains and mountains, were either consigned to the fire or abandoned in the tents which we left pitched.

[Passing through a great forest, Swain and his companions slowly worked their way up to the crest of the long mountain ridge between Mill and Deer Creek canyons. For the next fifty-odd miles the trail would lead along the high, rocky spine of this ridge, descending gradually into the Sacramento Valley.]

Night found us on the mountain in a forest of mighty pine and fir, making our best endeavors to shelter the teams from the storm, getting a frugal supper, and preparing for a final leave of the teams on the morrow.

November 6. Morning came and all but nine men, who were selected to stay with the teams, bade farewell to everything but a small pack of clothes and three or four days' rations, which each one packed on his back. . . . I carried a change of underclothes, both of flannel and of cotton, two pairs of socks, one coat, one pants, one neck handkerchief, my journal, pocket Bible, pocketbook and a few days' provisions.

We commenced our way in ten inches of snow, bidding adieu to those we left behind and casting a lingering look upon the teams and wagons, in full belief that it was the last time we should behold them.**

Cut loose from all hindrance and appreciating the importance of time, we journeyed on as fast as cord and muscle would carry us, raising at very short distances elevation after elevation of the mountain range and passing at every step the remnants of once fine trains fleeing like ourselves from the dangers of the increasing storm. Never shall I forget the scenes of that day.

The storm increased as the day advanced. The clouds were dark and lowering on mountaintops. The snow descended as it descends only in a

---

* *The diary entries for November 5, 6, 7 and 8 are created by using Swain's narrative recollection of those days written in his letter of March 15, 1850.*
** *Swain went with James Pratt and six other Rangers; Bailey and eight others stayed with the two wagons and would move ahead more slowly.*

mountainous region, and the thick foliage of the dark, mammoth firs and pines was loaded and bowed down with snowy crescents rising one above another, as limb succeeded limb, to the tops of those magnificent spires, among which the driving clouds frequently mingled. Snow fell deep and melted fast when fallen. Animals, already worn down by the journey of 2,800 miles, were poorly competent for the fatigue of toiling up hills and drawing vehicles through snow and water, especially too when deprived of food, and many were the noble animals which had performed their duty on that long journey that fell beneath their burdens this day, to be left a prey to the bear and wolf of that mountain desert.

Had manhood in its strength been doomed to surmount these dangers alone, human suffering would have been less. But there were the infirm and aged, for even here were gray heads. Many of the emigrants were palsied by that terrible disease, scurvy. Here too were females and children of every age. Here might be seen a mother wading through the snow and in her arms an infant child closely and thickly wrapped with whatever would secure it from the storm, while the father was close at hand exerting to the utmost in getting along his team, wagon, and provisions—the last and only hope of securing the life of the family. There might be seen a mother, a sister or a wife, winding along the mountain road, packing blankets and other articles, followed by children of every age, each with some article on his back or in his hands, hoping thus to enable the teams to get along by lessening the load.

During the whole afternoon our party waded through two feet of snow with no path, alternately leading an hour each, guided by the blazes on the trees by the sides of the road, while the fresh track of the grizzly bear plainly told the character of the mountain natives.

[Often the trail dropped abruptly into ravines, then climbed around giant rocks back to the precariously narrow crestline of the mountain ridge which one diarist called "the Devil's backbone."

["This ridge was . . . barely wide enough for a road. It was frightful to look down into the dark gaping gorges. . . . From this summit to the Sacramento Valley the descent is nearly 5,000 feet." "Between us and the promised land, the long ridges and intervening chasms stretch down their winding, tortuous lengths. . . . A few miles due west would land us in the Sacramento Valley, but that route is only possible for birds. . . . We are as inexorably bound to this ridge as is a locomotive to its iron track."]

The soaking of the melting snow had by afternoon compelled me to abandon half my pack, together with my rifle. I had left all else with but little regret, but when I leaned my rifle against a tree with my belt and sidearms, I felt I was leaving an old friend behind me.

Eight o'clock found us almost out of the line of snow, gathered around a blazing campfire, preparing our pinole and coffee.

We stood around the fire till morning, while the rain fell in streams.

November 7.   Daylight found us on bare ground and passing along the first oaks we had seen since leaving Missouri. We traveled all day in the most drenching rain that I ever saw and over the worst road that ever was. I was often in the mud up to my boot tops.

["On we went—on, on. We reached the Big Hollow in which many were encamped. Here we wound our way by footpath on a narrow ridge several thousand feet above the camps below.*

["Along the ridge on both sides are deep ravines. Rain and wind beat one almost unprotected, for the mountains here are bare of trees with the exception of scattering oaks. On we went, with sore feet, giving ourselves no time even to eat or rest, in the hope of reaching the settlement by night.

["We pressed on in line. In the darkness, wind, and rain, on we went. The road was muddy and rocky. . . . We kept on it with great difficulty. We finally turned out on wet and rocky soil to get a little rest. We sat until we became chilled through. It was dark and raining hard all the time. Then on we went, over the rocks and in the mud and water and in the storm for an hour longer, when we came to where we were hailed by voices under a tree. It proved to be Ladd and Swain. Then, worn out, we turned in. Snug together we sat under the tree in the rain—an awful night. We could make no fire, for the wet oak was the only timber. We suffered on through the night."]

Dark found me and several of the boys at the foot of the last hill, encamped in the Sacramento Valley under a live oak tree without fire and with every thread of clothes wet, sheltered from the rain by only my blanket, while on both sides and in front the mountain, torrents kept up their music to the tune of old Niagara.

I shall never forget that night! I had no fears for myself, for I knew that I could "stand the fire." But I expected the morning would see three

---

* *More generally called Deep or Steep Hollow, this tremendous ravine was a camping and resting place for those who had managed to bring their wagons this far. The trail left the ridgetop—too narrow and rocky to allow passage of wagons—and led steeply down the south side of the ridge, all the way to the bottom. There many wagons, animals and much equipment were abandoned, for after the long descent the trail climbed out of the hollow to the ridgetop—a struggle too great for many teams.*

Unencumbered with wagons or even pack animals, Swain and the other Rangers were able to follow a path which held to the crest above the depths of Steep Hollow.

of my companions in another world. Fortunately for them I had brought a pint bottle of "Number Six" with me from the train, and I administered it to them every hour through the night and compelled them to stir around frequently.

November 8.　　The moon rose and shone dimly through the clouds, and at three o'clock we could see where we could step. After considerable exertion I got them all up and started. ["Before daylight we arose, stiff and cold, and started our way in the wind and rain."]

The rain soon ceased. At dawn we arrived at Antelope Creek, eight miles from Lawson's, and found it not fordable. The sky cleared, and the sun shone warmly. We kindled a rousing fire, dried, and rested ourselves till noon, when General Wilson's son William, Frank Cannon and myself —with our clothes lashed to our shoulders—forded the stream with setting poles. None of the others would attempt it. It was the hardest job I ever had. When I stepped onto the opposite shore I thought my flesh would drop from my bones as high as the water came to my waist.*

We arrived at Lawson's at sundown, tired and worn with toil and exposure.

[Journey's end, twenty-five weeks from Independence, May 16, to Lassen's ranch, November 8.

[But Swain and all the others already at Lassen's and those coming in each hour were in no mood to celebrate. Whatever enthusiasm they had once felt in anticipating their first campfire in California had long since been sapped by fatigue, hunger, and sickness. "A more pitiable and rusty-looking set of footsore, lantern-jawed skeletons could not be found outside the ranks of the California emigrant army than came by this Lassen route."

["Our journey is done, and we hardly know what to do with ourselves. . . . There will be no more Indian alarms; no more stampedes; no more pulling, carrying, and hauling at wagons. . . . We are in rags, almost barefooted, without provisions. . . . But however sad for the fate of the poor fellows who fell by the way, we are glad to have got here at all."

---

* *General Wilson's son was hurrying to Lassen's Ranch to get some mules for his family, still far back on the trail. Franklin Cannon was one of the original Wolverine Rangers.*

　James Pratt wrote this day, November 8, that after Swain had crossed Antelope Creek with Wilson and Cannon, "the rest of us concluded to remain, since the weather was clearing and the stream was abating. . . . We passed the day quite comfortably." That afternoon Pratt and the others "felled a tree on this side of the stream, which fell across . . . making us a safe crossing." They reached Lassen's Ranch the next day.

[First letters sent home were often gloomy, even self-pitying. One young husband wrote to his wife: "I won't attempt to write [about the trip], but when you see my journal . . . you will shed tears when you come to know how much I have suffered and the hardships I have encountered. If it had not been for you and the children to think of, I should certainly have given up and died."

[The relief expedition commander, Captain Rucker, described the cut-off survivors as "a pitiable sight. There were cripples from scurvy and other diseases, women prostrated by weakness, and children who could not move a limb. In advance of the wagons were men mounted on mules who had to be lifted off their animals so entirely disabled had they become from the effect of scurvy. No one could view this scene of helplessness without commending the foresight which dictated that relief without which some of the recipients would inevitably have perished in the snows."

[At Lassen's Ranch "everything is a regular jam. Men going hither and yon, some in search of friends whom they are to meet here, others are those to be met. Some are buying provisions, some whiskey, some victuals, and others have nothing to buy with. . . .

["The tenements at Lassen's are three sun-dried brick houses, eleven by thirty, in which are kept a tavern, grocery, provision store, etc. . . . Along the road for half a mile are posted numerous tents and wagons at which provisions are for sale . . . to the poor, worn-down penniless emigrants." "Twenty-five cents for a drink of whiskey, fifty cents for brandy. . . . There is plenty of liquor. No lack of drink or drunkards, regular bloats. There are some dilapidated outbuildings and a log house in the course of erection. The whole establishment is on the bank of Deer Creek, the bank of which is here fifteen or twenty feet high and lined with alder, sycamore, willow, etc. Quarters and parts of beef hang on the trees and lie around on logs. The whole place is surrounded with filth. Bones, rags, chips, sticks, skulls, hair, skin, entrails, blood, etc. The steep bank, down which all must go for water, is paved with this offal."

[Through three days of heavy rain Swain waited at Lassen's Ranch, anxious for the arrival of Frederick Bailey and other Rangers still on the trail. A few came in each day, until all were at last safe from the mountain storms.

[On the morning of November 11, Swain and Bailey set out from Lassen's to walk the fifty-seven miles south to the nearest diggings on the Feather River, where they expected to meet Michael Hutchinson. The trail was deep in mud, the streams swollen and difficult to ford. On November 14 they reached Long's Bar, a mining camp where they met for the first time not emigrants, but miners—men who had dug gold from this very stream. Swain and Bailey looked for Hutchinson, impatient to stake their claim in El Dorado.]

Back Home

"Where you are or how you have fared we know not. . . ."

Sunday, 2 P.M.
Youngstown, November 4, 1849

Dear William,

Another month in time's swift calendar has rolled around and brought the time to write you again. But we have heard nothing from you since I last wrote you. Your last that we have received was dated "Fort Laramie, July 4," just four months ago. Where you are or how you have fared we know not, but hope you were in California by the 1st of October. If so, we expect to hear from you by the 15th of December, as your letter would not leave San Francisco till November 1. I see by telegraph there was an arrival at St. Louis from Salt Lake on the 25th October, bringing news to the 28th September from the Lake. I hope I shall get a line from you dated at that place by Tuesday or Wednesday of this week. There are stories in circulation here to the effect that there is great suffering on the desert beyond Salt Lake in consequence of the little grass there being burned up by emigrants ahead and that a great many will have to winter in Mormon settlements. These things make us feel anxious for you, and the fact that we don't hear from you does not contribute to lessen it at all. But I don't believe you could be kept at Salt Lake this winter if there was not a blade of grass on the desert. But we must bide our time until we hear from you. I hope you will hear from home as soon as you get to Sutter's Fort. I have written every mail and sent you three, four, or five papers at each time to keep you up with the times in the States. I shall send you some by this [mail].

We are all well and may this speedily find you the same. I think the health of Mother, Sabrina, and Little Sis is full as good as when I last wrote you. . . .

All of our friends are well, as far as I know. . . . We have had a fine autumn. . . . Our village is quite still just now, but we have had "great excitement" lately. Old grasswidow Parker has married a sergeant at the Fort, and Higby Clark and Rosa Weston were married last week. . . .

The people, especially the capitalists and enterprising men, are determined that we must have a railroad from St. Louis to San Francisco so that this generation will have use of it. Boston demands that it shall be made in five years. All assent that it is necessary, and it will probably be finished in ten or fifteen years. . . .

[continued on November 7]

November 7, 1849

Dear Will,

We are well this morning and send a thousand good wishes to you, and also we wish to be remembered to Mr. Hutchinson and to your other companions. Dr. Root's family are all well, saw him last night. Mrs. Bailey was still at her brother's beyond Buffalo the last we saw of her. . . .

I spent the evening with the Campbells last Saturday. . . . Mrs. Campbell said she had wanted to see you and bid you goodbye when you left last April. She said she felt as if one of her own family was leaving, and when you left she went to their chamber window and watched you get into Dr. Root's wagon and leave.

It is twenty minutes past eight o'clock now and the mail closes at 8:30, so goodbye and may God bless you. Mother sends all sorts of love to her poor boy.

> Your brother,
> George Swain

November 4, 1849—Youngstown

Ever dear William,

I am once more induced to drop a few lines to you, which is a very pleasant task involved upon me. The protecting hand of our heavenly Father has thus far been over us in your absence, and we have been preserved from dangerous illness and death. O, my dear, this anxiety of mind and the struggling of feelings to keep myself up is much greater than anyone is aware of. When I think of your absence, the long journey, sickness and dangers of every kind, I am ready to exclaim that none but an Almighty Creator could keep you from harm.

O that I could but see you one half-hour today and exchange one kind word and look, would it not be a consolation! And still, the pangs of separation would be greater. William, I hope you have not been as lonely this summer as I have been. But your cares without doubt have been much greater. Never, until your absence, had I learned the strength of my attachment. I frequently feel as though I could not live were you to be taken away. I feel that I am not prepared for the blow. Help me, O Lord, to say "Thy will be done."

We have a good deal of California news of late. Nothing very interesting, though some are making themselves rich by industry and hard labor and others by speculation. But the reports are very contradictory and therefore cannot be relied upon.

The shades of night have once more shed their darkening rays over us, and we as a family are comfortably seated around the fireside, numbering six in all, including Delia Barber and Martin D., who is working for us at present. Mother and George and Delia are reading. I have just got the chores done up and little Sister in bed and have seated myself to finish this imperfect epistle. . . .

My health is improving considerably from what it was in the summer. My back continues to trouble me yet, and I fear it always will. It is not quite as weak as it has been, but there is a great deal of pain below the shoulders and in the small of the back, which if I lift or exercise too much is much worse.

Eliza C. is tolerable well, but not by any means tough. She is pretty troublesome nights and is rather hard to tend and govern. . . .

Sis is crying, and I must leave the rest for another time. So, good night, William.

Tuesday, [November 6], 4 o'clock P.M.

I have again seated myself to finish out this sheet for tomorrow's mail. . . . We are looking for a letter from you from Salt Lake, as telegraphic dispatch brings news from August 17 stating that several thousand will remain there through the winter owing to the scarcity of grass, it having been burnt by a company of emigrants. I think there is no probability of your being there, not if there is a possibility of your getting through, which I hope you have been long enough now [to have done] and [that you know] something of what your prospects are by this time and have written a letter home and that ere you read this we shall have heard of your safety and arrival in California. And William, if God spares you to get home again, I shall henceforth and forever say "Where you go I go and where you stay I stay." If you get home with your health and make enough to clear your way, I shall be perfectly satisfied. May God add His blessing and return you to your family speedily.

My sheet is now full and I must close.

From your affectionate wife,
Sabrina Swain

CHAPTER X

In the Diggings

"You may rest assured that I have an older head on my shoulders by about 1,000 years than when I left the states."

On November 26, 1849, the last refugees from Lassen's Cut-off slumped down in the camps around Lassen's Ranch. Thanks to Rucker, Peoples, Todd, Rogers and the other men in the government relief expedition, the cut-off had been cleared of the last emigrants. They were all safe, ready to dig for gold.

Back on the trail, drifts of snow covered 200 miles of collapsed and mired wagons, flapping tents, bloated carcasses and treasured possessions scattered along that route which once had promised quick entry to the gold mines.

On the Carson and Truckee trails, those who crossed the Sierra Nevada in September and even October had an easy time compared to what had happened on Lassen's. But wherever and whenever they set up their first camps in California, the goldseekers had no way of knowing how many thousands had reached the mines ahead of them. They remembered the crowds at Independence or St. Joseph and the long lines of wagons along the Platte; they recalled reports of other trails to California and of ships sailing from New York crowded with goldseekers. But no one in the fall of 1849, including Military Governor Riley (Mason had resigned), sensed or foresaw the magnitude of the rush to California.

Far to the south of the Carson, Truckee and Lassen trails, some 10,000 more overlanders completed their unforgettable journeys after months on the Santa Fe trail or one of the several routes that led from Texas and Vera Cruz across Mexico. Many of these companies found themselves by fall in the West Coast ports of San Blas, Mazatlán and even

Acapulco, where they finally obtained ships to carry them to California.

By all the overland routes at least 42,000 goldseekers reached California between late July and the end of 1849. As well, about 6,000 Mexicans from Sonora emigrated to the mining region, where they added to the population of Sonorans—"foreigners"—who had come there in 1848.

Long before the first overlanders set out from the western frontier, other Americans had reached El Dorado by sea. In early October 1848, before the news of gold at Sutter's mill had spread the "gold fever," the steamship *California* sailed from New York bound for San Francisco with only a few passengers. By the time she had steamed around Cape Horn and anchored off Panama City on January 30, 1849, some 1,500 goldseekers had responded to President Polk's December 5 confirmation of the gold discovery by sailing from eastern ports to Chagres, where they crossed the Isthmus to Panama City, to wait for the *California*—each of them frantic to book passage for San Francisco. But the steamer had accommodations for only one hundred. Demand for tickets nurtured trickery, thievery and prices that soared to more than $1,000 for a bunk in steerage.

On February 28 the *California* entered San Francisco Bay, causing a wild celebration among the city's wintering miners. The passengers— about 450 of them—rushed ashore, as did the crew, leaving the ship abandoned. Some weeks later, on April 1, the *Oregon* and then the *Panama* on June 4 reached San Francisco, each jammed with goldseekers, many of whom had crowded on board at Panama City. Scores of ships from foreign ports brought Frenchmen, Chileans, Peruvians, Mexicans and the first of many Chinese.

By the end of December 1849, 697 vessels had entered the harbor, delivering more than 41,000 Americans and foreigners, of whom fewer than 800 were women. Most of those ships were deserted by their crews, left to rot on mudflats or to creak at anchor, until in later years some would be resurrected to carry thousands back to the States.

The 89,000 goldseekers were not settlers or pioneers in the tradition of America's westward migration. These people came as exploiters, transients, ready to take, not to build. Whether in the diggings or in San Francisco, Sacramento City, or Stockton, they found themselves surrounded by crowds of hurrying men concerned only with how to make the greatest amount of money in the shortest time. With that common motive, they also shared an indifference toward California and its future. No one knew where he might be next week, maybe headed home or working a claim on Sutter Creek. No one wanted to be tied down and burdened by social responsibility. There were no jails; justice was in-

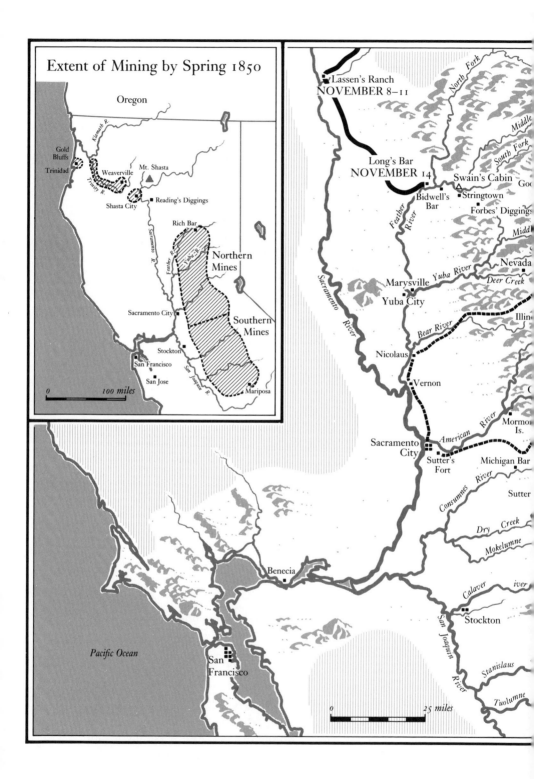

Extent of Mining by Spring 1850

Oregon

Gold
Bluffs
Trinidad

Klamath R.

Weaverville

Trinity R.

Shasta City

Mt. Shasta

Reading's Diggings

Rich Bar

Sacramento R.

Feather R.

Yuba R.

Northern
Mines

Sacramento City

Southern
Mines

Stockton

San Francisco

San Joaquin R.

San Jose

Mariposa

0   100 *miles*

Lassen's Ranch
NOVEMBER 8–11

North Fork

Middle

South Fork

Long's Bar
NOVEMBER 14

Swain's Cabin

Goo

Bidwell's
Bar

Stringtown

Forbes' Diggings

Feather

River

Midd

Sacramento

River

Marysville

Yuba River

Nevada

Deer Creek

Yuba City

Bear River

Illin

Nicolaus

Vernon

River

Mormo
Is.

Sacramento
City

American River

Michigan Bar

Sutter's
Fort

Sutter

Consumnes River

Dry Creek

Mokelumne

Benecia

Calaver   *iver*

San Joaquin

Stockton

River

Pacific Ocean

San
Francisco

Stanislaus

Tuolumne

0   25 *miles*

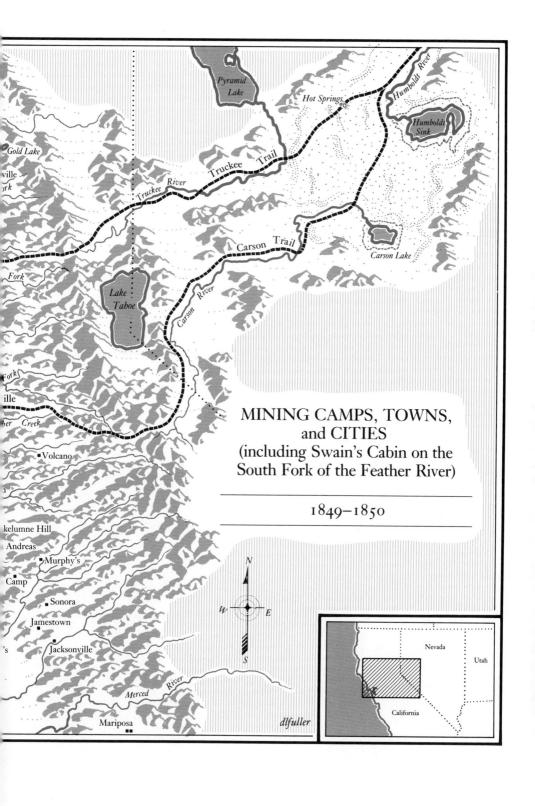

Pyramid
Lake

Hot Springs

Humboldt River

Humboldt
Sink

Gold Lake

ville
ork

Truckee Trail

Truckee River

Carson Trail

Carson Lake

Fork

Lake
Tahoe

Carson River

ork

ille

her Creek

Volcano

**MINING CAMPS, TOWNS,
and CITIES**
(including Swain's Cabin on the
South Fork of the Feather River)

1849–1850

kelumne Hill

Andreas

Murphy's

Camp

Sonora

Jamestown

Jacksonville

's

Merced River

Mariposa

N
W   E
S

Nevada

Utah

California

dlfuller

flicted quickly so as not to delay those called upon to pass judgment. In a world of strangers, in a place without evidence of government, religion or law, the goldseekers felt free to grasp for fortune. Like soldiers in a foreign land, it would be easy for many of them to slough off the social codes and moral precepts that had been enforced by family, friends and the influence of the church.

Arriving in California with their expectations still defined by what they had heard before leaving the States, hoping to achieve the quick successes that had been common and so widely reported in 1848, the men of '49 were dismayed to see so many miners along the banks of the American, Feather, Mokelumne and other rivers. They faced a reality that some must have anticipated and feared: too many goldseekers had come to El Dorado.

In 1848 a maximum of 6,000 worked the diggings. By December 1849 there were at least 40,000 miners in the same area. While the '48ers had always been able to find a place to dig and had usually been quickly rewarded, the crowds in the fall of '49 found many of the rivers and their tributaries already claimed. In San Francisco, Sacramento City and Stockton and in the hill towns of Placerville, Mokelumne Hill, Sonora, Nevada City, Volcano and other settlements, another 40,000 men and a few women prepared to go into the mines or sought their fortunes in burgeoning business opportunities. Each day several thousand gave up their hopes and made plans to return home.

The ignorance of the new arrivals and their confrontation with the realities of California were poignantly expressed by a Frenchman who wrote to a newspaper in Paris: "On our poor little maps of California printed in France, the San Joaquin is shown as a river flowing between the California mountains and the sea, a short distance from San Francisco, in the midst of a rich plain which its waters cover with gold dust every year. The editors had even taken the pains to gild that precious plain on their maps. . . . One could, as it were, go to the mines in the morning and return home each evening to sleep. Alas, the same is true of the map as with almost everything that is said about California: one can find out the truth only in the place itself."

For the thousands who came by sea, like the Frenchman, the first reality was San Francisco, a place of frantic growth. From the ship-crowded waterfront to the sandy hills, they heard the sounds of construction, the shouts of auctioneers and the music of gambling saloons. Boxes, bags, barrels, crates of foodstuffs and merchandise were stacked and piled in the mud and stagnant water of the streets. Scores of tents and canvas-covered structures flapped and swayed next to wooden and iron buildings shipped in from the states. A place without homes, a boom town of men, San Francisco was given over entirely to business, speculation and entertainment. Auction houses, hotels, bathhouses, groggeries, billiard rooms, boardinghouses, eating and drinking houses, two- and four-story office buildings, banks and scores of gambling saloons—all these, along with "dens of lewd women," crowded the steep and filthy streets.

With gambling the most obvious and profitable business, there was great demand for space, if only under canvas, where tables could be set up for monte, roulette, rouge et noire, with room for a bar, musicians and paintings of naked women. Rents in August at the Parker House attested to the booming economy. A small room on the second floor rented to a monte dealer for $1,800 per month, two other rooms on the same floor for $2,400 per month, with the hotel's annual revenue totaling $150,000. Next door a canvas tent fifteen by twenty-five feet, called El Dorado, rented to gamblers for $40,000 annually. Rents were paid in advance, as was interest on borrowed money at 8 to 15 percent *per month*—all paid in gold dust.*

In August, San Francisco's population was estimated at 6,000, by November 15,000. But it mattered little, so many were transients. Of the thousands who arrived each month by ship, most headed for the mines after a few days of San Francisco's temptations. From the Sierra mining camps hundreds of bearded miners landed each day, brought to the west's first boom town by a growing fleet of boats that sailed the Sacramento and San Joaquin rivers. Many wore money belts fat with gold dust. Others who had found disappointment came to work as carpenters, mechanics or laborers for wages that would have seemed munificent back home but would never provide what had been promised in California.

Not only thousands of would-be and former miners passed through San Francisco but everything that the new Californian needed, from whiskey to nails. Merchants in New York and other ports sent ships around Cape Horn loaded with whatever they thought would sell in the California market: tons of flour and pork, boxes of needles, bundles of shovels, axes and picks, thousands of yards of canvas, lumber in quantity and all sizes, boots, blankets, woolen clothing, mirrors, chandeliers, mahogany furniture, champagnes and wines, food of all kinds from canned oysters to cheeses. More important to the men of California than anything else, ocean steamers brought tons of mail. On August 26, 1849, the steamer *Panama* delivered to the overwhelmed San Francisco post office bags with 25,000 letters. Future shipments would double that number.

---

* To build a ten-room house in an eastern city in 1850 cost about $2,000.

Inasmuch as the gold region with scores of mining camps and several towns offered a far greater market than San Francisco, most of the imports were loaded onto smaller boats for the 150-mile passage up the Sacramento or San Joaquin rivers to Sacramento City or Stockton. Sacramento City served as the commercial and transport center for the northern mines scattered along the tributaries of the Sacramento River, while Stockton was equally important for the southern mines on the tributaries of the San Joaquin. From a few wooden shanties and canvas-covered structures in the spring, both settlements grew rapidly during the summer of 1849. Then in the fall they felt the impact of the overlanders' needs for food, tents, boots, blankets, and everything else abandoned on the trails. In both cities warehouses, hotels, stores, restaurants and gambling halls were built of logs, canvas, sheet iron, bricks—whatever could be found, purchased or cannibalized. Along the rivers' banks scores of ships were tied up, their cargoes stacked under the sycamore and cottonwood trees. As at San Francisco, many of these vessels had been abandoned by their crews, and merchants had taken them as storehouses and hotels.

Few if any of the miners, businessmen, merchants, shippers, speculators, bankers, gamblers—the thousands of men in the instant cities and scores of mining camps—paused that fall of 1849 to consider what wondrous changes had been accomplished in a matter of months: village to metropolis at San Francisco, wilderness to thriving ports at Sacramento City and Stockton, canyons and gulches to one-street mining towns, quiet rivers to commercial thoroughfares—everywhere the sounds of growth, business and high hopes. It had all been done without technology. Except for the oceangoing sidewheelers that came into San Francisco bay, there were few if any steam engines as yet in California. Mining techniques were primitive, building materials and methods simple; transport was by sail, muleback or wagon, and communication by interminable mail. The motive forces had been avarice, impatience, inventiveness and optimism.

Yankee enterprise and investment accelerated the transformation of California. Delivery of everything the mining region needed came by sailing vessels upriver from San Francisco, a voyage that took three to ten days. With demand so great and prices fluctuating wildly from day to day, merchants and speculators needed faster, more reliable transport for their merchandise. In response, East Coast businessmen shipped three disassembled steamboats to San Francisco. Launched in September, they replaced the uncertainty of sail with the dependability of steam; but they were too small to carry tons of freight and hundreds of passengers. Beginning in October, larger steamers that had sailed around Cape Horn established ten-to-twelve-hour scheduled service between San Francisco and the river ports. The first of what the San Francisco newspapers admiringly described as "floating palaces," the 750-ton *Senator* made a profit of over $60,000 each month during the first year of operation. Freight charges of $40 and more per ton from San Francisco to Sacramento City exceeded the cost of shipping the same goods from New York to the booming Pacific port.

While the river transport system was modernized, getting the barrels of flour, kegs of pork and liquor, bags of beans, bales, sacks and boxes from the river ports up to the mining camps and towns depended on wagons and pack mules. Each day throughout the dry season (May to October or November) hundreds of mule- and ox-drawn wagons set out from Sacramento City and Stockton over dusty roads, headed upcountry to the stores, hotels, and gambling saloons. In country too steep for wagons, long trains of pack mules followed trails that climbed high along narrow ridges and descended sharply to remote collections of miners' tents and shanties. Even the surefooted mules, "clipper ships of the mountains," were often delayed by storms, mountain slides or deep snowdrifts which made packing hazardous and sometimes impossible. But great profits could be made in this trade, with the packers charging as much as 75 cents per pound.

By spring 1850, competition among steamboats, freighters and packers would drive prices down, easing the risks of the small merchants and the living expenses of the miners. But meantime, with gold seemingly inexhaustible and the population vastly increased, the forces were obviously at hand to create a staggering inflation. A boiled egg cost 75 cents, a $2,000 steam engine sold for $15,000, a prostitute claimed to have made $50,000 in 1849, a farmer made $25,000 selling vegetables—blankets cost $12, boots $35, flour $35 per barrel. Whatever the price today or expected tomorrow, all depended on the miners' continued success and their increasing demand for food, shelter, transport, supplies and entertainment.

The economy was based on gold production, but no one knew just how much was being mined, put into circulation and shipped back to the States or to Europe, Mexico and South America. Such statistics were calculated in later years, but even then they would reflect considerable uncertainty. Estimates of gold production for 1848 ranged from $245,000 to $10 million, with similar imprecision for 1849: $10 million to $40 million. Whatever the actual numbers, the fact was that California boomed on gold, with production reaching a more accurate total of $81 million in 1852.

As with the sum, so the parts reported in 1849 contrasted widely, from the many miners who panned one or two ounces each day—$16 to $32—to the lucky few who struck it rich. Two men on the Yuba River reported November 4 that after two weeks' work "we have got $5,000." A company of miners on the American River as of August 30 "had raised in three days over $15,000." Not only the newspapers trumpeted these successes, they were reported and exaggerated by miners, packers and gamblers moving from one mining camp to another.

Everyone eagerly believed the stories of success, old-timers who had been mining since spring '49 and newcomers from ships or overland trails. They all needed reassurance that, despite the crowds of miners, California's rivers, creekbeds and dry diggings could still yield the sudden fortunes that would justify months of unrewarding work or weary travel. Especially anxious to hear of rich strikes were the thousands who arrived in November after the disasters on Lassen's Cut-off or after a voyage long delayed by a rough passage around Cape Horn.

William Swain was among those November latecomers—he and Frederick Bailey, Michael Hutchinson, John Root, James Pratt, Horace Ladd and the other Rangers, all trying to decide where to stake their claims in a world they had long anticipated and now entered with anxiety.

The gold mines were scattered through a vast area along the western slopes of the Sierra Nevada. While everyone used the word "mines," they were actually talking about the rivers, for most of the gold had been dug from the banks and flats and gravel-rock bars of the ten rivers that flowed through the foothills to join the two great rivers in the central valley.

Since 1848 it had been customary to speak of the mining region as two separate areas. The northern mines referred to the Feather, Yuba, Bear and American rivers, each with several forks and many lesser tributaries, all flowing through a mountainous country of deep canyons and gorges. Abundant winter rains and melting snow assured year-round water in all the streams.

In the southern mines the scene was quite different, so much so that the area was often described as "the dry diggings," meaning that gold had to be dug some distance from water during the summer because many smaller streams were dry. Here the main rivers—the Consumnes, Mokelumne, Calaveras, Stanislaus, Tuolumne, Merced and, farther south, the Mariposa—flowed through the foothills at a lower altitude, in a rolling, arid country sparsely covered with oak groves and madrones.

When the overlanders crowded in during the fall of '49, they looked for likely claims in the first mines they came to. If they had followed the Truckee trail, they first tried the North Fork of the American River or

the Bear River or the South Fork of the Yuba. If they came in on the
Carson trail, they first looked for gold along the South Fork of the American or the North Fork of the Consumnes. For those who hiked south
from Lassen's Ranch, the first mines were near the junction of the North
and Middle Forks of the Feather River. From the trails that ended in
southern California, the overlanders traveled north to reach the mines
along the Mariposa, Merced and Tuolumne. Also crowding into this
region were the Mexicans, who settled around a town called Sonora, on
a branch of the Tuolumne. As their number increased, the American
miners grew resentful of these intruders who "had no right" to gold that
belonged only to citizens of the United States.

The would-be miners who landed in San Francisco scattered
throughout both the northern and southern mines, for they could take a
boat upriver to Stockton, Sacramento City or the newest river port, the
booming town of Marysville at the mouth of the Yuba River. From these
centers, wagon and pack-mule trails led into the hills and to the many
mining camps.

When Swain and Bailey left Lassen's Ranch on November 11, they
set out over a well-marked trail for the Feather River. After a three-day
hike, they reached a mining camp called Long's Bar, a collection of
squalid shacks and tents along the Feather where some two thousand
miners crowded together, most of them driven from their claims by the
rising waters of the river and its forks. Swain and Bailey found Michael
Hutchinson there, and with two other Rangers they agreed to form a
mining partnership. Purchasing high-priced provisions at Long's Trading
Post, they packed their supplies and mining tools on their backs and
followed a muddy trail over a high ridge and down to the South Fork of
the Feather, where they staked a claim at the edge of the roaring stream.

Though they did not know it, Swain and his partners came to their
first claim well prepared for the rigors of mining life. They had been
toughened by having walked 2,000 miles; they were used to sleeping in a
blanket or two, where only the larger rocks had been kicked aside; they
had survived months of careless cooking which produced greasy flapjacks
and pork and beans or whatever else might be warmed with least effort.
How different the adjustment was for the thousands of men who had
spent five or six months confined to the narrow decks, stuffy, seasick
cabins and steerage of sailing ships and steamers. These men landed at
San Francisco soft, uncallused and unready for the work of miners that
would prove comparable to the sweaty toil of the Irish laborers who had
dug canals across New York, Ohio and other states.

While few of the words and phrases that had been used to describe

California would prove to be accurate, the most common was the most precise: in the diggings. Digging was the constant and endless task that faced every miner. Digging on a river bar in sand, gravel and rocks, between massive boulders, some of which had to be pushed aside. Digging in a dust-dry gulch hundreds of yards from the cool sounds of rushing water. Always digging, down and down through the eons of accumulation of rock and gravel that dulled pickaxes and bent shovels. Down six, eight, ten feet to reach bedrock, where the gold in flakes, granules or coarse nuggets—some several ounces large—would be found by weary miners whose hearts would leap and voices shout in triumph.

Even in 1848 when success came quickly to a few thousand miners and campfire stories sent men hurrying to the latest strike, even then the labor of digging had been universal. Whether at Mokelumne Hill in the southern mines or Rough and Ready to the north, the gold had to be dug from beneath the overlay of sand, gravel and rock. Through 1848 and most of 1849 the miners depended on the pan and the rocker to separate the gold. Simple to operate and easily portable, these "machines" remained dominant as long as the miners' nomadic impulse was sustained by new discoveries or the belief that such discoveries could be made by prospecting ever farther upstream. Thousands of newcomers were reluctant to give up the methods of their predecessors. No one wanted to invest time and money in complex machinery that would require months —maybe years—to achieve profitability, and, worse, would prevent joining the rush to the latest discovery.

By fall '49 there were few new discoveries and the old diggings were overwhelmed by miners. Gold could still be found, but no longer in such easy abundance. More efficient mining methods were called for—and so the long tom came into use.

It was simply an enlarged rocker, eight to fifteen feet in length. With its upper end attached to a flume or ditch which delivered a constant stream of water, the long tom allowed three or four men to wash great quantities of dirt dug by others at their claim. Because this primitive improvement in mining technology reduced the cost—the time and effort —of washing each cubic yard of dirt, miners could work claims that would have been unprofitable with only pan and rocker.

As important as was the tom, an even greater gain in efficiency came from the use of mercury or quicksilver, which was being mined south of San Francisco at New Almaden. Because this element has an affinity for gold, it was placed along the riffles or cleats, the obstacles on the bottom of the tom over which the water carried the gold-bearing sand and gravel. With this magnet, even the smallest specks of gold were held and amalgamated with the mercury. At the end of the day the men scraped the mercury from the riffles and heated it until it turned to vapor, releasing the gold. When cooled to its liquid form, the mercury was ready to be used the next day.

As science slowly replaced luck, as patience competed with impulse, other changes evolved during the fall of 1849. By far the most important was river mining. Living week after week along the rocky banks of the many rivers, looking at those roaring, winter-high waters that tumbled down from the Sierra Nevada, the miners believed—they knew—that for thousands of years the river bottoms had accumulated great deposits of gold, lodged in crevices, stored in potholes, piled up behind great boulders. Safe from all the digging of 1848, gold awaited the men who could devise a means of harvesting such a treasure. The concept satisfied both imagination and avarice. Building dams, flumes and races to divert the rivers would require steady labor for many months, some skill and considerable money to pay the costs of feeding the men and buying equipment. To meet this challenge, companies would have to be formed, not unlike those organized for the overland journey.

Thus a major change evolved—from individual, nomadic prospecting with simple, portable equipment to a commitment by a group of men on a single claim to invest months of effort in a complex, cooperative project. Here was Yankee enterprise and inventiveness at its best: move the Sierra's rivers, force them out of their ancient channels, lay bare the rivers' beds.

By January 1850, when Swain and his partners came to the South Fork, river mining had become the ambition of most miners. The great idea had been tried with encouraging success along the Feather and the American rivers in the fall of '49, before the winter rains turned those streams into raging torrents that swept away the miners' barriers. The Swain partners staked a claim where they believed they could build a dam after the snows had melted and the river receded. Meantime, they cut down pine trees and built a log cabin on the slope above the river. They did some prospecting in ravines and gullies some distance from the swollen river, washing a few shovels of dirt and gravel in their pans, searching for the specks of yellow that might justify a more serious effort, while waiting for the weather to allow the start of river mining.

Many of Swain's overland companions had also formed partnerships and chosen to stake claims along the South Fork and other branches of the Feather River. Continuing his role as journalist for the Wolverine Rangers, James Pratt wrote regularly to his old newspaper, the Marshall *Statesman*. The editors published each of his reports on his own life and on the doings of other Rangers. Horace Ladd and several others also wrote home telling of Ranger experiences and enterprises. Like thousands of families throughout the United States almost one year after their men had left home, the parents and wives of these Rangers shared their letters with neighbors and townsfolk by giving them to the *Statesman* and the *Democratic Expounder* for publication. Beginning in March (when the first letters from the mines arrived in Marshall) and continuing throughout 1850 and into early 1851, the two newspapers pridefully provided this welcome news for the many Ranger families.

The first letters told of the last days on Lassen's Cut-off. Pratt recalled that they "had expected to get into the mines with provisions enough on hand to last some time and then send down to Sacramento City and team up our supplies. But Fate, Fortune, everything went against us." After only a few days in the diggings, he packed up and went to San Francisco ($14 steerage passage on a schooner), where he rented an office and hung out his sign as a lawyer at the corner of Pacific and Montgomery. He wrote from there on December 20: "There is a world of legal business doing and to be done here. This is one of the most splendid cities for the legal profession in the world. . . . You see no women here. . . . It is a moving, jostling, busy tide of Man in his most earnest throes for sudden wealth. Rights of property are respected, for the interest of all effects this. But for tender sympathies . . . you must look in other lands where Woman has a more controlling and humanizing influence."

After describing San Francisco, Pratt told of the Rangers as he had left them in December. From his report and January letters by Horace Ladd and others, their folks back in Marshall learned that the Reverend Randall Hobart, his son William and five other Rangers had a claim on the South Fork where they planned to build a dam to mine the bottom of the river. The two Camp brothers and three others spent eighteen days building a stone house near their claim, "by far the best house in the mines, containing shelves, buttery and good substantial bunks and stools."

Five Rangers, including Horace Ladd, worked a claim where they lived in a tent they had bought for $75. Writing to his wife, Ladd advised that "there are a great many here that do not make a living. . . . They are men who calculated on finding gold put up in purses and ready for use, but when they find they have to work to get it, they back out. Any man who is willing to work can average his $100 per week in these old diggings where all the cream has been taken. Tom Manser and I have worked hard. The first day . . . we got six and a quarter ounces or $100 in this market at $16 per ounce.

"I should like very much to have been in Marshall during the holidays, but being where I could not play, I worked. On Christmas we took out $51 and New Year's $100. Better than working in Marshall at $1. . . . There was a ball at a trading post below here on Christmas and New Year's, tickets one ounce of gold. But they could not seduce me, I came here for the purpose of making money that we might enjoy it together and I shall not spend my money foolishly."

Horace Ladd sounded much like William Swain writing to Sabrina. The tone and the reassurances were echoed in scores of letters sent back home to women who came to be known as "California widows." In Marshall they learned that several Rangers gave up mining after only a brief effort. The Camp brothers built a store at Bidwell's Bar, the major trading center on the Middle Fork, where on January 19 they had "16,000 pounds of provisions to sell to the miners. . . . We are sure to make money faster than we can dig it." Another Ranger had a tent in Sacramento City which he used for a restaurant and boardinghouse. Unknown to Swain, Bailey and Hutchinson, their companion John Root was reported to have gone to San Francisco, where he "secured a controlling interest in a small boat and did a thriving business." The Rangers' captain, James Potts, speculated in real estate and ran a freight team near Lassen's Ranch, and another Ranger made $14 per day "playing the cornet and violin in a monte house in San Francisco."

Elmon Camp reported from his stone house that "the boys are all uncommonly fleshy and robust. We eat a great quantity of rice and sugar which is considered very healthy here. Mr. Allcott would be perfectly astonished could he see his son George, as I have seen him, scrambling up the steep rugged slope of the mountain with a pack of 50 pounds on his back and the rain pouring down in perfect torrents. His health is excellent and a tougher and more enduring boy I never saw." Less fortunate, two Rangers were accidentally shot but recovered; another became discouraged and left California altogether, "embarking for the Sandwich Islands." Two Rangers died within a month after reaching El Dorado.

Possibly James Pratt spoke for each of the Rangers and all the other husbands, sons and fathers who sent letters home from the Sierra foothills. "Over a month yet must pass before you get this letter. I know your anxiety, your love, your inquietude on my account. How gladly would I, if I could, relieve you by imparting with an electric current the news that I am here alive and well, for even that I know would be a relief to you. But thank Fortune, I am not now on the plains, and the steamer soon makes its trip of the many thousands of miles between us and will soon bear to the port of New York this letter where it will readily find its way to its destination."

William Swain wrote his first letter from California on December 13 —but this report of his safe arrival, so anxiously awaited in Youngstown, never reached the Swains. Sabrina, George and Mrs. Swain were without news of William for seven months, from September 10 when they received his last letter written on the trail at Fort Laramie until April 10, 1850. On that date his letter of January 6 from his claim on the South Fork was read in the Swains' cobblestone house. After their excitement quieted, the Swains shared the letter with the Roots and later with Mrs. Bailey. News of the letter quickly spread through Youngstown, and friends called at the Swain farm to learn what had happened to William, John, Frederick and Michael. Talk of the letter and of when the men would be coming home and hesitant expressions of hope for their success held the town's attention for several days. Similar feelings and questions would be aroused with the arrival of each letter in the months ahead. So it would be in Marshall and in villages and city neighborhoods from Missouri to Maine throughout 1850.

For Swain the silence from Youngstown would not end until March 3, when for the first time in almost a year he would read of home and know that Sabrina and Little Cub, George and his mother had all survived cholera, lesser diseases and imagined accidents. How slowly the mail passed, via Panama, from the cabin on the South Fork of the Feather River to the home in western New York, as it did from hundreds of cabins, tents and huts in the diggings to homes throughout the United States. During the weeks of waiting, fears and doubts gained strength. Except for talk of gold, how and where to get it, nothing commanded the miners' attention as much as their longing to hear from home. Writing to his wife in Illinois, a miner visiting Sacramento City lamented: "This long anxious waiting for news is one of the most corroding cares that trouble me." Then when the letters finally were delivered, what a change of mood! A young miner from Wisconsin set the scene: "If you could have seen us when we received our letters, you would have laughed and perhaps called us fools—such hoorahing, jumping, yelling and screaming. . . . You will take good care and write often when I tell you that I live upon your letters, with a small sprinkling of pork and bread."

As they longed for letters, they cursed the agency responsible for delivering them. The United States Post Office Department had failed utterly to prepare for the growth of California's population and the clamorous demand for mail service. The special agent sent to set up post offices did not arrive until February 1849; his instructions provided for offices at San Diego, San Pedro, Santa Barbara, Monterey and San Francisco. Month by month the Pacific Mail steamships' cargoes of letters increased. On October 31, 1849, more than 45,000 letters "besides un-counted bushels of newspapers" were piled into the San Francisco post office, where the clerks found it necessary to barricade themselves as protection from the shouting, pounding, threatening crowd. To prevent a general riot, the supplicants finally were persuaded to form lines "which extended all the way down the hill into Portsmouth Square and the man at the tail of the longest line might count on spending six hours in it before reaching the window. Those who were near the goal frequently sold out their places to impatient candidates for $10 and even $25. Indeed, several persons in want of money practiced this game daily as a means of living. Vendors of pies, cakes, and newspapers eatablished themselves in front of the office to supply the crowd, while others did a profitable business by carrying cans of coffee up and down the lines."

In November 1849 a post office was opened at Sacramento City, but the problem remained: How to get the letters to the mining camps up in the hills? Once again Yankee enterprise took over. Sensing a profit to be made, many miners left their claims to go into the business of collecting mail at the San Francisco and Sacramento City post offices and delivering it to the camps and towns. These expressmen traveled everywhere, to the most remote camps, wherever a merchant kept a list on which miners could record their names. Each month the expressmen took their lists to the post offices to collect letters and newspapers for their subscribers. They charged from $1 to $2 per letter delivered and usually 50 cents for a letter taken to the post office. Through this system, which became ever more competitive as the number of expressmen and express companies increased, the miners obtained their letters from the States.

Though frustrating and expensive, this mail system did provide, as Swain phrased it, "a line of communication . . . until we can converse with our tongues." He wrote to Sabrina, George, or his mother at least once each month, sending his letters by expressmen down to Sacramento City in time to reach San Francisco for the monthly steamer to Panama. Having packed away his diary to be preserved as the record of his over-land journey, Swain used his letters to tell of his California experiences. So it was with most overland diarists. After a few days, maybe a few weeks in the mines, they gave up diary-keeping; it was far easier and more satisfying to write a monthly letter. Back on the trail there had been a kind of rhythm to their lives, a new camp each evening, a starting and stopping each day, a sense of getting closer to California day by day, all of which provided a structure for the diary. Once in California, settled down to the daily work of mining, living week after week in the same place, they found diary-keeping an onerous task, no longer necessary.

Their diaries had told of the journey. The search for gold was just beginning and would be an experience they could share by mail.

■

January 6, 1850
South Fork of Feather River
25 miles from Long's Trading Post, and
16 miles above Bidwell's Trading Post

Dear George,

It is so long a time since I wrote you and I have passed through so
many scenes and changes of condition that I scarcely know what to say
among the multitude of things I wish to write. You have probably all had
much anxiety about my safe arrival in California, and as you have been
unable to hear from me for so long a time, you will be desirous of having
a lexicon of our journey. I wrote from Raft River by John Root [not
received] who packed through from that point, and I will commence my
letter at that point. But I can only give you a word in this letter as there
is so much to say about California and its mines of gold. . . .

We arrived at Lawson's Ranch on the 8th day of November, tired
and worn down with toil and exposure but hardy, healthy, and in good
spirits, buoyant with hope. We were in the Sacramento Valley in the
rainy season, destitute of provisions, without shelter, and everything eatable worth from $1 to $1.50 per pound. In fact, all was dear but rain and
mud which was everywhere.

We rested three days and put out for the Feather River mines, where
we arrived on the 14th of November at Long's Trading Post, the first
mines on this stream. ["Over two thousand people were living there in
tents, wagons, and small cloth houses. Many were fearful of starving.
. . . The roads were impassable for teams in the valley and consequently
the supply of provisions was small." The settlement was scattered on
both sides of the river. "Wherever the eye wandered on the slopes and in
the ravines close to the edge of the river, tents were pitched. . . ." "There
were fifteen to twenty stores" and the Batavia Hotel, "a comfortable house
of canvas and logs." "The river was about 100 yards wide, running like a
torrent through a narrow gorge in the mountains which are piled up on
either side to the height of one thousand feet."]

The swollen river prevented the miners from operating near its bed where gold is found most abundantly. Generally they were doing no more than boarding themselves, though occasionally one would make a lucky hit and find his thousands. During the fall, miners could average their ounce clear in working with rockers on the bars and edges of the streams, and those who were lucky enough to make dams across the streams before the rains often made large sums in a few days and frequently in a few hours.

["Last fall a small dam put in a short distance above Bidwell's Bar yielded a vast quantity of the precious metal. Two men and their two sons took out of it over $9,000 each and started home in October. They were from Oregon." "If the main stream of the Feather River could be dammed and turned out of its bed, the story of Aladdin's lamp would be eclipsed. The untold wealth of a few miles near Long's Bar would make the richest of the earth's nabob's comparatively poor." For example, on the North Fork of the American River "a company of men, thirty in number, turned the course of the river and took out $75,000. Their greatest yield for any one day was $6,040. . . . Although hundreds of such finds have been made, they are among the cases one reads about and are not of everyday occurrence."]

Mr. Hutchinson had packed through on his pony from the summit where we dissolved the joint stock company that we started with from Independence. He, Mr. Bailey, myself, and Mr. Samuel J. Moore of Calhoun County, Michigan, a Methodist preacher; and Lt. Franklin Cannon of Manchester, Michigan, have agreed to work in the mines on the joint [share equally] principle.

From all that Mr. Hutchinson had learned and that we could hear, we judged the South Fork of the Feather River to be the most likely to yield a pile another summer, for the following reasons: the main part of the Feather River and all the southern rivers have been overrun and consequently the best and richest placers found and worked. The South Fork of the Feather River was reported to be rich, and the gold on it coarse and not much worked. [In fact, the South Fork "had been but little prospected until late Fall, and as late as December there were but three or four cabins for the distance of twenty miles above Bidwell's Bar."] There is good timber for building (not the case on many of the streams of California), which with us is an important consideration as we believed our health next summer depended upon having dry, warm, and comfortable habitation during the rainy season.

[Many emigrants "rushed to the mines and went to work . . . without tents, many without blankets to shield them from the cold night air, living on pork and hard bread. . . . Hundreds have been stricken down by disease; many died, while others have been unfitted for work for the rest of the season. . . . Companies of ten to fifteen men who crossed the plains . . . were down sick at once, with no one to wait on them. Some recovered and some died. . . . When a man gets sick in the mines, even if he has a physician and medicine, the food he gets is not of the kind required and prices of medical attendance and of necessities are so high that a month's sickness sweeps off a big pile." "Physicians are all making fortunes in this country. They will hardly look at a man's tongue for less than an ounce of gold."]

In late November we bought provisions at Long's Trading Post and took packs of fifty pounds each. ["Nobody moves here without his bed on his back, takes a pick, pan, and shovel, firearms and ammunition."] We traveled over the mountains for twenty-five miles through rain, mud and clouds and arrived on the South Fork on the third day. ["The descent to the river is one mile and a half, from an altitude of 2,500 feet—rapid, rough, rocky, precipitous, slippery and sideling."]

After prospecting two days, we located a spot favorable for damming and draining the river. We made our claim and then built a house as soon as possible to shelter our heads from the soaking rains. So here we are, snug as schoolmarms, working at our race and dam. Whenever the rain will permit, a fall of the river will enable us to get into the bed of the river and know what is there. If there is no gold, we shall be off to another place, for there is an abundance of gold here, and if we are blessed with health, we are determined to have a share of it.

["As to the amount of gold which exists in this country, it has not perhaps been much exaggerated. There are great quantities, but the difficulty of obtaining it has not been properly understood at home nor the trials a man suffers in getting it. There are always exceptions. Some men seem born with a golden spoon in their mouths, but the great bulk of mankind has to labor for it."]

You may have some curiosity to know something about our location and dwelling. Our house is a log cabin, sixteen by twenty feet. It is covered with boughs of cedar and is made of nut pine logs from one to two feet in diameter, so that it is quite a blockhouse. It has a good door made of cedar boards hewn out of cedar logs, but no window. It faces the south and is on the north side of the river. In the east end is a family fireplace, in which large backlogs are burning night and day. At the west end is a bedstead framed into the logs of the cabin and running from side to side. The cords of the bedstead are strips of rawhide, crossing at every three inches, thus forming a bottom tight enough to hold large armfuls of dry breaks gathered from the sides of the mountains, which make a substitute for feather beds. On these are our blankets and buffalo skins. Altogether it makes a comfortable bed. Moore has a bunk in one of the other corners. Over the fireplace are our rifles, which are ever ready, cocked and primed, and frequently yield us good venison. In the other corner may be seen our cupboard with its contents, which consist of a few wooden and tin dishes, bottles, knives and forks and spoons, tin frying pan, boiler, and coffee pot.

Around the sides of the cabin at various points are the few articles of clothing belonging to the different members of the company. Under the bed are five cakes of tallow, under the bunk are three or four large bags of flour. Along the point of the roof is a line of dried beef and sixty or seventy pounds of suet. And out at the corner of the house in a large trough made of pine may be found salt beef in the pickle, in abundance.

At ten in the evening you might see in this cabin, while everything is still, a fire blazing up from the mass of fuel in the large fireplace, myself and Hutchinson on one end of the bedstead, Lt. Cannon on the other, Mr. Bailey stretched before the fire in his blankets on the ground floor, and Moore in his bunk. On the roof the incessant rain keeps up its perpetual patter, while the foaming stream howls out a requiem of the rushing torrent as it dashes on its way to the valley. And here, wakeful and listless, are the members of other circles too. But often the mind is far away, filled with other scenes, far distant homes, and relatives.

In front of our cabin a mountain rises from the edge of the river two thousand feet and hides the sun till ten o'clock in the day. Its top is often covered with snow. The live oak and numerous other mountain evergreens, besides the pine and cedar, green as spring, are loaded with snow near the mountain top and dripping with rain on its side and base. And this is only a specimen of the hills and scenery on all sides of us.

The following is a list of prices current per pound when we arrived at Long's Bar: pork, $1.25; beans from 75 cents to $1; sugar, 75 cents; coffee, 50 cents; tea, $2.50; saleratus, $6; vinegar, $5; pickaxes and tin pans, $8 apiece; coffee pots, $6 to $8; frying pans $6.

These prices were caused by the rains which commenced six weeks earlier this year than last and consequently found the merchants in the mines without having laid in their winter's stock. [Before the rains started in early November, supplies were shipped from Sacramento City by freight wagon and "hauling provisions and teaming generally paid more than well. Early in the season a man could get $800 to take three thousand pounds to the mines." But after the rains began, "the ground was so soft that it mired teams down so deep it was impossible to get them out, and they had to be left to die or to be shot." A man who saw freight wagons two miles above Sacramento City on November 13 reported "many teams stalled to their wagon beds in the muddy road and oxen firmly mired up to their bellies. Some were being pulled out with chains around their horns by other cattle, while bundles of hay before those waiting their turns showed them to have been mired some time."

[With supplies stalled in getting out of Sacramento City, "there were not provisions enough in these mines for those at work. . . . Hundreds left the mines on account of the scarcity. . . . Many of these were men who had come into the mines late and had barely accumulated a few hundred dollars. . . . The high price of provisions made them fancy that while they could not subsist in the mines, the more moderate rates in the cities would enable them to get through the winter with their slender means. Among them, however, were many who had made nothing and who depended on their labor for support. The consequence was, San Francisco and Sacramento City were soon filled with a needy crowd."]

At this time a small steamer comes up to the mouth of the Yuba River [where the town of Marysville is located] and merchandise is brought from there to the mining camps on pack mules. Since this mode of transportation was adopted in December, prices have fallen thirty percent.

["When a man is asked the price of anything here, he does not tell the price in dollars but will say an ounce, a half ounce, or two ounces, etc. Gold dust is the principal currency in this country. Every person has a small leather bag to hold his dust."]

We found the most extraordinary state of morals in the mines. Everything in this country is left where the owner wished to leave it, in any place no matter where, as such a thing as stealing is not known.

["The security we enjoy here would astonish dwellers in what are called well-organized societies where bolts and bars secure every door and safe, and vigilant watchmen are about. We leave our tents containing our gold and chattels with none to guard them, to be absent all day, without a thought. Prospectors are constantly traveling to and fro." "The general honesty . . . is usually attributed to the prompt and severe punishment always ready for offenders. . . . Arrest, trial and punishment rarely occupy more than a few hours. . . . No warrants, indictments, or appeals delay proceedings. . . . The miners are anxious to get back to their work and the prisoner is not long kept in suspense."

[In the absence of any governmental authority, police or jails, the miners on each river established their own laws. On the South Fork there were "two cases of theft. One of the men was flogged with 100 lashes and the other 150. The latter died from the flogging." Over the ridge on the

Yuba River, miners' law required that "if a man steals, they flog him for the first offense; second offense they crop his ears, and third, they hang him." On the North Fork of the American River "a man stole $300 and had both his ears cut off and the letter 'T' branded in his cheek. Theft consequently is of rare occurrence."]

Miners' rights are well protected. Disputes seldom arise and are settled by referees, as they would be at home. [When a disagreement arose "between two companies respecting the right to a claim or a portion of it, a general convention was called on New Year's day at Oregon Bar on the South Fork for the purpose of defining what constituted a claim and to have a general and mutual understanding with regard to each other's rights. . . ." "They divided the river into three districts, chose a president for each and decided that to hold a claim a company should post up a notice stating its bounds in writing, which should be good for ten days, after which the ground must be occupied by one or more of the company. All difficulties arising about claims made previously are to be settled by arbitration. Everyone is to have the privilege to work the banks of the river above a medium height of water—a provision to accommodate those who do not belong to any company. The river is mostly taken up in claims from twenty to seventy-five rods long."

[After posting a claim, each man or company "registers his name or bar on the books of the Association . . . and becomes a member. In the event of others attempting to drive him off, he is entitled to the protection of all the companies constituting the Association. . . . This is a general outline of the plan . . . which is looked to and spoken of along the river with as much deference and respect as if it was the law of the land. Indeed, as things are now situated in the mines, any action of Congress or of our own legislature is wholly unnecessary; and if either undertakes to erect a Miners' Code without practical experience, then look for difficulties, which will not occur so long as the miners are left to themselves."]

George, I tell you this mining among the mountains is a dog's life. A man has to make a jackass of himself packing loads over mountains that God never designed man to climb, a barbarian by foregoing all the comforts of civilized life, and a heathen by depriving himself of all communication with men away from his immediate circle. ["We see nothing here but hills, mountains and rocks . . . no farming operations, no meetings, no horses and carriages or cattle, no female society—hear no music except the occasional squeaking of a hoarse fiddle in some lone cabin, and the croaking of ravens, the chattering of woodpeckers and the roaring of the Rio de los Plumas. . . ."]

You can judge my feelings when I inform you that I have not had an

The artist (unidentified) titled this drawing "Sunday at Forbes diggings, Feather River." Note miner's pan on the log, foreground; to the left, a rocker with miner seated on it, playing cards; fiddler in the wagon; in front of the liquor store, a winch to hoist buckets of water; and to the right, domestic chores—cooking and washing.

CALIFORNIA HISTORICAL SOCIETY

opportunity to send to Sacramento City for my letters and papers and have no tidings from home since I received your last letter at Independence, and I have not seen a newspaper since I left the states. ["The sight of a late newspaper is rare among us and when one arrives . . . it is read and reread, with all its advertisements even, and then it passes from hand to hand till little is left to entitle it to the distinction of being a newspaper."]

Sutter's Fort changed its name to Sacramento City and postal arrangements are made to that place from San Francisco. I wish you to direct your letters to me at that place, for my business may call me there often during the summer and if not, I can get letters from there, for persons are going down and back every two weeks and I shall make arrangements to have my letters brought up.

["As it now stands the post office at San Francisco is a curse to the miners of California, as far as receiving letters through it is concerned. If there was no such office there, the people would depend on other and surer means of communicating with their friends. . . . There are hundreds and thousands of men in California who have not received a single letter from their friends, notwithstanding their application at the San Francisco office. They have tried and tried, in vain. Their letters have been in the post office, but so badly are matters arranged that they could not be found."]

There was some talk between us of your coming to this country. For God's sake think not of it. Stay at home. Tell all whom you know that are thinking of coming that they have to sacrifice everything and face danger in all its forms, for George, thousands have laid and will lay their bones along the routes to and in this country. Tell all that "death is in the pot" if they attempt to cross the plains and hellish mountains. Say to Playter [a Youngstown resident] never to think of the journey; and as for you, *stay at home*, for if my health is spared, I can get enough for both of us.

My health has been extremely good since I arrived here. I am fifteen pounds heavier than when I left home and measured six feet last evening. A slight attack of rheumatism in the left hip has given me some trouble for a few days.

You may think from the tenor of this letter that I am sick of my job, but not so. I have not seen the hour yet when I regretted starting for California, nor have any one of our little party ever regretted that we undertook the enterprise. I have seen hard times, faced the dangers of disease and exposure and perils of all kinds, but I count them nothing if they enable me to place myself and family in comfortable circumstances.

Now you will think that there is a contradiction in the advice that I gave you and others about coming to California and the declaration of my own satisfaction that I have performed the journey. The fact is that gold is plenty here and the accounts received before I left home did not exaggerate the reality. Therefore I am glad that I am here. But the time is past —if it ever existed—when fortunes could be obtained for picking them up. Gold is found in the most rocky and rough places, and the streams and bars that are rich are formed of huge rocks and stones. In such places, you will see, it requires robust labor and hard tugging and lifting to separate the gold from the rock. But this is nothing to the risk of life run in traveling to this country. Therefore, if I was at home and knew all the circumstances, I think I should stay at home; but having passed those dangers in safety, I thank God that I am here in so favorable circumstances.

[Other miners more easily discouraged, admitted after only a few days' work that "if there had been a vessel lying upon the Feather River bound for New Orleans, there was not one of us who would not rather have stepped on board than to have gone one step farther in search of gold, for our prospects are truly gloomy. . . . Almost every man we meet who has been in the mines is wishing himself out of this country." "Two-thirds of the people that are here would go home immediately if they had the means. . . . Generally speaking the gold fever cools down in a wonderful manner after a man has been here a week or two."]

I hope soon to send for my letters, and God grant that they may bring no sad intelligence from home, for I almost dread to hear from that happy home, fearing that our neighborhood may have been the theater of cholera.

You are better acquainted with the state of things around San Francisco Bay than I am, and therefore I say nothing about them.

I have felt great anxiety about my wife and child, as I left them no means to live upon for so long a time, expecting to send home means before this; and also, their necessities might embarrass you. I hope that you will see that they are provided for, and if I can remunerate you for any trouble you may have, I shall feel willing to do so and ever feel grateful for your kindness. Give my love to Mother, if she is yet living, and say to her that I often, very often, think of her. Tell Sabrina *not* to be overanxious about me, for I shall be careful of my health, and as soon as I can get the rocks in my pocket I shall hasten home as fast as steam can carry me.

Write often, for I may sometime or another get your letters.

[to be continued January 12, 1850]

[While Swain and thousands of other miners waited during January in the isolated mining camps of the Feather and Yuba rivers for the rainy season to end and the rushing waters to subside, hundreds of goldseekers chose to spend the winter in Sacramento City; others went there to buy supplies, enjoy a few days' spree or to seek out their mail. One of these was Isaac Lord, who had traveled overland near and sometimes with the Rangers. From the Feather River mines he paddled a small boat down the Sacramento River and arrived at the city the afternoon of December 22. In his diary he wrote that "the first view we had of the city was where a line of ships stretches along the river for nearly a mile, then a few houses loom up mistily in the fog among the trees. . . . The ships are fast to the shore and seem to be used as storehouses. . . . We paddled our craft into a kind of pool, tied up to a tree on the bank and stepped into the street. . . . The first that strikes one's attention . . . is the want of order—the utter confusion and total disorder which prevail on every hand. . . . The streets are not graded, nor is anything done to clear them out, except cutting down some of the scattering trees which five or six months ago were the sole occupants of the ground. The whole town plot is covered with boxes and barrels, empty or filled with all kinds of goods, in passable, indifferent, or bad order, or totally ruined; and wagons, lumber, glass bottles, machinery, and plunder of all sorts, heaped and scattered and tumbled about in the most admired confusion." "The streets are half a leg deep in filth and mud, rendering getting about awful beyond description. . . . The city is one great cesspool of mud, offal, garbage, dead animals and that worst of nuisances consequent upon the entire absence of outhouses."

["The whole city is literally stuffed, crammed with eatables of every description, so exposed that almost every kind must suffer more or less damage and hundreds of thousands of dollars' damage is already done. I saw at one establishment alone over 200 boxes of herrings rotting in one pile; any amount of spoiled pork, bacon, cheese, moldy and rotten; pilot bread; and most everything else. The destruction and waste of property here is almost or quite equal to that on the plains, with not half the necessity, and a thousand times the recklessness.

["There are a great number of dealers in produce or rather eatables here but more dealers of monte. The taverns have usually a large barroom in front, passing to which you will see, on one side, more display of glasses, bottles, cigars and liquors than in three or four of the largest liquor taverns in Chicago; and on the other, three or four or more tables and a man behind dealing monte, and this at all hours from breakfast to midnight."

["One of these public houses called 'The Plains' has its walls frescoed with scenes familiar to overland emigrants—Independence Rock, Devil's Gate, passes in the Rocky Mountains and in the Sierra Nevada, etc." Another "is a place made of a huge circular tent, like a small circus, and emblazoned with large letters 'City Diggins.' This during the day is almost unoccupied but at night music rings out and it is to excess crowded."

["The only object of many here appears to be to kill time and all kinds of amusements are invented to do the thing up as brilliantly as possible. For instance, the Young Men's Society Ball must have been decidedly rich. Fancy 150 hombres . . . each striving to secure one of the seventeen young ladies that were present. Tickets only $20."

["The door of many a gambling hall . . . stands invitingly open; the wail of torture from innumerable musical instruments peals from all quarters through the fog and darkness. Full bands, each playing different

tunes discordantly, are stationed in front of the principal establishments.
. . . Some of the establishments have small companies of Ethiopian
melodists, who nightly call upon 'Susanna' and entreat to be carried back
to Old Virginny. These songs are universally popular, and the crowd of
listeners is often so great as to embarrass the player at the monte table and
injure the business of the gamblers. . . . The spirit of the music is always
encouraging; even its most doleful passages have a grotesque touch of
cheerfulness—a mingling of sincere pathos and whimsical consolation,
which somehow takes hold of all moods . . . raising them to the same
notch of careless good humor.

["The southern part of Sacramento City, where the most of the
overland emigrants locate themselves, is an interesting place for a night
ramble. . . . The number of emigrants settled there for the winter
amounts to two or three thousand. . . . There on fallen logs about their
campfires might be seen groups that had journeyed together across the
continent, recalling the hardships and perils of the travel. The men with
their long beards, weather-beaten faces and ragged garments seen in the
red, flickering light of the fires make wild and fantastic pictures. Sometimes four of them might be seen about a stump, intent on reviving their
ancient knowledge of poker, and occasionally, a more social group filling
their cups from a kettle of tea or something stronger. Their fires, however, are soon left to smolder away. The evenings are too raw and they
are too weary with the day's troubles to keep long vigils. . . . The conversation is sure to wind up with a talk about home—a lamentation for
its missed comforts and frequently a regret at having forsaken them. The
subject is inexhaustible, and when once they commence calling up the
scenes and incidents of life in the Atlantic or Mississippi world, everything else is forgotten."

["People at home can have no conception of the amount of suffering
in the vicinity of this city. Many . . . are begging for employment, asking
only subsistence. Yesterday {December 22} there were twenty-five
deaths. Sickness does not arise from the severity of the climate . . . but
from a complication of causes. The intermittents {fevers} of autumn are
aggravated by overwork, scanty and bad food, disappointment, and
homesickness."

["*December 24.* Were it not that the whole country about us is
under water, business here would be almost unlimited. . . . There are
auction sales on the river bank at all hours of the day, where very many
articles are to be obtained at greatly—relatively—reduced prices. The
great drawback is the damaged condition of most of the goods. There are
hundreds of men here selling their 'traps' at auction and then bound for

home. Some have made enough already, and others are disgusted with the country and retire, homesick. Many are going to try their luck at San Francisco.

["*December 25.*   I noticed today a number of buildings going up, covered with sheet iron; and yet, a short joint of common, rusty, bruised four-inch stove pipe costs $4, and the new iron . . . is $1.50 a pound. Rents are extravagant. Water for a common boarding house costs $20 per week. As a kind of offset to this, I rather think that nobody pays taxes, as I am told that no one regards the city ordinances. All do as they please . . . taking possession of land where it was not actually occupied by improvements and building and improving in defiance of all show of authority or law. . . . Whoever wishes to build gets his lot surveyed and has it registered and up goes a house at once. They are running them up rapidly on Front Street, facing the river, and within a short stone's throw of the river and the shipping. A small house costing $2,000 will rent for $500 a month on this street.

["There are no well-filled blocks, but there are several very good, wood-covered buildings and two covered with zinc. On one corner two brick stores are going up. There is a large three-story, fine-looking building on Front Street, opening for a tavern. The buildings, intermingled with tents, extend almost a mile east and a half a mile south, and the tents as much farther. Large trees still stand towering up in the streets and among the buildings in the heart of the town.

["*December 26.*   The people here refrain from—from I hardly know what, unless it is common, vulgar stealing. I think there is less of what is ordinarily called stealing here than any place I was ever in; and yet there can be little difficulty in stealing to almost any extent. A vast amount of property, easily movable, is daily and nightly exposed without a watch, or even a lock.

["I was struck all aback when I saw the merchants receiving and handling gold. To examine the quality, they go through much the same maneuvers as the wheat buyers of Chicago when inspecting a sample of wheat. If the gold dust looks clean and fair, it is poured into the scales and weighed. If it looks dirty and has rock and sand in it, they take some in the palm, and stir it carelessly around with a forefinger and determine its value. Very seldom, however, except in exchanging for coin, is any deduction made. Every time it is weighed something is lost, and the business streets of Sacramento will, in a few years, be worth digging up and washing for gold. It is poured out and weighed almost as carelessly as rice or pepper in the States; and very few ever pick up any scattering flake, unless larger than a pinhead, and some pay no attention whatever

to so small matters. In the larger establishments the dust is dipped about in pint tin cups. In a word, it is an article of produce, as easily got as wheat or corn in the States, and handled with much the same feeling and comparatively with the same waste."

[On December 26 Isaac Lord left Sacramento City to return to the Feather River mines, taking passage on the steamer *Lawrence.* "Cast off at ten-thirty A.M. and in dropping in to the shore at the upper part of the city to take a scow load of lumber in tow, we ran against the limb of a big sycamore and broke down the smoke pipe. I should think that they would cut down the nuisances."

[Such nuisances were typical of the city's unconcern about municipal improvements. Indeed, there was not even a levee along the Sacramento and American rivers, which after the weeks of almost continuous rain had risen so rapidly that the danger of flood seemed imminent. But "the reckless spirit of speculation had declared an inundation as out of the question, if not physically impossible. The very air was tremulous with oft-repeated assurances that the town plot had remained free from floods

View of Sacramento City as it appeared during the great inundation in January 1850.

during the sojourn of the oldest Californians, and the headlong and un-reflecting career of the people showed them sufficiently credulous to be-lieve the really transparent story."

[In January, after a few days' clear weather, a storm brought a deluge of rain on the 8th, and soon muddy waters swirled through the fragile tents and ornate gambling halls. By the night of the 9th, Sacramento City was about four-fifths submerged.

[Three days later it was reported that "the water is still rising. Tents, houses, boxes, barrels, horses, mules, and cattle are sweeping by with the swollen torrent that is now spread out in a vast sea farther than the eye can reach. There are few two-story houses, and as the water rose, which it did at the rate of six inches an hour, men were compelled to get outside. Today there is no first floor in the city uncovered, and but for the vessels in the river, now crowded with people, there is no telling what numbers might have perished." To the upper story of a hospital "men come in boats, begging to be taken in, or bring some valuables for safekeeping. . . . A lone woman, sick and destitute, is curtained off in a corner of the room. . . . A few patients are muttering in delirium. Some are dying on the floor. Others, dead, are sewed up in blankets and sunk in the water in a room on the first floor.

["All sorts of means are in use to get about—bakers' troughs, rafts and India-rubber beds. There is no sound of gongs or dinner bells in the city. The yelling for help by some men on a roof or clinging to some wreck, the howling of a dog abandoned by his master, the boisterous revelry of men in boats who find all they want to drink floating free about them, make the scene one never to be forgotten. After dark we see only one or two lights in the second city of California.

["*January 13.* The weather is cooler and the water is falling a little. The vessels on the river are all crowded with people, and some cases of typhus or ship-fever have occurred. The high ground near Sutter's Fort is covered with tents, dogs, and cattle. . . . Cattle have perished in immense numbers." "It is a hard sight to see them swimming about or lying dead in heaps on some little hill."

["Hundreds of thousands of dollars in merchandise were wrested from the grasp of the merchants and traders of the city by the sweeping currents that ran through the streets, in some places with irresistible force." "Instead of the people wearing long faces as you would suppose, the city never was more lively. The streets were filled with boats, and everyone was for having a frolic." "Small boats brought almost any price on sale or hire. A common-sized whaleboat brought $30 per hour and sold readily for $1,000. But in an incredibly short time every particle of lumber that would answer for boat or raft-making was thus appropriated, and in a few days the people were enabled to emigrate to the adjacent hills." "Those who had boats have made nice fortunes with them by ferrying from town out to dry land, charging from $5 to $8."

[Contrary to the apparently frivolous reaction of many, the flood was in fact a major calamity—to be borne not only by the residents of Sacramento City but also by thousands of miners whose provisions would soon greatly increase in price. And the flood would leave another legacy: "What a smell! It certainly will be sickly here this summer."

[While the people of Sacramento City suffered and struggled in the aftermath of the great flood, William Swain, his friends and hundreds of other miners on the South Fork of the Feather River passed their time in their cabins when the weather was at its worst. On good days they worked on their claims to prepare for the time when the high water of the river would recede and they could at last dig for gold in the riverbed itself.

[On January 12 Swain continued the letter to George that he had started on the 6th.]

January 12

We have had heavy rains and high water, but the weather has now cleared off fine, like Spring. And spring is here, for the mountain oaks are putting out their leaves and all things are assuming a green hue. We are in hopes of having dry weather soon—then, "you see!"

["Many of the miners here are moving up the river to find locations for their summer's work, and we hear of thousands at Sacramento City who are all ready to come up as soon as the rainy season is over, which will probably be in the month of February. We see by the papers that there is a tremendous number of emigrants intending to come out to California this season from the States. Thousands will be disappointed."]

It is just for me to say that if my health is good and I do not have extraordinary good luck, I may not be home till next Fall. Mr. Bailey is well and sends his love to his family.

January 16

The rapidity with which this country is settling is only equaled by the change being made by Yankee enterprise. Three weeks ago but one steamboat plowed its way across San Francisco Bay and but one traversed the Sacramento River. Now four steamers may be seen making their regular trips from San Francisco to Yuba City, and flour which was then selling at 75 cents is now worth 40 cents per pound, as I have just heard from Mr. Hutchinson, who has come home from Long's Trading Post.

When we first located on this stream, no more than six houses were built on it. Now, within a distance of ten miles, 150 dwellings are built. [Some of the cabins "have cloth roofs, but others have quite decent clapboard roofs. Some are covered on the outside with green cowhides. Other miners have dug holes in the ground and covered them with pine brush and dirt." The largest camp or settlement "is called Stringtown, which is some forty buildings strung along . . . a sand or gravel bar on one side of the river. . . ." "Trading posts or stores are very numerous, and the traders appear to be doing a flourishing business. A large part of the trading is done on credit . . . with the expectation that the miners will pay as soon as they get to work in the bed of the river." "A miner can go into a store and get trusted for $1,000 in provisions."]

The "redskin" who four months ago roamed in his nakedness, the undisputed lord of these mountains and valleys, may now be seen on the hilltops gazing with surprise upon the scenes below—the habitations, the deep-dug channels and the dams built. The sound of the laborer's ax, shovel, pick and pan are sounds new to his ear, and the sight one to which his eye had never been accustomed.

The natives of these mountains are wild, live in small huts made of brush and go naked as when they are born. They subsist on acorns and what game they kill with their bows and arrows. They are small in stature, and their character is timid and imbecile. When they visit the camps of the miners, they evince the most timid and friendly nature. They are charged with killing miners occasionally when they find one alone, away among the hills hunting. The miners, especially the Oregon men, are sometimes guilty of the most brutal acts with the Indians, such as killing the squaws and papooses. Such incidents have fallen under my notice that would make humanity weep and men disown their race. [The men from Oregon "say they will kill or drive off every Indian in the country, and they will do it, for they had rather shoot an Indian than a deer any time."

["Indians are now frequently employed in the mines for a mere trifle. They generally contrive to get a shirt and a few get rich enough to buy a coat and pantaloons. But since the rains have set in . . . hundreds are seen wading the streams for fish or traveling on the plains, naked and paying no more regard to the wet, chilly storm than dumb beasts. In the valley they are now inoffensive, as the numbers of whites overawe them; but in the mountains they sometimes give miners trouble and some collisions have taken place."]

I send this by a man who is going to Sacramento City and to San Francisco on purpose for mails. He leaves here Saturday and will return in two weeks, when I shall probably get my letters by him, paying $2 apiece for bringing them up.

I shall write often as I can and shall fill my engagements to different persons to whom I promised to write as soon as I have gained sufficient knowledge of the country to do so understandingly. Say to Mr. Burge that this climate in the mines requires a constitution like iron. Often for weeks during the rainy season it is damp, cold, and sunless, and the labor of getting gold is of the most laborious kind. Exposure causes sickness to a great extent, for in most of the mines tents are all the habitation miners have. But with care I think health can be preserved.

Give my love to Sabrina and kiss little Cub for me.

Goodbye George,
William

P.S. I have wafered in some samples of gold found on the main branch of the Feather River. The coarse is a fine specimen found on this fork, but gold found here is often as coarse as a hickory nut.
P.S. An onion in the mines is worth a dollar, and boots $40 per pair. I have paid $8 for a jar of pickles.

P.S. All well, and I have sent this to San Francisco by a Mr. Tolles by paying 50 cents.

> February 17, 1850
> South Fork of Feather River
> Twenty-five miles from Long's Bar

Dear Sabrina,

I take advantage of an opportunity to send this letter to San Francisco to send you intelligence of my good health, but not of great fortune realized. You have probably ere this received both of my letters, the first in December and the other in January directed to George, by which you are apprised of my arrival in California, my health, and prospects up to that time.

Since I wrote I have enjoyed good health, as have all our company, which in this above all other countries is the greatest boon Heaven can bestow upon its inhabitants.

We have had much rainy weather and high water which has prevented us from doing much of any mining. But for the last two weeks we have had fine, clear weather. And such weather! So clear, so warm, such transparent skies. Such fine, soft, mild winds are seldom known, even in the land of my home. But I confess that this country with all its attractions has little but its gold that affords me gratification. I am a stranger in a strange land, with the bonds of friendship, the endearments of the home of youth and the fond ties of kindred all exerting their influences upon me, and like the pole to the needle, they attract all my thoughts and preferences back to the land of my home and family.

["Though there is a free, openhearted way with all here, yet there is not the same feeling of interest in one another as exists in society at home. Here all know and feel that our acquaintance is of short duration, and almost all expecting some day to return to the States, do not naturally feel desirous to become an intimate with those from whom they are soon to be separated. It is something like a stagecoach or steamboat acquaintance. . . . Probably nine out of ten of the miners are calculating someday to return to the States, and their stay here will be prolonged or shortened by their success or the demands of duty and love for those left behind them. Some will stay for years, adding gold to gold, and their avaricious souls will hardly be satisfied. Some will be content with a smaller amount and will hasten home to enjoy the pleasures awaiting them in the society of those they love. Some without a care or thought, gamble and lose their gold as fast as they obtain it."]

Were you and that dear little girl here, I think we might spend some years here very profitably, for certainly as I become acquainted with the country, the climate, and the great prospects of wealth and happiness, I deem them worthy of great consideration. But we are separated by what I consider the path of duty, marked by the providences of a kind, Heavenly Father, and these providences indicate that the separation must last for some months to come. In all probability the object of my journey cannot be accomplished before the commencement of the next rainy season, when I hope to bid adieu to the scenes of this land of glittering dreams and when turning my course homeward, Homeward Bound shall tell the place of my destination. If I shall ever see that day, it will be one of the happiest days of my life. May God grant us both health and life to enjoy a happy meeting in the home of our youth.

I cannot express the disappointment I have experienced in not as yet having received any letters from either you or George. I am as well satisfied that there is at least a dozen for me at Sacramento City as I am of my existence. I have sent after them by three express carriers, and failed to get any on account of the inability of the postmaster of that place to perform the duties of the office and no provision for clerks being made by the government. The enormous wages required by persons in this country will not permit the postmaster to employ help on his own responsibility. Nor has Mr. Bailey received any. Mr. E. received two from the San Francisco office.

I have seen two California *Tribunes*, the latest dated December 13. From these I have learned something of the affairs of the States. ["Newspapers are printed in New York especially for California and Oregon and sent by every steamer. And hundreds and thousands of them are sold throughout the mines by persons who make it a business to go to the Bay after letters and papers. . . . Books and papers meet with a ready sale. . . . The miners have more leisure and are longer in one place during the winter and consequently are more eager for reading of any kind than when wandering from place to place and rarely prevented from work by weather as is the case during the dry season. . . . We are shut out, as it were, from the world and have little that is new to attract our attention. And so when we get hold of a newspaper, it is read again and again, and every little incident forms the topic of conversation.

["Besides the occasional glimpses we thus get of civilized life through the papers and the common chit-chat of a neighborhood of miners, we have but little to occupy our attention except the all-absorbing talk about gold. . . ."]

As I left you but little money, I have felt great anxiety about affairs at home, fearing that you may not have received money sufficient to furnish the necessaries and comforts of life. Were it in my power to send you some few hundreds at this time, it would relieve my anxiety and afford me much pleasure; but the facts of my arriving here after mining had ceased, having to live at exceeding high rates, and having done but little during the wet weather have prevented me from laying up any amount. I can send money home by Adams & Co.'s Express to any city or village for ten percent, with insurance, and shall transmit you some as soon as I can.*

You will of course ask: Have you done nothing yet in mining? Yes, I have done considerable. I have panned along the banks of the river with various success. My first day's work in the business was an ounce; the second was $35, and the third was $92. I picked up a lump worth $51 which cost me no more labor than stooping down to take it up. But such days' work as these are not a common thing. To be sure, they give tone and character to all the affairs of California. They set prices on all kinds of provisions and merchandise and all kinds of labor. The merchant, when told that men find from $16 to $100 a day, very readily concludes they can easily pay $1 for a pound of potatoes, or $2 for a pound of dried apples, as in the state of New York they can pay half a cent for the former or four cents for the latter. So also with the rancher—his $200 is no price at all for his beef creature.

But the dry season and good roads are now here, and prices—these humbug prices—must cease. Already boots can be had for $16 per pair, and flour has fallen to 45 cents per pound. Although we do not live quite as high as we did, we live better at lower rates. It is also necessary to say that I have spent whole days in tramping along these rocky hills and shores and not found a shilling's worth of gold.

Our dam is finished, and the river, which is high and will probably be so for some months, is running through our race leaving its old channel bare. We have to remove some three feet of gravel and stone before we find the foundation rock where gold always lies. On account of the water which leaches from the race to the channel, we have not been able to test it but shall do it in a short time. We have found some gold, but in consequence of the thickness of the stones on the bedrock, it will not be so profitable as we expected.

---

* Founded in December 1849 (Wells Fargo entered California from New York in 1852), Adams & Company's Express had offices throughout the mining regions, providing express service for mail and a careful system of assays to determine the value of the different qualities of gold dust. The company purchased the dust from miners (paying between $14 and $16 per ounce) and for a fee transferred that value to its offices in the States where the miners' families could receive payment.

Daguerreotype of flume in the bed of a river, late 1850. Exact location is uncertain, but most likely in the Feather or Yuba River mines.

The whirling paddle wheels, turned by the flow of water in the flume, drove pumps to remove water from claims in deep parts of the river bed.

[To get at the gold in the bed of the river, other "companies are digging canals . . . while some are building flumes of planks saw-cut by hand . . . to carry the river high and dry above its natural bed. . . . Four or six plank flumes are in the process of construction on this branch of the river. They are built above the present level of the river and it is the intention to turn the river into them as soon as it is supposed they will contain it. . . ."

[To dig a canal or race or to build a plank flume "requires much labor of the hardest kind. . . . The general face of the country is such that digging a race is equivalent to blasting a channel through a ledge of flint and granite; and in order to make a flume, trees must first be felled, timber hewed, and boards sawed. Then the great spout is formed by patience and perseverance, all the while the miners living on Hope mixed with pork and flour in sufficient quantities, trusting to the bed of the river for pay!"]

Mr. Bailey and Hutchinson are both well. I have not heard from John Root since he went to the city. Lt. Cannon saw Stephen Eaton [from Youngstown] last week. Mr. Bailey sends his love to his family. He is certainly the best companion I have ever formed an acquaintance with. Give my love to Mother and George and kiss the girl for Father. I shall write as often as I can.

Yours as ever,
William

P.S. I want you to write me (as I suppose you have) a great deal about our little girl. I often think of her when night has hushed all sounds around me but the song of our noble river. Poor child! I shall never forget the expression of surprise on her countenance as she looked into my face as I took her in my arms and kissed her on the morning of leaving home. My prayer is she has been healthy, for if not I know that your task with her, already too great to bear alone, has been doubled. If alive and well, she must now be able to talk considerable and cut up many pranks from which you will draw some comfort. Do remember that her health during life depends much upon the manner in which she is fed and clothed. The kind of food she eats and manner of dress she wears requires your *particular attention*. You know my opinions upon this subject, and I conjure you by your hopes of heaven not to allow any influence of any persons to induce you to allow her physical energies to be crippled by dress, habit or food. Rely upon your own judgment, enlightened by a thorough acquaintance of the laws of the animal economy.

I feel much anxiety about you and Sis, and I would to God that our circumstances were such that we were together so that we might mutually assist each other in the task which unhappily you are compelled to bear alone!! But it will not always be thus with us.

Yours in affection,
William Swain

March 15, 1850.

Dear Sabrina and Mother,

Thanks to Almighty God I write in answer of letters received from home. Two in one envelope, one November 4 and one from Sabrina

December 7 [see pp. 292 and 338]. They came to hand March 3 and brought the glad news of the *life* and usual health of all our family circle! Thank God for His kind care over us! They were the most precious tidings I have ever known and double pay for the disappointment of looking and expecting anxiously the arrival of some note of absent and loved relatives while reason taught to dread the arrival of such note and instinct to hope even against hope. Thanks to kind Heaven that the blessings of life and health still surround us as a family, and may He graciously grant that those inestimable blessings may still be vouchsafed to us and that we may ere long be so happy as to be united in our home.

You have received my letters long ere this time, or at least two of them dated December and January and are apprised of my arrival in California, my health, which still continues good, and my prospects in the gold business; so that the line of communication between us is now open and will continue unbroken, I hope, till we can converse with our tongues instead of our pens.

The time during which we have had no correspondence has been a vexatious and tedious one!—and one of anxiety to us all. But now that it has passed and we are again enabled by the arrangements of government to hear from and know the circumstances surrounding each other, I look back upon it with satisfaction that we separated for mutual good, which I believe will be the result, as I have in my previous letters stated. However, I am not at all sorry that you were all ignorant of the circumstances which at different times surrounded me.

While you and George were comfortable seated in the family circle on Sabbath, November 4, addressing me, with Mother and Delia Barber reading and Cub sleeping on her bed by the stove, enjoying the comforts of home in a civilized land, the hand of fortune was dealing rudely with me—dealing out to me the bitterest pills of the journey. That day found me at Deer Creek valley, seventy miles from the abode of civilized man, to gain which I had still to ascend and descend the lower range of the Sierra Mountain desert. . . .*

During all the exposure of the journey I did not take the least cold nor last fall while exposed to the rain before building our cabin. I have never enjoyed better health than I did on the last half of the route, and have since I have been in California. I was weighed last week, 156 pounds, seven more than I have ever weighed in the States.

---

* *There follows a lengthy account of the last days of the Rangers' flight from the mountains to Lassen's Ranch. This part of the letter has been incorporated into Chapter IX.*

But I have spun out this letter so long that I have said nothing in it that I intended to say and must take another sheet.

So fare well in this,
William

March 17, 1850
Sabbath Afternoon, 4 o'clock
South Fork

Dear George,

How do you do, Mr. Officer at the Bridge!* Good luck to you and may joy surround you in your new business. By the by, I feel as though I was at home. The express man has just arrived and brought me all the letters you have written, at least a package for each month from May to October, also January containing yours and Sabrina's of that date, and yours of December, and some twelve November and December papers, for which I paid him an ounce. O!!

I have glanced over them all and two of the papers, and as the express man returns tomorrow morning I hasten to pen a few lines in answer to them, or rather to say that you may look for answers to them in the next mail, as there are many subjects upon which I have been intending to treat. For instance, the route across the plains; California, its prospects, its population and morals; the mines and the miners. I am now able to do so from observation and also now have the paper and ink to do it. In these letters I will give you a view of California as I understand it and shall try to send them by the next mail.

There are many subjects mentioned in your numerous letters which I would like to answer in this but cannot for want of time, so will answer them in my next. I appreciate your advice upon the principles of conduct and shall ever endeavor to be governed by them [George had urged William to read the fifth, sixth and seventh chapters of St. Matthew], for certainly this is a land of demoralization.**

---

* *This greeting acknowledges the news of George's appointment to the local customs office of the Niagara District at the Suspension Bridge, crossing the Niagara River near Youngstown to Ontario, Canada.*

** *Reports from California of sin in the mining camps and the cities brought forth admonitions from home to many husbands and sons. One nineteen-year-old from Wisconsin answered: "Your advice, Father, is in good time, for here a boy is truly in the very gates of destruction, as all kinds of vices hold unlimited sway in the cities and mines. But I hope and trust I shall be able to leave this country as pure and innocent as I came in—and that ain't anything to brag on, is it?"*

Last fall I was proud of the miners as a body, both for their honesty and their sobriety, but the rapidity with which they have retrograded only proves more clearly the necessity of religious restraint and the great influence of well-organized and moral society. Drinking has become very prevalent, swearing a habitual custom, and gambling has no equal in the annals of history. It has already reached as far as Feather River, and some of the boys who came across the plains in our train are at it, though they professed to be Christians when home.

["Vice seems more alluring here. It comes . . . to be a substitute for common amusement. The miner has not the society of the home circle to cheer and enliven him. He has no longer the friends, the innocent recreations to which he has been accustomed. On the Sabbath morning no church is open. . . . No mother or sister or beloved wife can cheer him." "Sabbath days here are spent by miners mostly hunting, prospecting for gold, and gambling. Very little attention is paid to morals. . . . From good authority we are told that there are several Methodist ministers at Sacramento City and San Francisco whose business is now dealing monte and playing at different games for the purpose of gain."

["Wherever rich diggings are heard of, gamblers are sure to go. They are always on the travel. They visit all the mining villages and set up their roulette and card tables and play euchre, brag, vincture {vingt-et-un} and monte, and in fact all kinds of games to suit their dupes."

["Their diggings are in the pockets of the miners and not in the pockets of the {river} bars. . . . They offer the simple and the foolish as good a chance to lose the results of months of labor and privation in an hour as is done in the more showy and magnificent hells in the city. . . . Generally a few days spent in one place is sufficient to drain the font of the gambling miner's stream, and when all have 'come down with the dust' who will pay tribute to folly, the gambler rolls up his blanket, shoulders his pile, and climbs to another bar."

["Almost everybody drinks. . . . The President of the Miners' Association was helped up the fork the other day so drunk that he went down every five rods in spite of all that a man hardly half as drunk as himself could do. Some days out of a hundred persons who pass, twenty or thirty go reeling. . . . A worthy doctor two miles below keeps a trading post, sells whiskey, etc. through the week, drinks brandy freely and preaches on Sunday. Who cares? Not the Devil. . . . Brandy retails for at least 25 cents a drink and for the most part 50 cents. And Feather River water is pure, soft, cool, handy, and plenty, and mixes readily . . . in the proportion of two to one, leaving quite a profit."]

I thank Heaven that *we* had parents who taught us to stand upon *principle* and that when adversity has darkened our way, we have still trod in our own shoes. It has taught us, when young, to rely upon ourselves and choose our own course of conduct irrespective of the influence and opinions of others. I would not part with that conscientiousness of self-reliance for all the gold of California or the popularity that our Union could afford. I shall read the passages in the Bible you have pointed out with great pleasure.

On the subject of religion, I have not paid the attention to it that I determined when leaving the States, but I have preserved my Bible and have read it often. ["There seems to be little disposition to maintain religious worship here. The thoughts of the people are entirely preoccupied with drinking, gambling, or getting gold out of the earth." "Religion and religious services, like everything else in California, is singular and unnatural. There is preaching occasionally by some Doctor of Divinity or gold-hunting minister; but all denominational cast or character is kept carefully out of view—in short, it is a kind of mongrel preaching, a little of everything and not much of anything. . . ."]

You have spoken of sending papers to me, but I think you had better not. They are already becoming very plenty and probably would not pay, and indeed I think speculation in any thing from the States here is very precarious and we had better not engage in anything of the kind at present. I will give you my reasons in my next. You also speak of Nelson's intention to send a steam engine for us to sell. My situation in the mines precludes me from knowing much about the business of the Bay, but I suppose that an engine with boilers, all the minutiae of fixings, together with the engineer's tools for putting it up, would be valuable property and would sell well. But I think that he had better correspond with someone at the Bay and ascertain the facts, for there is great hazard in sending anything to this country at this time.

[Reports from San Francisco "advise that the markets are so changeable that if you were to ship around the Horn goods that are now paying five and six hundred percent profit, perhaps by the time they arrived there, they might have to be sold for less than their cost and freight. . . . Shovels, spades, saddles and most kinds of hardware are a great drug there. Heavy clothing, boots, flannels, woolen hose, etc. are in great demand." "A most profitable trade is carried on between the Sandwich Islands [Hawaii] and California in sweet and Irish potatoes, onions, oranges, lemons—in short, all kinds of vegetables and fruits."]

Four weeks ago we thought the rain over, but March has been the worst month of the season. The waters are up, and our prospects for mining soon are dark, at least for two months to come. ["Very few on this river will be ready in that time, though some think that a week is sufficient to finish their work. On most of the claims the projected operations are entirely insufficient to drain the river. . . . Some, who will fail, are making extensive preparations—in talk—and really doing but very little. . . . The wildest schemes of human fancy are here mere common, every-day, matter-of-course speculations."]

I am very sorry to hear that little Sister was sick, and also that it was necessary that calomel should be given. I dread that medicine and hope you will not have to give her any more.

But I can write no longer if I send this by this mail, so farewell at present.

Your brother,
William

P.S. Mr. H. and B. are well and send their respects to their friends. I have not heard a word from John since last Fall. If you know where he is, send word. S. Eaton is at Bidwell's.

Back Home

"Little Eliza has grown nearly half . . .
and she has forgotten that she has or ever
had a father. . . ."

Youngstown, Friday, December 7, 1849

My own dear William,

Through the blessings and mercies of God I am again permitted to resume my pen in addressing a line to you. It is a most affecting thought to me and one that strikes me very forcibly, too, that while I am writing these lines to you, your body may be moldering back to its mother's dust from whence it came. To say the least, there is but little consolation derived from continual writing without any returns, and neither can there be a great deal of satisfaction to the one to whom they are addressed, to peruse about the same thing over and over again. Suffice it to say I will try to fulfill my promise and duty in writing, even if it be an old story.

We have not received even as much as a line from you since you left Fort Laramie and I can assure you the time seems very long. O William, how I want to hear from you and hope long ere this reaches you we shall have heard from you. We shall look for one by next Monday or Tuesday and if we do not get one, I shall be very much disappointed. It will be nine months the 11th of this month since you left home. How long to be separated from one we dearly love! My dear, if God spares your life to meet your family again, will it not be a happy meeting! (My blood chills within my veins when I think of the uncertainty of this.)

Little Eliza has grown nearly half in this time, and she has long ago forgotten that she has or ever had a father. As she grows older, the more I feel the need of a father's care and assistance in lightening the responsibility of governing and training her right, and I am placed in such circumstances that I do not govern her many times as I should if I were not by myself. She is a very smart, active child of her age, of a nervous temperament, rather quick-tempered, strong in her attachments and likes to have her own way when allowed in it. But by strict attention and a steady hand in training her incorrection, I trust there will be no serious trouble.

She is now asleep on her little bed by the stove. Mother is reading, and this constitutes the members in our family at present. George is at the Suspension Bridge in the Custom House office business, as you are aware ere this if you have received your letters. So you see, we are left in a rather lonely condition. As to a man for the winter to do chores, I do not know what we shall do yet. We do not know of anyone that would be faithful. I think if we could get William Swain we should be very well pleased. We must have someone immediately, as Mother and I cannot do both the out-chores and what there is to be done in the house.

Sis is tolerable well and rests better nights. She calls for "Uncy" very often and appears to be lonesome without him. We will ask her where "poor papa" is and she will raise her hand and say "way off" quite plain without knowing anything what it means. . . .

It is now nine o'clock and I must close till next month.

May the hand of Providence deliver us all during the remainder of your absence and bring you back speedily to the bosom of your family, is the prayer of your affectionate

Sabrina Swain

Excuse all the mistakes
for I write in a great
deal of noise from Sis.

Saturday morning: all well. I have got to go down to the office with these papers and letter. It is very cold this morning.

Goodbye
Sabrina

7 o'clock Evening
Suspension Bridge,
Dec. 7, 1849

Dear Brother William,

I just take my pen to write a few lines to you by this month's mail and send them to Youngstown for Sabrina to put with hers of this month. In the first place, and to me the most important, I am well, and may God grant that this will find you in the enjoyment of the same blessing. We are very anxious to hear from you, which we have not since your letter from Fort Laramie, dated July 4, a period of five months during which if you have been successful you must have experienced a great deal of labor and privation and anxiety; if unsuccessful God only knows what you have borne, or where you now are. But we hope to hear from you by the first of November mail from San Francisco, which will probably be here between the 12th and 15th of this month. . . .

Congress met last Monday and had not last night chosen a Speaker. The Democrats have a Majority over the Whigs. There are 111 Whigs, 112 Democrats, I believe, and several Free Soilers. The press think ex-Speaker Winthrop stands the best chance, but I am doubtful of it. We shall have wild work this winter in Congress. The South are said to be opposed to admitting California as a free state and will make a great deal of noise and try some hocus-pocus game over the North, but the North have their eyes open and will resist stoutly. . . .

The election in New York is nearly a draw game; the Whigs have rather the best of it, though but little. Most of the state elections in the South have gone against the administration because they thought the President and Cabinet were against admitting slavery into the territories. But I hope you Californians will stand your ground thus nobly taken and bide your time, if it is years; but it will *not* be long.*

---

* *In Congress the southern states bitterly opposed California's admission to the Union. The state's proposed constitution (overwhelmingly approved by the few thousand who had bothered to vote in November 1849) prohibited slavery. It was this noble stand that George applauded and southern orators denounced, leaving uncertain when California would become the thirty-first state.*

William, if I only knew that you were in California, at Sutter's or elsewhere, I should have sent you 1,200 or 1,500 New York papers, as I see they sell high there, from 50 cents to $1. If you will tell me what you think of such an operation and there is a chance for profit, I will send them to you per mail or express. Or if there are other small things that would pay, I can send them to you per steamer, as there is an express agent goes with each steamer to take things like our expresses here. Or if you want things sent for your own comfort, let me know it and I will start them forthwith, if possible.

Well, William, you are now in the land represented to be fatal to morals; tell me, is it so? If it is, William, be sure that you hold fast to those high principles of justice, honor, and righteousness that we have been taught from infancy and on which we have professed to act. Let whoever may, go astray and become reckless of morals. I believe you will still deck your character with virtuous actions, those brilliant badges of an order more noble than Napoleon's legions of honor or any other that the sons of ambition and price ever instituted. If you can't make quite so much money by a strict adherence to justice, let the gold go. You will feel better to come home and look us in the face as you always have done, with an honest conscience and moderate gain, than to meet our gaze and feel that wealth has been obtained by a single act of injustice. It would ever after mar the happiness of your triumph.

William, let me request you to read the fifth, sixth, and seventh chapters of St. Matthew, Christ's Sermon on the Mount. Read especially the fifth chapter, from the thirty-eighth verse to the end; the sixth chapter, ninth to fifteenth verses—the fourteenth and fifteenth particularly; and the seventh chapter, first, second and particularly the twelfth verses. I have read and reread them, and the more I read them the more I like them. You will discover that each verse or paragraph contains a great moral principle that requires a great deal of reflection to unfold and apply as extensively and constantly as we ought, and the grandeur and beauty of them are worthy of the teaching of God. No petty detail, but a general principle, which like all of God's other laws, physical or moral, we must apply to our own situation if we would be benefited by them. I do not make these remarks because I have not confidence in you; on the contrary, I have not a suspicion that you will forget the principles of home. I make them to strengthen you and direct you to go for support where Washington went for his. I have just been reading his religious opinions. They were of that sterling kind that needs no revisions, but supported him through evil and good report. They are well worth perusing.

I want you to write me *all* about California and yourself and your friends with you—don't fail. Many are waiting to hear what you write. George Allen, Alfred Canfield, William Decateur, and several others are thinking of coming out and want to know what William writes.

It is now past ten o'clock. May God bless, protect, prosper and return you safely home is the sincere wish of, dear William,

Your brother,
George

Youngstown, January 5, 1850
9:30 o'clock, evening

Dear Brother William,

Well, Will, a Happy New Year to you from one and all of us, and to Mr. Hutchinson, Mr. Bailey, and Mr. Root; and a right good, *lucky* year to you all. We have heard nothing from you yet and we await the arrival of this mail with much anxiety but hardly a hope of getting a line from you for this season. By the 1st of November mail Mr. Eaton received a line from Stephen dated October 15, stating that they were just arrived all well, nothing more. By date of your Fort Laramie letter Sabrina says you were nine days behind him, and if that distance were held you have barely time to get a letter into the present mail that left San Francisco November 16, arriving at Panama early in December. . . .

The State Constitution of California pleases the North, displeases the South. I hope Californians will maintain the stand. Perhaps much of their own and the Nation's fate turns on their firmness now.

The boat leaves New York on the 13th, and if this has good luck it will reach you there about the last of February.

Sunday morning, Jan. 6

Well, Will, here we all are, well except little Sis, and she is better and has quite an appetite and cackles considerable. I have just been carrying her around the floor, and she has been laughing and kicking in my arms and shows evident signs of being decidedly better. But, Will, I must quit to go to the bridge as I am not certain that there is anyone in my place and there is a great deal of crossing there. I came home last night on purpose to write and direct the papers. It is now almost ten o'clock and I ought to be there.

I should have said to Mr. Bailey that all his old friends, Doyle especially, are anxious to hear from him. Give my respects and best wishes to each of them. I wish them the realization of their highest wishes. Tell my friend, Mr. Hutchinson, that we want to see him and we'll do our best to help him hunt up a better half to take care of his "dust" and shanty and to do the agreeable to his friends, or anything else for which he may choose to call.

So goodbye, William. May God protect and bless you is the wish of your

Brother,
George Swain.

Youngstown, January 6, 1850
Sunday, one o'clock P.M.

My dear Husband,

With mingled sensations of joy and sorrow I address a few lines to you, my beloved husband—joy that I once more find myself enjoying comfortable health and the hope of once more seeing or at least hearing from you soon; sorrow that he who has been a participator in all my concerns for the last three or four years is not now at hand to participate with me in the joys and pleasures of the family circle. George has been writing and left me to finish this sheet; but he has written so extensively and I have written so lately that I have nothing of interest to write.

Monday evening, seven o'clock

Well, William, you see how much I wrote yesterday and how far this letter has gone today. Sis is asleep on her little bed by the stove. Mother is reading and George has gone up to Mr. Irish's, so we are alone as we usually are evenings and enjoy ourselves as well as can be expected in our loneliness. . . .

All our anxiety is about you, and God only knows where you are or what you are doing. I hope, however, you are at your journey's end long ere this and established in some kind of business. We learned by the papers that the rainy season has set in and all business at the mines thrown over until Spring; also that provisions are very high and scarce and mechanics' wages from $10 to $15 and as high as $25 per day. Now, William, is it so? You must have been there long enough to know something about how things stand.

And now, my dear, allow me to ask, are your most sanguine expectations realized or at least being so? Or do you find things very much exaggerated? Would you advise anyone to go to California? There are many anxious to hear from you and learn the prospects, and if favorable, there are some few that intend to leave Youngstown for California in February.

William, I am half asleep and cannot write any more tonight and shall not be able to write much in the morning. Before I close, however, I would like to ask you if the word of God is precious to your soul and if there is a pleasure in perusing it. O! I long to hear from you and learn how you are enjoying yourself, both in body and in mind.

Tuesday morning

Good morning, William—seven-thirty, and just got up from breakfast. All well except Cub, but she appears quite smart this morning.

William, I forgot to wish you a Happy New Year, which God grant may be a successful one too, at least enough to reward you for your long, tedious journey.

Goodbye till next month,

Sabrina Swain

Youngstown, Feb. 9, 1850

Dear Brother William,

May you be happy. We are not. We have not heard one word from you. And we are thus left to live on anxiety and conjecture alone. What the dickens is the reason you don't write, Boy? If you are all dead, it would be no more than civil to send us word. We have written to you every month since you left home as per agreement, but it is all like the handle of a jug so far. But I won't upbraid you, for I well know that you must have met with trouble and disappointment in no stinted measure or you would have written ere now, for I am full sure you will write as soon as you get where you can send home. It is this assurance that makes us feel so anxious. Everybody is inquiring about you, and many have given you up and think we never shall hear from you. But I tell you, I have no such idea, and am quite sure we will receive letters by the mail now due from the Isthmus. The *Empire City* came in to New York on the 7th with 290 passengers and $2,000,000 but brings no mail; that must come by the *Falcon*, which the Government, with admirable ingenuity, contrives to have always arriving behind private enterprise. There is a good deal of complaint about it. I wish I was mail agent on the Isthmus—I'd raise the devil with some of their ducks. Our big men at Washington don't know or care much about mail, if office and pay can be secured, apparently. But we have got to wait with patience to see what comes or don't come.

Sabrina is pretty well; her health is better now apparently than any time since she was married. She worries about William; and Mother dreams about him and talks with him. I have requested her to ask you how you get along and why you don't write the next time she has a talk with you—so that I expect to hear that way, if not by mail.

Little Cub is a *buster*. She grows fast, grows big, grows mischievous, grows fat, grows ugly, grows pretty; and already she is *Master of the house*, does what she pleases, and asks nobody's leave, hunts up mischief as fast as if she had a hundred eyes. You'd laugh to see her go upstairs and pay her respects to the preserves. The first time she did it I was upstairs dressing; she came up as usual. We had moved the hickory nuts out of the way, as she used to get them and bother us till we'd crack them for her. Cub went into the north chamber and was still for some time, *the usual sign that she is in mischief*. I looked in and there she stood in her glory. She had uncovered two pots and stood beside the one with a half-eaten pear in her fist and both hands and face covered with juice! Since then she has been up two or three times to see how the land lay. . . .

She must do everything that she sees others do. Must have her shoes blacked. Must fetch in wood. Must wash the stove and chairs with a wet rag. She still tends the wants of Nature on the floor, or rather lets them tend themselves. There a few minutes ago she scattered her water and her mother told her to go and get the mop and mop it up. Away she went and got it and tugged at it till she had dragged it several times over the place as sober as a judge.

Almost every time I come in she runs to me with both hands raised and sings out "Up! Up! Up!" And if she thinks I am going away she sets up a squall. And I tell you, if she thinks her Mother or Grandmother are going away, she raises a yell of agony that would startle a regiment of pirates. She has a set of lungs like a bull, and she uses them to fit in her laugh and fun and yell and scream and squeal, keeping the old stone house vocal with her noise. She is very full breasted and plump as a young quail, and as full of fun as an egg is of meat. She will laugh and slap her hands and stamp her feet if anything pleases her. But if she gets mad, she will throw herself on the floor and kick up her heels and squall like a wildcat. . . . But I will stop telling you about Sis, or I shall not have time for anything else. I hope you will be at home in less than a year to see her yourself and to wish us all the next Happy New Year. . . .

They are having warm times in Congress, and many think there is actual danger of what the South in great anger threatens, a dissolution of the Union. There is no doubt but many in the South hold the Union cheap and would rather be out than in it, but there are many there that will stand by the Union to the last. Henry Clay has introduced Compromise Resolutions that will most likely pass, though they are opposed now by both extremes, North and South.* He is still, as he always has been,

---

* *In late January 1850 the aging Henry Clay, Senator from Kentucky, sought to calm the crisis by proposing eight resolutions which he defended in a two-day speech, February 5–6.*

the great American Statesman. The noble sentiment he uttered the other day in the Senate was worthy of the Greatest Man of the Age, worthy of himself. When taunted by Foote of Mississippi and Mason of Virginia that he was deserting the South, he bravely answered, "I know my duty and coming from a slave state as I do, no power on earth shall ever make me vote for the extension of slavery over one foot of territory now free. Never.—No, Sir, NO." That single sentence electrified the Senate and perhaps saved the Union. If Clay were President instead of Taylor, the miserable quarrel about California would not now be cursing our country, threatening ruin. But I must refer you to the papers: the regular file of the New York *Express* that I send you regularly, and frequently the *Courier*.

I have joined the Sons of Temperance; we have a fine division here of some seventy or eighty members and do well. I wish you were here with us. . . .

The Ladies Sewing Society gave an oyster supper a week ago last Thursday evening and sold off the stock on hand to finish paying for the bell of the church, which they accomplished. Supper 50 cents each. Sabrina went down. We had a fine time. I enjoyed myself well and raised quite a breeze of fun. Some of the girls said next day that they didn't know George had so much vim in him. Poor coons, they never had a chance to see what he is!!! Sabrina, of course, did not feel so well: *her* man wasn't there, but she seemed to enjoy it as well as could be expected for a grass widow who don't like oysters.

Other things as usual. Mr. Hurlburt preaches to us yet. Dr. Root and family are well. I saw him today, and talked about the "boys" and the probability of getting a letter and when the mail would be in. They feel anxious about John. I got a line from Mrs. Bailey the other day, inquiring if we had heard from you and Mr. Bailey yet. . . .

O, forgot to tell you, I hear Mary Elliot is married, so my cake is all dough there again. But I take it easy; "good fish in the seas as ever swam."

If we knew anything about where you are or what you are about or what you want, I could do something for you, I think. If you can't make anything by staying there, *come home right off*; if you want money, let me know without hesitation, because I consider myself bound to share with you in misfortune as well as good fortune; and if you were at home we could work the farm to better advantage.

George

February 10

Sunday morning. All well. God bless you, William.

Youngstown
Sunday evening
March 10, '50

Dear William,

I have just been carrying little Sis about the house while Sabrina and Mother were cleaning off the table, and as I carried the little thing with her prattle and laugh and then with head laid over on my shoulder like a drooping flower seeking repose, I could not help thinking where her distant father was, or what was the reason we could not hear from him, for we have not yet heard a word from you since your Fort Laramie letter July 4. Now more than eight months and you may be assured that we are not easy about you. All about you is conjecture and every one conjectures to suit themselves as their fancy or information directs them. Some supposing you are dead; others that you are wintering at Salt Lake; others that you were among the companies that were caught in the snow and had to be extricated by the U.S. troops; others that you got into the mines late and went right at digging and did not bother your head about writing till you had got something to tell of, etc. etc. But the mischief take the luck, I am so confoundedly puzzled that I can't make a supposition that will satisfy myself. The only thing I'm certain of is that we've got no letter from you and that you are in some mean scrape and can't write. Of that I am satisfied.

I have written to you every month since you left, as per agreement, and sent your regular files of the New York *Express* and some other scattering ones; I have directed all to Sutter's Fort. And I only write this to keep my word good, for it seems like writing to the wind. Sabrina declines to write, for she thinks it will not be of any use. Be that as it may, I write till I know the worst or best, whatever it may be.

We have heard from most of the other young men that went from this region—Colt, McNeil, Stephen Eaton, John Eggleston, Belden, etc. —but nothing from you. The Lockport Company or part of it got home in February (the 14th). I went out there to see them and inquire for you, but they knew nothing. I saw Dr. M'Collum, but he did not know you had started till he got home. He had been on San Joaquin and Sacramento River and left the mines the forepart of November, but thought you had probably got through.*

---

* *William M'Collum, a practicing physician of Lockport, was one of the first of thousands to return from California. He had arrived in Lockport on February 15, 1850, after having spent the months between July and December of 1849 in the California mines. Almost immediately he began composing a narrative of his adventures, which must have been near*

I find the Lockport folks are willing to stay at home, not anxious to return to California. But there are others going from this county. Henry Hill starts this week and perhaps I shall send this by him, for I had put off writing in hopes to hear from you till today, thinking that this was the 9th and as the mail leaves on the 13th of each month that there would be time to get a letter to New York in time, but it is now doubtful. Therefore, I shall send either this or another by Mr. Hill if he will take it. Edwin Tower intends going with Henry and probably will.

Sabrina had a despairing fit after the last mail came in and brought no news from you. She felt worse than any time since your departure.

We have been expecting a mail from San Francisco, but the steamer *Philadelphia* that was expected in New York with the March mail is at the Isthmus. . . . I wish we had a telegraph to California or a streak of lightning in some of those mail carriers via the Isthmus. . . .

Goodbye, William.

> Anxiously yours in the bonds of affection,
> George Swain

---

completion by the time George saw him. Published in Buffalo in the spring of 1850, his narrative went under the imposing title of California As I Saw It. Pencillings by the Way of the Gold and Gold Diggers! and Incidents of Travel by Land and Water, *by William S. M'Collum, M.D., a Returned Adventurer. As well as being among the first to return, M'Collum was one of the first to recount his adventures for publication.*

CHAPTER XI

The Great California Lottery

*"Say to all my friends: stay at home. Tell
my enemies to come."*

By early April 1850, Swain, Hutchinson, Bailey and the other Rangers
had been in the diggings for five months; they had been a year away from
home. By their original expectations they should have been on their way
back to New York and Michigan with gold enough for triumphant home-
comings. That promise still seemed possible, but they knew its fulfillment
would require far more time and effort than once imagined. Along all the
rivers there were those who talked of giving up mining to look for work
in the cities. Swain, his friends and hundreds of similar mining partnerships in the muddy, winter-dark canyons waited for the rains to stop and
the high waters to recede so they could begin river-mining operations.

It had been a glum and lonely winter for the Youngstown men in
their dank cabin, only the doorway providing light and fresh air. The
weeks of rain had been far worse for other miners who survived in tents,
canvas-walled shacks or dugouts covered with brush. In this masculine
world of primitive housing, ignorance of cooking, and unconcern for
appearance and hygiene, with liquor, gambling and an occasional fight
the only distractions from their weary work or waiting, the great moment
came when they heard that the expressman was on his way. These enterprising mailmen not only found Swain's cabin on the banks of the South
Fork, they hiked to the most secluded clusters of habitations where miners dug for gold.

From their monthly trips by river steamers to stand in line at the
post offices in San Francisco and Sacramento City, they brought letters
from lonely wives and worried parents. They linked two worlds, the
farms and cities in thirty states and the mining camps nonexistent a few

FEATHER
and
YUBA RIVERS
MINING AREA

Summer 1850

months earlier—Long's Bar, Foster's Bar, Downieville, Mississippi Bar, Gold Springs, Shirtail Canyon, Spanish Diggings, Big Oak Flat and Nevada City, Sonora, Marysville, Yuba City. In both worlds, the letter-writers hoped for gold enough to end the lengthening separation.

Through the spring and summer of 1850 William Swain wrote home each month, sometimes more than one letter, to Sabrina, George and his mother, explaining his prospects and conditions in the mines, consoling Sabrina, fretting about his daughter for fear George would spoil her, and assuring his mother of his adherence to moral principles. More than most miners, he seemed to enjoy his monthly ritual; he wrote at great length and without complaint. Others told how difficult it was to find a smooth, flat place to write; tables were few and those made of rough planks. Candle or fireside light made daytime writing preferable. Worst of all, it was hard to hold a pen or pencil and write legibly with hands bruised, stiff, often cut, fingernails torn or missing from labor in the cold water amid rocks and gravel.

Yankee enterprise once again eased the way. By summer 1850 the miners could buy sheets of stationery on which were printed scenes of life in California—the great fire of May 5 which swept away several blocks of San Francisco's business district, the crowded waterfront at Sacramento City, or river-damming operations on the American River. Scores of different illustrated "lettersheets" were printed, sold by the tens of thousands to the miners and sent back to the States.

When the expressmen shouted their approach from the steep trails that led down to narrow canyons and rocky gorges where a string of cabins, huts, tents and other shelters housed the hairy miners, they brought not only letters from back home but newspapers as well, most common the New York *Herald* and the *Tribune*, which came to San Francisco by hundreds of copies to be sold on speculation in the mines. Reading hometown and national news lessened the miners' sense of isolation and gave them something other than gold mining to write home about. In May a miner at Bidwell's Bar told of buying a New York *Tribune* "dated March 13 which contains the important and gratifying news that Congress is becoming more *sober* and acting somewhat like statesmen."

In the eastern newspapers, especially those from New York, the miners read with growing concern about their world—the booming cities, the success of miners, the millions in gold delivered each month by steamers to the East Coast. This news compounded their anxiety—here they were living a harsh, comfortless life struggling to gain some part of what they had promised to bring home (Swain's goal was $10,000), and the eastern newspapers made California sound like a place where everyone was striking it rich. They were further astonished to read that great numbers of Americans planned to travel overland to California that summer—had no one read their letters?

What a dilemma they faced. They had to justify their staying in California far longer than ever expected, leaving wife and family with insufficient funds, dependent on parents and friends; had to argue that another season in the mines would surely produce success. At the same time, they had to explain why no one else should come to California.

While most letter writers admonished everyone to stay away from California, one cynical fellow held a different view: "I really hope that no one will be deterred from coming on account of what anybody else may say. The more fools the better, the fewer to laugh when we get back home."

For those already in the mines, with the dangers of the long journey behind them and with their experience in mining, the chance for some success seemed to justify their staying through the summer of 1850. That was Swain's argument, presented in his typically rational, calm manner. For others the decision was tormenting. "Oh, Matilda, oft is the night when laying alone on the hard ground with a blanket under me and one over me that my thoughts go back to Ohio and I think of you and wish myself with you. But I am willing to stand it all to make enough to get us a home and so I can be independent of some of the darned sonabitches that felt themselves above me because I was poor. Cuss them, I say. I understand they prophesy that I will never come back. Darn their stinking hides. If God spares my life, I will show them to be false prophets, for as sure as I live we will shake hands and give a warm embrace by spring anyhow, and before if you say so."

Striving for success in what many called "The Great California Lottery," the miners felt increasingly resentful of the California and eastern newspapers which reported gold being dug by the pound along all the streams from the Mariposa to the Feather. "Such stories are started by merchants and dealers in liquors and provisions, etc. to attract a crowd to their place and make a market for their goods." And it looked as though the newspaper stories were responsible for attracting thousands of new goldseekers to the already crowded mines.

As if to say "serves 'em right," a weary, embittered miner ended his monthly letter: "I understand by some letters from Iowa that there has been a Mountain of Gold found in this country, also a Lake of Gold. I should not wonder if the next news we get from the states would be that California has turned into a solid mass of gold."

No El Dorado, California seemed to all but a few of its temporary residents to have also been falsely praised for its climate and agriculture. "When I first heard of California I supposed it to be the Garden Spot of the World. I expected all kinds of vegetation and many tropical fruits growing in abundance. But I found here that the fair-named and far-famed California is but little better than a desert." "I have yet to find the first man . . . who does not feel himself deceived and disappointed in the character and appearance of the country. . . . Every description of it has been shamefully and corruptly overwrought."

In a remarkably lengthy and detailed analysis of California's economy, society, climate, soil and geology, Swain joined the chorus of disparagement, concluding with the judgments that the Sacramento Valley could not be irrigated and the gold mines would be exhausted in five years.

Very few disagreed. One who did realized that the goldseekers' jackpot psychology had blinded them to California's potential. "A great mistake has been made by people who have emigrated to California . . . in considering it merely as a temporary home, a sort of huge goose out of which a few feathers were to be plucked and then forsaken. . . . Never was there a more egregious error in regard to the character of the country. Gold is not the only product of California. Her fertile valleys and rich prairies are capable . . . of producing an untold store of agricultural wealth."

Farming seemed too slow a route to wealth in 1850 and for several years thereafter. Besides, it required settling down, staying in California. If they were ever to take up farming again, it would be back home, not in the Sacramento Valley where it never rained from April or May until October or November. As a consequence, the growing demand in the cities, towns and mining camps for all kinds of foodstuffs was largely supplied by imports—flour from Chile, oranges from Mexico, vegetables from Hawaii, cheese from Europe. Quantities of edibles were landed each day at Sacramento City. The *Placer Times* reported two schooners unloaded 3,000 pounds of butter in kegs, 2,000 pounds of pork, 5,000 pounds of cheese in tins, 2,000 pounds of sausage, 18,000 pounds of fresh chili beans, and 100 cases each of pickled oysters, clams, lobsters and scallops. Other ships delivered cargoes that included rubber tents with frames attached, 262 cases of boots, 10,000 cigars—and a large shipment of Vermont marble, for tombs and headstones.

For all that was shipped to California, the one import most wanted remained most scarce—women. The only estimates of how many had come to California were made by the harbormaster at San Francisco and by the newspapers, which tried time and again in 1850 to report "The Golden Emigration" by land and sea. Exemplary of their statistics: for the entire year, 1850, the count at San Francisco was 35,333 men and 1,248 women. From the main overland trail the figures came from the count at Fort Laramie: 39,560 men and 2,421 women with 609 children.

Unlike most of the women who came by ship, the overlanders were wives; most of them scattered with their husbands throughout the mining region. The women who landed at San Francisco stayed in that metropolis or settled in Sacramento City, for there was little reason to go out to the primitive mining towns and camps. In September a miner at Yuba City lamented that in that town of 2,000 "I don't suppose there are a dozen women anywhere in the vicinity. I know of only six and four of them are Mexicans." In April, a young man in Nevada City exclaimed:

"Got nearer to a female this evening than I have been for six months. Came near fainting."

Because there were very few women seen or heard about outside the big cities and because they were generally writing to wives and parents, the men of California made few references to the presence or absence of women. If they knew or had heard about prostitutes, they had every reason to obscure or ignore the subject. It was far more comfortable to express moral concern or outrage at the prevalence of gambling and drinking in every camp, town and city.

Those who did write about women did so as if commenting on another aspect of the speculative fever so epidemic in California. One of the Rangers observed in January: "Women here are doing full as well as men. They can get for cooking sometimes as high as $30 per day, and for washing they can get even as high as $50 to $60. One young lady who came in last fall now has over $3,000 clear. Another . . . is worth today $10,000." In one of the gambling halls in Marysville "there are eight young ladies dealing monte. One is reported to be a very handsome miss of about seventeen years old. . . ." Some of the women who pursued their fortunes as prostitutes dressed in men's clothes to ride horseback from camp to camp. "One celebrated character of this kind said she had made $50,000 and regretted that she had not double the capacity for increasing her gains."

Reporting not only the range of speculation but as well the laissez-faire attitude of the mining population, a man visiting Nevada City in August 1850 wrote to his brother back in Iowa: "The best house in this place is a two-story frame house about 30 by 40 and will be occupied as a whorehouse. It is looked on as an honorable business and a man goes into that as he would any other speculation. In fact, the whole business of the inhabitants of this country is to make money, no matter by what means."

Far more common than whores, professional gamblers tempted the miners at every cluster of tents and shacks. In the evenings and especially on Sunday when everyone left his claim, gambling and drinking offered the only escape from the toil and monotony of digging. With mining seen as a lottery in which a man's fortune was ruled more by luck than directed by perseverance, it was easy to turn to monte or roulette and hope that what thousands of shovelfuls had failed to turn up might be won on the single turn of a card or spin of a wheel. "There is a bar or gambling house at every step and . . . every attraction is offered and every trick practiced to get the miner's dust. We are thousands of miles from home and comfort ourselves by thinking that a knowledge of our indulgence in vice will never reach them."

While most writers concerned themselves with the moral consequences of vice, a few looked on the situation less seriously. In June 1850 a young miner by the name of Lucius Fairchild (in later years he would be a Wisconsin Supreme Court justice) wrote to a friend back home: "Gambling, drinking and *houses of ill fame* are the chief amusements of this country. Therefore you see that we have nothing but work, reading and writing to amuse us, as we are all nice young men and do not frequent such places."

Unlike Fairchild, William Swain did not jest about something as serious as sin—not around the fireside of his cabin nor in a letter to George, the only person to whom he might have revealed a deviation from the teachings of the Bible. For him California was not meant to be an adventure or an escape. Whatever others might do in their pursuit of fortune or in their disappointment, he would hold to the values of Youngstown—he even flaunted them, as he told in one letter. And he never forgot his obligation to Sabrina and George, to return home with a pocketful of rocks. For Swain and tens of thousands of miners in canyon camps and hillside towns, the return home was the pressing purpose of all their work.

The work that promised the greatest gains, that would surely send them home, was directed to river mining. For miles along the branches of the Feather, Yuba, American and other streams companies of men worked with axes and shovels and picks, here and there with dynamite, to build flumes and cut races for the moment when the water would be low enough for the dams to be closed and the rivers diverted. Allied with the miners in these great engineering feats were scores of merchants who provided food of all kinds and equipment, all on credit in the belief that the riverbed would pay for everything.

Sharing this expectation, Swain, Bailey and Hutchinson in March packed their supplies, pans and rockers on their backs and left their cabin on the South Fork of the Feather for a prospecting trip along the Yuba. They followed a steep trail over the ridge, still covered with drifts of snow, and scrambled down a steeper trail to the North Fork of the Yuba. Along the twisting course of this river, there were fifty-one large rock and gravel bars between Ousley's and Downieville, with uncounted smaller bars beyond that town. All three forks of the Yuba had scores of tributary creeks, gulches, flats, ravines and canyons. While his partners mined at Foster's Bar, Swain prospected farther up the North Fork. Though it was early in the season (the water was still high from the snow melting in the spring sun), he found "claimants" at every possible location. He would prospect yet farther upstream, all the way to Slate Creek.

Swain's letters from Foster's Bar, Slate Creek and the cabin on the

South Fork continued through the summer to record fundamental facts —where he was or had been, how much money he had been able to save despite the high prices, the state of his health, his relief and delight in receiving his first letters from home, and in most letters, the dark news that "nine tenths of the miners are sick at heart." Like everyone else who wrote home he sought to prepare his family for the inevitable choice: to give up on the great expectations that had brought him to California and head for home, with little more than when he had said goodbye—or to stay through the rainy season and try for a strike next summer, in 1851.

■

Sabbath, April 15, 1850
Foster's Bar, Yuba River
60 miles from Yuba City

Dear Sabrina and Mother,

When I last wrote you I was on the Feather River, but I now address you from the Yuba, about twenty-five miles from our cabin on that river. My absence from there has deprived me from receiving any letters since I last wrote and has also prevented me from writing as soon as I should, had I been at camp.

We have had considerable rain during the spring, and the rains in March became snow in the mountains. [The trail from the South Fork to the Yuba led "up to the top of the mountains nearly four miles and quite steep most of the way. . . . From the summit could be seen the immense bodies of snow that still lie at the head of the South Fork of the Feather and the North Fork of the Yuba. . . . In many places deep ravines were completely filled, to the tops of the pines only appearing above the snow. . . . The Yuba River runs through or beneath enormous beds of snow . . . where its muffled roar was so far beneath as to be scarcely heard."]

The great quantity of melting snow has caused very high water, which has thrown miners on their oars and really it has been a tiresome time. A great share of the weather is fine and pleasant, but the resting place of the "yellow boys" is far down in the waters. It is wearisome to one who is impatient to get at them and leave for a more congenial land, to mark the days as they drag their slow length along.

[Rather than wait for the rivers to subside, some impatient and imaginative miners sought their fortunes by the "use of submarine armor in working the channels of the rivers. Much money was expended and much time lost in making experiments, but to little advantage." One such experiment was "made by an old Georgia miner who had been accustomed to the use of the submarine suit which he had worn in recovering some treasure from a ship sunk in the Mississippi." Other miners tried "diving bells" to explore the depths of the rivers.]

I have occupied my time in prospecting over the miserable mountains and find it hard work which subjects a man to great exposure. The fact is, California has a miserable climate for mining: five months' rain, four months' high water, and three months' dry and good weather but very hot—almost too hot to work.

We are all here on the Yuba in good health. My health was never better and if it continues good through the summer I am confident of getting well paid for all my trouble on this long journey, and a little something handsome for the exposure and crucifixion of feeling I have undergone.

We finished our job on Feather River and tested it, although under great disadvantages. I am satisfied that it will *not pay* to work it out, but we intend to work part of it when the water goes down. Meanwhile, we shall prospect on this river till we find a place that suits us. We expect to go up this river soon and locate above here for the summer and hope to profit by the experience we have had. Our job [on the Feather River] cost us a great deal and much hard work. Many a one has acquired a large fortune with half the exertion we have made, but we are not discouraged; on the contrary, we are confident of success. However, it is rather provoking to be disappointed in high hopes.

["Many persons are returning home, tired of California. . . . That there is an immense amount of gold here none can deny, but it is much more difficult to obtain than it was last season. . . . In short, the cream has been taken off. . . .

["You will ask, What is the average amount daily made by the miners? This much is quite certain, that . . . every miner who has at least some experience expects to make an ounce a day, or else he is not satisfied with his placer and will prospect for a better one. Often we hear of men making on an average for several days from $50 to $100 to $300 per day; in fact, there is no doubt but such is the case. Many have certainly through the past year made from $5,000 to $10,000. . . . It must be understood that not all make this money by digging. Most of those who have done so well are those who brought capital with them and went directly to trading in the mines or in the city of San Francisco or Sacramento and other places. This gave them very great advantages, as everything sold at enormous profits. . . ." For example, a Wolverine Ranger who was in San Francisco reported a Captain Randolph "was making a very handsome little fortune on $2,000 worth of boots and shoes which he shipped around the Cape. He is selling common hip boots at $16 to $20 per pair. He will . . . clear at least $10,000."

["Some have made at the monte bank enough to go home. Others by a rare streak of good luck have made $6,000 to $8,000 by digging and working. But since the first of November the probability is that most have not made more than enough to pay the expense of living."]

But we are in good time for the mining season, and although we have no gold, we have our location on the Feather River, in which we might have sold a share for $1,000. But we would not cheat the fellow, as we did not believe the location to be worth much. I would rather have a clear conscience than $1,000. ["In many cases the grossest impositions have been practiced. Persons have scattered gold in the dirt of a claim they held, then have offered it for a high price, exhibiting a pan full of rich soil as a specimen. . . . Miners practice many arts to deceive others with regard to what they may be doing. Especially this is the case if they are doing well, when they generally say they are doing nothing." "In traveling around the mines for information, ten chances to one if you get the truth, unless you come across an acquaintance."]

We have been at work on this bar some days, averaging $12 per day, but it won't do while the high water lasts. Prices are reasonable: flour, 35 cents per lb.; fresh beef, 50 cents; salt pork, 60 cents; sugar, 70 cents; dried apples, $1. I have not eaten an apple since I left the Illinois River. All kinds of clothing is cheap here but boots and shoes. Boots are worth $25 to $30. I have two pair of J. Graves' boots yet and have not yet had to buy any clothing. We can board ourselves well here for $1.50 a day.

["Provisions are now obtained in the mines with much less difficulty than they were last fall and in greater variety, so that the meager diet of the miners can be replaced by that more healthful. Trading establishments keep pace with the crowds forcing their way into the mountain recesses, and competition is rapidly reducing the exorbitant prices which were common last fall." "Small towns are springing up on all sides of us, and the country is becoming more like our young states than a wild, unsettled land. Still it is a rough country after all. At the taverns in the mines there are no chairs, no beds, no bedclothes except blankets in which thousands have slept before, and all are full of body lice."]

I find this voyaging life disagreeable, as it is here today and there tomorrow and prevents me from hearing from home regularly or writing regularly and gives me a disagreeable feeling about the folks at home. I often feel as though I could not stay here, but reflection brings duty to my aid, and I solace myself with the thought that you are better off at home than I am here and that your wants will all be provided for. Still I feel very anxious to come home and see you all, little Sis in particular. May God grant that the long separation may prove to be for the comfort of us all through many years.

I am thankful to the Giver of good for the recovery of your health, Mother. May God grant that we may yet meet again and live for many years in the enjoyment of each other's society. I feel that I have not properly appreciated your kindness to me, and I have not properly estimated the value of a parent who has spent a life in caring for me and inculcating principles of justice, morality, and religion. Mother, I thank you for all those principles. Thanks can poorly pay for the years of trouble and hardship you have had, but it is all the tribute I can render at this distance from you.

I was sorry to hear of Sister's illness, but children are subject to such things, and I know that she will be taken care of. I am very sorry to hear, Sabrina, that you are troubled with your old complaint, spinal affection, and also with toothache. Be careful of yourself; do not lift or do hard work.

You have kindly asked in your last letter if my expectations are being realized. My specific answer to your kind question is that my expectations are not realized. We have been unlucky—or rather, by being inexperienced, we selected a poor spot for a location and staked all on it, and it has proved worth nothing. Had it proved as it was expected when we took it up, I should have more than realized my most sanguine expectation, and I should have today been on my way to the bosom of my family in possession of sufficient means to have made them and me comfortable through life. But it is otherwise ordered; and I mostly regret the necessity of staying here longer.

["You can scarcely form any conception of what a dirty business this gold digging is and of the mode of life which a miner is compelled to lead. We all live more like brutes than humans." "Not one man in a hundred . . . ever puts a razor to his phiz. The truth is, something looks wrong to see a white shirt or a shaven face. . . . With the help of shears to keep the road open to our mouths and a little trimming to keep our faces a little shipshape, we are at the top of fashion." Barbers "are about as useful here as would be a penny whistle under the falls of Niagara."]

I was in hopes to have sent home a good pile of money before this time, but I am not able to at present. Still, my expectations are high, and in my opinion the excitement about the gold mines was not caused by exaggeration. In fact, I believe that greater amounts of gold have been

Bruff titled this drawing "Repose of tired adventurers."

and will be taken from the mines this summer than the gold news have told, and I would not today take less than $10,000 for my summer's work. But I am of the opinion that the gold will soon be gathered from these washings and then will come the hardest part of this gold fever. I therefore would advise no one to come here, nor would I advise anyone who has good health *not* to come, unless it was George; and were his constitution iron and his body steel, I would not be willing he should come to this country to work in these mines. Nor would I again traverse the same route under the same circumstances, even were a princely fortune the sure reward. But were I to be unfortunate in all my business here and arrive at last at home without *one cent*, I should ever be glad that I have taken the trip to California. It has learnt me to have confidence in myself, has disciplined my impetuous disposition and has learnt me to think and act for myself and to look upon men and things in a true light. Notwithstanding all these favorable circumstances, it is a fact that no energy or industry can secure certain success in the business of mining; and it may perhaps be my lot after a summer of hardship and exposure to be but little better off than I am now. Be that as it may, I shall use my utmost endeavors to gain what money I can and do it honorably. Failing (if fail I should), I shall return home proud of honest and honorable effort.

In your letter, Sabrina, you have made frequent allusions to our little girl—her growth; her progress in walking, talking; her tricks of childhood; disposition; temper; attachments; etc., all of which are of great interest to me. I sympathize with you in the great responsibility devolving upon you alone in my absence, for with you I feel that the task of disciplining and guiding her mind is one of great care and anxiety and diligence, on which depends to great extent her disposition and happiness in future life. Be assured I would gladly share that task with you, knowing the weight of duty you feel, for I know that you properly estimate the relation of parent and child. And I also have the fullest confidence in your judgment and ability to train her aright. Having that confidence, I feel assured that you will do the best that can be done. I wish you always to be guided by your own judgment, irrespective of the opinions of either your own or my relatives in the discharge of duty to the child. . . .

In relation to the manner of discipline, it may be well to say that it is my belief that government of children should be effected by impressing upon the mind ideas of right and wrong, propriety and impropriety, and good and bad, and these principles once impressed upon the mind will constitute the most reliable means of directing the acts of infancy. But these are not always adequate to counteract the will and subdue the temper. . . . Restraints are necessary, especially in early infancy, and unless they are timely and judiciously resorted to, the omission may be the cause of great evil to the child and trouble to the parent. No less the good of the child than the duty of the parent requires restraints and punishments. . . .

Her physical development, too, I hope you will not neglect. It calls for far more care than parents usually bestow on their children's development. Be careful not to cripple the power of Nature by hampering it with close clothes; let them be such as will assist Nature in the creation of good physical system. Let her food be rather coarse and such that is easily digested, not too highly seasoned nor very salty. Milk is the best of all foods for young ones; and as little pork or grease as possible—it is the worst of all things for children except candies and sweets. Be sure not to allow her to sleep with a high pillow, for they cause round and stooped shoulders. Avoid anything that can have a tendency to induce curved spine. These will require your careful attention.

I am now bound hand and foot by high water, but it will not always last, and then I can do something worth talking about. I am not yet settled for the summer and shall not send to Sacramento City for any letters till I am. I have received a New York *Tribune* of February 7, in which I saw Henry Clay's resolutions and speech in the Senate. What fate the resolutions have met with I know not, nor how that vexed question will be settled. Certainly things at the seat of government are in a deplorable state. Henry Clay is still the great statesman of the nation, one of the immortal few who were not born to die. I trust that his wise counsel will prevail, and while Old Rough and Ready is there, there is a sound head at the helm. But certainly it appears that the Locos [Locofocos, or radical Democrats] are determined to do all the mischief they can. The aspect of the South looks dubious and shows that they have been caught by their own trap but have hit upon some new and undeveloped scheme to still hold the balance of power. What may come of the June convention [called by six southern states to meet at Nashville, Tennessee, to consider the advisability of secession], time alone may develop. But they may rest assured that not one foot of California will ever be the land of the slave. Freedom waves her banner here and that banner will never be replaced by the black banner of oppression. Harrigan, Foote, Calhoon, Davis and the host of Southerners may rave, but their peculiar institutions must and will wane before the frown of universal sentiment of mankind. . . .*

I have much to say upon California in respect to the habits, customs, and morals of the miners, which will be embraced in my next two letters. I am sorry to say that on the subject of morality and religion, the miners are losing principle. Cut loose from restraints of society, men's principles are put to the test, and where surrounding influence is their foundation, they fall like leaves before the autumn blast. Swearing is very prevalent, and drinking and drunkenness a prominent feature in the mines. Temperance men are disregardful of their solemn pledge, and Sons of Temperance of their secret oaths of abstinence. Yesterday in returning down the river, in a walk of ten miles, I was invited by acquaintances to drink

---

* *Though Swain's antislavery feelings were shared by the vast majority of miners, there were a few southern miners who brought slaves to work their claims. On the South Fork of the Feather River in April 1850: "There are Negroes here now laboring for their liberty, having contracted to give what they can earn in one, two or three years, or for a specified sum. On the Louisiana claim one is to pay $10,000 for himself, wife and child, and yet he is a free man here and knows it. His wife, like the wives of others, is held as a pledge of good faith."*

Opposition to slavery generally prevailed in the mines, as was emphasized by an Alabaman who wrote to his father in August 1850: "With twenty good Negroes and the power of managing them as at home, I could make from ten to fifteen thousand dollars per month. But here a fellow has to knock it out with his own fist or not at all."

brandy no less than three times. But I find it the easiest thing in the world to refuse. The reply, "I thank you, I never drink any liquor" delivered in an emphatic and decided tone, hardly ever fails to stop all importuning, besides administering a silent rebuke, and I often glory in the momentary confusion of the drinker.

["The amount drunk is perfectly astounding, appalling. The liquor sellers furnish tables and cards, and men sit down and play for drink. After one drink they must play another game, and the excitement of the play leads them on. . . . Then they must have cigars, nuts, pickles, etc. etc., so that in the course of the day many will spend $5 or $6, and even more, at the bar. . . . Old Alcohol in his palmiest days had not more faithful, loving subjects." "So much liquor is drunk that there is not a road nor a bypath but what you see empty bottles every few yards. . . ."]

Gambling too is another, I may say, of the prominent features of this country. It is now carried into the mines, and here in the mountains it is no unusual sight to see hundreds of dollars staked on the upturning of a certain card. I have known a gambler on this bar in one evening to rob the miners of $500 by their own wills. They are fools and need no pity. ["If the good people of the States could look in on these gambling dens for a minute or two, they would feel like calling home all foreign missionaries and turning them loose on this God-forsaken people."]

To such an extent does this vice exist that almost all participate in it. Many who were very careful to read a chapter in the Bible and pray every morning think it is no harm to deal monte in California; and one man, whom I am credibly informed was a Methodist minister at home, mines through the day and plays monte or some other game at night. Such men are not, thank heaven, the representatives of those principles taught in the Bible but rather of the depravity of human nature.

Slate Creek
[Tributary of the North Fork of the Yuba]
April 21

As I did not finish my letter last Sabbath, I shall finish it this afternoon and send it to Yuba City this evening, where I am just informed the government has established a post office. Yuba City is a small village situated on the Feather River at the mouth of the Yuba River, sixty miles or less from here. [In January it was reported that "several of the richest men in California were the originators and proprietors . . . of a large speculation in Yuba City. One of them had made a half-million dollars in Sacramento City speculation. . . . They offered . . . an eighth interest in Yuba City for $20,000."

[About a mile up the Yuba River at Marysville "you will see the go-ahead-iveness of the Yankee nation. In one fortnight's time $25,000 worth of lots at $250 each were sold. In ten days . . . seventeen houses and stores were put up, and what was before a ranch—a collection of Indian huts and a corral for cattle—became a right smart little city."

[A miner who was in Yuba City in March reported that "seven steamboats are plying between Sacramento City and those prodigies of Yankee enterprise. . . . These boats are mere scows of an ungainly build, with engines of forty horsepower, propelled by stern paddles. They are crowded with passengers every morning and evening. One of them, the *Linda*, changed hands to the tune of $40,000. They say she will bring the amount of purchase money in a half-dozen trips to Marysville."]

During the past week I have been over twenty-five miles prospecting on the Yuba. Was out four days—in sunshine, rain and snow—and found the river occupied by claimants at all the bars. Found gold all along the banks in small particles and on the slate base considerable, but found no location that suited me. Meantime, Messrs. Hutchinson and Bailey worked on this bar. We shall have to go higher than I have yet been, probably.

["Many of the mountain trails are already like great highways. You meet parties of men at every turn, sweating under heavy loads and scarcely able to speak for want of breath and toiling up the steep ascents —earning every dollar they get before they find it. And now instead of going armed as was necessary two or three months ago, we can traverse the mountain trails from the canyon to the valley with no other arms than a good jackknife to cut our raw pork."]

The Trinity River [about 200 miles to the northwest] is becoming all the rage, and I hope some of the miners will go there in place of everyone mining here, as they have all Spring.*

["It seems like June here. . . . The nights are warm, and the white oak is fully leaved out. . . . The growth of vegetation is inconceivably rapid. The most barren places are, almost in a night, covered with green grass and beautiful flowers. The river rises every night and falls again in the daytime, which indicates that the snow is melting high up the stream, as it takes from ten to twelve hours to reach here after it begins to melt in the forenoon."

---

* *Swain's hope was already a reality. The* Alta California, *April 10, 1850: "From the reports of persons lately come from an exploration of the country around the Trinity River, there remains no doubt of the great richness of the mines in that region. Already large bodies of practical and experienced miners are on the move in that direction."*

["The forest is full of splendid trees. In some places are groves of live oaks, their round symmetrical forms looking like large orchards of apple trees. . . . The tall pines, fir, cedar, spruce, manzanita and other trees all look splendid and are evergreen throughout the year. As fast as their foliage drops, new leaves take their place. The turpentine from pine trees is limpid and transparent when it first oozes out of the tree but hardens with age. . . . Miners keep bottles of soft turpentine to dress wounds and cuts, and its qualities are very healing. . . . Spruce tea is very conducive to health as an anti-dyspeptic and is sure to cure the scurvy. . . . Along the brooks are watercress and a sort of lettuce . . . and a small wild onion or garlic which flavors soups and stews. There is also plenty of wild mint which makes good tea. California soap grows in abundance: it is a root, in size and shape like a common onion, with one layer over another. . . . The bulb makes strong frothy suds which cleans clothes quicker than soap and is healing to sore hands."

["Other products of the country hereabouts are raspberries, goose-berries, and strawberries; wild peas; lizards and rattlesnakes, with occasionally a scattering of deer, grizzly bears, hare, squirrel, or Digger Indians. The turtledove and quail abound in this region, but on the whole game of every description is rather scarce." "There are so many people and so many engaged in hunting that . . . deer are probably fleeing to the mountains for safety as they cannot go to the river to drink, or graze among the neighboring hills without hearing the crack of some hunting rifle. . . ."]

George, I think it highly proper that Mother should go down to see her sister this spring, but I should hate to have her go down on that journey without your accompanying her. If you can command the means and time, you had better take her to Massachusetts and spend a few weeks in her company in the place of nativity.* I will be anxious to hear that she has gone, for Mother is aged and life's brittle thread may soon be severed. Such a visit in the evening of life would be gratifying to her, and duty to a kind and only parent calls upon us to enable her once more to visit the home of her youth and her relatives. Such an act on our part would ever be a source of gratifying recollection to us. Do not fail to go with her this spring or summer; I think it advisable not to delay. You can arrange your business at the office somehow. The expense would be almost nothing, and at any rate would not be a consideration in the matter. It will not be long before I shall be able to send home some funds and some I hope that will do some good.

---

* Patience (Mrs. Isaac) Swain was born August 1, 1780, in North Brookfield, Massachusetts, where her sister, Mrs. Phillip Deland, still lived.

Mr. Bailey sends his respects to all his friends and wishes you to write Mrs. Bailey, if she is still in Cattaraugus County, and let her know he is well. Mr. Hutchinson sends his best respects to all of you and says he is highly satisfied that he came to California and that you stayed at home. He thinks it was best of both. Give my best wishes to the Root family and write me if they have heard from John. Kiss little Sister for father, and when I come home, I will do it myself.

William

April —, 1850 [date left blank]
South Fork, Feather River

Dear George,

As I am to write you about California and its prospects, I shall be brief, giving you such facts as my limited opportunities will afford and drawing such conclusions as observations have induced. But I assure you at the start that my notion of California and its destiny is far from awarding to her the present or future greatness that many of the public prints of our country are foretelling for her through the pens of many of the correspondents in this land of "Glittering Dreams."*

The prosperity of any country depends mainly upon its innate and enduring ability to contribute to the happiness of a settled, abiding, and industrious population. In other words, it must possess the natural elements of an agricultural or manufacturing population, or unite them both. Without these elements no intelligent population will be abiding and permanent. Without permanency, industry (which contributes largely to the permanent happiness and comfort of a people and is in reality the real wealth of a prosperous nation) is not likely to exist, and therefore its all-creative power is not exerted in the conception and completion of great national arrangements and improvements which look to the well-being of the future equally with the present. . . .

California is divided by natural features into four parts: the Great Valley of the Sacramento and San Joaquin; the mountains; the narrow valley of the seacoast; and that of the Colorado. Of the valley of the Colorado, there is but little known, but all that is known tends to prove

---

* Though few, if any, launched forth on so broad and thoughtful an analysis of California and its future as Swain undertook in this letter, most diarists and letter writers had their opinions, generally disparaging or contemptuous. One miner snorted: "I am much amused at the sage remarks of some of the New York editors respecting California. . . . They dilate upon its agricultural capacities, its central position, etc. . . . It is no more fit for farming purposes than I am for preaching. Exhaust the gold and it will no longer attract ships to its shores, only to carry back the poor devils who are caught here in search of El Dorado. . . ."

that its advantages are small. The upper part is a sandy country with little or no timber and possessed of no advantages for *irrigation*, which in California agriculture is found to be absolutely necessary. It is beskirted by a desert, while the lower part is a desert of the worst kind which cuts all communication with other parts of the state except by passage on the desert or by water down the Gulf of California and up the coast. Thus situated, this portion of the state is but a counterpart of the basin [Great Basin] desert.

The seacoast valley, though extending along the coast 10°, is extremely narrow and has very few streams passing through it in the dry season. From this want of the means of irrigation, agriculture is a precarious business, but the mildness of the climate and the length of the rainy season renders it a fine grazing country, and that part below the Bay of San Francisco is justly noted for the number of its wild cattle and the deliciousness of its beef.

The Great Valley and the mountains are the divisions to which we must look to find the elements of prosperity and greatness of the state. First, then, to the mountains. These are the coast range of the Pacific shore, running along the whole western line of the valley, and the Sierra on the east, running near the coast range at the south end of the valley, comprising an area of one-half of all the territory of the state.

Of the coast range there is little known, except that parts of them are inhabited by hostile Indians and other portions covered with snow most of the year. However, many are sanguine of rich gold diggings being found among them. Their general characteristic is that of extreme roughness. They have no streams and hold out no inducement to enterprise; what exploration may develop of mineral wealth, time alone can tell.

The Sierra Nevada have been explored far more, and it is in these mountains that the mineral wealth of California as yet discovered exists. It is here that her great rivers rise, thread their way through hundreds of miles of mountain defiles, foaming and roaring along in their swift descent to the foot of the range, and then silently threading along the plain till they respectively unite with the two great arteries of the valley. Here too are the noble and far-famed forests of pine and fir which have no equal. In these—viz., the minerals, the power of the streams to drive machinery, and the wealth of the forests—we would naturally expect to find the enduring elements of national prosperity; but I am sorry to say that I am forced to conclude that the circumstances under which these resources exist counteract a great share of their intrinsic value. . . .

Therefore, for myself, I am satisfied that such a business [lumbering] will never be pursued in California. These forests thus situated and surrounded by obstacles which industry and enterprise cannot overcome, and which in other circumstances would constitute a source of unfailing wealth and attract the efforts of the industrious and enterprising, must ever stand incapable of furnishing any element to the permanent prosperity of the state; and these beautiful mountain streams, which in other circumstances would constitute the motive power of a world of machinery, are destined to flow on in their rocky channels, untrammeled by the schemes of genius and enterprise.

[In contrast to the mountain regions, in the Sacramento Valley enterprise and speculation "have wrought great changes. . . . The vast crowd that we learn is coming out this season will not experience the same hardship and destitution on their arrival that we did, although they will have enough, God knows, to curse the day they set out. On our arrival in the valley last year, there were but four ranches on the road for a distance of two hundred miles, from Reading's diggings {the Trinity River mines} to Sacramento City, and now there are stopping places and towns at convenient distances along the whole route, where necessaries of life can be obtained, although at exorbitant rates. . . . Towns are springing up along the banks of the navigable streams, with speculation rife in town lots where ninety days ago not a single house stood. . . . At Bear Creek . . . where late in the Fall only a ranch existed, the town of Nicolaus is laid out, houses going rapidly up and lots selling off like hot cakes . . . for from $500 to $3,000." "Probably the best town sites are already seized upon. . . . But if the lands are not cultivated, these towns will be but mushroom affairs. . . . The mines cannot support them, at least not steadily and permanently. Indeed, the existence of country towns that depend on gold mines must be sickly and precarious."

["Unlike any other country in the world's history, California has not been drawn together by the gradual aggregation of families and persons bound to each other by ties of kindred and relationship. It has not been peopled as other new countries have by a few hardy adventurers advancing into the wilderness, who through years of toilsome industry subdued it to cultivation, bringing around them others of a like character whose farmhouses gave place to rural hamlets, the hamlet to the thriving village, the village to a town and then a city. In those cases . . . newcomers became assimilated and bound to the older residents, families became interlocked and combined with other families, and society received a decided and fixed order.

["But here has been different. Large cities have sprung into existence almost in a day. The emigration to this country has been marked with a different stamp and character from any other emigration. It has generally been the emigration of individuals, not of families. The people have been to each other strangers in a strange land. Absorbed in the eager pursuit of wealth, they have not taken time for the cultivation of those affinities which bind man to man by a higher and holier tie than mere interest. Their hearts have been left at home. . . . They have considered that as this is but a temporary stopping place for them, they have not been called upon to do anything for California but all for themselves. . . . Hence, there has been an almost total lack of social organization." "All are here for money . . . for which every sacrifice will be made. The importance of the dollar and the might of the ounce are studied, sought for in every possible way. . . . In short, the sociable man is lost in the money-seeking, gold-hunting, selfish, acquisitive miser and conniving millionaire."]

This country may for some years attract the adventurers of other climes; she may hold out her glittering dust to excite the avarice of the speculator of other lands; she may, and in all probability will, become a great central point in the commerce of the two worlds; but in my judgment she lacks the essential elements of national prosperity and will be one of the poorest states of the Union.

As ever,
Your brother,
William Swain

June 15, 1850
South Fork, Feather River

Dear Brother George,

I embrace an opportunity to send a letter to you by a Mr. Chadwick of Illinois, who bought a part of Frank Cannon's interest in our location and established a small store here, intending to sell goods and work in the location, but he has been attacked with scurvy, become sick of California and is determined to cut dirt for the States. On his way home he passes through Buffalo and has offered to carry letters for us. So he will mail this at Buffalo, and you will be likely to get this from there, I hope. I might send $500 by Chadwick, but I prefer the responsibility of Adams & Company's Express to that of an untried stranger.

[Along with Chadwick, "many are leaving these diggings for home. Some are returning with large sums . . . but very few of them *dug* out their pile. Indeed . . . no one has carried away $4,000 of his own digging because there has been no weather for mining, and it costs a great deal to live. Those who have taken more home have probably made it by means that no honest man would resort to—by the sale of liquors, keeping gambling tables, gambling itself, or the more honorable employment of stealing cattle. . . . When a man is reported to have returned from this section to the States with $6,000 or $10,000 honestly acquired since the first day of November last . . . you may just post such a man as the ninth wonder of the world."]

I write this morning under great disappointment, and I will tell you the cause. On arriving at the cabin some three weeks ago, I found that Mr. Bailey had got your letter of March 10. On opening it, I found that at that late date you had not received my letters nor any intelligence from me since my Laramie letter. I have felt the greatest anxiety to get a letter stating that you have got my letters! My first was from Sacramento City on the 13th of December [never received], and the second on the 6th of January, both of which must have left San Francisco in the January mail, which if the mails were regularly conveyed ought to have been at Youngstown one month before you wrote. The truth is, there is shameful neglect of duty somewhere, and I think the Postmaster General should be held responsible. It is an evil which should be spoken of in proper terms by the press.*

Your letter contained so much of disappointment that I have felt more anxious about news from home than any time since I have been in California. Although I know you must have received my numerous letters long ere this time, I want to know it for certain and get an answer from some of them.

Well, last evening Captain Carley, a gentleman who came through in the Wolverine train with us, told me that Tolles, the expressman, had brought me two letters and that they were at Tolles' store a mile from here.** Being too tired to go after them last evening, I put it off till this

---

* With angry regularity California's newspapers did speak out against the Postal Service. But as the Alta California complained on January 9, "it has been in vain that remonstrances have been uttered, that anathemas have been hurled at the Postmaster General and all the subs in his department. Not a word or act has been drawn from that fountainhead." Continuing editorial attack and the universal outrage of the miners had no effect on the efficiency of the post office in California. In July 1855 the Alta declared the U.S. mail "a nuisance, a worse than useless institution that ought to be abolished."

** James S. Tolles, one of the three earliest expressmen, started his one-man business in December 1849. In his diary for February 7, 1850, he noted on his return to Long's Bar from San Francisco (the round trip took nineteen days): "Everyone is pleased with the manner in which I do my business as a mail carrier. I shall continue the business likely all summer if it pays." It did, despite competition at Long's Store. Tolles ran his operation until early 1852. His handbill advised: "James Tolles Express from the Feather River to San Francisco . . . calling at Brown's Bar, Boone's Bar, Stringtown, Fairfield Bar, Bidwell's Bar, Long's Bar, Marysville, Vernon and Sacramento . . . monthly to catch the steamer, starting from Mountain Cottage eighteen miles above Bidwell's Bar on the Ridge Road from Marysville to Slate Creek."

morn, when at daybreak I up and posted off and routed Tolles out of bed to get me my letters. The direction was not in any of your handwriting. One of them was postmarked New Orleans, the other San Francisco. However, they were directed to William Swain, and thinking that they might have been brought to the Bay by Henry Hill or that Mr. Hill addressed me, I paid the charge on them, expressing my doubt of their being my letters, and opened them. Lo! and Behold!! The New Orleans letter was from "A Kind Hearted Girl" whose heart was badly affected, to her "sweetheart" who was in California. It was a very affectionate letter, but it did not ease my pain any, except while we were having a hearty laugh over it. The other was from some illiterate father in Virginia to his son who had got into some scrape in California. Well, I resealed the letters, endorsing the fact that they were not my letters. I got off paying 40 cents postage on one of them and turned my steps homeward, disappointed and vexed, for I was sure of getting news that you had got my letters.

However, I shall soon get the letters, I expect, for there are so many of these confounded express men that if one does not bring you letters it's because the others have got to the office ahead of him. By some means or another they all get your name. I have received all your letters up to March 10, except February, which is in Burke's express office at Long's store.

I am now tolerably well, though I have been quite unwell for the last two weeks. I was taken with chill, fever and dysentery while on my tour to the source of the streams up under the summit range, of which I spoke in my letter written at Slate Creek. I had medicines with me and took opium and a large dose of quinine, which checked the disease.* I plodded on in the snow (which was from six to eight feet deep but packed hard and good traveling) for three days more, and then cut for home. I walked some twenty-five miles over those abominable hills and arrived at the cabin about six o'clock in the afternoon, where I found Mr. Hutchinson and Bailey per agreement.

I was not well next morning; took physic. That afternoon had some fever, the same the two following days but no chills. There was not

---

* Self-medication was common among the miners, with opium or the variant laudanum being widely used for almost any ailment. One miner told of taking morphine and charcoal to stop his dysentery, and another summed up the whole state of miners' diseases and the medical treatment for them: "Dierea, piles, gravel, chills, fever and scurvy begin to make their appearance and I ain't well myself. . . . There has been three doctors or things they call doctors working at me for some time. . . . Have now paid out all my gold to the doctors and they leave me worse in health."

apparently anything the matter with me, but my strength was all gone. I knew not what to do and called a doctor, who examined me and told us that my disease was subdued and all that was needed was strengthening. Accordingly, he gave me some powders which I took for two days and then commenced taking a tincture of iron in the form of drops, together with dogwood bitters, for two weeks. I was and am still weak, though I feel well and eat my meals regularly, but I do not work yet, for Mr. Bailey says I mustn't work until I am stout again. I tell you, I am a willing convert to that doctrine, for I don't intend to hurt myself by hard work, it's no use. I tell you, George, you would shake that 190 pounds heartily to see how easy a soul I have become.

["There are thousands of persons here who hardly ever saw a sick day in the States and are completely broken-down, and many of them, if they live, will never fully recover their health." Dr. J. D. B. Stillman, who started the first hospital in Sacramento City in November 1849, reported that "diarrhea was so general during the fall and winter months and degenerated so frequently into chronic and fatal malady that it has been popularly regarded as the disease of California . . . with the number of deaths greater than from any other disease."]

I am glad to hear of your health and of your being out among 'em. That's right, live while you love. Give Mother my love, and let me say that I yet hope to see her in our good, old comfortable home. I am glad to know that Sabrina and little Sis are well. I long to be at home and see you all, but Fortune just now says: No.

Our prospects are very good. We have bought out Chadwick for less than cost by paying cash down, which enables him to go home and will enable us to get our summer's provisions. We can replace all the money we paid him by selling part of the things at two-thirds the price they sell at here and have lots of traps to boot and plenty of "chicken fixins" among our store provisions. So you see that we are getting into trade a little. Perhaps you may hear from me in a few weeks to the tune of a thousand! I think my prospects for it are good, but I may be disappointed.

The waters are beginning to go down slowly and the miners are beginning to do a little work.

[In preparing to turn the South Fork from its bed, "the miners here are making a variety of dams. . . . Sacks of sand and stone walls filled between with earth and brush are most common. . . . Every kind of cloth is used for the sandbags. The coarsest hemp sacking, common sheeting, drill, and jeans are all the same price here, six bits; and it is almost impossible to get any in the city." One of the dams "was made by felling a large tree across one fork of the stream, then taking another and splitting

Daguerreotype of block-and-tackle system commonly used to remove rocks from a claim or to clear the way for construction of a dam or flume—late 1850.
BANCROFT LIBRARY, UNIVERSITY OF CALIFORNIA, BERKELEY

it into planks and putting them against the tree across the river and driving them into the bottom of the river and piling stones and earth against until it was tight. All the stones and earth and gravel had to be dug out of the hills and packed in handbarrows and walked out on the tree and tipped into the river above the dam." "Every stream in this country will be turned in all places practicable this summer, and you will hear of some big piles being taken out of the beds of some." At Deer Creek "the bed, bars, and all—every foot—is taken up from head to mouth. Nine pounds of gold were taken out behind a rock on Gold Run. A claim sold there at $30,000."

[Supplies—everything from sandbag cloth and shovels to whiskey and barrels of flour—"are packed in on mules. When mules can get no further, cargoes are transferred to the backs of men or Indians." At a mining camp above Foster's Bar, miners paid "men to pack in on their backs at the rate of $3 per pound . . . for a distance of twelve or fifteen miles."

["There are many Mexicans here with pack mules . . . some of them with three hundred pounds on them. . . . Whole barrels of pork are frequently mule-packed by the Mexicans. In fact, there is nothing which they cannot carry on a mule. The best loading is one-hundred-pound sacks of flour, two or three of them according to the strength of the mule." According to an American packer, mules "are rarely lazy and will travel the most dangerous mountain paths just as easily and unafraid as a somnambulist."]

Messrs. Hutchinson and Bailey are well. Mr. H. writes to his friend Milton by Chadwick, being the first time he has shook a pen since we arrived in California. Mr. B. has written once or twice to Mrs. B. He has received one letter from her. He declines writing now till he gets a letter which is at Bidwell's for him.

Your brother,
William Swain

P.S. Kiss all the family for me and give my respects to all inquiring friends.*

July 19, 1850
Bidwell's Bar

Dear Mother,

I received on the 12th of July Sabrina's and George's letters of April 10 which brought the glad news of your reception of my letters of January and February.** This was welcome intelligence to me, as it was the opening of correspondence since I arrived here, or rather it was the first answer to my many letters written home. But it gives me reason to believe that some of my later letters have miscarried, as my first two had; for I had written two previous to my January letter, the first dated December 13, a short letter, the other a sheet of foolscap, closely written and cross-written, dated January 6, in which I sealed a few scales of gold dust as specimens. It certainly is to be regretted that distant friends cannot have their correspondence properly and speedily forwarded by those who are commissioned to attend to that business.

I have written every three or four weeks since December, and if you

---

* Another young miner concluded a letter to his wife: "I wish I could find some little thing to send the children, but one sees nothing here of the kind, for everything here is for grownup children."
** The letters of April 10, 1850, are missing from the collection of Swain family letters.

have received all my letters, you have had to spend some time in reading them. The suspense we both have experienced in waiting so long for each other's letters is happily over, and we may probably hear from one another regularly hereafter. I get my letters now almost every four weeks and can get the New York newspapers in about six weeks or two months after print, so that I can know something about things at home in the States.

["The news that we get through the papers . . . is truly alarming. We hear of thousands and tens of thousands coming by sea and land this season. What is the meaning of it? Do the papers still continue to publish those exaggerated accounts of gold found here merely for the trouble of picking it up and fortunes made in a day?

["What will be the fate of those that are coming this season only time can tell. . . . The fact is, we are too late in this country to make a fortune and every season makes the matter worse. There are now no new rivers to be found in California. All have been explored from their mouths to their sources, from the Mariposa in the south to the Trinity in the north. All have been overrun with swarms of Sonorans and Americans. Not a foot of ground has not been prospected. . . . You at home had better buy lottery tickets with your money than come here expecting to be one of the lucky ones."

["Why do men stay in the mines, when these things must become evident at a glance? All do not stay. . . . Perhaps one-half of those who try the mines do not remain a month, but take up some other and more profitable operation in the cities. And those who do remain and dig through the season compose several classes, each of which is influenced by different motives. There are those to whom mining has all the excitement of gambling, and who, as they would buy a lottery ticket in the hope of drawing the highest prize, so now persevere, in spite of ill luck and the warning of others, fully expecting the advent of the day when they, and they alone, shall be rewarded with ample soil. There are thousands who at home would be obliged to work for a dollar a day and be under the eye of an overseer, and who, consequently, are not disappointed at being their own masters. There are others whose vicious temperament leads them to like a life in which, without fear of punishment, they can drink, fight and gamble, and, indeed, do anything except steal and murder. And lastly, there is a better class of men who, keeping aloof from all dissipation and disliking a life that cuts them off from most other society, yet having been decoyed by specious hopes, are obliged to continue as they have begun, because . . . no better lot opens before them. These four classes comprise a vast majority of the miners."]

Your letters brought news of your own and Sabrina's ill health and of your partial recovery, for which I sincerely thank Almighty God. From the tenor of George's letter I hope that those "better times" we have so long looked for have at last dawned. Thanks to Heaven that circumstances have been so overruled that he is placed in easy circumstances. You may all be assured that I have not the least doubt that all the wants of the family will be cheerfully supplied. Be assured of my perfect confidence that everything that will contribute to the comfort of family will be done. It is a source of great contentment to me to know that I have so kind and noble a brother, in whom I can place such confidence. I am sincerely grateful, as is Sabrina, for his and your kindness to her and Sis.

George mentioned that if he could keep his office through Taylor's administration, he would be able to pay the debts and lay up something. It is an important consideration to keep it, and he will probably realize the importance of keeping in good standing in the party.

Mr. Henry Hill has arrived here but had the misfortune to lose his valise, in which were letters, on the Chagres River [Isthmus of Panama]. He is twelve miles up the Middle Fork from here. I have not seen him, but S. Eaton, with whom I have been staying for two days, has been with him some two weeks. He tells me that Henry is outrageous homesick.

Henry and Eaton are going to work on the same bar all summer. Tomorrow I shall go by his place in returning to our cabin on the South Fork, as it will not be but five miles out of my way and I expect to get a great deal of news about things at home. Henry saw John Root at San Francisco.

In answer to George's suggestion in relation to speculation, I look upon it in this country as a precarious business, and while I am in the mines I think we had best not do anything about it. ["Some articles may be worth a great price one day and the next not half as much. So it is with long handled, round pointed shovels. Some are buying all they can get and selling them at $5 apiece. Last year the market was glutted with shovels and they were sold at auction for 8 cents apiece, and the same with picks." "Everything is wild here. Things are up and down quick. . . . The speculators, traders, gamblers, women and thieves keep their eyes on the mines and when the miners move, they all move. This spring there was but one house in Nevada City, now there is said to be 17,000 men in and about it. But perhaps there will be some new mines found or a new excitement got up, then away goes everybody and buildings that are worth $3,000 now will not be worth $500 then and provisions will be thrown away. . . . Everything is in a state of fermentation, rolling and tumbling about."]

Nevada City, late 1850.
CALIFORNIA HISTORICAL SOCIETY

Your request that I should not pay 10 percent for sending money home was a very agreeable one to me and came just at the time when I was anxiously debating whether I had better send money home or keep it here. The fact is that money will make more money here than in any other place in the world. ["Ten percent a month is the lowest figure that it lets for, and any amount can be safely invested. Money begins to seek investment, and it is said that considerable sums are sent from the States for that purpose."]

I think that by having money by me in the fall, I can—if fortune does not smile on me before—go into the cattle business and be sure of making a handsome fortune. It would require me to stay here till spring, which will be a *cross*, I tell you; but I must have the $10,000.

Last fall the price of emigrants' oxen, which usually came into the valley poor and worn down by their long journey, bore a price of $30 per yoke; and after being herded three or four months, sold for beef creatures at from $150 to $200 per head, a handsome percentage certainly. Could I do half so well on one hundred head, I'd start for home.

We have been at work in the bed of the river at our location on the South Fork for two weeks and have not made $2 per day. ["Generally the water is yet too high and comes into excavations so fast that it is impossible to get low enough to test the bed of the stream. In a few instances it has been done. Three or four claims are paying well." On a claim down the river "a flume is in and the whole stream running through it. This has been built by hand labor, including the sawing of about six thousand feet of lumber."

[In making claims "an unlooked-for difficulty has occurred. The levels on various rapids were not taken and the consequence is that many claims are overflowed by lower dams." "One dam has thrown the water back over three entire claims, and destroyed the prospects for this season of forty to fifty men. A decision before the Vice President of the Miners' Association was to the effect that the oldest claim had the RIGHT. Everybody up this way says that the decision is grossly unjust and that the judges are fools. Nothing further has been done. Those whom they flooded offered to dig their race deep enough to supersede the necessity of a dam, but they would yield to no compromise."

[At Shirt Tail Canyon in the American River mining region "nine men damming the stream . . . interfered with some men above who were digging in the river banks. They came to tear away the dam. The company told them they would defend the dam with their lives. Each party armed. The nine waited their return and shot thirteen who were in the act of tearing away the dam. . . . The nine were uninjured."]

Being convinced that our location will not pay for working, I have sold all my share but one-sixth, for which I have realized $650 down and a note for $225 due in one month, or the share is forfeited and comes back to my possession. The sixth I let out to be worked for one-half and the man supplies himself; but I hardly believe he will stick to his bargain. Messrs. Hutchinson and Bailey have sold one-quarter apiece of their share. They are working on the location but are sick of it and will, unless it should prove better, abandon the claim. Mr. Bailey has some $225, but Mr. Hutchinson has $300 more than he brought with him. I have $700 in gold dust, which I intend to hold onto like death. However, if we should find the location good yet, they would have the advantage of me. I think that we shall probably spend the mining season on the Middle Fork of the Feather, which will depend on circumstances. I shall go along the Middle Fork in search of some place to work, which is hard to find.

I am now a man at leisure for the first time since I have been in California, and I tell you when I let out my claim and got the man at work among the rocks for me, I felt that I had got rid of a heartless and ungrateful job. That was at noon, and at night I was here at this bar sixteen miles from home. I came here with the intention of buying a share in a claim, which undoubtedly is a rich one, but can never be drained and therefore is not worth a cent in my opinion. I have had too much experience to "go it blind." There is the greatest swindling, wild and visionary buying and selling in these claims and the gold business generally that ever existed. He who comes into the mines green runs great risk of being outrageously shaved.

["One report in circulation among the miners here . . . is with regard to a certain Gold Lake in this vicinity. One man who has been to these diggings says that he could take three ounces to the pan and average it nine out of ten. This man guided out a company of one hundred men, $50 each; but his searches for such diggings have proved a failure, like all other reports of this kind. Hundreds of miners have been running over the mountains in pursuit of these golden lakes."]

I wish to say to Sabrina that I wish her, and George also, to keep an account of her expenditures. Tell Ozro Barrett that I am in good spirits and believe that I shall yet realize good pay for all my trouble. Give my respects to all our family and friends.

Your son,
William

P.S. The weather is much hotter down here [at Bidwell's Bar] than up in the mountains, the thermometer standing generally at 115° in the shade at noon—too hot! I tell you, that's some pumpkins.

["Early morning . . . is the most valuable part of the day, for then it is cool, and from the rising of the sun until he shows himself over the mountains is often the equivalent to half a day, and in that half a day the work accomplished is equivalent to a whole day when the sun is pouring down with scorching heat. . . . It is not infrequently the case that before daybreak we hear rockers going and miners stirring to take advantage of the cool portion of the day. A great many miners who commence this early in the morning finish their work as soon as the sun appears and renew it as soon as he hides himself behind the mountains, till it is dark."]

August 12, 1850
South Fork of Feather River

Dear Mother,

As an expressman has just gone by our door and will return in an hour, I take my pen to write a line to let you know that I am and have been well since I last wrote; and as the sickly season is almost over, I am in hopes I shall escape any sickness this summer. There is considerable sickness of fevers and ague in the valley of Sacramento and some in the

mountains and some mountain fever, but generally the miners are well as to physical corporations—but nine-tenths of them are sick at heart! Aye!! Downhearted and discouraged!!! And many of them have great reason to be disheartened. Thousands who one month ago felt certain that their chances were sure for a fortune are at this time without money or any chance of any and hundreds of dollars in debt. Certainly such a turn of fortune is enough to sicken the heart of any man.

The cause of this is the failure of the claims on the rivers. All were induced to believe that a claim or place where the river could be turned and the river bed worked for gold would yield an ample reward to those who worked it. In keeping with that opinion, miners universally sought places in which to operate in that way and spent the winter and spring in cutting races, building dams, and preparing to reap an immediate fortune when the water fell! *That time has come!!* And nine out of ten of the locations have proved not working out, and the operators with dark forebodings behold their bright daydreams of golden wealth vanish like the dreams of night.

["Most all the canals have failed to drain the bed of the river for want of sufficient fall and on account of leakage. The cotton-duck flumes are almost a total failure. They were worn out in three or four days by the sand and small stones running through them. . . . Fourteen claims adjoining one another below here have been abandoned, except one." "A dozen companies in this vicinity erected dams at from $3,000 to $10,000 and after enduring the labor of prospecting in the winter rains, building cabins, making roads over mountains and suffering incredible hardships, they have relinquished their claims without getting a dollar, perfectly bankrupt and in debt for the very bread they ate while at work with high anticipations of a fair remuneration."

["From every direction reports come thicker and faster of the lean-ness of the river beds . . . and claims have assuredly fallen. Some men who refused $1,500 are now offering them for $500 and find no buyers."]

Since I wrote last from Bidwell's, I have been at work in company with Henry Hill on the Kanaka Bar [on the Middle Fork of the Feather River] and have done middling well, making some $200. So you see that I am plodding my slow length along toward a thousand. S. Eaton left that bar after being there a week and is badly discouraged; he is now at Bidwell's. He talks of going to Oregon. Henry Hill has done well, I think, and has $400 laid up; but he says everything is going to wreck in California and often tells how satisfied he would be if he was on his way home. Says he can afford to lose the summer for the sake of seeing and learning what he has learned and saw.

Hill and I came from Kanaka Bar over to our cabin yesterday, ex-pecting to find Messrs. Hutchinson and Bailey here, but the old hearth-stone is desolate. They, and all hands, have deserted the location, not having taken from it $100 apiece. Bailey has about $300 and Hutchinson may have $600, as he brought $300 with him. They left here last Monday for Nelson's Creek, where Henry and I started for when we left the Kanaka Bar and where we shall put for tomorrow morning in search of diggings or something to make money off.*

If it was two months later, I think I would bid these terrible hills a long farewell and vamoose to the cities. But not till the fall comes. Then I think if I am not doing extremely well, I shall quit this hellish life of a miner and try the valley, for I assure you I believe California has a little for me, anyway. I am quite satisfied with the way she has used me so far; and a satisfied mind is a great deal in this country. I think that *time* is all that is necessary in this country to get money—that is, if a man has his health; but it is a terrible place to be sick in.

I shall hang like death to what money I have got and get what I can. Time and circumstances only will enable me to say when I shall start for

---

* *Boomed by reports of miners who "took out in an hour or two over $100 in very coarse gold nuggets," Nelson's Creek attracted crowds of miners during the summer of 1850. Discovered by some of those who in June had joined the hunt for the mythical Gold Lake, Nelson's Creek (a tributary of the Middle Fork of the Feather River) was a rarity of California in the 1850s: a mining area that had not been worked in 1849.*

home. Hill says that he goes this fall if he has money enough to take him home.*

Mother, you must kiss little Sis for me. Tell Sabrina that I hope I shall be able to come home this fall with thousands. But the expressman is here and I must close. Tell George that he must save all the money he can from his office.

Yours with affection,
William Swain

Back Home

> "O! William, I cannot wait much longer. I want to see you so bad. . . . If you do not come soon, I shall get so poor and old that you will not own me when you do come."

[Surviving portion of a letter by George, probably written in early May 1850]

[Dear William],
. . . As things stand we are in a quandary. Don't know what to do.

---

* The anguish of trying to decide whether to give up on California or to stay another season was explained by a young miner writing to his sister back in Wisconsin: "It is hard for a man to leave here with nothing where there is so much money made. Still clinging to the hope that he will strike it soon, he hangs on until he spends what little he has and is then forced to stop. This I know to be the case in many instances. . . . I have no pile yet but you can bet your life I will never come home until I have something more than when I started."

Another miner revealed his torment to his wife: "O, Caroline, I can't bear the idea of going home with so little money as I have got now when there is a fortune so near. If I was to go now, I know I could never be contented. . . . In your letter you wrote that I must come back in the spring if I have not more than $5,000. If you could see these mines you would say it would take a man his lifetime to get that much."

We have written you everything as it transpired here and got no answer in return.*

Whatever you write about prospects there, be cool, weigh well the chances of success before you embark in an enterprise, and above all be careful of your health. Don't overdo. Stop when you find yourself unwell. If you get sick there, it will go hard with you. . . .

If you conclude to come home during the summer, take a comfortable passage on board the steamer and have your berth and board comfortable. I see it stated there is much sickness on steamers on the Pacific. Above all keep your courage up. If you fail there, you are not to blame. You have tried your best to do well, and if you can't do it there, you are better off than many who have gone there with their all and left nothing behind to fall back on. You have something, and friends who will meet you just as cordially unsuccessful as successful—and more so, for we are sure you have suffered, suffered, suffered in that terrible march of six months over land or rather through wilderness, desert and mountains. And as I write now, my heart almost stops beating for fear you may have fallen on that terrible way. And at times my anxiety so gets the mastery that I can hardly control myself. To tell the plain truth, I wish most sincerely you were out of that (if you are alive) and at home, no matter if you haven't got a single mill.

From present accounts from California there is much suffering, little success, and great chagrin. I want you to tell me the truth, the whole truth and nothing but the truth. I am convinced that digging is not the way to make money there. It is to trade. There, as here, the trader makes the money.

May God in His mercy protect and guide you, preserve you from evil and return you safe home, and permit us all to meet on earth in health and comfort, is the sincere prayer of your anxious brother,

George Swain

---

* *The sequence of communication between Swain and his family was as follows:*

March 3, 1850: Swain received his first letters from home.
April 10, 1850: George and Sabrina received their first letter from Swain in California, and on that date wrote to tell him that they had at last heard from him. Swain received the April 10 letters on July 12, 1850, but they are not reproduced, having been lost.

Suspension Bridge, June 6, 1850

Dear William,

I wrote a letter to send you by the last mail and went down home on foot with it on the ninth of May at night and found that Sabrina had sent her letter off that morning, so I concluded not to tax you with double postage by sending mine.

I don't think of anything new at Youngstown except that the "Sons" [of Temperance] are to have a celebration there on the Fourth of July, when I shall be there if I am well of course. And I wish you could be there. What an Independence *we'd* have! God grant that we may have many a one yet together. Wouldn't we celebrate in earnest? Wouldn't Mother and Sabrina have a jubilee? Wouldn't Cub and I kick up a rookery? Wouldn't we all celebrate to fits? Eh? Yet I hope we may all be thankful if we are permitted to meet again.

June 7

And now I have something to say of Little Cub, as I take it that you may *possibly* be a little interested in her welfare and growth and improvement. Well, she grows like a weed in every respect and talks dutch to fits, and it takes Sabrina and Mother to interpret it. . . . But she is so full of business out of doors that she doesn't have much time during the day to talk, and she is exceedingly fond of flowers. She plays "Ned" with Mother's flowers, and will frequently kick or pull all of the flowers and buds she can get hold of and bring them in to the great annoyance of Mother and Sabrina. . . .

When I was at home Monday morning, Cub came in with one hand full of blue flags, one stalk in blossom and the others buds just ready to burst. I got my face fixed to frown on her and make her know she had been doing wrong; but as she came in sight of me, she held up her hand and sang out with her little voice as high as the eighth note, "Putty, putty, putty," (pretty). and I tell you she took the starch out of me in a hurry, and I burst out laughing. That's the way she does it. If her mother is going to punish her, she will hug her and kiss her and the tears roll down her cheeks and she will plead the worst way for excuse, but will go right off and do it again. . . .

Be sure and write me every month. We feel much anxiety for you. The cholera is appearing in the South at different points along the Mississippi and Ohio, but not so bad as last year. I am well.

Affectionately your brother,
George Swain

Sunday nine o'clock in my room
Youngstown, June 9, 1850

My beloved Husband,

With a heart glowing with joy and at the same time rent with anxiety intolerable, I take my pen to address you. With joy that a day of rest has come and also the privilege of mingling with Christian friends and hearing from the sacred word of God, and more than all, the sweet pleasure of hearing from and addressing my dear husband, although it is epistolary. How little, my dear, we realize the privileges we enjoy. With anxiety for you, the greatest source of consolation this earth can afford me is to know your circumstances, which I know must be anything but pleasant. The change must be very great and must necessarily make a change in your health and constitution in one way or another which must tend to increase my anxiety—although you have been blessed since your arrival in California—but I am always looking for bad news in the next letter. Still I confess I should be unprepared for bad news. I own, my dear, that it is wrong for us to distrust the goodness of God; that we should place more confidence in Him, for He has told us that if we put our trust in Him, He will take care of us. What a promise, and how little we appreciate it.

O! that I could tell you the feelings and anxiety that I have had for you since you left home—none but God knows or ever can. Many and many a time in the stillness of the night have I imagined I saw you in the deepest trouble and distress, and without a doubt it was literally true. Never do I lay down on my bed at night but I last commit you to the care of God; and then sweet morn finds my thoughts in California where fain my bed would be with him whom my bosom holds dear; but it is otherwise, and I must make the best of it and wait patiently till God shall be pleased in His infinite goodness to return you in safety to your home and family. May God grant it.

Little Cub has been to the front door lately several times and called "Papa." I do not suppose she knew who she was calling, only we have told her that her Papa was off and she would make the reply that he must come home to "tee Lila." We ask her where Pa is. "In Tadaforna gity gol Gamma, Lila," meaning "In California getting gold for Grandma and Eliza." We ask her what her name is. She will say, "Lila Canny Pain. . . ."

On correcting her for any disobedience, she will turn to me and say: "I good gale" and put her arms around my neck and begin to kiss me. It softens my heart and I cannot punish her. I presume I feel more tender than I should if you were at home, but the thought comes up "poor child —Pa is gone. . . ."

She has just come into my room after waking up and says "write Pa." I took her in my arms and wrote on the bottom of this page a few words by letting her hold the pen and I guided her fingers. The words are: "Poor Pa. See Pa. Love Pa." Then she says "See Papa," so I wrote it again. The last: "Kiss Pa." These are words she frequently says when we are speaking about you. While she was holding the pen she seemed to realize what she was doing and wanted more ink in the pen to write more.

My dear, how often—O! how often—I think of various temptations you are surrounded with and how many men of good morals at home—yes, and professed Christians too—that have been led into all kinds of vice. O my dear, you cannot be too cautious—not that I distrust you, but rather on the contrary, perhaps I place too much confidence, knowing that we are all fallible creatures. But I know that my dear husband would not do anything to disgrace himself or his family. Be strictly moral, use no profane language. O, how often has my blood almost chilled in its veins to hear you use those bad words. Bear with me—and may God help you to do right, whatever it may be.

Kiss this sheet for me. O! William, I cannot wait much longer. I want to see you so bad.

Sabrina

Poor pa.   See Pa.   Love Pa.   See Papa.   Kiss Pa.

Suspension Bridge, July 8, 1850

Dear William,

As this is the last day I have to write for the mail that starts on the 13th from New York, I begin as best I can. I should prefer to wait till I could hear from you as we did not get a letter from you in June at all. The last we read was dated March 15 [p. 334], giving a description of that terrible passage of the Sierra Nevada to the valley, and Lawson's, etc. Thank God you were preserved, and I hope that ill health is not the cause of our not receiving a letter from you last month. I hope, Will, you will take a good deal of pains to be punctual in writing, for you have no idea of the anxiety we feel if we do not receive news from you as we expect. Your distance from home, the liability of disease, the state of society there, the probability that cholera will visit you this summer on its way westward round the world, and the many other uncertainties that exist there, contribute to make you an object of deep solicitude to us. Therefore, try and have your letters started in time for the mail, if there is not more than ten lines to let us know how you are.

We had a celebration at Youngstown on the fourth for the Sons of Temperance: a speaker from Buffalo, oration, and dinner in the grove south of the fort graveyard. We had a pretty good time, but we should have had much better if we had not got a heavy shower of cold water just after dinner that we did not bargain for and which drove us home in double-quick time and wet us some at that.

There has been celebrations all over the country this year. The health of the country is remarkably good, the weather fine, business pretty lively. There is more travel here at the Falls than ever before in the same part of the season. Many businessmen begin to fear a return of the times of '37, as real estate is very high and there is a general disposition to speculate. The California gold rush has already had its influence in this country, and I hear the June mail from California and $2,500,000 in gold has just arrived at New York; gold is already quite common in the travel enterprises.

The wheat crop will be below an average crop, and as there is no supplies in the country will be high this Fall most likely. Hay is rather light. Spring crops look pretty well. Apples bid fair; peaches are a failure; cherries about middling fair. I don't think of anything else around home to tell you. Dr. Root's wheat as usual looks well, and generally our town is ahead of the average in the country.

I hope we shall have something from you in a day or two; but this must go tomorrow, and so I will bid you goodbye, William; and may God bless and protect you and keep you in health and in the exercise of all those principles of honor, justice, and integrity that you were taught in childhood, is the wish of your brother

George Swain

P.S. Our weather is now pretty hot with frequent showers and thunder-storms.

I received a letter from Nancy Tisdale inquiring after you, saying several of her neighbors were going to California and one of her boys talked of it. I answered it and told her to keep her boy at home. I believe I told you in my last that I received a letter from Isaac saying his William and Isaac thought of going. I answered him in the same way.

Wednesday morn; half past seven
Youngstown, July 10, 1850

My Dear William,

I do not feel quite as well as usual this morning, being kept awake last night with Eliza, which you know is a death blow to me if I cannot have my regular sleep.

Sis seems to be quite smart this morning and is taking her breakfast with her Uncle. The cause of her restlessness I think was owing to her eating some cherries unbeknown to me. Her usual health is quite good. She improves, as far as signs of intellect, very fast; she can talk nearly as plain as children in general at three years old. As far as physical strength is concerned, I think she can hold her own with children in general her age. She made nothing of climbing this new fence you made between us and the log house; she crosses the road a dozen times a day, consequently making me together with the rest of the family rather more steps than we should have to take had we no Little Cub around. She will say "California" as plain as any one of us, and I assure you she may well have learned it, for the simple reason that she hears it so often that it has become as it were a byword to her. She will often sit down and sing the word over and over again.

Well, my dear, what are you doing amongst the gold of California? I hope by this time you can tell me when I can be looking for you home. We have great accounts of new discoveries of gold, and it is said that there will be more gold taken from Feather River this summer than was taken from all California last summer. May God grant that you may be one of the fortunate ones and soon be ready to come home; for if you do not come soon, I shall get so poor and old that you will not own me when you do come. I cannot express my disappointment in not receiving any letter from you last month. If we do not get any intelligence from you this month, I shall be very much concerned about you.

I must close for this time, as this must go to the office.

So goodbye in this

from your affectionate
Sabrina

Youngstown, Sunday
September 8, 1850

Dear William,

I snatch up my pen to fulfill the promise that I made to you when we parted. I received your letter of June 15 [p. 370] sent by Mr. Chadwick to Buffalo which he mailed at that place August 25 or 26, and we were very glad to hear from you, as we had not received anything by the mail that left San Francisco July 11 and got here August 10. (Whatever mail leaves

San Francisco on the first of one month gets here the tenth of the next month.)

We were very glad to hear that you were "tolerably well" but sorry to hear that you had chill fever. *Do be careful*, William, of your health, though this will not reach you till the sickly season is over and you will have been exposed to the worst part of California life. I hope you have been successful, for you have endured enough to command success.

You spoke of sending me some money. I hope you will not do it if you intend coming home this winter, for I can rub along comfortably till that time, if nothing happens, and the cost of sending it by express is considerable. But when you come yourself you had best effect an insurance on your money before leaving San Francisco, if you can do it reasonably, as several robberies have occurred on the Isthmus. The express company was robbed of several thousand dollars not long since.

I carried on the farm this summer myself by hiring a man which I would not have done had it not been for accounts from California stating that very few miners were making more than their board and that thousands would come home if they could only raise the means. Fearing that the same ill fortune that pursued you on your passage overland would still haunt you, I wrote that if you wanted to come home and could not raise the means, to let me know immediately and I would send them to you. Feeling sure that you would be at home during the autumn or winter and thinking it quite likely (in fact feeling sure) that you would want the farm another year, if you should live to get home safe, I thought it would be better for me to carry it on till you came than to let it out till you come, for if we had it in our own hands when you come, I could furnish the money to carry it on and you could make something off it. But it has given me "Alec" to do it and kept me dodging back and forth to the bridge all summer. I think I shall about make the farm clear itself and that is all.

I have paid out most of my wages to carry it on and to make the family comfortable and have not received anything yet. I have been at home threshing and getting ready for four days past. I have 78 bu. of oats and 316 bu. of wheat; I think it will hold out 300 bu., but I had an Irishman stack it and 100 bu. was so wet that I must have it turned and dried on the floor for several days to save it. This comes of having to trust hirelings when you are away from home. I have five acres of corn that I think may go 20 or 25 bu. to the acre and the stalks are pretty good. I have over an acre of potatoes that will yield but small, somewhere from 100 to 150 bu. But the quality is good, better than it has been for several years, dry and mealy. I wish I could send you some such as we had this afternoon. They'd make your mouth water. I dug some fine large Meshonicks this morning and we saved them to take for supper; there were two smashers among them and I rather thought one of them would be mine, *sure*. But when I came to wait on the table, I offered Mother one and she took it, and I asked Sabrina if she could shoulder the other, and she thought she could; so I took my share in smaller but reasonable-sized and first-rate potatoes. Mother and Sabrina cleared their plates in fine style.

Our apple crop will be pretty fair, but as I am obliged to be away from home I shall not be likely to make much of them. We have had but few peaches—not a bushel on the place. We have a bowl this afternoon with cream and sugar on them which I wish you could have shared.

The more I hear of foreign lands the better I like *our home* and think it will compare with most places, considering all circumstances. I have but little disposition to go to California at all, but I should like to go to Europe to see our fatherland and the places and people with which the great events of history are associated.

Little Sis is now quite smart, but since I last wrote you (immediately after) she has been very sick. For several days it was doubtful if she would live. The doctors disagreed; they did not know what ailed her, but thought at first it was bronchitis; then that it was inflammation of the lungs, and finally tried for worms and got but one from her. They doctored the poor little thing almost to death, but perhaps it did some good. They gave her calomel, which we would not allow for some time. I only withdrew opposition on Sabrina's account. I saw she began to think it best to follow their prescription as she did not know what to do, and I did not want her to think if Sis died that I perhaps was the cause or had prevented her cure by my obstinacy. You may be sure we all felt anxious and did not know what to do, the doctors ditto; and we were experimenting from one thing to another. But the poor little thing through the goodness of God lived through it and is now restored to us. . . .

Mr. Hill's people have received two letters from Henry Hill since his arrival in California, one from San Francisco, another from Sacramento City. He don't like the country and will come home next winter.

Considering it as I do of more importance than all the gold you can ever get, I hope you will not be offended with me for urging you again to a strict and stern adherence to those principles of honor and justice that the Bible teaches and which we were taught by our parents, approved by our conscience, and solemnly avowed as the guide of our manhood. Do not let the murder, violence, and injustice with which each paper is filled lead you astray and induce you to think more lightly of them. Prize them more dearly as you see the wickedness around you. Turn to the teachings of Jesus Christ and listen to the doctrines taught by Him of perfect justice, charity, love, and truth. Heed also the warning to violators of them. Read Proverbs; they are well worth it. May God grant that you may be kept from temptation and sin, delivered from evil, and made wise to know and do your duty as a man to men and to Him who made us and made laws for us to obey.

Good night, Will; it is now past eleven and the rest are abed long since.

September 9

We have this afternoon received your letter dated "Bidwell's, July 19, 1850" [p. 375], telling us that you were well, which gave us infinite pleasure, for which I hope we feel grateful to the Giver of health and all other blessings. And may He grant you a continuance of that great blessing.

You also tell us of H. Hill's arrival, of your selling out for $650 and letting out your remaining interest and going in search of another location. I hope you won't get bit in buying another location.

I hope Bailey and Hutchinson will succeed at their location and not lose their labor on that dam and race. Give my best wishes to them both. I have not heard from Mrs. Bailey since I last wrote. Dr. Root's all well. Mr. Eaton's and Hill's people all well. Give my respects to Stephen and Henry.

Cub makes great fun for us. When you get home, you will have your hands full.

May God bless and protect you.

Goodbye
George Swain

CHAPTER XII

Luck Is All

*"In no country of the world have I found
so much selfishness and such immense love
of money as in this El Dorado."*

When William Swain sold his interest in the river mining claim in the South Fork of the Feather River, he felt he "had got rid of a heartless and ungrateful job." His sense of escape for the moment offset his disappointment. Other miners knew his feeling. In early August a German sailor at Foster's Bar (where Swain and friends had prospected in March and April) wrote about his company giving up their claim after seventeen weeks of damming the river. Though he forlornly admitted, "Hope is gone now of making our pile," he and his partners had spirit enough to celebrate their escape. "We set our house on fire, gave several cheers. Our neighbors fired their guns and off we went."

Knowing the rivers, creeks and gulches were all claimed, most river companies resisted the impulse to quit. They stayed with their claims, hoping for lower water, working to stop the seepage through their dams, rigging pumps to empty the cavities in the riverbeds where gold surely would be found. Their determination and hope were reinforced by each report of another company's success. In mid-August nine men on a river claim near Bidwell's Bar took out $8,000 each, then sold their shares for $12,000 more and left for the States. Such news was heralded in the newspapers in Sacramento City and Marysville, even San Francisco, though they did not mention the thousands whose claims were barren.

As the reports of success testified, river mining remained the best chance to find great deposits. And not only the miners prayed for lower water so they could open up more of the riverbed. So did storekeepers in all the mining camps. By August these merchants and their creditors in the cities were impatient for their first payments.

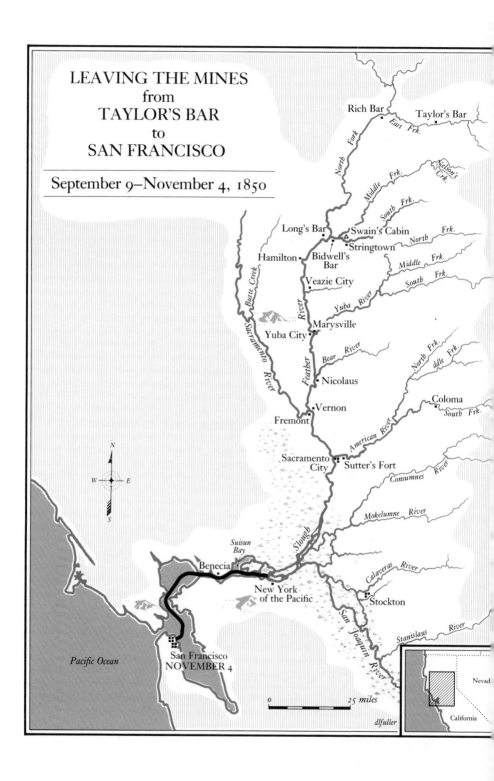

LEAVING THE MINES
from
TAYLOR'S BAR
to
SAN FRANCISCO

September 9–November 4, 1850

Rich Bar

Taylor's Bar

East Frk.

North Fork

Nelson's Crk.

Middle Frk.

South Frk.

Long's Bar

Swain's Cabin

Frk.

Stringtown

North

Hamilton

Bidwell's Bar

Middle Frk.

Butte Creek

Veazie City

South Frk.

River

Yuba River

Marysville

Yuba City

Sacramento River

Feather River

Bear River

Nicolaus

North Frk.

ddle Frk.

Coloma

Vernon

South Frk.

Fremont

American River

Sacramento City

Sutter's Fort

Consumnes River

Mokelumne River

N
W   E
S

Suisun Bay

Slough

Benecia

Calaveras River

New York
of the Pacific

Stockton

San Joaquin River

Pacific Ocean

San Francisco
NOVEMBER 4

Stanislaus River

0   25 miles

dlfuller

Nevad

California

September would be the crucial month, the last chance to work the riverbeds before the rains swept through the Sierra. On all the rivers the men knew their dams and flumes could not survive the sudden rise that would move downstream after the first rainstorm. That inevitable catastrophe might not come until mid-October or maybe, as in 1849, early November.

1850 did not favor such hopes. After months of cloudless skies, the evening of September 6 was overcast, gusts of wind chilled the air. A steady drizzle the next day warned of a possible storm higher in the mountains. The miners hurried the washing of their richest dirt through rockers and toms, hoping the rain would hold off a few more days. The storm broke on the 8th. Reports from upstream gave most companies along the forks of the Feather, Yuba and streams farther south time to remove their equipment. Then all they could do was climb the hillsides to wait and watch. Upriver a dam crumbled and in a few seconds the muddy surge of water four to six feet high swept away all their work—dams melted in the foaming water, canals disappeared, planks and logs were tumbled and tossed downstream. They heard a new and startling sound caused by large rocks rushing and grinding under water, borne by the tremendous power of the current. Watching the destruction, pointing to pieces of flumes and dams from upstream companies, the miners felt a peculiar satisfaction in knowing that so many others shared the same ruin, the same dashing of hopes and promises.

By nightfall their despondency had been eased by the companionship of drinking at the nearest saloon or around their campfires, talking of the summer's work, how much gold had been taken from the river, how much more might have been theirs if the rains had not come so early.

They had worked and slaved and strained through the scorching days of July, wading in icy water up to their waists, piling rocks at the dam sites, framing in the flumes, shivering and shaking until their turns came to stumble ashore for a cup of coffee or whiskey and the luxury of burying their aching legs in the hot sand along the river's edge. Rheumatic pains, boots that rotted and fell apart, crushed fingers, blistered hands, all had been suffered with a grin or a curse while visions of wealth eased the pain and weariness. Laboring with only the simplest tools, hurrying each day to be ready when the water was finally low, they had made a monumental effort to control miles and miles of mountain rivers. Their cooperation, inventiveness and sacrifice in the rivers of the Sierra far exceeded anything that had been demanded of them so long ago on the overland trails.

By mid-September the rivers flowed untroubled by the miners' restraints. Rainstorms drenched the mining region from the Feather to the Mariposa. The early start of the rainy season washed away all hope of getting back to the riverbeds. Even those that had been rewarding were beyond reach, until the summer of 1851.

What to do now? Maybe go to the southern mines where winter rains brought water to creeks and arroyos that had been dry all summer. But reports from Stockton and Sonora told of claim jumping and fights between Americans and foreign miners, some 15,000 of them, mostly Mexicans and Chileans. Another possibility would be to go to work at $100 per month as a laborer on someone else's claim that could be worked through the winter. Or look for a job in the city, but everyone knew that thousands of ex-miners and new arrivals were already in Sacramento City and San Francisco. Maybe stick with mining by prospecting back in the hills, along smaller creeks and narrow gorges where a claim might pay through the winter. Or—give up on California, sell the rocker and tools and tent and buy a ticket for home.

Letters from wives begged them to return. But the more they talked of leaving California, the more they wondered if they could. A man from Granville, Ohio, tried to explain to his wife: "You think that I and John and Mr. Hoyt would do better to come home and work on the railroad! Well, at what wages? Perhaps *one dollar*. Ha, talk to Californians about one dollar per day! It's true we sometimes work for two and three dollars per day and then again we make eight or ten as often, to make up. Your one dollar per day will have no charms for us now. Seriously, I heard a good working man express himself thus: 'I do not know what I shall do when I go back home if I cannot buy a good farm, for I don't think I will ever again be willing to work for fifty cents a day as I used to in Ohio.' "

Swain had a good farm; the temptation to give up, to return to Sabrina and Little Cub, troubled him through the summer of 1850. But his pride overcame his homesickness. In his letters he admitted his failure —it seemed everyone had failed. But he was confident that "California has a little for me," whether in mining or some other enterprise.

Swain stayed with mining. Others took what money they had to start a business. Forgetful or unknowing of the losses suffered by merchants who had trusted too many miners, they opened trading tents and eating houses, they put up hotels and bought wagons and teams to haul freight. But as in mining, "business of all kinds is overdone here. There are too many stores, too many teams, too many taverns for any one of them to make their pile right quick."

Some men could not survive their disappointment. A miner sadly noted, "It is not strange that there are so many disconsolate miners and that the majority of the inmates of the lunatic asylum in San Francisco are miners whose oft-disappointed hopes have made them mad."

For those who could see beyond the twists and turns of Fate in the mining region, who could believe in California's future, there were "princely fortunes" to be made in land speculation. With tens of thousands of emigrants arriving by land and sea, speculators set about selling lots in the many cities they had laid out "all over California and along the Pacific coast wherever they can find a bay or stream putting into the sea. Their cities on maps, suspended from offices of real estate agents, appear as large as New York and London."

Few of the 50,000 overlanders and the 35,000 who came by sea during 1850 cared one whit about California's future. Like the '49ers, most of them planned to dig for gold and return home.

The first overland companies reached the mines on July 3. By early September reports told of miles of dead animals along the Humboldt, thirst-crazed emigrants on the desert crossings, and starvation on the Carson and Truckee trails. Predictions that thousands far to the rear would not survive aroused concern. In Sacramento City and San Francisco, public meetings and newspapers called for contributions to a relief fund that would purchase supplies and animals to be sent to the mountain passes. With $40,000 to $50,000 raised from miners, city merchants and several wealthy private donors, relief parties established supply depots on the mountain trails and as far east as the Humboldt Sink. Though hundreds died—many more than in '49—the survivors hailed the relief campaign for having saved literally thousands of emigrants.

Once in the mines, the men of 1850 "saw the elephant." An old-timer wrote home that "many curse the day they ever started. They are not very satisfied with small wages and are inclined to run around just as we before them have done to our sorrow, and they will learn so."

Another '49er told of talking with "an industrious, worthy man, doing well back home. 'Why did you come here?' I asked. 'Did not all our letters discourage further emigration?' 'Yes, but you said there was gold here, and we thought we could get it if you could—that we could get it if anybody could. Besides, too, speaking frankly, we thought that as so many were getting rich, they only wrote such letters to keep others away.' "

Month by month it became more apparent to old-timers and to some new arrivals who could see beyond tomorrow that money could be made in the cities. Investment would be required and a commitment of time, but the city placers might be the richest of all. Sounds and sights of construction dominated San Francisco, the river ports and the hill towns.

The unloading of hundreds of tons of imports each day demanded new warehouses. Frequent fires destroyed buildings almost as fast as they were thrown up. Transient men overwhelmed the hotels and eating places. Gambling flourished—desperate miners hoping to make their pile with cards or chips.

The cities boomed, and some men saw in the rush and hurry a different opportunity, not wealth but advancement to influence and power in what would soon become the thirty-first state. Far from rockers and riverbeds, they pursued ambitions more familiar to the American experience—they worked in the world of politics.

They found plenty of ore—discontent and demands for change. Public meetings in December 1848 in San Francisco and San Jose had protested the continuance of the "inefficient, mongrel military rule" and complained that there were no legal, local governments to cope with the cities' increasing problems. What the political leaders, editors, property owners and businessmen wanted was immediate civil government to represent the interests of the people. Those interests required the creation of a lawful, trustworthy currency to replace the miners' gold dust and the increasing use of gold slugs. These crude coins, stamped with their presumed value, were turned out by enterprising individuals who made money by making money. The new government would have to pass laws to clarify the confusion of Mexican land titles, provide protection against the mountain Indians, and establish jails and hospitals. Military Governor General Bennett Riley had no authority, troops or experience to deal with these and other demands from an impatient and unruly citizenry.

Resolution of California's political problems should have come from Washington. But Congress had adjourned in March 1849, having failed in its constitutional duty to establish either a territorial or a state government for California. This delay, so exasperating to political leaders and businessmen in California, was the consequence of the continuing, angry debate between northern and southern states over whether slavery should be allowed in the vast territories recently acquired in the war with Mexico.

Faced with Washington's indecision and loud demands from San Francisco's self-proclaimed legislative assembly, Governor Riley took action. In June 1849 he issued a proclamation calling for an election of delegates from every part of the territory to assemble in Monterey in September. Their charge would be to draw up a territorial organization or a state constitution, to be ratified by the people and submitted to the United States Congress.

Forty-eight delegates were elected, including miners who were willing to leave their claims for the six weeks of political debate. After day-and-night sessions, the Founding Fathers on October 13, 1849, signed a constitution which established a state government (territorial status was clearly inappropriate, given California's population and wealth), outlawed slavery and, among other provisions, maintained the Hispanic tradition of the right of married women to own property, a decision designed not to appease but to attract.

Copies of the constitution were distributed to every mining camp and south to San Diego. On November 13 it was approved, 12,061 to 811, which suggests how few Californians cared one way or another.

In December 1849 the elected legislators assembled at the newly designated capitol, San Jose, and installed Peter Burnett as governor. He had come to the gold mines in 1848 from Oregon and had played a major role in promoting public demand for a civil government. They chose two United States Senators, William Gwin from Mississippi, who had arrived in California in June 1849, and John C. Frémont, who had returned in June to find that gold had been discovered on a large tract of land he owned on the Merced River. By fall he was a man of great wealth.

When California's two Senators-designate reached Washington early in 1850, Congress was still locked in sectional debate, now intensified by President Zachary Taylor's message requesting admission of California as the thirty-first state. Southern Congressmen and Senators argued that California's admission would upset the carefully maintained balance between slave and free states, permanently relegating the South to a minority position. Dissolution of the Union threatened; crisis gripped the nation. In late January the aging Henry Clay sought to resolve the conflict by offering a package of compromise resolutions which he defended in a famous two-day speech. Debates on these proposals dragged on for months. Finally, both houses approved the bill for admission on September 9, 1850.

The steamer *Oregon* brought the long-hoped-for news to San Francisco on October 18. The city exploded in celebration—guns boomed, bonfires blazed high, crowds cheered in Portsmouth Square, processions marched through the streets. Eastern papers with the news from Washington sold for $5. The next day the newspapers in Sacramento City proclaimed their delight at "the glorious intelligence."

Up in the hills, the news aroused a different response. "California has been admitted as a state at last. To read some of the San Francisco papers and some speeches in Congress, you would think the people here were very anxious and even indignant she was not admitted sooner. Humbug! There is not one man in a hundred that cares a damn about it one way or another. All they want is what gold they can get, and the state may go to hell, and they would vamoose for home."

For such men, and they were clearly in the majority, California was indeed a huge goose, to be plucked at will. As citizens of the United States, they could take all the gold they found without any restrictions or requirements whatsoever. The military governors, the lawmakers in San Jose and Washington had passed not a single law to control, regulate, tax or penalize Americans who dug and dammed wherever their prospecting led them. Although the gold-bearing lands were in the public domain, Congress had made no provision for the transfer of mineral rights to individual owners—therefore, everyone was a trespasser. If Congress did pass a law to restrict, regulate or tax the miners, who could or would enforce it in a wilderness of hills, in a society of wandering men?

When miners needed rules to protect their rights in the competition for mining claims, they drew up their own regulations. No one cared about owning the land, so there were no titles. A piece of ground belonged to a man or a company as long as it was worked, and generally tools could be left as evidence of possession. River claims involved greater complications, but there, too, disputes were generally resolved by arbitration. The rules varied from camp to camp, but in time, through practice and custom, they evolved into what was collectively called the Miners' Code.*

Left to themselves, as they were along the northern rivers, American miners were able to maintain reasonable order. But in the southern mines, where so many foreigners had gathered, simple rules could not control prejudice and jealousy. Responding to complaints that Mexicans (Sonorans) and Chileans outnumbered American miners along some of the rivers, that they had taken out of the country some $20 million in gold dust "which belonged to the people of the United States" and that the attraction of gold would cause California to be overwhelmed by an immigration of people "dangerous in character" from Mexico, South American countries, Australia and Europe—responding to the anger and fear of the people, the California legislature in April 1850 passed what was generally called the Foreign Miners' Tax. In brief, the law decreed that only native or naturalized citizens of the United States would be permit-

---

* *The effectiveness of these rules and the legislators' realization that it would be difficult to impose outside laws on the mining population are revealed by the fact that for eighteen years (1848–66) no legislation was enacted for the sale or transfer of mineral lands. During all that time when approximately $1 billion was mined without any congressional authorization, the regulations and customs of the miners constituted the only laws governing the mines and waters of the public land of the United States.*

ted to mine in California without a license, the cost of which would be $20 per month.

Foreign miners, including Peruvians and Frenchmen, announced their refusal to pay such an exorbitant tax. Several thousand gathered in Sonora and paraded in the streets, displaying their firearms. Three to five hundred American miners organized an armed force—a civil war threatened. A few arrests, a murder, the raising of "the brilliant star spangled banner" from a tall pine tree and a sullen quiet prevailed.

Far more than collecting a tax was at issue—nationalism and economic competition combined to strengthen old animosities. Stabbings, shootings, robberies were common in Sonora, Jamestown, Sullivan's Diggings and other mining settlements along the Tuolumne and Stanislaus rivers throughout 1850, with the Mexicans held to blame for "numerous cold-blooded murders." Merchants, editors and miners agreed that the tax had caused the dangerous times. They argued that if reduced to $5, it would be paid and peace would return.*

Tax or no tax, foreigners or no foreigners, crime of every kind, from skipping out on tavern bills to murder, was common throughout the mines by fall 1850 and thereafter. In the southern diggings everyone pointed to the Mexicans. In the north where there were few foreigners, the inefficiency of the laws and the courts recently established by the acts of the state legislature took the blame. The miners remembered the halcyon days of '49 when Judge Lynch assured speedy punishment and crimes were rare, life and property perfectly safe. With state authority replacing the improvised local justice of the miners, the criminals (if apprehended) "find some means of justifying their conduct or escaping conviction." So the *Alta California* complained in an editorial in September 1850.

Everything had changed since '49. Swain wrote of the moral decline, as did scores of other letter writers. A man from Missouri lamented: "Money is our only stimulus and the getting of it our only pleasure. Never was any country so well calculated to cultivate the spirit of avarice." Yet poverty and homesickness were epidemic. For many, California had become the elephant.

The true source of trouble and disappointment was the overwhelming number of miners. Gradually that harsh fact became apparent to everyone. The *Pacific News* on October 29, 1850, estimated that 57,000 miners were at work or prospecting on the forks of the Feather, Yuba,

---

* *In March 1851 the tax was repealed, but after pressure it was reenacted in 1852 at the reduced rate of $3, later raised to $4 a year, at which rate it was long sustained.*

402 / THE WORLD RUSHED IN

Bear and American rivers. And most were acknowledged to be earning barely enough to pay expenses. Many resorted to working for wages as laborers. Hundreds gave up the diggings to look for work in the cities. Many worked to earn enough to buy a ticket for home, via Panama. But pride held back the great majority—pride and the nagging hope, dream, sense of Fate, that another Nelson's Creek or a real Gold Lake would be found. This willingness to believe kept thousands of miners and men in the cities ready to pack their gear and rush to the most remote river or mountain lake.

In spring 1850, reports told of an exploring party that had found gold on the Trinity River in northwestern California. Swain had reported this news in his April letter. The San Francisco and Sacramento newspapers published stories about "vast quantities of gold." By summer, 10,000 miners had rushed overland and by ship to these new placers.

In the fall, restless believers responded to what came to be known as the Gold Bluffs excitement. News from the town of Trinidad near the Oregon border told of gold discovered in the sand of a beach, below lofty bluffs. Hundreds booked passage on a dozen ships from San Francisco. One of those who sailed to this fabulous El Dorado was J. Goldsborough Bruff, who had traveled close to the Rangers back in '49. Among the inducements that lured him and others: When the tide was out, the entire beach "is covered with bright and yellow gold." No digging required. In early 1851 the bubble burst.

William Swain resisted that temptation, as he had all others. Nor was he willing to work for wages or to risk his gold dust by purchasing one of the many claims daily offered for sale along the Feather or the Yuba. Instead, he traveled to Taylor's Bar on the east branch of the North Fork of the Feather, and there he took over part of a claim owned by one Daniel W. Currier, who was homeward bound for Lowell, Massachusetts, with $4,000. They made an agreement: in exchange for working as a member of the company, Swain would be entitled to a percentage of Currier's share of the gold mined.

During August and the first week of September, Swain and his new partners worked their claim, with results reported to Currier as follows:

September 9, 1850
Taylor's Bar

Mr. Currier, Sir,

In compliance with your request when leaving, we address you upon the subject of your business, left with us to attend to, with Mr. William Swain.

He has according to agreement, worked your share of this claim. The following is a true and correct account of the company business since you left, by which you will see the state of your and his business:

Sat. Aug. 31st. The Co. made a dividend of One
    Hundred & Ninety Two Dollars to the share $192.00
Mon. Sept. 9th. The Co. made a dividend of One
    Hundred & Eighty Four Dollars to the share 184.00

$376.00

In rendering the above account, we take the opportunity to say that Mr. Swain has executed his share of the labor on the claim in a satisfactory and faithful manner, and we hesitate not to express the opinion that you will settle with him justly.

> Yours truly,
> Cornelius Kelley
> James B. McMennomy

The tone of finality in this report suggests that as of September 9 Swain and his partners had given up their claim on Taylor's Bar—probably forced out by the storm of the 8th and resulting high water.

Possibly Swain wandered around the diggings along the North Fork during the last weeks of September. The rain and mud, his being alone with only wet blankets and the hope of a friendly miner's hospitality at night, and the talk on all sides of the destruction of river-mining operations must have left him deeply discouraged. By early October he was in the town of Hamilton, on the west bank of the Feather River.* "This place had about 400 inhabitants, four-fifths of whom were sick with chills and fever. I was taken sick, but I started for the hills and reached Bidwell's Bar, where I stayed all night. Next day I started for our cabin on the South Fork of the Feather River, to Hutchinson and Bailey. But I was so sick on the way that I could go no farther, so I stayed with a man named Snooks. Here I bought medicine and stayed all night. At three o'clock the next day I started for our cabin, about eight miles from Snooks'. Here were old friends, and they advised me to go home as soon as I could travel."

At last, the decision had to be made. Swain carried with him all the letters he had received from Sabrina and George. Surely he read them

---

* *The following statement was dictated by William Swain in 1889. It is the only record of his last days in the mines and of his decision to return home.*

once again, to reassure himself that he need not feel ashamed, that he had not failed, that it had not all been a mistake.

Sick, despairing of his promise to return with a pocket full of rocks, Swain must have felt a surge of gratitude when he reread George's May letter: "Above all, keep your courage up. If you fail there, you are not to blame. . . . You have friends who will meet you just as cordially unsuccessful as successful—and more so, for we are sure you have suffered, suffered, suffered. . . . To tell the plain truth, I wish most sincerely you were . . . at home, no matter if you haven't got a single mill."

What a brother. What a voice to hear in California.

■

["*October 17, 1850.**   The trail follows down the South Fork along the side of the mountains . . . when it passes over the mountains about two and a half miles to the top. From the summit . . . we soon lost sight of the deep, winding valley of the South Fork. After traveling about ten miles, we reached a ranch which is situated on the border of the valley where the road leaves the hills. This establishment being filled to overflowing with travelers, we took up our lodging in the stockyard. . . . We were up long before day and on our journey down the level Feather River valley. We stayed overnight at Veazie City, consisting of four or five good buildings. Here we had a bed and other good accommodations. We were, however, disturbed from sleeping by the usual noise kept up in such places in this country, such as fiddling, dancing, singing, yelling, etc.

["*October 18.*   We left Veazie City early in the morning and arrived at Marysville at noon. . . .

["*October 22.*   Yesterday we bought a ticket for Vernon by stage. . . .

---

* *After his goodbyes to Hutchinson and Bailey, who determined to try their luck at mining some time longer, Swain started his homeward journey. First he walked to Marysville, where he could buy riverboat or stagecoach passage to Sacramento City.*

Neither Swain's letters nor his 1889 reminiscences mention his trip from the cabin to San Francisco, where he arrived on November 4. However, another homebound miner, Amos Batchelder, who also had labored unsuccessfully with a river-damming company on the South Fork of the Feather, started within a few days of Swain. He kept a diary as far as Sacramento City.

Using Batchelder and then a combination of other diarists who wrote in October and November, a daily record has been created to describe what Swain probably saw and experienced.

Distance from here forty-five miles by land and eighty by water down the Feather River. . . . The stage for some reason went on its way without calling for us, so we concluded to take a whaleboat and were much pleased with the change. . . .

["Navigation down the river is rendered difficult for a few miles on account of the snags and stumps of trees, which are very numerous. . . . We arrived at Frémont, opposite Vernon, at eight o'clock in the evening.

["*October 23.* We are beginning to live again a little more like civilized beings. We had the best lodgings last night we have ever had in California. At two o'clock in the afternoon we took passage in the steamer *Governor Dana* for Sacramento City and are now having a glorious ride down that river. The weather is fine, the water and everything calm and beautiful, and we begin to enjoy life, after being shut out from the world in those mountains and living as we were obliged to while there for the space of a year. Here we feel almost at home and have an abundance of butter, cheese, milk, fresh beef, ham, venison, onions, turnips, melons, grapes, potatoes, beets and squash, with which the tables are supplied.

["Distance from Vernon to Sacramento, about fifty miles. As we approached the city of Sacramento, it presented a singular appearance. There is not much to be seen but the shipping lying along the bank of the river, the city being hid from view by the large trees that have been left standing on the levee. The bank is steep and about fifteen feet high and the levee is about ten rods wide."

["Along the bank of the river, fastened by chain and rope cables to the huge oaks and big sycamores, are a number of dismasted ships on which are built storehouses one to two stories high. . . . Steamers and ships and other craft haul up on the outside and pass the goods over the decks of these store ships, on to the levee. From thence they are carted to the stores and to the mines. . . . The levee is a tangled mass of Mexicans, Chinese, Chileans and Kanakas; also horses, mules, asses, oxen, drays, and lumber; flour, potatoes, molasses, brandy, pickles, oysters, yams, cabbages, books, furniture and almost everything that one can think of. . . ."

["The buildings are many of them substantial frames and bricks. The bricks are brought from the States. . . . The streets are not paved and in most places without sidewalks, but these are being built of boards in many places. Everything has the aspect of hurry and temporary. Everybody appears intent on his own business and generally lets others alone. Those who ride horseback go on a full run through the streets." "J Street, which is the principal one for business, extends back from the river about

two miles. This is completely filled with teams and people coming in from and going out to the mines, loaded with provisions and mining apparatus." "Many of the blocks are not inferior in appearance to eastern cities, with buildings painted to imitate granite."

[On October 21 the Sacramento *Transcript* carried a two-column story telling of the celebration on Saturday the 19th that greeted "the glorious intelligence of the admission of the State of California into the Union. . . . What with bonfires lit on the levee, the reports of guns and pistols, the cries of newsboys who ran through the city with 'Here's your Extra—California admitted! Here's your paper—Queen Victoria has got another baby,' the shoutings in the street and the thousand drinks of congratulations, the town was alive with excitement.

["At an early hour on Saturday evening, the citizens began to assemble . . . to express their feelings at the new position of the State. All were filled with enthusiasm and sought to show their patriotism in every conceivable manner. . . . One citizen threw his bar open to the public. . . . Fireballs filled the atmosphere, powder crackers were exploded in innumerable places and in numberless quantity. . . . Speech-making kept up till the night was far advanced. Whenever the names of the friends of California were mentioned, the most enthusiastic cheering arose. Among others, the mention of Henry Clay, Lewis Cass, Daniel Webster, Senator Douglas and some of the members from California created marked feel-

View of the steamboat landing, Sacramento City, from K Street —fall 1850.
HENRY E. HUNTINGTON LIBRARY

ing. . . . Thus did California take her position among the most influential of the thirty-one United States."

[*October 23.*   "The cholera has just commenced its ravages here, and the citizens are actively engaged in cleansing the city.* It is in a filthy condition—piles of rubbish are burning in the streets in every direction, filling the city with suffocating smoke." "The lurid fires, shining in the murky air, burn old shoes and boots and clothes by the ton and cartloads of bones and raw hides and putrid meat and spoiled bacon—so that the end of the matter is worse than the beginning. . . ."

["The number of people returning to the States . . . is somewhat astonishing. The steamers go crowded each day with living freight." "There is so much competition between the steamers that the fare has been reduced to 50 cents. The spirit of competition runs so high that they have employed the greatest brawlers to run for them and it is fun to hear them blackguard each other with thousands gathered around them, crying

---

* *The first case of cholera in Sacramento City was reported on October 18. The ubiquitous disease had been introduced to California on October 7, 1850, when a steamer from Panama arrived in San Francisco with twenty-two cases reported, including fourteen passengers who had died. The ship was not quarantined and the disease spread.*

   In Sacramento City deaths from cholera totaled 364 within the first month "and this was a most moderate calculation."

'one dollar in the bully *New World* or *Senator*,' and only 50 cents on the *Hartford*. There are now eight or more steamboats that run between here and San Francisco."

[*October 24.* "At two o'clock in the afternoon we took passage on board the steamer *Hartford* for San Francisco." The boat "steamed rapidly down the river, with Mount Diablo far before us. . . . The Sierra Nevada are faintly seen in the eastern sky, but between the Sacramento River and the mountains a great plain stretches out in a sweep which to the north and south runs unbroken to the horizon.

["We sailed along passing many vessels going up and down the river, many of them large brigs. . . . Several sloughs, as they are called, make out from the main river and join it again lower down. They often cut across bends and shorten the distance, some of them are eight and ten miles in length." Navigating the sloughs "was a matter of considerable nicety. The slough was but a few feet wider than the steamer and many of the bends occasioned her considerable trouble. Her bow sometimes ran in among the boughs of the trees, where she cannot well be backed without her stern going into the opposite bank." Further down "our steamboat kept to the main river channel, it being better. . . . We passed through one part of the river perhaps thirty miles in length where it was not more than three times as wide as the vessel. . . . We passed Monte-zuma City . . . one of the numerous cities that are daily being surveyed and laid out on paper and built up in men's imaginations so that a few may sell lots and make money. It is seldom that much is done, perhaps one or two houses are built, when the plan falls through, with the original stockholders having made a fortune in selling out their lands to the green ones who are unable to give them away. The next village was New York of the Pacific, situated near the junction of the two great rivers, the Sacramento and the San Joaquin. . . .

["In the straits leading to Suisun Bay the shore is abrupt with high hills on one side and rolling prairie on the other. Herds of cattle and of horses were roving unconstrained over the hills." "Suisun Bay was danc-ing to a fresh northern breeze as we skimmed its waters toward the town of Benecia . . . which appeared like a child's toy town. . . . At the upper end of town a church with a small white spire stood out brightly against the hills behind."

[As the riverboat steamed across the Bay for the wharves of San Francisco, the passengers pressed against the rail "to get a first sight of the city. . . . In a kind of crescent cove on the west side of the Bay with the land rising rather abruptly to the apex of high hills in the rear, San Francisco seems to be climbing up like a fledgling from its nest."]

CHAPTER XIII

Coming Home

At Panama City "passengers are weekly arriving in multitudes from California. . . . Some arrive poor and needy, others rich and greedy and all monstrous anxious to get home."

They came from everywhere, from mining camps on the Feather to those on the Mariposa; from hill towns and the great supply centers. Miners, merchants, speculators, expressmen, freighters, jobseekers—everyone at some time took passage on the sidewheelers that churned down the great waterways to San Francisco, the Pacific metropolis.

Some came on business: to order supplies from the East, to collect mail, speculate in real estate or try to make in a business enterprise what prospecting and mining had failed to produce in the foothills. Others came for pleasure: for a bath, a shave and a dinner in a new hotel, to have a portrait made at a daguerreotypist's studio, or for a spree at a gambling palace or bawdyhouse. Many more landed at the wharves anxious to leave El Dorado.

On November 4, William Swain with scores of scruffy miners stepped ashore and into the rush and noise of San Francisco's streets. Accepting that the $500 he carried in gold dust (plus what was owed him by Currier) would be all he could secure from the Sierra streams, he wrote to his family on the 6th—to tell them of his decision. "I have made up my mind that I have got enough of California and am coming home as fast as I can."

Difficult as it was to admit defeat, he felt better for knowing that in every mining camp, on every road and steamboat, in the streets, hotels, gambling halls and steamship ticket offices in San Francisco there were hundreds of others who had failed.

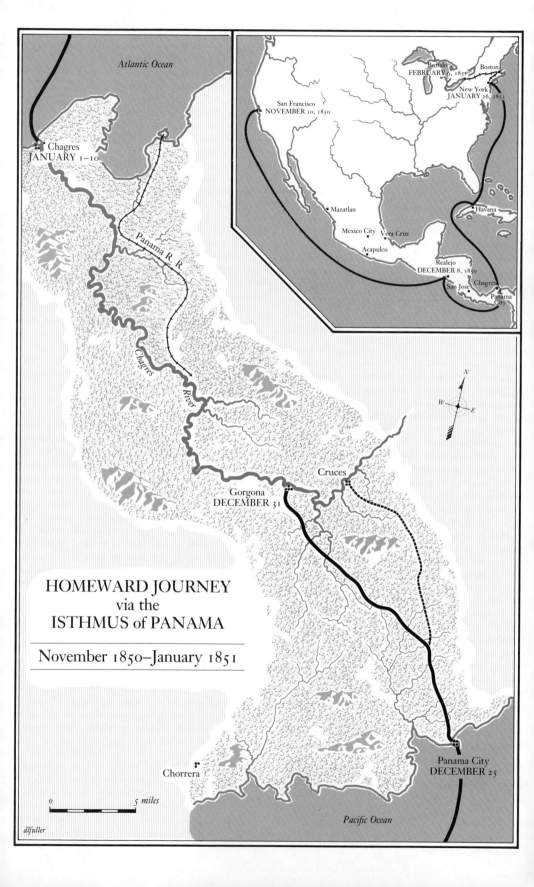

Atlantic Ocean

Chagres
JANUARY 1–10

Panama R. R.

Chagres River

San Francisco
NOVEMBER 10, 1850

Buffalo
FEBRUARY 6, 1851
New York
JANUARY 26, 1851
Boston

Mazatlan

Havana

Mexico City
Vera Cruz

Acapulco

Realejo
DECEMBER 8, 1850

San Jose

Chagres

Panama
City

N
W   E
S

Cruces

Gorgona
DECEMBER 31

HOMEWARD JOURNEY
via the
ISTHMUS of PANAMA

November 1850–January 1851

Chorrera

Panama City
DECEMBER 25

0   5 miles

dlfuller

Pacific Ocean

Frenchmen, Germans, English, Chinese, Chileans, Mexicans, Hawaiians, Yankees from Maine and slaveowners from Georgia walked the streets of this robust, booming place where "bustle, speculation and confusion, exhilaration and disappointment mingled together like sunshine and rain." The ships that brought them formed a forest of masts along the shallow shoreline: 526 vessels counted on July 1, 1850. Many were dismantled, deserted, left to rot at anchor. Enterprising merchants pulled more than a hundred high on the beach, where, embedded in the deep mud and connected to the streets by docks and wharves, they were converted to warehouses, saloons and lodgings. The brig *Euphemia* was used as the city's first prison. The famed *Niantic* as a storehouse earned for her owners a reported $20,000 a month.

By November 1850, San Francisco had suffered four major fires—December 24, 1849, and May 4, June 14 and September 17, 1850—each of which destroyed all or a large part of the business district. But the businessmen, like "the indefatigable spider," had replaced the charred ruins with new hotels, banks, gambling palaces and warehouses, many built of brick with iron doors and shutters as protection against the inevitable next conflagration. By the close of 1850, the permanent population was estimated at 25,000 to 30,000 (versus 2,000 in early 1849). Commenting proudly on the city's growth during 1850, one of the newspapers boasted that San Francisco compared favorably with New York or New Orleans, citing as evidence "forty-four steamers employed in river trade with Sacramento, Stockton and lesser towns; twelve oceangoing steamers connecting with Panama; semimonthly mail, seven daily newspapers, sixty brick buildings, eight or ten first-class hotels, 107 miles of street laid out and over seven miles of it substantially planked and most of that distance properly sewered."

Because the city fronted on a shallow cove, the merchants had built docks or wharves that reached out into the bay for large vessels to tie up and unload. Construction of these wharves (twelve completed by year's end) offered a carpenter named Wright from Connecticut an unusual opportunity. He specialized in driving into the mudflats the pilings on which the wharves were built. Much in demand, he earned a fortune of $60,000 to $70,000. An envious businessman commented: "Just imagine the pride and exultation with which he will meet his family and friends, and the deference which will be paid him in consequence of his altered position."

On the largest of these wharves, almost half a mile in length, "handcarts, porters, drays and now and then a fine carriage, rattle over the plank pavement in a sound of thunder, while at points along the wharf the thimblerigger, the French monte dealer and low gamblers are gathering crowds around them to practice upon the credulity of the unsophisticated. The pickpocket, the thief of all grades is in the crowd, and often, for want of other opportunity, a fight or excitement is got up to order so that these light-fingered gentry can practice their vocation. . . . Rows, fights and robberies are the order of the day, and the night too, and to see sin and depravity in its most glaring colors, the seeker after such pleasures has only to walk from one end of Long Wharf to the other."

Swain probably walked along Montgomery Street and passed Long Wharf. If he ventured out to its end, he must have watched steamboats constantly moving back and forth across the bay, taking out and bringing back men like himself.

But in his last letter from California, written on November 6, he told his family nothing about his four days and three nights in that city which symbolized California's wealth and sin. He was feeling unwell—chills and fever. Possibly he had a premonition. His letter had a somber tone; he wrote only to give the kind of information his family might need in case of his death on the homeward voyage.

But there were other reasons for his silence about San Francisco. More than any time since leaving home, he felt the seriousness of his commitment to the teachings of the Bible; he could almost hear the admonitions set forth in the letters from Sabrina and George—letters he had carefully placed in his slim baggage. Youngstown was as real to him as the tumultuous city that surrounded him. To write about what he saw and heard, to describe a place that shocked him, would have made him feel uncomfortable, embarrassed. If his San Francisco letter was to be his last, it should not tell of a way of life he disdained, even condemned.

But he was there, and what he saw was as much a part of his California experience as the mining camps along the Feather and the Yuba. You had not faced the elephant until you had spent some time in San Francisco.

More letters were written from San Francisco during gold rush years than from any other place in California. This was the New York of the Pacific: "The great place of the western continent, the heart, the brain, the focus, the main spring, the pinnacle, the extremity, the no more beyond of the New World."*

The only port for the gold region, the center for banking and commerce, San Francisco dominated California. And equally it held the atten-

---

* *Walt Whitman made this statement about New York City. How perfectly it described gold-rush San Francisco.*

tion and stimulated the avarice of exporters in New York, Boston, Philadelphia, New Orleans, European ports, Honolulu, Sidney, everywhere. No one had ever known of such a place as San Francisco, such a market as California. A shipload of ice—147 tons—from Boston arrived in San Francisco in July 1850 and quickly sold at 80 cents per pound. A ship from Mexico brought a cargo of cats. They sold readily for $8 to $12 as hoped-for protection against thousands of rats that infested the city and each month destroyed quantities of foodstuffs stored in tents and warehouses.

All mail came by ship to San Francisco. For the single month of August 1850, 45,000 letters were carried ashore—and 40,000 shipped out, all via Panama. If August was an average month, more than a million letters passed through San Francisco in 1850.

It was a city of men who slept in hotels, six, ten and more to a room, or in filthy lodging halls on rows of cots or in bunks hung from floor to ceiling. To escape such places, citizens of Rushville, Illinois; Nashville, Tennessee; Worcester, Massachusetts, visited drinking bars, billiard rooms and gambling saloons. Young men with money earned in the mines or money brought from home to pay for a start in the mines crowded into Portsmouth Square, where most of the gambling palaces were located. Immense and luxurious, these businesses mined the miners. Bedazzled and excited by life-size paintings of naked men and women "in almost every attitude" and by the reality of women leaning on the bars, talking and laughing with the men, sitting at card tables, or walking about with trays of cigars hanging in front of bosoms partially, thrillingly exposed, the goldseekers would never forget San Francisco.

After noting that "Americans much prefer French women who have the charm of novelty," a French goldseeker reported: "Some of the first in the field made enough in a month to go home to France and live on their incomes. All in all, the women of easy virtue here earn a tremendous amount of money. . . . To sit near you at a bar or at a card table, a girl charges one ounce an evening. For anything more, you have to pay a fabulous amount. A whole night costs from $200 to $400. Nearly all these women in Paris were streetwalkers of the cheapest sort. But out here, for only a few minutes they ask a hundred times as much as they were used to getting in Paris."

What Swain certainly would not have reported was daily grist for the local newspapers and for many other letter writers, all of whom wrote as observers, never as participants. On September 27, 1850, the San Francisco *Evening Picayune* commented on the moral condition of the city. "Drinking, gambling, debauchery far from being frowned upon have been patronized by men who in any other country would not risk their reputation by even the suspicion of contact with such scenes. . . . Bawdyhouses, if they have not been licensed, have been placed under no legal restraints and have been permitted to occupy the most conspicuous and central parts of the city."

What Swain shared with hundreds of ex-miners was an impatience to get away from California and start for home. Every day for months, sailing ships and steamers had passed through the Golden Gate bound for Panama, cabins and steerage crowded. Commenting on this exodus, a doctor in San Francisco wrote to his wife in Connecticut: "More people seem to be returning to—than coming from—the Atlantic states. Some 250 persons went on the small steamer *Antelope* and some 300 now go on the *Tennessee*." For the period August 1 through September 13, 4,672 men —not one woman—left San Francisco. The final count for the year was 26,593 men and eight women.*

Rich or poor, there was only one way to go home: by sea. Overland travel eastward across the Sierra and the deserts was out of the question. Everyone had either experienced that suffering and toil or had learned of it in convincing detail. Only occasional Mormon parties bound for Salt Lake City traveled eastward from California. In the late summer of 1850 and again in 1851, they passed thousands of new recruits for El Dorado trudging down the Humboldt.

The water route was the way, by ship from San Francisco to Nicaragua or Panama, across the jungled isthmus by foot and canoe to an Atlantic port and then by ship again to New Orleans or New York. Those who could afford the best bought cabin passage on one of the Pacific Mail Steamship Company's steamers for the voyage to Panama City. Ticket prices in fall 1850 and early winter 1851 ranged from $275 to $300. For those with more limited means, the steamers offered steerage quarters, dark, dirty and crowded, at $125. Many more ex-miners turned to sailing ships, which offered a ticket for $50 to $85. While the steamers scheduled the trip for fourteen days, the sailing ships were often delayed by unfavorable weather or lengthy calms and might take anywhere from thirty to more than fifty days to reach Panama City.

As merchants at the frontier towns of Independence and St. Joseph had taken advantage of ignorant city boys and speculators at Lassen's Ranch had charged destitute emigrants outrageous prices for survival food, shipowners in San Francisco grasped at opportunity. With hundreds of ships out of use or actually abandoned along the waterfront,

* *The lure of El Dorado had not diminished. Between August 1 and September 13, 5,940 men and fifty-seven women landed at San Francisco.*

many old vessels were refitted (new rigging supplied or the old patched up) and advertised as ready to receive passengers. Most miners had never seen a sailing ship. They were easily persuaded by agents' promises of good food, clean quarters and skilled crews. Once at sea there was no escaping the unsanitary quarters or improving the daily serving of putrid food. Of the men still maintaining their diaries who returned home in the fall of 1850 and early '51, most complained bitterly about conditions on sailing ships and steamers. Several reported their ships ran out of food and water and had to be aided by passing vessels. In several cases, the passengers signed petitions or resolutions condemning the captains and owners of their ships. At least one passenger told of bringing a lawsuit.

Most graphic in his outrage was Isaac Lord. He had traveled close to the Rangers and mentioned them several times on the overland trail. In early 1851 he was traveling steerage on board the steamer *Oregon*, bound for Panama. He said of the ship: "The passengers were fed like hogs. . . . Some of the hard bread was of good quality, some moldy, and much of it was infested with black bugs burrowing into it like woodchucks in a sandbank. A cold-water soak would drive them out of their holes and cause them to vamoose, and you had the supreme gratification of knowing how many escaped; but you got no satisfaction as to how many remained to be eaten. It was altogether better to soak them in hot water or in your tea, as they cooked as easily as oysters, and you didn't have to eat them raw. They were not numerous enough to be full substitute for fresh meat.

"If the bread was bad, the pork was worse. Not that it was wormy. No, no, it was too strong for that. Worms know what is palatable and take good care not to get into such pork barrels. . . . Many and many a savory ten-pound morsel of ox carrion was tossed overboard that must have proved a vomit for a shark. If not disposed of in some such effectual way, it would appear at the next table.

"Another favorite dish, at least with the cooks, was Indian pudding. . . . Dark molasses would hide the mold and strangle the bugs and tangle the worms. As to the tough beef. . . , the Lord is not to be blamed because the Mexicans raise such little, tough, sinewy, cockfighting bundles of rattan and rubber done up in calfskin for beef, or that they . . . release them on shipboard to starve or be killed to keep them from starving.

"The owners of the line are to be held accountable. . . . None but a rich man would ever think of starving the poor to increase his gains, of making money by cheating a man out of his dinner after he had paid two prices for it. . . . One who has been in the mines . . . will hardly complain if treated halfway decently."

For once, it was Swain's fate to be treated decently. He bought a ticket on a new sailing ship, the *Mosconome*. Possibly he had read an advertisement which ran that week in the *Alta California:* "From Central Wharf—Realejo and Panama—the splendid New York packet ship Mosconome . . . 2,000 tons burthen, 18 months old and most magnificent ship in the harbor. She has splendid accommodations for eighty passengers, besides a commodious second cabin. Her between decks are eight feet in height, with single berths furnished with new mattresses. A list of stores can be seen on board."

In his November 6 letter, Swain warned his family that he might encounter "sickness on the route." It was the old enemy, cholera. There were deaths in San Francisco, and on overcrowded, unsanitary ships the virulent disease sometimes swept through the passengers' quarters. In October a steamer bound for Panama buried thirty-seven men at sea!

Though conditions on board steamships might be dangerous and uncomfortable (especially in steerage), at least the steamers would drop anchor off Panama City within a day or so of their scheduled arrival. On sailing ships a calm could leave the sails slack as days passed and the water supply was rationed. Fearful of cholera, revolted by moldy food, miserable with seasickness and belowdecks stench, some passengers chose to leave their ships when they put in for supplies at Mazatlán, Acapulco or Realejo. From these remote places they risked the uncertainties and discomforts of overland travel through Mexico and Nicaragua to a Gulf Coast port. The great majority of homebound men stayed on board their ships until they could escape at Panama City.

The ancient Pacific port had no harbor as such. The ships anchored some distance offshore and native canoes pushed alongside so baggage and passengers could be lowered (sometimes dropped) into the narrow hulls. Thousands of Americans were paddled ashore, to experience for the first time a foreign people and culture. The American impact on the economy and life of Panama would be profound and permanent. Though the isthmus was part of the Republic of New Granada, and Panama City's history went back to the very beginnings of Spanish control of the New World (the city was founded in 1519), the Americans quickly scorned what they found and with Yankee superiority and moral indignation set about making changes.

By December 1850, when Swain arrived, the place was in reality run by Americans. Beginning in 1849, with the first rush to California, they had simply taken over from the Panamanians, who seemed so lazy and incapable of managing the transport, hotels, bars and other facilities and services immediately demanded by Americans. A British traveler noted that "the natives appear to dislike Americans in general. . . . The

Yankees hurry them and cannot endure their slow, lingering ways." Quarreling, street fights and a riot were reported in the San Francisco newspapers and in Panama's two papers, both owned by Americans. A goldseeker on his way to California forecast: "There will be serious trouble if the emigration continues. I should not be surprised at any time to hear that the Americans have taken over the place. . . . They are fast working themselves into the business of the place, and it will not be long before it will be monopolized by them."

In truth, Panama became America's first colony, organized to serve the hurrying travelers who each year passed to and from California as quickly as their fellow countrymen could arrange and at as high a price as competition would allow.

Swain landed at Panama City on Christmas Day, 1850. On the 29th he wrote a cursory note to his family. Like most other men on their way home, he took no time, had no inclination to write about what he expected to report in person in a matter of days. Fortunately, a few of the homeward-bound, with journalists' zeal, did keep descriptive records of the sights and circumstances in this country preempted by hurrying Americans.

Panama City was jammed not only with those eager to get home but also with hundreds of men (and a few women) waiting to board the steamers and sailing ships that would take them to San Francisco. The two sharply different crowds—those who had seen the elephant and those expecting to find El Dorado—encountered each other in that steamy, jungled country, halfway between home and California.

Throughout 1850 and most of 1851 the number of California-bound emigrants far exceeded available berths on the steamships. Everyone knew of the dangers and uncertainties of the sailing ships, so they tried in every way to secure the more comfortable passage. Frequently the steamships sailed north with one thousand passengers pressed into space designed for a maximum of six hundred. The chance to be one of those hundreds required standing in line at a ticket office, "sweating, panting, pushing, snarling" and then waiting three or even five weeks before boarding one of the overbooked ships. One stranded goldseeker fumed, "I get more tired of Panama every day . . . I should like to see an earthquake or revolution."

For those on their way across the isthmus to the miasmal port of Chagres, an ancient trail opened the way through dense jungle. With their baggage packed on mules, the homebound Americans walked to the town of Gorgona, "a most miserable place" on the Chagres River, where they climbed onto flat-bottomed boats with protective awnings, to float downstream to the coast. On the trail and the river they could see only a few feet into the tropical forest, but they could hear the loud cries of monkeys and parrots.

While floating downstream they passed construction crews at work building a railroad, another example of American domination of Panama. In 1849 a group of New York businessmen had obtained a charter from the New Granada government for the building and operation of a trans-isthmus railroad. In 1850 the Panama Railroad Company started work; progress was slow and very costly. The line would not be completed until 1855, but during the ten years thereafter, close to 400,000 people rode through the jungle, ocean to ocean, in only three hours—an achievement that nurtured American pride, brought immense profits to the railroad company and stimulated early interest in an American canal.

Swain and those with him spent three days crossing the isthmus, landing at Chagres the evening of January 1, 1851. Some travelers never reached the port; numerous reports told of brigands who attacked from the jungle darkness, robbing, stabbing, overturning boats. The hundreds who came ashore from the riverboats found that Americans had taken over there as well, turning the swampy port into a western boom town with crowded streets, hotels, bars and gambling dens. Chagres' notoriety was earned as "the most unhealthy place in Christendom. Many passengers had their lives insured . . . and there was a clause in each policy stating that remaining at Chagres overnight would be a forfeiture."

Whatever the dangers for travelers, however great the resentment and distrust between native and invader, Panamanians and Americans were locked in an economic and geographic interdependence. For the people of Panama City and Chagres, today's and tomorrow's profits depended far more on San Francisco and New York than on Bogotá. For Californians, the sixty-mile isthmus was the indispensable link with the States—the fastest and safest travel route and, of supreme importance, the place of transshipment for all business and personal mail.

Like all the men in San Francisco in November 1850 who waited for passage home, William Swain heard stories about Panama. They made the place sound both exotic and dangerous. To avoid the dangers, crossing from Pacific to Atlantic via Nicaragua was discussed. But that route would not be a practical alternative until a few years later when it was developed by Cornelius Vanderbilt.

Panama it would be—and then home.

Deserted ships along San Francisco waterfront; late fall 1850.

November 6, 1850
San Francisco

Dear Friends,

Here I am in this city on my way home, thank God. It is a long time since I have written home. The cause has been my being in the mountains where I could not send letters till within three weeks past, when I came down to the valley and was attacked with chill fever, which I am nearly recovered from.

I have made up my mind that I have got enough of California and am coming home as fast as I can.

I am traveling in company with Messrs. Noble and Sears of Ann Arbor, Michigan, who I think are companions I can depend upon in case of sickness on the route, of which there is some danger as cholera is existing to a considerable extent in this place and will probably be on the route at the Isthmus. But I think there is little danger from it if persons live carefully, and even in case of attack I think it yields readily to timely and judicious treatment. We have procured medicines to take on shipboard and shall do all to avert the fatal effects of the disease in case each other is attacked. Mr. Noble has been engaged in the druggist business and is acquainted with the use of medicines, and I put great confidence in him as a companion; besides, we have a surgeon attendant on the ship.

We have taken cabin passage in a large and convenient New York packet by the name of *Mosconome*. Her accommodations are very good and the number of passengers going will not exceed one hundred in both cabins and on deck. I think we shall be much less liable to disease on her than on the steamers, as she is newly fitted out.

We were to have sailed yesterday, and shall "positively" haul out in the Bay this afternoon and put to sea tomorrow. May the winds of heaven waft us along like the clouds. I think there is a probability of good fare and attention on the voyage. Passage, $85.

["From information gathered in conversation with many who have traveled over them, the routes principally traveled by emigrants are three —across the Isthmus of Darien from Panama to Chagres; through Central America from Realejo to San Juan; and across Mexico from Acapulco to Vera Cruz."

[The port of Acapulco, some 1,500 miles south from San Francisco, "is described as a place of no ordinary beauty. Its harbor is safe and commodious and is made the refuge of all vessels that are disabled in the gales that prevail along the coast at certain seasons, besides many others which are run in for the purpose of replenishing their exhausted supplies or of being condemned as unseaworthy. . . .

["The majority of emigrants reembark at Acapulco for Panama; but a few, prompted either by curiosity or mistaken motives of economy, purchase mules and in parties of five or more strike out across the country. The road generally traveled leads them through a sparsely settled portion of Mexico, where but indifferent accommodations are extended to the traveler. . . . The road leads also through the City of Mexico, whence the journey to the seaboard is more easily accomplished. The average expense attendant upon this land passage is about $150."]

We intend taking the Nicaragua route in case we find it properly organized on arriving at Realejo. Our ship stops there and then goes to Panama; fare to either place is the same. I think that I may reasonably expect that the sickness of the Isthmus will have greatly diminished by the time I arrive, as it will be December, and with great prudence I think I have little danger to fear from it. I have not allowed myself to eat any vegetables yet, although they are plenty in market; and I have not tasted an apple since I left the Illinois River. If prudence is a guarantee against southern diseases, I shall escape them.

I think I shall be at home by the 1st of January, 1851. Business will call me from New York City to Lowell, Massachusetts, before I come home. A Mr. Daniel W. Currier of that place owes me $279 and I have his obligations and the documents to get it. He had $4,000 when he went home. I will write from New York City.

I left Messrs. Hutchinson and Bailey a week ago last Monday [October 28] at our cabin at Feather River in good health, and I saw S. Eaton at Marysville. He is working at his trade. I sent $200 for Mr. Bailey to Mrs. Bailey by Adams & Company's Express and wrote her a letter with the certificate, day before yesterday. I got your August and September letters at Sacramento, and wrote a letter to S. Eaton with the news Sabrina wrote from his people, as he has never got a letter from them at this place. I shall get home with only $700 or $800 [including the Currier debt], but I am thankful for small favors. Also I trust Heaven has blessed me beyond my expectations. If I arrive home with health unimpaired, I have no regretting that I left home on this journey. Hurray for home.

> *Wheresoe'r I roam,*
> *There is one land beloved*
> *Of Heaven above the rest;*
> *One spot above all others blessed.*
> *That land is My Country,*
> *And that spot is my home.*

I write in a great hurry and must close. If any accident should happen to me on the route, the Messrs. Noble and Sears will be on hand to assist me and send all necessary intelligence to you. Hoping that I may be on hand to wish you a Merry Christmas,

> I remain, as ever,
> Your Son, Brother, and Husband,
> William S.

P.S. Kiss Little Cub and tell her that the original of that baby picture is coming to see her and have many fine things for her.

> November 14, 1850
> Packet Ship *Mosconome*
> 500 m. from San Francisco

Dear George,

As I am on my passage home on this ship and there is cholera on board, there is a possibility that I may be attacked by it, and as I am in bad health, not having recovered from the attack of fever and chills of which I wrote you in my letter from San Francisco, I deem it a matter of prudence that I make a statement of my affairs in writing, seal it and direct it to you per Mr. Henry Noble, in whose care I shall leave what articles I have here, both of money and other articles. These articles are,

Late 1850. Looking east to San Francisco's waterfront crowded with hundreds of ships, many abandoned.

BANCROFT LIBRARY, UNIVERSITY OF CALIFORNIA, BERKELEY

however, not worth anything unless I should be able to see to them myself and be able to carry them home with me; that is, if circumstances should require me to leave anyone to attend to my affairs.

I have with me now about $500 in gold dust and $10 in specie. I also have a very fine double-barrel fowling piece which I should take great pride in bringing home with me, if I get home. I also have an Agreement between myself and Daniel W. Currier of Lowell, Massachusetts, and a statement of the business done by the stipulation of the Agreement. It is signed by persons who were agreed upon in the Agreement, and so drawn that I think there can be no trouble in getting the money. Mr. Currier's address is Daniel W. Currier, No. 19 Laurence Corporation, Lowell, Massachusetts.

I told you in my last letter that Mr. Noble of Ann Arbor, Michigan, is my traveling companion, and I repeat it here so that you may be sure to be informed of his whereabouts. He has had good success in California, and I think he is an honorable man.

I have two other friends on board. One of them, Mr. Oliver Gold-smith, was one of the Wolverine Rangers and crossed the plains with me. He is a young man and unsettled in life.* The other is Mr. Sibley, whom

---

* *Oliver Goldsmith, also unsuccessful in his gold-mining efforts, returned to Detroit, Michigan, where in 1896 he published* Overland in Forty-Nine! The Recollections of a Wolverine Ranger. *This book includes an account of the return voyage but does not mention William Swain.*

I became acquainted with last winter by being located near him on the South Fork of the Feather River; he also is a young man and resides near Boston, Massachusetts. In case necessity requires, I shall request these persons to address you. I believe that I have said all that is necessary, and may God grant that there will be no necessity for any of these few lines to have been written.

Be assured, dear brother, that in these times when death and danger surround me, there is a consolation in the consciousness of having lived a moral life and in having lived a life in which principle has been the rule of action, principle founded upon justice and morality. This is not what we were taught to believe Christianity to be, and probably many of our Christian friends would think it not worthy of being harbored as a reflection of consolation in such an hour as this. But to me the reflection of having lived morally even amid all the influences which have surrounded me during my absence and of having done justly by my fellow man is a consolation that I would not exchange for any earthly benefit. Thus far on this journey, even ever since I left home, the protecting hand of a merciful God has been my shield. Through the dangers of this terrible pestilence along the Missouri and on the route of the plains for 800 miles, His care has protected me; through the toils and perils of the mountain land He has sustained me, and I still have confidence to trust His gracious will.

Dear brother, I have already said far more than I thought of saying when I commenced; but one word more. I have seen many hardships, dangers and privations, and made nothing by it, i.e. accumulated no property; but if I arrive at home with my health, I shall ever be glad that I have taken this trip. Absence from my friends has given me a true valuation of them, and also it has taught me to appreciate the comforts and blessings of home. Above all, the circumstances attendant upon the journey, combined with reflection, have impressed upon my mind a proper appreciation of the overruling hand of an all-wise and kind Being in the affairs of mankind.

This just estimation of things, as also of principles, will abundantly repay all my toils and privations, and if life is spared me, will be a source of contentment and happiness both to myself and family and friends. Its influence will be to impress more deeply in my mind the goodness of my Creator, and to more firmly establish my reliance upon the principles of religion and morality so carefully taught us by our parents in childhood. It will, I trust, enable me to discharge in a proper manner the duties of a member of society, a brother, son, husband, and father.

May God in His mercy graciously deign to hear the prayers of a pious mother and wife, which I know are daily offered for my safety, and may He also grant the fervent prayers of a sinful creature of creation offered here in this "speck" on the ocean's bosom; and may it please the Almighty to grant us all a happy meeting in our joyful home, is the prayer of your

Brother,
William Swain

December 23, 1850
At sea near Panama

Dear Mother and Sabrina,

Through the mercy of God I am here in safety and in good health, having had a pleasant passage from San Francisco from whence we sailed on the 10th of November about noon. A fine gentle land breeze wafted our noble ship from her moorings towards the entrance of the Bay, six miles distant. We were soon passing safely through the narrow and rock-bound channel with the wind and tide in our favor, and standing out on the broad surface of the great Pacific. As we passed the entrance, we had a fine opportunity of observing the great capability of the Bay, its great security, and the absolute control a good fortification on either side would have of it. The entrance of the Bay is two miles wide from shore to shore. The channel is near the center, and the banks on both sides are high.

The breezes of heaven favored our voyage, and we dashed on our trackless course in majestic style, passing on our outward course one brig bound in and two ships anchored off the Bay, while ten other ships which sailed from the Bay loaded with passengers for Panama in company with us kept us company, specking the bounding billow with their dark hulks and imparting life to the scene by their broad and glittering canvas. Off the Bay we had the pleasure of seeing a number of whales, some near and others far from us, spouting and throwing their huge backs above the surface of the water. Schools of blackfish—small whales—also were rolling about like so many cattle rolling in the deep; porpoise in great number, puffing and blowing, would occasionally pass our path. This was the first time I had looked forth upon ocean, and altogether it was far more gratifying than I had expected, and I considered myself greatly favored by having an opportunity to see so many of the beauties and wonders of the deep in so short a time.

For three days and nights did the free breezes drive us along. ["One of the luxuries was to stand in the shadow of the sails, when a fresh breeze, cool and reviving, was driving us along at the rate of ten knots an hour and gaze out upon the blue waves."]

Our craft traversed her watery way for a distance of near 600 miles before our fine breeze failed and we traversed the rest of the journey with light winds, while many calms have wearied us out.

[On board another sailing ship crowded with men returning home, "the miners gathered on deck and told some pretty hard yarns. Many of them said they would rather be on the Humboldt desert with only two days provisions than to be on board ship. . . . There was a row between the steerage and cabin passengers. The cabin passengers wanted the captain to keep the steerage folks off the quarter deck. The steerage would go where they pleased. The cabins stretched a rope across the deck. The steerage went below, got out their revolvers and butcher knives and swore they had paid their money and would go where they pleased. The cabin folks had to knock under. . . ."]

Few of our number got seasick and indeed all were usually well, myself more so than I had anticipated from the feeble state of health when I embarked.

But all was not well. A kind Providence saw fit to visit even our small company with affliction. That dire pestilence, cholera, was among us!—and from its dreadful effects we consigned two of our number to a watery grave. Many others were sick, but with the blessings of heaven upon the means used, they were restored and the scourge removed from among us. Certainly when I reflect upon the gauntlet I have passed in this deadly disease, I am constrained to recognize the preserving care of a kind Providence.

I take great pleasure in saying that we have a very roomy, clean and commoding ship, and a captain who is a gentleman and, I think, a Christian.

On our voyage nothing of more than everyday interest occurred. We arrived at Realejo in 28 days from San Francisco [on December 8].* Here we stopped three days. The village is eight miles from the bay, and on the second day at daybreak I left the ship in company with a boat. The passengers for the village and the boatman plied the oars to the tune of *Cheerily O!* and we passed quickly across the small bay and soon entered

---

* As a supply port for ships bound to Panama and as a landing place for passengers who intended to cross the Isthmus of Nicaragua to the Caribbean port of San Juan, Realejo became an important port during the gold rush years. A large bay, protected at its entrance by an island, afforded safe harbor; and here a dock was built as a coaling depot for steamers. The town itself, numbering about 1,200 people, was situated some miles up a tidewater stream and could be reached in native canoes.

the narrow arm that leads to the village. Twilight was fading into the light of day, and animal nature was awaking from the repose of the night. Here I had my first near view of a tropical forest in all its depth and verdure. From its thickets rose the early notes of hundreds of the feathered tribe, and among its boughs gamboled from bough to bough the monkey in all its caprice. Here while we gently glided along the smooth watery mirror, enjoying the bracing coolness of the morning air, I saw and heard the first parrots squalling and flitting along in their native wilds. That beautiful morn! Those gay scenes were well calculated to awaken merry and lively feelings, and I can truthfully say that *that* morning was the first that brought to my bosom the glad and joyous feelings of my youth since I left the door of my loved home.

We arrived at Realejo in time for breakfast, where I regaled my breadbasket upon fowl and eggs for the first time since leaving home. ["The town exhibited the result of Yankee enterprise by way of perhaps a dozen framed houses which constituted the American Hotel, Eureka House, Travellers Home, California Hotel, etc. Everything in the shape of eatable or rather takeable had risen in price. . . . The prevailing opinion seemed to be that the hungry Californians cared nothing about price if their appetites and desires were gratified. . . . The chickens and eggs became scarce in a short time. A man would sit down to a table with a good chicken and a half dozen eggs with bread and cooked plantain in abundance and leave it thoroughly cleaned of everything save the dishes. This is to be accounted for by examining into the stinted manner in which the passengers live on board the boats running from California to the States. . . . The manner they are fed on these boats sharpens the traveler's appetite to a wonderful extent, so much so that the Americans are considered by Central Americans to be the greatest eaters in all the world."]

I made a tour of Realejo and found much to admire. The character of vegetation, the tropical fruit of all kinds which was in great plenty, the place in general with its buildings and architecture, the church and the ruins of an old nunnery in particular, the natives and their habits and customs, with many things of minor importance, served to engross my attention and mind.

At noon I dined on chicken and eggs, and after dinner walked a few miles into the country to view the cultivated lands: the fields of plantain, bananas, and corn in all stages—i.e., ripe, roasting, tasseling, knee-high, and just planting. I bought a half-bushel of oranges for 63 cents, a few dozen eggs at 50 cents per dozen, some limes, and a few bananas, and at 4 o'clock took a boat for the ship where we arrived at dusk. I shall be able

to tell you much more about this visit in a strange land that will be of
interest.

I found that the route from this place consisted of 140 miles of travel
to Granada and then the lake and river to San Juan on the Atlantic. ["It
was supposed at San Francisco that a line of steamers had been established
from New Orleans to San Juan . . . and that the connection with Realejo
had been completed. Very many being deceived by these representations
took passage to Realejo. Upon arriving here nothing definite could be
ascertained concerning the arrangements for crossing the Gulf. However,
many who landed had become so heartily tired of the sea that they pre-
ferred crossing to San Juan, even upon uncertainties, rather than to reembark for Panama."*

[For the trip across Nicaragua "there are two modes of conveyance.
One is by a clumsy two-wheeled vehicle called a *carretta*, covered with
rawhides and drawn by four oxen. The wheels are transverse sections of
large trees about six inches thick. . . . Six men are furnished with one of
these and a driver who sits on the *carretta* armed with a long, sharp goad
which he thrusts into the animals until they bleed . . . while a boy ten or
twelve years old precedes as a guide carrying a machete or long knife
. . . without which it would be difficult to penetrate the thickets. In this
manner transportation is performed to Granada, and the price asked for
each person is $6. The other mode is on horseback, and the charge made
is the full value of a horse."

[According to reports, "the traveler proceeds from Realejo through a
country unrivaled for the wild grandeur of its romantic scenery . . . to
the beautiful city of Granada. . . . There he prepares for his trip across
Lake Nicaragua and down the San Juan River. Instead of finding, as he
expected, a steamboat ready to convey him on his way, he is informed
that she has been wrecked in the river and that he must either take passage
in a bungo, or find his way across by land. Some take the land route,
traversing forests in which dwell myriads of bright-plumaged birds, chattering monkeys, and numerous other animals. By far the greater portion
embark in bungoes, a clumsy kind of canoe made of the trunks of immense trees, partly covered with an arch of palm leaves and managed by

---

* *Among those discouraged by the lengthy sea voyage was William Swain's traveling
companion, Oliver Goldsmith, who later wrote: "After twenty-eight days on the water
. . . I was quite fascinated by the idea of a trip under such different conditions. I therefore
decided to leave the ship at this port and secure a passport, hiring a horse, and engaging my
guide, I started on the journey."*

    The Panama Star *reported November 14, 1850, that "about two thousand persons"
had crossed Nicaragua, traveling from Realejo to San Juan.*

a pole or paddle. After a while they find themselves in the insignificant little town of San Juan. Here they find that it is all humbug about the 'regular line,' and they are compelled to take passage on some little sloop bound to Chagres or Havana if they are so fortunate as to find any there, or else wait for the semimonthly British steamer which touches at Chagres on her passage home."]*

I didn't like the journey in the hot sun in this latitude, as I was yet weak from the effects of an attack of diarrhea, so I concluded to come on down to Panama.

We left Realejo on the twelfth of this month and have had a tedious passage on account of calms, but shall soon be on land again, I hope.

I intend to spend two or three days at Panama and its vicinity, and then take passage for New York City by way of Havana, where I intend spending a few days; I feel anxious to see this country now that I am here.

I shall write when I get to New York City. Give my love to all inquiring friends. Tell George that I'll soon be at home again. Ah!! Home again. Kiss Sis for me. I tell you all, I feel as though I was almost home, for I know that the steamer will make distance short.

William

[The *Mosconome* dropped anchor off Panama City on Christmas Day, 1850. Swain came ashore and stayed four days in the ancient Spanish city. While there, he wrote a few lines to his family advising them of his arrival and plans to cross the Isthmus. Nothing more. Why his silence, when he knew that George would delight to read about so historic a place, with ruins of great cathedrals? He would be home in a few weeks—he would wait and tell everything then.**

["The celebrated city of Panama from the anchorage looks like most old Spanish towns, dingy and antiquated—the dilapidated walls crumbling into the sea, somber-looking rows of houses with red-tiled roofs, numerous old churches, the tall towers of the Cathedral, whose lofty spires glisten in the sun with a coating of pearl-oyster shells. . . .

---

* On December 1, 1850, the Panama Star carried a story that "a British steamer arrived at Chagres a few days since, bringing down 480 passengers from San Juan."

** Three other homeward-bound goldseekers traveling at almost the same time as Swain wrote extensive accounts of all they saw while crossing the Isthmus: Isaac Lord, who landed at Panama City in March 1851; J. Goldsborough Bruff, who landed in June; and E. H. N. Patterson, who was there in December 1850, the same month as Swain. By combining these descriptive records with other diaries and letters written in late 1850 and early '51, an eyewitness narrative has been created to recount what Swain probably saw and experienced.

Ship Niantic receiving her
Passengers at
Panama.

Panama City as seen by tens of thousands of goldseekers journeying to or from California. This drawing, reproduced from the log book of the *Niantic*, was dated June 1849. Later beached, used as a warehouse and then as a hotel, the *Niantic* became one of San Francisco's most famous landmarks.

NATIONAL MARITIME MUSEUM, SAN FRANCISCO

["Now there is excitement and confusion on board—getting out baggage and leaving the ship. Swarms of boats and canoes come alongside, with a war of words in many languages, English and Spanish predominating. . . ." "The boats come to the ships to convey the passengers ashore and charge $2. . . . On approaching the landing, the natives wade out to meet the boats. . . . The passengers mount the backs of the natives and are carried through the surf to the landing for 50 cents more."

["The natives attach themselves like leeches to each particular thing and seem to regard it as their own property for the time being. They want a dollar for carrying each parcel into the city. . . .

["From the narrow beach . . . you ascend a few feet to a dilapidated platform of stone masonry . . . which seems to have been an arcade-front to a boat landing at high tide. The whole was once roofed over and must have been very pretty, if not grand and imposing. . . . A shattered fragment of roof which once sheltered the proud, lordly Don from sun and rain now only overshadows displays of greasy-looking bar soap . . . and all kinds of tropical fruit and cheap trinkets and fancy goods and bolognas and watches, hats and shoes, beads and cakes, red peppers and ribbons, knives and cattle entrails, men and women, dogs and babies, parrots and monkeys, and nondescripts."

["The main portion of the city, in which are located the public buildings, churches, etc., is surrounded by a massive wall, with a gate opening upon the sea on the east and one towards the country on the west. . . . Most of the business of the city is done within the walls, the circumference of which is from one and a half to two miles and which contains perhaps 3,000 inhabitants.

["The buildings of the city are mostly brick and stone, three stories high. . . . Three-fourths of the front rooms of the basement stories are occupied as small stores or grog shops, which . . . are mostly kept by Spanish women, all vivacious and rather pleasing in their manners. . . . Americans can address them only in their newly acquired Spanish and, of course, make awkward work of it."

["The streets run at right angles, or nearly so. They are narrow, and some of them not the cleanest, while the alleys, courts, and by-places are filthy beyond description. Licentiousness walks the streets unblushingly and is the rule. . . . The whites are very indolent, lounging in their hammocks all day, and the browns are lazy. Some few are busy a part of the time." "Everybody—man, woman, and child—smokes cigars and drinks wine and liquor; but seldom is a native seen drunk, though it is quite common to see a drunken foreigner. . . . Most of the Americans appear to have thrown aside all restraint and give loose rein to evil practices. . . . All, with scarcely one exception, appear to be actuated by no other principle than selfishness or passion."

["American traders have stores along the principal streets where goods of all kinds are kept, but at prices ranging at a very high rate." "All the hotels are kept by Americans except one, and that by a Negro who was once a servant in a hotel in New York, and he keeps the best hotel in the place. But they are all miserable, poor affairs—poor food, badly cooked; no beds, eight to twelve dirty cots in a room and everything else to match. Board from $8 to $12 a week." "One might easily imagine himself in New York from the signs he will read both day and night, for the streets are hung with transparencies behind which is placed a light and all sorts of familiar names are displayed: The Corporal, Uncle Sam, Washington House, New York Hotel, etc. etc." "The Mansion House has a first-story canvas ceiling, second story no ceiling; partitions ten feet high, then nothing forty feet to the crisscross, crotched timbers of the roof on which tile are laid. Sleep on canvas berths." But efforts to sleep "are in vain, what with the infernal barking of long-tongued curs, the monotonous yet melodious song of a bevy of señoritas not far off, the tiresome hum-drum of a fiddle and bones at a neighboring fandango, the rowdy yells of a crowd of drunken emigrants . . . and the clock of the old cathedral chiming out the hours. . . ." "The bell-ringers attached to the different churches seem to vie with one another to see which can produce the most outrageous noises on their cracked bells. Morning, noon, and night there is a constant clang and clatter of iron tongues. . . ."

[Almost every day goldseekers bound for California "come into the city from Chagres; some òn mules, some on foot, muddy and weary, and some dejected and apparently homesick, and occasionally one swung in a hammock tied to a stake, borne on the shoulders of two natives: that is when they are sick and unable to ride. . . . Every steamer now brings some females, many of them bad characters. Frequently these females, for convenience in crossing the mountains, put on men's clothes.

["Most of the emigrants seem borne up with the prospect of golden reward, thinking no doubt that their troubles on the Isthmus are ended and that they will speedily embark on some swift-gliding steamer for El Dorado. But, alas, many have to wait for weeks before they can get away. The agents in New York represent to all that they will not have to stop here more than one or two weeks at the farthest. Yet many do not get away for eight to ten weeks, and they perhaps sell their tickets at a sacrifice on steamers that they have found out too late will not be here for weeks and buy tickets on other steamers at enormous prices, or go on sailing vessels with the prospect of being at sea seventy-five to ninety days. . . . While the tickets are low, speculators buy them and hold on until the steamer comes in and then sell them for one or two hundred percent, which puts them out of the power of the majority to buy.

["The number of persons here waiting for passage . . . at times has been at least two thousand. . . . There is very great complaint at the wrong done to passengers by owners of the steamers in New York in sending them on here when they know they will be detained for weeks, endangering their lives and at heavy expense. A majority of those who come after they have bought their tickets in New York have hardly enough to pay their expenses across the Isthmus, and that is soon consumed here."

["It may be said of Panama with almost as much truth as it is of California: 'tis distance lends enchantment to the view. In wandering about the city, the miserable poverty everywhere manifest; the degeneracy of the race who occupy rude huts near the substantial mansions erected by the early settlers; the ignorance which characterize the populace—these sober, practical realities are not compatible with the romance with which the city was invested at first view."

["The traveler has the choice of three modes of transportation to cross the Isthmus from Panama to Cruces or Gorgona {the heads of navigation on the Chagres River}. He may go on foot and pay a native for toting his baggage, a duty which one man will perform if the weight he is required to sole-cart be less than two hundred pounds; or he may hire a mule to pack his baggage; or, again, if too feeble to walk across, he may ride a mule. . . . As for crossing in a vehicle of any kind, unless it be a hammock suspended from a pole resting on the shoulders of a couple of natives, it is a matter of utter impossibility. . . .*

["Great numbers of natives with their framework packs run hither and yon about the hotels, eagerly . . . indicating their willingness to make pack horses of themselves for a reasonable remuneration." "Mules, which abound, congregate around the Plaza, and all is bustle and noise and confusion. . . . Most of the packing is now done by the Americans, who hire all the mules and pack them through, making a dollar or two on each for their trouble and risk. This is designed to prevent a heap of mistakes and many difficulties, as a foreigner with three or four words of Spanish usually deems himself fit for a government interpreter at least, and never stops to consider whether the natives understand him or not. . . ."

["The rainy season has entirely passed and for the next three or four months the weather will be hot and dry. . . . This dry season is the best time for crossing the Isthmus. During this period the road between Panama and Gorgona becomes dry and the travel good. After May the heavy rains make it sloughy and slippery, causing danger from mules falling or sinking into a slough from which very frequently they cannot be extricated. During the dry season the Cruces road is seldom traveled, as it is much rougher and more rocky."]

Panama, December 29, 1850

Dear Friends,

I arrived at this place on Christmas and have been waiting for the arrival of the steamers at Chagres, which will be about the 6th of January.

We leave here in the morn for Gorgona and thence to Chagres, from

---

* *Not quite an impossibility, for a Mrs. Gillingham in September 1850 employed an unusual vehicle when traveling from Panama to Cruces. "Having neglected to provide herself with a Bloomer costume, she had either to ride a mule attired in her usual dress . . . or submit to the novel mode of riding on the back of a nude native, lashed in a chair. She adopted the latter mode of conveyance. . . ."*

whence we shall probably leave for New York on the 8th, via Havana. I am well, and the health of this place is good. Considerable sickness in Chagres.

Goodbye,
William

[After five days in Panama City, Swain resumed his journey on December 30, heading for Gorgona about twenty-two miles distant.

["We move off up a narrow street—a long, straggling train of mules and men, women and children, natives and horses and dogs, etc. . . . We soon pass out at one of the gateways of massive stone masonry, and crossing a broad ditch, emerge . . . into the suburbs, bigger by half than the walled city. . . . It seems to be inhabited entirely by Negroes and mixed brown races. They dress for the most part in white, generally sprigged with blue or pink; the houses are, if possible, more dilapidated than in the city. . . .

["As we pass on, the houses are slighter and slighter, the people more and more naked, and the road more out of repair, while the land is more uneven. On the left is a considerable mountain. At short distances you find warm water, liquors, and sometimes three or four kinds of unpalatable bread. Many a good temperance man here finds in the bad water, already poisoned, an excuse for taking some dirty poisonous spirit, to neutralize it. . . .

["A few miles out, the street runs almost imperceptibly into a paved road, seven feet wide, with rough curbstones on each side. It leads to Cruces, and we are to follow it several miles before we turn off to the left for Gorgona. It is generally very well preserved, in some places much broken and in some places almost obliterated—nothing but the mule trails showing its course." "It is stated that Pizarro, the conqueror of Peru, ordered the paving of this road, which was done with large round stones sometimes a foot-and-a-half in diameter. Since Panama sank into insignificance, this pavement has been entirely neglected and is now completely broken, and the big stones are lying loose and in great disorder. . . . It is only astonishing that the mules are capable of passing at all over these loose heaps of round stones with a load on their backs."

["The road is shaded nearly half the time and gets better as we progress. . . . There is a lingering and lagging behind—sore feet and lame legs, weary backs. A great many wayfarers stop at the Half-way House, fagged out. The hard pavement with its washboard surface and

On the trail to Gorgona.

broken grade is passed and the road becomes more rough and hilly. . . . Sometimes we find the path cut down almost perpendicularly on each side, ten feet or more, ascending and descending through banks of red and yellow clay . . . deep enough to hide a mule or horse. . . ." "These ravines gradually widen to twenty or thirty feet at the top. At the bottom, such has been the constant tread of mules that their feet have worn tracks in the solid rock, four or five inches deep. In going over this route they appear to understand every track in which to put their feet. When mule-teers are about to enter these gorges or gullies, they raise a halloo to prevent others who may chance to be at the opposite end from entering, as it would be impossible to pass each other should they meet. In fact, persons on foot in order to pass each other, one party has to submit to be clambered over, which is often done. Such is the depth and narrowness of these trails and the density of growth overhanging the top that a man's voice is conveyed as through a tin tube."]

[Beyond these gorges "one can hardly get more than a yard or two from the path without a cutting instrument. . . . The forest is one mass of tangled vines, thorns, trees and leaves." "Indeed, the growth . . . is such that it is said to be the lurking places of tigers, wolves, monkeys and anacondas that can wind themselves on the branches and reach down and take up an ox or mule with ease. . . ."

[The jungle trail came to the banks of the Chagres River at Gorgona, the head of navigation "with two or three American frame buildings which are used for hotels and warehouses. The rest, amounting to about 150 Indian dwellings, consists of huts made of canes and covered with long dried leaves commonly taken from palm trees. The number of inhabitants changes with the season and during business time is about five hundred. . . ." Here the native boatmen waited to carry passengers downriver in canoes and flat-bottomed boats—fare, $2 to $5.

[After a night's rest at a Gorgona hotel, "we had our baggage down to the landing, a beautiful gravel bar or beach of some thirty or forty acres on the bend of the river where the boats lie. After a great deal of getting on board and off and moving and shifting and fretting and crowding and scolding and swearing, we finally shoved off . . . in a long, flat-bottomed boat. Before we got ten rods, we ran ashore. The boat does not mind her rudder more than a spoiled child does its mother. . . .

["After four hours out, our boat has been aground three times. Passed a steamer fast on a bar, tugging and twisting with steam, rope and pole to get loose; she turned round and ran stern foremost awhile. . . . Now we leak. Landed, caulked, and tallowed and off we drift again. . . ."

[On another boat, "a good strong launch with awning fore and aft . . . rowed by four yellow, half naked natives and owned and commanded by a Long Island Negro named Williams," the five passengers "were cheerful and agreeable and drifted on as pleasantly as possible, having to aid them . . . a box of ale, several bottles of claret and a couple of brandy, with crackers, cheese, cigars, pipes and tobacco."

["We have met a number of boats . . . going downriver but none coming up. The tide will turn the other way when the steamers come in at Chagres.

["Passed a tent-town on the right bank with a large wooden building, where Americans are at work on the railroad. . . . Twenty-four miles from Gorgona we passed a wooden city on the right bank, another railroad depot, where the grade lies directly along the river for a mile or more and is mostly done except for the culverts. . . . The whole will soon be done to the crossing above Gorgona. . . ."*

["The river is exceedingly crooked and enclosed between high hills, covered with thick forests and dense shrubbery down to the water's edge.

---

* *In fact, work progressed slowly on the Panama Railroad. As of December 1850, some 600 men were employed on the project, but working conditions, desertion, and disease took a heavy toll. Mortality among the workers ran at 50 percent at the end of three months' work and 80 percent after four months.*

Palms, bananas, rich vines, reeds, majestic plants, and beautiful flowers crowd upon the stream in lavish luxuriance, and the reflection of this mass of verdure gives the water a rich green and gorgeous aspect. . . . Herons, blue and white, and vultures with white shoulders, occasionally add to the diversity of the scene."

["This country is infested with large numbers of Chileans, Peruvians, Costa Ricans and other South Americans whose chief occupation for years past has been plunder and raping—and as this Isthmus now presents the richest field for operations, they are flocking here in numbers too great for the safety of life and property." One report told of the theft of $120,000 in gold dust.

["Some time after dark the captain ordered our boat ashore on the right bank, where from the lights there appeared to be several houses. . . . Discovered a large, one-story building or shed kept by an American. . . . There were quite a number of passengers here from New Orleans for California—several women and some children. Supper was served at least decently . . . but there were no beds. . . . A few men slept on the boat.

["Rose at 4 A.M. . . . and all is instantly bustle, so that very soon we are again drifting down the river. . . . We came to the railroad again, and here the rails are down and the road in operation, for just as we dropped alongside a handcar came rattling along the track and was loudly cheered by our passengers. There are quite a number of American houses here. They tell us that many of the hands are sick. Our informants were sitting on a low ledge of rocks fishing, and looked sickly enough, sure."

["On the banks of this river, along which hundreds of boats are daily passing and where the solitude of the forest is continually broken by the voices of men, we see parrots swinging upon the branches, monkeys chattering among the trees with an air of impudence and self-security, alligators sunning their unwieldy carcasses on logs, and even a South American tigress {jaguar}, followed by numerous progeny, walking boldly down to the water's edge, as our boat glides along near the shore."

["Landed at Chagres. It is located on both sides of the river, at its very mouth." "It has grown into temporary importance, like all other points on the Isthmus, from its connection with the immense amount of travel to and from California. It has no natural advantages whatever to recommend it . . . having no harbor whatever and being the very pesthouse of disease. The completion of the railroad to Gorgona . . . will deprive it not only of fame but of inhabitants, for the population will remove en masse to Navy Bay six miles distant, the eastern terminus of the railroad.

["The original town, now called the 'native town,' is situated on the south bank of the river on a sloping hillside. . . . The houses are all of the palm-thatched order except a few frame buildings, one occupied by the British Consul and another by a Yankeeized native hotelkeeper. . . . The principal street is lined with shops. . . . There are also a number of billiard rooms which are well patronized, for the natives are madly addicted to play.

["The emigrants, to and fro, always stop on what is called the American side, located on a low flat over which are scattered a large number of frame houses occupied as stores, warehouses or hotels. The place has sprung into existence as it were in a night, and when the stimulus that is now its life shall be withdrawn, it will wither as speedily." "The hotels, which have assumed the names of the crack houses in New York, as the Irving House, United States Hotel, etc., are perfect hog-holes and hardly fit for a dog to eat at—furniture, food, and everything filthy."

["Passengers down the river are constantly arriving. They complain of hard fare and being swindled at every turn." "Stories of murders and robberies on the river and thefts perpetrated on mule trains crossing from Panama are rife in the town all the time. We were told that stragglers had been waylaid, dragged into the thick copse that lined the road, there robbed of everything; that organized bands infested the whole route, embracing every opportunity for highway robbery. . . . Only a few weeks before a specie train had been attacked and a large amount of dust stolen. Rumors were afloat of murders very recently committed on the river. But no investigation was instituted by the American Consul to discover the perpetrators."

["Here at Chagres the shores on either side of the river, which is here 200 to 300 yards wide, are lined with boats and canoes of all sizes and descriptions, covered, half-covered, and open. . . . A large sign in one street is very conspicuous and reads thus: 'No Nuisance!' On a high rocky point is an old fort, a miniature Gibraltar, on and in solid rock. It must have cost a mint of money, but is now in ruins—everything crumbling down. The cannon are there, but useless; and the town is there, but not worth defending if anybody should be foolish enough to want it.

["The mass of the inhabitants in the American town (and there may be a daily average of 800 or 1,000) are natives, who are mostly Negroes, the descendants of Spanish slaves . . . and mulattoes from different parts, mostly Jamaica. These last are as saucy, impudent, active and strong as white men and know as well the worth of money. They are the workies of the country, though the railroad employs some of the natives (a very inoffensive race) at 50 cents a day. The great manager and prime mover here is the citizen of the United States. Much of the smaller business is carried on by foreigners, mostly Jews."

["You cannot turn a corner here or enter a hotel or grocery without encountering a roulette table, with its ever-revolving wheel, or a monte bank with its little pile of specie, and the hangdog look of the banker who is constantly endeavoring to attract customers. Small deposits, it is true, are made here, for of all gambling this of Chagres is the most contemptibly mean in point of risks ventured. Around a table you can at all times see a complete, practical amalgamation of the races: the sooty Negro who risks his dime on 'de turkee buzzard,' as they term the eagle in the roulette; the native and Negro halfbreed who ventures the earnings of a week on a single card; the moody and discontented emigrant who perchance may risk a XX {"double sawbuck," i.e., $20} in an effort to retrieve his fallen fortunes; the ferocious and villainous-looking boatman who recklessly wins or loses with equal indifference—assured that if unsuccessful, his craft will put up the fare next day, especially if the steamer is about to sail.

["The boatmen are, for the most part, the roughest specimens of humanity imaginable—American, Irish and Dutch, with a sprinkling of England's freemen. They rule with such rigid sway that the natives dare not enter into competition with them; even the owners of the small river-steamboats fear personal violence and the destruction of their property if they should offer to carry passengers to and from the ocean steamers. The steamers' own boats are not even permitted to land emigrants. The result of all this is that the emigrants to and from the steamers are necessarily subjected to most extortionate charges; and the American national name is brought into disrepute by the mongrel crowd who claims to be and are recognized as Americans. . . .

["A fever of excitement pervades among the numerous emigrants here . . . when a faint outline of smoke is discovered seaward a long way off on the horizon, denoting the approach of a steamer. Some emigrants hold tickets for the *Cherokee* for New York; some for the *Philadelphia* direct to New Orleans; others for the *Pacific* for New York and New Orleans by way of Havana. Which boat is it? Eager eyes watch her approach. Eager hearts await her coming. All desire to be the first away.

["When she reaches her anchorage, a small boat is dispatched with the purser, who comes ashore to countersign and register tickets. When this is announced, a rush for tickets is occasioned at the reception window. . . . You have seen crowds—at elections, in barrooms, around the tavern fire on a cold night, at the table on the ringing of a dinner bell, at a horse race or a dog fight—well, just condense these, imagine their united pressure increased by the power of a hydraulic press, and you begin to approximate . . . the jams that weekly occur about the steamer offices at Chagres."]

Chagres, January 8, 1851

Dear Friends,

I arrived here on New Year's evening and have been here since, waiting for arrival of steamers. The *Cherokee* arrived yesterday morn and leaves tomorrow, and I send this by A. M. Nichols, who is from Ranals Basin on the [Erie] Canal below Lockport. He leaves in the *Cherokee* and will probably arrive in New York two days before I do, from which place he will transmit it by mail. The *Falcon* is due today, and I will sail in her for New York via Havana on the 10th or 11th. I have taken a ticket and with good luck may be in New York on or by the twenty-second or third instant.

I have had a pleasant trip on the Isthmus and have found much to interest me, employing my time as well as possible in seeing and observing. I shall have something to say about this country and its inhabitants.

I expect much from my visit to Havana, and I am almost in fidgets for fear Jenny [Lind] may leave before I arrive; but I shall have a time there anyhow, if the steamer lays long enough.*

I have had excellent health since I arrived on the Isthmus, in fact I am getting boyish in my spirits. I have enjoyed myself more since I arrived here than on all this tramp before and have the prospect of getting home!! with good health and high spirits and some money in pocket, for all of which I feel that I am very lucky. I feel that as I cast off the cares of toil and business while on this route home, the spirit of youth is still o'er me. Yes, I believe I shall arrive at home the same person in spirit and *principle* as when I left the home of youth. No—absence, time and distance have not cooled the attachment of relatives; exposure and toil have not injured my health, and no temptation nor circumstance has ever for one moment induced me to *violate principle*, the conscientiousness of

---

* *Jenny Lind's itinerary included Havana in the early part of January 1851. Heralded by P. T. Barnum as the "Swedish Nightingale," she had arrived in New York on September 4, 1850, and her reception suggests that Swain was not alone in having the "fidgets" at the prospect of hearing her. "Tickets for her first concert [in New York] were sold at auction. . . . They were mostly bought up by speculators who subsequently sold them at from $25 to $225! The gross sales yielded upwards of $26,000. New Yorkers have gone stark raving mad about the nightingale."*

Looking toward the mouth of the Chagres River and the town of Chagres, to the right.
HENRY E. HUNTINGTON LIBRARY

which I would not yield for any compensation this world could give.

I shall write as soon as I arrive in New York. Give my love to all.

William

P.S. The booming of a cannon has just passed over this silent place and probably the *Falcon* has dropped anchor in the bay.

["Boats loaded with passengers are going to or coming from the different ships all the time, though the wind is quite fresh and the surf rolls in strong, so that some of the boats are two or three hours in rowing out. . . . From the shore the passage looks perilous, but it is safe with a sober crew. There is real danger, however, in getting on board, the boats rising and falling some five to ten feet and the ship's rolling and pitching sometimes brings the iron stairs with a crash onto the bow of the boat, nearly overturning it."

[The dangers and excitement that Swain probably experienced in boarding the *Falcon* were described by another passenger headed for New York. "Our ship was lying at least two miles from the shore, and when our boat reached her, we found ourselves on the outside rank of some eighty or a hundred similar crafts and numerous others crowding in upon

old Town   New Town,

us. The steamer rolling heavily from side to side; the boats crashing against each other as they alternately rose and fell with the waves; the boatmen swearing, expostulating, and explaining; the rushing for the step across the boat-bridge; cries; threats; yells—all served to render worse-confounded the confusion caused by the winds and waves.

["At length all were aboard, baggage stowed away, and a partial calm prevailed among the excited throng. The last boat had left the steamer's side. The anchor was hauled in. The paddles revolved and we are—not off yet, quite. We thought we were, but all at once it was recollected that the United States mail was not yet on board.

["So eager are emigrants to proceed on their journey when they have progressed thus far on their return that they seldom stop to demur at the treatment they receive, or the dangers and risks they incur in taking passage upon one of these crowded vessels. Steerage passengers particularly (and these are the great majority) are compelled to stifle their feelings of pride and succumb to treatment which under other circumstances they would revolt at. They must sit around their little victual tub and swallow their beef and potatoes without a murmur, they must meekly yield to be crowded together like so many cattle, and to sleep without complaint upon a single blanket. If they are sick, they must not expect any attention —and they are wise if they call not upon the ship's surgeon, for it is sometimes very convenient to pay professional fees with the dead stranger's money.

["This is a very faint sketch of the realities of a trip, but it is nothing in comparison with the real danger that the passenger is always in of sacrificing his life to the culpable negligence of the owners of the vessel. A more complete mantrap could not be devised than one of these steamers. . . . The marine laws of the United States require passenger vessels to carry boats sufficient to carry all the passengers in case of any disasters. Yet . . . for 600 persons our ship carries two boats that would hold about fifty men. What then, in case of accident, are the other 550 to do? This is a matter upon which the minds of the officers are at rest—the passage money has been paid and every man must look out for himself."

[On board the *Falcon* a passenger found that 483 others had bought tickets for New York, at $80 each. "There ought not to have been more than 150 passengers on board." Between Chagres and Havana cholera took the lives of thirteen passengers, all buried at sea.

[Like most ships bound for New York, the *Falcon* regularly stopped at Havana, where the passengers went ashore to seek a brief respite from the ship's discomforts and dangers. More than Panama, Cuba aroused the nationalism of Americans, for unlike most Central and South American countries which had achieved independence, the island remained under the rule of Spain. Talk of overthrowing Spanish despotism was common in the United States, as it was in the letters and diaries of goldseekers who landed at Havana on their way to or from California.

[A passenger on the steamer *Pacific*, bound from Chagres to New York, wrote in his diary: "We steamed under the frowning gray walls of Moro Castle which stands gloomily at the entrance of the harbor to protect the lovely and affluent city. Who in these days when Cuban invasion has been so prolific a theme for fireside gossip and newspaper paragraphs has yet to hear for the first time the name of this world renowned fortification? The Spanish look upon it as being impregnable. Let them beware how they tamper with Yankee Doodle or they may see their mistake! The topic most indulged in by passengers entering this port is—what a country this would be if it was only in the Union. And how easy a matter it would be for the United States to make themselves master of this Garden Spot of the world."

[Sharing this judgment, another goldseeker proclaimed: "Cuba belongs to the United States by the ties of contiguity and natural relation. It is a beautiful island, in fact everything is perfect in our view but the government. The people are very civil to Americans as we, of course, think they ought to be. . . . We only need one man to ten Spaniards to Yankeeize man, woman and child, island and all."]

January 28, 1851
Lovejoy Hotel, New York City

Dear Sabrina,

I arrived here by the *Falcon* in bad health, as you have probably learned by my telegraphic dispatch to George at the Falls.

I was attacked with Chagres fever the day before I left Chagres and was very sick all the passage.

[The symptoms and distress of Chagres fever tormented another emigrant, stricken a few days before his departure for New York on board the *Crescent City:* "I had a slight chill, followed by burning fever." As the ship steamed across the Caribbean, "I was quite indifferent to the things around me, having a burning fever and raging thirst. Whatever I took, I immediately threw up, except water. . . . My bones ached so that I had no comfort."]

Through the Goodness of God I am now recovering slowly. I was so low when I arrived here that I had to be assisted from the boat to the carriage, and that you know for me is very low.

I took room at this tavern where I have had the attention of a good physician (though I have needed very little advice or medicine) and the very attentive care of the landlord. I am now quite free from all pain or disease, feel well and enjoy what I eat with good taste and can get anything that the doctor and landlord think best for me to eat at very low prices and of the very best kind.

I shall very likely be strong enough to start for home in three days. My severe weakness was mostly the result of exposure and inability to get any suitable nourishment on the steamer.

Now, do not any of you be at all worried about my being injured by my journey home by railroad, for I shall not travel when it will injure me. I shall be at home as soon as prudence will allow. So do not be at all worried about me. I shall, with the blessing of God, be once again in the family circle at home. Give my love to all. Kiss the child for me. This writing tires my hand, so goodbye for two or three days.

Your affectionate husband,
William

P.S. If I receive any pullback in my health, I will let you know of it.

Friday, January 31, 1851
Lovejoy House, New York
10 1/2 P.M.

Dear Mother and Sister,

I got here yesterday about 2 o'clock and found Will about 4 o'clock, half an hour after I started to look for him. When I arrived, he had gone out into the street two or three doors for the first time. He looked pretty thin in flesh, dark in color, and shabby in dress, and taken by and large was a hard-looking customer. But he is rapidly on the mend. They had kept him on very light food, but we took supper together, and this morning he ate some raw oysters, and at supper, buttered toast, fried onions, buckwheat cakes, cabbage and vinegar, and a couple of raw oysters.

He has felt well all day. We have been strolling around the city most of the day and this evening took a shoot through Barnum's Museum. He has just gone to bed and says he feels well, without being tired.

He tells me he wrote home on Wednesday and told you all about his sickness. He was taken with Chagres fever the day before he sailed on the *Falcon* and was sick all the way here. When he got here he was very weak and low, and had been very sick. But now his disease is gone and he seems in a fair way to soon be well again.

We intend to start from here for Boston tomorrow morning at 8 o'clock, get there about 5 o'clock, stay there over Sunday, go to Lowell Monday, and Tuesday start for home; and we hope to get there on Thursday but may not, for we may be longer at Lowell. We both want to get home soon as we can. I want to be back in my place, as I had no opportunity of seeing Mr. Cook before I left. I should like to stay here three or four days but can't.

I should have telegraphed to you last night but I was so busy talking to Will that it was too late before I thought of it, and today we were busy and forgot it till too late—probably because I thought you would get this letter as soon as a telegraph.

If anything happens we will telegraph you. If I telegraph from here tomorrow before I start, you would not get it before Monday's mail. I am quite well. Kiss "Lila" for Uncle George and for Pa too, though he is asleep now.

Now don't be in a sweat. I have told you exactly the truth. Since yesterday, Will has gained as fast as any person I ever saw.

May God bless you all, and a blessed night.

Yours as ever,
George Swain

Wednesday afternoon, February 5, Sabrina received George's telegram from Boston—he and William would arrive by train in Niagara Falls, Thursday morning.

By noon almost everyone in Youngstown had heard the news. Neighbors and friends from as far as Lewiston came to the cobblestone house to wait with Sabrina, Mrs. Swain and Eliza. Dr. and Mrs. Root were there, the Bullocks who lived on River Road just south of the Swain farm, Mr. Burge who owned the village store, and other Youngstown friends. Sabrina's parents, Mr. and Mrs. Barrett, and her sister Harriet were there. Through the past two years they had all shared Sabrina's anxiety, welcomed her reading William's letters and vicariously experienced the great adventure. Now he was coming home and they wanted to be part of the closing scene.

Friends and relatives reminded Eliza again and again that her father was coming home. Usually a friendly child, she felt shy as more and more people crowded into the house, and she missed Uncle George. She cried for attention and clung to Sabrina, for whom the hours passed with painful slowness.

Sabrina's brother, Ozro, had driven the Barretts' sleigh to the train station in Niagara Falls to meet William and George. By noon they were approaching Lewiston. The snow had turned to slush after a day of sunshine. The horses moved at a quick pace without urging.

Ozro reined in the team at the top of Lewiston Hill, not far from the Barretts' farm. William stood in the sleigh and looked across the forested plain below, bordered on the west by the gorge of the Niagara River, north to the village of Youngstown, and beyond he could see the blue of Lake Ontario. A moment to savor. He put his hand on George's shoulder and, feeling a surge of emotion, he spoke. "I have been many miles and seen many places, but this is the finest sight I have ever seen."

For the last few miles from Lewiston Hill to Youngstown, Ozro drove the team at an ever faster pace. Familiar sights slipped past; farmhouses and great walnut trees reminded William of the many times he had ridden along River Road to the Barrett farm to see Sabrina before their marriage.

As the sleigh glided up to the house, a score of people shouted their welcome. Sabrina stood alone; she felt self-conscious when she looked into William's eyes; she waited for him to jump down and come to her. Relatives and friends were quiet as they watched the '49er embrace his wife.

By dark the house was quiet. William sat in the kitchen with his mother, Eliza on his lap, while Sabrina nervously prepared dinner. George had gone outside to talk with Harriet and Ozro before they drove the sleigh back to Lewiston. He came in with a large box, which he handed to William. A few minutes later Sabrina held up a black satin dress her husband had purchased in New York.

Twenty-two months after he had left, William Swain returned from San Francisco. In the years ahead, Sabrina and George would share February 6 as the end of their long vigil, while for William that date marked the renewal of his life as a husband, father and farmer.

Across the United States in villages, towns and cities, hundreds—eventually thousands—of wives and their returning husbands felt the emotions of welcome and anxiety. After years when letters had provided the only reassurance of love and faithfulness, they returned to marriage. More than a sense of uncertainty or alienation might separate them for a time. Like soldiers home from far places, the goldseekers came back with new ideas and changed values, and within a few weeks or months many felt restless and impatient. Remembering the pace of life in California, the ease of obtaining credit from merchants, the anonymity which assured freedom to act as one wished, they resented old-fashioned rules of business and hometown curiosity and gossip. In California cities and mining camps they had learned to accept what once they would have judged unacceptable, and some had behaved in ways they knew would be judged harshly by relatives and neighbors.

Everyone who had stayed home had read about the wild ways of California; therefore they thought they knew something about that western world. Their eager curiosity sought answers and stories that would validate their worst assumptions. Most of all, they wanted to ask: "How much gold did you bring home?"

Some gave the answer by paying off a mortgage or old debts, buying a new house, a new business or acreage to enlarge the farm. For these men, California's promise had been fulfilled and their new status in the community obscured problems of personal relationships and made their return a triumph.

Others, anticipating the questions that awaited them, created excuses for empty pockets. In an editorial about homebound goldseekers, the *California Daily Courier* in San Francisco reported that "robberies often occur on the Panama isthmus, of Americans returning from California. We know that most of them have been traced to our own countrymen. And we are aware also that many of these stories of robberies are mere sham. One man reported a loss of $10,000 and made a great story about it, when we *know* he had to borrow the money to get out of San Francisco. Another man got up a good deal of sympathy by reporting that he had been robbed of his 'little all' while asleep at his hotel."

An ex-miner while crossing the Isthmus in late 1850 was crowded from the jungle trail by a train of mules. Forced to step into the underbrush, he saw there a folded blanket—and opening it, he found $4,000 in gold dust. Did he upon his return home admit the truth or pridefully claim to have earned his fortune in the mines?

For most, there were no last-minute twists of fate, no lies to hide failure. There would be no new life, often not even gold enough to ease the transition back to the old life. Disappointed wives and defensive husbands faced questions from creditors (who were often parents or in-laws) about what the goldseekers had accomplished during their months in California. That they returned from the land of gold with little to show gave some neighbors and relatives a chance to question and to whisper.

Swain's family had no doubts, nor anyone else in Youngstown and Lewiston. They knew William. And his letters, with the few that came from Bailey and Hutchinson, had kept the entire neighborhood aware of, even involved in, the California story. So for Swain the return home was comfortable. He and George were quickly back at work as partners on their farm.

Frederick Bailey and Michael Hutchinson gave up their California expectations in late 1851 and, with no greater success than Swain, returned to Youngstown and Buffalo. With his wife and child, Bailey moved to eastern New York and out of the Swains' lives. Hutchinson returned to his farm near Buffalo, remarried and through the years remained a close friend of the Swains, the families exchanging visits once or twice a year. In 1886 Hutchinson sold his farm and bought a house in Eden. That same year he donated $2,000 for the establishment of a town hall, which was named in his honor. He died in 1891 at the age of eighty-five, leaving an estate of $10,000.

John Root came home in 1853. Two years later he was living on a farm he had purchased near Battle Creek, Michigan. But his interests were not in farming. His letters written between 1855 and 1860 were largely concerned with his efforts to perfect a "trunk engine." His debts included a mortgage on the farm. In 1857 he married a woman from Vermont, Maria Boardman. By 1862 they had moved with their daughter to New York City, where he founded the Root Steam Engine Works. His "trunk engine" won first prize in 1867 at the Paris Exposition. An industrialist of some success, Root lived with his family in Europe for several years. He died at age fifty-six in 1886.

Among the Wolverine Rangers, several chose to stay in California. James Pratt found San Francisco to be an ideal city for the practice of law. He formed a partnership with a young attorney from Ithaca, New

York, Cornelius Cole, who had come overland in the summer of 1849. In later years Cole told in his memoirs of their office "in the fine Gothic Hall at the corner of Montgomery and Jackson streets." Reflecting the rough, frontier character of life in San Francisco at that time, Cole recalled that he and Pratt not only practiced law in their office but were accustomed to lodge there as well, "wrapped in blankets on the floor." Pratt died in San Francisco in 1865 at the age of forty-five.

The Reverend Randall Hobart, with his son William, persevered at several mining claims along the South Fork of the Feather River until the early 1860s, when he went into politics and was elected sheriff and then auditor of Nevada County. Later he edited a newspaper. In 1905 his son William achieved some prominence as president of the Society of California Pioneers.

Like Randall Hobart, other Rangers gained success in California politics. Warren T. Sexton (who delivered the major address when the Rangers celebrated the Fourth of July near Fort Laramie) turned from mining on the Yuba River to be elected clerk of Butte County, which encompassed a large area of the northern mines, including the towns of Oroville, Bidwell's Bar and Long's Bar. Oliver Goldsmith, who returned to Detroit after leaving the *Mosconome* at Realejo, made a nostalgic trip to California in 1899. While there, he searched out his Ranger friend Al Frary, whom he found working at a railroad depot in Los Angeles in the winter. Frary spent his summers in the Sierra foothills working his mining claim.

A few Rangers achieved financial success, at least for a time. One, George Van Brunt, made "a fortune" in business in Marysville, but as of May 1851 he had lost most of it "by loaning and giving credit to miners." The most successful Ranger, Morgan Rood, was reported to have accumulated $6,000 by summer 1851.

What happened to Horace Ladd, who wrote so many letters, and to F. C. Cannon and Samuel Moore, Swain's cabinmates on the South Fork, and to Herman and Elmon Camp? Possibly the Camp brothers remained in California, for in the fall of 1850 Herman was operating a muleback express company carrying mail between Marysville and Rich Bar. But more likely they, like the others, returned to "the slow, sure but real business of home." The Marshall newspapers made general references in 1851 and 1852 to various Wolverine Rangers who returned to southern Michigan—none with pockets full of rocks.

J. Goldsborough Bruff arrived home, Washington, D.C., on July 20, 1851. The closing line in his remarkable diary read: "Never before did I so devoutly appreciate the heart-born ballad 'Home! Sweet home!'

. . . and nonetheless that I had 'seen the elephant.' " Isaac Lord and E. H. N. Patterson safely reached their homes in Milwaukee, Wisconsin, and Oquawka, Illinois. So it was in the 1850s—goldseekers returning by the thousands to homes across the nation.

At the Swain farm, William and George in 1855 bought ninety-one adjacent acres and each year thereafter planted more peach trees. As the years passed, the Swain brothers became the major peach farmers in Niagara County. George built himself a home on the new acreage following his marriage in 1852 to Cornelia Cornwall.

Sabrina thrived. She helped William with farm chores, and when time allowed they worked together in their garden by the willow trees in the front yard. In 1854 she gave birth to a son, George. A third child, Sara Sabrina, came in 1860, and their last, Lincoln Fremont, was born in 1863.

When Eliza grew up, she pursued a musical career. She founded a school of music in the town of St. Catherine across Lake Erie in Ontario, Canada. At age thirty-three she married George Raglan Simpson of Toronto, in a ceremony under the willows, June 1881.

George and Cornelia had three children. Always active in Republican politics, George was elected to various local offices, including sheriff of Niagara County in 1860. He died in 1892, age seventy-one, with William and Sabrina at his bedside.

All the Swain children remembered, as highlights of their youth, sitting on the porch of the cobblestone house on summer evenings or inside by the fireplace in winter, listening to William's stories of the overland journey—the hailstorm on the Platte, the Fourth of July celebration at Fort Laramie, the final ascent of the Sierra Nevada, and always the blizzard on Lassen's Cut-off. There were also tales of mining on the South Fork and of San Francisco or the jungles of Panama. Like all '49ers, William relived his great California adventure through the ritual of telling and retelling his stories, sometimes at the request of his and Sabrina's friends or under the urging of George, who would help William remember. The diary was often brought out and consulted for dates and details, and as part of the family's Fourth of July celebration, William's Fort Laramie letter was read for many years. But it was the children as they grew older who most often persuaded William to recollect. The diary remained in the desk drawer as the stories took on dramatic embellishments—until like so many other '49ers, William recalled the gold rush as a grand and glorious moment in history when young men, brave and strong pioneers, had traveled to California where as builders they had helped make the thirty-first state.

Through the many years of their marriage, William and Sabrina were known in Niagara County for their hospitality and the celebrations at The Willows following political victories. On many such occasions, Sabrina wore her black satin dress. Her second daughter, Sara, recalled the most gala occasion of all. On July 6, 1897, her parents celebrated their fiftieth wedding anniversary. Before family and surviving friends, Sabrina stood in that dress and softly proposed a toast: "To my '49er."

On the evening of August 16, 1904, William—aged eighty-three—went out to pick some Concord grapes for Sabrina. He died in his garden. Sabrina lived at The Willows until her death at eighty-seven, in 1912.

Eliza died in the cobblestone house in 1926. Sara stayed on, the last Swain to live in that house built by Isaac and his two sons.

Epilogue

*"California was settled by a sudden rush
of adventurers from all parts of the world.
This mixed multitude, bringing with it a
variety of manners, customs and ideas,
formed a society more mobile and unstable,
less governed by fixed beliefs and principles. . . ."*

The California gold rush made America a more restless nation—changed
the people's sense of their future, their expectations and their values.
Suddenly there was a place to go where everyone could expect to make
money, quickly; where life would be freer, where one could escape the
constraints and conventions and the plodding sameness of life in the
eastern states.

This new California offered more than a chance to dig for gold. Tens
of thousands of men who returned throughout the 1850s—husbands,
sons, fathers, brothers, neighbors, business partners—told of their successes or failures in the mines, but they also talked about businesses that
produced fabulous profits and farmers who sold their produce at unheard-
of prices and a society where no one cared about your background, only
about what you would be doing tomorrow. How sharp the contrast
seemed, between San Francisco and Philadelphia, Marysville and Milwaukee, Sonora and Circleville. Along with stories told and retold and
newspaper accounts, books were being published about the Golden State,
at least fifteen in 1850, thirty by 1855, with more to follow each year.

In the everyday consciousness of the American people, California
could scarcely be believed—immorality openly accepted, cities destroyed
by fire and rebuilt in a matter of weeks, stagecoach and steamship companies competing to carry thousands of miners to and from hill towns and
port cities, traditional rules of personal and business conduct tossed aside
in the hurly-burly of making money. For an ever-increasing number of
Americans, the thirty-first state seemed to offer a robust alternative to
their slow, conventional life in the old thirty.

Always in the past, going west had offered an escape, a new life to farmers, frontiersmen, pioneers, settlers—to the people already on or near the frontier who could cope with an isolated, primitive life; rough men and women willing to struggle for years to own cheap land. California was a new kind of West, not only a place with gold and all it promised, but also a place with business opportunities and new ways of farming. It was suddenly a place of cities and wealth, with newspapers, hotels, theaters, first-class transportation, comforts, even luxuries; a place where city folk could go—men who had never followed a plow, did not know how to shoot a gun, had no calluses on their hands.

For the first time in American history, the West—California—appealed to everyone. That appeal was nurtured not only by what was known and expected of California, but also by the fact that going west no longer was equated with danger and deprivation. One of the consequences of more than 100,000 goldseekers' having traveled overland to California by the fall of 1851 was the presence of blacksmith shops, trading posts, bridges and ferry services along the trails. Shipboard transport had improved as well, with a score of steamers and sailing ships offering passage to Panama or Nicaragua and then to San Francisco in three weeks for a few hundred dollars.

Most susceptible to the new lure of California were the ex-goldseekers who, after six months or maybe a year on their farms in North Carolina or in factories in Pittsburgh, felt "nailed down to inactivity and a life of picayunes." California's new opportunities, remembered freedom and mild climate beckoned to the men who had gone there once for gold and now were ready to return as builders. Their families, their friends, and the men with whom they worked through the long, dreary winters listened to what they said about farming in the Sacramento Valley, about booming cities, new towns being built, and the wages in the mines—$5 to $8 per day versus $1 to $1.25 in eastern coal mines.

In Marshall, Michigan, the *Statesman* reported that Wolverine Rangers were returning to California with their families in 1851. So it was across the country.

But those who returned were few compared to the many California-bound for the first time. Year after year the emigration continued via the year-round Panama and Nicaragua routes and the summer overland trails. The lure of California gold remained so great through the 1850s that more than 30,000 men and a few thousand women from the British Isles, Germany and France sailed around Cape Horn to land in San Francisco. From Asia, an estimated 25,000 Chinese landed by the end of 1852. California and its gold had caused the first worldwide mass migration.

1852 saw the climax of overland travel from the United States. More than 50,000 emigrants, including many more wives and children than in previous years, followed the well-developed trails. While hopes for gold persisted, encouraged by reports of continuing success in the mines, most of the emigrants had heard or read about the realities of life in the diggings. What appealed to farmers and businessmen was the growing awareness that the needs of more than 100,000 miners and the growth of cities had created an astonishing market. *Hunt's Merchants Magazine* in 1852 published a letter from a woman who claimed to have made $18,000 selling pies to the miners. Two acres of onions sold for $2,000. Apples imported from Oregon sold in the mines for $1.50 each. Demand for beef, flour, potatoes, pickaxes, wagons, lumber and more lumber had powered a growth in farming, industry, commerce and services that defied measurement.

Among those tempted by the new world on the Pacific were the California widows who had been waiting for their husbands to return. After two, three, five years of receiving letters that ended with promises of a return "before the next rainy season," after reading about opportunities for women to make money and their right to own property, many of these wives decided to go to California to join or to find their men, with or without their permission. They emptied family savings, borrowed from relatives, or may have received money from the mines. They packed a few possessions and alone or with children traveled with an overland company or by ship.

The experience of one such woman may have exemplified the gumption and newfound independence of others whose stories were never recorded. Lucinda Mann had said goodbye to her gold rush husband, Henry, in spring 1849. Left with four children, the youngest born the previous October, she waited in Albion, Michigan. In February 1851, Henry wrote: "Were it in the nature of things for me to send for you and the children, how gladly would I do so. . . . But this is idle. You cannot come without I am with you."

In spring 1852, Lucinda decided she could wait no longer. With her children, she traveled overland with a company from Michigan. She reached the mining town of Jackson in September, where she learned that Henry had died on May 22. Lucinda stayed; she took over as proprietress of his store. In May 1853, she married a miner named William McKim.

Back in her hometown, the news of Lucinda's good fortune so soon after her sad arrival in California was carried beyond her family circle to other towns. It was news that helped other women break free from the nature of things—from the ingrained judgment that a wife should wait for her husband, no matter how long he was gone.

On the other side of the continent, in the man's world of San Francisco and up in the mining country, an increasing number of "virtuous females" were trying to tame the wild life of the cities and mines. Editorials in San Francisco newspapers boasted that "the arrival of every steamer brings the wives and families of our most respected citizens. Such a thing as HOME is becoming known in San Francisco!" In December 1854 the *Butte Record*, a newspaper printed in Oroville (a town with sixty-five saloons not far from Bidwell's Bar), reported a project that must have aroused the miners' anticipations. "Miss Sarah Pellet is in the up-country regions vigorously pursuing her plans for the amelioration of the condition of Californians. She contemplates the importation to California of 5,000 young ladies from New England. They are to be recommended by the Sons of Temperance in New England as worthy girls, and in advance of their shipment, the different divisions of the Sons of Temperance in California are to agree to receive a certain number of consignments so that each lady will be provided for immediately on her arrival."

The failure of Miss Pellet's endeavor (too few worthy girls willing to be shipped) left the miners—Temperance men and drinkers alike—dependent on the widows, orphans and daughters among the annual immigration: 20,000 overland and 35,000 by sea in 1853. How many women was unknown.

But there were records of other imports, and those records suggest that the Sons of Temperance had failed abysmally in their more traditional endeavor. In the year 1853 California received and presumably drank 20,000 barrels of whiskey; 400 barrels of rum; 9,000 casks, hogsheads and pipes, 13,000 barrels, 2,600 kegs and 6,000 cases of brandy; 34,000 casks and hogsheads, 13,000 barrels and 23,000 cases and boxes of beer; and 5,000 pipes and casks, 6,000 barrels, 5,000 kegs, 8,000 cases and 1,600 packages of "unspecified liquors."

Whatever such consumption said about the moral tone of California (a subject of continuing concern to the editors of newspapers in San Francisco and Sacramento), it did accurately reflect the circumstances of a society of lonely men who—like soldiers and sailors on leave—sought companionship in taverns, grog shops, hotels, and gambling palaces or tents. In all those public places, from the Trinity to the Mariposa, drinking was the common bond—and talking of money-making and home. Many bought rounds of drinks to celebrate their decision to return. More than a few of those with tickets for the voyage drank a toast to the day when they would return to California. Many others watched and listened, wistful, knowing that in their hearts they had come to accept "home" as the symbol of their pre-California life. They felt as one man wrote: "The independence and liberality here and the excitement attending the rapid march of this country make one feel insignificant and sad at the prospect of returning to the old beaten path at home."

Whether with pockets full of rocks or with the burden of failure, whether intent on coming back with their families or swearing to settle down in Maryland, they sailed from San Francisco each year—31,000 men (presumably no women) in 1853, 22,800 in 1855, 27,900 in 1858, 14,500 in 1860.

Throughout the 1850s and later decades, the annual exodus never came close to equaling the influx from the eastern states and around the world. California's population increased 2,500 percent from 1848 to 1852; the 1860 census totaled 380,000 and in 1870 the count came to 560,000. Everyone knew what the census of 1850 affirmed—that women were rare in California: only 8 percent of the population. By 1860 the count of women had increased to 30 percent, but only 2 percent in the mining counties. Most significant in appraising California's uniqueness was the fact that 24 percent of the population in 1850 had come from foreign lands, and that percentage increased to 39 percent in 1860. All previous frontiers had been settled (after the initial advance by hunters, trappers and Indian traders) by agriculturalists, men and women with the same social and cultural backgrounds. Oregon's immigrants (Anglo-Saxon Protestants) had come largely from western farm states. In California, the diverse elements that made up the nation were thrown together for the first time in American history—northern and southern, slave and free, New England townspeople and Iowa farmers, Europeans and now Asians.

California's dynamic intermingling was colorfully reflected in the names of mining camps and towns: German Bar, Iowa Hill, Irish Creek, Cape Cod Bar, Tennessee Creek, Chinese Camp, Georgia Slide, Dutch Flat, French Corral, Michigan Bluffs, Illinoistown, Nigger Hill, Washington, Boston, Bunker Hill, Italian Bar, Dixie Valley, Vermont Bar and Kanaka Bar. And where else in all the world could Irish (33,000 in 1860) and Chinese (35,000) have competed for jobs?

Given the pattern and velocity of change, it was inevitable that rapid advances should be made in mining methods and technology. From the hand-operated machines and the efforts of individual miners and partnerships which had worked the placer deposits during the years 1848–51, mining operations expanded to include large-scale enterprises which developed expensive machinery requiring significant investment. From the years when no capital and little experience were required to work river bars, even to get at riverbeds, the time had come when gold was mined from tunnels, quartz veins, shafts and hydraulic claims.

The first capital-intensive venture was directed at quartz or vein mining. Following pioneer efforts on Frémont's property at Mariposa in 1849, quartz mining attracted a frenzy of investment during 1851–53. Californians and easterners organized a number of companies to finance development and construction of what came to be known as the California stamp mill, to crush quartz into powder and thereby begin the process of separating the gold. The first of these massive machines cost as much as $50,000 to $100,000. To promote the sale of stock, one quartz-mining company issued a circular which promised "the contemplated machinery" would crush enough quartz annually to produce "$240,000,000, a sum sufficient to revolutionize the commercial relations of the world."

Nine out of ten quartz operations failed, leaving behind not only graveyards of complex, costly machinery but thousands of disappointed stockholders from California to England.

In 1853 a far more simple and immediately profitable mining method was developed by a Yankee from Connecticut, a miner named Edward M. Matteson who had been working in the Yuba River diggings. He came up with a simple but dynamic idea: direct a powerful stream of water against a hillside so that the gold-bearing dirt, even though hundreds of feet below the surface, would be disintegrated by the force of the water and washed down to where it could be caught in a series of sluices. The labor-saving advantages of what was called hydraulic mining were profound, as explained by the Sacramento *Weekly Union* in March 1857: "A few years ago men did the work, using water merely as an auxiliary, and the amount of work done depended on the number of men employed. But now the water is used as the laboring agent, and like machinery in manufacturing, only men enough to keep the machinery properly directed are required. Thus banks of earth that would have kept a hundred men employed for months in its removal will now be removed by three or four men in two weeks."

To meet the hydraulic mining companies' insatiable demand for water, companies were formed to finance the construction of ditches, canals and flumes that carried water, often for miles, from a source in the hills down to a point where the water entered a hose connected to a cast-iron nozzle which directed the high-pressure stream against a gold-bearing hillside. With hundreds of miners put out of work by hydraulicking, there were plenty of laborers available to dig ditches, tunnel through ridges and construct flumes. By 1857 they had completed 4,405 miles of these aqueducts at a cost of $11,890,000.

Despite the financial difficulties of quartz mining, the risks and disappointments of river mining, the wastefulness of hydraulicking, and the small returns earned by tens of thousands of individual miners who stubbornly worked their rockers, long toms and dry and river diggings, mining continued to be remarkably productive. By 1857, just ten years after that seminal moment at Sutter's Mill, the total value of gold production exceeded $500 million. And not one dollar had been paid to the Federal Treasury.

Gold financed development of mining, farming, manufacturing, shipping, gambling, banking—the diversity of opportunity that made California universally attractive. By 1860 the value of the state's manufactures far exceeded the value of that year's gold production, and 20,000 farms produced the food supply. Never had there been such a frontier—by 1855 more newspapers were published in San Francisco than in London, more books were published than in all the rest of the United States west of the Mississippi. The per capita wealth exceeded that of any other state.

With the wealth there was as well the dash, daring and recklessness of a society of young men whose vigor and unsatisfied passion dug and blasted tunnels far into the earth, constructed flumes that hung on the face of a cliff and spanned a valley by resting on the tops of trees, cheered opera stars and celebrated every holiday and occasion from the Fourth of July and Washington's Birthday to the British victory over the Russians in the Crimean War, with elaborate parades and drunken sprees.

Such explosive energy could not be contained within the state's boundaries. California sent its men in search of new El Dorados to the most remote reaches of the Far West and at the same time served as the financier, manufacturer and supplier for the new mining frontiers.

In 1852, California miners found gold in southern Oregon, in 1855 on the upper Columbia River, in 1858 in British Columbia. That year more than 23,000 Californians rushed to the Fraser River just across the Canadian border. In 1859–60 they finally did strike it rich—on the east side of the Sierra Nevada. Prospectors working in barren ravines not far from the emigrant trail along the Carson River discovered not only encouraging amounts of gold but great quantities of bluish-black sand which clogged their rockers. After weeks of exasperation, someone shipped a sample to an assay office in Nevada City and learned that the sand was silver, in dazzling concentration. The news caused a stampede from California's northern mines across the Sierra Nevada to what would become known as the Comstock Lode, with Virginia City as the center. More than men, California money crossed the mountains to create companies that would cope with a far more complex geology than anything encountered in California. The gold and silver in the Comstock Lode was mined from massive veins about two miles long, from a dozen to one hundred feet wide, reaching down into the earth a tantalizingly uncertain distance. California's wealth would finance the development of the Comstock, the production of silver worth many millions annually, the trans-Sierra roads and finally the railroads.

California's miners also traveled to Colorado in 1859 and 1860 to join the rush to the fabulous gold discovery at Cripple Creek. So it was throughout the Far West, from British Columbia to Baja California, "everywhere present, everywhere respected, everywhere vital . . . the adopted sons of California—youngest begetter of colonies—carried with them the methods, the customs, the ideas of the mother region."

A mother who fostered get-rich-quick materialism at home and encouraged the rifling of treasures wherever they could be found, California aroused the fears of eastern states' preachers, educators and editorial writers. They warned against the temptress with her bawdy ways and social instability. They held California responsible for changing many Americans from conservative, contented citizens, satisfied with a reasonable return on their investment and toil, to excitable, insatiable speculators who sought "to realize on the resources of the universe in a day." Henry David Thoreau epitomized this concern when he declared in 1862: "The rush to California . . . reflects the greatest disgrace on mankind. That so many are ready to live by luck and so get the means of commanding the labor of others less lucky, without contributing any value to society—and that's called enterprise!"

Few listened to Thoreau and the others, that first generation of California's critics. Their dour judgments and warnings were like whispers against the shouts of success from San Francisco businessmen and Sacramento Valley farmers, stageline and lumber-mill operators, clipper-ship and riverboat owners, lawyers, quicksilver smelters, cattlemen and bankers. These men and thousands more had never heard of Queen Calafia, ruler of an island kingdom. The California they knew looked to the '49ers as heroes of a mythical past, the pan and rocker as symbols of a primitive age. The California they knew had become a place that gave new meaning, even reality, to the most American of myths—the pursuit of happiness.

■

Appendix

One of the most significant characteristics of the rush to California—a journey motivated by individual monetary ambition—was the goldseekers' practice of forming joint-stock companies and partnerships. Seemingly at odds with the highly personal motives which impelled so many thousands to leave their homes, these collective organizations provided a sense of security or safety in numbers for men who faced a journey by land or sea that would last four, five, even six months.

Most goldseekers had spent their lives within a few miles of their farms, villages or neighborhoods. Facing a journey of thousands of miles, they felt a sense of impending loneliness, while their families worried about Indians and disease. Of more immediate concern, city men and farmers alike knew little if anything about preparing for the long sea voyage or about what supplies and equipment would be needed for the overland journey. While some had worked with horses, mules or oxen on their farms, most were ill prepared to select and manage teams. The handling of pistols and rifles was foreign to many—yet everyone assumed that such arms would be necessary.

These and other uncertainties and problems were resolved by organizing or joining companies which promised companionship and most important, assigned to men with experience in the wilderness or at sea the responsibility for selecting the best wagons and teams or the best ship and necessary supplies. Thus city men and other greenhorns gained as members of joint-stock companies the skills and know-how they lacked. As well, they could more easily obtain money from family or creditor if it was to be invested in a joint-stock company that provided not only the means to get to California but also part ownership in the company's

459

assets, which often included merchandise to be sold at profit in the California market. Such businesslike practicality countered the skeptics who scorned the rush to California as a wild adventure.

With their economic advantages, the companies also provided a moral tone that was reassuring to the goldseekers' families. Company by-laws, constitutions or articles of association usually prohibited liquor and swearing and often required strict observance of the Sabbath.

Clearly gold rush companies were an important and interesting dimension of the national experience. And yet with few exceptions, diarists and letter writers at the time, and historians and others in later years, ignored the subject. That the goldseekers failed to write about their companies is not surprising; they often left out what we now want to know. As for the historians, the explanation comes from the only one who made an effort to analyze these organizations—David Potter. In his remarkably informative introduction to *Trail to California*, he suggests that very little is known about these companies because so few of their constitutions have survived. (He knew of only two.) Nonetheless, Potter discussed (pp. 7–43) the economics, leadership and management of overland companies with great perception and intelligence.

As to the companies that chose the sea routes, there are only two studies: Octavius Howe, *The Argonauts of '49;* and Oscar Lewis, *Sea Routes to the Gold Fields.*

In the course of my research, I have seen or found reference to a considerable number of many overland company constitutions, by-laws or articles of association. The following list is probably the most complete yet published and should serve as both a stimulus and a guide to those interested in exploring this vital aspect of the gold rush.

Diaries which include company constitutions (or whatever the organizing document was called) are: Ashley, Churchill, Clapp, Bryarly-Geiger, Gish, Hardy, John A. Johnson, Langworthy, Lorton, McCall, McKinstry, Newcomb, Page, E. D. Perkins, Pritchard, and Joseph W. Wood.

Company constitutions were published in the St. Louis *Daily Union*, March 24, 1849; the Oquawka *Spectator*, February 14, 1849; and the *Frontier Guardian* (microfilm #N21, Huntington Library), May 30, 1849; and in *Iowa Journal of History* 30, 315–17 and 343; and *Missouri Historical Review* 39, 149.

R. W. G. Vail, *Gold Fever, A Catalogue of the California Gold Rush Centennial Exhibition* (New York, 1949), 29–30, cites the publication of by-laws and/or constitutions of fifteen companies from eastern states.

■

ARTICLES OF ASSOCIATION AND AGREEMENT
as published in the Marshall Statesman,
January 17, 1849

At a meeting of the "Wolverine Rangers," held at the office of the Secretary, in Marshall, on the 13th inst., it was, on motion,

Resolved, That the publishers of the Marshall *Statesman,* and *Democratic Expounder* be requested to publish the Articles of Association and Agreement in their papers for the information of the public.

The Books of the Company are open at the office of the Secretary [James Pratt], where any one wishing to join can make application at any time before the first day of March next. It would be well for those who intend to go, to join as soon as convenient, so as to have a voice in the selection of the Agents of the Company, and of its officers under the Articles of Association.

The present temporary officers, for the purpose of completing the organization of the Company, are, Randall Hobart, Chairman; Jas. Pratt, Secretary; Lucius G. Noyes, Treasurer.

Articles of Association and Agreement entered into, and made by the undersigned, for the purpose of mutual safety and advantage in prosecuting an overland route to California from Independence on the Missouri River, and after arriving at the place of destination.

1st, This company shall be called the "Wolverine Rangers."

2nd, Its officers shall be a Board of five Directors, a Captain, Lieutenant, Secretary, Treasurer, and Steward, to be elected by a majority of the members.

3d, Each member shall pay into the Treasury, by the 20th day of March next, the sum of eighty five dollars in current funds—ten dollars of the above sum must be paid on signing these Articles of Association, to be forfeited in case the balance is not paid as above specified—provided, also that the Board of Directors shall have power to raise by an equal assessment upon the members an amount not exceeding in all the sum of one hundred dollars, including the eighty five dollars required to be paid in, should the said Directors deem it necessary to do so.

4th, By the tenth day of March next, an Agent to be selected by the Company, shall be sent to inquire into and ascertain the points where supplies can be purchased the cheapest and best—and by the first day of April, two members, to be chosen in like manner, shall be sent to join the said Agent, with the funds of the Company, and assist him in purchasing said supplies, and forwarding them to Independence, the starting point of the Company, where a settlement shall be made with the said Committee, by the Board of Directors, and submitted to the Company for their action—the said last mentioned agents to give bonds to the satisfaction of the Director for the faithful discharge of the trust reposed in them.

5th, All supplies and property purchased with the Company funds shall be joint property—belonging to those who start from Independence together for the route, and who there shall be considered as constituting said company. The members shall be present at Independence by the first day of May, and any person not there by the time the company leaves that place shall forfeit all he has paid in—and have no interest in the company property—unless such person shall be reinstated by a vote of a majority of the company.

6th, After arriving at the gold regions in California, any member of the company may retire therefrom, on giving two weeks notice to the Directors, or any three of them, of his intention to do so. Whereupon the said Board of Directors shall settle with such person equitably, allowing him his share of the company avails, taking his receipt, and ordering his retirement to be entered in the company record.

7th, Each member binds himself upon his honor to fulfill as far as he can his duties as a member of this association—to be orderly, temperate and faithful—obedient to the will of the majority, properly expressed—and to stand by and relieve, so far in his power, any member in peril or distress.

8th, The Board of Directors shall hold their offices for six months—shall have charge of the expedition and the interests of the company—settle accounts—hear and adjust grievances—report monthly to the company the state of the finances, and the condition of the company affairs—recommend when necessary appropriations, draw drafts on the Treasury for such sums only as are appropriated by a majority of the company, a certificate of the Secretary of the vote, to accompany the draft. From any decision, or order of the Board, an appeal may be taken to a majority of the company by any member who may consider such appeal proper or desirable. And such Board shall report as soon as possible to the company the name of such person as may have given notice of his wish to retire from the company.

9th, The Captain shall hold his office for three months. It shall be his duty to conduct and command the expedition, pursuant to the orders and suggestions of the Board of Directors—and to preserve order and decorum on the members.

10th, The Lieutenant shall hold his office for three months—and it shall be his duty to aid and assist the Captain in the performance of his duties.

11th, The Secretary shall hold his office for six months—shall keep a record of the proceedings of the Board of Directors, and of the company—shall certify to the chairman of the Board of Directors, the vote appropriating monies for the use of the company—and do all other acts incident to his office.

12th, The Treasurer shall hold his office for three months. He shall pay all orders drawn on him by the Board of Directors, which are accompanied by a certificate of the Secretary of the vote appropriating the money—he shall report to the Board of Directors, monthly, the state of the Treasury—and shall deliver up all effects, monies and other things belonging to his office, when directed to do so by a vote of the company; and he shall give bonds to the Secretary and his successors in office in an amount to be fixed by the Board of Directors and to their satisfaction.

13th, The Steward shall hold his office for six months. He shall have charge of the provisions, and serve up and distribute the company's rations. He shall report monthly the state of his department.

It is understood that in case of the death of a member, his share of the company property shall be settled by the Board of Directors, and kept by them for his next of kin, or for those whom the deceased may have expressed a wish should receive it, and be paid over to them as soon as practicable.

Each member shall provide himself with a good rifle, 3 lbs. powder, 10 lbs. lead, and a good hatchet, and such other things as he may deem desirable, or useful.

These articles, or any of them, may be amended, and others added, by a vote of two-thirds of the members.

The Board of Directors, or a majority of them, shall have power to call meetings upon sufficient notice.

These articles shall bind the undersigned, their heirs, executors, administrators and assigns.

WOLVERINE RANGERS' ROSTER
as published in the Marshall Statesman,
April 11 [Wednesday], 1849

The Wolverine Rangers take their final leave of Marshall on Tuesday or Wednesday of next week. We have been furnished with the following list of officers and members of the company, and the residence and occupation of each, as far as could be ascertained:

Jesse J. Baker, Captain
S. S. DeArman, Lieutenant
George B. Allcott, Secretary
Thomas E. Cook, Treasurer
Herman Camp, Steward

BOARD OF DIRECTORS: Randall Hobart, Thos. Rawson, Horace C. Ladd, Wm. Carley, George W. Hoag.

AGENTS: James Pratt, J. D. Potts, Randall Hobart

NAMES OF MEMBERS	RESIDENCE	OCCUPATION
James Pratt	Marshall	Lawyer
E. C. Noyes	Plymouth	
James D. Potts	Marshall	Saddler
Horace C. Ladd	Marshall	Saddler
Thomas Manser	Marshall	Saddler
George W. Hoag	Marshall	Blacksmith
Jesse G. Baker	Marshall	Machinist
Randall Hobart	Marshall	Local Preacher
Chauncy Nichols	At Large	Daguerrean
Charles A. Barton	Marshall	Carpenter
George B. Allcott	Marshall	Student
S. S. DeArman	Marshall	Tinner
Joseph Rogers	Clarendon	Farmer
Thomas Rawson	St. Joseph	Local Preacher
L. Brooks	Bellevue	Blacksmith
Almon P. Frary	Lansing	
J. C. Climper	Lansing	Millwright
Julius A. Kent	Marshall	Clerk
Herman Camp	Marshall	Speculator at Large
J. A. Sutherland	Marshall	Blacksmith
Benjamin Givin	Marshall	Joiner
John Warren	Marshall	Blacksmith
William Carley	Allegan	Lt. House Keeper
S. H. McClellan	Galesburg	Farmer
William Highly	St. Joseph	
Samuel D. Moore	Battle Creek	Local Preacher
Frederick Mills	Gull Prairie	Farmer
A. H. Blakesly	Marshall	Tanner
Henry Gray	Hastings	
D. D. Fralick	Plymouth	Blacksmith
H. A. Bently	Plymouth	Blacksmith
Joseph Henry Palmer	Vermontville	Physician
Oliver Goldsmith	Detroit	Tobacconist
Ira Vits	Albion	Farmer
John McAlister	Battle Creek	Lawyer
George Van Brunt	Athens	Farmer
F. C. Cannon	Manchester	
Thomas E. Cook	Marshall	Clerk
S. G. Noble	Unadilla	Carpenter
C. B. Carr	Manchester	Physician
Volney Chapman	Manchester	Farmer
William J. Magoon	Manchester	
H. B. Seymour	Saugatuc	

Names of Members	Residence	Occupation
James McCormick	Allegan	
Noah E. Ives	Plainfield	
George H. Ives	Plainfield	
A. S. Lyon	Manchester	
Thomas Delong	Lansing	
Hugh M. Phillips	Detroit	Miner
John Campbell	Manchester	
Morgan L. Rood	Bellevue	Gunsmith

■

Notes

PROLOGUE

As a brief survey of California history prior to 1849, the Prologue is based on information drawn from a variety of sources, in addition to those cited below. As everyone has discovered in writing about California, Hubert Howe Bancroft's six-volume history remains the most fertile source of information. Also of special value in preparing the Prologue: John W. Caughey, *Gold Is the Cornerstone;* William H. Hutchinson, *California . . . ;* David Lavender, *California . . . ;* Rodman Paul, *California Gold Discovery;* Leonard Pitt, *Decline of the Californios;* and Irving Richman, *California Under Spain and Mexico.*

PAGE
25 Epigraph: Larkin, VII, 303.
26 "not to look . . .": Garr, 134. This quote has been slightly changed to clarify its meaning. Information on the character of immigrants from Mexico is drawn from this valuable essay. Also Pitt, 6.
27 Vancouver quoted: Bancroft, *History*, I, 529.
27 "to speak of California . . .": Pitt, 6.
27 Statistics on ranchos (acreage and cattle) and Indians: Pitt, 10; Lavender, 76.
28 "no angry words . . .": Bancroft, IV, 310–11.
29 380 foreign residents: Bancroft, IV, 117. Stearns, Fitch and Spence: Rolle, 113.
30 "Those men who . . .": Bernard DeVoto, *The Year of Decision 1846* (Sentry Edition, Boston, 1961), 58.
30 "horses that retain their vigor . . .": I am embarrassed to admit, I cannot identify this source.
30 "Miserable people who sleep . . .": statement by Thomas Jefferson Farnham, 1839 or 1840; quoted in James D. Hart, *American Images of Spanish California* (Berkeley, 1960), 13.
        Valuable comment on the judgmental attitude of Americans and Europeans is offered by Pitt, 14–19, including a description of Californios as "a thieving, cowardly, dancing, lewd people, generally indolent and faithless."
30 "In the hands of an enterprising . . .": Richard Henry Dana, *Two Years Before the Mast* (New York, 1936), 193.
        Another comment by Dana deserves quoting: "There are no people to whom the newly invented Yankee word 'loafer' is more applicable than to the

Spanish Americans." This comes from the valuable essay by Hart, *New Englanders in Nova Albion*, 9, which discusses American attitudes toward California from the 1790s to 1890s.

30   Emigrants to California, 1841–48: Unruh, 119.

31   Information on Yerba Buena/San Francisco, the Mormons and Brannan comes from Bancroft, VI, 6; and Lavender, 142–43.

32   Sutter's Fort: Bancroft, VI, 13–14.

33   "My eye was caught . . .": Lavender, 150.

33   "Boys, I believe . . .": Bancroft, VI, 33.

33   "I have made a discovery . . .": Bancroft, VI, 43.

The story of Marshall's discovery has been told so many times, with variations and differing quotations, that the event has become institutionalized folklore. My recounting is based on Bancroft, VI, 32–34, 38–41. Another account should be noted and recommended as the definitive collection of every known source, document, account and memoir relating to the discovery: Paul, *California Gold Discovery*.

34   "Gold!": Bancroft, VI, 56.

Newspaper articles relating to the discovery and the growing public interest published in the *Californian* and the *California Star* in spring 1848 are reprinted in Paul, 69–80.

34   "A frenzy seized my soul . . .": Bancroft, VI, 56.

35   "The whole country . . .": Paul, 71.

35   "Doubts still hovered . . .": Paul, 101.

35   "Another bag of gold . . .": Paul, 102.

35   "For the present . . .": Bancroft, VI, footnote 65.

37   Brannan's store: Paul, 95.

This and subsequent information from Paul is taken from what is generally referred to as "Mason's Report," which was in fact a letter written by Colonel Richard B. Mason, Military Governor of California, dated Monterey, August 17, 1848, addressed to the Adjutant General, Washington, D.C. This "report" is reprinted in Paul, 91–100.

38   Humphrey and ranchers, $16,000.: Paul, 95.

38   "We can hear of nothing . . .": Larkin, 278 and 287.

39   "I have to report . . .": Larkin, 285–86.

39   "If our countrymen . . .": Larkin, 303.

39   273 pounds of gold: Paul, 97.

40   "a small gutter . . .": Paul, 93.

40   "I was surprised . . .": Paul, 96.

40   "Many private letters . . .": Paul, 97.

40   Angelenos' mining success: Bancroft, VI, 80.

41   "Some of those . . .": Larkin, 321–22.

41   "If you can have . . .": Larkin, 316.

42   "There are no shoes . . .": Larkin, 341.

42   "almost the entire male population . . .": Bancroft, VI, footnote 112. From a variety of sources, I have judged 4,000 to be the most reasonable guess as to the number of Oregonians in California by December 1848. Bancroft gives information on the several parties of Oregonians who came by ship and overland.

42   Estimates of the number of miners in the diggings by the end of 1848 have been made by everyone who has written on the subject, with Bancroft's judgment—8,000 to 10,000 (VI, 89)—being my source.

43   "We in this country . . .": Letter by J. F. Reed, dated "Pueblo de San Jose, August 1, 1848," published in the *Illinois State Register*, Springfield, July 5, 1849.

CHAPTER I

All dates pertain to the year 1849 unless otherwise cited.

PAGE

45   Epigraph: Little, January 1.
45   "collected at random . . .": *California Star*, Paul, *California Gold Discovery*, 78.
45   N.Y. *Journal of Commerce:* Bancroft, *History*, VI, footnote, 115.
45   "Your streams have minnows . . .": Caughey, *Gold Is the Cornerstone*, 40.
48   "I have no hesitation . . .": Paul, 97.
49   "You know Bryant . . .": Letter signed M. T. McClellan, "October 28, 1848, San Francisco," published in the *Missouri Republican*, St. Louis, April 16, 1849.
50   "Joseph has borrowed . . .": quoted by Oscar Lewis, *Sea Routes*, 10.
50   Massachusetts companies: Howe, 175.
52   Ann Arbor newspaper: Bidlack, 12–13.
52   The Ann Arbor man who sold his home and the farmer who sold his farm are from article in Detroit *Daily Advertiser*, April 16.
53   The journey from various parts of the United States to the western frontier was an important part of the gold rush experience. But most diarists did not start writing—at least with any detail—until they reached the jumping-off points.
      Several of the best who did describe their travel through the states: Kendrick (from Boston to St. Louis via Pittsburgh and the Ohio River, citing costs); Little (from Boston via sailing ship, railroad, canal boat and river steamer, twenty-three days to St. Louis at cost of $23 per person); John A. Johnson (MS diary), Parker and Barnard (riverboat travel down the Ohio to St. Louis, up the Missouri to Independence); Watrous (from Marshall, Mich., by railroad to Chicago, down Illinois-Michigan Canal to St. Louis and on to St. Joseph); and Reeve (by flatboat down the Ohio and Mississippi to St. Louis and then on to Independence).
54   Information about William Swain and his family is derived from extensive interviews with his third child, Miss Sara Swain, from correspondence with her (1948–50), from family papers and records provided by Miss Swain, and from visits to the Swain farm and the town of Youngstown.
56   "Many men who . . .": Buffalo *Morning Express*, January 26, 1849.
59   "It is impossible . . .": Letter by Dr. C. N. Ormsby, July 24, 1849, in Bidlack, 29.
62   "About twenty steamers . . .": MS letter by James Drew, July [n.d.], 1845, at Buffalo. New York Historical Society, New York City.
      While the information quoted comes from an earlier period, it is doubtful that commercial shipping in and out of Buffalo would have changed significantly by spring 1849. Drew mentioned the *London;* in fact he sailed on it to Detroit.
      Another diarist, Hislap, described Buffalo and his lake trip to Chicago in August 1850. Lorton was in Buffalo in September 1848; he stayed at Huff's Hotel (no description) and then took the lake steamer to Chicago, writing a good account of life on board.
66   "The dock is full . . .": Lorton, diary September 28, 1848.
66   "purifies the blood . . .": advertisement, *Illinois Journal*, Springfield, December 19, 1848.
69   "It is a large . . .": James Pratt, Wolverine Ranger, letter, "Chicago, March

8 . . . ," published in the Marshall, MI, *Statesman*, March 14. Pratt, former editor of the *Statesman*, played an important role in the overland company Swain joined, and the *Statesman* published many letters and accounts by him and other members of the company, as is explained in a later note.

69 "When I told him . . .": Swain, MS Reminiscence.

70 "Sleep, eat, and live . . .": Cunynghame, 35–36.

Webster traveled the Illinois-Michigan Canal and described the trip, April 25.

70 "We have amused ourselves . . .": Barnard, letter "On board steamer *Paris*, Cincinnati, April 1."

71 For an eyewitness report of cholera victims on Missouri River steamboats, see Pearson, 13. He described visiting the *Grand Turk* when it docked at St. Louis in mid-April, with thirteen dead passengers on the deck.

For an informative study of cholera and its prevalence and prevention in 1849, see "Cholera Epidemics in St. Louis," Missouri Historical Society, *Glimpses of the Past* (1936). Also James T. Barrett, "Cholera in Missouri," *Missouri Historical Review*, LV (July 1961).

72 "looks beautiful . . .": Pratt, letter "St. Louis, March 20," *Statesman*, April 4.

72 "Every boat that comes . . .": Kerr, letter "St. Louis, April 8."

72 "Steamboats are discharging . . .": Randall Hobart, Wolverine Ranger, letter "Steamboat Amelia, Missouri River, May 1," published in the Marshall, MI, *Democratic Expounder*, June 1. The *Democratic Expounder*, like the *Statesman*, published letters and accounts from members of Swain's company.

73 "St. Louis is a great city . . .": Pratt, letter "St. Louis, March 20."

73 "is tremendous. Hundreds . . .": "The California Fever," *Missouri Republican*, April 9.

73 "has given a wonderful . . .": Hobart, letter "Steamboat *Amelia*."

74 "Four Negroes for Sale . . .": Advertisement, *Missouri Republican*, April 13.

75 "The upper part of the city . . .": Decker, April 10.

76 "a dense medley of Hoosiers . . .": Bruff, I, 438.

76 "Every berth was full . . .": Delano, *Life*, 14–15.

76 "Geese, ducks, turkeys . . ."; "Speaking of game . . .": C. W. Smith, April 10, 1850.

76 "two Californians . . .": Newcomb, April 15, 1850.

Shombre, March 1849, told of gambling, drinking and rowdiness on Missouri riverboats; and Decker, April 7, reported "fiddling, dancing, card playing and gaming" and concluded that "steamboats are wicked places."

76 "Many passengers engage . . .": John A. Johnson, MS diary, March 18, on board steamer *Independence*.

77 "The Missouri is decidedly . . .": Coke, June 1, 1850.

77 "with great violence . . .": Cross, 34.

This abandoned steamer was probably the *James Monroe* "which left St. Louis with about 100 cabin passengers . . . and before reaching Jefferson City, 150 miles, seventy of them died. At the city the boat was deserted and all fled for their lives. . . . One company from Indiana was on board. Of twenty-seven men . . . only two were spared. . . . The graves of passengers ranged along the shore for about half a mile." From E. D. Perkins, 2.

Cholera on board steamers between St. Louis and Independence is reviewed by Barry, 807, 827, 829–30.

77 "with virulence,"; "Under the unfavorable . . .": Wistar, 43.

Jagger, May 9, on board the *Mary Blum* described that steamer as "a floating carnal house." Two other reports of cholera victims bound for Independence and St. Joseph: John A. Johnson, "Preparation," April 29; and Mendall Jewett, April 3–4, 1850.

78   "It is surprising . . .": Rothwell, May 11, 1850.

    On May 2, 1849, Page wrote: "Doctors are more numerously represented . . . than any other part of the community. Every company will have one or more."

79   "walk, in order to . . .": Newcomb, April 28, 1850.

    Mendall Jewett, April 1, 1849, told of the *Salida* being stuck on a sand bar with the passengers going ashore to lighten the load. Hagelstein, April 1850, gives a full account of a hundred passengers going ashore to assist freeing a steamer from a sand bar. Other steamer mishaps and serious accidents: Hillyer, 216; Tiffany, April 17.

    Excellent accounts of riverboat travel from St. Louis to Independence: Berrien, Burbank, Chalmers, Delano's *Correspondence*, and Mendall Jewett.

CHAPTER II

All dates pertain to the year 1849 unless otherwise cited.

PAGE

87   Epigraph: J. C. McBride, letter May 12, 1850, at Council Bluffs.

    Lyne, letter Independence, May 4: "I could not have imagined so many going had I not seen it. My only wonder is if any are left in the settlements."

88   The best summary of the rivalry between Independence and St. Joseph and its implications for the emigrants is presented by Unruh, 68–73. Other studies of these frontier towns as jumping-off points in 1849–50: Gregg, and Wyman.

    For detailed description of the operation of the ferries at St. Joseph in 1849: Pearson, 13. Excellent description of the commotion at St. Joseph: MacBride, April 24, 1850. Descriptions of Independence: letters to "Editors of the Reveille," *Weekly Reveille*, St. Louis, April 30 and May 14.

88   "many thousand lies . . .": Unruh, 70.

88   The number of emigrants at Independence and St. Joseph: To prove how many gathered at the jumping-off points in the spring of 1849 is not possible —only estimates can be made. From evidence in the frontier newspapers, the diaries and letters of goldseekers and reports of military officers, I have calculated what seems to me a very reasonable, indeed minimum estimate: 35,000 *by mid-May.*

    To review the situation: First we must assign estimates to each of the possible routes the emigrants could follow westward from the Missouri frontier. There were four basic trails. First, the Santa Fe Trail southwest from Independence. Second, the Oregon–California Trail—often called the South Pass route—which also started at Independence. (Emigrants from smaller outfitting towns—Weston, Westport Landing and to the north Old Fort Kearny—also set out on the Oregon–California Trail.) Third, the trail from St. Joseph and its nearby crossings of the Missouri River which led west to join the Oregon–California Trail. And fourth, the Mormon Trail from Council Bluffs west along the north side of the Platte River to Fort Laramie, where it joined the main Oregon–California Trail.

    So, the starting points were rather dispersed. But because of the necessity of crossing the Missouri River at St. Joseph, Council Bluffs and intermediate ferries, it was possible to count the number of wagons at those crossings. St. Joseph and St. Louis newspapers published reports of the wagons counted at those ferry crossings. From these reports and the scores of estimates by diarists and letter writers, the total number of wagons crossing on the ferries between St. Joseph and Council Bluffs came to 4,850. Figuring an average of four men per wagon (a few companies included women and children), the total for the emigration north of Independence was 19,400 people.

No such mathematical precision is possible for the crowd around Independence, because the companies from there rolled westward from campsites sprawling for miles along the frontier. They did have to cross the Kansas River farther west, and wagon counts were made there. From various diaries and letters, and gauging the Independence crowd at about two-thirds the total to the north, some 3,200 wagons or 12,800 people set out from Independence on the Oregon–California Trail.

As to the number on the Santa Fe Trail, Bancroft, *History*, VI, 159, estimated 8,000. But that figure has generally been considered excessive; more acceptable is the judgment of Ralph P. Bieber, who estimated the Santa Fe emigration at 2,500–3,000, with contemporary observations supporting the higher figure. For example, at a river crossing on the trail southwest of Independence, an emigrant on May 31 counted 187 wagons, and he estimated "the teams in advance" at 700. Another traveler heading toward Independence on the trail on May 8 met "one unceasing, everlasting flood" of emigrants (Barry, 825).

So, the total: 19,400 from St. Joseph and Council Bluffs; 12,800 from around Independence; and 3,000 on the Santa Fe Trail—for a grand total of 35,200. Some of these gave up while still in camp, others died in camp, and still more, as we shall see, turned back within a few days or weeks after starting their journey.

A final comment on this rather lugubrious subject—but one of importance, because the size of the emigration is central to understanding the impact of the rush on the American people and to the circumstances of life on the overland trail. Just as diarists and letter writers in 1849 differed sharply in their estimates of the crowd (Swain thought 10,000 an excessive number while others confidently judged the total to be at least 35,000), modern historians have come up with widely varying estimates. For the Oregon–California Trail (therefore excluding the 3,000 who went via the Santa Fe Trail), George R. Stewart estimated 22,500 (*California Trail*, 232), John W. Caughey suggested 36,000 ("Transit of the Forty-niners," 27), Georgia W. Read and Dale Morgan agreed on 30,000 (Morgan, Introd. to Pritchard, footnote, 17), Ray Billington estimated 45,000 (*Far Western Frontier*, 226), and Bancroft often cited 50,000.

88 *Consignee:* Barry, 804.

89 cholera on board the *Monroe:* E. D. Perkins, 2.

89 "they would be as handy as sheep": Ingalls, April 30, 1850.

Referring to the problem of "taming" their newly purchased mules, an observer in Independence on May 27 noted: "The Mexicans in town have reaped a fine harvest by breaking these wild mules." Letter Independence, May 27, *Missouri Republican*, June 3.

89 packing: Diaries which best describe the difficulties and tribulations of traveling with pack mules are Webster, Batchelder and Stuart—all members of the Boston Pack Company. Stansbury, MS diary June 20, described this company. Other good accounts of pack companies: James W. Evans, Coke.

90 "twenty elliptic spring wagons . . .": From the Pioneer Line's prospectus, quoted by Bernard J. Reid, diary, 3. Reid traveled with the line and recorded the entire, tragic journey.

For the best summary of information on the Pioneer Line and other stage companies, see Unruh, 101–04.

91 "Almost every village . . .": Detroit *Daily Advertiser*, April 16.

Another example of editorial concern about the transfer of money and population to California was expressed as early as January 11 by the New York *Herald:* "What will this general and overwhelming spirit of emigration lead to? Will it be the beginning of a new empire in the West, a revolution in the commercial highways of the world, a depopulation of the old states for the new republic on the shores of the Pacific?"

91 The Wolverine Rangers and James Pratt: Information about the Rangers, from their first organizing efforts in January to the final formation of the company and departure from Marshall, Michigan, on April 18, is set forth in articles and letters published in the Marshall *Statesman.* The only complete file of this newspaper is preserved at the William L. Clements Library, Ann Arbor. All pertinent material in the newspaper relating to the Rangers was collected and published in 1974 in *The Gold Rush, Letters from the Wolverine Rangers to the Marshall Statesman, 1849–51.*

Inasmuch as I made use of the Rangers' letters in the *Statesman* file at the Clements Library many years prior to 1974, most citations relate to the newspaper rather than the book. This excellent book offers in its introduction an extensive review of the Rangers, i-xii.

James Pratt took the key role in leading and reporting the organizational efforts of the men who joined to form the Wolverine Rangers. At the first two meetings in early January, it was agreed they would go overland via the California–Oregon Trail, that all equipment should be purchased at the frontier, and that $10,000 should be raised by $100 payments from 100 men to pay for equipment and supplies and to cover expenses for a period of time after arrival in California. At the next meeting, held in Pratt's office, temporary officers were appointed and "Articles of Association and Agreement" drawn up and submitted to the two newspapers for publication.

On February 28 the thirty-six men who had paid and finally joined the Wolverine Rangers selected their board of directors (five), the several officers and the first agent.

On April 11 the *Statesman* published the roster of Wolverine Rangers, a total of fifty-one, listed by name, residence and occupation. (Complete roster is reproduced in the Appendix.) Seventeen Rangers came from Marshall, the others from small towns in southern Michigan.

Most communities in Michigan, as in other states, sent to California their groups of men organized into companies, some of them financed by investors who stayed home but expected to share in the profits from gold mining. The Wolverine Rangers were the largest and best organized of Michigan's gold rush companies.

The letters of Pratt and several other Rangers, published in the *Statesman* and the *Democratic Expounder,* have been used extensively to augment the Swain diary from the outset of the journey through the months in California.

91 "The reports here . . .": Letter by George Winslow, published in "A Tragedy on the Oregon Trail," *Collections of the Nebraska State Historical Society,* v. 17, 1913; 118.

91 "Governor Boggs has written . . .": Pratt, letter Independence, April 26,

Statesman, May 16. John A. Johnson, "Preparation," April 29, also quotes this Boggs letter at length.

92 "who scratched off the following . . ." and the song: Pratt, letter Independence, April 9, *Statesman*, May 2.

93 Specific information and drawings of typical overland wagons can be found in Stewart, *California Trail*, 107–12.

93 arguments, fights, shootings, dissension: John A. Johnson, "Preparation," April 29; letter signed "California," *Missouri Republican*, April 29; and letter Newark *Daily Advertiser*, April 13.

94 New York Life Insurance Co. and policy for $2,500: Bidlack, 7; Gill, 10.

95 "It is known . . .": Georgia Willis Read, letter April 14, 1850.

Coy, *Great Trek*, has this description of the Upper Landing or Wayne City: "The most miserable of all wretched collections of log huts ever inhabited by pickpockets, grog vendors, and vagabonds of every shade, name and nature."

95 "The Noland and Independence Houses . . .": Letter Independence, April 23, *Weekly Reveille*, St. Louis, April 30. Sprague, April 5, described the Noland House.

95 "You have only . . .": Lorton, letter St. Joseph, May 9, New York *Sun*, June 8.

Speaking of the merchants in the outfitting towns, McDiarmid, May 22, 1850, wrote: "I have found sharpers before, but I have never found before a more heartless set of *scoundrels*."

95 "Considering the large number . . .": Letter signed "California," Independence, April 21, *Missouri Republican*, May 1.

96 "There are two gambling . . .": Pratt, letter Independence, April 9, *Statesman*, May 2.

96 "One of these establishments . . .": Letter signed "California," Independence, April 21, *Missouri Republican*, May 1.

Other reports of gambling: Tiffany, April 19; *Weekly Reveille*, April 30; and Shombre, May 3, said that in addition to the temptations of gambling there was "a groggery" on the outskirts of Independence "which has been full all day of emigrants taking their last spree. Some of our boys were tite all day."

96 "The little seven-by-nine . . .": Pratt, letter Independence, April 9, *Statesman*, May 2.

96 "They have rather singular rules . . .": Hall, letter Independence, May 11.

96 "recommends a dose of . . .": Lord, May 6 at Independence.

97 "They can be managed . . .": Letter signed "Mifflin," May 15, *Weekly Reveille*, June 11.

97 "Mules are so stubborn . . .": Fairchild, letter St. Joseph, April 23.

97 "The Indians will not . . .": John A. Johnson, "Preparation," letter Independence, March 23.

For extensive information from scores of diaries/letters, 1849 and 1850, relating to promotion of oxen vs. mules, the number of oxen used vs. mules and horses, arguments between oxen and mule advocates, praise of oxen as superior to mules both for handling and ability to pull heavier loads, comparison of lengths of time required by oxen vs. mule companies to reach California: contact the author.

For an excellent general discussion of the advantages of oxen and mules, see Potter, 40–48.

97 "The alarm among the people . . .": Letter near Independence, May 11, St. Louis *Weekly Reveille*, May 28.

97 "Cholera is the prevailing . . .": Letter signed "California," Independence, May 13, *Missouri Republican*, May 17.

97 "All hands are making . . .": Randall Hobart, Wolverine Ranger, diary May 5, *Democratic Expounder*, June 1.

97 "You would be amused . . .": Lyne, letter near Independence, May 4.
      Delano, *Correspondence*, letter April 21, has an amusing comment that the emigrants will "find out that women are worth something after all."

103 "noise and confusion reigned . . .": Johnston, April 21.
      Other descriptions of Independence crowded with Californians: Pratt, letter April 9; Wistar, 45–46; Sprague, April 6.

103 "are made of osnaburg . . .": Decker, May 4.

104 "mustachios are becoming . . .": Hamelin, May 7.

105 "wagons perfectly rammed . . .": Lorton, diary May 8.

105 "Fighting for precedence . . .": Bruff, I, 7.

105 "There are only two . . .": Lorton, diary May 8.
      For an exceptional description of the emigration at St. Joseph in spring 1850: "Pencillings by the Way . . . ," *Alta California*, September 24, 1850.

105 "By noon our steers . . .": Hobart, May 11, *Democratic Expounder*, June 1.

105 "had quite a rich . . .": Hamelin, May 8.

105 "A wild, unbroken mule . . .": Webster, May 5 and 27.

105 "had a high old time . . .": Wistar, 44.
      Webster, May 26, reported that despite all efforts to train their mules, they remained "wild and vicious." Bernard Reid, diary, 7, described breaking 300 mules to harness, and E. D. Perkins, July 25, became so angry at his mule "that I picked up the rifle barrel instantly and without a minute's thought struck her over the head with it, bending it to a beautiful curve."

106 "He is being rubbed . . .": Horace Ladd, Wolverine Ranger, letter May 14, *Statesman*, May 30.

106 "has two wagons . . .": Goldsmith, 13.

106 "Each mess has a . . .": Pratt, diary May 18, *Statesman*, June 27.

108 "Dr. Wells and E. S. Camp . . .": Ladd, May 14, *Statesman*, May 30.
      Descriptions of emigrants suffering and dying from cholera are rare; presumably diarists did not want to report so tragic a scene, knowing their families would later read the account. I have found two poignant, graphic reports: one by Delano, *Life*, 17–18; and the other, a remarkably eloquent, gentle, yet doctor-like report of a cholera victim's symptoms, reactions, pain and death, by Hoover, describing his younger brother, age twelve, who died on the trail on June 18.

CHAPTER III

All dates pertain to 1849 unless otherwise cited.

PAGE
111 Epigraph: John A. Johnson, "Preparation," letter May 23.
      Ramsay, July 4, complained about crowded conditions on the trail: "The immense numbers of emigrants . . . makes it doubly tiresome from the fact that they are constantly in each other's way and more particularly at the crossings of rivers and difficult places on the road."

114 "We are armed to the teeth . . .": Pratt, diary May 5, *Statesman*, June 27.
      In 1849 and 1850 fear of the Pawnees was far out of proportion to any

actual danger. A good example of experience with this tribe is found in the diary of Bruff, I, 18. On June 10, his company met a band of Pawnees: "Alas, the great warriors, Arabs and terror of the plains turned out to be a sadly reduced, starving, contemptible race. They begged me for bread. . . . As they were actually starving, famine might drive them to rob and break up some small party. . . ." Bruff's judgment proved true; another '49er wrote on May 6 (in the *Weekly North-Western Gazette*, July 4): "We are in the heart of Pawnee country. The Indians are not very hostile but are nearly starved, which will cause them to rob lone wagons and small companies. Yesterday I with several others went seven miles back to the relief of two ox-wagons who were about to be taken by the Indians. On seeing us coming well mounted, they were taken with leaving. . . ." Lorton, diary, June 2, told of an emigrant who was killed by the Pawnee; and Hillyer, 226, gives a most graphic account of his company's encounter with Pawnee and consequent killing and mutilation of a member of his company.

Most companies passed through Pawnee country without seeing the tribe, even at a distance. For extensive records of emigrants' comments on the Pawnee, contact the author.

115   "so eager for sport . . .": Langworthy, June 19.

Brown, 13, concluded that there was far more danger "from the carelessness of arms among fellow emigrants than from the hostile Indians." Same opinion by McCall, May 26; J. E. Armstrong, July 15; and others.

As to the number of emigrants killed by Indians: in his study of the subject Unruh, 185, calculated that in 1849 only thirty-three emigrants lost their lives, while sixty Indians were killed by emigrants. In 1850 the ratio was about the same: forty-eight to seventy-six. Clearly the emigrants were the aggressors.

Unruh emphasized, and the diaries for both years support his contention, that the first party of the journey was far safer than west of the South Pass: 90 percent of all emigrant deaths caused by Indian attack occurred *west* of South Pass.

Thus the emigrants passed through Pawnee and later Sioux country with only minimal risk; as a consequence, their system of guard duty and other protective measures were abandoned long before they reached the area of danger west of the South Pass.

115   Cholera deaths: The frightening persistence of cholera was mentioned by almost every diarist in 1849 and 1850. Jagger, who was traveling within a few days of the Rangers, stated that three to six fresh graves were seen each day, May 31; Prichet on May 14 told of a company from Mississippi that had lost five out of twenty-eight men since leaving Independence. Hoover, June 9, saw ten graves from one company, and DeWolf, June 17, told of one company wiped out by cholera, six of seven members dead. Webster, June 10, stated that at many campsites there were twelve to fifteen graves.

But it is not possible to compute with accuracy from such records just how many emigrants died of cholera in 1849, 1850 or later years. Obviously many of the diarists who reported graves counted the same ones. What is to be the estimate of cholera deaths? The figure most often cited for 1849 (more by habit than from evidence) comes from Bancroft, *History*, VI, 149. He estimated that 5,000 '49ers died of the disease while traveling to South Pass. The frequency with which this number is quoted reflects not only the weight given to Bancroft as an authority but as well the tradition of dramatizing the dangers faced by goldseekers.

Clearly Bancroft's 5,000 is excessive, an impossible toll given the total number at the frontier and on the trails. A far more reasonable estimate is 1,500 deaths by cholera, in the frontier camps and on the trails east of Fort Laramie. (Cholera was practically unknown west of the fort.)

115   "It was generally . . .": Shepherd, 44.

     McKeeby, July 24, 1850, advised "$50 in cash to each man," and Delano, *Life*, 106, stressed the need for money.

116   "a farmer who had . . .": William Weber Johnson, 80.

     Hammond and Layton comment on the origins and uses of the expression.

116   "I wish you were . . .": Barnard, letter May 6.

117   Count at Fort Kearny: 5,516 wagons is from letter signed "Pawnee," June 23, *Missouri Republican*, August 5. Major Osborne Cross and George Gibbs, who was with Cross, both observed that four men per wagon was "less than average" (Cross, 79 and 301). Webster on June 19 said that 5,400 wagons had passed Fort Kearny; many other diarists gave similar or varying counts. Barry, 871, has an excellent summary of the count of wagons at Fort Kearny.

118   "This California movement . . .": Pratt, letter May 28, *Statesman*, July 4.

118   "Tell Charles that . . .": letter, Oquawka *Spectator*, June 13.

118   "the wagon covers are . . .": "Pencillings by the Way," diary May 11, 1850, *Alta California*, September 21, 1850. Similar descriptions for 1849, see: Banks, June 10; Delano, *Life*, June 8; and Lorton, diary May 8.

119   "Last night our wagons . . .": Pratt, diary May 18, *Statesman*, June 27.

120   "We are traveling . . .": "Here at Bull Creek . . .": Pratt, diary May 20, *Statesman*, June 27.

120   "We were joined . . .": Pratt, diary May 20, *Statesman*, June 27.

122   "Many of them obtain . . .": Thompkins, MS diary, 30. Other Indians along the western frontier sought to charge a toll for passage through their land: Hutchings, June 9; and Kilgore, May 20, 1850.

122   "saw more than one . . .": McKinstry, diary May 17, 1850.

122   "Such was the amativeness . . .": Foster, April 6.

     This reference and the one by McKinstry are the only explicit statements I have seen that tell of emigrant fraternization with Indians along the trail. Such activities were undoubtedly common but propriety prohibited comment.

123   "It is said by . . .": Hosmer, letter May 5.

123   "had adopted a set . . .": Goldsmith, 12.

123   "Our . . . choice for . . .": Goldsmith, 12–13.

124   "This Indian, a Shawnee . . .": Pratt, diary May 25, *Statesman*, June 27.

126   "contains fifteen or . . .": Jagger, May 26.

     For extensive emigrant commentary of Uniontown and the ferry operation there, see Barry, 795–96. Also Sprague, May 16 and 17.

126   "The shops are kept . . .": William Kelly, I, 59.

126   "Two boats are . . .": Pratt, letter Kansas Ferry, May 28, *Statesman*, July 4.

127   "This land of . . .": Pratt, May 28.

127   "news arrived that . . .": Jagger, May 26.

127   "The stories have . . .": Pratt, letter May 28.

127   "The whole emigration . . .": James W. Evans, June 30.

128   "The duties of the cooks . . .": Goldsmith, 23.

131   "In looking behind . . .": Johnston, May 9.

131   "They have seen . . .": Horace Ladd, Wolverine Ranger, letter June 7, *Statesman*, July 11.

131   "see worse times . . .": Rothwell, letter May 17, 1850.

132   "are very useful . . .": Letter signed "W.R.R.," May 21, 1850, quoted in Wyman, 100.

      Speaking of the "backtrackers," Webster, June 10, wrote: "To meet so many who have been farther westward and who have turned backward . . . has its influence upon a large number and causes them to also reverse their course." Discouraged emigrants returning home, some giving up as far west as Fort Laramie, are mentioned by many diarists: Cross, 42 and 46; Farnham, May 29; and Staples, July 9.

132   "We are traveling . . .": Pratt, letter June 10, *Statesman*, July 18.

132   "every bone or horn . . .": Buffum, May 19. Banks, May 23, along the Little Blue mentioned the same.

132   "We are now . . .": Pratt, letter June 10, *Statesman*, July 18.

133   "His wound will . . .": Pratt, letter June 13, *Statesman*, August 15.

      Many diarists reported shooting accidents, including Ladd, letter June 10, *Statesman*, July 18; Berrien, April 29; Farnham, June 16, told of victim abandoned by the trail; McCall, May 26; Armstrong, July 15. Other accidents included severe to fatal lacerations from falling beneath wagon wheels: Bidlack, 22.

134   "It created quite . . .": Pratt, letter June 13, *Statesman*, August 15.

135   "Some of the . . .": Anonymous, June 14.

135   "There is a store . . .": Letter signed "Mifflin," May 31, St. Louis *Weekly Reveille*, June 25.

135   "The sutler's store . . .": E. D. Perkins, June 14. Operations at the sutler's store described by Sprague, May 30.

      Fort Kearny played an important role in westward migration and Indian affairs: see Mantor, 175–207; and Willman, 215–45.

137   "There was a rumor . . .": Pratt, letter June 13, *Statesman*, August 15.

137   "The great majority . . .": Letter signed "Pawnee," May 26, *Missouri Republican*, June 16.

137   "men come in . . .": Gibbs, May 29.

137   "Every state, indeed . . .": Letter signed "Pawnee," May 18, *Missouri Republican*, June 13.

138   "The great California . . .": Letter signed "Pawnee," June 23, *Missouri Republican*, August 5.

CHAPTER IV

All dates pertain to 1849 unless otherwise cited.

PAGE

143   Epigraph: Batchelder, August 25.

145   "were plastered with . . .": Wilhelm Hoffman, 18.

146   "Not a buffalo . . .": Long, May 15.

      Messages seen along the trail were mentioned by many diarists, including: Bruff, I, 36; Parker, May 23, 1850; Pratt, June 26; and Joseph Wood, June 2.

146   "It would make . . .": Dewolf, July 7. Similar comment by Parsons, July 18, 1850.

      A few diarists copied the inscriptions on headboards—name, age, date, cause of death. Best such records by Bruff and Littleton.

      Some of the graves seen in the Platte Valley were actually caches of

supplies, camouflaged in this manner by companies which intended to return to retrieve their goods. Such caches mentioned by Bruff, I, 27; Middleton, June 19; and Stansbury, *Exploration*, August 6.

A number of diarists told of companies abandoning their sick companions along the trail: Staples, July 7, found a man "deranged and sick with
very bad diarrhea, entirely naked and sunburnt." Lord, June 6, wrote of a
similar case; also Thissell, 48; Farnham, June 17; Ingalls, July 11, 1850;
Bidlack, 22–23; and F. F. Keith, August 23, 1850.

Several companies were so determined not to lose time that they refused to stop long enough to bury their dead. The bodies were carried in
the wagons until evening camps: Thissell, 58; Loveland, May 29, 1850.

146   "If there is any . . .": Thissell, 37. The same theme was repeated by Lord,
August 14; Banks, June 10; Downer, letter October 12 (in Ressler, 248);
and Wilkins, August 25.

147   "To be the leader . . .": Farnham, September 12.

Evidence of the troubles that plagued most captains is abundant in
1849 and 1850 diaries: Bruff suffered continual exasperations, and Pritchard
presented a classic example of a captain's tribulations, June 4. Also Lorton
on fickleness of emigrants in choosing their captains, diary February 7.

For extensive examples of dissension—quarreling, feuding, fights,
stabbings, shootings, gambling arguments—which often led to the breakup
of companies, contact the author.

147   "Oh, if I could . . .": E. D. Perkins, June 16.

147   "They are much wilder . . .": Foster, June 23.

The Sioux who asked for payment of tribute were mentioned by
Sprague, June 8.

147   "the pretty young squaws . . .": Griffith, June 3.

Scores of diarists wrote lengthy, admiring descriptions of the Sioux
and told of visiting their villages. For many of the emigrants, the Sioux
seemed to be handsome examples of James Fenimore Cooper's "noble savage." Their friendliness and pretty women commanded considerable attention. Contact author for numerous references, 1849 and 1850.

148   "good light biscuits . . .": Ladd, letter June 10, *Statesman*, July 18. Goldsmith, 23, also described cooking arrangements, particularly the making of
flapjacks.

149   "We had a pail . . .": Ingalls, July 4, 1850. Parke told of ice cream and
Watson of explosives.

149   "fired a gun . . .": Lorton, diary July 4.

150   "Antelope are very . . .": Parke, May 23.

150   "It is the duty . . .": Packard and Larison, 6–7.

150   "It takes an average . . .": John King, letter June 16, 1850.

151   "The chips burn . . .": Wistar, June 4.

151   "They emit . . .": Pratt, letter July 1, *Statesman*, September 12.

153   "Not less than . . .": Sawyer, May 21, 1850.

154   "As far as . . .": McCall, June 10 and 1.

154   "races between trains . . .": Rothwell, May 15, 1850.

154   "The excitement of . . .": Joseph Wood, May 25.

158   "All the wagon covers . . .": James D. Lyon of the Plymouth Company,
traveling with the Rangers, letter July 4, Detroit *Daily Advertiser*, September 10.

159   "When we halt . . .": Goldsmith, 28–29.

159   "sometimes of several . . .": McCall, June 3.

159   "come out of . . .": Langworthy, May 28.

159 "They are very . . .": Stansbury, *Exploration*, June 30.
159 "To plunge the wagons . . .": Wistar, June 6.
160 "A fairly good . . .": Goldsmith, 29.
161 "During the forenoon . . .": Pratt, June 26, *Statesman*, September 12.
161 "All the accessible . . .": Bruff, I, 36.
162 "a proud, noble-looking . . .": Farnham, June 5.
162 "Mosquitoes can't be beat . . .": Stine, July 5 and June 20, 1850.
     Forty-niners told of swarms of mosquitoes along the Platte: Banks,
     June 11; Hamelin, June 15; Gould, July 1; Hoover, June 22.
164 "There is but one . . .": Hutchings, July 16.
     Others told of climbing Chimney Rock: Millington, May 7; Sprague,
     June 13; Pigman, May 16, 1850; and Clark W. Thompson, April 29, 1850,
     recounted how he climbed with one arm immobilized by a broken collar-
     bone!
165 "a government express . . .": Pratt, June 29, *Statesman*, September 12.
165 "We frequently meet . . .": Lyon, letter July 4, *Daily Advertiser*, September
     10.
166 "A man has a . . .": Pratt, July 2, *Statesman*, September 12.
166 "a Frenchman . . .": Lyon, July 4, *Daily Advertiser*, September 10.
166 "lives in an Indian . . .": Stansbury, *Exploration*, July 9.
     This trading post and Robidoux were described by many diarists. The
     most important new information on the subject is found in Darwin, June
     26; also E. D. Perkins, June 30, and Gorgas, May 25, 1850, give excellent
     reports. For modern survey, see Mattes, "Robidoux's Trading Post."
167 "It has been burnt": Hobart, letter July 4, *Democratic Expounder*, September
     14.
167 "the Board decided . . .": Pratt, July 3, *Statesman*, September 12.
167 "At sunrise . . .": Herman Camp, Wolverine Ranger, letter July 8, *States-
     man*, September 5.
169 "While many other . . .": Anonymous Wolverine Ranger, letter July 5,
     Democratic Expounder, September 7.
170 "The site of the fort . . .": Johnston, May 29.
170 Footnote: "Arose with a bursting . . .": Hamelin, July 5.
170 "this is a great . . .": Wilkins, June 24.
170 "Every mode of conveyance . . .": William Wilson, June 19.
170 "You see piles of . . .": Foster, June 16.
170 "Rifles are thrown . . .": Cephas Arms, letter June 29, *Knoxville Journal*,
     October 17.
170 "must either lighten . . .": Long, June 7.
171 "Bushels of letters . . .": John A. Johnson, diary June 11.

CHAPTER V

All dates pertain to 1849 unless otherwise cited.

PAGE
175 Epigraph: Delano, *Correspondence*, letter October 12.
176 "The number of . . .": Langworthy, June 27, 1850.
     Most 1849 diarists frequently mentioned wagons and other gear aban-
     doned along the trail west of Fort Laramie: Spooner, June 16; Reid, diary
     July 18.

178 "a Yankee turned . . .": James W. Evans, June 28.

Geiger and Bryarly, June 28, told of sending letters back to the States via "a party of trappers . . . 50 cents a letter. They had some thousands of letters." The Burlington, IA, *Tri-Weekly Telegraph* on August 27 told of 3,000 letters delivered from the trail.

178 "The Mormons . . . have . . .": Prichet, June 22.

The Mormon ferry was a subject of great interest to many diarists, most of whom expressed envy of the Mormons' financial success. The establishment and operation of this ferry was described by Dale L. Morgan in his definitive article "The Ferries of the Forty-niners," 12–31.

180 "There are but few . . .": Richard May, August 1848. Though written the year prior to the rush, the judgment remains accurate and relevant for the '49ers.

For a most informative commentary on mules vs. oxen and proper management of animals on the trail, see Potter, Introduction, 40–48.

180 "Everywhere within six or eight . . .": Frémont, 57.

181 "The trappers say . . .": May, July 26, 1848.

181 "Their mode of . . .": Geiger-Bryarly, June 29.

As the first tourists in the West, '49ers expressed a sense of appreciation of the wilderness world. Horace Ladd wrote home from the Black Hills: "When I get back home, I am going to fit out a nice train and take about six men and their wives and come out as far as this point on a pleasure excursion. It would be one of the greatest places in the world to travel—roads good, feed abundant, game plenty, and O! such magnificent scenery." Lyne, letter July 23, enthused: "You cannot imagine the life we lead. I have gained by the trip by nearly stopping the use of tobacco. . . ."

184 "In some trains . . .": Delano, *Life*, May 30.

184 "boiled tar and . . .": Parke, June 21.

Similar reports by William Watson, June 17; Lorton, diary June 22; Chalmers, June 6, 1850; and McDiarmid, July 11, 1850.

184 "As with few . . .": Wistar, June 22.

187 "a general crossing . . .": Burbank, June 27. He added that along the river emigrants were "making canoes, others caulking their wagon beds, and others crossing at the ferries."

188 "men are daily drowned . . .": Langworthy, June 20, 1850.

188 "six men . . . drowned . . .": Prichet, June 21.

188 "swimming about in . . .": Chamberlain, June 20.

Hoover, July 4–9, tells of five days' effort to get their oxen across the river. Many '49ers reported the difficulties and dangers of ferrying the North Platte at the Deer Creek crossings: Farnham, June 24; Foster, June 22; Joseph E. Wood reported several drownings in two days, June 21; Reid (diary) gave an extensive, highly personal account of almost drowning and the rescue of another man swept downstream, July 4; Tinker, July 11, a remarkable report; Stansbury, *Exploration*, reported twenty-eight deaths at the Deer Creek Crossings as of July 25; and Banks summed up by observing on June 22: "It seems a little like a battlefield."

For extensive survey of 1849 and 1850 diarists' reports on Deer Creek and Mormon ferry crossings of the North Platte, contact the author.

188 "Some thirty or forty . . .": E. D. Perkins, July 15.

One of the Mormons reported that each of the ten men working the ferry made $646.50 by the end of July. Spooner, June 22, observed: "While others are chasing wealth, the Mormons are catching it, no dream."

189 "This water seems . . .": Goldsmith, 49–50. E. D. Perkins says the same, July 16.

189 "Mules instinctively . . .": Jagger, June 30.
189 "mineral spring and lake . . .": *Latter-Day Saints' Emigrants Guide*, 14.
189 "were immediately unyoked . . .": Goldsmith, 49.
189 "it is impossible . . .": Stansbury, *Exploration*, July 28.
190 "is an Eden spot . . .": Shields, June 8, 1850. Forty-niners were equally praising of this spring: Castleman, July 11; Staples, July 18; Dewolf, July 23.
190 "There are several . . .": Middleton, July 20 and 19.
190 "from the summit . . .": Bruff, I, 501.
191 "more than one hundred . . .": Castleman, July 10.
191 "As soon as . . .": McKinstry, July 19, 1850.
192 "Independence Rock . . .": Bruff, I, 54.
192 "some huge monster . . .": Cross, July 8.
192 "is about two hundred . . .": Shields, June 10, 1850.
192 "Thousands of names . . .": Bryarly-Geiger, June 25.
192 "It is indeed hard . . .": Delano, *Life*, July 29.
193 "a very narrow . . .": Bruff, I, 58.
     One of the major topographic features on the trail, Devil's Gate invariably attracted the curiosity and challenged the descriptive powers of the passing emigrants. One of the most colorful descriptions: Lorton, diary July 13.
193 "a morass perhaps . . .": Delano, *Life*, June 26.
193 "The surface is dug up . . .": Bruff, I, 59.
193 "the view is beautiful . . .": MacBride, June 9, 1850.
194 "A Mormon from the Salt Lake . . .": Middleton, July 28.
     This Mormon undoubtedly was John D. Lee, who, according to his journal, was at this time "on a picking up expedition." (Picking up from the vast assortment of equipment, food and tools abandoned by the emigrants.) On August 3 he told of the hundreds of emigrants he met along the Sweetwater. He and his companion were "hailed almost every fifteen minutes by some company or other. . . . Very frequently some twenty or thirty persons would surround our wagon and plead for a moment's instructions [about the trail ahead]."

CHAPTER VI

All dates pertain to the year 1849 unless otherwise cited.
     In the first part of this chapter, I have frequently used Bruff's remarkable diary to provide details lacking in Swain's record. Bruff is especially reliable and pertinent at this point on the trail because he and his Washington City Company are traveling only forty hours behind the Rangers.

PAGE
199 Epigraph: H. Merrill, August 5 (written at the west end of Hudspeth's Cut-off).
199 "between two low hills . . .": Frémont, 60.
199 "This elevated and notable . . .": Bruff, I, 62.
199 "the summit of the continent . . .": Wistar, June 30.
199 "to take a . . ."; "long trains of wagons . . .": Delano, *Life*, June 29.
199 "I got out the . . .": Decker, June 16.
203 "They had mastered . . .": DeVoto, 66 and 67.
203 "Changed my underclothes . . .": Chamberlain, July 22.
203 "We feel puzzled . . .": Banks, July 30.

204 "Senator Benton and other . . .": William Wilson, August 6.
206 "The marsh and road . . .": Bruff, I, 64.
207 "At the forks . . .": Bruff, I, 68.
208 "This kind of . . .": E. D. Perkins, July 25.

At the forks most gold rush companies chose to travel westward via Sublette's Cut-off, first traveled with wagons in 1844. Spooner, July 19, estimated that three-quarters of the emigration had chosen the cut-off. However, an increasing number of the later companies turned south to Ford Bridger and on to the Mormon's oasis, Salt Lake City, 220 miles from the forks. This route was best described in 1849 by Doyle, Gray and Hamelin; and in 1850 by Langworthy, Lorton, McDiarmid and Newcomb.

208 "A beautiful mountain . . .": Bruff, I, 67.
208 "is a nasty, dirty . . .": Middleton, July 31.
208 "Quite a sandy . . .": Bruff, I, 71.
208 "There is something . . .": E. D. Perkins, July 25. This quote has been slightly changed to clarify meaning.
208 "thirsty and dusty . . .": Bruff, I, 71–72.
208 Footnote quote, "broke up a wagon . . .": Bruff, I, 69.
209 "Such a rough . . .": H. Merrill, July 14.
209 "smoking with dust . . .": Bruff, I, 515.
209 "very high . . ."; "appeared like a . . .": Bruff, I, 72.
209 "Before we reached . . .": Goldsmith, 51.
209 "over high, narrow . . .": Bruff, I, 76.
209 "the beautiful valley . . .": Bruff, I, 76.
210 "Crowds of wagons . . .": Middleton, August 6.

Along the creek crowds of passing emigrants sometimes produced sounds that echoed strangely in the desert wilderness. Burbank, July 14: "We are entertained this evening with various kinds of music. On both sides of the stream, drum, fife, key bugle, etc. beside various voices talking, laughing, halloing, and crowing. From the noise and bustle, one would fancy himself to be on the levee at St. Louis."

210 "a camp of some . . .": Goldsmith, 51–52. Middleton wrote of these trappers, August 4.
210 "The camp was . . .": Bruff, I, 76 and 78.
211 "and was well . . .": Bruff, I, 78.
211 "deep sand and dust . . .": Bruff, I, 81.
212 "the finest-looking 'redskins' . . .": Goldsmith, 53–54.
212 "speak many English words . . .": Bruff, I, 92 and 94.
213 footnote on mountain fever: Discussed in "Diseases, Drugs, and Doctors . . . ," by Georgia W. Read.

Best diarist statements about the fever: Nevins, letter December 2; Frush, July 2; McBride, July 15; McCall, July 5; and McKeeby, June 16, 1850; Rothwell, July 14, 1850.

214 "The descent down gravel . . ."; Burbank, July 20.
214 "Pegleg Smith . . .": Chamberlain, July 8.
214 "His squaw is . . .": Israel Hale, July 16. Decker also described Smith, June 16. And Goldsmith mentioned meeting Smith, 52–53.

As a fascinating footnote to the role of Pegleg Smith in the gold rush story, I was delighted to discover in the *Daily Alta California*, March 8, 1858, an article or rather notice which reported that Pegleg had submitted a petition to the California legislature seeking $8,000 as recompense for aid he had extended to overland emigrants.

His evaluation of his support to California emigrants was apparently a fair one, for the legislature later (date uncertain) passed a recommendation to the U.S. Congress requesting from that source (rather than from California funds!) an appropriation of $8,000 for Mr. Smith.

215 "There were at . . .": E. D. Perkins, August 9. This quote is taken from the original manuscript diary and reads somewhat differently from the published version in *Gold Rush Diary*, ed. Thomas D. Clark, 94.

The Rangers, like most companies after July 19, chose to follow Hudspeth's Cut-off, also known as Emigrants' Cut-off and sometimes Myers' Cut-off—the only part of the entire trail to California that was opened in 1849. From the diaries of Parke, Farnham, Armstrong, Joseph W. Wood, and an anonymous Granville, Ohio, diarist, I have established the date on which Benoni M. Hudspeth and John J. Myers first traversed this new trail: July 19. For extensive information on this subject, contact the author.

Dale L. Morgan in his brilliant editing of the diary of James A. Pritchard identified Benoni Hudspeth: Note 7, 144.

The best accounts by diarists who traveled via Fort Hall are Biddle, Bruff, Chamberlain, Prichet, Sprague, and Tiffany, all 1849. Bruff, I, 107, included a great quote by Richard Grant, the Hudson's Bay Company agent: "There is no place where you Yankees cannot carry a wagon that I ever saw."

215 "The road having . . .": Searles, 57–58.
215 "Whether it is . . .": Steele, August 2, 1850.
216 "When we commenced . . .": Ingalls, July 6, 1850.
216 "The dust is one . . .": E. D. Perkins, August 12.
216 "The soil is of . . .": Bennett, August 11, 1850.
217 "The lake looks white . . .": Lord, August 13.
218 "arid and dusty . . ."; "wonderfully realistic . . ."; McCoy, August 14.
219 "discouraged by our . . .": Goldsmith, 50.
219 "fresh-water lobsters . . .": Batchelder, August 24. Similar reports of eating trout, clams and mussels along the Raft: H. Merrill, August 5; Wilkins, August 16; Murrell, August 3.
219 At Cassia Creek where Hudspeth's Cut-off and the road from Fort Hall joined, the emigrants had a chance to compare distance and traveling time on the two routes. While the distance proved to be about the same and diarists reported considerable argument as to the merits of the cut-off (Burbank, August 2; Darwin, August 4; Evans, August 1; Farnham, September 11; Hale, July 28; Stuart, August 22; and Tate, July 31), nonetheless, the cut-off virtually superseded the Fort Hall route in 1850.

However slight the saving in distance, the cut-off served a psychological need—it offered a more direct, westward route, and it was *new*. The combination was irresistible.

220 "two ponies . . . and . . .": Goldsmith, 50.
221 "two tall and sharp-pointed . . .": Langworthy, September 9, 1850.
221 "Opposite these two . . .": Sawyer, June 22, 1850.
221 Footnote on Mr. Rice: For the goldseekers who traveled to Salt Lake City, there were three possible routes from there to California: westward across the desert south of the Great Salt Lake on a trail known as Hastings' Cut-off, northward around the lake and then west to rejoin the main California Trail at Steeple Rocks, or south via the Old Spanish Trail to Los Angeles.

Very few gold rush companies chose Hastings' Cut-off in 1849; the tragedy of the Donner party crossing in the Salt Desert in 1846 was well known. The great majority from Salt Lake City traveled north around the lake, 185 miles to the junction with the main trail at Cassia Creek. Best accounts are: Doyle, Hutchings and Johnston for 1849; McKeeby and Newcomb for 1850. Also see Korns and Fleming-Standing for modern studies.

In 1849 only ninety-five emigrants chose to travel south from Salt Lake City on the Old Spanish Trail to Los Angeles. Some of them became famous for the tragedy of their experience in Death Valley, particularly Manly; also Nusbaumer. The most readable, graphic recounting of this ordeal was written by diarist Lorton, 1849. His explanation for choosing this route reveals one of the tormenting choices (based on rumors) that faced the '49ers. August 14 at Salt Lake City: "No one knew what to do. To cross the trackless desert [Hastings' Cut-off] was burning yourself alive and to go the northern route was rushing into a graveyard and riding over dead bodies. . . ."

221 "This evening . . .": Middleton (traveling near the Rangers), August 26.

CHAPTER VII

All dates pertain to 1849 unless otherwise cited.

PAGE

225 Epigraph: John Wood, August 26, 1850.
225 "meanest and muddiest . . .": Belknap, 94.
225 "nothing but horse broth . . .": Ingalls, July 28, 1850.
225 "Humbug River": Joseph Henry Merrill, August 10; E. D. Perkins, September 7; and Tiffany, July 20.
229 "rancid bacon with . . .": Searls, August 19.
229 "We have a great . . .": Hale, August 18.
229 "Conversed with some . . ."; "very politely invited . . .": Bruff, I, 168 and 171.
230 "Overtaken by our fellow . . .": Hamelin, June 29.
230 "My God, McKinstry . . .": McKinstry, August 21, 1850.
     John Wood, 109, complained of the difficulty of keeping his diary each day.
230 "I looked in one . . .": Keith, August 23, 1850.
231 "the Sierra Nevada Mountains . . .": Delano, *Life*, August 10.
     Like much of Delano's "diary," this statement was obviously written after the date indicated, because the first wagons did not enter Lassen's Cut-off until August 11. However, Delano's idea and phrasing are here, as elsewhere, valid.
231 "would not have been practicable . . .": Farnham, July 31.
232 "Those who came by . . .": Banks, August 10.
     What Swain learned from Mr. Rice of the Mormons and their wilderness city was probably much the same information as that in the reports of other gold rush emigrants who passed through Salt Lake in 1849 and 1850. With few exceptions their diaries and letters speak favorably of the Saints. Three of the most vivid and observant accounts are those (all 1849) of Doyle, Hamelin (a delightful, zesty diary) and Lorton. Also good: Griffith, Millington and Newcomb, 1850, and Parsons, who stayed there from September 1850 to February 1851. Also "Letters by Forty-niners written from Great Salt Lake in 1849," *Western Humanities Review*, April 1949. Informative but decidedly hostile: Langworthy, 1850.
232 "How times change . . .": McCall, August 7.

232   "took it into his head . . .": Middleton, August 28.
233   "is about thirty-five miles . . .": Street, 74.
233   "marshes, sinks, ponds . . .": Bruff, I, 160.
233   "Clouds of steam rise . . .": Sawyer, June 25, 1850.
234   "several feet below . . .": Wistar, July 27.
234   "a grassy and willowy rivulet": Bruff, I, 161.
234   "long looked forward to . . .": Rothwell, July 21, 1850.
234   "the sterile, barren and sandy . . .": Tiffany, July 31.
234   "often struck out ahead . . .": Stuart, September 2.
234   "would serve supper . . .": Goldsmith, 56.
234   "It is too deep . . .": Wistar, August 1.
235   "never tie up their . . .": Middleton, July 27.
235   "how the Indians . . .": Goldsmith, 56.

      This incident was reported by Batchelder and Middleton on September 4; and Stuart, 59, wrote that "two members of the Wolverine Rangers came into our camp this evening [September 3] stating they had been fired at by three Indians." He reports further details and that the Rangers stayed the night with them. An unimportant event, except for the fact that it ended up in four different diaries.

235   "These birds are . . .": Bryarly-Geiger, July 25.

      Delano, *Life*, July 30, told of shooting ducks, geese and cranes along the Humboldt, while Biddle, July 29, Chalmers, August 9, 1850, and Moorman, August 16, 1850, wrote of eating frogs.

235   "Eight wagons . . .": Bruff, I, 164.

      Many diarists report meeting this band of Mormons and tell of being encouraged by their news of gold in California: Batchelder, September 5; Dewolf, 209; Foster, 50; Gould, September 3; Hackney, August 20; and Webster, 79.

235   "Every emigrant feels . . .": Ramsey, August 4.
236   Footnote on Hastings' Cut-off: Named for its promoter, Lansford W. Hastings, who in 1846 influenced several emigrant companies, including the Donner party, to travel his new shortcut to California. Leading across ninety searing miles of "the most desolate stretch of desert in America" (Korns), this route ended at the Humboldt. Reports of the few 1849 companies that followed this cut-off were given by Bruff, I, 562; Hutchings, September 25; and Lord, October 21. In contrast, hundreds of emigrants took Hastings' Cut-off in 1850. Diarists include Bloom, Chalmers, Moorman, Shinn, Skinner, Udell and John Wood. Of all the diaries written on this tragic trail, the most graphic and observant is that of McDiarmid, July 29–August 26, 1850.

      McKinstry, August 14, 15, and 29, 1850, mentioned packers along the Humboldt who had come via the cut-off; also Langworthy, September 18 and 21, 1850.

      General studies of Hastings' Cut-off: Paden, *Detours;* Kelly, *Salt Desert Trails;* and most thorough, Korns, "The Salt Lake Cut-off."

236   "The heat is fiery . . .": Lord, September 6.
236   "an ox fell down . . .": Middleton (traveling with the Rangers), September 7.
236   "There is not . . .": Middleton, September 7.
236   "The heat today . . .": Lord, September 7.
237   "The river is very . . .": Middleton, September 18.

      While it was not uncommon in 1849 for the emigrants' animals to get mired in the sloughs and mud along the Humboldt, this danger increased greatly in 1850 when rainfall was abnormally heavy and the river flooded the lowlands: Ingalls, July 7; Branstetter, July 17–August 4; Sawyer, July 2 and 4 described the unpleasant task of having to wade into the river to cut grass to feed the animals kept at a safe distance from the sloughs; Loomis, July 24; and Stine, September 6, told of many dead animals "stuck fast" in the mud.

237   "Our grass has been . . .": Middleton, September 10.

237   "They each took . . .": Middleton, September 12.

237   "marching by night": Goldsmith, 57. Goldsmith wrote in detail of his pack trip down the Humboldt and meeting John Root, 57–85.

239   "Bore the horn and . . .": Hale, August 28.

241   "The sand hills . . .": Darwin, August 17.

241   "scarcely a night . . .": Delano, *Life*, August 6.

242   "These fellows are . . .": Lord, September 2.

242   "They are seldom seen . . .": Hale, August 15 and 16.

Most diarists told of attacks, real or rumored, by the Diggers. Newcomb, August 3, 1850, summed up the emigrants' attitude: "The Digger Indians are a low-lived, mean, filthy, thieving race of beings."

Doyle, August 20, 1849, reported his company lost "thirty-four or thirty-five of our cattle during the night." A party of twenty-three armed men chased the Indians, without success. Other companies sent out armed parties in pursuit of the Diggers, some reporting emigrants wounded, Indians killed: Israel Hale, August 20; Armstrong, August 15; Willis, July 28; Banks, August 15; and Charles Turner, August 6. Wistar, July 30 and August 3, told of night guards killed by the Diggers. Troubles with the Diggers continued in 1850, with Moorman reporting August 23: "The emigrants have resolved to shoot down every Indian that makes his appearance on this river. . . ."

242   "A man can get used . . .": Langworthy, October 5, 1850.

242   "We see some of the most . . .": Batchelder, September 7.

242   "Well, they say misery . . .": Ingalls, July 28, 1850.

Similar observations on the changed appearance and mood of the emigrants were written in 1849: Clark, July 29; Lord, September 6; and letter signed "Mifflin," September 18 from California, *Weekly Reveille*, December 10.

CHAPTER VIII

All dates pertain to 1849 unless otherwise cited.

Once again the Bruff diaries have been used with great frequency. Bruff was traveling very close to the Rangers and unfailingly provided specific, graphic detail. Another diarist, Joseph Middleton, was traveling on some days with, and other days close to, the Rangers, and his account is also quoted frequently.

PAGE

247   Epigraph: John Wood, August 26, 1850.

252   "the two trails or roads . . .": Bruff, I, 179. Also Banks, August 25.

The scene at the forks where conflicting notices praised or damned the two routes was one of uncertainty and torment, with some companies engaged in serious argument: Darwin, August 16; and Doyle, September 5. Elisha Lewis, August 30, reported that his company divided, some going south to the sink, others west on the cut-off.

The tracks that led west from the forks and became known as Lassen's Cut-off were those of a company of California-bound settlers led in 1848 by Peter Lassen, who had a ranch in the northern part of the Sacramento Valley. Hoping to open a trail across the Sierra to his ranch, he led the emigrants west from the Humboldt. He followed tracks made in 1846 by emigrants bound for Oregon. Thus, for the first half of his so-called cut-off to California, Lassen led his unsuspecting emigrants north to Oregon, until at last at Goose Lake near the Oregon border he turned south into an interminable maze of mountains, finally to reach his ranch.

It was this route that the '49ers followed, beginning August 11.

Prior to August 11 all the emigration traveled south along the Humboldt River to its sink, where the muddy, alkaline water spread out in a desert slough. From there two trails led west and south to the Sierra Nevada, one to the Truckee River and the other to the Carson. Each river offered a route into the mountains, where the trails crossed the summit and led down to the Sacramento Valley. There are scores of diaries (published and manuscript) for both the Truckee and Carson routes.

252   "people are driving . . .": Middleton, September 22.
252   "are mere drippings . . .": Bruff, I, 180.
253   "I had associated with . . .": Goldsmith, 137.
253   "Two of these springs . . .": Bruff, I, 182.
256   "in the sun looks . . ."; a "very beautiful mirage . . .": Bruff, I, 183–84.
256   "parties sleeping under . . .": Goldsmith, 138–39.
256   "the great basaltic promontory . . .": Bruff, I, 571.
256   "is a deep, circular pit . . .": Middleton, September 26.
      This description is a remarkably accurate picture of Black Rock Springs as I saw it in 1953.
257   "Half an hour before . . .": Middleton, September 25.
258   "Thermometer 94° . . .": Middleton, September 28.
258   "This produced quite . . .": Bruff, I, 187 and 572.
259   "like thunder close . . .": Stuart, September 20.
260   "At one time we hear . . .": Hale, September 12.
260   "Some of the travelers . . .": Bruff, I, 188.
261   "The Wolverine Rangers are . . .": Middleton, October 3.
262   "Thank Jupiter! . . .": Bruff, I, 198.
262   "A very cold night. . . .": Middleton, October 4.
262   "Got a present of about . . .": Middleton, October 4.
263   "Thermometer at sunrise . . .": Middleton, October 5.
263   "Last night flocks of . . .": Middleton, October 8.
265   "In the center . . .": Bruff, I, 203. Israel Hale also wrote an excellent description of crossing the summit, September 3.

CHAPTER IX

All dates pertain to 1849 unless otherwise cited.

For this rather complex chapter, I have once again relied on Bruff and Middleton, because they both traveled so close to the Rangers. James Pratt's diary is the major resource, carrying on the story after Swain's diary ends. And I have extensively used the official reports of the government relief party sent to Lassen's Cut-off to rescue the emigrants. Identified as "Relief Report," these communications include letters sent by the members of the relief party who met and assisted the Rangers.

PAGE

269 Epigraph: Bruff, I, 240–41.

271 "I have just come . . .": Letter Sacramento City, September 17, Relief Report, 108.

271 "and remember that . . .": Relief Report, Peoples to Todd, 103; Rucker to Peoples, 102 and 101.

272 "it is useless . . .": James Pratt, "Notes by the Way by a Wolverine Ranger," diary entry of October 14, Marshall *Statesman*, April 17, 1850. The *Statesman* on this date printed Pratt's notes, in the form of a diary, covering October and early November. For the rest of this chapter quotations from Pratt's diary will be identified only by Pratt's name and the date of his diary entry.

272 "The government agents . . .": Pratt, October 14.

273 "the emigrants have such . . .": Bruff, I, October 3.

274 "You must tell . . .": Relief Report, Rucker to Peoples, 104.

275 "rendering it impossible . . .": Relief Report, 131.

275 "In justice to the men . . .": Relief Report, Peoples to Rucker, 122.

276 "Capt. Potts & Comp. . . .": Records of the War Department, Adjutant General's Office, letters received S–120–1850. Copy in author's possession.

277 "The teams were . . .": Pratt, October 14.

277 "The papers and records . . .": Goldsmith, 88.

277 "All feel well . . .": Pratt, October 15.

277 "the water has nearly . . .": Batchelder, September 26.

277 "The whole shore is . . .": Delano, *Life*, August 28.

278 "posted on trees . . .": Batchelder, September 29.

Reporting on the Pit Indians, Lieutenant R. S. Williamson of the U.S. Topographical Engineers wrote: "They act with a great deal of caution, never showing themselves during the day. They have no other arms than bows and arrows. . . ." (From Williamson, "Report," 20.) Many companies lost some or all of their surviving teams to the night-raiding Pits. Typical reports of such losses: Farnham, September 6; Castleman, September 29; Israel Hale, September 6; and Granville Ohio Company, September 6.

On October 18, Middleton reported the death of two emigrants on guard duty killed by the Pits. Keller in 1850 told of eight emigrants killed in a fight with these Indians. As well, the Pits harassed the government relief parties (Relief Report, 105, 117, and 119).

Though of only peripheral interest as a further example of the Pit Indians' depredations, their September 26 attack on a party of Topographical Engineers near Goose Lake allows me to mention that the U.S. government as early as 1849 had authorized exploration to find the most practicable route for a railroad to California. The commander of this railroad survey, Captain William H. Warner, and two of his men were killed in the ambush. (See Williamson, 21; and Bruff, I, 228.) The northernmost reaches of the Sierra Nevada were later named the Warner Range in memory of the captain.

A number of emigrant diarists wrote of meeting Captain Warner's party prior to his death, including Biddle, September 6; Gray, September 13; Howell and Pond, September 14; Doyle, September 20 and Stuart, September 27. On October 4, Lord wrote of Warner's death and on October 5, Austin told of treating one of Warner's wounded men.

It is interesting to note that Peter Lassen acted as guide for Captain Warner, Lassen having persuaded Warner that the most practicable route for a railroad lay along Lassen's Cut-off—to his ranch (see Williamson Report, 19). The survey, in fact, proved that such a route was decidedly impractical. Biddle, September 6 and Gray, September 13, both mention meeting Lassen as guide of the Warner party.

278 "Frequent deep pits . . .": Middleton, October 18.
278 "They are some ten . . .": Castleman, October 1. Also B. W. Evans, September (n.d.).
278 "After dark when . . .": Pratt, October 17.
279 "Far to the west . . .": Pratt, October 18.
279 "Last night Mr. McClellan . . .": Pratt, October 19.
279 "We have a good . . .": Pratt, October 19.
280 "were vestiges of . . .": Bruff, I, 209.
280 "because we saw . . .": Pratt, October 21.
280 "killed a beef . . .": Middleton, October 21.
281 "Evidences of a large . . .": Pratt, October 26 and 27.
282 "the Indians carried . . .": Bruff, I, 217.
282 "They wanted us . . ."; "It is now evening . . .": Pratt, October 26.
282 "Our duck soup . . .": Pratt, October 27.
282 "as a last . . .": Doyle, October 6.
282 "Many emigrants were . . .": Middleton, October 26.

As to scurvy, Doyle on October 9 reported: "Scurvy very prevalent. . . . Many men have died with it in the last ten days." For a graphic description of the disease among the emigrants on the cut-off, see Hoppin, 1.

283 "Sacred to the memory . . .": Bruff, I, 228.
283 "an Irishman and . . .": Bruff, I, 218.

Delano, *Life*, September 12, tells an amusing, richly graphic tale of trying to eat "hard, dry beefsteak."

283 "very nearly round . . .": Doyle, October 5.
284 "begins twenty miles . . .": Pratt, October 31.
284 "It is not . . .": George Jewett, October 2.
284 "Water occurs . . .": Pratt, October 31.
285 "sold bread at . . .": Bruff, I, 219.
285 "was surrounded by . . .": Bruff, I, 222.
285 "We remain here . . .": Pratt, October 31.
285 "In fourteen miles . . .": Bruff, I, 597.
285 "It rained hard . . .": Pratt, November 1.
286 "the banks are . . .": Bruff, I, 228.
286 "It is night . . .": Pratt, November 1.
286 "This morning . . .": Pratt, November 2.
286 "For twenty miles . . .": Relief Report, Peoples to Rucker, 133.
286 "This evening we . . .": Pratt, November 2.
286 "It rained and . . .": Pratt, November 3.
286 "Daylight dawned . . .": Swain, letter March 15, 1850.
286 "The rest of . . ."; "Rogers and one . . ."; "The evening clears . . .": Pratt, November 4.
288 "the Devil's backbone": Doyle, "Table of Distances and Guide to Lassen's Trail."
288 "This ridge was . . .": Doyle, October 11.
288 "Between us and . . .": Lord, October 29.
289 "On we went . . ."; "Along the ridge . . ."; "We pressed on . . .": Pratt, November 7. Bruff, II, 634, on this day reported that other members of the scattered Ranger company camped near him.
290 "Before daylight we . . .": Pratt, November 8.

Another Ranger who told of the company's flight from the mountains and snow and of the suffering on the trail was James D. Lyon, letter December 24, Detroit, *Daily Advertiser*, February 22, 1850.

290   "A more pitiable . . .": Stuart, October 19.
290   "Our journey is done . . .": Wistar, August 26, 1849.
291   "I won't attempt . . .": Orvis, letter February 15, 1850.
291   "a pitiable sight . . .": Relief Report, Rucker to Smith, December 20, 1849; 139.
291   "everything is . . ."; "The tenements at Lassens . . .": Doyle, October 14.
291   "Twenty-five cents . . .": Lord, October 31 and November 1.

CHAPTER X

All quotations by Wolverine Rangers (Pratt, Camp, Ladd and Hobart) are cited by the page on which they are reprinted in *The Gold Rush, Letters from the Wolverine Rangers to the Marshall Statesman, 1849–51*, given below on the short form *Gold Rush Letters Statesman*.

All quotations from Delano, unless otherwise cited, are from *Alonzo Delano's California Correspondence*, with date and page.

PAGE
296   Epigraph: William Wells, October 21, 1850.
296   10,000 overlanders via southern routes: Egan, 280.
297   6,000 Sonorans: William Perkins, 29–30.
297   697 vessels entered San Francisco Harbor: Joan Margo, 90.
        401 were ships from American ports and 296 foreign. On February 1, 1850, Derbec, 77, reported at San Francisco: "There is no end to the number of ships entering the port . . . overloaded with emigrants. . . . The ships enter twenty at a time, one behind the other."
297   41,000 Americans and foreigners, including 800 women: Soule, 243.
300   "On our poor little maps . . .": Derbec, 97–98.
301   Parker House rentals and revenue: William Perkins, footnote, 87.
301   canvas tent: Bayard Taylor, 44.
        Taylor, 45, told of other "buildings" in San Francisco in June 1849 with annual rents of $75,000, and a one-story, twenty-foot-wide store at $40,000. From such properties one San Franciscan derived an income of $50,000 *monthly;* another, who died insolvent in fall 1848 with debts of $41,000, left real estate with rentals that advanced so rapidly that after his debts were paid, his heirs received a yearly income of $40,000. Soule, 254, tells of similar astonishments.
301   interest rate: Soule, 254. Pratt, 107, said interest at 10% per month "is the lowest figure money lets for."
301   San Francisco population: Bayard Taylor, 153.
301   25,000 letters: Winchester, August 26, 1849. Double that number: Bayard Taylor, 156.
303   *Senator*'s profit: McGowan, "San Francisco-Sacramento Shipping . . . ," 49–50.
303   packers' 75 cents per pound: Joan Margo, 49.
303   eggs: *Gold Rush Letters Statesman*, December 12, 1849, 76.
303   steam engine: Bayard Taylor, 153.
303   prostitute: Garniss, 17.
303   farmer: Bayard Taylor, 163.
303   blankets, boots and flour: *Gold Rush Letters Statesman*, 81, 73, 87.
        Throughout letters, diaries and narratives telling of San Francisco and other towns in 1849, there are scores of examples of "high prices," listed to

astonish the reader and describe the character of California's economy.

303   annual gold production: Paul, *California Gold*, appendix.

304   "we have got $5,000": A. Dunn, postscript to letter, November 4, 1849, Kalamazoo *Gazette*, February 1, 1850.

304   "had raised in . . .": *Alta California*, August 30, 1849.

Reports of great success in mining during 1849 were common: Bayard Taylor, 172, said that $10,000 was "frequently made"; an overlander who arrived in October made $6,000 by December, *Gold Rush Letters Statesman*, 85.

308   "had expected to . . .": Pratt, December 20, 1849, 70.

308   "There is a world . . .": Pratt, December 20, 1849, 72 and 74.

308   "by far the best . . .": E. S. Camp, January 9, 1850, 93.

308   "there are a great . . ."; "I should like . . .": Ladd, January 9, 1850, 88 and 90.

309   "16,000 pounds . . ."; Ladd, January 19, 1850, 96.

Information on other Rangers: *Gold Rush Letters Statesman*, 97, 119 and 154.

309   "the boys are . . .": E. S. Camp, February 17, 1850, 119 and 96.

Less fortunate Rangers: *Gold Rush Letters Statesman*, 97 and 121.

309   "Over a month . . .": Pratt, December 25, 1849, 75.

310   "This long, anxious . . .": Page, December 29, 1850.

310   "If you could . . .": Fairchild, January 1, 1850.

311   "besides uncounted . . ."; "which extended all . . .": Bayard Taylor, 156 and 158.

312   "Over two thousand . . ."; Doyle, November 3, 1849.

312   "Wherever the eye . . .": Gerstaecker, 162.

312   "There were fifteen . . .": *Gold Rush Letters Statesman*, December 12, 1849.

From the same report: "This place [Long's Trading Post] contains about 1,500 inhabitants, both sides of the river. With the exception of a few log cabins covered with sailcloth and beef hides [for roofs], they live in tents."

312   "a comfortable house . . .": Lord, January 3, 1850.

Others who described Long's: Castleman, October 26, 1849; Kimball Webster, October 19, 1849; and Pond, December 2, 1849.

312   "The river was . . .": Doyle, November 11, 1849.

313   "Last fall a . . .": Doyle, January 20, 1850.

313   "If the main stream . . .": Lord, February 11, 1850.

313   "a company of men . . .": John A. Johnson, "Letters," November 20, 1849.

313   "had been but a little . . .": Delano, March 2, 1850, 40.

313   "rushed to the mines . . .": Delano, November 19, 1849, 31 and 30.

Batchelder in November 1849 told of "many miners without shelter of any kind except their India-rubber clothing."

314   "Physicians are all . . .": Letter by William Royall, quoted in Wyman, 158. This writer went on to say: "I have known doctors charge a patient as much as $100 for one visit and prescription."

314   "Nobody moves here . . .": Delano, March 22, 1850, 57.

Main, March 18–19, 1850, gave a vivid account of packing in supplies on his back through deep snow.

314   "The descent to . . .": Lord, February 19, 1850.

Batchelder, January 7, 1850, gave a good description of traveling from Long's Trading Post to his claim six miles up the South Fork of the Feather; and Baker, May 1850, gave a detailed account of traveling from Marysville to Stony Point on the South Fork.

314 "As to the amount . . .": Batchelder, January 7, 1850.
    An excellent discussion-survey of the northern mining region and of mining methods is found in Delano, 24, 57–58.
315 "hauling provisions paid . . .": Delano, October 12, 1849, 24.
    Albert Lyman, October 16, 1849, described the road from Sacramento City to the American River diggings as "fairly thronged with teams and trailers. Vast numbers of heavy teams with goods for the mines leave daily and pack mules for the same destination are to be seen in caravans."
    Also, Pritchard told of profits from hauling, 140.
315 "the ground was so . . .": Hover, letter, November 29, 1849.
316 "many teams stalled . . .": Stuart, November 13, 1849.
    Difficulties of hauling and packing and consequent increase in prices: Delano, 25 and 34; Stillman, November 19, 1849; Fairchild, December 8, 1849; Hall, letter November 25, 1849.
316 "there were not . . .": Delano, November 19, 1849, 32, and March 12, 1850, 50.
    Faced with California prices, one recent arrival wrote home February 15, 1850, advising how best to prepare for a trip to El Dorado: "What is needed above all else are pockets full of money." Derbec, 84.
    With the pockets of would-be miners quite empty, most everyone depended on credit—and to a surprising extent throughout the mining regions miners could buy supplies and equipment on credit. Pratt told of Rangers buying at Long's Trading Post on credit, December 20, 1849; Castleman, October 27, 1849, told of credit offered at Bidwell's Bar; Patterson, August 29, 1849, reported easy credit at Hangtown.
    Without credit offered at the stores in mining camps, most miners could not have bought provisions while working their claims. Pratt, December 20, 1849, 73, reported that Ranger Herman Camp "buys all provisions —flour, pork, molasses, sugar, etc.—on credit." His bill at Long's Trading Post totaled $1,200.
316 "When a man . . .": Hall, letter November 25, 1849.
316 "The security we enjoy . . .": McCall, October 13, 1849.
316 "The general honesty . . .": Wistar, 123.
    Comments on the safety of personal possessions, including gold, were commonplace. Of greater interest is the miners' assumption, sometimes protestation, that the "general honesty" was directly attributable to "Lynch Law." Many diarists and letter writers wrote home, often with a tone of boastfulness, to tell of the swiftness and severity of punishment inflicted for robbery. A good example, by Parke, September 18, 1849, at Bidwell's Bar: "No great Criminal Lawyer is allowed to humbug in this country, thereby creating the hope of escape. . . . Miners' Laws are swift and certain in their execution." Lord said the same, January 5, 1850.
316 "two cases of theft . . .": Ladd, February 6, 1850, 97.
317 "if a man steals . . .": Letter on Yuba River, October 21, 1849, Kalamazoo *Gazette*, February 1, 1850.
    Lord, November 1, 1849, told of a flogging of thirty lashes for theft of a revolver. Lyman gave a good account of a crime, resulting arrest, trial and verdict in summer 1849, 121–22.
317 "a man stole . . .": John A. Johnson, "Letters," August 26, 1849.
    Bayard Taylor in September 1849, 71, told of a man near Stockton whose head had been shaved and his ears cut off after receiving a hundred lashes for stealing "ninety-eight pounds of gold."
317 "between two companies . . .": Delano, March 2, 1850, 40.

317 "They divided the river . . .": Batchelder, December 4, 1849, writing from the South Fork of the Feather River.

Delano, 40–41, explained these same requirements, and Lord, February 24, 1850, told of another dispute at Oregon Bar, South Fork, and its settlement by the miners' association.

317 "registers his name . . .": Delano, March 2, 1850, 41.

317 "We see nothing . . .": Batchelder, December 4, 1849, writing from the South Fork of the Feather.

318 "The sight of a late . . .": Delano, February 16, 1850, 37.

318 "As it now stands . . .": Harker, "Morgan Street," letter February 2, 1850, 75–76.

320 "if there had been . . .": Ramsey, September 13, 1849.

Similar laments: Abrams, September 16, 1849; E. D. Perkins, October 6, 1849.

320 "Two-thirds . . .": Nash, letter February 27, 1850, *Statesman*, April 10, 1850.

Theodore T. Johnson, 2, summed up the plight of many: "Day after day we saw parties filing down from the mountains filled with disgust and disappointment at the climate, the country and the inaccessible nature of the gold regions to which thousands had been assured their vessels could sail, furnishing them with a home on board while they were engaged in gold digging on the shady banks of the beautiful rivers."

321 "The streets are half a leg . . .": Winchester, November 19, 1849.

321 "The whole city . . ."; "There are a great number . . .": Lord, December 22, 1849.

321 "One of these . . .": Johnston, September 9, 1849.

Gray, November 9, 1849, gives names and descriptions of Sacramento gambling halls.

321 "is a place made . . .": Darwin, September 2, 1849.

321 "The only object . . .": Anonymous letter, Sacramento City, January 29, 1850, *Michigan Expositor*, March 26, 1850. Though written after the destructive flood of January 8, this letter specifically referred to conditions prior to the flood.

321 "The door of many . . ."; "The southern part . . .": Bayard Taylor, 205–06, 208–09.

322 "People at home . . .": Stillman, December 23, 1849.

Speaking of sickness and death in the mines and the cities, Delano, March 22, 1850, said that most emigrants, even if they had come through their journey in good health, "must be sick after arrival. Exposure and bad diet contribute much to producing sickness." Lord, May 23, 1850, told of a company of thirty-two men who came overland safely but by that date "more than one third are dead." Scurvy was common: Shufelt, March 3, 1850; Batchelder, September 10, 1850; Fairchild, 63; Letts, 122; Joseph C. Buffum, 97; and Hoppin, November 25, 1849.

Even more prevalent was diarrhea. Dr. J. D. B. Stillman, "Observations," 299–300.

Lord summed it up, April 3, 1850: "Rheumatic pains are rife, scurvy is as common as damaged flour, and diarrhea haunts the dwellers of this famous land."

A final comment from an anonymous letter writer, November 29, 1849 (Wyman, 85): Many of the miners "have gotten well of the gold fever but have been suddenly taken ill with homesickness. . . . Suicides caused by disappointment are numerous." Bruff, June 29, 1850, II, 800, told of suicides also.

322 "December 24 . . ."; "December 25. . . ."; "December 26. . . .": Lord, same dates.

324 "the reckless spirit . . .": Morse, 58.

325 "the water is still . . ."; "then come in . . ."; "All sorts of means . . ."; "January 13 . . .": Stillman, January 12 and 13, 1850.

In this most famous of Sacramento's floods, the water rose an average of four feet within the city, the consequence of a total rainfall of 36 inches.

326 "It is a hard . . .": Buck, 60.

326 "Hundreds of thousands . . .": Morse, 62.

A wonderful example of California's optimism was offered by Coit, 101, when he told of the mood in Sacramento during the January 1850 flood. Speaking of the value of real estate ("at the most unheard-of prices"), he said that even the flood did not affect those prices. "As people could not get about with ordinary convenience to attend to business, they made a sort of real estate exchange of their house tops where many lots, then under water, changed hands."

326 "Instead of the people . . .": Buck, 59.

326 "Small boats brought . . .": Morse, 62.

326 "Those who had . . .": Letter January 28, 1850, *Michigan Expositor*, April 2, 1850.

326 "What a smell! . . .": Orvis, February 15, 1850.

327 "Many of the miners . . .": Ladd, January 9, 1850, 88–89.

327 "have cloth roofs . . .": Pond, December 2, 1849.

327 "is called Stringtown . . .": Lord, February 20 and 19, 1850. Baker also described Stringtown, June 1850.

327 "Trading posts . . .": Batchelder, South Fork of the Feather, February 17, 1850.

327 "A miner can . . .": Letter by Ranger George Allcott on the Feather River, December 1849, Kalamazoo *Gazette*, March 29, 1850.

328 "say they will kill . . .": Fitch, letter Coloma, April 29, 1849.

Miners' cruelty to and abuse of any and all Indians encountered is reflected in only a few diaries; generally the subject is avoided. Fitch in his April 29, 1849, letter told of "Oregon men" who had killed "about 40 Indians and burned their rancheros." Hall, January 1851, also told of the Oregonians' "great antipathy" for Indians "whom they frequently murder when out of sight of other miners." John A. Johnson, August 26, 1849, told of miners' shooting "every Indian they could find." William I. Morgan gave numerous examples of his and other miners' casual cruelty to Indians.

As with prostitution, very few miners mentioned Indian women, a subject beyond the pale of Victorian morality and sensibilities. But in a mining region with 40,000 to 50,000 men, plenty of liquor and few women, it was inevitable there would be many sad instances of indignities, abuse and violence.

328 "Indians are now . . .": Delano, November 19, 1849, 28.

Batchelder on the South Fork of the Feather, December 22, 1849: "We see Indians almost every day traveling up and down the river. Some are employed in the mines by the whites. . . ." Also Banks, December 9, 1849.

329 "Though there is . . .": Page, letter January 27, 1850, 230–31.

330 "Newspapers are printed . . ."; "Besides the occasional . . .": Page, 230, 244.

332 "companies are digging . . .": Batchelder, January 7, 1850.

332 "requires much labor . . .": Baker, June 1850.

Hobart, a Wolverine Ranger, with his son and five others, dug a race along the South Fork of the Feather. He described the work in a letter, May 24, 1850, *Statesman*, August 21, 1850. For two months they worked at cutting a canal about 25 rods long, into which the river would be turned. "We cut through granite rock from five to six feet deep the whole length. Our tools cost us a great deal together with our provisions." Howland, 359, also described digging a canal or race along the Feather.

335   Footnote, "your advice . . .": Fairchild, 53–54.
336   "Vice seems more . . .": Daniel Woods, 187.
336   "Sabbath days here . . .": Hoppin, letter June 16, 1850.
336   "Wherever rich diggings are . . .": Howland, 485.
336   "Their diggings are . . .": Delano, *Pen-Knife Sketches*, 25–26.
336   "Almost everybody drinks . . .": Lord, April 4 and 28, 1850.
337   "There seems to be . . .": Lord, April 28, 1850.
337   "Religion and religious . . .": John A. Johnson, "Letters," October 21, 1849.
337   "advise that the . . .": Ingalls, letter December 13, 1849.
337   "A most profitable . . .": John A. Johnson, "Letters," December 18, 1849.
337   "Very few on . . .": Lord, March 14, 1850.

The risks and losses encountered by the merchants in San Francisco, and Sacramento too, were discussed by Derbec, who on February 15, 1850, 84, wrote of merchants "crushed under exorbitant rents" and wildly fluctuating prices who gave up business to go into mining—an ironic twist, for the miners believed the merchants were making the fortunes in California.

In an editorial entitled "Fluctuations in the Market," *Alta California*, February 25, 1850, argued that the wild swings in commercial prices were caused by rumors. "San Francisco is a great whispering gallery" where rumors of surplus and shortage spread quickly.

CHAPTER XI

PAGE
350   Epigraph: Dutton, December 28, 1850.
352   "dated March 13 . . .": Parke, May 4, 1850.
352   "I really hope . . .": Lord, August 11, 1850.
353   "Oh, Matilda . . .": Dewolf, letter July 30, 1850, 221.

The subject of the emotional relationship between miners and their families is one that (like so many others in the gold rush experience) has not been adequately explored and studied. Hidden, or rather obscured, amid extensive factual diaries and letters, I have found maybe twenty poignant, nakedly revealing statements and laments by miners telling of their loneliness, their wounded pride and their hope that they can return home without embarrassment. Far more difficult to find, because so few of their letters have survived, are the revelations of anxiety and doubt written by wives and other relatives, sent to their men in California. The gold rush was in many respects a national tragedy, much like a war, with families separated not only by distance but equally by fear and silence. I am hopeful one day of preparing an adequate survey of this most emotional dimension of the gold rush. Meantime, the following quote offers a hint of the pent-up emotions.

Writing to his wife in Illinois, William Peacock in the mining town of Ophir ended his letter of January 5, 1851: "I would come home if I was not ashamed to, as I feel you and my friends would have just cause to reproach me with folly in coming here against your advice. I hope you will forgive me and receive me kindly if I come home, which I fear will be the case. I shall stay and try it this summer and if I can do nothing, I will be satisfied to return and spend my days in peace and poverty with my family."

353 "Such stories are . . .": Charles Nash, letter July 10, 1850, *Statesman*, September 4, 1850.

353 "I understand by some . . .": Wilson, letter November 24, 1850.

353 "When I first heard . . .": Hall, November 25, 1849.

353 "I have yet . . .": John A. Johnson, diary September 28, 1849.
Delano, *Correspondence*, says the same, 26–27.

354 "A great mistake . . .": Joseph C. Buffum, 112–13.

354 *Placer Times* information on imports comes from the issue of October 10, 1850. Some of this information is also from the Sacramento *Transcript*, December 25, 1850. See McGowan and Joan Margo for extensive studies of imports and freighting to the mines.

354 Count at San Francisco of immigration by sea during 1850: from the *Pacific News*, January 6, 1851; p. 2.
Exemplary of the ratio of men to women, the *Alta California*, August 2, 1849, reported 3,565 men and 49 women had landed during the month of July.
Count of the overland immigration as estimated at Fort Laramie.

354 "I don't suppose . . .": Kent, letter September 7, 1850.

355 "Got nearer to . . .": Crackbon, April 2, 1850.

355 "Women here are . . .": Allcott, letter (n.d.; probably January 1850), Kalamazoo *Gazette*, March 29, 1850.

355 "there are eight . . .": Main, July 16, 1850.

355 "One celebrated character . . .": Garniss, 17. The women who rode horseback dressed as men were mentioned by Decker, October 17, 1850.
As previously observed, there were very few diarists who mentioned prostitutes: Darwin, 158 and 190; Anderson, July 25, 1851; and William Brown, July 25, 1850.

355 "The best house . . .": Clark W. Thompson, letter August 24, 1850.

355 "There is a bar . . .": E. D. Perkins, 195.

356 "Gambling, drinking and . . .": Fairchild, letter June 1, 1850.

357 "up to the top . . .": Lord, April 28, 1850.

357 "use of submarine . . ."; "made by an old . . .": Daniel Woods, 186.
Carnahan, letter on South Fork, July 29, 1850, told of miners "trying diving bells, while others have submarine dresses to work the bottoms of the streams." Also Knower, 161; DeGroot, 273–80.

358 "Many persons are . . ."; "You will ask . . .": Three letters dated November 29, 1849; n.d.; and January 24, 1850, quoted in Wyman, *California Emigrant Letters*, 85, 86 and 87–88.

359 "was making a very . . .": Pratt, letter December 20, 1849, *Statesman*, February 20, 1850.

359 "Some have made . . .": Letter January 24, 1850, quoted in Wyman, 87.

359 "In many cases . . .": Daniel Woods, 90 and 109.

359 "In traveling around . . .": Fairchild, letter February 12, 1850, 61.
Letts said the same, 101–02.

359 "Provisions are now . . .": Delano, *Correspondence*, April 4, 1850, 61.

359 "Small towns are . . .": Fairchild, June 1, 1850.

360 "You can scarcely . . .": Harker, "Morgan Street," letter February 2, 1850, 74–75.

360 "Not one man . . .": Page, letter December 16, 1849, 212.

360 "are about as useful . . .": Lord, July 29, 1850.

363 Footnote, "There are Negroes . . .": Lord, April 30, 1850; and "With twenty good . . .": Milner, letter August 15, 1850, 538.

364 "The amount drunk . . .": Lord, South Fork, Feather River, June 1, 1850. Letts, 120–22, wrote of liquor as the miner's "first consolation" and, 128, said: "Our bottle was a universal panacea."

364 "So much liquor . . .": Cosad, August 5, 1849.

364 "If the good people . . .": Parke, September 9, 1850.

364 "several of the richest . . .": Winchester, letter Sacramento City, January 1850.

365 "you will see . . .": Buck, letter February 12, 1850.

365 "seven steamboats arc . . .": Letter signed "E.C.K.," Sacramento City, March 23, 1850, *Alta California*, March 28, 1850.

365 "Many of the mountain . . .": Letter Marysville, April 25, 1850, *Placer Times*, April 29, 1850.

365 Footnote: Rush to the Trinity River described by deMassey who told of his voyage from San Francisco to Trinity Bay, difficulties of reaching the mines from the coast, and his mining disappointment through August 1850 when he returned to San Francisco. Also Pritchard, 139–40.

365 "It seems like . . .": Lord, South Fork, Feather River, April 4 and 14, 1850.

366 "The forest is . . .": Howland, 473.

366 "Other products of . . .": Isaac Baker, South Fork, May 1850.

366 "There are so many . . .": Batchelder, South Fork, February 17 and January 7, 1850.

367 Footnote: "I am much amused . . .": Delano, *Correspondence*, March 2, 1850, 44.

369 "have wrought great changes . . .": Delano, *Correspondence*, March 12, 1850, 46–47. And March 2, 1850, 43–44.
    Baker, May 23, 1850, wrote of real estate speculation and of "paper towns."

369 "Probably the best . . .": Lord, November 8, 1849.

369 "Unlike any other . . ."; "But here has been . . .": Editorial entitled "The State of Society in California," Marysville *Herald*, August 20, 1850.

370 "All are here . . .": Decker, October 2, 1850, 235.

370 "many are leaving . . .": Lord, South Fork, May 25, 1850.
    John A. Mason, letter near Sonora, November 17, 1850, said much the same: "There is some men makes money digging but they are few. Merchants and gamblers make all, and so soon as they start home, they tell you that they dug it. But not so, not one word of it is truth."

371 Footnote on Tolles: Wiltsee, *The Pioneer Miner*, 43 and 45.

372 Footnote: Love, November 3–7, 8–13 and 25 and December 28, 1849.

373 "There are thousands . . .": Ingalls, 16.

373 "diarrhea was so . . .": Stillman, "Observations," 299–300.

373 "the miners here . . .": Lord, July 16 and June 11, 1850.
    Sandbag dams: Delano, *Correspondence*, April 4, 1850; 61. Stuart, June 22, 1850, described in detail how a sandbag dam was built on the South Fork; and Bishop, June 15, 1850, told of building a dam with 700 bags of white cotton drill filled with sand.

373 "was made by felling . . .": Main, South Fork, March 28, 1850.

374 "Every stream in . . .": Fairchild, May 20, 1850, 69.

374 "the bed, bars and . . .": Decker, May 18, 1850, 213.

374 "are packed in . . .": Lord, May 10, 1850.

374 "men to pack in . . .": Letter, North Fork of the Yuba River, April 14, 1850, Sacramento *Transcript*, April 25, 1850.

375 "There are many . . .": Joseph W. Wood, October 20, 1850. Wood wrote

extensively on Mexican mule packers. Others: Albert Lyman, 118; Lord, May 8, 1850; Isaac Baker, May 22, 1850.

375 "are rarely lazy . . .": Meyer, 74–75.

375 Footnote: Page, letter September 29, 1850, 295.

   Edwin G. Hall at Sacramento, October 26, 1849: "The stores instead of being filled up with calicos, laces, and silks are filled with pick axes, spades, shovels, etc. etc."

376 "The news that . . ."; "What will be the fate . . .": Charles Nash, letter July 10, 1850, *Statesman*, September 4, 1850.

376 "Why do men . . .": Kip, 33–34.

377 "Some articles may . . .": Sweetser, May 24, 1850.

377 "Everything is wild . . .": Clark W. Thompson, letter Nevada City, September 23, 1850.

378 "Ten per cent . . .": Letter by "a Wolverine Ranger," February 27, 1850, *Statesman*, April 17, 1850.

378 "Generally the water . . .": Delano, *Correspondence*, letter Stringtown, July 29, 1850, 86.

379 "a flume is in . . .": Batchelder, July 23, 1850.

379 "an unlooked-for . . .": Delano, *Correspondence*, 86.

379 "One dam has . . .": Lord, July 16, 1850.

379 "nine men damming . . .": Banks, August 25, 1850.

380 "One report in . . .": Hoppin, June 16, 1850.

   Bruff gave an extensive accounting of the Gold Lake excitement, July 14–August, 1850. Also Parke, June 18, 1850; and Lord, June 18 and 27, 1850.

380 "Early morning . . .": Osborn, July 29, 1850.

381 "Most all the canals . . .": Batchelder, South Fork, August 15, 1850.

381 "A dozen companies . . .": Delano, *Correspondence*, South Fork, September 1, 1850, 92.

382 "From every direction . . .": Lord, July 20, 1850.

   Scores of reports told of bitter disappointment among the river-damming companies. Anguished, angry, despairing men told of their failures: Sawyer, 113; Windeler, August 4, 6 and 13, 1850; Gorgas, September 9, 1850; Fairchild, 86; Lord, August 1, 1850.

   Daniel Woods, 170–76, prepared the most extensive survey of the success or failure of river mining operations, covering fourteen companies. As well, he surveyed miners who made money by gambling, in trade, and by various other means. This unique record covers mining in the Tuolumne River area and south to Mariposa, November 1849–April 1850.

382 Footnote, "took out in an hour . . .": Parke, June 26, 1850.

383 Footnote, "It is hard . . .": Fairchild, letters March 19, 1851, and October 18, 1850; and "O, Caroline . . .": Orvis, letter September 15, 1850.

CHAPTER XII

PAGE

393 Epigraph: Schliemann, 56.

393 "Hope is gone . . ."; "We set out . . .": Windeler, August 13, 1850, 88.

   Bitter disappointment and angry denunciations of California are common in the diaries and letters of late summer and fall, 1850, reflecting the failure of river mining. Sawyer, 113; Gorgas, September 9; Fairchild, October 18; Plummer, September 2; Edmund Booth, 30; Batchelder, August 15. Clark W. Thompson summed up on November 30, 1850: "California is a grand humbug!"

393 Bidwell's Bar, $8,000 for each miner: From E. S. Camp, Wolverine Ranger, letter August 20, 1850, *Statesman*, December 4, 1850.

Other reports of success in river mining sustained the many less lucky through the summer of 1850: miners on Spanish Bar on the American River took from their river claim $6,796 in just three days; another miner on that river sent to his family in New Jersey $5,376 (Fitch, September 8, 1850).

Another method of mining attracted a growing number of miners in the late summer of 1850. In the northern mines of the Yuba River and in the area around Nevada City there developed what was called coyote or "kiota" diggings "named from a small species of wolf that burrows like a fox" (Kent, letter December 8, 1850). This mining effort required digging a shaft, like a well, down to bed rock where horizontal tunnels were excavated to follow on or near the bed rock where gold was found. Timbers had to be set to prevent collapse of the tunnels. The miners "crawl on their hands and knees and work in this way. The gold-bearing dirt is drawn up by windlass to be washed. The kiota gold is very fine dust." (Sawyer, 118–20). Some of these shafts reached down as deep as ninety-seven feet. In all of them the air was foul, dust thick, danger great. Reports of success, as always, sustained those at work and attracted those disappointed in other areas. A letter from Nevada City, August 9, 1850, published in the Sacramento *Transcript* August 15, reported that two men had dug from a kiota claim "their pile of $18,000 in four or five weeks."

395 Descriptions of dams collapsing, or raging rivers tossing aside the miners' summer-long efforts, are best set forth by Daniel Woods, 152; Mulford, "The Bed of the River," 396; Derbec, 150.

396 "You think that . . .": Ellis, letter December 29, 1850.

396 "business of all kinds . . .": Dutton, December 28, 1850.

Same: Lew B. Harris, June 26, 1850; Delavan, letter August 6, 1850, *Michigan Expositor*, October 1, 1850. As early as the first summer of mining, 1848, Chester Lyman warned, 273: "Everyone cannot get rich trading."

396 "It is not strange . . .": Osborn, July 25, 1850.

397 "all over California . . .": Sawyer, letter Sacramento City, September 13, 1850.

397 "many curse the day . . .": Fairchild, letter September 1850, 84–85.

397 "an industrious, worthy man . . .": Delano, *Correspondence*, letter September 1, 1850.

398 "inefficient, mongrel . . .": Bancroft, *History*, VI, 268.

399 November 13, 1849; number of voters: Bancroft, VI, 305.

399 "California has been . . .": Dart, letter December 26, 1850.

400 "which belonged to . . .": William Perkins, 34.

For an informative, sensitive study of the causes and consequences of the Foreign Miners' Tax, see Dale L. Morgan, Introduction to William Perkins, 29–44. Also Pitt, 54–68.

401 "the brilliant star spangled banner": William Perkins, 41.

"Money is our only . . .": I am embarrassed to admit, I cannot identify this source.

402 "vast quantities . . .": *Alta California*, April 15, 1850. 10,000 miners: reported January 11, 1850, by Andrew Bradbury in San Francisco, in a letter printed in Decker, 18–19.

Further information on the rush to the Trinity mines: see Massey whose diary offers an extensive account; also Pritchard, 139–40.

402 "is covered with . . .": Bruff, II, 1113.

    See Bruff, II, 1112–13 for a report on this "excitement."

402 The letter addressed to Mr. Currier is part of the Swain Family Papers at the Beinecke Rare Book and Manuscript Library.

403 Swain's 1889 statement is in the Beinecke Library.

404 Entries dated October 17 through 23, 1850: Batchelder, same dates.

405 "Along the bank . . .": Lord, November 26, 1850.

    An astonishing variety of imports destined for the mines was listed in almost every issue of the Sacramento *Transcript* under "Goods Just Landed." A random assortment noted October 22: 200,000 feet of lumber, 41 plows, 100 boxes of sperm candles, 14 cases of Mrs. Kidder's Cordial, 30 cases of dried peaches—and more.

    In contrast to the above items which sold quickly and profitably to meet the needs of the miners, a merchant (Sweetser, November 27, 1850) complained of there being no market whatsoever for a shipment of hairbrushes.

405 "The buildings are . . .": Parker, September 3, 1850.

405 "J Street . . .": Batchelder, October 23, 1850.

406 "Many of the blocks . . .": Sweetser, letter May 24, 1850.

407 "The cholera . . .": Batchelder, October 23, 1850.

407 Footnote, "and this was . . .": Quoted in Bruff, II, 1100.

407 "The lurid fires . . .": Lord, October 23, 1850.

    Lord commented extensively on the spread of cholera in Sacramento City, October 20 through November 11, 1850. He noted on November 2: "The streets are almost deserted . . . the eating houses almost empty and all, except for some loading for the mines, is at a dead standstill."

407 "The number of . . .": Marysville *Herald*, October 29, 1850.

407 "There is so much . . .": Sweetser, September 25, 1850.

    The Marysville *Herald*, September 13, has an article on this subject, entitled "Competition."

408 "At two o'clock . . .": Batchelder, October 24, 1850.

408 "steamed rapidly down . . .": Bayard Taylor, 220.

408 "We sailed along . . .": Peters, May 17, 1850.

408 "was a matter . . .": Bayard Taylor, 220.

    Though Taylor wrote of his trip down the Sacramento River in December 1849, his description remains essentially accurate for fall 1850.

408 "our steamboat kept . . ."; "In the straits . . .": Peters, May 17, 1850.

408 "Suisun Bay was . . .": Bayard Taylor, 220.

408 "to get a first . . .": Delano, *Pen-Knife Sketches* . . . , 33.

CHAPTER XIII

PAGE

409 Epigraph: *Panama Star*, December 31, 1850.

411 "bustle, speculation and . . .": Gardiner, 154.

411 Deserted ships and *Euphemia* and *Niantic:* Soule, 281, 355, 233; and M'Collum, 75.

411 "the indefatigable spider": Soule, 345.

411 "forty-four steamers . . .": *Pacific News*, January 6, 1851.

411 "Just imagine the . . .": Coit, 95.

411 "hand-carts, porters, drays . . .": Delano, *Pen-Knife Sketches*, 39–40.

413   Shipload of ice: *Alta California*, September 29, 1851.

413   Cats from Mexico: Plummer, May 7, 1851.

413   Number of letters, month of August 1850: *Panama Star*, October 4, 1850.

      Throughout the mining regions and especially in San Francisco, letter writers and newspaper editorials damned the United States' postal system for its inability to cope with the mass of mail. Further, there were cries of outrage at the high cost of mail delivery. The *Alta California*, November 2, 1850, published an angry editorial advocating "Cheap Postage."

413   "in almost every attitude": Lord, February 14, 1851. He wrote at length, with a tone of moral outrage, about the gambling palaces.

413   "Americans much prefer . . ."; "Some of the first . . .": Russailh, 28–30.

      1849–51 accounts of vice in San Francisco, in other cities or in the mines are rare. Newspapers, diaries and letters often reflect shock and outrage but give no details or facts. Russailh arrived in San Francisco in March 1851, three months after Swain's departure. But because there were no major fires during this interval, it is safe to assume that the circumstances Russailh described were similar to those observed by Swain.

      Soule, 642, and Darwin, 158 and 190, tell of prostitution, the latter in 1849.

414   "More people seem . . .": Coit, 98.

414   Statistics on people leaving California, August 1 through September 13, 1850: *Alta California*, September 14, 1850. Total number of men and women who left in the year 1850: *Pacific News*, January 6, 1851. Footnote information: *Alta California*, September 14, 1850.

      (More than offsetting the departures by sea during 1850 were the approximately 50,000 immigrants who reached California by the several overland trails: Unruh, 119.)

      The rush to return to the states was described by several diarists in San Francisco: Main, September 28; Lord, February 24, 1851; Tiffany, December 12 and 14; Stillman, October 24; and the *Alta California* regularly reported on the exodus.

      An engineer on board one of the Pacific Mail Steamship Company's ships reported that the demand for accommodations was so great that the men returning shipped on as crew members. So great was the demand for any kind of berth on these ships that "we were compelled to keep guard on shipboard to prevent overloading the ship with stowaways." (From Kemble, *Panama Route*, 130.)

      Howland told of working for his passage home, as an officer on board the PMSC's *Tennessee*, 487.

414   Price of tickets on steamers and sailing ships: Foster, September 11; Bannington, November 6; Tiffany, December 12; Pierce, October 8; Page, December 29; Boyden, December 20 (all 1850); and Lord, February 14, 1851; and Kingsley, February 26, 1851.

414   Length of voyage to Panama City: Beyond the average reported thirty to fifty days, Boyden told of a seventy-two-day voyage; similarly, McCoy, April 6, 1851; Isaac Baker and Ness, October 1850, both on the same ship; and Osbun, October–January 1851.

415   Complaints about conditions on sailing and steam ships: Patterson, October 27, 1850; *Pacific News*, October 29, 1850; Mobley, December 1850, told of a long voyage marked by sickness, shortage of water, storms, days adrift without wind and his ship being condemned as unseaworthy when they reached Acapulco; and Isaac Baker and Ness told of abandoning their ship at Acapulco, October 1850.

415 "The passengers were fed . . ."; "If the bread . . ."; "Another favorite dish . . ."; "The owners of the line . . .": Lord, February 15 and 16 and March 4, 1851.

   While Lord described conditions on board his ship with more gusto and anger than most, there were other diarists and letter writers on their way to Panama who voiced bitter complaints about shipboard food: Letts, 177–178; Johnston, December 1849; Parke, October 15, 1850; Tiffany, February 1851; and Gorgas, March 11, 1851, called the food on his ship "wholesale and filthy manure." In a number of cases, passengers got up petitions or resolutions condemning the captains of their ships. Watts told of passengers on his ship bringing a suit against the ship owners.

416 "From Central Wharf . . .": *Alta California*, October 29, 1850, p. 3.

416 Deaths on board Panama-bound ships: The thirty-seven buried at sea were reported by Pierce, October 8, 1850. Batchelder, November 1850, told of seven deaths in thirty days on his ship. Other records of death and sickness: Parke, December 21, 1850; Gorgas, February 9, 1851; Pigman, February 6, 1851; McCoy, October 29 and December 1, 1850. W. W. Miller told of burials at sea, October 1850; and then Miller himself died on board his ship, off Realejo, December 30, 1850.

416 "the natives appear . . .": Wortley, 319.

417 "There will be . . .": Fish, October 21, 1849.

417 "sweating, panting, pushing . . .": Letter by returning Wolverine Ranger at Panama City, June 7, 1850, *Statesman*, July 3, 1850.

417 "I get more . . .": Crackbon, April 29, 1849.

   Other accounts of tiresome waiting at Panama City for passage to San Francisco: Pangborn, June–July 1850; M'Collum, 98–113; and Goss, letter June 18, 1850.

417 "a most miserable place": Schliemann, 36.

418 "the most unhealthy place . . .": Letts, 14.

420 "From information gathered . . ."; "is described as . . ."; "The majority of emigrants . . .": Patterson, October 1850, Part VI.

   This is the first of several quotations from E. H. N. Patterson, who was one of the most observant and persistent diarists on the Panama route. His record, October 26–December 12, 1850, was published in the Oquawka *Spectator*, March 5–July 23, 1851, entitled "The Isthmus Route," Parts I–XVI. Quotations are cited by the appropriate date they were written, followed by the part in the series.

   Patterson's statements about Acapulco point up the fact that a considerable number of homebound goldseekers either went ashore there or some decided to leave their ships and travel overland through Mexico to reach Vera Cruz and another ship for the east coast. Descriptions of Acapulco include Wolcott, January 1851; Stimson, 430; Tyson, 40–41; Steuben, June 1850; an especially vivid account of the city by Bruff, II, 970–73; E. C. K., letters in *Alta California*, December 17, 1850; and Upham, 362–64.

   A description of the contrast between goldseekers traveling *to* California and those returning *from* El Dorado is given by Schliemann on his way to California, March 1851.

   An unusually candid social commentary by Bannington, November 23–26, 1850, tells of his sojourn in Acapulco and his "fine times" and "still better fun" with the "senorettas," also cockfights, betting and drinking.

   Like soldiers away from home for the first time, like arrogant tourists ("ugly Americans"), some goldseekers caused trouble for the Mexican authorities in the ports of Mazatlán and Acapulco. Baxter, August 26–27, 1850, told of a fight between homebound Americans and Mexican gamblers, with the United States Consul finally involved.

Homebound goldseekers who left their ships at Acapulco include: McCoy, December 1850; Mobley, December–January 1851; and Ness, October 1850.

424   "One of the luxuries . . .": Patterson, October 1850, Part VI.

425   "the miners gathered . . .": Baxter, August 17 and 20, 1850.

426   "The town exhibited . . .": Albert C. Wells, letter June 4, 1850.

Other descriptions of Realejo: Letts, 145; Stillman, December 1850; Goldsmith, 126; and especially Stevens, March 30–April 1, 1849.

427   "It was supposed . . .": Patterson, November 1850, Part VI.

427   Footnote, "After twenty-eight days . . .": Goldsmith, 126.

427   "there are two modes . . .": Stillman, December 1, 1850.

427   "the traveler proceeds . . .": Patterson, November 1850, Part VI.

A surprising number of returning goldseekers chose to take the Nicaragua route, before Vanderbilt had established his steamship service and other amenities for this route which would compete with Panama for the California business. An excellent report of crossing Nicaragua is found in a letter, November 9, 1850, in the *Panama Star*, November 14, 1850. Other accounts of the journey from Realejo to San Juan on the Gulf coast: *California Daily Courier*, September 2 and October 29, 1850; Goldsmith, 126–31; Letts, 146–67; Pierce, November–December 1850; Wolcott, January–April 1851; and an especially vivid account by Stillman, 201–36. Parke, November–December 1850, and Weed, November 1850, both told of the trip, with Weed also providing a table of distances.

428   "The celebrated city . . ."; "Now there is . . .": Bruff, II, 975.

Patterson, November 1850, Part VI, gave a similar description of Panama City.

429   "The boats come . . .": Pigman, February 20, 1851. Also Foster, September 24, 1850; and Upham, *Notes of a Voyage*, 367.

429   "The natives attach . . ."; "From the narrow beach . . .": Lord, March 5, 1851.

430   "The main portion . . ."; "The buildings . . .": M'Collum, 100 and 103.

430   "The streets run . . .": Lord, March 5, 1851.

430   "Everybody—man, woman . . .": Horn, letter June 1850, 547.

Horn's letter provides an exceptionally detailed record of life in Panama and the goldseekers' experiences there, as well as a fine description of the river trip to Chagres.

Also critical of Americans in Panama City was Goss, June 18, 1850: "Rioting and debauchery in all its different forms prevail here. . . . Drinking and gambling and all kinds of sin are committed with boldness."

430   "American traders have . . .": Patterson, November 1850, Part VI.

430   "All the hotels . . .": Horn, letter June 1850, 544.

430   "One might easily . . .": Peters, March 4, 1850. Also Letts named six American hotels, 186; and Albert C. Wells, December 5, 1849, wrote about American businesses in Panama City.

430   "The Mansion House . . .": Lord, March 5, 1851.

430   "are in vain . . .": Patterson, November 1850, Part VI.

431   "The bell-ringers attached . . .": Hecox, letter February 28, 1849; in M'Collum, 185.

431   "come into the city . . ."; "Most of the emigrants . . ."; "The number of persons . . .": Horn, 545, 548 and 549.

431   "It may be said . . .": Patterson, December 1850, Part VII.

For most goldseekers Panama was their first exposure to a foreign people and culture. They responded with a predictable attitude of Yankee superiority and nationalism. The Panamanians' lack of "git-up-and-go" and their Catholicism aroused scorn and disgust and seemed to many diarists and letter writers to explain the poverty of the country: Gorgas, March 26, 1851; Lord, March 1851; Batchelder, December 3, 1850; Hecox, February 28, 1849 (M'Collum, 183–86); and Horn, June 1850.

American arrogance inevitably led to trouble. Horn, June 1850, told of a riot, and the *California Daily Courier* in San Francisco on July 1, 1850, reported that the Panamanians "have resorted to pistols and knives . . . driven to desperation by the cruelties practiced on them and the open contempt with which they have been treated." The paper reported a riot in which two Americans were killed.

Animosity between Americans and Panamanians was commented on by an English traveler, Wortley, II, 319 and 279; III, 291.

432   "The traveler has . . ."; "Great numbers of . . .": Patterson, December 1850, Part VIII.

432   "Mules, which abound . . .": Lord, March 6, 1851.

     Charge for packing varied: Patterson paid a native $5 to carry sixty pounds of luggage from Panama to Gorgona; Tiffany, March 4, 1851, hired a mule for $10; and Upham, September 1850, hired two mules for $16 each.

432   "The rainy season . . .": *Panama Star*, December 31, 1850. Also February 11, 1851.

432   Footnote, "Having neglected . . .": Upham, 371.

433   "We move off . . ."; "As we pass . . ."; "A few miles out . . .": Lord, March 6, 1851.

433   "It is stated . . .": Autenrieth, 12–13.

     Other descriptions of this part of the trail: Patterson, Parts VIII and IX; Hovey, May 1851; and Bruff, July 5, 1851 (II, 980–84) gave an especially detailed account of the road to Cruces.

433   "The road is shaded . . .": Lord, March 6, 1851.

434   "These ravines gradually . . .": Letter entitled "Crossing the Isthmus," *Illinois Journal*, June 6, 1849, p. 2, column 3.

     Foster, 94, also described this tunnel-like trail, as did Schliemann, March 11, 1851.

434   "one can hardly . . .": Lord, March 6, 1851.

434   "Indeed, the growth . . .": Foster, 94.

435   "with two or three . . .": Autenrieth, 14; same in Horn, 537.

     Schliemann, 36, described Gorgona in March 1851, stating that it consisted of "a few wooden houses with the gorgeous denominations of Union Hotel and Panama Railroad Hotel." Also Pangborn, June 15, 1850.

435   "we had our baggage . . ."; "After four hours . . .": Lord, March 7, 1851.

435   "a good strong launch . . ."; "were cheerful . . .": Bruff, July 1851 (II, 987).

435   "We have met . . ."; "Passed a tent-town . . .": Lord, March 7, 1851.

435   Footnote on Panama Railroad: John Haskell Kemble, *Panama Route*, 191–92.

     In April 1852, Schliemann, returning from California, described the progress and problems of the railroad, which was then in operation for part of the route.

     A thorough and detailed narrative of the building of this remarkable railroad is given by David McCullough, *The Path Between the Seas* (New York, 1977).

435   "The river is exceedingly . . .": Bruff, II, 987–88.

436   "This country is . . .": *Panama Star*, December 31, 1850.

     The *Star* reported the robbery of $120,000, same date, and on March

5, 7 and 11, 1851, gave a lengthy accounting of the murder of eight Americans who were traveling down the river.

436   The *California Daily Courier* in San Francisco, July 1, 1850, reported robberies but judged most of them committed by Americans against their fellow countrymen. Schliemann, 38–39, reported crimes against travelers, including stabbings, boats overturned, and bodies thrown into an abyss.

436   "Some time after . . ."; "Rose at 4 A.M. . . .": Lord, March 7–8, 1851.

436   "On the banks . . .": Patterson, December 1850, Part X.

     Schliemann gave a most descriptive account of travel on the Chagres: scenery, villages, railroad workers, and "lazy" natives, March 1851. Also, Pangborn, June 1850; and Peters, February 1850.

436   "Landed at Chagres . . .": Lord, March 9, 1851.

436   "It has grown . . ."; "The original town . . ."; "The emigrants . . .": Patterson, December 1850, Part XI.

437   "The hotels, which . . .": Horn, June 1850.

437   "Passengers down the river . . .": Lord, March 10, 1851.

437   "Stories of murders . . .": Patterson, December 1850, Parts XII and XIII.

     Sickness and men left to die in the streets were described by Pierce, December 21, 1850—about the same time Swain was in Chagres. Pigman, February 21, 1851, told of a physician who poisoned patients to steal their gold.

437   "Here at Chagres . . ."; "The mass of the . . .": Lord, March 9 and 10, 1851.

438   "You cannot turn . . ."; "The boatmen are . . ."; "A fever of excitement . . ."; "When she reaches . . .": Patterson, December 1850, Parts XIII and XIV.

     Pierce, December 21, 1850—same time as Swain—reported, "There are perhaps one thousand in Chagres. . . . A tremendous rush is going on for tickets. . . . Men actually fainted in the crowd."

439   Footnote, "Tickets for her . . .": *Panama Star*, September 27, 1850.

440   "Boats loaded with . . .": Lord, March 10, 1851.

     Pierce, December 24, 1850, reported "some were drowned and others lost their baggage by the upsetting of the boats" in being transported from beach to steamer.

440   "Our ship was . . ."; "At length all . . ."; "So eager are . . ."; "This is a very . . .": Patterson, December 1850, Part XV.

     Passenger accommodations on board the *Falcon* were apparently very much the same as those described by Patterson. Upham, *Notes of a Voyage*, 376, reported accommodations on the *Falcon* were "most miserable."

     For a descriptive account of returning goldseekers' discomforts and dangers during the voyage across the Caribbean (with stopover at Havana) and up the Atlantic coast to New York City, including the passengers manning the pumps of their leaking ship, see Weed, December 1850.

     For an unusually lengthy and descriptive account of the trip from Panama via Kingston, Jamaica, to New Orleans and up the Mississippi River to Illinois, see Lord, March 11–April 3, 1851.

442   "There ought not . . .": Baxter, September 13, 1850.

442   "We steamed under . . .": Patterson, January 1851, Part XVI.

442   "Cuba belongs to . . .": Albert C. Wells, letter December 5, 1849.

443   "I had a slight . . ."; "I was quite . . .": Pierce, December 24–29, 1850.

445   "I have been . . .": From interview with William Swain's daughter, Sara Sabrina Swain.

     All information about William's homecoming is based on interviews, letters and family documents provided by Miss Swain. She took great pride in having preserved every scrap of information about her father.

446 "robberies often occur . . .": *California Daily Courier*, July 1, 1850.

447 $4,000 found in the underbrush: Ness, October 23, 1850.

447 Disappointed wives and defensive husbands: The impact of the gold rush on the personal relations of returning goldseekers is a subject that has not yet been explored. I have found a number of poignant, revealing letters exchanged between husbands and wives, fathers and children written during the gold rush years, 1849–52. They provide additional evidence that the gold rush for most men and their families was a disruptive, often tragic experience.

447 Information about Frederick Bailey, Michael Hutchinson and John Root: From family papers, county records, newspaper obituaries, and Miss Swain.

447 Report on Pratt: Cole, 78.

Report on Reverend and William Hobart: *The Gold Rush, Letters from the Wolverine Rangers*, xi–xii.

Report on Sexton: Mansfield, *History of Butte County*, 114.

Report on Goldsmith and Frary: Goldsmith, 143.

Report on Van Brunt and Rood: Letter by E. S. Camp, *The Gold Rush, Letters from the Wolverine Ranger*, 153–54.

Report on Herman Camp: Clappe *(The Shirley Letters)*, 63.

448 "Never before did . . .": Bruff, II, 997.

449 Information about William, Sabrina, George and family members comes from family records and interviews with Miss Swain and other descendants.

EPILOGUE

PAGE

451 Epigraph: James Bryce, *The American Commonwealth* (New York, 1916), II, 428.

452 "nailed down to inactivity . . .": Wooster, letter Yuba River, October 26, 1850; 30.

452 Number of immigrants, 1850s: Doris Wright, 326; Unruh, 119.

453 *Hunt's Merchants Magazine* quote and price of onions and apples: Pomeroy, 48–49.

453 "Were it in the nature . . .": Mann, letter February 14, 1851.

Lucinda Mann's story: Letters, 1852–53.

454 "the arrival of every steamer . . .": *San Francisco As It Is*, September 27, 1850; 55. This book gathers together editorials from the San Francisco *Picayune*, August 1850–April 1852. They provide a superbly detailed record of life in San Francisco for those years.

454 "Miss Sarah Pellet . . .": quoted from the *Butte Record* by Mansfield, *History of Butte County*, 96–97.

454 Statistics on whiskey, etc., imported: Soule, 495.

454 "The independence and liberality . . .": Plummer, letter March 14, 1851.

455 Statistics on people leaving San Francisco: Doris Wright, 331.

455 Statistics on growth of California population and percentage of foreigners: McWilliams, 66–67 and 75.

455 Comparison of Irish and Chinese: McWilliams, 68.

McWilliams offers a brilliantly original, forceful interpretation of the impact of the gold rush on California's development.

456 "$240,000,000, a sum sufficient . . .": Article about the Rocky Bar Mining Company, *Michigan Expositor*, November 19, 1850.

Other articles in this newspaper on the development of this quartz mining company on the Middle Fork of the American River: February 19 and September 24, 1850. Also Carl L. Wheat, "The Rocky Bar Mining Company."

For an excellent survey of quartz-mining operations in 1850 and later years: Paul, *California Gold*, 130–146.

456 "A few years ago . . .": Paul, *California Gold*, 163.

456 Information on hydraulic mining and aqueducts: Paul, *California Gold*, 164.

457 Statistics and general information on California manufacturers, farms, newspapers, etc.: McWilliams, 33, 58.

458 "everywhere present, everywhere respected . . .": Paul, *California Gold*, 194.

458 "to realize on the resources . . .": William E. Connelley, *Kansas and Kansans*, I, 183.

The full 1891 statement by Connelley, a Kansas pioneer, offers a unique perspective on the impact of the Gold Rush: "The California Gold Fever was a disease that spread to all the world. It revolutionized America. . . . It changed the American from a conservative, contented citizen satisfied with a reasonable return upon his investment and toil to an excitable, restless, insatiable person who wished to realize on the resources of the universe in a day. It was the beginning of our national madness, of our insanity of greed. It marks the advent of character decadence and American moral degeneracy. In California a man might wash from a placer more gold in a week than he could accumulate in a life of business. When the placer gold was exhausted, he turned to other natural resources, and his greed increased." This is a full echo of Henry Thoreau's condemnation of the Gold Rush.

458 "The rush to California . . .": Henry Thoreau, essay "Life Without Principle," *Atlantic Monthly*, October 1863.

Sources

The purpose of this bibliography is, first, to provide identification of every source cited in the Notes as well as many other informative sources I used in my research; and second, to organize all primary sources, published and manuscript, into a system that will provide significant information about each, and thereby facilitate the research of others interested in the gold rush experience.

There are five sections:

I: Overland to California, 1849–50
II: Life in the Mines and Cities, California, 1849–51
III: Homeward Journey via Panama, 1850–51
IV: Newspapers
V: Secondary Sources

Each primary source is listed in one or more of the first three sections. If a diary or letter collection ends on arrival in California, it will appear only in Section I. If it continues in California, it will also appear in Section II. Generally, diarists and letter writers who described their return home had previously written about California—therefore, sources in Section III usually also appear in II. And a few appear in all three sections.

This system provides simple identification of the subject area(s) of each primary source. As well, the time span of each is identified in each section. For instance, if a goldseeker kept a diary on the overland trail in 1849 and then wrote letters from California in 1850 and more letters about his return in 1851, those dates appear with the listing of the diary and letters in Sections I, II, and III.

Each primary source is identified as: diary, journal, letters, diary-narrative, narrative, or reminiscence.

DIARY: Day-to-day personal record with date assigned to each entry written on that date or shortly thereafter. Written without time for revision or embellishment, without expository structure and without self-conscious literary pretensions (in most cases).

JOURNAL: Used in titles of published diaries; suggests some revision or improvement of the original diary by the diarist. Many diaries edited for publication are titled "journal." The word should refer to a record kept as part of a job, for official purposes, rather than to a diary. Nonetheless, the two terms are often used interchangeably. I should note that the first page of Swain's diary carries the title, "The Journal of . . ." Certainly he did not revise his diary.

LETTERS: This category indicates at least two, generally three or more, and often as many as twenty. Though scores of single letters (as opposed to a

508

series by the same writer) are preserved in the various collections of gold rush material, I have not listed single letters unless they have unusual value or are cited in the Notes.

NOTES: A brief, casual record, more perfunctory than a diary.

GUIDE: An aid to travel on the overland trail, with descriptive information as to trail conditions and mileage from water hole to river crossing to mountain pass to fork in the trail, etc.

TABLE OF DISTANCES: Less descriptive listing of mileage from point to point along the trail.

DIARY-NARRATIVE: Daily entries are of such length and style as to achieve narrative quality, thereby evidencing that the entries were rewritten or revised at some later date. Thus the diary structure may prevail but is almost incidental to the narrative force of the entries. A good example of a diary expanded and rewritten into lengthy narrative entries is Alonzo Delano, *Life on the Plains and Among the Diggings*.

NARRATIVE: A continuous record—not interrupted by dates—written some time after the events described. Though lacking the regular chronology of a diary or a diary-narrative, a narrative does have sufficient reference to days or months to provide a reliable time sequence (in contrast to a reminiscence). A narrative generally reflects conscious effort by the author to achieve story quality or readability not possible in the start-stop format of a diary. One of the best examples is Howard C. Gardiner, *In Pursuit of the Golden Dream*.

REMINISCENCE: May also be called a recollection or memoir. Written for the purpose of publication many years after the events described, these accounts are generally unreliable, both because they lack dates or chronological structure and because of their tendency to romanticize/dramatize "the days of yore." The few listed here provide specific, verifiable information.

This bibliography makes no attempt to be definitive. New diaries and letters are discovered and new publications appear each year. I have excluded scores of diaries which are so brief, perfunctory and/or repetitive as to be of little value. Many publications with enticing titles have also been excluded because they proved to be, at best, of only peripheral interest.

In the course of developing this bibliography, I have built up a mass of specific information about each entry and about several hundred diaries, reminiscences, reports, guides and secondary sources which do not appear here. Knowing how much time and hope can be invested in reading through such records, I want to make available to others the results of my years of research. Therefore, I will place with the Bancroft Library, University of California at Berkeley, all my notes and bibliographical information, along with copies of several versions of the text. These versions include considerable specific information in footnotes and notes which could not be included in this book. Copies of these versions will also be available at the Henry E. Huntington Library, San Marino, California. Until all this material is permanently located in these major research centers (probably in 1982), I will try to be helpful to those who may need specific information about a given diary or other source: does it contain a description of certain places or circumstances on the trail, does it report life at a specific mining camp, town or city in California at a certain time, and so on.

■

Libraries and historical societies frequently cited are abbreviated as follows:

BL: Bancroft Library, University of California, Berkeley, CA
CAHS: California Historical Society, San Francisco, CA
CASL: California State Library, Sacramento, CA
COHS: Colorado Historical Society, Denver, CO
HL: Henry E. Huntington Library, San Marino, CA
ILHS: Illinois Historical Society, Springfield, IL
INHS: Indiana Historical Society, Indianapolis, IN
INSL: Indiana State Library, Indianapolis, IN
KSHS: Kansas Historical Society, Topeka, KS
Lilly: Lilly Library, University of Indiana, Bloomington, IN
MAHS: Massachusetts Historical Society, Boston, MA
MNHS: Minnesota Historical Society, Minneapolis, MN
MOHS: Missouri Historical Society, St. Louis, MO
NBHS: Nebraska Historical Society, Omaha, NB
NYHS: New York Historical Society, New York, NY
NYPL: New York Public Library, New York, NY
ORHS: Oregon Historical Society, Portland, OR
UTHS: Utah Historical Society, Salt Lake City, UT
WAHS: Washington Historical Society, Tacoma, WA
WIHS: Wisconsin Historical Society, Madison, WI

CAHSQ and similar abbreviations incorporating those above refer to quarterly publications. Some other obvious abbreviations: MS, manuscript; TPS, typescript or other manual copy; MF, microfilm or other photocopy.

Section I:
OVERLAND TO CALIFORNIA, 1849–50

Although a fair number of diaries have survived which describe gold rush travel to California via the southern trails—the Santa Fe Trail and those from Fort Smith (Arkansas) and from Gulf ports of Texas and Mexico—I have not included any of these records.* Swain traveled the trail followed by the great majority of overland emigrants, the South Pass route.

Therefore, diaries, letters, *et al.* in this section tell of travel via the several variants of the South Pass route: trails westward from Independence, St. Joseph and other jumping off points; the Mormon trail along the northside of the Platte River, to Fort Laramie; the cut-off trails: Sublette's, Hudspeth's and Lassen's; via Fort Bridger and Salt Lake City; and the Carson and Truckee trails into California.

With few exceptions, all diaries and letter collections (a total of 339) were written in 1849 or 1850. I was, of course, primarily interested in records of 1849 because Swain traveled that year. But I also studied 1850 accounts and include them because conditions on the South Pass route in that year differed but slightly

---

* *For information about travel to California via the several southern routes during the gold rush years, see Ferol Egan,* The El Dorado Trail; *also Grant Foreman,* Marcy and the Gold Seekers *(Norman, OK, 1939).*

Of course thousands reached California in 1849, 1850 and later years after voyages around Cape Horn or via the Isthmus of Panama: see Oscar Lewis, Sea Routes to the Gold Fields; *and Octavius T. Howe,* Argonauts of '49.

from 1849, albeit there was far more rain in '50 than in the previous summer. After 1850 conditions changed significantly, with bridges, blacksmith shops and other amenities easing the dangers and difficulties. (Unruh gives an excellent evaluation of how conditions and travel changed each year on the South Pass route, 1849 through the 1850s.)

NOTE: An asterisk indicates that the diary or letter collection continues after arrival in California—therefore the same author will appear in Section II.

Abbey, James. [Diary] *California: A Trip Across the Plains in the Spring of 1850.* New Albany, IN, 1850.

Anderson, William Wright. Diary, 1848 [to Oregon]. TPS: Lilly.

Anonymous [Sagamore Company, Lynn, Mass.] Diary, 1849. MS: MNHS; MF: BL.

Anonymous. Diary, 1850. MS: INHS.

Appleby, William I. Diary, 1849. MS: Historian's Office, Salt Lake City.

————. Letters, 1849. *Frontier Guardian,* Kanesville, IA, June, July, Sept. 1849.

*Applegate, George W. Letters, 1849. MS: Yale.

Arms, Cephas. [Diary, 1849, southern route from Salt Lake City] *Illinois Journal,* Knoxville, Oct.–Nov. 1849, Jan.–Feb., May–June 1850.

Armstrong, J. Elza. [Two diaries, 1849; also John E. Banks] *The Buckeye Rovers in the Gold Rush,* ed. Howard L. Scamehorn. Athens, OH, 1965.

*Ashley, Delos R. Diary, 1849. TPS: BL.

Athearn, Prince A. [Diary, 1849] "Log Book . . . ," ed. Lovelia Athearn. *Pacific Historian* 2(1958), 3(1959).

Austin, Henry. Diary, 1849. MF: BL.

Backus, Gordon. Diary, 1849. MS: Yale.

Badman, Philip. Diary, 1849. MS: Yale.

Bailhache, John. "Overland Diary, 1850." Napa *Journal,* CA, April 20, 1952.

Baldwin, J. F. [Diary, 1850] *The California Patron and Agriculturist.* San Francisco, 1887.

Baldwin, Lewis. Diary, 1849 [to Oregon]. MS: Fred A. Rosenstock, Denver.

*Ballew, Horace M. Letter, 1850. MS: BL.

*Banks, John E. [Two diaries, 1849] See J. Elza Armstrong.

Barnard, Frederic W. Letters, 1849 [from Maryland to St. Joseph, Missouri]. MS: Yale.

Barry, Louise. *The Beginning of the West* . . . Topeka, KS, 1972.

Bartholomew, Jacob. Diary, 1850. MS: Lilly.

*Batchelder, Amos. Diary, 1849. MS: BL.

Beck, Morris H. Letters, 1850. MS: BL.

Bennett, James. [Diary, 1849] *Overland Journey to California.* New Harmony, IN, 1906.

Benson, John H. Diary, 1849. MF: BL.

Berrien, Joseph W. [Diary, 1849] "Overland from St. Louis to the California Gold Field . . . ," ed. Ted and Caryl Hinckley. *Indiana Magazine of History* 56 (1960).

*Bickford, William H. Diary, 1849. MS: BL.

Biddle, B. R. [Diary, 1849] *Illinois State Journal,* Springfield, June, Dec. 1849.

*Bidlack, Russell E. [1849] *Letters Home; The Story of Ann Arbor's Forty-Niners.* Ann Arbor, MI, 1960.

Blood, James A. Diary, 1850. TPS: CASL.

*Bloom, Henry S. Diary, 1850. TPS: CASL (from Kankakee *Daily Republican,* IL, May–June 1931).

Boggs, John. Diary, 1849. MF: BL.

Booth, Caleb. Diary, 1850. MS: Yale.

*Booth, Edmund. [Diary and letter, 1849] . . . *Forty-Niner*. Stockton, CA, 1953.

*Bourne, Ezra. Diary, 1850. TPS: BL.

Boyle, Charles Elisha. Diary, 1849, Columbus *Dispatch*, OH, Oct., Nov. 1849.

*Bradley, A. B. Diary, 1850. MS: BL.

Branstetter, Peter L. Diary, 1850. MF: MOHS.

*Breyfogle, Joshua D. Diary, 1849. MS: Dartmouth College; MF: BL.

*Bridgeford, Jefferson. Letters, 1850. MF: CAHS.

*Brouster, George W. Letters, 1850. MS: MOHS.

Brown, John Evans. [Diary, 1849] "Memoirs of an American Goldseeker," ed. Katie E. Blood. *Journal of American History* 2(1908), New Haven, 1909.

*Bruff, J. Goldsborough. [1849] *Gold Rush; The Journals, Drawings, and Other Papers* . . . , ed. Georgia W. Read and Ruth Gaines. New York, 1944; 2 vols.

Bryarly, Wakeman. [Diary, 1849] *Trail to California: The Overland Journal of Vincent Geiger and Wakeman Bryarly*, ed. David M. Potter. New Haven, 1945; reprint, New Haven, 1962.

*Buffum, Joseph C. Diary, 1849. MS: CASL; TPS: BL.

*Burbank, Augustus R. Diary, 1849. MS: Library of Congress; MF: BL.

Burrall, George. Diary, 1849 [to South Pass]. TPS: Newberry Library, Chicago; MF: BL.

Bush, C. W. Letters, 1849. MS: BL.

Cagwin, N. A. Diary, 1850 [to Bear River]. MS: CASL.

Cain, Joseph, and Aireh Brower. [1850] *Mormon Way-Bill, to the Gold Mines from Pacific Springs*. Salt Lake City, 1851.

Caldwell, Dr. [T. G.]. "Notes of a Journey to California by Fort Hall Route [May] to October 1849." In Bruff, *Gold Rush*, II.

"California." Letters, 1849. *Missouri Republican*, St. Louis, Apr., May 1849.

Call, Asa C. Diary, 1850. TPS: CAHS.

Campbell, James. Diary, 1850. MS: BL.

*Castleman, P. F. Diary, 1849. TPS: BL.

Chalmers, Robert. "The Journal . . . April 17–September 1, 1850," ed. Charles Kelly. *Utah Historical Quarterly* 20(1952).

Chamberlain, William E. Diary, 1849. MS: CASL; MF: BL.

Child, Andrew. [1850] *New Guide for the Overland Route to California*. Milwaukee, 1852; reprint, Los Angeles, 1946.

Christy, Thomas. [Diary] . . . *Road Across the Plains . . . Compiled from . . . Personal Observations During the Spring and Summer of 1850*, ed. Robert H. Becker. Denver, 1969.

Churchill, Stillman. Diary, 1849. MS: Fred A. Rosenstock, Denver; MF: BL.

Clapp, John T. [1850] *A Journal of Travels to and from California*. Kalamazoo, MI, 1851.

Clark, Bennett C. [1849] "Diary of a Journey from Missouri to California," ed. Ralph P. Bieber, *Missouri Historical Review* 23(1928).

*Clark, Jonathan. [1849] "The Diary. . . ." *The Argonaut*, San Francisco, August 1925.

Clayton, William. *The Latter Day Saints' Emigrants Guide: Being a Table of Distances from Council Bluffs to the Valley of the Great Salt Lake*. St. Louis, 1848.

Coke, Henry J. [Narrative/diary 1850] *A Ride over the Rocky Mountains to Oregon and California*. London, 1852.

*Cole, Cornelius. [1849] *Memoirs. . . .* New York, 1908.

*Cone, Gordon C. Diary, 1849. MS: Fred A. Rosenstock, Denver.

Cook, William A. Diary, 1850. Unionville *Republican*, MO, July 17, 1935.

Coquillard, Alexis. Diary, 1849 [to Independence Rock]. MS: Indiana State Library.

*Cosad, David. Diary, 1849. MS: CAHS.

Cross, Osborne. [1849] "The Journal. . . ." *The March of the Mounted Riflemen*, ed. Raymond W. Settle. Glendale, CA, 1940.

Cunynghame, Colonel A. T. [Diary, 1850, of trip on Illinois–Michigan Canal] *A Glimpse at the Great Western Republic*. London, 1852.

Daggy, Elias. Diary, 1850. MS: MNHS.

*Darwin, Charles B. Diary, 1849. MS: HL.

*Decker, Peter. *The Diaries . . . : Overland to California in 1849 and Life in the Mines, 1850–1851*, ed. Helen S. Giffen. Georgetown, CA, 1966.

*Delano, Alonzo. [Diary/narrative, 1849] *Life on the Plains and Among the Diggings: Being Scenes and Adventures of an Overland Journey to California*. Auburn, NY, 1854.

*———. [Letters, 1849] . . . *California Correspondence*, ed. Irving McKee. Sacramento, 1952.

Democratic Expounder, Marshall, MI. 1849–50.

Denver, Gen. James W. Diary, 1850. TPS: NYPL.

*Dewolf, Captain David. [1849] "Diary of the Overland Trail . . . and Letters . . ." *Transactions*, ILHS [n.p.], 1925.

Dowell, B. F. Diary, 1850. MS: Yale.

*Doyle, Simon. Diary, 1849; and "Table of Distances and Guide to Lassen's Trail." MS: Yale.

*Dressler, William. Letters, 1850. MS: BL.

Dundass, Samuel Rutherford. [1849] *Journal . . . , Including . . . Entire Route to California. . . .* Steubenville, OH, 1857.

*Dutton, Jerome. "Across the Plains in 1850; Journal and Letters . . . ," ed. Claude W. Dutton. *Annals of Iowa* 9(1910).

Edmundson, William. [1850] "Diary Kept . . . While Crossing the Western Plains. . . ." *Annals of Iowa* 8(1908).

Emigrant's Guide, Being a Table of Distances . . . from Great Salt Lake City to San Francisco. [n.p., n.d.; apparently early summer 1850] Yale.

Evans, Burrelle W. Narrative, 1849. MF: BL.

Evans, James W. Diary, 1850. MS: BL.

Everts, F. D. Diary, 1849. MS: Yale.

*Fairchild, Lucius. [Letters, 1849] *California Letters . . .* , ed. Joseph Schafer. Madison, WI, 1931.

Farnham, Elijah B. "From Ohio to California in 1849: The Gold Rush Journal . . . ," ed. Merrill J. Mattes and Esley J. Kirk. *Indiana Magazine of History* 46(1950).

*Finch, Hampden G. Letters, 1850. MS: INSL.

*Foster, Isaac. [Diary and letters, 1849] *The Foster Family, California Pioneers*, ed. Lucy Foster Sexton. Santa Barbara, CA, 1925.

Frémont, John C. *Report of the Exploring Expedition to the Rocky Mountains in the Year 1842, and to Oregon and North California in the Years 1843–44*. Washington, 1845.

Frink, Margaret A. [1850] *Journal of the Adventures of a Party of California Goldseekers . . . During a Journey across the Plains. . . .* Oakland, CA, 1897.

Frush, William H. Diary, 1850 [to Oregon]. MS: Yale.

Gapen, William. Letters, 1850 [near Missouri frontier]. MS: INSL.

Gardner, D. B. Diary, 1850. MS: Library of Congress.

Gaylord, Orange. "Diary [1850] . . . to California. . . ." *Transactions of the Forty-fifth Annual Reunion, Oregon Pioneer Association*. Portland, 1920.

Geiger, Vincent. [Diary, 1849] See Wakeman Bryarly.

Gelwicks, Daniel W. Diary, 1849 [to South Pass]. TPS: BL.

Gibbs, George. [1849] "The Diary. . . ." *March of the Mounted Riflemen*, ed. Raymond W. Settle. Glendale, CA, 1940.

*The Gold Rush, Letters from the Wolverine Rangers to the Marshall Statesman, 1849–51. Mt. Pleasant, MI, 1974.

*The Gold Rush, Letters [including 1850 diary] *of David Wooster, from California to the Adrian, Michigan, Expositor, 1850–1855.* Mt. Pleasant, MI, 1972.

*Goldsmith, Oliver. [1849] *Overland in Forty-Nine: The Recollections of a Wolverine Ranger*. . . . Detroit, 1896.

*Gorgas, Solomon. Diary and letters, 1850. MS: HL.

Gould, Charles. [Two diaries, 1849; also David J. Staples] *The Boston-Newton Company Venture: From Massachusetts to California*, ed. Jessie Gould Hannon. Lincoln, NB, 1969.

Graham, Henry M. Diary, 1850. MF: INHS.

Granville, Ohio Company. Diary, 1849. MS: Yale.

*Gray, Charles Glass. [1849] *Off at Sunrise, the Overland Journal . . .* , ed. Thomas D. Clark. San Marino, CA, 1976.

Griffith, Andrew J. Diary, 1850. MS: David L. Hill, Baltimore.

Grindell, John. Diary, 1850. TPS: WAHS.

*Gros, Christian. Letters, 1850. TPS: INHS.

Grow, S. L. Diary, 1850. MS: Yale.

Gunnison, John. Diary, 1849–50. MS: National Archives.

———. Letters, 1849. MS: HL.

Hackney, Joseph. [Diary, 1849] *Wagons West . . .* , ed. Elizabeth Page. New York, 1930.

Hagelstein, George M. [1850] "The Hagelstein Diary," ed. Walter V. Kaulfers and LaVern Cutler. *American German Review* 6(1936).

Hale, Israel F. "Diary of Trip to California in 1849." *Society of California Pioneers Quarterly* 2(1925).

*Hale, John. [Reminiscence, 1849] *California As It Is: Being a Description of a Tour by the Overland Route and South Pass of the Rocky Mountains. . . .* Rochester, NY, 1851.

*Hall, Edwin G. Letters, 1849. TPS: CASL.

Hamelin, Joseph P., Jr. Diary and Table of Distances, 1849–50 [southern route from Salt Lake City]. MS: Yale.

Hansen, George W. [Letter, 1849] "A Tragedy of the Oregon Trail." *Collections of the NBHS* 17(1913).

Hardy, Francis. Diary, 1850. MS: Yale.

*Harker, George Mifflin. [Letters, 1849] "Morgan Street to Old Dry Diggings." MOHS, *Glimpses of the Past* 6(1939).

Harlan, Aaron W. [1850] "Journal . . . While Crossing the Plains. . . ." *Annals of Iowa* 11(1913).

Harmon, Appleton M. [Diary at North Platte Ferry, 1849–50] *Appleton Milo Harmon Goes West*, ed. Maybelle Harmon Anderson. Berkeley, 1946.

Hastings, Lansford W. *The Emigrant's Guide to Oregon and California*. Cincinnati, 1845.

*Hill, Jasper S. *The Letters [April–June 1849] of a Young Miner, Covering the Adventures . . . During the California Gold Rush . . .* , ed. Doyce B. Nunis, Jr. San Francisco, 1964.

Hill, John B. [1850] "Trip by Land from St. Jo to California." TPS: Yale.

Hillyer, Edwin. "From Waupun to Sacramento in 1849: The Gold Rush Journal . . . ," ed. John O. Holzhueter. *Wisconsin Magazine of History* 49(1966).

Hinds, T. W. Diary, 1850. MF: BL.

*Hinman, Charles G. [Letters, 1849] *A Pretty Fair View of the Eliphent* . . . , ed. Colton Storm. Chicago, 1960.

*———. Diary, 1849. MS: Denver Public Library.

Hislap, Thomas. Journal, 1850 [of trip on Great Lakes, Buffalo to Milwaukee]. MS: HL.

Hittell, John S. "Reminiscences of the Plains and Mines in '49 and '50." *Overland Monthly*, series 2, 9(1887).

Hixson, Jasper M. Diary, 1849. TPS: CAHS.

Hoffman, Benjamin. [Diary, 1849] "West Virginia Forty-Niners," ed. C. H. Ambler, *West Virginia History* 3(1941).

*Hoffman, Wilhelm. Reminiscence, 1849. Trans. TPS: Yale.

Hoover, Vincent A. Diary, 1849 [southern route from Salt Lake City.]. MS: HL.

Horn, Hosea B. [1850] *Horn's Overland Guide, from . . . Council Bluffs . . . to the City of Sacramento.* . . . New York, 1852.

*Hosmer, Charles A. Letters, 1849. MS: Stanford University.

*Hover, Austin A. Letter, 1849. TPS: CASL.

Howell, Elijah Preston. Diary, 1849. TPS: BL.

Hutchings, James M. Diary, 1849. MS: Library of Congress; MF: BL.

Ingalls, Eleazer. [1850] *Journal of a Trip to California by the Overland Route Across the Plains.* . . . Waukegan, IL, 1852.

Isham, G. S. [Diary, 1849] *Isham's Guide to California Compiled from a Journal.* . . . New York, 1850.

*Jagger, D. Diary, 1849. MS: CAHS.

Jefferson. T. H. *Map of the Emigrant Road from Independence, Missouri to San Francisco, California.* [New York, 1849.] Reprint, San Francisco, 1945.

*Jewett, George E. Diary, 1849. TPS: BL.

*Jewett, Mendall. Diary, 1850. TPS: Denver Public Library.

*Johnson, John A. Diary, 1849. MS: Yale.

*———. [Letters, 1849] "Preparation for the Overland Journey to California. . . ." *Pioneering on the Plains.* Kaukauna, WI, 1924.

Johnson, Joseph H. Diary, 1849 [to Mormon Ferry on the North Platte]. MS: HL.

*Johnston, William G. [Diary, 1849] *Experiences of a Forty-Niner.* Pittsburgh, 1892.

*Josselyn, Amos P. [Diary, letters and table of distances, 1849] *The Overland Journal* . . . Baltimore, 1978.

Keith, F. F. [1850] "Journal of Crossing the Plains . . ." *Two Argonauts on the Oregon Trail* (mimeograph). Amargosa Memorial Library, Menlo Park, CA [1961]. See also Shoemaker.

*Keller, George. [Diary, 1850] *A Trip Across the Plains and Life in California.* Massillon, OH, 1851; Reprint, Oakland, CA, 1955.

*Kelly, William. [Narrative, 1849] *Across the Rocky Mountains, from New York to California.* London, 1852.

*Kendrick, Benjamin F. Letters, 1849. MS: Yale.

*Kerr, John M. Letters, 1849. MS: CASL; and *Southwestern Historical Quarterly*, Jan. 1926.

Kilgore, William H. [1850] . . . *Journal of an Overland Journey to California* . . . , ed. Joyce R. Muench, New York, 1949.

King, John N. Diary, 1850. MS: Yale.

*———. Letters, 1850. MS: ILHS; MF: CAHS.

*Kirkpatrick, Charles A. Diary, 1849. MS: BL.

*Kiser, Joseph C. Diary and letters, 1850. MS photostat: WIHS.

*Krepps, Bolivar G. Letters, 1849. MS: Denver Public Library; MF: BL.

Krill, Abram. Diary, 1850. MS: Yale.

Lampton, William. Diary, 1850. MS: MOHS; TPS: BL.

Lane, Samuel A. Diary, 1850. MF: BL.

*Langworthy, Franklin. [1850] *Scenery of the Plains, Mountains and Mines, or a Diary Kept upon the Overland Route to California.* Ogdensburg, NY, 1855.

Lee, John D. *A Mormon Chronicle: The Diaries . . . , 1848–1876,* ed. Robert G. Cleland and Juanita Brooks. San Marino, 1955; 2 vols.

Lewis, Elisha. Diary, 1849. TPS: WIHS; MF: BL.

*Lewis, John F. Diary, 1849. MS: Yale.

Lindsey, Tipton. Diary, 1849. MS: BL.

*Little, Moses F. Diary, 1849. MS: Yale.

Littleton, Micajah. Diary, 1850. TPS: CASL.

Locke, Dr. Dean J. Diary, 1849. TPS: CAHS.

Long, Charles. Diary, 1849. MS: Yale.

Loomis, Leander V. [1850] *A Journal of the Birmingham Emigrating Company,* ed. Edgar M. Ledyard. Salt Lake City, 1928.

*Lord, Dr. Isaac. Diary, 1849. MS and newspaper clippings: HL.

Lorton, William B. Diary, 1848–49 [southern route from Salt Lake City] MS: BL.

———. Letters, 1849. New York *Sun,* June 8; Sept. 7, 1849.

*Love, Alexander. Diary, 1849. MS: Yale.

Loveland, Cyrus C. [1850] *California Trail Herd: . . . Missouri to California Journal . . . ,* ed. Richard H. Dillon. Los Gatos, CA, 1961.

*Lowry, Dr. James T. Letters, 1850. Indianapolis *Star,* Oct. 1930.

*Lyne, James. Letters, 1849. MS: Yale.

Lyon, James D. [Wolverine Ranger]. Letters, 1849. Detroit *Advertiser,* Sept. 1849, Feb. 1850.

MacBride, W. S. Diary/narrative, 1850. MS, TPS: HL.

McBride, J. C. Letters, 1850. TPS: NBHS and CAHS.

———. Reminiscence-diary, 1850. TPS: CAHS.

*McCall, Ansel J. [Diary and letters] *The Great California Trail in 1849.* Bath, NY, 1882.

McCoy, Samuel F. [1849] "The Diary. . . ." *Pioneering on the Plains.* Kaukauna, WI, 1924.

*McDiarmid, Finley. Letters, 1850 [to Salt Lake City and via Hastings' Cut-off]. MS: BL.

*McElroy, Thornton. Letters, 1849. MS: University of Washington Library.

*McKeeby, Lemuel C. [Diary, 1850] "The Memoirs. . . ." *CAHSQ* 3(1924).

*McKinstry, Byron N. [1850] *The California Gold Rush Overland Diary . . . ,* ed. Bruce L. McKinstry. Glendale, CA, 1975.

*Mann, Henry Rice. Diary, 1849. TPS: CAHS.

Markle, John. Diary, 1849. MF: BL.

Marshall, Philip C., ed. [Narrative, 1849] "The Newark Overland Company." *Proceedings of the NJHS* 70, 1952.

May, Richard M. Diary, 1848 [*sic*]. MS: BL.

Merrill, H. Diary, 1849. TPS: J. S. Holliday, San Francisco.

*Middleton, Joseph. Diary, 1849. MS: Yale.

Miller, Reuben. Diary, 1849. MS: Historian's Office, Salt Lake City; TPS: HL.

Milliken, Samuel. Letters, 1850. TPS: Lilly.

*Millington, D. A. Diary, 1850. MF: BL.

Mitchell, Lyman. Diary, 1849. MF: BL.

Monroe, Michigan Company. Diary, 1849. TPS: BL.

Montgomery, William. Diary, 1850. MS: HL.

*Moorman, Madison B. [1850] *The Journal* . . . , ed. Irene D. Paden, San Francisco, 1948.

Morgan, Dale L. [ed.] "Letters by Forty-Niners Written from Salt Lake City in 1849." *Western Humanities Review* 3(1949).

———. Introduction: see Pritchard, James A.

Morgan, Martha M. *A Trip Across the Plains* . . . [to Salt Lake City in 1849 and California in 1850]. San Francisco, 1864.

Moses, A. C. Letter, 1849. MS: Floyd E. Risvold, Minneapolis.

*Moxley, Charles G. Letters, 1849. MS: Yale.

Murphy, A. Lapp. Diary, 1849. MS: University of Kansas Library; TPS: BL.

*Murrell, George M. Letters, 1849. MS: HL.

Muscott, John M. Letters, 1849. *Sentinel*, Rome, NY, May 30 and July 4, 1849.

*Ness, Richard. Narrative, 1849. MS: Yale.

*Newcomb, Silas. Diary, 1850. MS: Yale; MF: BL.

*Nixon, O. W. Letters, 1850. *Clinton Republican*, Wilmington, OH, Apr.–May, Oct., 1850.

Nusbaumer, Louis. [Diary, 1849 to Salt Lake City] *Valley of Salt, Memories of Wine: A Journal of Death Valley* . . . , ed. George Koenig. Berkeley, 1967.

*Orvis, Andrew M. Diary, 1849. MS: Yale.

Packard, Wellman, and Greenberry Larison. [Reminiscence, 1850] *Early Emigration to California* . . . , ed. Milo Custer; reprint. Bloomington, IL, 1928.

*Page, Henry. [Letters, 1849] *Wagons West* . . . , ed. Elizabeth Page. New York, 1930.

Park, Edmund B. Letters, 1849 [near Independence, Missouri]. TPS: BL.

*Parke, Charles R. Diary, 1849. MS: HL.

*Parker, William T. Diary, 1850. MS: HL.

Parsons, Lucena P. Diary, 1850 [to Salt Lake City; on to California in 1851]. TPS: Stanford University.

*Patterson, E. H. N. Diary, 1850. Oquawka *Spectator*, IL, May–Nov. 1850.

"Pawnee." Letters, 1849. *NBHS Publications* 20(1922).

———. Letters, 1849. *Illinois State Journal*, Springfield, June 1849.

———. Letters, 1849. *Missouri Republican*, St. Louis, June, Aug. 1849.

*Peacock, William. [1850] . . . *Letters*. . . . Stockton, CA, 1950.

Pearson, Gustavus C. [Reminiscence] *Overland in 1849: From Missouri to California by the Platte River and the Salt Lake Trail* [to Los Angeles], ed. Jessie H. Goodman. Los Angeles, 1961.

Pease, David E. Diary, 1849 [to Oregon]. TPS: NBHS; MF: BL.

"Pencillings by the Way of Life on the Plains." [Diary, May 8–20, 1850] *Alta California*, San Francisco, Sept., Oct. 1850.

Peoples, John H. [Relief Report from Lassen's Cut-off, 1849] "General Smith's Correspondence, California." 31st Congress, first session. *Sen Ex Doc 52*, Washington, 1850.

*Perkins, Elisha Douglas. [1849] *Gold Rush Diary: Being the Journal* . . . *on the Overland Trail* . . . , ed. Thomas D. Clark. Lexington, KY, 1967.

Persinger, James B. Diary, May 8–June 8, 1850 [to Ash Hollow]. TPS: MOHS.

*Pigman, Walter G. [1850] *The Journal* . . . , ed. Ulla S. Fawkes. Mexico, MO, 1942.

Platt, P. L., and Nelson Slater. *Traveler's Guide Across the Plains upon the Overland Route to California*. Chicago, 1852. Reprint, San Francisco, 1963.

Pomroy, H. B. Diary, 1850 [to Bear River]. MF: BL.

*Pond, A. R. Diary, 1849 [begins on Humboldt River]. MS: HL.

Potter, David M. Introduction: see Bryarly, Wakeman.

Price, Joseph. [Letters, 1850] "The Road to California . . . ," ed. Thomas Marshall. *Mississippi Valley Historical Review* 11(1924).

*Prichet, John. Diary, 1849. MS: INSL.

Pritchard, James A. [1849] *The Overland Diary . . . from Kentucky to California*, ed. Dale L. Morgan. Denver, 1959.

*Ramsay, Alexander. ". . . Gold Rush Diary of 1849," ed. Merrill J. Mattes. *Pacific Historical Review* 18(1949).

Read, George Willis. [Diary, 1850] *A Pioneer . . .* , ed. Georgia W. Read. Boston, 1927.

*Reeve, Clayton. [Letter Apr. 1849 from Independence] "From Tennessee to California in 1849: Letters of the Reeve Family of Medford, New Jersey," ed. Oscar O. Winther. *Journal of the Rutgers University Library* 11(1948).

*Reid, Bernard Joseph [1849] "A California Gold Rush Letter . . . ," ed. James D. Van Trump and Alfred D. Reid, Jr. *Western Pennsylvania Historical Magazine* 44(1961).

———. Diary and letter, 1849. TPS: HS of Western PA, Pittsburgh.

Relief Report. See Rucker, Daniel.

Rhodes, Joseph. [Diary, 1850] ". . . the California Gold Rush," ed. Merrill J. Mattes. *Annals of Wyoming* 23(1951).

*Riggin, James C. Letters, 1850. TPS: INSL.

Robinson, Zirkle D. [Diary] *The Robinson-Rosenberger Journey to the Gold Fields of California, 1849–1850*, ed. Francis C. Rosenberger. Iowa City, 1966.

*Rothwell, William R. Diary, 1850. MS: Yale.

Rucker, Daniel. [Relief Report from Lassen's Cut-off, 1849] "General Smith's Correspondence, California." 31st Congress, first session. *Sen Ex Doc 52*, Washington, 1950.

*Sawyer, Lorenzo. [Diary, 1850] *Way Sketches: Containing Incidents of Travel Across the Plains from St. Joseph to California . . .* , ed. Edward Eberstadt. New York, 1926.

Scheller, John J. Diary, 1850. TPS: CASL.

Searls, Niles. [1849] *The Diary of a Pioneer . . .* , ed. Robert M. Searls. San Francisco, 1940.

Sedgley, Joseph. [Diary] *Overland to California in 1849*. Oakland, CA, 1877.

*Senter, Riley. [Letters, 1849] *Crossing the Continent to California Gold Fields*. [Lemon Grove, CA, 1938.]

Shepherd, Dr. J. S. [1850] *Journal of Travel Across the Plains to California and Guide to the Future Emigrant*. Racine, WS, 1851. Reprint, 1945.

Shields, James G. Diary, 1850. MS: Yale.

Shinn, John R. Diary, 1850 [west from Salt Lake City on Hastings' Cut-off]. MF: BL.

Shoemaker. "The . . . Diary of 1850." *Two Argonauts on the Oregon Trail* (mimeograph). Amargosa Memorial Library, Menlo Park, CA [1961]. See also F. F. Keith.

Shombre, Henry. Diary, 1849. MS: KSHS; MF: BL.

*Skinner, H. A. Diary, 1850 [west from Salt Lake City on Hastings' Cut-off]. MS: University of Kansas; MF: BL.

*Sleight, Morris. Letters, 1850. MS: Chicago Historical Society.

Smith, Bathseba W. Diary, 1849. MS: UTHS.

Smith, C. W. [1850] *Journal of a Trip to California*, ed. R. W. G. Vail. New York [1920].

Sponsler, A. C. "An 1850 Gold Rush Letter from Fort Laramie. . . ." *Nebraska History* 32(1951).

*Spooner, E. A. Diary and letters, 1849. MS: Fred A. Rosenstock, Denver.

Sprague, Royal T. Diary, 1849. TPS: Frances E. Luby, Port Washington, NY.

Stackpole, William T. Diary, 1849 [to Green River]. MS: Yale.

Stansbury, Howard. Diary, 1849. MS: National Archives; MF: BL.

———. [1849] *An Exploration to the Valley of the Great Salt Lake of Utah.* . . . Philadelphia, 1852.

Staples, David J. [1849 to Humboldt River] "The Journal . . . ," ed. Harold F. Taggart. *CAHSQ* 22(1943). See also Charles Gould.

Starr, Franklin, Diary, 1849. MS: ILHS; MF: BL.

Starr, Henry W. Diary, 1850. TPS: J. S. Holliday, San Francisco.

Statesman, Marshall, MI. 1849–1850. William L. Clements Library, Ann Arbor, MI.

Stauder, John A. Diary, 1850. TPS: University of Missouri.

Steck, Amos. Diary, 1849. MS: COHS.

*Steele, John. [Diary/narrative] *Across the Plains in 1850,* ed. Joseph Schafer. Chicago, 1930.

———. *The Traveler's Companion Through the Great Interior: A Guide for the Road to California by South Pass . . . and Sublett's and Headpath's Cut-offs.* . . . Galena, IL, 1854.

*Steuben, William N. Diary, 1849. MS: BL.

*Stimson, Francher. [Diary, 1850] "Overland Journey to California. . . ." *Annals of Iowa* 13(1922).

Stine, Henry A. Diary and Letters, 1850. TPS: CASL.

Stitzel, Jacob. Diary, 1849. MF: BL.

Stover, Samuel M. *Diary [1849] . . . Enroute to California.* Elizabethton, TN, 1939.

*Street, Franklin. [1850] . . . *A Concise Description of the Overland Route . . . Including a Table of Distances.* Cincinnati, 1851.

*Stuart, Joseph A. [Diary, 1849] *My Roving Life,* vol. 1. Auburn, CA, 1895.

*Swain, William. Diary and Letters, 1849. MS: Yale.

———. Reminiscence, 1886. MS: J. S. Holliday, San Francisco.

*Swan, Chauncey. [1849] "Letters of a Forty-Niner," ed. Mildred Throne. *Iowa Journal of History* 47(1949).

Tappan, Henry. [1849] "Gold Rush Diary . . . ," ed. Everett Walters and George B. Strother. *Annals of Wyoming* 25(1953).

Tarbell, J. *The Emigrant's Guide to California: Giving a Description of Overland Route . . . Including a Table of Distances.* . . . Keokuk, IA, 1853.

Tate, James. Diary, 1849. TPS: CAHS; MF: BL.

Thissell, G. W. [Narrative/diary, 1850, *sic.] Crossing the Plains in '49.* Oakland, CA, 1902.

Thomasson, A. H. Diary, 1850. MS: CASL.

Thompkins, Dr. Edward A. Diary/narrative, 1850. MS: HL.

———. [Diary, 1850, excerpts] in Coy, *The Great Trek.*

*Thompson, Clark W. Letters, 1850. TPS: Library of Congress.

Thompson, W. P. Diary, 1850. MS: Yale.

*Tiffany, P. C. Diary, 1849. MS: Yale.

Tinker, Charles. [1849] ". . . Journal: A Trip to California," ed. Eugene H. Roseboom. *Ohio State Archeological and Historical Quarterly* 61(1952).

*Tolles, James S. Diary, 1849. *Appeal Democrat,* Marysville, CA, Feb.–Mar. 1930.

Trowbridge, May E. [Diary, 1849] *Pioneer Days: The Life Story of Gershom and Elizabeth Day.* Philadelphia, 1895.

*Turner, Charles, Diary, 1849. MS: Charlotte Paterson, Cleveland.

Turner, William. Diary, 1850. TPS: WIHS.

*Tuttle, Charles A. Letters, 1849. MS: BL.
*Udell, John. [Diary, 1850] *Incidents of Travel to California*. Jefferson, OH, 1856.
Vivian, Martin. Diary, 1850. TPS: NBHS.
Ware, Joseph E. *The Emigrant's Guide to California, 1849*. Reprint, ed. John Caughey. Princeton, 1932.
Waterhouse, Loyal N. Diary, 1850. MS: Princeton University Library.
Watrous, R. [1850] "Notes of a Trip to California." *Democratic Expounder*, Marshall, MI, Jan.–Mar. 1851.
Watson, B. A. Letters, 1849. *Illinois State Journal*, Springfield, May, June, Aug. 1849.
Watson, William J. [1849] *Journal of an Overland Journey to Oregon. . . .* Jacksonville, IL, 1851.
*Webster, Kimball. [Diary, 1849] *The Goldseekers of '49: A Personal Narrative of the Overland Trail and Adventures in California*. Manchester, NH, 1917.
Weir, John B. [Diary, 1849] "From Where the Gold Diggers Go." *Missouri Courier*, Hannibal, Feb. 7, 1850.
*Wells, Epaphroditus. Letters, 1849. TPS: BL.
*Wells, William. Letters, 1849. TPS: CASL.
*Weston, Francis F. Diary, 1849. MS: Henry Clifford, Los Angeles.
*Wheeler, George Nelson. Diary, 1850. MS: HL.
Whitman, Abial. Diary, 1850. MS: Yale.
Wilkins, James F. [Diary, 1849] *An Artist on the Overland Trail . . .* , ed. John F. McDermott. San Marino, CA, 1968.
*Williams, James. Letter, 1850. TPS: Ohio State Archeological and Historical Society.
Williamson, Lieut. R. S. "Report of a Reconnaissance . . . of a Route through the Sierra Nevada. . . ." Report of the Secretary of War for 1849. 31st Congress, first session. *Sen Ex Doc* 47, Washington, 1850.
Willis, Edward J. Diary, 1849. MS: Yale.
*Wilson, William. Diary and letters, 1850. MS: Yale.
*Wistar, Isaac J. [Diary, 1849] *Autobiography. . . .* Philadelphia, 1914. 2 vols. New edition, New York, 1937.
*Wolcott, Lucian M. Diary, 1850. MS: HL.
Wood, John. [1850] *Journal . . . from Cincinnati to the Gold Diggings. . . .* Chillicothe, OH, 1852.
*Wood, Joseph W. Diary, 1849. MS: HL.
*Woods, James M. Letters, 1850. TPS: MOHS.
Woodward, Thomas. [1850] "Diary . . . While Crossing the Plains to California." *Wisconsin Magazine of History* 17(1934).
*Wyman, Walker D. [ed.]. [1849–50] *California Emigrant Letters*. New York, 1952.
Young, Sheldon. [Diary, 1849] "The . . . Log." *In the Shadow of the Arrow*, ed. Margaret Long. Caldwell, ID, 1941.

Section II: LIFE IN THE MINES AND CITIES, CALIFORNIA, 1849–51

Once they reached California, most diarists lost interest in their daily records. Many quit the first day in the mines, others tried to keep up their entries every few days or once a week. Why bother with a diary when letters could be sent from even the most remote mining camps, letters reporting safe arrival in California and news of first efforts at digging for gold? Letters that would reach home in a few weeks. Except for the most persevering, diarists put their trail records away, to be saved for that time when they could be read by family and friends.

In this California section, I have limited my research to diaries, letters, newspaper reports, et al. that were written in California during 1849 and 1850, with a few extending into early 1851. Circumstances of life in mining camps and cities, the moods and attitudes of the miners and city merchants all changed so rapidly, so dynamically, that what was written in 1850 should not be applied to 1849 and certainly post-1851 should never be used to characterize or describe 1850 or earlier. By fall 1850 the goldseekers themselves referred to 1849 as "the good old days." And yet many modern writers indiscriminately use accounts of 1855 as if they told of life in California in 1849 and 1850.

The fact is that the *gold* rush should be considered to have ended by 1852. After that date the rush to California continued, certainly—but no longer did the immigrants arrive expecting to find El Dorado, hoping for quick success. The jackpot psychology of 1848–1850 had been dissipated, if not swept aside, by the thousands of letters from California telling of the miners' disappointments and hardships. As the realities of mining became known, so did the burgeoning opportunities in California agriculture, business and transportation—with mining offering a wage-paying job.

NOTE: An asterisk identifies those overlanders listed in Section I who continued to report from California, either as diarists or letter writers. Those without asterisks came to California by ship (Cape Horn or Panama) or via one of the southern overland trails; and a few simply started their writing after reaching California.

■

Abbe, Alanson. Diary, 1849. MS: HL.

Abbott, Carlisle S. [1850] *Recollections of a California Pioneer*, New York, 1917.

Abrams, William Penn. Diary, 1849. MS: BL.

Allsop, J. P. C. Reminiscence, 1849–50. MS: BL.

Annis, Isaac. [Letters, 1849–51] "A Grandfather in the Gold Rush . . . Writes Home from Auburn Dry Diggins," ed. John E. Parsons. *NYHSQ* 41(1957).

[Anonymous/Anderson]. Diary, 1851, MS: BL.

Ansted, David T. *The Goldseeker's Manual.* New York, 1849.

*Applegate, George W. Letters, 1849. . . .

*Armstrong, J. Elza. [Two diaries, 1849–52] *The Buckeye Rovers.* . . .

Armstrong, William. Reminiscence, 1849–50. MS: BL.

*Ashley, Delos R. Diary, 1849–50. . . .

Audubon, John W. *Audubon's Western Journal 1849–1850.* . . . , ed. Frank H. Hodder. Cleveland, 1906.

Baker, George H. Diary and Letters, 1849–50. MS: Society of California Pioneers.

———. "Records of a California Residence." *Society of California Pioneers Quarterly* 3(1931).

Baker, Isaac. Diary, 1850. MS: BL.

*Ballew, Horace M. Letters, 1850–51. . . .

*Banks, John E. [Two diaries, 1849–52] See J. Elza Armstrong.

Bannington, Alexander P. Diary, 1850. MS: HL.

Barker, Isaac Jr. Diary, 1850. MS: HL.

Barnes, James S. Letters, 1849–57. TPS: BL.
*Batchelder, Amos. Diary, 1849–50. . . .
Baxter, Benjamin. Diary, 1850. MS: HL.
*Bickford, William H. Diary, 1849–50. . . .
*Bidlack, Russell E. [1849] *Letters Home.* . . .
Bishop, Leander H. Diary, 1850. TPS: BL.
*Bloom, Henry S. Diary, 1850–52. . . .
*Booth, Edmund. [Reminiscence and letters, 1850–53] . . . *Forty-Niner.* . . .
Borthwick, J. D. [Narrative, 1851–54] *Three Years in California.* London, 1857.
*Bourne, Ezra. Diary, 1850. . . .
Bowles, Issac. [Letter, 1850] "A Minister Joins the '49 Gold Rush," *Amateur Book Collector* 5(1955).
Boyden, Seth. [Diary, 1849–50] ". . . Days in California." *NJHS Proceedings* 12(1927), 13(1928).
*Bradley, A. B. Diary, 1850–51. . . .
*Breyfogle, Joshua D. Diary, 1849–50. . . .
*Bridgeford, Jefferson. Letters, 1850–51. . . .
*Brouster, George. Letters, 1850. . . .
Brown, William. Letters, 1849–55. MS: HL.
*Bruff, J. Goldsborough. [1849–51] *Gold Rush* . . .
Buck, Franklin A. [1849–51] *A Yankee Trader in the Gold Rush, the Letters* . . . , ed. Katherine A. White. Boston, 1930.
Buffum, E. Gould [1848–49] *Six Months in the Gold Mines.* Reprint, ed. John W. Caughey. Los Angeles, 1959.
*Buffum, Joseph C. Diary, 1849–51. . . .
*Burbank, Augustus R. Diary, 1849–51. . . .
Canfield, Chauncey de Leon. [1850–51] *The Diary of a Forty-Niner* [fiction but valuable], ed. Chauncey L. Canfield. New York, 1920.
Carson, James H. [1848–49] *Early Recollections of the Mines,* 2nd ed. Stockton, CA, 1852.
Carter, Henry. Diary, 1849. MS: Yale.
*Castleman, P. F. Diary, 1849–50. . . .
Chaffee, Joseph Bennett. Letters, 1850–51. MS: NYHS.
Christman, Enos. [1850–52] *One Man's Gold: The Letters and Journal of a Forty-Niner,* ed. Florence M. Christman. New York, 1930.
Churchill, William C. Letters, 1849–54. Published as *Fortunes Are for the Few: Letters of a Forty-Niner,* ed. Duane A. Smith and David J. Weber. San Diego, 1977.
Clappe, Louise A. K. S. ["Dame Shirley"]. *The Shirley Letters from the California Mines: 1851–1852,* ed. Carl I. Wheat. New York, 1949.
*Clark, Jonathan. [1849–50] "The Diary. . . ."
Coit, Daniel W. [Letters, 1849–51] *Digging for Gold Without a Shovel* . . . , ed. George P. Hammond. Denver, 1967.
*Cole, Cornelius. [1849–60s] *Memoirs.* . . .
Colton, Walter. [1846–49] *The California Diary.* . . . Oakland, 1948.
*Cone, Gordon C. Diary, 1849–50. . . .
Cook, S. H. Letter, Jan. 28, 1850. *Michigan Expositor,* Adrian, April 2, 1850.
Cornelison, John H. Diary, 1849. MS: NYPL.
*Cosad, David. Diary, 1849–50. . . .
Cowden, John. Letters, 1849. MS: Yale.
Cowley, Richard B. Diary, 1849–51. MS: HL.
Crackbon, Joseph. Diary, 1849–50. TPS: CASL.
Craven, John J. Letters, 1849–50. MS: HL.

Crosby, Elisha O. [1849] *Memoirs* . . . , ed. Charles A. Barker, HL, 1945.

Cutter, James R. Letters, 1850. MS: Boston Public Library.

Dart, John P. "A Mississippian in the Gold Fields: The Letters . . . , 1849–1856," ed. Howard Mitcham. *CAHSQ* 35(1956).

*Darwin, Charles B. Diary, 1849. . . .

Davis, Stephen C. [1850–54] *California Gold Rush Merchant, the Journal* . . . , ed. Benjamin B. Richards, San Marino, 1956.

*Decker, Peter. [1850–51] *The Diaries*. . . .

DeGroot, Henry. [Narrative] "Six Months in '49." *Overland Monthly* 14(1875).

*Delano, Alonzo. [Letters, 1849–52] . . . *California Correspondence*. . . .

*———. [Diary/reminiscence, 1849–51] *Life on the Plains*. . . .

———. *Old Block's Sketch Book: Or, Tales of California Life*. Sacramento, 1856.

———. *Pen-Knife Sketches: Or, Chips off the Old Block*. San Francisco, 1934.

Delavan, James. Letter, Aug. 12, 1850. *Michigan Expositor*, Adrian, Oct. 8, 1850.

———. *Notes on California and the Placers: How to Get There, and What to Do Afterwards, by One Who Has Been There*. New York, 1850.

Denver, A. St. Clair. Letters, 1850. Clinton *Republican*, Mar. 20, 1850, Jan. 10, 1851. Wilmington, OH.

Derbec, Etienne. [Letters, 1850–51] *A French Journalist in the California Gold Rush* . . . , ed. Abraham P. Nasatir. Georgetown, CA, 1964.

DeWitt, Alfred, wife and brothers. Letters, 1849–50s. MS: BL.

*Dewolf, Captain David. [Letters, 1849–50] "Diary of the Overland. . . ."

Doble, John. . . . *Journal and Letters from the Mines* . . . *1851–1865*, ed. Charles Camp. Denver, 1962.

Dougal, William H. [1849–50] "Letters of an Artist in the Gold Rush," ed. Frank M. Stanger. *CAHSQ* 22 (1943)

Downie, Major William [Recollections, 1849–58] *Hunting for Gold*. San Francisco, 1893.

*Doyle, Simon. Letters, 1849–53. . . .

*Dressler, William. Letters, 1850–53. . . .

*Dutton, Jerome. [Letters, 1850] "Across the Plains. . . ."

Dwinelle, John W. [1849] "The Diary. . . ." *Society of California Pioneers Quarterly* 8(1931).

Eastland, Joseph G. and Thomas B. Eastland. Letters, 1850–51. MS: CAHS.

Elder, John. Letters, 1850–51. MS: INHS.

Ellis, William. Letters, 1850–53. MS: Yale.

Evans, George W. B. [1850] *Mexican Gold Trail: The Journal of a Forty-Niner*, ed. Glenn S. Dumke. San Marino, 1945.

*Fairchild, Lucius. [1849–55] *California Letters*. . . .

Fay, Caleb T. [1849–50s] Reminiscence. MS: BL.

*Finch, Hampden G. Letters, 1850–51. . . .

Fish, L. I. Diary, 1850–52. MS: HL.

Fisher, Jacob. Letter, 1850. MS: Louisiana State University.

Fitch, John R. Letters, 1849–52. MS: HL.

*Foster, Isaac. [Diary and letters, 1849–50] *The Foster Family*. . . .

Gardiner, Howard C. [Narrative] *In Pursuit of the Golden Dream, Reminiscence of San Francisco and the Northern and Southern Mines 1849–1857*, ed. Dale L. Morgan. Stoughton, MA, 1970.

Garniss, James R. [1849–50] Reminiscence. MS: BL.

Gerstaecker, Fredrich. [1849–50] . . . *Travels* . . . *California and the Gold Fields*. London, 1854.

Gill, William. [1850–51] *California Letters* . . . , ed. Eva T. Clark, New York [1922].

Gish, John. Letters, 1850–51. MS: Yale.

Godard, H. B. Letter, 1850. MS, TPS: CASL.

*The Gold Rush, Letters from the Wolverine Rangers [1849–51]. . . .

*The Gold Rush, Letters of David Wooster. . . .

The Gold Rush, Letters of Thomas S. Myrick from California to the Jackson, Michigan, American Citizen, 1849–55. Mt. Pleasant, MI, 1971.

*Goldsmith, Oliver. [Reminiscence, 1849–50] Overland in Forty-Nine. . . .

*Gorgas, Solomon. Diary and letters, 1850–51. . . .

Goss, Milo J. Letters, 1851. TPS; J. S. Holliday, San Francisco.

*Gray, Charles Glass. [1849] Off at Sunrise. . . .

Grimshaw, William R. [1848–50] . . . Narrative, ed. J. R. K. Kantor. Sacramento, 1964.

*Gros, Christian. Letters, 1850–52. . . .

*Hale, John. [Reminiscence, 1849–50] California As It Is. . . .

*Hall, Edwin G. Letters, 1849–51. . . .

Hammond, Worthington and Nicholas Hammond. Letters, 1849–50. MS: CASL.

*Harker, George Mifflin. [Letters, 1849–50] "Morgan Street. . . ."

Harris, Lewis B. Letters, 1850. TPS: CASL.

*Hill, Jasper S. [Letters, 1849–52] The Letters of a Young Miner. . . .

Hills, Thomas. Letters, 1849. MS: BL.

*Hinman, Charles G. [Letters, 1849–50] A Pretty Fair View. . . .

*———. Diary, 1849–50. . . .

*Hoffman, Wilhelm. Reminiscence, 1849–50. . . .

Hoppin, Charles R. [1849–1850s] . . . Some of His Letters Home. Oakland, CA, 1948.

Horn, Daniel A. Letters, 1850–53. MS: Southern Historical Collection, University of NC.

*Hosmer, Charles A. Letters, 1849–51. . . .

*Hover, Austin A. Letter, 1849. . . .

Hovey, John. Diary, 1849–51. MS: HL.

Howland, Captain. [1849–50] Reminiscence. TPS: Book Club of California, San Francisco.

Ingalls, John. California Letters of the Gold Rush Period . . . 1849–1851, ed. W. G. Vail. Worcester, MA, 1938.

Jackson, Charles P. Letter, 1850. MS: CASL.

*Jagger, D. Diary, 1849–50. . . .

*Jewett, George E. Diary, 1849–50. . . .

*Jewett, Mendall. Diary, 1850–51. . . .

*Johnson, John A. [1849] "Letters from the California Gold Mines." Pioneering on the Plains. Kaukauna, WI, 1924.

*———. Diary, 1849–50. . . .

Johnson, Kenneth M. San Francisco As It Is [excerpts from the San Francisco Picayune, 1850–1852], Georgetown, CA, 1964.

Johnson, Theodore T. [Narrative, 1849] Sights in the Gold Region and Scenes by the Way. New York, 1849.

*Johnston, William G. [Reminiscence, 1849] Experiences. . . .

*Josselyn, Amos P. Letters, 1850. . . .

*Keller, George. [Narrative, 1850] A Trip Across the Plains. . . .

*Kelly, William. [Narrative, 1849–50] A Stroll Through the Diggings of California. London, 1852.

K[emble], E. C. Letters, 1850. Alta California, San Francisco, Mar., Dec. 1850.

*Kendrick, Benjamin F. Letters, 1849–50. . . .

Kent, George F. Letter, 1850. MS: HL.

———. "Life in California in 1849 as Described in the 'Journal' . . . ," ed. John W. Caughey. *CAHSQ* 20(1941).

*Kerr, John M. Letters, 1850–52. MS: CASL.

Kerr, Thomas. [Diary, 1849–52] "An Irishman in the Gold Rush . . . ," ed. Charles L. Camp. *CAHSQ* 7(1928).

Kettelle, William G. Diary, 1849. MS: Columbia University, Butler Library.

Kincade, John T. Letters, 1850–60s. MS: HL.

*King, John N. Letters, 1850. . . .

King, Thomas B. [1849] *California: The Wonder of the Age: A Book for Everyone Going to or Having an Interest in the Golden Region*. New York, 1850.

Kingsley, Nelson. [1849–51] "Diary of . . . a California Argonaut of 1849," ed. Frederick J. Teggart. *Publications of the Academy of Pacific Coast History* 3(1913–14).

Kip, Leonard. [Reminiscent narrative, 1849] *California Sketches with Recollections of the Gold Mines*. Los Angeles, 1946 (1st ed., Albany, 1850).

*Kirkpatrick, Charles A. Diary-reminiscence, 1849–51. . . .

*Kiser, Joseph C. Diary and Letters, 1850–51. . . .

Knower, Daniel. [Reminiscence, 1849–50] *The Adventures of a Forty-Niner*. Albany, NY, 1894.

*Krepps, Bolivar G. Letters, 1849. . . .

*Langworthy, Franklin. [Narrative, 1850–53] *Scenery of the Plains*. . . .

Larkin, Thomas Oliver. [1848–49] *The Larkin Papers, Personal, Business and Official Correspondence . . .* , ed. George P. Hammond. Vols. 7 and 8. Berkeley, 1960 and 1962.

Leonard, J. P., MD. "Medical Observations . . . San Francisco and Sacramento, 1849," ed. Robert T. Legge. *CAHSQ* 29(1950).

Letts, John M. [Narrative, 1849] *California Illustrated: Including a Description of the Panama and Nicaragua Routes*. New York, 1852.

Lienhard, Heinrich. *A Pioneer at Sutter's Fort, 1846–50*, ed. Marguerite E. Wilbur. Los Angeles, 1941.

*Lewis, John F. Diary, 1849. . . .

*Little, Moses F. Diary, 1849–50. . . .

*Lord, Dr. Isaac. Diary, 1849–51. . . .

*Love, Alexander. Diary, 1849–52. . . .

*Lowry, Dr. James T. Letters, 1850–51. . . .

Lyman, Albert [1849] *Journal of a Voyage to California and Life in the Gold Diggings*. Hartford, CT, 1852.

Lyman, Chester S. [Diary, 1847–1850] *Around the Horn to California*, ed. Frederick J. Teggart. New Haven, 1924.

*Lyne, James. Letters, 1849–50. . . .

*McCall, Ansel James [Rewritten diary, 1849] *Pick and Pan*. . . . Bath, NY, 1883.

McClellan, James. Letter, 1850. MF: Southern Historical Collection, University of North Carolina Library.

M'Collum, William. [Reminiscence, 1849] *California as I Saw It: Pencillings by the Way of Its Gold and Gold Diggers*. Buffalo, 1850. Reprint, ed. Dale L. Morgan, Los Gatos, CA, 1960.

McDermott, John Francis. [1849] "Gold Fever: The Letters of 'Solitaire,' Gold Rush Correspondent." *MOHS Bulletin* 6(1949).

*McDiarmid, Finley. Letters, 1850–51. . . .

*McElroy, Thornton. Letters, 1850. . . .

McFarlan, John R. Diary, 1850–51. MS: HL.

McIlhany, Edward W. [1849–50s] *Recollections of a '49er*. Kansas City, 1908.

*McKeeby, Lemuel C. [Diary/narrative 1850–51] "Memoirs. . . ."
*McKinstry, Byron N. [Diary, 1850–52] *The California Gold Rush*. . . .
Main, Charles. Diary, 1849–51. MS: BL.
*Mann, Henry Rice. Letters, 1849–51. Mimeograph, Mrs. William Cox, Alameda, CA. Copy at BL.
Mann, Lucinda. Letters, 1852–53. See mimeograph by Mrs. William Cox at BL.
Marryat, Francis Samuel. [1850–52] *Mountains and Molehills: Or Recollections of a Burnt Journal*. New York, 1855. Reprint, intro. Robin W. Winks, Philadelphia, 1962.
Mason, John A. Letter, 1850. MS: CASL.
Massey, Ernest de. [Diary/narrative, 1849–50] *A Frenchman in the Gold Rush* . . . , trans. and ed. Marguerite E. Wilbur. San Francisco, [1927].
Meredith, Samuel Caldwell. Letters, 1850. MS: INHS.
Megquier, Mary Jane. *Apron Full of Gold, the Letters* . . . *from San Francisco, 1849–1856*, ed. Robert G. Clelland. San Marino, CA, 1949.
Meyer, Carl. [Reminiscence, 1850–51] *Bound for Sacramento*, trans. Ruth F. Axe. Claremont, CA, 1938.
*Middleton, Joseph. Diary, 1849–50. . . .
Miller, Samuel and Solomon. Letters, 1850–53. MS: CAHS.
Miller, William K. Letters, 1849–50. MS: NYPL.
Miller, William W. Diary, 1849–50. MS: Yale.
*Millington, D. A. Diary, 1850–51. . . .
Milner, John T. [Letters, 1849–50] ". . . Trip to California . . . ," *Alabama Historical Quarterly*, XX, 1958.
Mobley, C. C. Diary, 1850. MS: HL.
*Moorman, Madison B. [1850] *The Journal*. . . .
Morgan, Dale L. Introduction, see Perkins, William.
Morgan, William I. Diary, 1850–53. TPS: BL.
Morse, E. W. Diary, 1849–50. MS: HL.
*Moxley, Charles G. Letters, 1849–50. . . .
*Murrell, G. M. Letters, 1849–53. . . .
Nash, Charles. Letters, 1850. *Statesman*, April 10 and September 4, 1850.
*Ness, Richard. Narrative/diary, 1849–50. . . .
Nevins, Julius M. Letters, Dec. 1849, March 1850. MF: BL.
*Newcomb, Silas. Diary, 1850. . . .
*Nixon, O. W. Letters, 1850–51. *Clinton Republican*, Dec. 1850, Mar.–Aug. 1851.
Norton, Edward. Letters, 1850–53. TPS: Henry Clifford, Los Angeles.
Noyes, George N. Reminiscence, 1850–51. MS: BL.
Odall, Rodney P. Jr. Letters, 1850–51. TPS: BL.
*Orvis, Andrew M. Diary, 1849–50, and letter, 1850. . . .
Osborn, Timothy C. Diary, 1850–55. MS, TPS: Bl.
Osbun, Albert G. [Diary, 1849–50] *To California and the South Seas* . . . , ed. John H. Kemble. San Marino, CA, 1966.
*Page, Henry. [Letters, 1849–50] *Wagons West*. . . .
*Parke, Charles R. Diary, 1849–51. . . .
*Parker, William T. Diary, 1850–52. . . .
*Patterson, E. H. N. Letters, 1850. . . .
Paul, Rodman W. *The California Gold Discovery, Sources, Documents, Accounts and Memoirs*. . . . Georgetown, CA, 1967.
Payson, George. [Narrative, 1849–51] *Golden Dreams and Leaden Realities*. New York, 1853.

*Peacock, William. [1850–52] . . . *Letters.* . . .

*Perkins, Elisha D. [1849–50] *Gold Rush Diary.* . . . Also letters, 1849–50 (in *Gold Rush Diary* appendix).

Perkins, Isaac. Letters, 1850–52. MS, TPS; CASL.

Perkins, William. *Three Years in California . . . Journal of Life at Sonora 1849–1852,* ed. Dale L. Morgan and James R. Scobie. Berkeley, 1964.

Peters, Henry H. Diary, 1850. MS: NYPL.

Pierce, Hiram D. [Diary, 1849–50] *A Forty-Niner Speaks,* ed. Sarah W. Meyer. Oakland, CA, 1930.

*Pigman, Walter G. [1850–51] *The Journal.* . . .

Pittman, Amos S. Letters, 1849–52. MS: Yale.

Plummer, Charles. Diary, 1850–51. MS: HL.

Pomeroy, Charles. Letter, 1851. Published, n.d., n.p. Southwest Museum, Los Angeles.

*Pond, A. R. Diary, 1849–52. . . .

Pownall, Joseph. Letters, 1850–54. MS: HL.

*Prichet, John. Diary, 1849–50. . . .

Prindle, Samuel L. Diary, 1849–50. TPS; BL.

Quinton, John B. Letters, 1850–52. MS: New Brunswick Museum, St. Johns, Canada.

*Ramsay, Alexander. [Diary, 1850] ". . . Gold Rush Diary. . . ."

Reed, Gardner K. Letters, 1850–51. MS, TPS: Yale.

Reed, William F. Diary, 1849–53. MS: BL.

*Reeve, Clayton [Letter, December 30, 1849, from Sacramento City] "From Tennessee. . . ."

*Reid, Bernard Joseph. "Diary of . . . 1850." *Pony Express Courier* 4(1937), Placerville, CA.

*Riggin, James C. Letters, 1850–51. . . .

———. Letter, December 1850. MS: HL.

"Robert." Letter, 1850. MS: HL.

*Rothwell, William R. Letters, 1850. . . .

Russailh, Albert de Benard. [Narrative] *Last Adventure: San Francisco in 1851,* intro. and trans. Clarkson Crane. San Francisco, 1931.

*Sawyer, Lorenzo. [Letters, 1850–51] *Way Sketches.* . . .

Schliemann, Heinrich. [Diary, 1851–52] . . . *First Visit to America, 1850–51,* ed. Shirley H. Weber. Cambridge, MA, 1942.

*Senter, Riley. [Letters, 1850–53] *Crossing the Continent.* . . .

Shaw, William. [Narrative, 1849] *Golden Dreams and Waking Realities: Being the Adventures of a Gold-Seeker in California and the Pacific Islands.* London, 1851.

Sheppard, Ebenezer. Diary, 1849–51. TPS: CAHS.

"Shirley, Dame." See Louise A. K. S. Clappe.

Shufelt, S. [1850] *A Letter from a Gold Miner: Placerville California . . . ,* intro. Robert G. Clelland. San Marino, CA, 1944.

*Skinner, H. A. Diary, 1850–51. . . .

*Sleight, Morris. Letters, 1850–51. . . .

Smith, Seth. Letters, 1850–51. MS: BL.

"Solitaire." See John Francis McDermott.

*Spooner, E. A. Diary and letters, 1849–50. . . .

*Steele, John. [Narrative, 1850–53] *In Camp and Cabin: Mining Life and Adventure in California.* . . . Lodi, WI, 1901.

*Steuben, William N. Diary, 1850. . . .

———. Letter, 1849. *Sentinel,* Rome, NY, Feb. 27, 1850.

Stevens, G. B. Letters, 1849. MS, TPS: Yale.

Stillman, Jacob D. B. *The Gold Rush Letters* . . . , ed. Kenneth Johnson. Palo Alto, 1967.

———. "Observations on the Medical Topography and Diseases of the Sacramento Valley . . . 1849–50." *New York Journal of Medicine* 7(1851).

———. [Reminiscence/diary, 1849–50] *Seeking the Golden Fleece*. San Francisco, 1877.

*Stimson, Fancher. [Reminiscence, 1850–51] "Overland Journey. . . ."

Street, Franklin. [essay] *California in 1850, Compared with What It Was in 1849* . . . Cincinnati, 1851.

*Stuart, Joseph A. [Diary, 1849–51] *My Roving Life*. . . .

*Swain, William. Letters, 1850. . . .

*Swan, Chauncey. [1849–51] "Letters . . ."

Swan, John A. [Reminiscence, 1848] *A Trip to the Gold Mines of California* . . . , ed. and intro. John H. Hussey. San Francisco, 1960.

Sweetser, A. C. Letters, 1850–51. MS: HL.

Taylor, Bayard. [Narrative, 1849] *El Dorado: Or Adventures in the Path of Empire*. New York, 1949.

Taylor, Renaldo R. [1849–50] *Seeing the Elephant: Letters* . . . , ed. John W. Caughey. [Los Angeles] 1951.

Taylor, William. [1849–50] *California Life Illustrated*. New York, 1858.

Teller, Woolsey. Letters, 1850. MS: Yale.

*Thompson, Clark W. Letters, 1850–53 . . .

*Tiffany, P. C. Diary, 1849–50. . . .

*Tolles, James S. Diary, 1850. . . .

Townsend, Beeson. Letters, 1850. MS: CASL.

Tracy, Frederick P. Letter, 1849. TPS: CASL.

*Turner, Charles. Diary, 1849. . . .

*Tuttle, Charles A. Letters, 1850. . . .

Tyson, Dr. James L. [Narrative, 1849] *Diary of a Physician in California*. . . . New York, 1850.

*Udell, John. [Diary, 1850–51] *Incidents*. . . .

Upham, Samuel C. [Narrative, 1849–50] *Notes of a Voyage to California* . . . *with Scenes in El Dorado*. . . . Philadelphia, 1878.

———. Letters, 1850. MS: Boston Public Library.

Upton, Eugene A. Letters, 1849–50. Published in *Boston Traveller*, n.d.; bound in scrapbook, CAHS.

Varnell, William M. Letters, 1849–50. MS: Louisiana State University Library.

Varney, Jotham. Letters, 1850. TPS: CAHS.

Waite, E. G. "Pioneer Mining in California." *Century Magazine* 42(1891).

Wardwell, William H. Diary, 1850–51. MS: New England Historic Genealogical Society, Boston.

Weber, John B. Diary and letters, 1849. *Illinois State Journal*, Springfield, Jan., Mar. 1850.

*Webster, Kimball. [Diary/reminiscence 1849–50] *The Goldseekers*. . . .

Weed, L. N. Diary, 1850. MS: Yale.

Welch, Adonijah S. [1850] "Three Gold Rush Letters . . . ," ed. William H. Hermann. *Journal of History* 57(1959).

*Wells, Epaphroditus. Letters, 1849–51. . . .

*Wells, William. Letters, 1850. . . .

*Weston, Francis F. Diary, 1849–51. . . .

*Wheeler, George Nelson. Diary, 1850–51. . . .

Wheeler, Osgood Church. [1849–51] "Selected Letters. . . ." *CAHSQ*, 27 (1948).

White, James. Diary, 1849–50. MS: MAHS.

Williams, Henry Fairfax. Diary, 1849 and 1851. MS: BL.
———. Letters, 1848–50 and 1852–60s. MS: BL.
*Williams, James. Letter, 1850. . . .
*Wilson, William. Letters, 1850. . . .
Winchester, Jonas. Letters, 1849–50. MS: CASL.
Windeler, Adolphus. [1850–53] *The California Gold Rush Diary of a German Sailor*, ed. W. Turrentine Jackson. Berkeley, 1969.
*Wistar, Isaac J. [Reminiscence, 1849–57] *Autobiography*. . . .
*Wolcott, Lucian McClenathan. Diary, 1850–51. . . .
*Wood, Joseph W. Diary, 1849–53. . . .
Woodin, Stephen, Letters, 1849–50. MS: HL.
Woods, Daniel B. [Narrative/diary, 1849–50] *Sixteen Months at the Gold Diggings*. New York, 1851.
*Woods, James M. Letters, 1850. . . .
Woodward, E. Morrison. Diary, 1849. MS: BL.
Wright, William. Co-partnership Agreement, Constitution and Records of Wright's Company of Gold Diggers, 1849. MS: BL.
*Wyman, Walker D. [ed.]. [1849–52] *California Emigrant Letters*. . . .
Yale, Gregory. Letter, 1850. MS: HL.

SECTION III: HOMEWARD JOURNEY VIA PANAMA, 1850–51

In contrast to the known 518 diaries, letter collections and reminiscent records which described the overland journey to California in 1849 and 1850, I know of only eighty-eight recountings of the journey from California to the eastern states during the years 1849–51. Approximately 90,000 men returned via Panama (only several hundred through Nicaragua and Mexico) during that three-year period. Possibly many more of them wrote diaries and letters which have been lost; some may yet be found. Nonetheless, the evidence is overwhelming that very few made the effort to write about their return journey.

For the past 130 years, historians and general writers have been equally inattentive to the final phase of the gold rush cycle—the departure month after month throughout the gold rush years of the thousands who sailed from San Francisco, bound for home in the "old thirty."

It was the rush to El Dorado, the spectacle of 30,000 people—50,000 in 1852—walking across the wilderness half of the continent, that commanded attention at the time and has done so ever since. More important, the drama of events in California during the gold rush years, the velocity of change in that dynamic society and the mystique of the place have combined to challenge the curiosity and intellect of historians and novelists alike.

The return home is the untold part of the great gold rush experience, and the accounts that were written—seventy are here listed (with eighteen reminiscences and sketchy diaries excluded)—offer ample detail, colorful and accurate, to nourish the writing of a major book about the denouement.

My final chapter, "Coming Home," is a brief re-creation of what happened to William Swain, geared to the pace and balance of his story. He was hurrying home, like everyone else—no time for homebound goldseeker or modern historian to linger and explore. But given the existing records that I have seen and the many more that I am sure can be found (especially in the two Panama City newspapers, the *Star* and the *Echo*), I believe that the return home is a subject of great potential, involving the impact of thousands of Americans on Panama as well as on their home towns. Once back in Savannah, Indianapolis or Worcester, how well did those men who had seen San Francisco adjust to the old ways, the picayunes of daily life? Like veterans home from war, were they impatient with traditional mores and rules? Did their discontent cause them to seek change? How many gave up on home and returned to California?

One of the most poignant dramas of the entire gold rush occurred month after month in the cities and jungles of Panama—the meeting of thousands of men returning from California and those heading to California. They had to meet, as they traveled the same trails through the jungle, moved up or down the Chagres River, and walked the streets of Panama City and Chagres. And yet Hubert Howe Bancroft in his robust book devoted entirely to the gold rush, *California Inter Pocula* (San Francisco, 1888), described it only briefly (p. 173): "Narrowly they eyed one another, the going and the returning . . . brave men . . . meeting here in the heart of a tropical wilderness . . . some sick to death of goldseeking, others burning for it."

The only goldseeker who told of this interplay between those who had seen the elephant and those yet to be initiated was Heinrich Schliemann, who described the contrasting scene on board two ships that paused in the harbor at Acapulco, one crowded with singing men bound for the gold fields, the other silent with the disappointment of those who had dug there.

Beyond these two vignettes, the drama has been ignored. Not even the most descriptive diarists of 1850 and 1851—E. H. N. Patterson and Isaac Lord— commented on the confluence of those migrations.

The men who wrote diaries and/or letters describing their journey home were with few exceptions the same men who had written while in California—as they were generally the same who had written during the overland trip to California. Thus to a far greater degree than has been recognized previously, the eyewitness, I-was-there record of the gold rush—overland, California and return home—was written by the same men.

Whether writing or not, the vast majority—more than 90 percent—who returned to the states did so via Panama. A few chose to leave their ships at Realejo, to cross Nicaragua to the Gulf; a smaller number disembarked at Acapulco for the journey through Mexico to Vera Cruz or another Gulf port.

Did anyone return home by the overland trails? From the diaries and letters written in 1849, 1850, 1851 and fewer in 1852 which I have read, I know of only one man who chose to return overland. Peter Branstetter left California on July 2, 1851, and traveled the Humboldt, South Pass and Platte River route eastward against the westward tide of that year to Missouri, where he arrived September 2.

The other possible route home was by ship around Cape Horn. I know of two diarists who reported their return by that lengthy voyage: Lorenzo D. Sargent, diary, 1850 (MS: Yale); and Charles Tinker.

I have excluded a considerable source of information about the Isthmus of Panama during the gold rush years—the diaries and letters written by emigrants on their way *to* California. They reflect a point of view quite different from that of the returning goldseekers. Therefore, I have used only a few such records to provide specific information as needed in Chapter XIII.

With few exceptions, all diarists and letter writers listed in this section have appeared in either Section I or II, or both. Therefore, full bibliographical information for each can be found in one of those sections. Those listed here for the first time have full bibliographical information.

The time span—months and year—during which a diarist or letter writer traveled from California to the states via Panama (or Nicaragua) is cited in each case.

■

Anonymous. Letter, May, 1851. *Michigan Expositor*, July 1, 1851.

Autenrieth, E. L. *A Topographical Map of the Isthmus of Panama* [with text describing the Isthmus crossing]. New York, 1851.

Baker, Isaac. Diary, Sept.–Nov. 1850. . . .

Bannington, Alexander P. Diary, Nov.–Dec. 1850. . . .

Batchelder, Amos. Diary, Oct.–Dec. 1850. . . .

Baxter, Benjamin. Diary, Aug.–Sept. 1850. . . .

Boyden, Seth. [Diary, Dec. 1850—Jan.–Mar. 1851] ". . . Days in California. . . ."

Bradley, A. B. Diary, Feb.–May 1851. MS: BL.

Bruff, J. Goldsborough. [Diary, June–July 1851] *Gold Rush.* . . .

Buffum, Joseph C. Diary, Sept.–Oct. 1851 [via Nicaragua]. . . .

Burbank, Augustus R. Diary, April–May 1851. . . .

Carter, Henry. Diary, April–May 1849; Dec. 1849–Jan. 1850. . . .

Chaffee, Joseph Bennett. Letters, Mar.–May 1850. . . .

Cosad, David. Diary, Jan.–Feb. 1850. . . .

Crackbon, Joseph. Diary, Apr.–July 1849. . . .

Darwin, Charles B. Diary, Dec. 1849–Apr. 1850. . . .

DeWitt, Alfred, wife and brothers. Letters, 1849–1850s. . . .

Ellis, William. Letters, Feb.–Oct. 1850. . . .

Fish, L. I. Diary, Oct. 1849. . . .

Foster, Isaac. [Diary, Sept. 1850] *The Foster Family* . . .

Goldsmith, Oliver. [Reminiscence, Jan.–Mar. 1850, via Nicaragua] *Overland in Forty-nine.* . . .

Gorgas, Solomon. Diary, Feb.–Mar. 1851. . . .

Goss, Milo J. Letters, May–June 1850. . . .

Gregory, Joseph W. . . . *Guide for California Travelers Via the Isthmus of Panama.* New York, 1850.

Griswold, Dr. Chauncey D. *The Isthmus of Panama, and What I Saw There.* New York, 1852.

Hecox, W. H. [Feb.–Mar. 1849] "Five Letters from the Isthmus," in William M'Collum, *California As I Saw It.*

Horn, David. [Letter, June 1850] "Across the Isthmus . . . ," ed. James P. Jones and William W. Rogers. *Hispanic American Historical Review* 41(1961).

Hovey, John. Diary, May, 1851. . . .

Howland, Captain. [Sept., 1850] *Reminiscence.* . . .

Johnston, William G. [Narrative, Dec. 1849–Jan. 1850] *Experiences.* . . .

Kingsley, Nelson. [Feb.–Mar. 1851] "Diary of . . ."

Knower, Daniel. [Reminiscence, Jan. 1850] *The Adventures* . . .

Letts, John M. [Nov.–Dec. 1849, Jan. 1850, via Nicaragua] *California Illustrated.* . . .

Lord, Dr. Isaac. Diary, Feb.–Mar. 1851. . . .

Lyman, Chester S. [Diary, Mar. 1850] *Around the Horn.* . . .

M'Collum, William. [Narrative, Feb.–May, 1849] *California As I Saw It.* . . .

McCoy, A. W. "The Journey Home through Nicaragua." [April 1851] *Pioneering on the Plains.* Kaukauna, WI, 1924.

McCoy, [Samuel]. [Diary, Sept.–Dec. 1850] "The Journey Home Through Mexico." *Pioneering on the Plains.* . . .

McIntosh, Thomas. Diary, July 1850. MS: MAHS.

Miller, William W. Diary, Oct.–Dec. 1850. . . .

Millington, D. A. Diary, Sept. 1851. . . .

Mobley, C. C. Diary, Nov.–Dec. 1850, Jan. 1851 [via Nicaragua].

Ness, Richard. Diary/narrative, Sept.–Nov. 1850.

Osbun, Albert G. [Diary, Sept.–Dec. 1850, Jan. 1851; through Mexico.] *To California.* . . .

Panama Star, Sept.–Dec. 1850, Jan.–Mar. 1851.

Pangborn, David. [Diary, June–Aug. 1850] "A Journey from New York to San Francisco. . . ." *American Historical Review*, 9(1903–04)

Parke, Charles R. Diary, Sept.–Dec. 1850 [via Nicaragua].

Patterson, E. H. N. Diary, Oct.–Dec. 1850, Jan. 1851. Oquawka *Spectator*, IL, Mar.–July 1851.

Peters, Henry H. Diary, Feb.–Mar. 1850. . . .

Pierce, Hiram D. [Diary, Oct.–Dec. 1850, Jan. 1851; via Nicaragua] *A Forty-niner.* . . .

Pigman, Walter G. [Diary, Feb. 1851] *The Journal.* . . .

Prichet, John. Diary, Jan. 1851. . . .

Schliemann, Heinrich. [Diary, Mar. 1851; April, 1852] *First Visit.* . . .

Sheppard, Ebenezer. Diary, Mar.–May 1850, via Nicaragua.

Steuben, William N. Diary, June–Aug. 1850. . . .

Stevens, G. B. Letters, Feb.–June, 1849. MS: Yale.

Stillman, Jacob D. B. [Reminiscence/diary, Oct.–Dec. 1850, via Nicaragua] *Seeking the Golden Fleece.* . . .

Stimson, Fancher. [Narrative, Dec. 1850] "Overland Journey. . . ."

Taylor, Bayard, [Narrative, July–Aug. 1849 via Panama; Dec. 1849, Jan.–Feb. 1850 through Mexico] *El Dorado.* . . .

Thompson, Clark W. Letter, 1850.

Tiffany, P. C. Diary, Dec. 1850–Mar. 1851. . . .

Tyson, Dr. James L. [Narrative] *Diary of a Physician.* . . .

Udell, John. [Diary] *Incidents.* . . .

Upham, Samuel C. [Narrative, Aug.–Sept. 1850] *Notes of a Voyage* . . .

Van Wyck, Sidney. Diary, Feb. 1851. MS: CAHS.

Watrous, R. [March 1851] "Notes of a Trip. . . ."

Weed, L. N. Diary, Sept.–Dec. 1850 [via Nicaragua]. . . .

Wells, Albert Chipman. Letters, Dec. 1849–1851, Panama and Nicaragua. MS: NYHS.

Wolcott, Lucian McClenathan. Diary, Jan.–April 1851 [via Nicaragua]. . . .

Woodward, E. Morrison. Diary, Jan.–March 1850. . . .

Wortley, Emmeline Stuart, Lady. *Travels in the United States, 1849–1850*, vols. 2 and 3. London, 1851.

Section IV: NEWSPAPERS

Scores of newspapers published in towns and cities of the United States during the gold rush years have been preserved on microfilm in public, college/university and historical society libraries. (See *Newspapers in Microform, United States*, Washington, D.C., 1973.) With few exceptions these weeklies and dailies during spring 1849 published advertisements reflecting the "gold fever" and reported the companies of men organizing for the journey to California. By summer and for many months thereafter, newspapers frequently published letters from the overland trails and from California's mines and cities. Sometimes complete diaries were published serially.

California newspapers carried extensive information throughout 1849–52 about mining activities and all attendant matters. By the early 1850s many mining towns had their own weekly newspapers. They offer an honest, often poignant picture of mining-camp life. Easy and rewarding access to these newspapers is provided through a remarkable Ph.D. thesis: Chester B. Kennedy, *Newspapers of the California Northern Mines, 1850–1860: A Record of Life, Letters and Culture* (Stanford University, 1949).

As Mr. Kennedy has revealed, newspapers offer a rich source of information. But as in digging for gold, the prospector must work through a vast amount of throwaway material to find the letters and diaries.

Future discoveries of eyewitness accounts will not be made by chance in attics or old trunks but by persevering search through reel after reel of microfilmed newspapers. There are no diggings more certain to provide reward for hard work.

The following list of newspapers is certainly not intended to be more than a scattering sample of newspapers that carried reports, letters and/or diaries of the gold rush years. To avoid endless repetition of the same dates, it can be generally assumed that each newspaper was published in one or more of the years 1849, 1850, 1851 and 1852, and that each newspaper is available on microfilm. However, both generalizations are not always applicable: Dates of publication should be checked in *American Newspapers, 1821–1936*, ed. Winifred Gregory (New York, 1937), and/or *Newspapers in Microform*.

Many of the following newspapers have been cited in the Notes.

■

Alta California: See *Daily Alta California; Tri-Weekly Alta California*
Baltimore *Sun*, MD
Boston *Traveller*, MA
Buffalo *Daily Courier*, NY
Buffalo *Morning Express*, NY
Burlington *Gazette*, IA
Burlington *Hawkeye*, IA
Burlington *Tri-Weekly Telegraph*, IA
California Evening Picayune, San Francisco, CA
Chicago *Daily Record*, IL
Cincinnati *Enquirer*, OH
Clinton Republican, Wilmington, OH
Columbia *Statesman*, MO
Columbus *Dispatch*, OH
Daily Alta California, San Francisco, CA
Daily California Courier, San Francisco, CA
Daily National Intelligencer, Washington, D.C.
Democratic Expounder, Marshall, MI
Detroit *Daily Advertiser*, MI
Frontier Guardian, Council Bluffs, IA
Illinois Daily Journal, Springfield, IL
Illinois Gazette, Lacon, IL
Ithaca *Journal*, NY
Jersey City *Sentinel*, NJ
Jersey City *Telegraph*, NJ
Kalamazoo *Gazette*, MI
Kankakee *Daily Republican*, IL
Knoxville *Journal*, IL
Logansport *Weekly Journal*, IN
Marshall *Statesman*, MI
Marysville *Appeal Democrat*, CA (1930)
Marysville *Herald*, CA

Michigan Expositor, Adrian, MI
Missouri Courier, Hannibal, MO
Missouri Republican, St. Louis, MO
Missouri Statesman, Columbia, MO
Napa *Journal*, CA (1952)
New Orleans *Daily Picayune*, LA
New York *Herald*, NY
New York *Sun*, NY
Newark *Daily Advertiser*, NJ
Niagara Cataract, Lockport, NY
Niagara Courier, Lockport, NY
Ohio State Journal, Columbus, OH
Oquawka *Spectator*, IL
Pacific News, San Francisco, CA
Panama Star, Panama City, New Grenada
Peoria *Democratic Press*, IL
Pittsburgh *Gazette*, PA
Sacramento *Placer Times*, CA
Sacramento *Transcript*, CA
St. Joseph *Adventurer*, MO
St. Joseph *Gazette*, MO
St. Louis *Daily Intelligencer*, MO
St. Louis *Weekly Reveille*, MO
Scioto Gazette, Chillicothe, OH
Sentinel, Rome, NY
Tri-Weekly Alta California, San Francisco, CA
Weekly North Western Gazette, Galena, IL

Section V: SECONDARY SOURCES

Adams, Dorothy Q. "Life in the Mining Camps of the Yuba Valley." Master's thesis, University of California, Berkeley, 1931.

Alger, Horatio. *The Young Miner: Or, Tom Nelson in California*. Reprint. Intro. John Seelye. San Francisco, 1965.

Allen, William W., and Richard B. Avery. *California Gold Book*. San Francisco, 1893.

Altrocchi, Julia C. "Paradox Town: San Francisco in 1851." *CAHSQ* 28(1949).

Angel, Myron. *History of Placer County*. Oakland, 1882.

Aucutt, Lucile. "Life in the California Mining Camps: A Type Study." Master's thesis, University of California, Berkeley, 1931.

Bancroft, Hubert Howe. *California Inter Pocula*. San Francisco, 1888.

———. *History of California, 1848–1859*, vols. 1–6. San Francisco, 1888.

Barrett, James A. "Cholera in Missouri." *Missouri Historical Review* 55(1961).

Baur, John E. "The Health Factor in the Gold Rush Era." *Rushing for Gold*, ed. John W. Caughey. Berkeley, 1949.

Bean, Edwin F. *History and Directory of Nevada County, California*. Nevada City, CA, 1867.

Bieber, Ralph P. *Southern Trails to California in 1849*. Glendale, CA, 1937.

Biggs, Donald C. *Conquer and Colonize, Stevenson's Regiment and California*. San Rafael, CA, 1977.

Billington, Ray Allen. *The Far Western Frontier, 1830–1860,* New York, 1956.
———. "Books That Won the West: The Guidebooks of the Forty-Niners and Fifty-Niners." *The American West,* IV (1967).
Blumenthal, Henry. "The California Societies in France, 1849–1855." *Pacific Historical Review* 25(1956).
Buckbee, Edna B. *Pioneer Days of Angel's Camp.* Angel's Camp, CA, 1932.
———. *The Saga of Old Tuolumne.* New York, 1935.
Caughey, John W. *Gold Is the Cornerstone.* Berkeley, 1948.
———. [ed.]. *Rushing for Gold.* Berkeley, 1949.
———. "The Transit of the Forty-Niners." *University of Wyoming Publications* 37.
Chinard, Gilbert. "When the French Came to California: An Introductory Essay." *CAHSQ* 22(1943).
"Cholera Epidemics in St. Louis." MOHS, *Glimpses of the Past* 3(1936).
Collyer, Gilbert A. "Early History of El Dorado County." Master's thesis, University of California, Berkeley, 1932.
Coman, Katherine. *Economic Beginnings of the Far West.* New York, 1912.
Cook, Sherburne F. "The Conflict Between the California Indian and White Civilization, part 3, 'The American Invasion, 1848–1870.' " *Ibero-Americana* 23(1943).
Coy, Owen C. *Gold Days.* Los Angeles [1929].
———. *The Great Trek.* Los Angeles, 1931.
———. *In the Diggings in 'Forty-Nine.* Los Angeles, 1948.
———. "Paper Towns and Easy Money." *Proceedings of the American Historical Association,* Pacific Coast Branch, 1928.
Crampton, Charles G. "Gold Rushes Within the United States, 1800–1900: A General Survey." Master's thesis, University of California, Berkeley, 1936.
Cronise, Titus Few. *The Natural Wealth of California.* San Francisco, 1868.
Cushing, Charles S. "The Acquisition of California, Its Influence and Development. . . ." *California Law Review,* 1920.
Dornin, May. "The Emigrant Trails into California." Master's thesis, University of California, Berkeley, 1922.
Duffus, R. L. *Queen Calafia's Island: Facts and Myths about the Golden State.* New York, 1965.
Dyke, Dorothy J. "Transportation in the Sacramento Valley, 1849–1860." Master's thesis, University of California, Berkeley, 1932.
Egan, Ferol. *The El Dorado Trail.* New York, 1970.
Egenhoff, Elisabeth L. "The Elephant as They Saw It: A Collection of Contemporary Pictures and Statements of Gold Mining in California." *California Journal of Mines and Geology, Centennial Supplement* 45(1949).
Eldredge, Zoeth S. *The Beginnings of San Francisco,* 2 vols. San Francisco, 1912.
Ellison, Joseph. "The Struggle for Civil Government in California, 1846–1850." *CAHSQ* 10(1931).
Ellison, William H. *A Self-Governing Dominion: California, 1849–1860.* Berkeley, 1950.
Eyring, Rose. "Portrayal of the California Gold Rush in Period Imaginative Literature from 1848 to 1875." Ph.D. dissertation, University of California, Berkeley, 1944.
Farley, Charles A. "The Moral Aspect of California: A Thanksgiving Sermon of 1850." *CAHSQ* 19(1940).
Faragher, John M. *Women and Men on the Overland Trail.* New Haven, 1979.
Fleming, L. A. and A. R. Standing. "The Road to 'Fortune': The Salt Lake Cutoff." *UTHSQ* 33(1965).

Feller, David. "The Profitability of California Gold." Master's thesis, University of California, Berkeley, 1965.

Garr, Daniel J. "A Rare and Desolate Land: Population and Race in Hispanic California." *Western Historical Quarterly* (Apr. 1975).

Garrett, Lula May. "San Francisco in 1851: As Described by Eyewitnesses." *CAHSQ* 22(1943).

Gates, Paul W. "California's Embattled Settlers." *CAHSQ* 41(1962).

Grant, Phil S. "The Songs of the Forty-Niners: A Collection and Survey." Master's thesis, University of California, Berkeley, 1924.

Gray, Helen B. "Beginnings of Nativism in California, 1848–1852." Master's thesis, University of California, Berkeley, 1948.

Gregg, Kate L. "Boonslickers in the Gold Rush to California." *Missouri Historical Review* 41(1947).

———. "Missourians in the Gold Rush." *Missouri Historical Review* 39(1945).

Groh, George W. *Gold Fever: Being a True Account, Both Horrifying and Hilarious of the Art of Healing (So-Called) During the California Gold Rush.* New York, 1966.

Gudde, Erwin G. *California Gold Camps.* Berkeley, 1975.

———. *California Place Names: A Geographic Dictionary.* Berkeley, 1949.

Guinn, James. "The Sonoran Migration." *Southern CAHS Publications* 8(1909–10).

Hammond, George P. *Who Saw the Elephant.* San Francisco, 1964.

Hanchett, William F. Jr. "The Question of Religion and the Taming of California, 1849–54." *CAHSQ* 32(1953).

———. "Religion and the Gold Rush, 1849–54: The Christian Churches in the California Mines." Ph.D. dissertation, University of California, Berkeley, 1952.

Hanson, George E. "The Early History of the Yuba River Valley." Master's thesis, University of California, Berkeley, 1924.

Harris, Henry. *California's Medical Story.* Springfield, IL, 1932.

Hart, James D. *New Englanders in Nova Albion: Some 19th Century Views of California.* Boston, 1976.

Hazard, Lucy L. *The Frontier in American Literature.* New York [1927].

Hill, Jim D. "The Early Mining Camp in American Life." *Pacific Historical Review* 1(1932).

Hittell, Theodore H. *History of California,* vol. 2. San Francisco, 1886.

Holliday, J. S. "The California Gold Rush Reconsidered." *Probing the American West: Papers from the Santa Fe Conference.* Santa Fe, 1962.

———. "The Influence of the Family on the California Gold Rush." *Proceedings of the 3rd Annual Meeting of the Conference of CAHS.* Stockton, CA, 1957.

———. Foreword, *Valley of Salt, Memories of Wine . . . ,* Louis Nusbaumer. Berkeley, 1967.

Howe, Octavius T. *Argonauts of '49, History and Adventures of the Emigrant Companies from Massachusetts, 1849–50.* Cambridge, 1923.

Hubach, Robert R. "Unpublished Travel Narratives on the Early Midwest, 1720–1850: A Preliminary Bibliography." *Mississippi Valley Historical Review* 42(1955).

Huffman, Robert E. "Newspaper Art in Stockton, 1850–92." *CAHSQ* 34(1955).

Hughes, Marshall. "The Argonaut Mining Companies of 1848–1850." Master's thesis, University of California, Berkeley, 1939.

Hulbert, Archer B. *Forty-Niners: The Chronicle of the California Trail.* Boston, 1931.

Hunt, Rockwell D. "Pioneer Protestants of Early California." *Rushing for Gold,* ed. John W. Caughey. Berkeley, 1949.

Hutchinson, W. H. *California: The Golden Shore by the Sundown Sea.* Palo Alto, 1980.

Jackson, Joseph Henry. *Anybody's Gold: The Story of California's Mining Towns.* New York, 1941.

———. *Gold Rush Album.* New York, 1949.

Johnson, William Weber. *The Forty-Niners.* New York, 1974.

Jones, J. Wesley. ". . . Pantoscope of California." *CAHSQ* 6(1927).

Kelly, Charles. "Goldseekers on the Hastings Cutoff." *UTHSQ* 20(1952).

———. *Salt Desert Trails.* Salt Lake City, 1930.

Kemble, John Haskell. *The Panama Route: 1848–1869.* Berkeley, 1943.

———. "The Gold Rush by Panama, 1848–1851." In John W. Caughey, ed., *Rushing for Gold.* Berkeley, 1949.

Kennedy, Chester B. "Newspapers of the California Northern Mines 1850–1860; A Record of Life, Letters and Culture." Stanford University, 1949.

Korns, J. Roderic. "The Salt Lake Cut-off." *UTHSQ* 19(1951).

———. "West from Fort Bridger: The Pioneering of the Immigrant Trails Across Utah, 1846–1850." *UTHSQ* 19(1951).

Kroll, Helen B. "The Books That Enlightened the Emigrants." *ORHSQ* 45(1944).

Lapp, Rudolph M. "Negro Rights Activities in Gold Rush California." *CAHSQ* 45(1966).

———. *Blacks in the Gold Rush.* New Haven, 1977.

Lavender, David. *California, Land of New Beginnings.* New York, 1972.

———. *Westward Vision, the Story of the Oregon Trail.* New York, 1963.

Layton, Thomas N. "Stalking Elephants in Nevada." *Western Folklore* 35(1976).

Lewis, Marvin [ed.]. *The Mining Frontier: Contemporary Accounts from the American West in the Nineteenth Century.* Norman, OK, 1967.

Lewis, Oscar. *The California Mining Towns.* San Francisco, 1933.

———. *Sea Routes to the Gold Fields: The Migration by Water to California in 1849–1852.* New York, 1949.

———. *Sutter's Fort: Gateway to the Gold Fields.* Englewood, NJ, 1966.

Lorch, Fred W. "Iowa and the California Gold Rush of 1849." *Iowa Journal of History and Politics* 30(1932).

McCullough, David. *The Path Between the Seas: The Creation of the Panama Canal, 1870–1898.* New York, 1977.

McDermott, John Francis [ed.]. *Travelers on the Western Frontier.* Urbana, IL, 1970.

McGowan, Joseph A. "Freighting to the Mines in California, 1849–1859." Ph.D. dissertation, University of California, Berkeley, 1949.

———. "San Francisco–Sacramento Shipping, 1839–1854." M.A. thesis, University of California, Berkeley, 1939.

McMurtrie, Douglas C. "An Introduction and Supplement to a History of California Newspapers." *CAHSQ* 7(1928).

McWilliams, Carey. *California: The Great Exception.* Santa Barbara, 1976.

Mansfield, George C. *The Feather River in '49 and the Fifties.* Oroville, CA, 1924.

———. *History of Butte County, California.* Los Angeles, 1918.

Mantor, Lyle E. "Fort Kearny and the Westward Movement." *Nebraska History* 29(1948).

Margo, Elisabeth. *Taming the Forty-Niner.* New York, 1955.

Margo, Joan. "The Food Supply Problem of the California Gold Mines, 1848–1855." Master's thesis, University of California, Berkeley, 1947.

Mattes, Merrill J. *The Great Platte River Road: The Covered Wagon Mainline Via Fort Kearny to Fort Laramie.* Publication of NBHS 25(1969).

———. "Chimney Rock on the Oregon Trail." *Nebraska History* 36(1955).

———. "Fort Laramie, Guardian of the Oregon Trail." *Annals of Wyoming* 17(1945).

———. "Hiram Scott, Fur Trader." *Nebraska History* 26(1945).
———. "Robidoux's Trading Post at 'Scott's Bluffs,' and the California Gold Rush." *Nebraska History* 30(1949).
———. "The Sutler's Store at Fort Laramie." *Annals of Wyoming* 18(1946).
Merriam, J. Chester. *Bars on the Yuba River.* Dobbins, CA, 1951.
Miners' Own Book . . . Various Modes of California Mining. San Francisco, 1858.
"Mining for Gold in California." *Hutchings' Illustrated California Magazine* 2(1857–58).
Morefield, Richard H. "Mexicans in the California Mines, 1848–53." *CAHSQ* 35(1956).
Morgan, Dale. *Overland in 1846, Diaries and Letters of the California-Overland Trail,* vol. 1. Georgetown, CA, 1963.
———. "The Ferries of the Forty-Niners." *Annals of Wyoming* 31(1959), 32(1960).
———. "The Mormon Ferry on the North Platte." *Annals of Wyoming* 21(1949).
Morse, John F. *The First History of Sacramento City.* Sacramento, 1945.
"The Mountaineers of California." *Hutchings' Illustrated California Magazine* 4(1859).
Mulford, Prentice. *Prentice Mulford's Story: Or, Life by Land and Sea.* London, 1913.
———. "The Bed of the River" and "California Culinary Experiences" in *California Sketches,* ed. and intro. Franklin Walker. San Francisco, 1935.
Nasatir, Abraham P. [ed.] "The French in the California Gold Rush." *Franco-American Pamphlet Series,* no. 2. New York, 1934.
———. "The French Consulate in California, 1843–1856: The Moerenhout Documents." *CAHSQ* 13(1934), 27(1948).
Neasham, Aubrey. "Sutter's Sawmill." *CAHSQ* 26(1947).
Nunis, Doyce B., Jr. "The Enigma of the Sublette Overland Party, 1845." *Pacific Historical Review* 28(1959).
O'Brien, Robert. *California Called Them: A Saga of Golden Days and Roaring Camps.* New York [1951].
Otis, Dr. F. N. *Illustrated History of the Panama Railroad.* New York, 1862.
"Packing in the Mountains of California." *Hutchings' Illustrated California Magazine* 1(1856–57).
Paden, Irene. *Prairie Schooner Detours.* New York, 1949.
———. *The Wake of the Prairie Schooner.* New York, 1943.
Paul, Rodman W. *California Gold: The Beginning of Mining in the Far West.* Cambridge, 1947.
———. *The California Gold Discovery, Sources, Documents, Accounts and Memoirs. . . .* Georgetown, CA, 1967.
———. *Mining Frontiers of the Far West, 1848–1880.* New York, 1963.
Petty, Claude R. "Gold Rush Intellectual, the California of John S. Hittell." Ph.D. dissertation, University of California, Berkeley.
Peterson, Richard H. *Manifest Destiny in the Mines: A Cultural Interpretation of Anti-Mexican Nativism in California, 1848–1853.* San Francisco, 1975.
Pitt, Leonard. *The Decline of the Californios: A Social History of the Spanish-Speaking Californians, 1846–1890.* Berkeley, 1966.
Pomeroy, Earl. *The Pacific Slope, A History of California. . . .* New York, 1965.
Quaife, Milo Milton [ed.]. *Pictures of Gold Rush California.* Chicago, 1949.
"Quartz Mining in California." *Hutchings' Illustrated California Magazine* 2(1857–58).
Ramey, Earl. "The Beginnings of Marysville." *CAHSQ* 14(1935), 15(1936).
Read, Georgia Willis. "The Chagres River Route to California in 1851." *CAHSQ* 8(1929).
———. "Diseases, Drugs, and Doctors on the Oregon–California Trail." *Missouri Historical Review* 38(1943–44).

————. "Women and Children on the California Trail in the Gold Rush Years." *Missouri Historical Review* 39(1944–45).

Ressler, Theodore C. "Trails Divided: A Dissertation on the Overland Journey of Iowa Forty-Niners of the 'Sacramento Mining Company.' " TPS: Author, Williamsburg, IA.

Richman, Irving B. *California Under Spain and Mexico.* Boston, 1911.

Richmond, Robert W. "Developments Along the Overland Trail from the Missouri River to Fort Laramie, Before 1854." *Nebraska History* 33(1952).

Robinson, Henry. "Pioneer Days of California." *Overland Monthly* 8(1872).

Rogers, Fred B. "Bear Flag Lieutenant: The Life Story of Henry L. Ford, 1822–1866." *CAHSQ* 30(1951).

Rolle, Andrew F. *California, A History.* New York, 1963.

Root, George A. "Ferries in Kansas, Part II, Kansas River." *KSHSQ* 2(1933).

Roske, Ralph J. "The World Impact of the California Gold Rush 1849–1857." *Arizona and the West* 5(1963).

Royce, Josiah. *California from the Conquest in 1846 to the Second Vigilance Committee in San Francisco,* intro. Robert Glass Cleland. New York, 1948.

Savage, W. Sherman. "The Negro on the Mining Frontier." *Journal of Negro History* 30(1945).

Shaffer, Leslie D. "The Management of Organized Wagon Trains on the Overland Trail." *Missouri Historical Review* 55(1961).

Shinn, Charles H. *Mining Camps: A Study in American Frontier Government,* intro. Joseph Henry Jackson. New York, 1948.

Soule, Frank, et al. *The Annals of San Francisco.* San Francisco, 1855.

Stanley, Reva H. "Sutter's Mormon Workmen at Natoma and Coloma in 1848." *CAHSQ* 14(1935).

Starr, Kevin. *Americans and the California Dream, 1850–1915.* New York, 1973.

Stewart, George R. *The California Trail.* New York, 1962.

Strong, Phil. *Gold in Them Hills: Being an Irreverent History of the Great 1849 Gold Rush.* Garden City, NY, 1957.

Sudweeks, Leslie L. "The Raft River in Idaho History." *Pacific Northwest Quarterly* 32(1941).

Swartzlow, Ruby J. "Peter Lassen, Northern California's Trail-Blazer." *CAHSQ* 18(1939).

Thomas, M. Robert. "The Buckeye Argonauts." *Ohio State Archeological and Historical Quarterly* 59(1950).

————. "The Impact of the California Gold Rush on Ohio and Ohioans." M.A. thesis, Ohio State University, 1949.

Underhill, Reuben L. *From Cowhides to Golden Fleece.* Stanford, CA, 1939.

Unruh, John D., Jr. *The Plains Across.* Urbana, IL, 1979.

Watkins, Albert. "History of Fort Kearny." *Collections of the NBHS* 16(1911).

Watkins, Thomas, and Roger Olmsted. *Mirror of the Dream.* Oakland, 1976.

Webb, Todd. *The Gold Rush Trail and the Road to Oregon.* Garden City, NY, 1963.

Webb, W. L. "Independence, Missouri, A Century Old." *Missouri Historical Review* 22(1927).

Wheat, Carl I. *Books of the California Gold Rush.* San Francisco, 1949.

————. *Mapping the Trans-Mississippi West,* vol. 3. San Francisco, 1959.

————. "The Rocky-Bar Mining Company: An Episode in Early Western Promotion and Finance." *CAHSQ* 12(1933).

White, Stewart Edward. *The Forty-niners.* New Haven [1918].

Willman, Lillian M. "The History of Fort Kearny." *Publications of the NBHS* 21(1930).

Wiltsee, Ernest A. *Gold Rush Steamers of the Pacific.* San Francisco, 1938.

————. *The Pioneer Miner and the Pack Mule Express.* San Francisco, 1931.

———. "The City of New York of the Pacific." *CAHSQ* 12(1933).

Winther, Oscar O. *The Trans-Mississippi West: A Guide to Its Periodical Literature (1881–1938)*. Bloomington, IN, 1942.

———. "Stage-Coach Service in Northern California, 1849–52." *Pacific Historical Review* 3(1934).

Wright, Doris M. "The Making of Cosmopolitan California: An Analysis of Immigration, 1848–1870." *CAHSQ* 19(1940).

Wright, Flora Alice. "Richard Barnes Mason, Governor of California." Master's thesis, University of California, Berkeley,

Wright, Louis B. *Culture on the Moving Frontier*. New York, 1961.

Wyman, Walker D. "Council Bluffs and the Westward Movement." *Iowa Journal of History* 47(1949).

———. "The Outfitting Posts." *Pacific Historical Review* 18(1949).

Acknowledgments

This book has grown with me for many years. Through those years librarians, historians, professional colleagues, typists, editors and close friends have been involved with and supportive of what we called "the book." Some have expressed astonishment that I've taken so long to finish; some have died, including four whose names appear on the dedication page.

At last the time has come to acknowledge the encouragement, assistance and criticism that have helped me persevere and finally know when I should stop rewriting and revising.

At the start there was Edward Eberstadt, who introduced me to the William Swain diary and persuaded me to start what was to be a year's work. And Miss Sara Sabrina Swain, who preserved the diary for forty years, with her parents' letters, which she gave me as a testament of her belief in me and this book.

Next there was Bernard DeVoto, master historian of the West. He read an early version, then called *Pocket Full of Rocks*, and sent me a four-page, single-spaced letter of admonition and encouragement. His judgment strengthened my confidence and my commitment.

James Babb, Yale University Librarian, gave me special access to the newly acquired William R. Coe Collection of Western Americana. For more than a year I worked in that magnificent collection, always encouraged by Jim and by Archie Hanna, who became the collection's first curator and continues today in charge of that greatly expanded resource.

Two other men in charge of great libraries befriended and encouraged me—Randolph Adams at the William L. Clements Library, University of Michigan, and Robert Miller at the University of Indiana Library.

Throughout the 1950s and the early 1960s, my good friend and editor at Houghton Mifflin Company, Craig Wylie, patiently and forbearingly accepted the many delays caused by my insistence on revising and expanding a book he wanted to publish. In 1952 when I made a difficult decision to give up a business career to attend graduate school, thereby to be better prepared to complete my book, and at other times

541

when my delays and failures to meet deadlines might have angered a person less patient and understanding, Craig wrote one of his many thoughtful letters. I am deeply indebted to him.

At the University of California, Berkeley, professors Lawrence Kinnaird and John D. Hicks not only guided me as a graduate student but believed in my book as it slowly progressed. My research in those years centered on the wealth of the university's Bancroft Library, where Director George P. Hammond was always helpful, as were members of the staff: Robert Becker, Elizabeth Gudde and her husband Erwin, Julia McCloud, Estelle Rebec and Barr Thompkins. At Bancroft and beyond no one helped me more than Dale L. Morgan. No one knew as much about the diaries and other records of overland travel as Dale. As historian, wise critic and friend he was indispensable to this book.

The present director of the Bancroft Library, James D. Hart, first helped me when I was a graduate student in his classes and most recently when he read the manuscript and made a number of insightful suggestions and corrections.

As a research fellow at the Henry E. Huntington Library, I gained support from Director John Pomfret and Leslie Bliss, manuscripts librarian. Several scholars working at the Huntington that year and in later years were helpful, in particular Earl Pomeroy. And through all the years that I have come back to the Huntington, Carey Bliss has been wonderfully kind.

At the California Room of the California State Library in Sacramento, Allen Ottley helped me find whatever seemed most elusive. William N. Davis, state archivist, always found time to listen and advise.

At the Library of Congress, Gary Kohn (Manuscripts Division) was most helpful.

The library at the California Historical Society has a great collection of gold rush material, and the staff has been generous in assisting me. Special thanks to Maude Swingle, who has been there longest and carries on decade after decade in her cheerful, knowledgeable way.

I want to thank Munson Baldwin for his meticulous work in checking sources and verifying notes, way back in the 1960s. And Bruce Hamilton for helping me organize and prune my ever growing bibliography.

Through the book's evolution, there have been more than seven complete revisions, requiring typing and retyping of thousands of pages. The person who did most of that work was Mildred Johnson. Her care and patience will never be forgotten.

Pamela Seager at the California Historical Society typed more than one version of several chapters, and she helped keep me at work when other pressures made it seem easier to give up.

I met Virginia Gerhart when she was a graduate student of mine; then she worked for more than a year full time, helping me when it looked as if I was ready to finish the book—that was back in 1969–70. Virginia was important for more than one year; in fact, she helped in many ways for many years. Her loyalty and unfailing attention to every detail are deeply appreciated.

Next, I want to thank those who read the manuscript at different stages of its development, offering criticism and reactions that nurtured new ideas and helped to restrain my enthusiasm. Tom Watkins and Roger Olmsted, friends and experts in California history, understood my ambition and helped refine it. Oscar Lewis, dean of California historians, gave me his wise counsel and admonished me to hurry up and finish. Henry Mayer persuaded me to cut out sections that had once seemed inviolate. His knowledge of American history and his editorial judgment were of great value. Anne Galloway read the manuscript with great care and interest and suggested a number of important changes. Carol Sweig saw the book as if it were a novel and from that perspective gave me some welcome and new ideas. Jeanne Hopper made many important suggestions in the fall of 1980 which led to major improvements.

Of all those who have worked closely with me, no one has been more supportive and wisely critical than Doris Ober. Throughout 1980 and the first months of 1981 I worked with her on every detail of the final revision. This book has been significantly improved by Doris's rejection of many pages that I thought were great but she said must go.

I most gratefully thank friends and colleagues who agreed to read the manuscript so that I might gain from their thinking at the very end of this long process. First Ray Allen Billington, who in December 1980 gave me eight pages of specific corrections of phrase, date, name, reference—invaluable improvements. And he wrote me a letter of such generous praise and encouragement that I knew all the years had been truly rewarded.

Others who made suggestions I used and wrote letters that I shall always prize: John Caughey, William Hutchinson, Howard Lamar, Rodman Paul, Kevin Starr and Wallace Stegner. I am deeply grateful to each for his encouragement and thoughtfulness.

I wish to express my great appreciation of John Dodds. He was my editor at Simon and Schuster through 1980. His ideas and his perception of this book provided the basis for a major and final revision. He wisely persuaded me to cut and cut some more. I also thank at Simon and Schuster my editor Tom Wallace who has been an enthusiastic advocate. And Edith Fowler, designer, who understood and achieved everything I have wanted visually for this book. And Ted Johnson, copy editor, who did a superb job.

Rather than list a score and more historical societies and libraries and all those who helped me over many years, I sincerely hope that the officers and staffs of those institutions will know of my respect and lasting appreciation.

Index

544